BUSINESS ORGANIZATIONS

ASPEN CASEBOOK SERIES

BUSINESS ORGANIZATIONS

A TRANSACTIONAL APPROACH

William K. Sjostrom, Jr.
James E. Rogers College of Law
The University of Arizona

Wolters Kluwer
Law & Business

ISBN 978-1-4548-0291-4

Library of Congress Cataloging-in-Publication Data

Sjostrom, William K.
  Business organizations : a transactional approach / William Sjostrom, Jr., James E. Rogers
      College of Law, Professor Law, University of Arizona College of Law.
      pages cm. — (Aspen casebook series)
  Includes index.
    ISBN 978-1-4548-0291-4
  1. Business enterprises — Law and legislation — United States. I. Title.
    KF1355.S59 2013
    346.73'06—dc23

                                                                                                2012050746

SUSTAINABLE
FORESTRY
INITIATIVE

Certified Sourcing
www.sfiprogram.org
SFI-01234

SFI label applies to the text stock

About Wolters Kluwer Law & Business

Wolters Kluwer Law & Business is a leading global provider of intelligent information and digital solutions for legal and business professionals in key specialty areas, and respected educational resources for professors and law students. Wolters Kluwer Law & Business connects legal and business professionals as well as those in the education market with timely, specialized authoritative content and information-enabled solutions to support success through productivity, accuracy and mobility.

Serving customers worldwide, Wolters Kluwer Law & Business products include those under the Aspen Publishers, CCH, Kluwer Law International, Loislaw, Best Case, ftwilliam.com and MediRegs family of products.

CCH products have been a trusted resource since 1913, and are highly regarded resources for legal, securities, antitrust and trade regulation, government contracting, banking, pension, payroll, employment and labor, and healthcare reimbursement and compliance professionals.

Aspen Publishers products provide essential information to attorneys, business professionals and law students. Written by preeminent authorities, the product line offers analytical and practical information in a range of specialty practice areas from securities law and intellectual property to mergers and acquisitions and pension/benefits. Aspen's trusted legal education resources provide professors and students with high-quality, up-to-date and effective resources for successful instruction and study in all areas of the law.

Kluwer Law International products provide the global business community with reliable international legal information in English. Legal practitioners, corporate counsel and business executives around the world rely on Kluwer Law journals, looseleafs, books, and electronic products for comprehensive information in many areas of international legal practice.

Loislaw is a comprehensive online legal research product providing legal content to law firm practitioners of various specializations. Loislaw provides attorneys with the ability to quickly and efficiently find the necessary legal information they need, when and where they need it, by facilitating access to primary law as well as state-specific law, records, forms and treatises.

Best Case Solutions is the leading bankruptcy software product to the bankruptcy industry. It provides software and workflow tools to flawlessly streamline petition preparation and the electronic filing process, while timely incorporating ever-changing court requirements.

ftwilliam.com offers employee benefits professionals the highest quality plan documents (retirement, welfare and non-qualified) and government forms (5500/PBGC, 1099 and IRS) software at highly competitive prices.

MediRegs products provide integrated health care compliance content and software solutions for professionals in healthcare, higher education and life sciences, including professionals in accounting, law and consulting.

Wolters Kluwer Law & Business, a division of Wolters Kluwer, is headquartered in New York. Wolters Kluwer is a market-leading global information services company focused on professionals.

To Nancy, Liam, Oliver, and Simon

· SUMMARY OF CONTENTS ·

· PART I ·
PREFATORY MATTERS

· CHAPTER 1 ·
BUSINESS FORMS OVERVIEW

· CHAPTER 2 ·
AGENCY LAW

· CHAPTER 3 ·
CHOICE OF FORM CONSIDERATIONS

· PART II ·
UNINCORPORATED ENTITIES

· CHAPTER 4 ·
PARTNERSHIPS AND LIMITED LIABILITY PARTNERSHIPS

· CHAPTER 5 ·
LIMITED PARTNERSHIPS AND LIMITED LIABILITY LIMITED PARTNERSHIPS

· CONTENTS ·

PART II: UNINCORPORATED ENTITIES

CHAPTER 4: PARTNERSHIPS AND LIMITED LIABILITY PARTNERSHIPS

CHAPTER 5: LIMITED PARTNERSHIPS AND LIMITED LIABILITY LIMITED PARTNERSHIPS 153

CHAPTER 6: LIMITED LIABILITY COMPANIES 179

PART III: CORPORATIONS   221

CHAPTER 7: THE INCORPORATION PROCESS   223

CHAPTER 8: CORPORATE FINANCE   257

Contents

Contents

CHAPTER 12: MINORITY SHAREHOLDER PROTECTIONS 533

· PREFACE ·

I designed this book for those who want to teach business organizations (or corporations) from a transactional perspective. In that regard, the book's key attributes are as follows:

- *Content selected through a corporate lawyer lens*: I was a corporate lawyer[1] for many years before entering the academy, both at a law firm and in-house, and have drawn on this experience in selecting the book's content and topic depth. The book covers the business organizations law that every budding corporate lawyer should know.
- *Emphasis on real-world provisions*: The book is loaded with actual provisions from various documents corporate lawyers draft and review so that students get to see how the covered legal concepts are documented. The provisions also give students a sense of what corporate lawyers do in practice.
- *Teaching through exercises*: The book includes numerous exercises, all of which require students to apply what they've learned from the readings. This involves analyzing contractual language in light of statutory provisions and case law and applying this language in various situations encountered by a corporate lawyer. Many of the exercises involve reviewing a complete document, such as an LLC operating agreement, and answering questions regarding it. As a result, students get to see how various provisions excerpted or described in the book fit together in a single document. The exercises are designed to reinforce the covered material and help students develop the planning and problem-solving skills of a corporate lawyer as well as expose students to the documents and issues at the heart of a transactional practice.

---

1. For those of you unfamiliar with the label, a corporate lawyer (also called a deal or transactional lawyer) has a transactional practice as opposed to a litigation practice. In other words, a corporate lawyer works on deals, not cases. Examples of deals include acquiring or selling a business, selling stock to investors, and borrowing money from a bank. A corporate lawyer advises the client as to the best way to structure a deal, negotiates the legal terms of the deal, and drafts or reviews the contract(s) to document the deal. The phrase corporate lawyer is somewhat of a misnomer because his or her work is not limited to corporations. Deal or transactional lawyer is more accurate but less used.

- *More narrative, fewer cases*: I cover many legal concepts through concise explanatory text instead of judicial opinions. This enables me to keep the book a manageable size while providing more depth in areas central to a corporate law practice. It also frees up student preparation and class time for focusing on the exercises instead of case crunching. Each case is followed by a series of straightforward questions to get students to zero in on the key aspects of the case, leading to efficient class discussion. Additionally, unlike most casebooks, the book does not include "notes." Instead, I have integrated the note-type material into the text which enhances readability by making the book flow better.

A couple of points for students who are concerned about this book because they want to be litigators or otherwise have no interest in practicing corporate law:

1. The provisions and documents you will learn about are often at the center of business organization related disputes. Thus, familiarity with them, as well as the planning behind them, is invaluable to a business litigator.
2. The book covers most, if not all, of the business organizations topics tested on the bar exam. Thus, you should have no worries on that front.
3. The book will give you a good sense of what corporate practice is all about and may inspire you to become a corporate lawyer after all.

One final note, the provisions and documents included in the book are not meant to serve as model forms. In several instances I have deleted language from the provision or document on which the item is based to shorten or simplify it for pedagogical reasons. With that said, the items do generally serve as examples of good legal drafting as I spent some time cleaning up drafting errors.

William K. Sjostrom, Jr.

January 2013

· ACKNOWLEDGMENTS ·

I want to thank my research assistants Kyle Overs, Matthew Palfreyman, George Vescovo, and Cheyenne Walsh for their help on this book. Thanks also to Cathy Smith, Kimball Smith, Katie Sullivan, Andrew Vanell, and Omar Vasquez.

BUSINESS ORGANIZATIONS

· PART I ·

PREFATORY MATTERS

· CHAPTER ONE ·

BUSINESS FORMS OVERVIEW

People can choose from a variety of legal forms under which to operate a business. In this chapter, I introduce the fundamental characteristics of various legal forms. Below are separate sections for the six most common business forms (sole proprietorship, partnership, limited liability partnership, limited partnership, corporation, and limited liability company). Then follows a section providing a brief description of some less common or specialized business forms. The last section of the chapter covers some key foundational concepts. Many of the points made in this introductory chapter are elaborated on later in the book.

A. SOLE PROPRIETORSHIP

1. Definition

A sole proprietorship (also called a proprietorship) is a business owned by a single person (a sole proprietor) who has not filed the paperwork to operate the business in some other legal form. In other words, a single-owner business is a sole proprietorship by default, but the owner can opt into some other form by filing paperwork, typically with a secretary of state office.[1]

---

1. A secretary of state office is a governmental office that, among other things, processes, files, and maintains documents related to businesses formed or operating in the state (for example, articles of incorporation, the document you file to create a corporation). The office is headed by the secretary of state, an elected position of the executive branch. Many states have a specific section or division within the office to handle business filings. For example, California has a "Business Entities Section" and Delaware has a "Corporations Division." In some states, the equivalent of the secretary of state office is called something else. For example, in Florida the office is called the Department of State. In this book, I use the term "secretary of state" generically to refer to a state office that handles business filings, regardless of what the office is actually called.

The defining feature of a sole proprietorship is that there is no legal distinction between the owner and the business. This means that all of the assets of the business are owned by the individual in the same way that the individual owns his or her non-business assets (house, car, boat, etc.). For example, say Smith runs a plumbing business as a sole proprietorship. The pipe wrenches, soldering torch, drain cleaner, and other equipment he buys for the business are owned by him. They are not owned by the business because the business is a sole proprietorship and thus there is no legal distinction between Smith and the business.

2. Governing Law

By definition, a sole proprietorship has a single owner with complete management authority. Thus, there is no need to provide rules governing the rights and duties of owners and managers, which is the primary purpose of a business entity statute. Hence, unlike the other business forms covered in this book, there is no separate body of sole proprietorship law.

3. Management

As sole owner, a sole proprietor is entitled to make all business decisions. Thus, there are no formalities (meetings, votes, etc.) involved. Whatever the sole proprietor says goes. A sole proprietorship can have employees and can delegate decision-making authority to them if the sole proprietor so chooses.

4. Liability Exposure

Because the business and the sole proprietor are one and the same, a sole proprietor is personally liable for the obligations of the business in the same way and to the same extent that the sole proprietor is liable for his or her personal obligations (home mortgage loan, car loan, boat loan, tort judgment). For example, if Smith's plumbing business defaults on its office rental lease, the landlord can seek recovery from the business assets (plumbing equipment) and non-business assets (house, car, boat, etc.) of Smith. Smith will also be personally on the hook for any torts arising out of the business. For example, if a Smith employee negligently performs a plumbing job and as a result a client's home suffers water damage, the client can sue Smith personally.

5. Taxation

A sole proprietor is entitled to any income generated by the business and bears any losses. A sole proprietor reports net income or net loss from the business on his or her personal federal income tax return (usually by attaching Schedule C to his or her Form 1040). The business does not file a federal income tax return nor does it pay federal income tax.

6. Legal Name

Because the business and the sole proprietor are one and the same, the official legal name of a sole proprietorship is the sole proprietor's legal name. For example, the official legal name of Smith's plumbing business is "Robert B. Smith." Using an individual's name usually is not preferable from a marketing perspective. Thus, most sole proprietorships will use a more catchy name. For example, Smith may want to call his business AAA Plumbing so that it is listed first in the yellow pages. Operating a business under a name that differs from the business's legal name is referred to as using a "DBA" (stands for "doing business as"), assumed name, or fictitious name (depending on the state). The legal name of AAA Plumbing remains Robert B. Smith and that is the name Smith would use on legal documents relating to the business (for example, contracts and checks). However, to avoid confusion, it is common for a sole proprietorship to include a "DBA" designation in the signature line of a document. For example, the signature line of the office lease for Smith's plumbing business would read "Robert B. Smith, DBA AAA Plumbing."

B. PARTNERSHIP

1. Definition

A partnership (also called a general partnership to distinguish it from a limited partnership) is a for-profit business with two or more owners who have not filed the paperwork to operate the business in some other legal form. In other words, a multi-owner, for-profit business is a general partnership by default, but the owners can opt in to some other form. The owners of a partnership are referred to as partners.

2. Governing Law

A partnership is governed by the partnership statute of the state in which it is organized.[2] Each state has its own partnership statute based either on the

---

2. Usually, partners will agree upfront under which state's partnership laws they are forming the partnership and this is what I mean by the state of organization. However, as discussed in Chapter 4, sometimes people do not realize they are forming a partnership and therefore obviously do not know to agree on a state of formation. In this situation, the common law rule is that the partnership law of the jurisdiction of where the contract of partnership is made governs. Uniform Partnership Act (1997) (RUPA), however, includes a

Uniform Partnership Act (UPA) or the revised Uniform Partnership Act (RUPA), with the exception of the Louisiana statute. These statutes address the relationship among the partners and between the partners and the partnership.

The National Conference of Commissioners on Uniform State Laws (NCCUSL)[3] adopted the UPA in 1914, and each state other than Louisiana enacted it into law. The NCCUSL adopted RUPA in 1994 and amended it in 1996 and 1997. The convention is to reference the adoption or amendment year in the title to distinguish the various versions. Thus, the official name of the current version of RUPA is the Uniform Partnership Act (1997) (note that although this Act is often referred to as RUPA, the word "revised" is not in the official name).

A majority of states have repealed their UPA-based partnership statutes and replaced them with RUPA-based statutes. You should not assume that a state has adopted UPA or RUPA verbatim. States are free to make changes or not adopt NCCUSL amendments. Thus, in practice, when a partnership issue comes up you should consult the applicable state partnership statute and not the UPA or RUPA.

3. Partnership Agreement

Most partnerships have a written partnership agreement signed by each partner. A partnership agreement typically addresses, among other things, management structure, allocation of profits and losses among the partners, partner taxation, admission and withdrawal of partners, and dissolution. It is important to understand that partnership statutes are composed largely of default rules that a partnership can alter or opt out of through appropriate language in its partnership agreement.[4] In other words, a partnership agreement allows the partners to tailor the rules to their specific needs and preference. Tailoring will undoubtedly be necessary, because it is highly unlikely that all of the default rules will correspond with what the partners want. For example, the default rule under both the UPA and RUPA is that partners share profits equally.[5] Thus, each partner in a four-person partnership would be allocated to 25 percent of the partnership's profits, absent a provision in the partnership agreement allocating profits differently. This outcome may be the one desired by the four partners if they all contributed an equal amount of money to the partnership. If they contributed unequal amounts, sharing profits equally is probably not the

---

governing law provision that provides: "[T]he law of the jurisdiction in which a partnership has its chief executive office governs relations among the partners and between the partners and the partnership." RUPA §106(a).

3. NCCUSL is a nonprofit organization founded in 1892 composed of more than 300 uniform law commissioners, including state legislators, practicing attorneys, judges, and law professors from across the country. The NCCUSL drafts and proposes statutes in areas of law where it believes state uniformity is desirable. It has drafted more than 200 uniform laws, including the UPA, RUPA, the Uniform Limited Partnership Act, the Uniform Limited Liability Company Act, and the Uniform Commercial Code.

4. *See, e.g.,* RUPA §103.

5. *See* UPA §18(a); RUPA §401(b).

desired outcome. In such a case, the partners will provide for some other rule in the partnership agreement.

As a result, the starting point for providing advice to a partnership on partnership law issues is usually a review of the partnership agreement and not the applicable statute. The statute does, however, remain relevant because it contains some rules that partners cannot contract around.

While a partnership agreement does not have to be in writing, going with an oral agreement is inadvisable. A written agreement will lessen the likelihood of future disputes between the partners as to what was agreed. It will also allow the partners to tailor the rules in much greater depth than is realistic with an oral agreement.

4. Management

The management structure of a general partnership is typically specified in the partnership agreement. Common approaches include the following:

- The partners select a managing partner generally vested with the authority to make all decisions.
- The partners select a management committee composed of partners generally vested with the authority to make all decisions.
- The partners all get a say in managing the business, with each partner having an equal vote.
- The partners all have a say in managing the business with each partner having voting power in accord with the partner's capital contribution to the partnership.

If a partnership goes with the managing partner or committee structure, the partnership agreement will typically require a partnership vote on matters outside of the ordinary course of business (for example, admitting a new partner, expelling a partner, or selling the business). The partnership agreement will specify the required vote for approval (for example, majority, supermajority, or unanimous).

The default rule for partnership management, which would apply if the partnership agreement is silent on the issue, is that each partner has equal rights in the management of the partnership business.[6]

5. Liability Exposure

Each partner is personally liable for the obligations of the partnership.[7] Thus, for example, if a general partnership's business fails and it defaults on

---

6. *See* UPA §18(e); RUPA §401(f).

7. *See* UPA §15; RUPA §306(a). Under the UPA, partners' liability is joint and several for torts and joint but not several for contracts. Under RUPA, partners are jointly and severally liable for all partnership obligations.

a loan it took from a bank, the bank can sue any of the partners personally to collect on the loan. These partners will then have to pay the judgment out of their personal assets. Similarly, if one partner commits a tort while carrying out partnership business, the tort victim can sue and recover from any of the partners. Technically, the bank or tort victim would have to exhaust the partnership's assets before executing a judgment against a partner, although this is of little consequence if the partnership's business has failed. The bottom line is that a partner's personal assets are at risk of being reached to satisfy obligations of the business.

6. Taxation

A general partnership is normally taxed under Subchapter K of the Internal Revenue Code (IRC). Subchapter K (Sub-K) is comprised of provisions specifically designed for the taxation of a business organized as a partnership. Under Sub-K, a general partnership is not required to pay federal income tax. Instead, it allocates its profits and losses to its partners pursuant to the partnership agreement (or the applicable partnership statute if there is no agreement or provision allocating profits and losses). Each individual partner[8] then reports his or her share of the profits or losses on the partner's personal federal income tax return (usually by attaching Schedule E to his or her Form 1040) and pays any resulting tax liability. This sort of taxation is referred to as "pass-through" because the business's profits or losses are passed through to the owners' tax returns. The IRS requires a partnership to file an annual information return (Form 1065) specifying, among other things, the partnership's income and deductions and each partner's allocation of profits or losses.

Note that, as discussed in more detail in Chapter 3, it is possible for a general partnership to opt out of Subchapter K taxation and into Subchapter C or Subchapter S taxation.

Exercise 1.1

1. Ando setups a lemonade stand on the boulevard in front of his house to make money in the hope of buying a go-cart. Assuming Ando hasn't filed any paperwork with the secretary of state, in what legal form is his lemonade stand business operating? What is the official legal name of the business?

---

8. By individual, I mean a partner that is a natural person. Corporations, limited liability companies, and other entities can be partners in a general partnership. An entity partner would be allocated profits and losses just like an individual partner, but would not report them on Form 1040 because entities do not file Form 1040.

2. The next weekend, Ando decides to have his friend Bae join his lemonade stand business with the understanding that they will divide any profits between them. Assuming they haven't filed any paperwork with the secretary of state, in what legal form is their lemonade stand business operating?
3. Ando constructed the stand and provided the lemonade powder, paper cups, and ice. Bae provided a cash box she borrowed from her dad. Ando worked at the stand for six hours. Bae had to leave for a T-ball game so she only worked for three hours. The stand generated $38 in sales. Legally, how is the money to be divided between the two?
4. Assuming Bae insists on the full share to which she is legally entitled, what should Ando have done differently?

C. LIMITED LIABILITY PARTNERSHIP

1. Definition

A limited liability partnership (commonly called an LLP for short) is a for-profit business with two or more owners that has filed a "statement of qualification" with a state's secretary of state office.[9] A key feature of this form is that, unlike a general partnership, LLP partners are not personally liable for the obligations of the partnership. In other words, a limited liability partner's liability on partnership obligations is limited as opposed to unlimited.

2. Governing Law

States created the limited liability partnership form by adding LLP provisions to their general partnership statutes. An LLP is simply a general partnership that has elected LLP status under the applicable provisions of the general partnership statute. Hence, an LLP is governed by the general partnership statute of the state in which it is organized, namely, the state in which it filed its statement of qualification. Put differently, states do not have discrete limited liability partnership statutes.

3. Partnership Agreement

Most LLPs have a written partnership agreement signed by each partner. The agreement typically addresses the same matters covered in a general partnership's partnership agreement. Because LLPs are governed by the same statute as

---

9. *See, e.g.,* RUPA §1001(c).

general partnerships, what was said above about the partnership agreement of a general partnership applies equally to the partnership agreement of an LLP.

4. Management

Again, because limited liability partnerships are a type of general partnership, what was said above about the management structure of general partnerships applies equally to LLPs.

5. Liability Exposure

Partner liability exposure is the distinguishing feature of a limited liability partnership from a general partnership. Originally, states provided limited liability partnership partners with a "partial shield." Specifically, LLP provisions in states' general partnership statutes provided that an LLP partner was not liable for obligations of the LLP arising from negligence or misconduct committed by another partner, but remained liable for all other partnership obligations (e.g., contractual obligations).

As of 2012, all but two states (Louisiana and South Carolina) have amended the limitation of liability language in their general partnership statute LLP provisions to provide a full liability shield. Under a full shield, an LLP partner is not liable for any obligations of the partnership solely because he or she is a partner. A partner does, however, remain liable for his or her own negligence, wrongful acts, or misconduct.

6. Taxation

The Internal Revenue Code treats an LLP exactly the same as a general partnership. Hence, as you probably guessed, what was said about the federal taxation of general partnerships applies equally to LLPs.

Exercise 1.2

The following two provisions are from two different partnership statutes. These provisions address the liability of a partner for limited liability partnership obligations. Specifically, it's the language from the particular statute that specifies what I referred to as the "liability shield" of the LLP form. Does provision A provide for a full shield or a partial shield? What about provision B? Which provision would you prefer if you were a partner in an LLP? Which provision would you prefer if you were a contract creditor of an LLP? What about if you were a tort creditor of an LLP?

Provision A

A partner in a limited liability partnership is not liable, directly or indirectly, including by way of indemnification, contribution or otherwise, for a debt, obligation, or liability chargeable to the partnership arising from negligence, wrongful acts, or misconduct committed while the partnership is registered as a limited liability partnership and in the course of the partnership business by another partner, or an employee, agent, or representative of the limited liability partnership.

Provision B

An obligation of a partnership incurred while the partnership is a limited liability partnership, whether arising in contract, tort, or otherwise, is solely the obligation of the partnership. A partner is not personally liable, directly or indirectly, by way of contribution or otherwise, for such an obligation solely by reason of being or so acting as a partner.

D. LIMITED PARTNERSHIP

1. Definition

A limited partnership is a partnership with one or more general partners and one or more limited partners that has filed a "certificate of limited partnership" with a state's secretary of state office.[10] General partners in a limited partnership are the same as general partners in a general partnership—they have management rights but no liability shield. In other words, they are personally liable for the debts and obligations of the limited partnership. Limited partners have no management rights but do get a liability shield. In other words, they generally are not liable for the debts or obligations of the limited partnership.

2. Governing Law

A limited partnership is governed by the limited partnership statute of the state in which it is organized; namely, the state in which it filed its certificate of limited partnership. Each state has its own limited partnership statute based on some version of the Uniform Limited Partnership Act, with the exception of the Louisiana statute.

---

10. *See, e.g.,* Uniform Limited Partnership Act (2001) §201(a).

3. Limited Partnership Agreement

Most limited partnerships have a written limited partnership agreement signed by each partner. The agreement typically addresses the same matters covered in a general partnership's partnership agreement plus additional provisions addressing the rights and obligations of the limited partners. As is the case with general partnership statutes, limited partnership statutes are composed largely of default rules. Thus, a limited partnership agreement tailors the statutory rules to the specific needs and preferences of the partners. Hence, when advising a limited partnership on a limited partnership law issue, you should probably start by reviewing the limited partnership agreement.

4. Management

A distinguishing feature of the limited partnership form is that it is managed by the general partner(s) with the limited partners having no rights to participate in the control of the business. If there is more than one general partner, the limited partnership agreement will specify how management rights are allocated among the general partners. For example, the agreement could provide for a managing partner elected by the general partners or one of the other partnership management structures discussed in Section B.4 above.

5. Liability Exposure

Liability exposure is another distinguishing feature of the limited partnership form. As noted above, general partners of limited partnerships are personally liable for the debts and obligations of the limited partnership, while limited partners are not. If a business organized as a limited partnership fails, limited partners will lose whatever they paid into the partnership in exchange for their limited partnership interests, but their personal assets will not be on the hook for any unpaid obligations of the limited partnership, unlike the personal assets of the general partners. However, as discussed in Chapter 5, the limited partnership statute of many states recognizes an exception to the limited liability of a limited partner that participates in the control of the limited partnership's business.

6. Taxation

The Internal Revenue Code treats a limited partnership exactly the same as a general partnership. Thus, what was said about the federal taxation of general partnerships applies, for the most part, to limited partnerships.

E. CORPORATION

1. Definition

A corporation is a business that has filed "articles of incorporation" (also commonly called a "charter") with a state's secretary of state office. Key features of a corporation include limited liability for all of its owners (called shareholders or stockholders), and management authority vested in a board of directors elected by the shareholders.

2. Governing Law

A corporation is governed by the law of the state in which it is incorporated (organizing a corporation is referred to as "incorporation"), namely, the state in which it filed its charter. Each state has its own corporate law statute. The following 32 states have corporate law statutes based on some form of the Model Business Corporation Act (MBCA): Alabama, Alaska, Arizona, Arkansas, Connecticut, Florida, Georgia, Hawaii, Idaho, Indiana, Iowa, Kentucky, Maine, Massachusetts, Mississippi, Montana, Nebraska, New Hampshire, New Mexico, North Carolina, Oregon, Rhode Island, South Carolina, South Dakota, Tennessee, Utah, Vermont, Virginia, Washington, West Virginia, Wisconsin, and Wyoming. The remaining 17 states developed their own statutes, although many of them have adopted select provisions of the MBCA.

The MBCA was promulgated in 1950 by what is now the Section of Business Law of the American Bar Association (ABA). The Section has amended the MBCA on numerous occasions throughout the years and promulgated a complete revision in 1984 (sometimes referred to as the Revised Model Business Corporation Act or RMBCA). From time to time, the Section puts out a new edition of the MBCA that incorporates all amendments adopted since the last edition. The latest edition is the fourth, which the ABA published in 2007. As is the case with all business entity statutes, you should not assume that a state has adopted the MBCA verbatim. States are free to make changes or not adopt amendments. Thus, in practice, when a corporate law issue comes up with respect to a corporation incorporated in an MBCA state, you should consult the applicable state's corporate law statute and not the MBCA (although you may want to look at the official MBCA commentary on the particular provision at issue). For non-MBCA states, you should likewise consult the applicable state's corporate law statute.

Delaware is unquestionably the most important non-MBCA state, because it by far attracts the most incorporations by out-of-state businesses and is the state of incorporation for over 50 percent of U.S. publicly traded companies. Hence, we will study both the MBCA and Delaware's corporate law statute, the Delaware General Corporation Law (DGCL).

3. Governing Documents

A corporation is required to have a charter and bylaws. These documents are collectively referred to as a corporation's governing (or organic) documents. Other governing documents include shareholders' agreements and corporate governance principles. Various provisions of corporate law statutes provide default rules that a corporation can vary or opt out of by including appropriate language in one or more of its governing documents. These documents do not necessarily address or mention default rules that a corporation does not want to vary or mandatory rules that the statute does not permit a corporation to alter. Thus, it is critical to consult a corporation's organic documents *and* the applicable corporate law statute when advising a corporation on a corporate law issue.

A corporation's charter, among other things, specifies the corporation's name, the types of stock (e.g., common stock and preferred stock) it is authorized to issue, the rights and preference of any preferred stock, and an office and agent for the service of process in the state of incorporation. The initial charter of most corporations is pretty bare-bones and is oftentimes only one or two pages long (we look at charters in more detail in Chapter 7).

A corporation's bylaws specify rules regarding the governance of the corporation. These rules address, among other things, notice and quorum requirements for board and shareholder meetings, number and qualifications of directors, voting standards, proxy voting, appointment of officers, and stock certificates.

Shareholders' agreements are common for closely held corporations and may address a myriad of issues. Typical provisions include stock transfer restrictions, employment of shareholders, board representation, and buy-sell rights with respect to the corporation's shares.

Corporate governance principles are common for publicly held corporations. They typically address, among other things, director responsibilities, board committees, content and frequency of board and committee meetings, and director compensation.

4. Management

As mentioned above, corporate law statutes vest ultimate management authority in a corporation's board of directors.[11] The number of people on the board is set by the corporation, and its shareholders elect the directors. This structure is referred to as centralized management because the authority to manage the corporation is centralized in the board of directors as opposed to decentralized among the business's owners. Unlike partners, a corporation's shareholders have no statutory authority to manage the corporation.

---

11. *See, e.g.,* MBCA §8.01(b); DGCL §141(a).

Typically, a board of directors does not make day-to-day decisions with respect to a corporation's business. Instead, it appoints officers to run the business, subject to board oversight. In a corporation with a small number of shareholders (often called a closely held corporation), it is common for all shareholders to be on the board of directors and to serve as officers. Thus, they wear three hats simultaneously: shareholder, director, and officer. Such a structure obviously frays the concept of centralized management, but oftentimes makes sense for a closely held corporation. Conversely, at public corporations, the overwhelming majority of shareholders are neither on the board nor officers of the corporation.

Many states allow a corporation with fewer than a specified number of shareholders to opt out of having a board of directors and be managed by its owners, as is the default for partnerships.[12]

5. Liability Exposure

As mentioned above, the corporate form provides its shareholders with limited liability. Specifically, a shareholder is not personally liable for the debts or obligations of the corporation. For example, MBCA §6.22(b) provides, "Unless otherwise provided in the articles of incorporation, a shareholder of a corporation is not personally liable for the acts or debts of the corporation. . . ." If a corporation fails, a shareholder will likely lose what he or she paid for her shares, but the shareholder's personal assets are protected. All states provide a full liability shield regardless of whether a shareholder takes part in the corporation's management.

6. Taxation

For federal income tax purposes, a corporation is taxed under Subchapter C of the Internal Revenue Code unless it has elected to be taxed as a "small business corporation" under Subchapter S. A corporation that is taxed under Subchapter C is commonly referred to as a C-corporation, and one taxed under Subchapter S is commonly referred to as an S-corporation. Note that the "S" and "C" designations are only relevant to taxation. In other words, the same corporate laws apply regardless if a corporation is a C-corporation or an S-corporation.

A C-corporation is considered a separate taxpaying entity. Thus, it must file an annual income tax return (usually on Form 1120) reporting its income, deductions, and credits for the year and pay any resulting income tax at corporate income tax rates. If a C-corporation distributes money to its shareholders, the shareholders must include the distribution in their taxable incomes. Thus, a

---

12. *See, e.g.,* MBCA §7.32(a)(1).

corporation's profits are taxed when earned and then taxed again when distributed to shareholders, resulting in so-called double taxation.

Subchapter S taxation is similar to partnership taxation. Like a partnership, an S-corporation is not required to pay federal income tax. Instead, it passes through its profits and losses to its shareholders pursuant to their ownership interests. Each individual shareholder then reports his or her share of the profits or losses on the shareholder's personal federal income tax return (usually by attaching Schedule E to his or her Form 1040) and pays any resulting tax liability. The IRS does, however, require an S-corporation to file an annual information return (Form 1120S) specifying, among other things, the corporation's income and deductions and each shareholder's allocation of profits or losses.

F. LIMITED LIABILITY COMPANY

1. Definition

A limited liability company (commonly called an LLC for short) is a business that has filed "articles of organization" (or a similarly named document) with a state's secretary of state office. An LLC provides its owners (called members) with a full liability shield and pass-through taxation.

2. Governing Law

A limited liability company is governed by the law of the state in which it is organized; namely, the state in which it filed its articles of organization. Unlike partnership and corporate law statutes, there is a not a lot of uniformity among LLC statutes. Although the National Conference of Commissioners on Uniform State Laws promulgated a Uniform Limited Liability Company Act in 1995 and a revised version in 2006, neither version has been widely adopted.

3. Operating Agreement

Because LLC statutes are composed largely of default rules, most LLCs have a written agreement tailoring the rules to the specific needs and preferences of the LLC's members and managers. As a result, the starting point for providing advice to an LLC on LLC law issues is usually a review of this agreement (which is referred to under many states' LLC statutes as the LLC's "operating agreement," although Delaware calls it a "limited liability company agreement") and not the applicable statute. The statute does, however, remain relevant because it contains some rules that the parties cannot contract around. The typical operating agreement addresses, among other things, management structure, allocation of profits and losses among the members, member taxation, transfer of membership interests, and dissolution.

4. Management

An LLC can be either member-managed or manager-managed. Under most LLC statutes, the LLC will be member-managed unless its articles of organization state it is to be manager-managed. Member management is similar to partnership or decentralized management — the statute vests the members with the authority to manage the LLC. Manager management is similar to corporate or centralized management — the statute vests management authority in a board of managers elected by the LLC members.

5. Liability Exposure

As mentioned above, the LLC form provides its members with limited liability. Specifically, a member is not personally liable for the debts or obligations of the LLC. If an LLC fails, a member will likely lose what she paid for her membership interests, but the member's personal assets are protected. All states provide a full liability shield.

6. Taxation

The Internal Revenue Code treats a two-member LLC exactly the same as a general partnership. Thus, what was said about the federal taxation of general partnerships applies equally to two-member LLCs. A single-member LLC is typically taxed like a sole proprietorship (the IRS classifies a single-member LLC as a "disregarded entity"). Thus, what was said about the federal taxation of a sole proprietorship generally applies to a single-member LLC.

Questions

1. An LLC is often called a corporate/partnership hybrid. Why is that?
2. What is the difference between a member-managed LLC and a manager-managed LLC? Which type is the default under the ULLCA (2006) (make sure you note the statutory provision that supports your answer)? How does an LLC opt in to the other type of management?
3. What does LLC stand for?

G. BUSINESS FORM STATISTICS

Below is a table listing the number of businesses in the United States and business revenues by form for 2007 (based on data published by the IRS). For whatever reason, the IRS lumped together limited partnerships and LLPs in the data source used for the table. Following the table is an IRS chart that shows

Number of Businesses and Business Receipts by Form, 2007 Tax Year
(All figures are estimates based on samples.)

Form	Number	Percent of total	Business Receipts (in thousands)	Percent of total
C-corporations	1,878,956	5.9%	$18,243,198,903	62.1%
S-corporations	3,989,893	12.4%	5,974,197,102	20.3%
General partnerships	741,509	2.3%	570,783,438	1.9%
Limited partnerships & LLPs	536,145	1.7%	1,213,767,079	4.1%
LLCs	1,818,681	5.7%	2,062,483,341	7.0%
Nonfarm sole proprietorships	23,122,698	72.1%	1,324,403,080	4.5%
Totals	32,087,882	100.0%	$29,388,832,942	100.0%

Number of Partnerships by Type of Entity, Tax Years 2000-2008

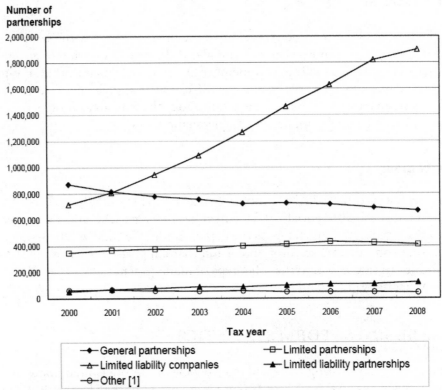

[1] Data for "other" partnerships include foreign partnerships, as well as partnerships which checked the "other" box, Form 1065, Schedule B, line 1, Type of Entity, or did not check a box.

the number of U.S. partnerships by type for 2000 through 2008 that does not lump together limited partnerships and LLPs.[13] The chart includes LLCs because the IRS classifies them as partnerships for tax purposes.

H. WHY ARE THERE SO MANY DIFFERENT FORMS?

Answering this question requires a brief history lesson on business forms. Originally, there were only three business forms in the United States: sole proprietorships, partnerships, and corporations. The limited partnership arrived on the scene in 1822 when New York enacted the first limited partnership statute. The form was established to address some of the shortcomings of the existing forms. Specifically, with the onset of the U.S. industrial revolution, business became more capital intensive, and thus many businesses needed to raise significant amounts of equity financing. By definition, a sole proprietorship could not raise equity financing without converting to a partnership. Yet a partnership was not a great vehicle for raising equity capital because many people were reluctant to invest given the partnership's lack of a liability shield. The corporate form offered a liability shield, but, at the time, incorporation required the business to obtain a charter from a state legislature. This involved lobbying, campaign contributions, etc. and was therefore expensive and time consuming. The limited partnership form made it much easier for a business to raise equity capital as compared to a partnership, because it could do so by selling limited partnership interests to investors that came with a liability shield. Additionally, forming a limited partnership simply required the business to make a short filing (at the time, usually with the county clerk's office) as opposed to getting legislative approval.

Pennsylvania adopted the first general incorporation statute in 1836 allowing a business to incorporate by making a filing instead of obtaining legislative approval. By 1890, all states had adopted similar corporate law statutes. This opened the door to the widespread use of the corporate form.

Congress added Sub-S taxation to the mix in 1958. Up until that time, most small businesses operated as sole proprietorships or partnerships to avoid corporate double taxation. The enactment of Sub-S allowed these businesses to incorporate and gain a liability shield, while still avoiding double taxation.

Wyoming adopted the first LLC statute in 1977. The motivation was to create an entity that provides its owners with a liability shield and could be taxed under Sub-K. LLCs did not immediately catch on because of uncertainty concerning taxation. In 1988, the IRS resolved the uncertainty when it stated definitively that it would treat Wyoming LLCs as partnerships for tax purposes.[14]

---

13. See IRS, Partnership Returns 2008, available at http://www.irs.gov/pub/irs-soi/08pareturnsnap.pdf.
14. See Rev. Rul. 88-76.

A number of states enacted LLC statutes in the wake of this ruling, and by 1996 every state had one.

Limited liability partnerships arrived on the scene in Texas in 1991. Their genesis was the savings and loan (S&L) crisis of the late 1980s. Specifically, banking regulators began bringing malpractice suits against Texas law firms that did work for failed S&Ls. Because damages sought in these suits often exceeded the assets and malpractice insurance of these firms, the firms' partners, many of whom had no involvement with S&L work, were very concerned about the potential personal liability they faced given that the firms were organized as partnerships. Hence, lawyers convinced the Texas legislature to amend the Texas partnership statute to limit the liability of partners with respect to the misconduct of their fellow partners. By 2000, all states had added LLP provisions to their partnership statutes.

As you can see, there are so many different forms because of a natural progression. We started with only three forms, but each of them had shortcomings that became more apparent as the world changed. Thus, states added limited partnerships to the mix and the IRS later adopted Sub-S taxation. This worked for a while, but then new shortcomings emerged, resulting in the LLC and LLP. States really have no motivation to eliminate older forms because it would create transitional issues, and an older form may still be the best form for a particular type of business. Hence, over time we end up with more and more forms.

I. OTHER FORMS

Below is a brief description of some less common or specialized business forms. For the most part, I do not elaborate on these forms elsewhere in the book, but you should at least have a general idea of what they are.

1. Limited Liability Limited Partnership

A limited liability limited partnership (commonly called an LLLP for short) is a limited partnership where the limited partners *and* the general partner(s) get a full liability shield. In some states, to become an LLLP, a limited partnership makes a filing with the secretary of state pursuant to LLLP provisions added to the state's limited partnership statute. In other states, it makes a filing pursuant to the LLP provisions of the state's general partnership statute.

2. Professional Corporation

A professional corporation (commonly called a PC for short) is a business incorporated under a professional corporation statute. States enacted these statutes to provide some level of liability protection to the owners of professional firms (law, medicine, accounting, etc.) whose professional rules prohibit them from incorporating under a regular corporate law statute. Typically, a professional corporation can be organized only for the purpose of rendering professional services, and all of its shareholders must be licensed to render those specific services. For example, all shareholders of a law firm that is organized as a professional corporation must be licensed attorneys. Use of PCs has significantly declined with the emergence of LLPs and PLLCs (discussed below). In some states, PCs are called professional service corporations or professional associations.

3. Professional Limited Liability Company

A professional limited liability company (commonly called a PLLC for short) is a business organized under a professional limited liability company statute or provision. As with a PC, typically a PLLC can be organized only for the purpose of rendering professional services, and all of its members must be licensed to render those specific services. Currently, 35 states have PLLC statutes or provisions.

4. Close Corporation

A close corporation (not to be confused with a closely held corporation) is a corporation that has elected to be governed by a state's close corporation statute or provisions. Typically, an eligible corporation makes the election by including in its charter a statement along the lines of "this corporation is a statutory close corporation." These statutes and provisions vary widely from state to state, but eligibility is usually based on having no more than a specified number of shareholders (such as 25). Close corporations statutes are more flexible than regular corporate statutes, and address problems common to corporations with a small number of shareholders. Historically, few eligible corporations have elected close corporation treatment.

5. Series Limited Liability Company

A series LLC is an LLC that segregates its business into separate "series." For example, the owner of five apartment buildings could form a series LLC and then put each of the five buildings in a separate series. The advantage of this structure is that the assets of a particular series are insulated from claims against a different series. For example, say faulty wiring at one of the five apartment buildings caused a fire that injured a number of tenants. There is a good chance that the tenants will only be able to sue the series that holds the particular building (let's call it "Series 1") and not the series LLC generally. Further, they will only be able to recover against the assets of Series 1 and not against the assets of any other series or the series LLC generally. Even if their judgment exceeds the assets of Series 1, they will not be able to seize the other four apartment buildings because these buildings are in separate series.

As of 2012, eight states (Delaware, Illinois, Iowa, Nevada, Oklahoma, Tennessee, Texas, and Utah) have amended their LLC statutes to provide for series LLCs. To date, the form has not been widely used because of uncertainty regarding taxation and treatment by non-series LLC states.

6. Nonprofit Corporation

A nonprofit corporation is a corporation formed under a state's nonprofit corporation statute. These statutes generally limit the form to companies organized for the public benefit, religious purposes, or the mutual benefit of its members. Nonprofit corporations typically do not issue stock and are usually exempt from federal income taxation.

7. Low-Profit Limited Liability Company

A low-profit limited liability company (commonly called an L3C for short) is an LLC whose primary purpose is not to earn a profit but to pursue a socially beneficial objective. The form was created in Vermont in 2008 by adding L3C provisions to the Vermont LLC statute. As of 2012, eight states (Illinois, Louisiana, Maine, Michigan, North Carolina, Utah, Vermont, and Wyoming) provide for the form.

8. Benefit Corporation

A benefit corporation (B corp for short) is a corporation incorporated in a state with a benefit corporation statute that elects to be a benefit corporation by including a provision to that effect in its charter. Additionally, a benefit corporation must have a purpose of creating "general public benefit." A general public benefit is "[a] material positive impact on society and the environment, taken as a whole, assessed against a third-party standard, for the business and operations of a benefit corporation."[15] As of 2012, eleven states have adopted such statutes (California, Hawaii, Louisiana, Maryland, Massachusett, New Jersey, New York, Pennsylvania, South Carolina, Vermont, and Virginia). These statutes explicitly require a benefit corporation's directors in making a decision to consider not only the best interests of its shareholders, but those of its employees, customers, community and society, and the local and global environment, among other things.

---

15. Mod. Ben. Corp. Leg. §102(a).

9. Business Trust

A business trust is a business organized under a state's business trust statute or trust law. Under this structure, the business is managed by trustees pursuant to a trust agreement or declaration of trust for the benefit of the business's owners (called beneficiaries). Many investment companies such as mutual funds are organized as business trusts.

10. Joint Venture

A joint venture is really more of a business concept than a legal concept. It is when two or more businesses or individuals combine resources to pursue a discrete business opportunity or venture. For example, Sony Corporation and Ericsson, a Swedish telecommunications company, currently have a joint venture for making mobile phones. Sony brings consumer electronics expertise and Ericsson provides telecommunications technology know-how. It is common for the parties to form a joint venture entity, typically an LLC or corporation, to house the joint business. Otherwise, the relationship will likely fall under the definition of a general partnership, triggering application of a general partnership statute.

J. SOME KEY CONCEPTS

1. Internal Affairs Doctrine

As mentioned above, each state has its own statutes for the various business entities, and the statute that applies to a particular business entity is the statute of the state in which the business is organized (or incorporated). This is known as the internal affairs doctrine, a doctrine that is technically a choice of law rule. It is so named because business entity statutes generally address the internal governance of the business entity, that is, the rights and duties of owners and managers.

A consequence of the internal affairs doctrine is that a business entity can choose which state's statute it wants to be governed by. This is because a business can organize as an entity in the state of its choosing even if it does not do business in the state. For example, say two individuals have decided to start a new internet company that will be based in Tucson, Arizona. They have decided to go with the LLC form, but for several reasons prefer Nevada's LLC statute over Arizona's. All they need to do is organize their LLC under the Nevada LLC statute, and it will then be governed by that statute and not the Arizona statute (or, for that matter, the LLC statute of any other state).

In *Vantage Point Partners v. Examen, Inc.*,[16] the Delaware Supreme Court explained the policy behind the internal affairs doctrine, at least in the corporate context, as follows:

> The internal affairs doctrine developed on the premise that, in order to prevent corporations from being subjected to inconsistent legal standards, the authority to regulate a corporation's internal affairs should not rest with multiple jurisdictions. It is now well established that only the law of the state of incorporation governs and determines issues relating to a corporation's internal affairs. By providing certainty and predictability, the internal affairs doctrine protects the justified expectations of the parties with interests in the corporation.
>
> The internal affairs doctrine applies to those matters that pertain to the relationships among or between the corporation and its officers, directors, and shareholders. The Restatement (Second) of Conflict of Laws §301 provides: "application of the local law of the state of incorporation will usually be supported by those choice-of-law factors favoring the need of the interstate and international systems, certainty, predictability and uniformity of result, protection of the justified expectations of the parties and ease in the application of the law to be applied." [17] Accordingly, the conflicts practice of both state and federal courts has consistently been to apply the law of the state of incorporation to "the entire gamut of internal corporate affairs."[18]

Questions

1. XYZ, Inc. is incorporated in Ohio, headquartered in Kentucky, and does 90 percent of its business in Indiana. An XYZ, Inc. shareholder brings a suit against the XYZ, Inc. board of directors for breach of fiduciary duty stemming from a decision made by the board at a board meeting held in Hawaii. The corporate breach of fiduciary duty claim will be governed by the law of which jurisdiction?
2. An XYZ, Inc. employee negligently runs down a client with her car when arriving at a business meeting in Indiana. As a result, the client brings a tort suit against XYZ, Inc. Assuming the same facts as in Question 1, which jurisdiction's tort law applies?

2. Default vs. Mandatory Rules

A default rule is one that can be altered by agreement between the parties. Thus, it applies only if the parties have not otherwise agreed to a different rule.

---

16. 871 A.2d 1109 (Del. 2005).

17. Restatement (Second) of Conflict of Laws §301 (1971). *See* Restatement (Second) of Conflict of Laws §303 cmt. d (stressing importance of uniform treatment of shareholders).

18. *McDermott Inc. v. Lewis*, 531 A.2d at 216 (quoting John Kozyris, *Corporate Wars and Choice of Law,* 1985 Duke L.J. 1, 98 (1985)). The internal affairs doctrine does not apply where the rights of third parties external to the corporation are at issue, for example, contracts and torts. *Id. See also Rogers v. Guaranty Trust Co. of N.Y.,* 288 U.S. 123, 130-31, 53 S. Ct. 295, 77 L. Ed. 652 (1933).

A mandatory rule is one that applies regardless of a contrary agreement by the parties. In other words, the parties cannot contract around a mandatory rule; an agreement that purports to do so has no effect.

As alluded to above, business entity statutes are composed largely of default rules. For example, RUPA §103(a) essentially provides that all RUPA rules are default rules except those rules listed under RUPA §103(b). There is no similar blanket-type provision under corporate law statutes. Instead, the statutory language of an individual rule will dictate whether it is a default rule. For example, MBCA §8.08(a) provides: "The shareholders may remove one or more directors with or without cause *unless the articles of incorporation provide that directors may be removed only for cause*" (emphasis added). Hence, the default rule is that shareholders can remove directors without cause, but the corporation and its shareholders can agree to a for-cause requirement by including language to that effect in the corporation's charter. The clause in italics is what signifies that this is a default rule. If the clause was not there, the rule would be mandatory because the provision does not specify a way for the rule to be altered nor does some other provision of the MBCA. In other words, unless a corporate law statutory provision specifies that a rule can be altered, the rule is a mandatory rule.

When it comes to corporate law default rules, you need to pay attention to the means by which the rule can be overridden. Specifically, some rules can only be overridden by a provision in the corporation's charter (MBCA §8.08(a) provides an example of this), while others can be overridden by a provision in a corporation's charter or bylaws and still others in a corporation's bylaws or by resolution of the board of directors. For example, MBCA §8.02 provides, "A director need not be a resident of this state or a shareholder of the corporation *unless the articles of incorporation or bylaws so prescribe*" (emphasis added). Thus, a corporation can override this rule by, for example, including a provision either in its articles or bylaws along the lines of the following: "Each director must be a resident of the state of _____ and a shareholder of the corporation." As we will discuss, there are typically more formalities associated with amending a charter as compared to amending bylaws and therefore you should think of default rules that can only be altered in corporation's charter as more "sticky" than those that can be altered in a corporation's bylaws or by some other means.

The basic idea behind default rules is to establish a set of rules that work well for most businesses. Parties for whom all the rules are a good fit can take them off the rack without having to bargain over them. Parties for whom not all the rules work can alter some of the rules. Mandatory rules reflect a judgment by the drafters that for public policy reasons parties should not be able to contract around a rule even if they think it would be more efficient for them to do so. Note, however, that in the business entity context, parties may be able to get around a mandatory rule by choosing a different organizational form. In other words, mandatory rules differ across forms.

Exercise 1.3

1. Identify two RUPA provisions that specify mandatory rules.
2. Identify two MBCA provisions that specify default rules. Also, state how a corporation would opt out of each of these rules.

---

3. Majority vs. Minority Owner Perspective

Whether altering a particular default rule makes sense often depends on whose perspective we look at it from. For example, under default corporate law rules, a person that owns a majority of a corporation's voting shares (a majority shareholder) has complete control over the corporation. This is because although ultimate decision-making authority resides in the board of directors and not the shareholders, under default rules a majority shareholder can elect, and at any time remove, the entire board of directors. Thus, if a majority shareholder is unhappy with a board decision, he or she can replace the board with people who are willing to do the majority shareholder's bidding or even reduce the size of the board to one and elect himself or herself as the sole director. Because of this level of control, a majority shareholder does not have to alter the default rules to include protections like preemptive rights[19] or veto power over specified corporate actions. For a majority shareholder, these rights are implicit in complete control.

Conversely, unless a minority shareholder insists on alterations to the default rules, for example, as a condition to buying shares in a corporation, he or she will have zero say on how the corporation is run. In other words, he or she will not be entitled to representation on the board of directors, to buy additional shares in the corporation, to cause the corporation to distribute profits to its owners, etc. Thus, changes to default rules are often driven by minority shareholders in an effort to have some say in how the corporation is run.

The same dynamic is often present in partnerships and LLCs as well, even though the default rules under these statutes generally are not as majority owner-favorable as is the case with corporations. This is because it is normally the person who will be the majority owner who takes the lead in forming the entity and thus has the partnership or operating agreement drafted so that he or she has the same sort of control as a majority owner of a corporation.

The bottom line is that whether a particular change to a default rule is in your client's best interest usually depends on whether your client is a majority or minority owner of the entity.

---

19. Preemptive rights give an existing shareholder the opportunity to purchase a proportionate part of a new issue of shares before it is offered to other persons. Preemptive rights are covered in Chapter 12.

4. Public vs. Private Companies

A public company is one whose shares (or other ownership interests) are traded on a public secondary market such as the New York Stock Exchange (NYSE) or the NASDAQ Stock Market.[20] In other words, its shares are publicly traded. A private company is one whose shares are not publicly traded.

The overwhelming majority of public companies are organized as corporations, although there are some publicly traded limited partnerships and LLCs. Private companies come in all forms. Public companies are generally much larger than private companies in terms of assets, revenues generated, and number of employees. There are, however, some very large private companies, including Cargill, Incorporated (estimated 2010 revenues of $109.8 billion and 130,500 employees) and Koch Industries, Inc. (estimated 2010 of $100 billion and 70,000 employees).

Private companies are sometimes referred to as "closely held" because they often have a small number of owners. Conversely, a public company will have hundreds, thousands, or even hundreds of thousands of owners. In many public companies, this results in a so-called separation of ownership and control. Specifically, the company is owned by numerous and dispersed shareholders, but controlled by an essentially self-perpetuating board of directors and its handpicked senior executives.

Note that the same corporate law statute applies to a corporation regardless if it is public or private. As discussed in Chapter 13, a public company is also subject to additional regulation under federal securities laws, in particular the Securities Exchange Act of 1934, and the rules of the exchange (if any) on which its shares are traded.

A company starts out as private and then may later choose to go public. A company generally goes public by hiring an investment banking firm to market and sell its common stock to the public in an initial public offering, or IPO. A primary advantage of going public is that it leads to a secondary trading in the company's stock on a public market such as the NYSE or NASDAQ, also known as liquidity. This trading allows company founders, early-stage investors, employees, etc., to cash out some or all of their shareholdings in the company by selling shares into the public market. Conversely, by definition, there generally is no active secondary trading market for the shares of a private company, and thus private company shares are considered illiquid, or difficult to resell.

Question

A Corp. and B Corp. are identical in all respects except that A Corp. is public and B Corp. is private. You are offered the choice of a 1 percent stake in either company. Which stake would you choose and why?

---

20. *See* MBCA §1.40(18A).

· CHAPTER TWO ·

AGENCY LAW

Every corporate lawyer needs to know at least a little bit about agency law, because agency law dictates when a business will be bound by a contract with a third party that someone entered into on the business's behalf. This contracting happens all the time at virtually every business, regardless of size or form — an assistant places an order for office supplies, a manager hires a new employee, a CEO signs a merger agreement, etc.

More formally, agency law "encompasses the legal consequences of consensual relationships in which one person (the 'principal') manifests assent that another person (the 'agent') shall, subject to the principal's right of control, have power to affect the principal's legal relations through the agent's acts and on the principal's behalf."[1]

With this formal definition in mind, let's look at an example. Say Monet is the sole proprietor of a house-painting business and has set up an account with a paint store to buy paint on credit. Monet has a number of painting crews, so it wouldn't be practical for him to handle all the purchases of paint. Hence, Monet has delegated to each crew chief the task of buying paint at the paint store and charging it to Monet's account. This makes a lot of sense for Monet, because it prevents him from having to waste his valuable time buying paint.

But should the paint store be comfortable letting others charge to Monet's account? That is where the law of agency comes in. As we shall see, the paint store is generally protected, even if Monet later claims a purchase of paint was made improperly by a crew chief. And, of course, the law should encourage (or not discourage) the paint store to allow these types of arrangements, because otherwise we are looking at a lot of inefficiencies (in this case, the waste of Monet's valuable time).

---

1. RESTATEMENT (THIRD) OF AGENCY Intro. (2006).

This chapter covers aspects of agency law most relevant to a corporate attorney. Unlike business entity law, which is heavily statutory-based, agency law consists largely of state common law. In discussing this common law below, I draw on the Restatement (Third) of Agency, given that judges routinely apply the Restatement in this area.

A. CREATION OF AGENCY RELATIONSHIP

An agency relationship is created when an agent-to-be and a principal-to-be consent to their association with each other. Specifically, the relationship arises when (1) a principal "manifests assent" to the agent that (2) "the agent shall act on the principal's behalf and subject to the principal's control," and (3) "the agent manifests assent or otherwise consents to so act."[2]

In this context, a "manifestation" is written or spoken words or other conduct. Thus, when Monet tells a crew chief job candidate at the end of an interview that "I'd like to hire you to serve as crew chief with the responsibilities I just discussed," and the candidate nods her head in agreement, we have the requisite manifestations—spoken words by Monet, the principal-to-be, and conduct by the candidate, the agent-to-be—to create an agency relationship. This exchange is an example of the most common way in which an agency relationship is created in the business organizations context: the business hires a person as an employee.

All employees are agents of their employers because employment is a consensual relationship where the employee (agent) is subject to the control of the employer (principal). Some employees may have very little authority to bind their employers, but that is a separate issue. As a corollary, not all individuals hired by a business are employees. Oftentimes a business will hire someone as an "independent contractor" instead of an employee, because doing so means that numerous employment laws do not apply to the relationship, saving the business money. The person will nonetheless be an agent if the relationship meets the above-specified three elements of agency, as exemplified by the next case. The Restatement (Third) of Agency refers to such people as "nonemployee agents."[3]

(handwritten margin note: Actual Auth)

Frawley v. Nickolich
41 S.W.3d 420 (Ark. App. 2001)

BAKER, Judge.

This is an administrative appeal from the Arkansas Professional Bail Bond Company and Professional Bail Bondsman Licensing Board. The appellant,

---

2. *Id.* §1.01.
3. *Id.* §1.01, cmt. c.

Elizabeth Frawley, is a licensed bail bondsman who was employed by appellant, J & J Bonding, Inc., on December 16, 1997. Appellant Frawley was notified by the Board that she solicited business or advertised for business in or about a place where prisoners were confined in violation of Ark. Code Ann. section 17-19-105(2). Appellant J & J Bonding, Inc. was notified that it was responsible for Ms. Frawley's actions pursuant to Ark. Code Ann. section 17-19-210(b) because she was acting within the scope of her authority as a J & J bondsman. The statutory prohibition against solicitation reads as follows:

> No professional bail bondsman or professional bail bond company, nor court, nor law enforcement officer nor any individual working on behalf of a professional bail bondsman or professional bail bond company shall: . . . (2) Solicit business or advertise for business in or about any place where prisoners are confined or in or about any court. . . .

Ark. Code Ann. §17-19-105(2) (Supp. 1999).

This prohibition was amended in 1997 with an effective date of July 1, 1997. The amendment inserted the language "nor any individual working on behalf of a professional bail bondsman or professional bail bond company" in the introductory language. *Id.* (commentary).

The charges in this case were based upon allegations that Dixie Hinerman, a friend of Ms. Frawley's, accompanied Ms. Frawley to the Pulaski County jail and distributed business cards of Ms. Frawley's to a trusty and others at the facility. A hearing was held before the Board on March 13, 1998, and the Board found appellants guilty of the charges. The Board suspended Ms. Frawley's license for ninety days and imposed a fine of $2,500 against J & J Bonding. Appellants timely appealed the Board's decision and argued to the circuit court, and again in this appeal, that there was no evidence of an agency relationship between Ms. Hinerman and Ms. Frawley. They urge that without evidence of an agency relationship, Ms. Hinerman's actions on December 16, 1997, should not have been imputed to Ms. Frawley. . . .

The following facts were largely undisputed. On December 16, 1997, Ms. Hinerman accompanied Ms. Frawley to the Pulaski County jail. Ms. Frawley left her cellular phone with Ms. Hinerman outside the facility and entered the jail on a bond matter. While Ms. Frawley was inside the facility, Ms. Hinerman gave several of Ms. Frawley's business cards to an inmate with trusty status and told him to take the cards into the jail and pass them out to anyone who needed them. She also passed out cards to other individuals. At least one of these cards had Ms. Hinerman's name handwritten with "Sec." to indicate secretary. All of the cards had both Ms. Frawley's and J & J Bonding's names imprinted. The cards also listed Ms. Frawley's cellular phone number. Although not paid by Ms. Frawley, Ms. Hinerman helped Ms. Frawley by driving around with her and answering her cellular phone. When answering the telephone for Ms. Frawley, Ms. Hinerman would gather the caller's name, phone number, and information about the person for whom a bond was sought. She denied giving specific information about fees for obtaining a bond and claimed she only answered a few phone calls. Both Ms. Frawley and J & J Bonding would receive the financial benefit of any bail bond business solicited by Ms. Hinerman through the distribution of cards on December 16, 1997, in or about the premises of the Pulaski County jail. Ms. Frawley denied knowing that Ms. Hinerman was distributing the cards at the time of distribution, but said she was upset with Ms. Hinerman when she found out and told her never to do it again.

The Arkansas Supreme Court adopted the definition of agency contained in the Second Restatement of the Law of Agency, §1, comment a, which provides that the relation of agency is created as the result of conduct by two parties manifesting that one of them is willing for the other to act for him subject to his control, and that the other consents so to act. The principal must in some manner indicate that the agent is to act for him, and the agent must act or agree to act on the principal's behalf and subject to his control. *Evans v. White*, 284 Ark. 376, 682 S.W.2d 733 (1985) (citing *Crouch v. Twin City Transit*, 245 Ark. 778, 434 S.W.2d 816 (1968)). The two essential elements of the definition are authorization and right to control. *Id.*

There is substantial evidence from which the Board could conclude that Ms. Hinerman was acting on behalf of Ms. Frawley when distributing her business cards at the jail. Ms. Frawley left Ms. Hinerman with access to her business cards and cellular phone and gave instructions to obtain certain information from the callers regarding their bonding needs. The cards had Ms. Frawley's cellular phone number on them. Ms. Frawley left Ms. Hinerman outside the detention facility while she was inside preparing a bond on behalf of J & J Bonding. Appellants fail to demonstrate how a fair-minded person could not reach the conclusion that Ms. Frawley in some manner indicated that Ms. Hinerman was to act for her. Neither have appellants demonstrated that a fair-minded person could not reach the conclusion that Ms. Hinerman acted on appellants' behalf. It is logical to conclude that someone who received a business card could contact Ms. Frawley and J & J Bonding for a bond and therefore the distribution of the card was on appellants' behalf. Even if no one contacted appellants as a result of the distribution, Ms. Hinerman's action were still on behalf of appellants in that she was providing individuals with the name and number of a bail bondsman. Similarly, Ms. Frawley's instruction to Ms. Hinerman to never pass out the cards again at a jail supports the conclusion that Ms. Hinerman was subject to appellants' control in some way, whether or not appellants had prior knowledge of this specific distribution of cards by Ms. Hinerman. Therefore, Ms. Frawley is accountable for Ms. Hinerman's actions. In addition, substantial evidence supports the finding that Ms. Frawley was acting within the scope of her employment as a J & J bondsman, and J & J was properly held accountable pursuant to statute. . . .

Accordingly, we affirm.

Questions

1. Who is the principal and who is the agent?
2. Why does the case turn on the existence of an agency relationship?
3. What facts does the court point to in finding an agency relationship?
4. Why was J & J Bonding fined?
5. What could Frawley have done differently to avoid liability? What about J & J Bonding?

Parties to a business relationship often do not want to create an agency relationship, because they do not want the legal consequences that flow from it (like being charged with violating a non-solicitation statute) imposed on the relationship. Thus, it is fairly common for a contract between two businesses to include a clause along the lines of the following:

Relationship. It is understood that neither party is an agent, employee, or servant of the other for any purpose whatsoever. Buyer and Seller shall each conduct its business in its own name and shall each be solely responsible for its own acts, conduct, and expenses and the acts, conduct, and expenses of its employees and agents. Nothing in this Agreement shall create a partnership or joint venture between Buyer and Seller.

Note, however, that how the parties characterize a relationship, although relevant, is not controlling. As the Restatement (Third) explains:

> The parties' agreement may negatively characterize the relationship as not one of agency, or as one not intended by the parties to create a relationship of agency or employment. Although such statements are relevant to determining whether the parties consent to a relationship of agency, their presence in an agreement is not determinative and does not preclude the relevance of other indicia of consent.[4]

Questions

1. Is the relationship between a professor and the students in his or her business organizations class an agency relationship?
2. What about between a professor and a student he or she has hired as a research assistant?

---

4. *Id.* §1.02, cmt. b.

B. WHEN IS A PRINCIPAL BOUND TO A CONTRACT?

The basic agency law rule is that a principal is bound to a contract made on the principal's behalf by an agent if the agent acted with actual or apparent authority.[5]

1. Actual Authority

According to the Restatement (Third) of Agency, "[a]n agent acts with actual authority when, at the time of taking action that has legal consequences for the principal, the agent reasonably believes, in accordance with the principal's manifestations to the agent, that the principal wishes the agent so to act."[6] Continuing with our painting business example, assume Monet says to crew chief Arroyo that "I authorize you to charge paint to my account at the paint store." This statement would be a manifestation by Monet (the principal) to Arroyo (an agent) that Monet wants Arroyo to charge paint on Monet's behalf. Thus, Arroyo has actual authority to do so, and therefore when she charges paint for a job to Monet's account, Monet is bound to the contract (paint in exchange for a promise to pay). Note that the focus is on communication by the principal to the agent, and the agent's reasonable interpretation of that communication.

Incidentally, whether Arroyo is bound on the contract depends on whether the paint store has actual or constructive knowledge that Arroyo is acting for a principal and that Monet is the principal. If the paint store so knows, Arroyo is not bound on the contract.[7] If the paint store does not know Arroyo is acting for a principal or even if the paint store knows she is but does not know the principal's identity, Arroyo is bound on the contract.[8]

Actual authority can be express or implied. The above scenario provides an example of express actual authority. Monet expressly told Arroyo that she had authority to buy paint. Implied actual authority includes authority to do acts necessary or incidental to achieve the principal's express objective. For example, a crew chief that is expressly authorized by Monet to "run the business while I'm on vacation" likely has implied actual authority to sign contracts for new jobs on behalf of Monet, as doing so would be incidental to running the business. Implied actual authority can also arise from manifestations by the principal that reasonably lead the agent to believe he or she has authority to take a particular action. For example, say Arroyo from above has repeatedly charged paint brushes, roller heads, and masking tape to Monet's account at the paint store. Arroyo mentions to Monet that she is doing this, and Monet just shrugs

---

5. Restatement (Third) of Agency §6.01.
6. *Id.* §2.01.
7. *Id.* §6.01.
8. *Id.* §§6.02 & 6.03.

his shoulders. Monet's manifestation (the shoulder shrug) likely gives rise to implied actual authority for Arroyo to charge these items.

2. Apparent Authority

Per the Restatement (Third) of Agency, "[a]pparent authority is the power held by an agent or other actor to affect a principal's legal relations with third parties when a third party reasonably believes the actor has authority to act on behalf of the principal and that belief is traceable to the principal's manifestations."[9] Hence, continuing our painting business example, say Monet calls the paint store and tells the manager that "I have authorized Arroyo to buy paint on my account." This statement would be a manifestation by Monet (the principal) to the paint store (a third party) that Arroyo has authority to charge paint on Monet's account. The focus here is on communication by the principal and the reasonable interpretation of this communication by the third party. Note that apparent authority and actual authority often coincide. In our example, this would happen if Monet tells Arroyo she is authorized, and he tells the paint store Arroyo is authorized.

The existence of apparent authority is clear-cut in the above example given Monet's direct and unambiguous communication with the paint store, but direct and unambiguous communication is not required for finding apparent authority, as demonstrated by the next case.

H.H. Taylor, C.A. v. Ramsay-Gerding Construction Co.
196 P.3d 532 (Or. 2008)

BALMER, J.

This breach of warranty action requires us to determine when an agent has apparent authority to bind a principal under Oregon law. Apparent authority arises when actions of a principal cause a third party reasonably to believe that an agent has authority to act for the principal on some particular matter. While constructing a hotel, plaintiffs became concerned about the possibility that their new stucco system might rust, and their contractor organized a meeting with the stucco installer and an agent of the stucco manufacturer, among others. At that meeting, the agent made a number of representations to plaintiffs, including that they had a five-year warranty, which he later confirmed in writing. A jury found that the agent had apparent authority to provide the warranty and that the principal had breached that warranty, and the trial court entered judgment for plaintiffs. The Court of Appeals reversed, holding that the agent

---

9. *Id.* §2.03.

did not have apparent authority to bind the principal. For the reasons set out below, we reverse and remand to the Court of Appeals.

We state the facts in the light most favorable to plaintiffs, because they prevailed before the jury. In 1998, plaintiffs, H.H. (Todd) Taylor and his wife, C.A. Taylor, began construction of a hotel in Lincoln City. They hired Ramsay-Gerding Construction Company as their general contractor. In turn, Ramsay-Gerding hired a subcontractor to install stucco plaster exterior siding and accompanying accessories. Pursuant to the stucco installer's recommendation, Ramsay-Gerding proposed using a stucco system called "SonoWall," manufactured by ChemRex, Inc., and plaintiffs approved that proposal.

During construction, plaintiff Todd Taylor grew concerned about possible rusting of the galvanized fittings that were included in the stucco system. In September 1998, Ramsay-Gerding halted construction until the problem could be solved and organized a meeting to discuss the situation. Among those present at the meeting were Taylor, a representative of Ramsay-Gerding, and a representative of the stucco installer. Additionally, Ramsay-Gerding's representative, pursuant to communications with the stucco installer, brought Mike McDonald, ChemRex's territory manager for Oregon, to the meeting as a ChemRex "representative." In response to Taylor's concerns, McDonald asserted that the SonoWall system was "bullet-proof" against rust but noted that a corrosion inhibitor would provide further protection. When Taylor was still unconvinced, McDonald stated, "Mr. Taylor, did you know you're getting a five-year warranty?" By the end of that meeting, Taylor agreed to go forward, with the addition of the corrosion inhibitor.

In July 1999, after construction had been completed, but before all construction funds had been disbursed, McDonald sent a letter to the stucco installer on ChemRex letterhead. The letter stated, in part, "This letter is to confirm that [ChemRex] will warrantee the Sonowall stucco system for five years covering the material and labor on this project starting in March of 1999," and was signed "Mike McDonald, Territory Manager OR." The stucco installer eventually sent that letter to Ramsay-Gerding, who sent it to plaintiffs, and McDonald stated at trial that he had intended the warranty to extend to plaintiffs.

At some point in late 1999, an employee of plaintiffs' company noticed discoloration on the exterior walls of the hotel. By the spring of 2000, the employee had realized that the discoloration was rust and contacted Taylor. In the summer of 2000, Taylor informed Ramsay-Gerding of the problem, and representatives from ChemRex and the stucco installer came to the hotel to examine the stucco system. However, no one ever fixed the problem.

In 2001, plaintiffs initiated this action against Ramsay-Gerding for breach of the construction contract. In April 2002, Ramsay-Gerding filed a third-party complaint against ChemRex, alleging, among other things, that ChemRex had breached its warranty of the stucco system. Ramsay-Gerding also sought indemnity and contribution from ChemRex for any damages that plaintiffs might recover from them. In August 2003, plaintiffs amended their complaint to add a claim against ChemRex for breach of express warranty.

In 2004, plaintiffs and Ramsay-Gerding moved to bifurcate their breach of express warranty claims against ChemRex from the other claims and defenses in the case. The trial court granted that motion, and, in July 2004, the express warranty claims were tried to a jury. At the close of the evidence, ChemRex moved for a directed verdict, arguing that there was insufficient evidence for the jury to find that McDonald had authority to act for ChemRex in giving the warranty. The trial court determined that the evidence did not support a finding of actual authority but allowed the jury to determine whether McDonald had apparent authority. The jury found for plaintiffs on the breach of warranty claim, which necessarily included a determination that McDonald had apparent authority to provide the warranty. . . .

. . . ChemRex . . . appealed, arguing, *inter alia,* that the trial court had erred in denying its motion for a directed verdict on the issue of apparent authority. The Court of Appeals agreed with ChemRex that its motion for a directed verdict should have been granted. . . . As to the apparent authority issue, the Court of Appeals applied this court's decision in *Badger v. Paulson Investment Co., Inc.,* 311 Or. 14, 803 P.2d 1178 (1991), reasoning that McDonald's role as selling agent and his title of territory manager were insufficient to establish apparent authority to provide a warranty on ChemRex's behalf. Instead, to establish apparent authority, the Court of Appeals concluded that plaintiffs were required to offer evidence

> (1) [of] further conduct by ChemRex conferring on [McDonald] the authority to perform the specific function at issue here—warranting the product sold—or
> (2) that persons in McDonald's position *customarily* have such authority and that plaintiffs knew that McDonald was a person in that position.

Taylor, 215 Or. App. at 685, 172 P.3d 251 (emphasis in original). Finding no such evidence in the record, the Court of Appeals held that the trial court had erred in denying ChemRex's motion for a directed verdict. *Id.* at 690, 172 P.3d 251. We allowed plaintiffs' petition for review. . . .

We begin with a review of some basic principles of agency law. Generally speaking, an agent can bind a principal only when that agent acts with actual or apparent authority. Restatement (Second) of Agency §140 (1958). Actual authority may be express or implied. When a principal explicitly authorizes the agent to perform certain acts, the agent has express authority. However, most actual authority is implied: a principal implicitly permits the agent to do those things that are "reasonably necessary" for carrying out the agent's express authority. In contrast, a principal also may be bound by actions taken that are "completely outside" of the agent's actual authority, if the principal allows the agent to appear to have the authority to bind the principal. Such a circumstance is called "apparent authority."

For a principal to be bound by an agent's action, the principal must take some affirmative step, either to grant the agent authority or to create the appearance of authority. An agent's actions, standing alone and without some action by the principal, cannot create authority to bind the principal. Thus, "'[a]pparent authority to do any particular act can be created only by some conduct of the principal which, when reasonably interpreted, causes a third party to believe that the principal consents to have the apparent agent act for him on that matter.'" *Wiggins v. Barrett & Associates, Inc.*, 295 Or. 679, 687-88, 669 P.2d 1132 (1983). Additionally, the third party must "'rely on that belief'" when dealing with the agent. *Id.*, 295 Or. at 688, 669 P.2d 1132.

Here, the key issue is whether the principal—ChemRex—took sufficient action to create the appearance of authority on the part of McDonald. Apparent authority requires that the principal engage in some conduct that the principal "'should realize'" is likely to cause a third person to believe that the agent has authority to act on the principal's behalf. Although the focus of that inquiry is on the principal's conduct, the third party need not receive information respecting either the nature or the extent of that conduct directly from the principal:

> "The information received by the third person may come directly from the principal by letter or word of mouth, from authorized statements of the agent, from documents or other indicia of authority given by the principal to the agent, or from third persons who have heard of the agent's authority through authorized or permitted channels of communication." *Badger v. Paulson Investment Co., Inc.*, 311 Or. 14, 24-25 n.9, 803 P.2d 1178 (1991).

Thus, information that has been channeled through other sources can be used to support apparent authority, as long as that information can be traced back to the principal.

A principal can create the appearance of authority "by written or spoken words or any other conduct. . . ." Restatement at §27. For example, when a principal clothes an agent with actual authority to perform certain tasks, the principal might create apparent authority to perform other, related tasks. Similarly, when a distant principal places an agent "in charge of a geographically distinct unit or branch[,]" that may lend weight to a finding of apparent authority, depending on the circumstances. Restatement (Third) of Agency §3.03 comment d (2006). For example, if the principal structures its organization so that the "branch manager"—or territory manager—"makes decisions and directs activity without checking elsewhere in the organization[,]" that may create apparent authority to commit the principal to similar transactions. *Id.*

Holding [We turn to the application of those principles to the actions of ChemRex at issue here. Using the standards discussed above, we conclude that there is sufficient evidence in the record to support the jury's finding that McDonald acted with apparent authority when he warranted the stucco system to plaintiffs. The first issue is whether ChemRex took sufficient steps to create the apparent authority to provide a warranty. Significantly, ChemRex gave McDonald actual authority to help in processing warranties and to communicate with customers—about warranties—using ChemRex letterhead. Indeed, McDonald used that authority to confirm, in his July 1999 letter, that plaintiffs had a five-year warranty. Furthermore, ChemRex clothed McDonald with the title of "territory manager" and gave him the actual authority to visit job sites and to solve problems, such as plaintiffs' rust problem, that he found there. McDonald also had the authority to sell an additional product intended to address the very performance at issue here and to answer plaintiffs' questions about the system, which he did in response to plaintiffs' stated concerns.

The next issue is whether there was evidence from which the jury could have concluded that those actions by ChemRex reasonably led plaintiffs to believe that McDonald was authorized to provide the warranty. ChemRex argues that McDonald's title could not have led plaintiffs to believe that McDonald was so authorized, because plaintiffs were unaware of that title until after construction was completed. However, Taylor testified that he believed that McDonald "was the person that was in charge of or supervising this area, the coastal area. He was the guy that you had to get your answers from." He also stated that he knew that McDonald "represented" ChemRex. It is not necessary that plaintiffs knew McDonald's exact title; they knew generally that McDonald was in charge of the geographical area in which their project was located and that he represented ChemRex. In any event, McDonald used his title of territory manager for Oregon when signing the July 1999 letter confirming the five-year warranty. Because, as discussed below, the jury was permitted to find that plaintiffs relied on that letter, it is further evidence that plaintiffs knew of McDonald's position.

ChemRex also implies that McDonald's position is irrelevant because ChemRex did not directly inform plaintiffs of that position. But it was not necessary that plaintiffs learn of McDonald's position directly from ChemRex; receiving that information through an intermediary, such as a contractor, would be sufficient. The general contractor knew that McDonald was the territory manager for Oregon, or "[ChemRex] for Oregon, so to speak," and the stucco installer knew that he was in charge of the "Oregon area." It was permissible for the jury to infer that plaintiffs learned the information from the general contractor and the stucco installer.

Because of McDonald's position and his actual authority to help allay plaintiffs' concerns about rust, it was reasonable for plaintiffs to infer that one of the ways in which McDonald had authority to allay their concerns was by warranting the system for five years. That is particularly true here, because there was evidence in the record that five years was a reasonable length of time for such a warranty.

The third issue is whether plaintiffs reasonably relied on McDonald's apparent authority to provide the warranty. ChemRex does not dispute that plaintiffs relied on McDonald's statements and conduct at the September 1998 meeting in moving forward with the construction project. However, ChemRex argues that the evidence was insufficient to show that plaintiffs had relied on the 1999 letter, because construction already had been completed when plaintiffs received the letter. We disagree. Plaintiffs' general contractor testified that it was customary to obtain all warranties in writing before completing the "close-out" process and paying the retainage. Although he could not recall specifically whether that had happened here, he was confident that that procedure had been followed. Further, plaintiffs' stucco installer testified that he had asked for the warranty in writing because of plaintiffs' concerns, and Taylor testified that obtaining the warranty in writing was "important" to him. Although the evidence does not conclusively demonstrate that plaintiffs relied on the letter from McDonald, the jury was entitled to find, from the evidence discussed above, that plaintiffs did so rely.

In sum, plaintiffs presented sufficient evidence for the jury to find that McDonald had apparent authority to provide the warranty on ChemRex's behalf. We therefore reverse the Court of Appeals decision on that issue. As noted, because the Court of Appeals concluded that ChemRex's motion for a directed verdict should have been granted, it did not address ChemRex's other assignments of error or plaintiffs' argument that the trial court erred in submitting ChemRex's comparative fault defense to the jury. We therefore remand to the Court of Appeals so that it may consider those issues.

The decision of the Court of Appeals is reversed, and the case is remanded to the Court of Appeals for further proceedings.

Questions

1. What was the contract at issue in the case?
2. What was the plaintiffs' argument as to why ChemRex was bound?
3. What manifestations of ChemRex did the court say created apparent authority?

Note that the court in *H.H. Taylor* imposes a reliance element for finding apparent authority. Specifically, the court states that the third party must rely on its belief that the agent had authority. Although a number of courts impose a reliance requirement, the Restatement (Third) of Agency does not.[10]

As the court alludes to, the appointment of an agent by a principal to a particular position or office constitutes a manifestation by the principal. Thus, if a third party knows an agent is in a particular position and this knowledge is traceable to the principal, the agent has apparent authority to do what a person in the agent's position would customarily have authority to do. For example, say Monet hires Bose as an additional crew chief, but specifically tells him that he is not authorized to charge anything on Monet's account at the paint store. Bose goes to the paint store wearing a Monet Painting shirt with "crew chief" embroidered on the front given to him by Monet and charges some paint. The

---

10. *See* RESTATEMENT (THIRD) OF AGENCY §2.03, cmt. e.

paint store employee notices the "crew chief" embroidery and lets Bose charge paint on Monet's account. Monet would be bound on this contract because Bose had apparent authority. The paint store's knowledge that Bose was a crew chief was traceable to Monet (Monet gave Bose the crew chief shirt), and a crew chief, as the paint store well knows, customarily has the authority to charge paint.

You probably deduced from the last example that the apparent authority of an agent can be broader than his or her actual authority. Bose lacked actual authority to charge paint, but possessed apparent authority to do so. In fact, a person who is not even an agent of a principal and therefore has no actual authority can nonetheless possess apparent authority and bind the principal. For example, say Monet fired Arroyo, terminating their agency relationship, yet never told the paint store. (Remember, Arroyo was a crew chief, and Monet told the paint store she had authority to charge paint.) Arroyo thereafter charges some paint to Monet's account. Monet will be bound on this contract, because Arroyo had apparent authority. The last the paint store heard from Monet regarding Arroyo was that she was authorized to charge paint, so, as far as it knew, she was still authorized. (This is sometimes called "lingering authority," because it lingers after the agency relationship has ended.) Now, if the paint store somehow knew or had reason to know that Arroyo was no longer an agent of Monet, Arroyo would not have apparent authority, because the paint store would not be able to successfully claim it reasonably believed that Arroyo had authority.

Incidentally, you may be wondering how exactly a paint store has knowledge given it is not an actual person. Well, per the Restatement (Third) of Agency, "[o]rganizations are treated as possessing the collective knowledge of their employees and other agents. . . ."[11] This is called imputed knowledge. Hence, Monet could defeat a claim of apparent authority by the paint store by proving an employee of the paint store knew Arroyo was no longer Monet's agent.

3. Estoppel

A business may be bound to a contract entered into on its behalf by an agent or other person lacking both actual and apparent authority under the doctrine of estoppel. Here is the Restatement (Third) of Agency formulation of the rule:

> A person who has not made a manifestation that an actor has authority as an agent and who is not otherwise liable as a party to a transaction purportedly done by the actor on that person's account is subject to liability to a third party who justifiably is induced to make a detrimental change in position because the transaction is believed to be on the person's account, if
>   (1) the person intentionally or carelessly caused such belief, or
>   (2) having notice of such belief and that it might induce others to change their positions, the person did not take reasonable steps to notify them of the facts.[12]

---

11. *Id.* §5.03, cmt. c.
12. *Id.* §2.05.

Notice that unlike apparent authority, finding estoppel (1) does *not* require a manifestation traceable to the principal regarding the purported agent's authority, but (2) does require detrimental reliance by the third party (but recall that some courts have imposed a reliance element for finding apparent authority).

The Restatement (Third) of Agency provides the following illustration with respect to estoppel:

> P has two coagents, A and B. P has notice that B, acting without actual or apparent authority, has represented to T that A has authority to enter into a transaction that is contrary to P's instructions. T does not know that P's instructions forbid A from engaging in the transaction. T cannot establish conduct by P on the basis of which T could reasonably believe that A has the requisite authority. T can, however, establish that P had notice of B's representation and that it would have been easy for P to inform T of the limits on A's authority. T detrimentally changes position in reliance on B's representation by making a substantial down payment. If it is found that T's action was justifiable, P is estopped to deny B's authority to make the representation.[13]

T cannot successfully argue actual authority because P has specifically forbidden A from engaging in the transaction. Nor can T successfully argue apparent authority, because there is no conduct or other manifestation received by T and traceable to P that T can use to support the argument. P nonetheless seems in the wrong here, because P knew that B was misleading A, and could have easily remedied the situation, but did nothing.

4. Inherent Agency Power

A business may be bound to a contract entered into on its behalf even in the absence of actual authority, apparent authority, or estoppel under the doctrine of inherent agency power. The Restatement (Second) of Agency describes inherent agency power as follows:

> Inherent agency power is a term used in the restatement of this subject to indicate the power of an agent which is derived not from authority, apparent authority or estoppel, but solely from the agency relation and exists for the protection of persons harmed by or dealing with a servant or other agent.[14]

Courts invoke inherent agency power when fairness dictates holding a principal liable on a contract even though the purported agent lacked authority and one or more estoppel elements is missing. As the Restatement (Second) of Agency explains:

---

13. *Id.* §2.05, cmt. d, illust. 1.
14. RESTATEMENT (SECOND) OF AGENCY §8A.

Partnerships and corporations, through which most of the work of the world is done today, depend for their existence upon agency principles. The rules designed to promote the interests of these enterprises are necessarily accompanied by rules to police them. It is inevitable that in doing their work, either through negligence or excess of zeal, agents will harm third persons or will deal with them in unauthorized ways. It would be unfair for an enterprise to have the benefit of the work of its agents without making it responsible to some extent for their excesses and failures to act carefully. The answer of the common law has been the creation of special agency powers or, to phrase it otherwise, the imposition of liability upon the principal because of unauthorized or negligent acts of his servants and other agents. These powers or liabilities are created by the courts primarily for the protection of third persons, either those who are harmed by the agent or those who deal with the agent. In the long run, however, they enure to the benefit of the business world and hence to the advantage of employers as a class, the members of which are plaintiffs as well as defendants in actions brought upon unauthorized transactions conducted by agents.

The court applies the doctrine of inherent agency power in the following case.

Menard, Inc. v. Dage-MTI, Inc.
726 N.E.2d 1206 (Ind. 2000)

SULLIVAN, J.

Menard, Inc., offered to purchase 30 acres of land from Dage-MTI, Inc., for $1,450,000. Arthur Sterling, Dage's president, accepted the offer in a written agreement in which he represented that he had the requisite authority to bind Dage to the sale. The Dage board of directors did not approve and refused to complete the transaction. We hold that as president, Sterling possessed the inherent authority to bind Dage in these circumstances.

BACKGROUND

Dage-MTI, Inc., is a closely held Indiana corporation which manufactures specialized electronics equipment. At all times relevant to this appeal, Dage was governed by a six-member board of directors ("Board"), consisting of Ronald and Lynn Kerrigan, Louis Piccolo (a financial consultant retained by Ronald Kerrigan), Arthur and Marie Sterling, and William Conners. In addition to being a Board member, Arthur Sterling ("Sterling") had served as president of Dage for at least 20 years at the time of the trial on this matter. Of the six directors, only Arthur and Marie Sterling resided in Indiana.

For many years, Sterling operated Dage without significant input from or oversight by the Board. Over the course of the summer and early fall of 1993, however, Kerrigan took steps to subject Dage management to Board control. Kerrigan hired New York-based financial consultant and future Board member

Piccolo to assess the company's performance. Kerrigan also retained New York attorney Gerald Gorinsky to represent his interests concerning Dage.

In late October of 1993, the Dage shareholders met in New Jersey to discuss an offer by Sterling to purchase the Kerrigans' shares of Dage. During the course of the meeting, Sterling first informed other directors that Menard, Inc., had expressed interest in purchasing a 30-acre parcel of land owned by Dage and located in the Michigan City area. Menard is a Wisconsin corporation that owns and operates home improvement stores in the Midwestern region of the United States.

On October 30, 1993, Menard forwarded a formal offer to Sterling pertaining to the purchase of 10.5 acres of the 30-acre parcel. Upon receipt of the offer, Sterling did not contact Menard to discuss the terms and conditions of the offer. Instead, on or about November 4, 1993, he forwarded the offer to all the Dage directors with a cover note acknowledging that Board approval was required to accept or reject the offer. Ultimately, this offer was rejected: Kerrigan, Piccolo, and Gorinsky determined that the offer should be rejected due to the collective effect of certain sections of the purchase agreement submitted by Menard, as well as co-development obligations that the offer imposed on Dage. This rejection was communicated to Sterling, and although he viewed the offer to purchase favorably, he let the offer lapse. Later, he informed Menard's agent, Gary Litvin, that members of Dage's Board objected to various provisions of the offer.

On November 30, 1993, Sterling called Kerrigan and informed him that Menard would make a second offer for the entire 30-acre parcel. Sterling presented a two-part proposed resolution ("consent resolution") to the Board: the first part authorized Sterling to "offer and purchase" another parcel located immediately to the north of the 30-acre parcel and referred to as the "Simon property"; the second part authorized Sterling to "offer and sell" the 30-acre parcel. Sterling, Kerrigan, Piccolo, and Gorinsky discussed the offer and Sterling was told to change the "offer and sell" provision to "to offer for sale." He was also instructed that he could purchase the Simon property on behalf of Dage, but could only "offer" the 30-acre parcel to Menard at a particular price. Additionally, Sterling was told that in soliciting offers for the 30-acre parcel, he was not to negotiate the terms of a sale. Gorinsky reminded Sterling that any offer from Menard would require Board review and acceptance, and he instructed Sterling to forward any offer to the Board for approval or rejection.

Finally, Sterling was told that if Menard submitted an agreement with the same objectionable provisions as the first offer, it would be rejected. Sterling agreed to follow the instructions of the Board "as long as I don't have to pay for" Gorinsky's and Piccolo's services in reviewing the offer. Based upon the discussion, Sterling drafted a new resolution, which stated that he was authorized "to take such actions as are necessary to offer for sale our 30 acre parcel ... for a price not less than $1,200,000."

On December 6, 1993, Sterling informed Piccolo that Menard had agreed to make another offer. Piccolo reminded Sterling of his obligation to secure Board approval of the offer. Menard forwarded a second proposed purchase agreement to Sterling. This agreement contained the same provisions that the Board found objectionable in the first proposed agreement. However, this offer differed in that it was for the purchase of the entire 30-acre parcel for $1,450,000.

During a week-long series of discussions beginning December 14, 1993, and unknown to any other member of the Dage Board, Sterling negotiated several minor changes in the Menard agreement and then signed the revised offer on behalf of Dage. Menard also signed, accepting the offer. Under Paragraph 5(c)(I) of the agreement, Sterling, as president of Dage, represented as follows: "The persons signing this Agreement on behalf of the Seller are duly authorized to do so and their signatures bind the Seller in accordance with the terms of this Agreement." (R. at 916; Finding of Fact No. 47.) (R. at 1144, 1149.) No one at Dage had informed Menard that Sterling's authority with respect to the sale of the 30-acre parcel was limited to only the solicitation of offers.

inherent agency power

Upon learning of the signed agreement with Menard, the Board instructed Sterling to extricate Dage from the agreement. Later, the Board hired counsel to inform Menard of its intent to question the agreement's enforceability. However, it was not until March 29, 1994, that Dage first gave notice to Menard of this intent.

Menard ultimately filed suit to require Dage to specifically perform the agreement and to secure the payment of damages. . . . Following a bench trial, the trial court ruled in favor of Dage. The Court of Appeals affirmed, finding that Sterling did not have the express or apparent authority to bind the corporation in this land transaction.

DISCUSSION . . .

I

Two main classifications of authority are generally recognized: "actual authority" and "apparent authority." Actual authority is created "by written or spoken words or other conduct of the principal which, reasonably interpreted, causes the agent to believe that the principal desires him so to act on the principal's account." *Scott v. Randle,* 697 N.E.2d 60, 66 (Ind. Ct. App. 1998). Apparent authority refers to a third party's reasonable belief that the principal has authorized the acts of its agent; it arises from the principal's indirect or direct manifestations to a third party and not from the representations or acts of the agent.

On occasion, Indiana has taken an expansive view of apparent authority, including within the discussion the concept of "inherent agency power." *See Koval v. Simon Telelect, Inc.,* 693 N.E.2d 1299, 1301 (Ind. 1998) (certifying answer to a federal court that retention of an attorney confers the inherent power on that attorney to bind the client to an in court proceeding).

"'Inherent agency power is a term used . . . to indicate the power of an agent which is derived *not* from authority, apparent authority or estoppel, but solely from the agency relation and exists for the protection of persons harmed by or dealing with a servant or other agent.'" *Id.* at 1304 (quoting Restatement (Second) of Agency §8A (1958)). This "'status based' . . . [form of] vicarious liability rests upon certain important social and commercial policies," primarily that the "'business enterprise should bear the burden of the losses created by the mistakes or overzealousness of its agents [because such liability] stimulates the watchfulness of the employer in selecting and supervising the agents.'" *In re Atlantic Fin. Management, Inc.*, 784 F.2d 29, 32 (1st Cir. 1986). And while "representations of the principal to the third party are central for defining apparent authority," the concept of inherent authority differs and "originates from the customary authority of a person in the particular type of agency relationship so that no representations beyond the fact of the existence of the agency need be shown." *Cange v. Stotler & Co.*, 826 F.2d 581, 591 (7th Cir. 1987).

In *Cange*, the Seventh Circuit explained this concept's genesis:

> Judge Learned Hand articulated this concept of inherent agency power when he upheld a jury verdict for plaintiff based on a contract the jury found to be an unconditional engagement for a singing tour despite the principal's instructions to its agent to engage the singer only for such recitals as he could later persuade record dealers to book her for, instructions which were not told to plaintiff. *Kidd v. Thomas A. Edison, Inc.*, 239 F. 405 (S.D.N.Y.). He reasoned that the scope of an agency must be measured "not alone by the words in which it is created, but by the whole setting in which those words are used, including the customary powers of such agents" and thus the contract was enforceable because "the customary implication would seem to have been that [the agent's] authority was without limitation of the kind here imposed." *Id.* 239 F. at 406. The principal benefits from the existence of inherent authority because "[t]he very purpose of delegated authority is to avoid constant recourse by third persons to the principal, which would be a corollary of denying the agent any latitude beyond his exact instructions." *Id.* 239 F. at 408; *see* Restatement (Second) of Agency §§8A comment a, 161 comment a (1958).

Cange, 826 F.2d at 590-91.

We find the concept of inherent authority—rather than actual or apparent authority—controls our analysis in this case. Menard did not negotiate and ultimately contract with a lower-tiered employee or a prototypical "general" or "special" agent, with respect to whom actual or apparent authority might be at issue. Menard dealt with the president of the corporation, whom "'"[t]he law recognizes . . . [as one of] the officers [who] are the means, the hands and the head, by which corporations normally act."'" *Community Care Ctrs., Inc. v. Indiana Dep't of Pub. Welfare*, 468 N.E.2d 602, 604 (Ind. Ct. App. 1984). In so finding, we consider significant the "'"distinction . . . between a corporate act, performed through the intermediation of a person specially empowered to act as its agent, and a like act done immediately by the corporation through its executive or administrative officers, which may be termed its *inherent agencies*."'" *Community Care Ctrs., Inc.*, 468 N.E.2d at 604.

II

Our determination that the inherent agency concept controls our analysis does not end the inquiry, however. The Restatement (Second) of Agency §161 provides that an agent's inherent authority

> subjects his principal to liability for acts done on his account which [(1)] usually accompany or are incidental to transactions which the agent is authorized to conduct if, although they are forbidden by the principal, [(2)] the other party reasonably believes that the agent is authorized to do them and [(3)] has no notice that he is not so authorized.

Distilled to its basics, we find that Sterling had inherent authority here if: (1) first, Sterling acted within the usual and ordinary scope of his authority as president; (2) second, Menard reasonably believed that Sterling was authorized to contract for the sale and purchase of Dage real estate; and (3) third, Menard had no notice that Sterling was not authorized to sell the 30-acre parcel without Board approval. . . .

A

As to whether Sterling acted within the usual and ordinary scope of his authority as president, the trial court found that Sterling, a director and substantial shareholder of Dage, had served as Dage's president from its inception; had managed the affairs of Dage for an extended period of time with little or no Board oversight; and had purchased real estate for Dage without Board approval. However, the trial court reached the conclusion that "[t]he record persuasively demonstrates that the land transaction in question was an extraordinary transaction" for Dage, which manufactures electronic video products. (R. at 921; Conclusion of Law No. 11.) Thus, the court concluded that "Sterling was not performing an act that was appropriate in the ordinary course of Dage's business." *Id.*

We initially note that the Restatement looks at whether the acts "usually accompany or are incidental to transactions which *the agent* is authorized to conduct." Restatement (Second) of Agency §161(emphasis added). On the other hand, our analysis of inherent agency in *Koval* was focused on whether "'a general agent . . . acted within the usual and ordinary scope of *the business* in which he was employed.'" 693 N.E.2d at 1304 (emphasis added). There is a difference.

The Restatement looks at the agent's office or station in the company to gauge the scope of the agent's authority, whereas our analysis in *Koval* looked to the purpose and scope of the business in which the general agent (i.e., attorney) was employed. We find the Restatement, which is focused "solely [on] the agency relation," is more appropriate in the current situation involving corporate officers, who are "natural persons who hold and administer the offices of the corporation." *Community Care Centers, Inc.*, 468 N.E.2d at 604.

Given that the trial court found that Sterling, as president of the company since its inception, had managed its affairs for an extended period of time with little or no Board oversight and, in particular, had purchased real estate for Dage in the past without Board approval, we conclude that Sterling's actions at issue here were acts that "usually accompany or are incidental to transactions which [he was] authorized to conduct." Restatement (Second) of Agency §161.

B

Next, we must determine whether Menard reasonably believed that Sterling was authorized to contract for the sale and purchase of Dage real estate. While Sterling's *apparent authority* to bind Dage was "vitiated" by Menard's knowledge that the sale of Dage real estate required Board approval, this information did not defeat Sterling's *inherent authority* as Dage president to bind the corporation in a "setting" where he was the sole negotiator. *Cange,* 826 F.2d at 591.

Because the inherent agency theory "originates from the customary authority of a person in the particular type of agency relationship," *id.,* we look to the *agent's indirect or direct manifestations* to determine whether Menard could have "reasonably believe[d]" that Sterling was authorized to contract for the sale and purchase of Dage real estate. *Koval,* 693 N.E.2d at 1304 n.7. And considering that the "agent" in this case is a general officer of the corporation (as opposed to an "appointed general agent" or "company general manager"), we find that Menard "should not be required to scrutinize too carefully the mandates of [this] permanent . . . agent[ ] . . . who [did] no more than what is usually done by [a corporate president]." Restatement (Second) of Agency §161 cmt. a.

Here, the facts establish that Menard reasonably believed that Sterling was authorized to contract for the sale and purchase of Dage real estate. We begin with the premise that "'the acts of a corporation done through its officers are acts done per se.'" *Community Care Ctrs., Inc.,* 468 N.E.2d at 604. Next, we note that at all times "Sterling held himself out as president of Dage." (R. at 919; Finding of Fact No. 67.) In fact, "Sterling ha[d] served as president of Dage since its inception"; as noted in the preceding section, he was a substantial shareholder and member of the six-person Board of Directors; he had managed the affairs of Dage for an extended period of time with little or no Board oversight; and he had purchased real estate for Dage without Board approval. (R. at 911, 912; Findings of Fact Nos. 7-9, 16.) And although "early in the transaction, Sterling advised [Menard] that he was required to go back to his 'partners' to obtain authority to sell the entire thirty acres[, Sterling later] confirmed that he had the authority from his Board of Directors to proceed." (R. at 922-23; Conclusion of Law No. 19.)

We find it reasonable that Menard did not question the corporate president's statement that he had "authority from his Board of Directors to proceed" with the land transaction. *Id.*

We also find it reasonable for Menard not to scrutinize Sterling's personal "acknowledge[ment]" that he signed the agreement for the purchase and sale of the real estate by authority of Dage's board of directors." (R. at 919; Finding of Fact No. 67.) We believe this especially to be the case where (1) Sterling himself was a member of the Board; (2) the agreement contained an express representation that "[t]he persons signing this Agreement on behalf of the Seller are duly authorized to do so and their signatures bind the Seller in accordance with the terms of this Agreement," (R. at 916; Finding of Fact No. 47); and (3) Menard was aware that Dage's corporate counsel, Patrick Donoghue, was involved in the review of the terms of the agreement.

C

Finally, we consider whether Menard had notice that Sterling was not authorized to sell the 30-acre parcel without Board approval. The record does not indicate that Menard was aware of the existence of the consent resolution, much less that it limited Sterling's authority as president. Nor was there evidence that either the Board or Sterling informed Menard that Sterling's authority with respect to the sale of the 30-acre parcel was limited to only the solicitation of offers. And, as discussed *supra,* Sterling personally acknowledged that he signed the agreement by authority of Dage's Board of Directors, of which he was a member.

It is true, as the Court of Appeals noted, that Menard was advised early in the transaction that Sterling had to go to the Board to obtain approval. This knowledge would have vitiated the apparent authority of a lower-tiered employee or a prototypical general or special agent. But we do not find it sufficient notice that Sterling, an officer with inherent authority, was not authorized to bind Dage at the closing.

The trial court found that Sterling signed the agreement with Menard during the week of December 14, 1993; that he represented in the agreement that he was authorized to sign it and that his signature bound Dage; and that when Dage's lawyers contacted Menard on March 29, 1994, it "was the first notice given by Dage to Menard that there was any issue regarding the enforceability of the agreement." (R. at 916, 919; Findings of Fact 46, 47, 63.) Indeed, Sterling wrote to Menard on February 7, 1994, indicating that Dage was performing as required by the agreement. We conclude that Menard had no notice that the Board had limited Sterling's authority with respect to 30-acre parcel.

D

In *Koval,* this Court said: "if one of two innocent parties must suffer due to a betrayal of trust—either the principal or the third party—the loss should fall on the party who is most at fault. Because the principal puts the agent in a position of trust, the principal should bear the loss." *Koval,* 693 N.E.2d at 1304.

That maxim has particular resonance here. The record fails to reveal a single affirmative act that Dage took to inform Menard of Sterling's limited authority with respect to the 30-acre parcel, and the Board did not notify Menard that Sterling had acted without its authority until 104 days after it learned of

Sterling's action. By this time, Sterling had taken additional steps to close the transaction. Dage's failure to act should not now form the basis of relief, penalizing Menard and depriving it of its bargain.

CONCLUSION

We ... vacate the opinion of the Court of Appeals, and ... remand to the trial court for further proceedings consistent with our conclusion that Dage was bound by Sterling's actions.

SHEPARD, C.J., dissenting.

I think today's decision will leave most corporate lawyers wondering what the law actually is.

A board of directors authorizes the president to sell some real estate but requires that the sale be submitted to the board for approval or disapproval. The president understands that he must submit any sale to the board. He tells the potential buyer that he must submit it. The buyer knows that its offer must be submitted to the board after the president signs the sales agreement. The agreement is in fact submitted to the board and disapproved. Our Court holds that the agreement is binding anyway.

The majority calls this "an expansive view of apparent authority." Facially, this seems like an understatement.

On the other hand, the Court embarks upon its discussion of "inherent authority," which it rightfully describes as a specie of apparent authority, after endorsing the conclusions of the trial court and Court of Appeals that the corporation's president did not possess apparent authority to sell the land without board approval.

In the end, it is difficult to know how lawyers will advise their clients after today's decision. Where all parties to a corporate transaction understand that board approval is required and that it may or may not be forthcoming, the black letter law cited in today's opinion points toward a conclusion that the buyer's offer was not accepted by the seller.

While I agree with the general legal principles laid out by the majority, those principles seem undercut by the resolution of this case.

Incidentally, Menard could have sued Sterling in his individual capacity. As the Restatement (Third) of Agency provides: "A person who purports to make a contract, representation, or conveyance to or with a third party on behalf of another person, lacking power to bind that person, gives an implied warranty of authority to the third party and is subject to liability to the third party for damages for loss caused by breach of that warranty, including loss of the benefit expected from performance by the principal...."[15] It appears that Menard did not sue him.

---

15. RESTATEMENT (THIRD) OF AGENCY §6.10.

Note that the drafters of the Restatement (Third) decided not to use the term "inherent agency power" observing that "other doctrines stated in this Restatement encompass the justifications underpinning §8A, including . . . the doctrines of apparent authority [and] estoppel." Courts, of course are not bound by the Restatement and therefore are free to continue to use the term, and many do.

Questions

1. Why didn't the fact that Sterling was Dage's president create actual authority or apparent authority in Sterling to enter into the real estate transaction on behalf of Dage?
2. Why wasn't Paragraph 5(C)(I) of the agreement Sterling signed with Menard sufficient to create apparent authority?
3. Do you agree with the court's decision?
4. The dissenting judge says: "In the end, it is difficult to know how lawyers will advise their clients after today's decision." What does he mean?
5. Why do you think Menard sued Dage instead of Sterling?

5. Ratification

Finally, a business may be bound to a contract entered into on its behalf even in the absence of actual authority, apparent authority, or estoppel under the doctrine of ratification. The Restatement (Third) of Agency defines ratification as "the affirmance of a prior act done by another, whereby the act is given effect as if done by an agent acting with actual authority." It provides that "[a] person ratifies an act (a) by manifesting assent to be bound by the act, or (b) through conduct that justifies a reasonable assumption that the person so consents."[16] For example, say Arroyo of Monet's painting business fame knows that Monet is looking to buy a used basket crane for the business. While driving home from work, she notices one for sale on the side of the road. After testing it, she realizes it is a great deal, but fails in her efforts to reach Monet. Thinking the crane will be snapped up by the next person noticing it, Arroyo tells the owner she is buying it on behalf of Monet, and writes the owner a check for the down payment. The next day when Arroyo tells Monet about the deal, Monet responds, "Thanks for getting me such a great deal!" Monet has thus manifested assent to be bound to the deal and therefore is bound under the doctrine of ratification.

example

---

16. *Id.* §4.01.

Exercise 2.1

Refer to the Monet-Bose example on pages 40-41 above, but assume Bose was wearing an Ozzy Osbourne t-shirt instead of a Monet Painting shirt.

1. Given this change in shirts, would Monet still be bound on Bose's paint purchase? Would Bose be bound?
2. Assume that Bose had charged paint to Monet's account in the past even though he was not authorized to do so, and Monet always paid the bill without objection knowing that the charges were incurred by Bose. Would Monet be bound to the latest Bose transaction?
3. Assume that when Bose went to charge paint, the paint store called Monet to inquire about Bose's authority, got Monet's voicemail, and left him a message asking if Bose had authority. Monet promptly listened to the message but never called the paint store back, and so the next day the paint store let Bose charge some paint. Would Monet be bound on this transaction?
4. Assume that Bose told the paint store that he was authorized to charge paint. The paint store believed him, so let him do it. Would Monet be bound?
5. What could Monet do to minimize the risk of being bound on unauthorized transactions entered into at the paint store by Bose, Arroyo, and the like?

Exercise 2.2

Tee is in the market for a recreational vehicle, so goes to RV World, LLC to check out her choices. Tee zeros in on the Elite Deluxe model, but is concerned about reliability. Arain, an RV World sales person, tells Tee not to worry, because the Elite Deluxe comes with a lifetime warranty. Unknown to Tee, the standard warranty is only two years, and RV World's sales manager has specifically told Arain that he is not authorized to say anything different. Tee decides to purchase the Elite Deluxe, in part because of Arain's statements regarding the warranty.

1. Is RV World obligated to provide a lifetime warranty on Tee's RV?
2. Same facts as above, but the RV Purchase Agreement Tee signed to finalize her purchase included the following clause:

> NO AGENT, EMPLOYEE, OR REPRESENTATIVE OF SELLER HAS ANY AUTHORITY TO BIND SELLER TO ANY AFFIRMATION, REPRESENTATION, OR WARRANTY EXCEPT AS STATED IN THIS AGREEMENT.

"Seller" was defined earlier in the Agreement as RV World, LLC, and the Agreement provides for a one-year limited warranty. Does this change your answer for Question 1?

6. Entity-Specific Rules

Up until now, we have been discussing agency law generally and all of the examples have involved Monet's painting business, a sole proprietorship. We now turn to some entity-specific rules regarding the authority to bind the entity that supplement the general rules we discussed above.

a. Partnerships

RUPA §301(1) provides as follows:

> Each partner is an agent of the partnership for the purpose of its business. An act of a partner . . . for apparently carrying on in the ordinary course the partnership business or business of the kind carried on by the partnership binds the partnership, unless the partner had no authority to act for the partnership in the particular matter and the person with whom the partner was dealing knew or had received a notification that the partner lacked authority.[17]

Hence, the default rule is that each partner has actual authority to bind the partnership. Furthermore, when it comes to apparent authority, there is no requirement of a manifestation traceable to the partnership to the third party, as is the case under the common law of apparent authority discussed above. This statutory provision essentially serves as a manifestation to all third parties that every partner has the authority to bind the partnership when it comes to partnership business in the ordinary course. As with the common law of apparent authority, if the third party's belief that a partner has authority is not reasonable because the third party knew or had received a notification from the partnership that the partner lacked authority, the partnership is not bound.

RUPA specifies that a person has received a notification when it "(1) comes to the person's attention; or (2) is duly delivered at the person's place of business or at any other place held out by the person as a place for receiving communications."[18] Thus, if a partnership is worried about a partner entering into an unauthorized contract with a third party, the partnership can send to the third party a notification of a restriction on the partner's authority. As the statutory language indicates, such a notification is effective upon delivery, whether or not it actually comes to the third party's attention.

Note that the common law of agency applies to partnerships and partners notwithstanding RUPA §301. For example, say a partnership manifests to a third party that a partner has authority to bind the partnership to something outside of the ordinary course. The partner and third party then enter into a contract on behalf of the partnership consistent with such manifestation. The

---

17. RUPA §301(1). The analogous UPA provision is §9.
18. RUPA §102(d).

partnership is bound on the contract under common law apparent authority even though it is not bound under RUPA §301 (because the contract is outside the ordinary course).

b. Corporations

As discussed in Chapter 9, shareholders have very limited decision-making authority. This authority does *not* include authority to bind the corporation. In other words, shareholders are not agents of the corporation. A corporation acting through its board of directors or an officer or other employee could confer actual or apparent authority on a shareholder (and for that matter, anyone else), for example, by telling the shareholder or a third party he or she has authority; but the mere fact that someone is a shareholder does not imbue him or her with any authority to bind the corporation.

Ultimate decision-making authority resides in a corporation's board of directors; and, as indicated in the preceding paragraph, it includes the power to authorize people to act on behalf of the corporation. An individual director cannot, however, confer actual or apparent authority. Directors can only act collectively as a board. (The mechanics of board action are discussed in Chapter 9.) Further, an individual director as such is not an agent of the corporation. In other words, the position confers no actual or apparent authority to bind the corporation. Of course, as with shareholders, the corporation could confer actual or apparent authority to a director.

One of the board's responsibilities is to appoint executive officers (e.g., the president and CEO) to manage the day-to-day business of the corporation, subject to board oversight. Unlike shareholders and individual directors, officers are by definition agents of the corporation. Usually, this is pursuant to a state's corporate law statute. For example, MBCA §8.41 provides:

> Each officer has the authority and shall perform the functions set forth in the bylaws or, to the extent consistent with the bylaws, the functions prescribed by the board of directors or by direction of an officer authorized by the board of directors to prescribe the functions of other officers.[19]

It is typical for a corporation's bylaws to specify the authority of at least some of its executive officers. Here is a sample bylaw provision specifying the authority of the corporation's chief executive officer:

5.6 Chief Executive Officer.

Subject to such supervisory powers, if any, as may be given by the Board of Directors to the chairman of the board, if any, the chief executive officer of the

---

19. MBCA §8.41(a).

Corporation shall, subject to the control of the Board of Directors, have general supervision, direction, and control of the business and the officers of the Corporation. He or she, or his or her designee, shall preside at all meetings of the stockholders and, in the absence or nonexistence of a chairman of the board, at all meetings of the Board of Directors and shall have the general powers and duties of management usually vested in the office of chief executive officer of a corporation and shall have such other powers and duties as may be prescribed by the Board of Directors or these Bylaws.

The board should adopt a resolution specifying the authority of any executive office it has created if such authority is not specified in the bylaws, as contemplated by the above statutory language. Non-executive officers are normally appointed by the relevant executive officer. For example, a corporation's chief financial officer (CFO) would appoint the vice president of finance.

I do not mean to imply that only a corporation's officers have actual authority to bind the corporation. Included within an officer's authority is typically the authority to confer authority to bind the corporation on a subordinate, which conferral may authorize that subordinate to confer authority to a person below him or her in the hierarchy. Hence, authority is conferred down the line all the way to the office clerk who has the authority to buy office supplies on behalf of the corporation.

c. LLCs

It is hard to generalize about the authority rules for LLCs. Some state statutes follow RUPA and limit member authority of a member-managed LLC and manager authority of a manager-managed LLC to acts apparently carrying on the business of the LLC. Other states follow the corporate rule and provide that a member is not an agent of an LLC. Basically, you will need to check the applicable LLC statute and the LLC's governing documents (e.g., its operating agreement).

Exercise 2.3

Aoki, Biton, and Chiba are each one-third owners in XYZ LLP. XYZ is organized in a state that has adopted RUPA verbatim. XYZ's partnership agreement provides, among other things, as follows: "No partner shall, without the prior written consent of the other two partners, (i) borrow money on behalf of the partnership except in the ordinary course of partnership business; (ii) lease, rent, purchase, sell, mortgage, or otherwise create a lien upon any partnership real estate or any interest therein, or enter into any contract for any such purpose; or (iii) make or incur any expenditure on behalf of the partnership in excess of $50,000." XYZ's business consists of owning and operating three gas stations.

Unbeknownst to Aoki and Biton, Chiba buys a new 2012 top-of-the-line Cadillac Escalade in the name of XYZ for $78,000. She trades in her 2000 Saturn LW and finances the $76,500 balance through a loan from the dealership in the name of the partnership. Chiba then promptly skips town in her new ride, never to be heard from again. Neither Aoki, Biton, nor XYZ had any contact or dealings with the car dealership.

1. Is XYZ obligated on the loan?
2. Assume that XYZ is not an LLP but instead an LLC (XYZ, LLC) organized in a state that has adopted the ULLCA (2006) verbatim and that XYZ's operating agreement includes the same sort of provision quoted above. Would XYZ LLC be obligated on the loan?
3. What changes would you need to make to the quoted provision to adapt it for an operating agreement as opposed to a partnership agreement?

7. Ensuring Authority

As the above discussion demonstrates, there are a number of arguments a third party can make when a business claims it is not bound to a contract because the person signing it on the business's behalf lacked authority. There is, however, a risk that none of these arguments will prevail. Going back to our paint store example, say Johnson has zero connection to Monet or his business, but has observed Monet's crew chiefs charging to Monet's account. Johnson uses this knowledge to convince the paint store cashier that he's authorized by Monet to charge on the account. Johnson has no actual authority because Monet has manifested nothing to him. Johnson has no apparent authority because Monet does not even know he exists, so there is no manifestation regarding Johnson to the paint store traceable to Monet. Estoppel is inappropriate because Monet did nothing to cause the paint store to believe Johnson was authorized nor did Monet have knowledge of such belief. Inherent agency power will not work, either, because there is no agency relationship between Monet and Johnson.

In this scenario, the obvious way for the paint store to eliminate the risk that Johnson is not authorized to charge on Monet's account is to call Monet and ask him whether Johnson is authorized. However, it might not always be practical for the store to do this, and Monet might not want to be bugged with these calls because the whole point of setting up the account was to avoid getting involved in buying paint. In balancing these and other considerations, the paint store may conclude it only makes sense to call Monet for purchases above a specific dollar amount.

For more significant transactions, such as the acquisition of a business, the parties will conclude it makes sense (given the amount of money involved) to take some steps to ensure authority. These steps often include requiring the delivery of two documents at closing[20] that address authority: a secretary's certificate and an opinion letter; and, if a partnership or LLC is involved, a party may also require the filing of a certificate of authority. Each of these is discussed below.

a. Secretary's Certificate

A secretary's certificate is a document signed by an entity's secretary certifying that certain actions were approved by the governing body of the entity (board of directors, managing partner, board of managers, etc.). In this context, a secretary is the officer of the business entity responsible for maintaining the books and records of the entity. Here is a sample secretary's certificate from the acquisition of a business (the acquisition is structured as an asset purchase) delivered by the seller's secretary to the buyer.

ABC CORP.
SECRETARY'S CERTIFICATE

The undersigned hereby certifies that he is the duly elected, qualified, and acting Secretary of ABC Corp., a Delaware corporation (the "**Corporation**"), and that, as such, he is authorized to execute and deliver this certificate on behalf of the Corporation and has access to and is familiar with the corporate records of the Corporation, and that:

1. Attached hereto as **Exhibit A** is a true and correct copy of the resolutions duly adopted by the Board of Directors of the Corporation on October 24, 2011. None of such resolutions has been amended, modified, or repealed in any respect. All of such resolutions are in full force and effect on the date hereof.
2. The following individuals are duly elected, qualified, and acting officers of the Corporation holding on the date hereof the offices set forth opposite their names, and the signature set forth opposite their names and titles are their true signatures.

Name	Office	Signature
Joan K. Hernandez	President	_____
Keith T. Adams	Chief Financial Office	_____
Jerome W. Peters	Executive Vice President	_____

---

20. A closing is when the parties to a contract exchange consideration. For example, if the acquisition of a business is structured as an asset purchase for cash consideration, at closing the buyer will deliver the cash to the seller (typically by a wire transfer) and the seller will sign various documents transferring the title to its assets to the buyer.

IN WITNESS WHEREOF, the undersigned has executed this certificate as of November 16, 2011.

By: _____

Name: Michael T. Phelps

Title: Secretary

Exhibit A

WHEREAS, the Corporation desires to enter into an Asset Purchase Agreement (the "Purchase Agreement") by and among the Corporation and XYZ LLP, a Nevada limited liability partnership ("Purchaser"), pursuant to which the Corporation will sell to Purchaser all of the Corporation's assets; and

WHEREAS, the directors of the Corporation deem it to be advisable and in the best interest of the Corporation to enter into the Purchase Agreement and to consummate the transactions contemplated thereby.

NOW, THEREFORE, BE IT RESOLVED, that the Corporation is hereby authorized, directed and empowered to enter into the Purchase Agreement, with substantially the terms set forth in the summary reviewed by the directors of the Corporation; and

FURTHER RESOLVED, that each of the President, Chief Financial Officer, and Executive Vice President of the Corporation are authorized, directed, and empowered in the name and on behalf of the Corporation, to enter into, execute, deliver and perform the Purchase Agreement and any and all amendments and modifications thereto.

By signing the above certificate, Phelps is certifying that the ABC board of directors adopted a resolution conveying actual authority on ABC's president, CFO, and executive vice president to sign and carry out the asset purchase agreement on behalf of ABC. It is common for this type of resolution to authorize more than one officer so that the closing can proceed, if for example, ABC's president is out of the country. Item number 2 is called an "incumbency provision" and sometimes is instead included in a separate document called an incumbency certificate. It confirms the positions of the listed individuals, which, as you know from our discussion above, can give rise to implied actual authority, apparent authority, or inherent authority. The signature part is to protect against forged signatures. In theory, a person could compare the signatures on the secretary's certificate to those on the various closing documents, although I have never heard or seen anyone actually doing this at a closing

Most corporations provide for the office of a secretary in their bylaws, and some states' corporate law statutes require a corporation to have one (neither the MBCA nor the DGCL does). A partnership or LLC may find it convenient to provide for such an office in its partnership/operating agreement for the primary purpose of providing secretary certificates like the one above.

b. Opinion Letters

An opinion letter is a letter from the attorney or law firm of one party to a transaction to the other party to the transaction that addresses various legal issues with respect to the transaction. Thus, in connection with the closing of the asset purchase deal reflected in the above secretary's certificate, the law firm representing ABC would deliver an opinion letter to XYZ, and the law firm representing XYZ would deliver an opinion letter to ABC (this requirement would be reflected in the Asset Purchase Agreement signed by ABC and XYZ). Below is an excerpt from an opinion letter relevant to authority.

> 2. The execution and delivery of the Purchase Agreement and the performance by the Company of its obligations thereunder, have been duly authorized by all necessary action, and the Purchase Agreement has been duly executed and delivered on behalf of the Company and constitutes the valid and binding obligation of the Company, enforceable in accordance with its terms, except as enforceability may be limited by bankruptcy, insolvency, or other similar laws of general application affecting the enforcement of creditors' rights or by general principles of equity limiting the availability of equitable remedies. . . .

The opinion is designed to address authority, among other things. Specifically, in order to render it, the law firm will draft resolutions along the lines of those in Exhibit A to the Secretary's Certificate and have them adopted by the ultimate decision maker for the entity (board of directors, managing partner, board of managers, etc.). These resolutions will confer actual authority on one or more individuals to close the transaction on behalf of the entity. For example, as indicated in Exhibit A, the board of ABC authorized ABC's President, Chief Financial Officer, and Executive Vice President "to enter into, execute, deliver and perform the Purchase Agreement and any and all amendments and modifications thereto" on behalf of ABC. The law firm will verify that the resolutions were adopted, in this case in accordance with ABC's charter and bylaws, and will use this as a basis for its opinion that "the Purchase Agreement has been duly executed and delivered on behalf of the Company. . . ."

Requiring a secretary's certificate and legal opinion may seem like holding up your pants with a belt and suspenders. When it comes to a multi-million dollar transaction, however, the parties want to make sure that no one's pants fall down.

c. Statement of Authority

RUPA §303 authorizes a partnership to file an optional statement of partnership authority with the secretary of state specifying the actual authority of its partners. A partner is then deemed to have such actual authority to bind the partnership, even if he or she does not, in a transaction with a third party who gave value and had no knowledge that the partner was acting without actual authority (if the transaction involves the transfer of real estate, the statement must also be recorded in the office for recording transfers of real property). In light of this provision, it is fairly common for a third party engaging in a significant transaction with a partnership to require the partnership to file a statement of authority with respect to the transaction. For example, in the ABC/XYZ transaction referenced above, it may be prudent for ABC to require XYZ (if you didn't notice, XYZ is an LLP) to file a statement of partnership authority specifying that the partner or partners who will be signing transaction documents on XYZ's behalf have the authority to do so.

The ULLCA provides for a similar filing by an LLC.[21] There is no equivalent for corporations under the MBCA or DGCL. Some corporate statutes do, however, contain a somewhat similar provision that deems a document signed by certain specified officers as binding on the corporation even if the officers lacked authority. For example, California Corporations Code §313 provides:

> [A]ny note, mortgage, evidence of indebtedness, contract, share certificate, initial transaction statement or written statement, conveyance, or other instrument in writing, and any assignment or endorsement thereof, executed or entered into between any corporation and any other person, when signed by the chairman of the board, the president or any vice president and the secretary, any assistant secretary, the chief financial officer or any assistant treasurer of such corporation, is not invalidated as to the corporation by any lack of authority of the signing officers in the absence of actual knowledge on the part of the other person that the signing officers had no authority to execute the same.

Exercise 2.4

Refer back to the facts of Exercise 2.3. In addition to those facts, assume XYZ LLP filed a statement of partnership authority with the secretary of state and recorded it in the property transfer office for the county in which all of its real estate is located. This statement included the following:

5. If applicable, state the authority, or limitations of authority, of some or all partners to enter into transactions on behalf of the partnership (attach separate sheet if necessary):

No partner shall, without the prior written consent of the other two partners, (i) lease, rent, purchase, sell, mortgage, or otherwise create a lien upon any partnership real estate or any interest therein, or enter into any contract for any such purpose, or (ii) make or incur any expenditure on behalf of the partnership in excess of $100,000.

---

21. *See* ULLCA §302.

1. Would the statement of partnership authority filing change your answer to Question 1 of Exercise 2.3?
2. Would your answer to Question 2 of Exercise 2.3 be different if XYZ, LLC filed a statement of authority with the same limitations as above?
3. In addition to buying the Escalade, Chiba also entered into a real estate sale contract pursuant to which she agreed on behalf of XYZ LLP to sell a lot owned by XYZ to Doyle for $45,000. Upon signing the contract, Doyle gave Chiba a down payment of $4,500. Is XYZ LLP bound to the contract?

C. LIABILITY OF A PRINCIPAL FOR AGENT TORTS

Under the common law of agency, a principal can be directly or vicariously liable for torts committed by an agent. A principal is subject to direct liability if, among other things, the principal was negligent in selecting or supervising the agent. Thus, say Perez owns a piano store and hires Acosta to deliver pianos to customers. Acosta assaults Tabin while in Tabin's home delivering a piano. Perez did not conduct a background check on Acosta prior to hiring him. If Perez had, Perez would have discovered that Acosta had multiple assault convictions and, as a result, would not have hired Acosta to make deliveries. Perez is directly liable to Tabin.[22] The justification for holding a principal liable in this situation is that the principal's own fault contributed to the agent's commission of the tort.

A principal is vicariously liable for a tort committed by an agent if the agent is an employee of the principal and committed the tort while acting within the scope of employment. This is known as the doctrine of respondeat superior (Latin for "let the master answer"). Hence, respondeat superior liability turns on whether the agent was an employee and then on whether he or she was acting within the scope of employment.

We touched on the distinction between an employee and a non-employee agent above, a distinction that is important not only for agency law vicarious liability but tax, employee benefits, and employment law as well. Each of these areas has similar but differing definitions of employee, and here we are only going to discuss the agency law definition. Restatement (Third) of Agency §7.07(3) defines employee as "an agent whose principal controls or has the right to control the manner and means of the agent's performance of work."[23] The following comment to this section provides guidance on applying the definition:

Numerous factual indicia are relevant to whether an agent is an employee. These include: the extent of control that the agent and the principal have agreed the

---

22. *See* RESTATEMENT (THIRD) OF AGENCY §7.06, cmt. b, illust. 1.
23. *Id.* §7.07(3).

principal may exercise over details of the work; whether the agent is engaged in a distinct occupation or business; whether the type of work done by the agent is customarily done under a principal's direction or without supervision; the skill required in the agent's occupation; whether the agent or the principal supplies the tools and other instrumentalities required for the work and the place in which to perform it; the length of time during which the agent is engaged by a principal; whether the agent is paid by the job or by the time worked; whether the agent's work is part of the principal's regular business; whether the principal and the agent believe that they are creating an employment relationship; and whether the principal is or is not in business. Also relevant is the extent of control that the principal has exercised in practice over the details of the agent's work.[24]

As mentioned above, under the Restatement (Third) of Agency, an agent that is not an employee is called a nonemployee agent.

As to whether an employee was acting within the scope of employment, Restatement (Third) of Agency §7.07(2) provides the following: "An employee acts within the scope of employment when performing work assigned by the employer or engaging in a course of conduct subject to the employer's control. An employee's act is not within the scope of employment when it occurs within an independent course of conduct not intended by the employee to serve any purpose of the employer."

The Restatement (Third) of Agency offers the following justifications for the doctrine of respondeat superior:

> Respondeat superior creates an incentive for principals to choose employees and structure work within the organization so as to reduce the incidence of tortious conduct. This incentive may reduce the incidence of tortious conduct more effectively than doctrines that impose liability solely on an individual tortfeasor.
>
> Respondeat superior also reflects the likelihood that an employer will be more likely to satisfy a judgment. Moreover, an employer may insure against liability encompassing the consequences of all employees' actions, whereas individual employees lack the incentive and ability to insure beyond any individual's liability or assets.[25]

Note that the Restatement (Second) of Agency used different labels in applying the doctrine of respondeat superior. Specifically, it used the term "master" instead of principal, "servant" instead of employee, and "independent contractor" instead of nonemployee agent. Thus, it provided that "[a] master is subject to liability for the torts of his servants committed while acting in the scope of their employment."[26] Hence, you will likely run into this language in judicial opinions, especially those that predate the Restatement (Third) of Agency.

---

24. *Id.* §7.07, cmt. f.
25. *Id.* §2.04, cmt. b.
26. Restatement (Second) of Agency §219.

Incidentally, an agent is subject to liability for his or her torts even if a principal is also liable under respondeat superior or some other theory. As the Restatement (Third) of Agency provides, "[A]n actor remains subject to liability although the actor acts as an agent or an employee, with actual or apparent authority, or within the scope of employment."[27] Hence, if an employee commits a tort within the scope of employment, the victim could, and often does, sue the employee and the employer. In some instances, a principal has a duty under agency law to indemnify an agent. However, this duty to indemnify "does not extend to losses that result from the agent's own negligence, illegal acts, or other wrongful conduct."[28]

Note that an agent owes a principal a duty of good conduct,[29] among other duties. Thus, if a principal has to pay money to a victim of a tort committed by an employee, it is likely that the principal could sue to recover this money from the employee, arguing that the employee breached this duty of good conduct. This rarely happens in practice, because most businesses have liability insurance that covers any costs related to torts committed by employees; and, if the employee is otherwise valued by the principal, the principal does not want to damage the relationship by suing the employee.

D. THE PRINCIPAL-AGENT PROBLEM AND FIDUCIARY DUTIES OF THE AGENT

1. The Principal-Agent Problem

Say Clare's Conery, Inc. (CCI), an ice cream shop business, hires Durand as an hourly employee to work its ice cream counter. Durand has some concern with CCI's success, because if CCI fails, she would be out of a job. However, like most people, Durand is more concerned with her own self-interest than the success of CCI. Thus, sometimes she comes in late, leaves early, takes long breaks, and does not exert her best efforts. Other times she helps herself to free ice cream and does not charge her friends when they come in for ice cream. One time she even stole from the cash register. Obviously, none of these things are in the best interest of CCI.

The above is an illustration of what economists call the principal-agent problem. The gist of the problem is that the interests of a principal (in this case, CCI) and those of an agent (in this case, Durand) will invariably diverge; that is, an agent will not always act in the best interest of the principal. It is simply human nature to sometimes put your own self-interest ahead of the interests of someone else.

---

27. RESTATEMENT (THIRD) OF AGENCY §7.01.
28. *Id.* §8.14, cmt. b.
29. *Id.* §8.10.

CCI can take steps to keep Durand in line. For example, it could install a punch clock and surveillance cameras. A punch clock would likely keep Durand from arriving late, leaving early, or taking extended breaks, because she would know that CCI would then know and dock her pay or maybe even fire her. Surveillance cameras would likely keep Durand from helping herself to ice cream or giving it away to her friends, because she knows someone may be watching. Implementing these measures will, of course, cost CCI some money — at a minimum, it will have to buy, install, and maintain the punch clock and surveillance system. Economists refer to these types of costs as agency costs. Specifically, agency costs are defined as monitoring costs, bonding costs, and residual loss. Monitoring costs refer to expenditures incurred by a principal to minimize divergent behavior by an agent. CCI's costs for the punch clock and surveillance system would fall into this category. Bonding costs refer to expenditures incurred by an agent to bond itself to the principal that the agent will limit its divergent behavior. For example, Durand could get "bonded," meaning she could buy a bond from an insurance company that would reimburse CCI if Durand stole from the ice cream shop. Residual loss is loss resulting from the divergence notwithstanding monitoring and bonding.

Residual loss reflects the fact that no matter what a principal does, it probably will not be able to totally eliminate divergent behavior by an agent. In our example, for instance, a punch clock and surveillance system will likely not prevent Durand from occasionally slacking off, for example, not scooping ice cream as efficiently as she could. Costs of this slacking off — or shirking — fall into the residual loss category.

In theory, a business would not spend the money on things like punch clocks and surveillance systems unless it thought doing so would reduce total agency costs; in other words, unless the business believes that the resulting decrease in residual loss would be greater than the cost of implementing the systems. For example, say CCI estimates that installing a punch clock will save it $3,000 a year in labor costs, because it will cause employees to work their full shifts or at least be paid less if they show up late, leave early, or take an extended break. CCI also estimates that going with a punch clock will cost it $1,000 a year (includes depreciation of the clock, amortization of the installation expenses, and yearly maintenance). It should therefore go ahead and do it, because doing so reduces total agency costs by $2,000 per year ($3,000 decrease in residual loss less $1,000 increase in monitoring costs). Of course, in most situations, estimating the resulting decrease in residual loss will be speculative, at best.

Note that economists define an agency relationship "as a contract in which one or more persons (the principal(s)) engage another person (the agent) to perform some service on their behalf which involves delegating some decision-making authority to the agent."[30] This definition is broader than the legal definition of agency relationship and thus encompasses relationships that do not

---

30. Michael Jensen & William Meckling, *Theory of the Firm: Managerial Behavior, Agency Costs and Ownership Structure*, 3 J. FIN. ECON. 305, 308-09 (1976).

fall under that definition. For example, economists routinely characterize the shareholder-executive officer relationship in a public corporation as an agency relationship — the shareholders are principals and the executive officers are their agents. This relationship, however, is not a legal, or true, agency relationship because shareholders do not have the requisite control over the executive officers.

The primary way the law addresses the principal-agent problem is by imposing a fiduciary duty of loyalty on agents. The duty of loyalty has different formulations depending on the context, but all the formulations boil down to essentially the same thing: a duty to act in the best interests of the principal as opposed to the best interests of the agent.[31]

2. Fiduciary Duties of the Agent

As for agency law, the Restatement (Third) of Agency provides: "An agent has a fiduciary duty to act loyally for the principal's benefit in all matters connected with the agency relationship."[32] It then specifies that this duty includes the following:

- "a duty not to acquire a material benefit from a third party in connection with transactions conducted or other actions taken on behalf of the principal or otherwise through the agent's use of the agent's position";[33]
- "a duty not to deal with the principal as or on behalf of an adverse party in a transaction connected with the agency relationship";[34]
- "a duty to refrain from competing with the principal and from taking action on behalf of or otherwise assisting the principal's competitors";[35] and
- "a duty (1) not to use property of the principal for the agent's own purposes or those of a third party; and (2) not to use or communicate confidential information of the principal for the agent's own purposes or those of a third party."[36]

As you can see, the duties an agent owes a principal are fairly extensive. In the real world, however, they are not a primary factor for keeping agents in line. Most people strive to do what is right, to work hard, and to be honest because of their moral codes or cultural values. These moral codes are reinforced by ambition and reputational concerns. Ambition drives people to work hard in an effort to get ahead. Reputational concerns constrain people from misbehaving

---

31. Note that in this sentence the terms "principal" and "agent" are used as in the economist definition of agency, that is, more broadly than the legal definition of these terms.
32. RESTATEMENT (THIRD) OF AGENCY §8.01.
33. *Id.* §8.02.
34. *Id.* §8.03.
35. *Id.* §8.04.
36. *Id.*

out of fear of others thinking poorly of them or getting fired. There are other factors at play as well (altruism, norms, etc.) but you get the idea.

Thus, agency law fiduciary duties serve more as a backstop. They only come into play when these other factors have failed and then only if the agent's misbehavior has, or likely will, cost a business a significant amount of money. In other words, typically when a manager discovers an employee is misbehaving, the manager will reprimand or fire the employee as opposed to the employer suing him or her for breach of fiduciary duty. If, however, there is a lot of money involved, a business is much more likely to pursue a breach of fiduciary duty claim, as the next case illustrates.

Foodcomm International v. Barry
328 F.3d 300 (7th Cir. 2003)

WILLIAMS, J.

Foodcomm International sought and received a preliminary injunction against its former employees, Patrick Barry and Christopher Leacy, and Outback Imports, Inc., the company Barry and Leacy formed with Empire Beef, Inc., Foodcomm's former customer. The preliminary injunction prohibits Barry and Leacy from providing any services to Outback or Empire. In an order dated January 23, 2003, we affirmed the district court's granting of the preliminary injunction; this opinion explains the basis for our earlier decision.

I. BACKGROUND

Foodcomm is an importer of chilled Australian beef. Patrick Barry and Christopher Leacy were senior sales representatives at Foodcomm and oversaw its dealings with Empire Beef, one of Foodcomm's largest customers. Leacy and Barry were not executives with Foodcomm, but were two of Foodcomm's four highest-paid employees, and together had exclusive control over Foodcomm's purchasing and sales of Australian chilled beef.

In 2001, Empire approached Foodcomm with a business proposal to redistribute market fluctuation risk between the companies (the "redistribution deal"). Although both sides initially expressed interest in the arrangement, negotiations broke down following a meeting between Empire's Scott Brubaker and Foodcomm's Greg Bourke in March 2002. Leacy, who had been present at the meeting, asked Bourke to leave it to him (Leacy) to "smooth things over" with Empire. During this "smoothing over" process, Leacy learned from Brubaker how badly damaged the Foodcomm-Empire relationship had become when Brubaker informed Leacy that Empire would not conduct further business with Foodcomm. Leacy did not relay this information to anyone at Foodcomm, and Foodcomm's business with Empire dropped roughly 75 percent.

Meanwhile, Barry and Leacy's relationship with Foodcomm also took a downward turn. In May 2002, Barry and Leacy decided to "seek alternative employment together," and contacted Brubaker at Empire Beef to inquire whether it would be interested in their services. Brubaker requested a written business plan; Barry and Leacy used their Foodcomm computers and PDAs to prepare a business plan for a new company (Outback Imports) that would import Australian chilled beef for Empire. Barry and Leacy never informed Foodcomm about their plans with Empire and Outback, and Leacy continued to maintain to Foodcomm that he was "smoothing things over" with Empire.

Outback was incorporated in July 2002, but Barry and Leacy did not resign from Foodcomm until late August 2002. In September 2002, Outback began operating as a division of Empire with Barry and Leacy, now Empire employees, at its helm. Upon learning about Outback and its ownership by Empire and operation by Barry and Leacy, Foodcomm filed a complaint in district court seeking a preliminary injunction enjoining Barry and Leacy's continued employment with Empire and Outback. Following a four-day hearing, the district court made a preliminary finding that Barry and Leacy had . . . breached their fiduciary duties to Foodcomm when they approached Empire with a business plan and formed a company to compete against Foodcomm. The district court enjoined them from directly or indirectly providing services of any kind to or for Empire or Outback or any of their affiliates and agencies. Barry and Leacy brought an expedited appeal. Following oral argument, we affirmed the injunction in an unpublished order because, as we now explain, the district court did not abuse its discretion in granting the injunction.

II. ANALYSIS

We review the grant of a preliminary injunction for an abuse of discretion. . . .

The district court determined that Barry and Leacy's secret negotiations with Empire Beef to create Outback Imports were actions against the interests of Foodcomm and constituted a breach of Barry and Leacy's fiduciary duty of loyalty. It is a fundamental principle of agency law that agents owe fiduciary duties of loyalty to their principals not to (1) actively exploit their positions within the corporation for their own personal benefits; or (2) hinder the ability of the corporation to conduct the business for which it was developed. Officers and directors have been found to have breached their fiduciary duties when, while still employed by the company, they (1) fail to inform the company that employees are forming a rival company or engaging in other fiduciary breaches, (2) solicit the business of a single customer before leaving the company, (3) use the company's facilities or equipment to assist them in developing their new business, or (4) solicit fellow employees to join a rival business.

Barry and Leacy contend that since they were not titled as "officers" of Foodcomm, they do not owe fiduciary duties to Foodcomm. We disagree. Barry and Leacy were two of Foodcomm's highest paid employees, they were compensated based on the company's net profits, together they had exclusive charge over all of Foodcomm's purchasing of Australian chilled beef, and their job descriptions at Foodcomm involved significant autonomy and discretion. These are the hallmarks of a fiduciary, and employees, as agents of their employer, do not fall outside the purview of a breach of fiduciary duties. *Mullaney, Wells & Co. v. Savage,* 402 N.E.2d 574, 580 (Ill. 1980). "*Mullaney* ... is a case in which defendant was neither an officer nor a director of the plaintiff corporation. Nevertheless, the defendant in *Mullaney* was found to owe a fiduciary duty to the corporation because there was an agency relationship." *Radiac Abrasives, Inc. v. Diamond Technology, Inc.,* 532 N.E.2d 428, 434 (Ill. App. 1988) (internal citation omitted).

In the present case, Leacy was privy to the collapse of negotiations between Foodcomm and Empire regarding the redistribution deal and offered to "smooth things over." The evidence adduced at the hearing supports the finding that instead of "smoothing things over," Leacy conspired with Barry to present Empire with a business plan to create an Empire-owned entity that would provide the same services as were already being provided by Foodcomm, and directly compete with Foodcomm. Such efforts to actively exploit their positions within Foodcomm for their own personal benefits, and to hinder Foodcomm's ability to conduct its business with Empire, if proved at trial, constitute a breach of fiduciary duty. The evidence likewise supports a finding that Barry and Leacy also failed to inform Foodcomm of each other's plan to join Empire and form Outback, a rival company to Foodcomm; they solicited Empire's participation in their business plan while keeping their negotiations hidden from Foodcomm; and they used Foodcomm resources to draft and communicate the business plan to Empire. These actions, if proved at trial, also constitute breaches of their fiduciary duties. . . .

III. CONCLUSION

For the foregoing reasons, we AFFIRM the district court's grant of a preliminary injunction.

Questions

1. Would the case have come out differently if Barry and Leacy were not two of Foodcomm's highest paid employees and did not have significant autonomy and discretion?
2. Would the case have come out differently if Barry and Leacy were independent contractors for Foodcomm instead of employees?
3. What should Barry and Leacy have done differently?

An agent's fiduciary duties owed to a principal end upon the termination of the agency relationship. The problem for Barry and Leacy is that they started maneuvering to get the Empire business while still employed by Foodcomm. Had they waited until they quit, the case may have come out in their favor.

As noted above, the Restatement (Third) of Agency includes within the duty of loyalty an agent owes a principal "a duty to refrain from competing."[37] This does not mean, however, that an agent cannot, for example, seek employment with a competitor while still employed by the principal. Specifically, the "refrain from competing" section states that "an agent may take action, not otherwise wrongful, to prepare for competition following termination of the agency relationship."[38] Although the *Foodcomm* court did not explicitly address whether Barry and Leacy's maneuvers were "wrongful," presumably they were.

In light of the fact that agent fiduciary duties end upon termination of the agency relationship, it is common for a business to essentially extend portions of them beyond termination by contract. Specifically, many businesses routinely have at least their upper-level employees sign an agreement containing some or all of the following types of provisions:

---

6. NON-COMPETITION AND NONSOLICITATION COVENANTS. In consideration of the compensation and other benefits provided to Employee under this Agreement, Employee agrees to be bound by the covenants in this Section 6.

6.1. Non-Competition Covenant. Employee agrees that, during his employment by Company and for a period of one year after the termination or resignation of his employment for any reason whatsoever, he will not become employed, affiliated or associated (whether as an officer, director, employee, consultant, partner, joint venturer, or independent contractor), except as a customer, with any financial institution located in Arizona.

6.2. Covenant Not to Solicit Customers. Employee agrees that Company has a legitimate business interest in protecting its clients from solicitation by Employee if he ceases to be employed by Company. Accordingly, for a period of one year after the termination or resignation of his employment for any reason whatsoever, Employee shall not solicit, nor assist anyone else in the solicitation of any Company customer, for the purpose of selling or servicing the customer with any product or service that directly competes with the products or services of Company that were designed, developed, manufactured, sold, leased, distributed, or marketed by Company during the Employee's employment.

6.3. Covenant Not to Solicit Employees. Employee acknowledges that Company's employees, consultants, and other contractors constitute vital and valuable aspects of its business and missions. In recognition of that fact, for a period of one year after the termination or resignation of his employment for any reason whatsoever, Employee shall not solicit, nor assist anyone else in the solicitation of any of Company's then current employees, consultants, or other contractors, to terminate their respective relationships with Company and to become employees, consultants, or contractors of any entity or business with which Employee may then be associated, affiliated, or connected.

---

37. RESTATEMENT (THIRD) OF AGENCY §8.04.
38. *Id.*

6.4. **Injunctive Relief.** Employee acknowledges and agrees that the obligations he assumes under this Section 6 are of critical importance to Company and that any breach or threatened breach of the restrictive covenants in this Section 6 would be highly injurious to Company and that it would be extremely difficult to compensate Company fully for damages Company would incur due to any such violation. Accordingly, Employee specifically agrees that Company shall be entitled to temporary and permanent injunctive relief to enforce the provisions of the restrictive covenants in this Section 6, and that such relief may be granted without the necessity of proving actual damages and without necessity of posting any bond. This provision with respect to injunctive relief shall not, however, diminish Company's right to claim and recover damages, or to seek and obtain any other relief available to it at law or in equity, in addition to injunctive relief.

Notice that the above language includes a subsection addressing injunctive relief. Lawyers for employers include this type of provision because, as in *Foodcomm*, oftentimes injunctive relief will be the principal's preferred remedy. Recall from your contracts class that normally a court awards money damages as opposed to specific performance (e.g., an injunction) for breach of contract unless the remedy available at law (i.e., money damages) is inadequate. A provision like 6.4 above is included in a contract to make it more likely that a court will conclude that money damages are inadequate. That is why the provision, among other things, says "it would be extremely difficult to compensate Company or an Affiliate fully for damages." Such a provision is by no means definitive on the issue, but lawyers figure it does not hurt to include it.

· CHAPTER THREE ·

CHOICE OF FORM CONSIDERATIONS

Chapter 1 introduced the various legal forms in which people operate business-es. We now turn to considerations that drive the choice of form. These consider-ations include tax treatment, liability exposure, and attractiveness to investors.

A. TAX TREATMENT

For many business owners, federal tax treatment is the most important con-sideration for choosing a form. While a lot of the details regarding business taxation can be left to business tax classes, we cover three tax issues that are (or can be) particularly relevant to business form selection: minimizing federal in-come tax liability, minimizing federal employment tax liability, and allocating profits and losses among owners.

1. Minimizing Federal Income Tax Liability

a. Overview

Federal income tax liability for a business depends largely on how the busi-ness is classified for tax purposes, an issue that is related to, but not wholly de-termined by, the form in which the business is operated. Possible classifications are Subchapter C (Sub-C for short), Subchapter K (Sub-K for short), Subchap-ter S (Sub-S for short), or disregarded entity. (Recall that a reference to "Sub-chapter" is to a subchapter of the Internal Revenue Code.) A business generally gets to pick its classification, but the choices available vary by form.

The following table sums up the federal income tax classification choices for the various entities.

Entity	Choices
Multi-owner unincorporated entity other than a limited partnership (general partnership, LLP, LLC)	Sub-K* Sub-C Sub-S (if eligible)
Limited partnership	Sub-K* Sub-C
Corporation	Sub-C* Sub-S (if eligible)
Single-member LLC	Disregarded* Sub-C Sub-S (if eligible)

Each entity has a default tax classification, that is, a classification that applies unless the entity opts in to some other classification. The "*" in the above table denotes the default classification for the applicable business entity. An entity opts in to a different classification by filing a form to that effect with the IRS.[1]

I included "(if eligible)" after the three references to Sub-S in the table because the particular entity can opt in to Sub-S taxation only if it meets the following eligibility requirements as specified in Subchapter S:

- It is a domestic entity, that is, it is incorporated or organized in one of the 50 states or the District of Columbia;
- It has 100 or fewer owners;[2]
- All of its owners are individuals, estates, certain types of trusts, or tax-exempt organizations;
- None of its owners are nonresident aliens; and
- It has only one class of ownership interests outstanding (disregarding differences in voting rights).[3]

An entity must continually meet the above criteria to qualify for Sub-S taxation. If, for example, it inadvertently ends up with more than 100 owners, it will no longer qualify for Sub-S taxation, and therefore its tax classification will immediately change to the default classification for the particular entity.

---

1. The specific form is either IRS Form 8832 (commonly called the "check-the-box form") or Form 2553 (commonly called the "S-election form").

2. Family members (as defined in IRC §1361(c)(1)(B)) and their estates are treated as one owner for the count.

3. A corporation is generally considered to have only one class of stock if "all outstanding shares of stock of the corporation confer identical rights to distribution and liquidation proceeds." IRC §1.1361-1(l).

For example, a corporation's classification will change to Sub-C, and an LLP's classification will change to Sub-K. Thus, Sub-S taxation is often described as "fragile" because eligibility is easily inadvertently lost.

Note that per IRC §7704, a publicly traded unincorporated entity is taxed under Sub-C unless at least 90 percent of its gross income consists of "qualifying income," in which case it can be taxed under Sub-K. "Qualifying income" includes interest, dividends, real property rents, gain from the disposition of real property, income and gain from commodities or commodity futures, income and gain from mineral or natural resources activities mining and natural resource income, and gain from the disposition of capital assets. An unincorporated entity is considered publicly traded if its ownership interests are traded on an established securities market (for example, the New York Stock Exchange or NASDAQ) or are readily tradable on a secondary market.[4]

A corporation taxed under Sub-C is often referred to as a C-corporation, and one taxed under Sub-S is likewise referred to as an S-corporation. Confusingly, tax professionals sometimes refer to an LLC, LLP, or other unincorporated entity that has elected to be taxed under Sub-S as an S-corporation even though under state law the entity is not actually a corporation. Along similar lines, do not be thrown off by the fact that Sub-S is explicitly designed for "small business corporations," and thus Sub-S rules and forms refer to the entity as an S-corporation. An unincorporated entity can nonetheless elect to be taxed under Sub-S if it meets the Sub-S criteria.

b. Sub-K and Sub-S Taxation

As mentioned in Chapter 1, both Sub-K and Sub-S provide for pass-through taxation, meaning that the entity calculates its income/loss for the tax year and then allocates it to each owner. For a Sub-S entity, allocations have to be based on percentage ownership, meaning if you own 40 percent of the entity, you are allocated 40 percent of its income or loss each year. For a Sub-K entity, allocations can be based on something other than percentage ownership as discussed in Section A.3. below. Here is an example of pass-through taxation in action. We use a corporation that has elected to be taxed under Sub-S (often called an S-corporation), but the calculations would be the same if it were instead an unincorporated entity taxed under Sub-K.

Example 1.

Clare's Conery Inc. (CCI) is a single shareholder corporation owned by Clare. CCI earns $100,000 for its 2012 fiscal year.

CCI meets the Sub-S eligibility requirement so elects to be taxed under Subchapter S.

---

4. *See* Treas. Reg. §1.7704-1(c) for the definition of "readily tradable on a secondary market."

Because CCI is taxed under Subchapter S, it does not pay tax. Assume that CCI distributes the entire $100,000 to Clare. Clare includes this amount on her personal federal income tax return. Assume that Clare's income tax filing status is single and that she had no other income, tax credits, deductions, etc for 2012.[5] The 2012 tax rates for a single taxpayer were as follows:

2012 Individual Tax Rates — Single Taxpayer

Taxable income over	Not over	Tax rate
$ 0	$ 8,700	10%
8,700	35,350	15%
35,350	85,650	25%
85,650	178,650	28%
178,650	388,350	33%
388,350	—	35%

The above tax rates are applied to taxable income incrementally. In other words, an individual pays tax at a rate of 10 percent on his or her first $8,700 of taxable income, 15 percent on his or her next $26,650 of taxable income, 25 percent on his or her next $50,300 of taxable income, etc. Thus, Clare will pay $21,460.50 in federal income tax on the $100,000 distribution calculated as follows: ($8,750 × .1) + ($26,650 × .15) + ($50,300 × .25) + (14,500 × .28).

End result: IRS gets $21,460.50, and Clare is left with $78,539.50.

Note that the end result would be the same even if CCI did not distribute the $100,000 to Clare but instead retained it in the business. Under both Sub-S and Sub-K, owners of a business are taxed on business income allocated to them even if the business did not distribute any money to them.

As I mentioned above, an unincorporated entity can elect to be taxed under Sub-S if it meets the Sub-S criteria.[6] This raises the question of why a business that decides on Sub-S taxation would, for example, organize as an LLC instead of as a corporation. One reason is that LLC statutes are generally more flexible when it comes to tailoring rules to the preferences of the owners and require fewer formalities than corporate law statutes. Going with an LLC over a corporation may also be attractive if the business anticipates becoming ineligible for Sub-S taxation in the future (e.g., if it plans to solicit equity investments from business entities) or is worried about inadvertently blowing its Sub-S eligibility (e.g., by mistakenly selling an ownership interest to a nonresident alien). This is

---

5. For simplicity, the calculations in the example do not take into account the standard deduction Clare would be able to subtract from her income before calculating her federal income tax liability

6. Note that a limited partnership will never be able to meet the criteria, because by definition it has two classes of ownership interests — general partnership interests and limited partnership interests.

because a Sub-S LLC defaults to Sub-K taxation when it loses Sub-S eligibility, while an S-corporation defaults to the double taxation of Sub-C. One downside to going with a Sub-S LLC over an S-corporation is that a number of states do not recognize S-elections by LLCs for state tax purposes.

c. Sub-C Taxation

In contrast to Sub-K and Sub-S taxation, an entity taxed under Subchapter C is treated as a separate taxpayer. Thus, the entity must file an annual income tax return (usually on Form 1120) reporting its income, deductions, and credits for the year and pay any resulting income tax at corporate income tax rates. For 2012, these rates were as follows:

2012 Corporate Tax Rates

Taxable income over	Not over	Tax rate
$ 0	$ 50,000	15%
50,000	75,000	25%
75,000	100,000	34%
100,000	335,000	39%
335,000	10,000,000	34%
10,000,000	15,000,000	35%
15,000,000	18,333,333	38%
18,333,333	—	35%

As with individual rates, the above tax rates are applied incrementally. In other words, a Sub-C entity pays tax at a rate of 15 percent on its first $50,000 of taxable income, 25 percent on its next $25,000 of taxable income, 34 percent on its next $235,000 of taxable income, etc.

If a Sub-C entity distributes money to its owners (such a distribution is normally referred to as a dividend), the owners must include the distribution in their taxable incomes. Dividends paid by C-corporations are generally taxed at the capital gains rate (as opposed to ordinary income rates), which was 15 percent in 2012.[7] Thus, a Sub-C entity's profits are taxed when earned and then taxed again (but at least generally at a lower rate) when distributed to owners.

---

7. Actually, the 2012 capital gains rate was 0 percent if the taxpayer's total income placed him or her in the 15 percent tax bracket (for Clare, this would be the situation if her income was $50,000 or less) or 15 percent if the taxpayer's total income placed him or her in the 25 percent tax bracket or higher (Clare falls under this because her total income in the example exceeds $50,000).

This "double taxation" typically results in more money paid to the IRS in taxes and less money ending up in owner pockets as compared to pass-through taxation. To illustrate this point, I redo the CCI example from above with CCI being taxed under Sub-C instead of Sub-S:

Example 2.

Assume Clare's Conery Inc. (CCI) earns $100,000 for the fiscal year.

CCI does not qualify to be taxed under Sub-S so it is taxed under Sub-C.

Thus, CCI pays $22,250 in corporate income tax [($50,000 x .15) + ($25,000 x .25) + ($25,000 x .34)]. Assume it then distributes the remaining $77,750 to Clare.

Clare is required to include this $77,750 on her tax return. Clare has to pay tax on this amount at 15 percent, so she will pay $11,662.50 in taxes ($77,750 x .15) on this dividend, leaving her with $66,087.50 after tax.

End result: IRS gets $33,912.50 ($22,250 from CCI + $11,662.50 from Clare), and Clare is left with $66,087.50 ($100,000 – $33,912.50 paid to the IRS).

Hence, the fact that CCI is taxed under Sub-C instead of Sub-S results in an additional $12,452 being paid to the IRS,[8] an amount that comes straight out of Clare's pocket.

Exercise 3.1

1. CCI earns $150,000 for the its 2012 fiscal year. CCI does not qualify to be taxed under Sub-S (Clare, its sole shareholder, is a nonresident alien), so it is taxed under Sub-C. Clare decides to leave all the money in the business. In other words, unlike the example from above, CCI does not distribute its profits to Clare. How much does CCI have to pay in federal income tax on the money? What about Clare?

2. Same facts as Question 1, but CCI has made an S-election. How much does CCI have to pay in federal income tax on the money? What about Clare?

3. A Inc. (AI) has 84 shareholders, all of whom are individuals, reside in the United States, and are U.S. citizens. AI is incorporated in Iowa and its charter authorizes it to issue up to 1,000,000 shares of common stock and 10,000 shares of preferred stock. AI's shareholders collectively own 600,000 shares of common stock and 200 shares of preferred stock. Is AI a C-corporation or an S-corporation?

---

8. Here's the calculation: 78,539.50 – 66,087.50 = 12,452.

d. Disregarded Entity Taxation

As the above table indicates, a single-owner LLC is taxed as a "disregarded entity" (an entity "that is treated as an entity not separate from its single owner for income tax purposes"[9]) unless it opts for Sub-C or Sub-S taxation (assuming it meets the S-election eligibility criteria). A disregarded entity is taxed essentially the same as a sole proprietorship. The owner reports net income or net loss from the business on his or her personal federal income tax return. A single-member LLC cannot elect to be taxed under Sub-K, because Sub-K taxation is only available to unincorporated entities with two or more owners.

e. Summation

In sum, business owners (like most people) want to pay as little tax as possible, so they will choose a business form that allows them to elect the tax treatment that will result in the lowest tax liability. From this perspective, Sub-C taxation is generally the worst because it results in "double" and therefore generally greater taxation of the business's earnings. Thus, for many business owners, going with Sub-C taxation is immediately eliminated from contention.[10]

With Sub-C taxation currently out of contention, the federal income taxation choice generally reduces to Sub-K versus Sub-S taxation for multi-owner businesses and disregarded entity versus Sub-S for single-owner businesses. Sub-K and Sub-S both provide for pass-through taxation, but there are a number of differences between the regimes. While the bulk of the differences can be left to business tax classes, in the next subsection we discuss one difference that sometimes tips the balance in favor of Sub-S.

2. Minimizing Federal Employment Tax Liability

The owners of a business taxed under Sub-K are subject to self-employment tax (commonly called SE tax) on the business's income if they participate actively in its business affairs. They are also subject to SE tax on any wages paid to them by the business. For 2012, the federal self-employment tax is 13.3 percent of the first $110,100 of an individual's self-employment income and 2.9 percent thereafter. The $110,100 ceiling is adjusted annually for inflation, so it typically

---

9. IRS Form 8832, General Instructions.

10. The relative unattractiveness of Sub-C taxation varies with applicable tax rates. Sub-C taxation is currently unattractive, because corporate rates plus the dividend rate exceeds individual tax rates on ordinary income. For example, assume the applicable corporate rate is 35 percent and the dividend rate is 15 percent. The effective income tax rate on earnings distributed as dividends to shareholders is 44.75 percent (.35 + [(1 − .35) × .15]) which is significantly higher than the top individual tax rate of 35 percent. If instead the effective rate on earnings was lower than the applicable individual tax rate (which could happen if Congress lowers corporate and/or dividend rates, and/or increases individual rates), business owners would generally prefer Sub-C taxation over Sub-K or Sub-S taxation.

goes up every year. The 13.3 percent rate is normally 15.3 percent but was temporarily reduced as part of an Obama Administration economic stimulus plan. SE tax is used to fund Social Security and Medicare.

Conversely, owners of a business taxed under Sub-S are not subject to self-employment tax on the business's income. A Sub-S business and its owners are subject to Social Security and Medicare taxes (often called FICA) on wages paid by the business to its owners at a combined rate of 13.3 percent, that is, the same rate as the SE tax. However, income retained by a Sub-S business or distributed to owners as dividends is not subject to FICA tax. Thus, Sub-S taxation can substantially reduce employment taxes.

For example, assume Gray and Smith own AAA Pool Services (APS), a successful pool cleaning and maintenance business. They agree to split profits 50/50, both work there full time, and are each paid $80,000 in salary. In 2012, the business generated $140,000 in net income which Gray and Smith decide to leave in APS to fund equipment upgrades and expansion.

If APS is taxed under Sub-K, Gray and Smith will each have to pay self-employment tax on $150,000. This amount is composed of their $80,000 salaries plus the $70,000 of net income allocated to each of them ($140,000 net income split 50/50). In 2012, federal self-employment tax on $150,000 is $15,800,[11] so the two of them will pay a combined total of $31,600. Note that APS pays nothing.

If APS is instead taxed under Sub-S, the $80,000 salaries paid to Gray and Smith will be subject to FICA tax at a rate of 13.3 percent (APS pays half and Gray and Smith pay half). Thus, the combined total of employment taxes paid by APS, Gray, and Smith will be $21,280, which is $9,634 less than would be paid in employment taxes if APS is taxed under Sub-K. The difference comes from the fact that under Sub-S, no employment taxes are imposed on the $140,000 retained by APS. Gray and Smith could further save on FICA tax by decreasing the amount they take in salary and correspondingly increasing the amount they take as distributions from APS. The IRS, however, is well aware of this strategy and therefore requires that salaries paid to employee-owners of Sub-S businesses be reasonable. Thus, if Gray and Smith were to drop their salaries from APS to $30,000 to avoid FICA on another $50,000 each, they run the risk that the IRS will audit them or APS and conclude the $30,000 salaries were unreasonably low. In such an event, the IRS would recharacterize a portion of the APS distributions received by Gray and Smith as salaries, meaning that they would have to re-do their taxes to reflect an increased salary, pay the resulting increase in the amount they owe plus interest, and perhaps have to pay a penalty.

Note that employment tax savings from Sub-S versus Sub-K taxation only materialize if the business is profitable. For example, if APS had zero profits for the year, Gray and Smith would still pay self-employment tax on their $80,000 salaries but no APS net income would be allocated to them because it

---

11. Here is the calculation: ($110,100 × .133) + [($150,000 − $110,100) × .029] = $15,800.40.

had none. Thus, total employment taxes paid would be the same under Sub-S and Sub-K.

The same dynamic is present for a single-owner LLC deciding between disregard entity taxation and Sub-S taxation. Specifically, if the LLC is taxed as a disregarded entity and its owner participates actively in its business affairs (which is likely always the case), the LLC's income and any wages paid by the LLC to the owner are subject to SE tax. If a single-owner LLC is instead taxed under Sub-S, only wages paid by the LLC to the owner are subject to employment tax (in this case, it would be FICA tax). Hence, the single owner of a profitable LLC will likely save on employment taxes if he or she goes with Sub-S taxation for the business instead of disregarded entity taxation.

Exercise 3.2

You are the sole owner and employee of a dog-walking business organized as an LLC. The business generated profits of $10,000 for its latest fiscal year after paying you a $30,000 salary and has decided to retain these profits.

1. Assume the LLC has not made an S-election or checked the box to be taxed under Sub-C. How much do you owe in employment taxes? How much does the LLC owe in employment taxes?
2. Assume the LLC has made an S-election. How much do you owe in employment taxes? How much does the LLC owe in employment taxes?

For the following two problems, assume instead that the LLC lost $10,000 for its fiscal year after paying you a $30,000 salary.

3. Assume the LLC has not made an S-election. How much do you owe in employment taxes? How much does the LLC owe in employment taxes?
4. Assume the LLC has made an S-election. How much do you owe in employment taxes? How much does the LLC owe in employment taxes?

---

3. Allocating and Using Losses

It is not uncommon for a business to be started by two different types of people: those with a great idea, passion, and energy but no money, and those with a lot of money that like the idea and admire the passion and energy of the other person. For example, say you have a great idea, no money, but a rich aunt who has always been fond of you. You convince her to provide you funding to develop your idea. You form EFG, LLC and take a 60 percent ownership interest in exchange for transferring the idea to EFG. Your aunt gets a 40 percent ownership interest in exchange for investing $500,000 in EFG. It will take some time to develop and commercialize your idea so you expect the company to lose $300,000 in its first year of business. As you know, under both Sub-K and Sub-S, losses are passed through to the owners of the business. Thus, if the losses of EFG are allocated based on percentage ownership, you would be allocated $180,000 in losses ($300,000 × .6) and your aunt would be allocated $120,000 ($300,000 × .4). As someone with no money, you will not be able to use $180,000 in losses because you drew a very modest salary from the company, which income was completely offset by other deductions (home mortgage interest, property tax, etc.) on your tax return. Put differently, passed-through losses reduce a person's tax burden only to the extent that the person has income against which the losses can be subtracted.

It is a different story for your aunt. She has a lot of income from various investments, and therefore could use not just $120,000 in losses but the entire $300,000 if they were allocated to her. In other words, she has more than $300,000 in income against which she could subtract the losses on her income tax return, thereby reducing the amount of tax she owes. Thus, it probably makes sense to allocate all the losses from the business to your aunt. Even if you could use some of the losses, your aunt is presumably in a higher tax bracket than you, so the losses will reduce the dollar amount of her tax burden more than they would reduce the dollar amount of your tax burden if allocated to you. You could even ask your aunt to take a slightly smaller ownership stake in the company (say, 39 percent instead of 40 percent) to compensate you for agreeing to allocate all losses to her.

Allocating losses (and profits) on a basis other than percentage ownership is possible under Sub-K but not Sub-S. Thus, your company would need to go with Sub-K in order to get extra losses to your aunt. More generally, if a multi-owner business desires to allocate profits and losses on some basis other than percentage ownership (doing so is commonly referred to as "special allocations"), it will need to go with an unincorporated entity and stick with Sub-K taxation. The business cannot be organized as a corporation because a corporation is taxed under Sub-C or Sub-S, neither of which allows special allocations.

A business puts special allocations in place by including appropriate provisions in its partnership, operating, or similar agreement. Because special allocations have been at the heart of numerous schemes by high-income taxpayers to use business losses to offset or shelter their business and other income, a number of IRS rules designed to thwart abusive tax shelters come into play.

While we leave the bulk of the details related to special allocations to business tax classes, you should be familiar with the concept of substantial economic effect and the three primary limitations on an owner deducting losses on his or her individual federal tax return, so these topics are discussed briefly below. Note that the IRS refers to owners of a business taxed under Sub-K as partners even if the business is an LLC (under state law, owners of an LLC are called members, not partners). Thus, we will do the same in the following subsections.

a. *Substantial Economic Effect*

Generally speaking, a special allocation is valid for tax purposes only if it has "substantial economic effect,"[12] or SEE for short. It would be nice if I could now give you a short and concise description of what this means. Unfortunately, it is not possible, because SEE is one of the most complex subjects in all of tax. Nonetheless, here is my attempt to sum up the gist of SEE in one sentence: For a special allocation to have substantial economic effect, it has to at least appear that the partners agreed to it for economic reasons rather than to merely minimize the partners' tax obligations. Let's look at some examples to give you a flavor for this.

Say you and your cousin decide to start a hot dog stand, split ownership 50/50, operate it as an LLC, and go with Sub-K taxation. Your cousin contributes cash for his ownership stake. You are short on cash, so your cousin agrees that you can pay for your ownership stake at the end of year one. The LLC's operating agreement provides that your cousin will receive 90 percent of the profits and losses during year one. After year one, you and your cousin will split profits and losses equally. This special allocation likely has substantial economic effect, because it reflects the economic fact that your cousin has more money than you invested in the business for the first year.

Conversely, say you contributed cash for your ownership stake at the same time as your cousin, but still agreed that 90 percent of the profits and losses would be allocated to him during year one. You agreed to this allocation largely because you both expect the business will lose money its first year, and your cousin is in a higher tax bracket than you. Thus, the losses will reduce his tax obligation by a greater dollar amount than they would yours. This special allocation likely has no substantial economic effect.

If the IRS determines an allocation does not have substantial economic effect, it will disregard it and generally tax each partner based on his or her percentage ownership. If that occurred in the example above, you and your cousin would have to redo your tax returns with the hot dog stand's losses allocated 50/50.

To reiterate, IRS regulations on substantial economic effect are lengthy, complicated, and well beyond the scope of this book (and my expertise). The above discussion is meant only to introduce you to the concept so that you are aware of it. In practice you will likely need to consult a partnership tax expert (lawyer or accountant) when including special allocations in an operating or partnership agreement.

---

12. I.R.C. §704(b).

b. Deduction Limitations

Even if the special allocation provisions put in place by a partnership have "substantial economic effect," an individual may nonetheless be prevented from deducting losses allocated to him or her by the basis, at-risk, or passive loss limitation.

(1) Basis Limitation

The basis limitation caps the deduction a partner can take for partnership losses allocated to him or her in any particular year to the partner's adjusted basis in his or her partnership interest at the end of that year before taking into account a partner's share of the loss. Roughly speaking, a partner's initial basis equals the amount of money and the value of any property he or she contributed to the partnership. A partner's basis is increased by, among other things, any additional contribution made by the partner to the partnership and partnership income allocated to the partner. A partner's basis is decreased by, among other things, money and the value of any property distributed to the partner by the partnership and the partnership losses allocated to the partner. Thus, a partner's adjusted basis equals his or her initial basis plus any of the foregoing increases and less any of the foregoing decreases.

For example, say you contributed $10,000 to a partnership in exchange for a partnership interest in a startup business. The business loses money during its first year of operation so it makes no distributions to its partners, but $4,000 of losses are allocated to you under the partnership agreement. At the end of year one, your adjusted basis in your partnership interest would be $6,000 ($10,000 – $4,000). The next year, the business turns a profit so it distributes $1,000 to you. Additionally, $2,000 of profits are allocated to you under the partnership agreement. At the end of year two, your adjusted basis in your partnership interest would be $7,000 ($6,000 – $1,000 + $2,000). In year three, the partnership loses money, and you are allocated $6,000 of loss. You would be able to deduct the full $6,000 (subject to the at-risk and passive loss limitations). Your adjusted basis in your partnership interest would be $1,000. In year four, the partnership again loses money, and you are allocated $3,000 in losses. You would only be able to deduct $1,000 in losses (subject to the at-risk and passive loss limitations), and your adjusted basis would decrease to zero. (IRS rules provide that adjusted basis can never be less than zero.) You can, however, "carry forward" your $2,000 in unused losses and deduct them in a future year in which the adjusted basis in your partnership interest is greater than zero.

(2) At-Risk Limitation

The at-risk limitation caps the deduction a partner can take for partnership losses allocated to him or her to the amount the partner has "at risk" in the business. This limitation is similar to the basis limitation, because both limitations take into account the amount a partner has invested in the business, but the amount at risk can differ from a partner's adjusted basis because of loan guarantees, stop-loss agreements, or nonrecourse loans.

For example, a partner's adjusted basis is increased for his or her share of any nonrecourse loan taken out by the partnership. A nonrecourse loan is a loan for which no partner is personally liable. Because the partner is not personally liable on the loan, he or she is not considered "at risk" on it.[13] Hence, the partner's amount at risk will be less than his or her adjusted basis by an amount equal to the partner's share of the nonrecourse loan.

A partner can carry forward losses that are disallowed as a result of the at-risk rules and deduct them in future years in which the partner has a sufficient amount at risk.

(3) Passive Activity Loss Limitation

The passive activity loss limitation allows a taxpayer to deduct losses from "passive" activities only to the extent of the taxpayer's passive income from his or her other passive activities for that year. Passive activities include: (1) Ownership of a business in which the taxpayer does not materially participate during the year, and (2) rental activities, even if the taxpayer materially participates in them, unless the taxpayer is a real estate professional. In general, a taxpayer materially participated in a business for a tax year if he or she was involved on a regular, continuous, and substantial basis in its operations.[14]

Thus, for example, if your aunt from above did not materially participate in the operations of EFG, the EFG losses allocated to her will be considered passive. As a result, she will only be able to deduct them against passive activity income she had for the year (assuming the deduction was not otherwise disallowed by the basis or at-risk limitation). Say your aunt was (1) allocated $100,000 in income from some other investment she made in a pass-through entity in whose business she did not materially participate, and (2) had $50,000 in rental income from an apartment building she owns. She thus has $150,000 of passive activity income and therefore could deduct the full $120,000 of EFG losses allocated to her (assuming the deduction was not otherwise disallowed by the basis or at-risk limitation).

A taxpayer may carry forward unused passive losses to deduct against future passive income. Thus, if your aunt instead had only $50,000 of passive activity income for the year, she would be able to deduct, or use, only $50,000 of the EFG losses allocated to her but could carry forward the unused $70,000 of passive activity losses to deduct against passive activity income in a future year.

---

13. IRS rules do allow a partner's share of certain nonrecourse loans secured by real estate that is used in the business to increase a partner's amount at risk.

14. *See* Treas. Reg. §1.469-5T(a) for a list of seven different tests for what constitutes material participation.

Since you materially participated in EFG's business, the $180,000 in EFG losses allocated to you are characterized as ordinary. As a result, you can offset this amount against your ordinary income (e.g., your EFG salary), subject to the basis and at-risk limitations. If you have insufficient ordinary income to use the full $180,000, you can carry forward for up to 20 years any unused portion to offset against your future ordinary income.

c. Summation

If business owners want to allocate profits and losses for tax purposes on some basis other than percentage ownership, they will have to organize the business as an unincorporated entity (LLC or partnership) so that the business can be taxed under Subchapter K. They can then include provisions in the business's operating or partnership agreement providing for "special allocations." These allocations, however, must have "substantial economic effect," or they will be disregarded by the IRS. Even then, the deductibility by a partner of partnership losses is subject to basis, at-risk, and passive loss limitations.

B. LIABILITY EXPOSURE

Liability exposure is a significant choice of form consideration. There are two aspects of liability exposure relevant to form selection: (1) the extent to which the owners of a business operated in a particular legal form face potential personal liability on the business's obligations (I refer to this exposure as "inside liability exposure"); and (2) the extent to which the creditors of the owners of a business operated in a particular legal form can recover against the business's assets (I refer to this exposure as "outside liability exposure").

1. Inside Liability Exposure

a. Overview

As we touched on in Chapter 1, owner exposure for inside liabilities varies across forms. Corporations and LLCs provide full inside liability shields to all owners regardless of the state of incorporation/organization. Most LLPs provide their partners with full inside liability shields but LLPs organized in Louisiana and South Carolina provide only partial shields. Limited partnerships afford limited partners full liability shields, but in many states this shield can be partially lost under the control rule. General partners of a limited partnership get no liability shield regardless of the state of organization, and neither do sole proprietors or partners of a general partnership.

For many business owners, the fact that neither a general partnership nor a sole proprietorship provides an owner with any inside liability protection immediately eliminates these forms from contention as a possible choice for a business. Liability exposure concerns often eliminate limited partnerships from contention too. The story with limited partnerships, however, is a little more complicated.

Lawyers figured out early on that they could get all owners of a limited partnership a liability shield simply by incorporating the general partner. Specifically, instead of an individual serving as the general partner of a limited partnership, the individual would become the sole shareholder of a newly formed corporation, and this corporation would serve as the general partner. Because the individual controls the corporation, the individual controls the limited partnership to the same extent as if he or she were actually the general partner. However, the individual is now protected against personal liability for the obligations of the limited partnership by the liability shield of the corporation. Limited partnerships with corporate general partners were once a fairly prevalent structure. In part because of the rise of LLCs and LLPs, this is no longer the case. LLCs and LLPs are taxed the same as limited partnerships, but provide liability shields to all their owners without the additional complication and expense of having a second entity (the corporate general partner) in the mix or any equivalent of the control rule.

For some business owners, liability exposure concerns even eliminate an LLP from contention. This is largely because in three states (California, Oregon, and New York) the LLP form is limited to professional practices, for example, law, accounting, and medicine. While a non-professional business operating in one of these states is free to organize as an LLP in a state without a professional practice restriction, there is a good chance that a professional restriction state will treat such an LLP as a general partnership, meaning no liability shield for its partners.[15] The justification for this treatment is that a foreign[16] LLP should not be able to engage in business that is not allowed of a domestic LLP.[17] The strength of the LLP liability shield is also weakened by the existence of the two partial-shield states mentioned above. While a business operating in one of these states is likewise free to organize as an LLP in a full-shield state, some uncertainty remains as to whether a court in a partial-shield state will honor the full-shield provided by the state of organization. Furthermore, at one time there were many more partial-shield states (a number of states have since amended their partnership statutes to provide for a full shield). Thus, there may be some lingering bias among attorneys in or near former partial-shield states against recommending the LLP form.

15. *See, e.g.*, RUPA §1101 cmt.
16. A business operating in a state that is not its state of organization is referred to by that state as a "foreign" LLP, LLC, corporation, etc., as the case may be.
17. A business operating in its state of organization is referred to by that state as a "domestic" LLP, LLC, corporation, etc., as the case may be.

The bottom line is that corporations and LLCs provide the best protection for owners against inside liabilities. The corporate law and limited liability company statutes of all states provide full inside liability shields and no state limits their use to professional practice (although the professional practice regulations of many states prohibit various professions from operating in the corporate or LLC form).

b. Veil Piercing

No type of entity provides an impenetrable liability shield, because all shields are subject to veil piercing, a judicially created exception to limited liability. Under this exception, a court disregards the liability shield of a corporation, LLC, or other limited liability entity and holds its owners personally liable for the entity's obligations. Veil piercing is a heavily litigated issue. Nonetheless, the law in the area is murky, because no bright line test exists for when a court will pierce. The next case discusses various factors courts consider in deciding whether to pierce. This case is included to provide an *example* of a piercing case and not because it is the leading case on piercing. There is no leading case on piercing.

Kansas Gas & Elec. Co. v. Ross
521 N.W.2d 107 (S.D. 1994)

LOVRIEN, Circuit Judge.

This is an appeal by Kansas Gas & Electric Company (KG & E) from summary judgment granted to Jeff Ross in an action by KG & E to "pierce the corporate veil" of Ross Service Company, Inc. (Ross Service) and hold Jeff Ross individually liable for outstanding corporate debt. We affirm.

FACTS

Ross Service is a South Dakota corporation engaged in the scrap metal and wire salvaging business. KG & E is a Kansas corporation engaged in the supply of natural gas and electric power.

This controversy arose from a transaction initiated on June 27, 1990, when Ross Service submitted a bid of 38 cents per pound to KG & E for the purchase of approximately 1.9 million pounds of surplus wire. Ross Service was to provide trucking and pay KG & E weekly for wire received.

The bid was signed "Jeff Ross, Owner, Ross Service Company, Inc." KG & E accepted this bid on July 2, 1990. Pursuant to the agreement, KG & E, according to their records, provided Ross Service with surplus wire worth $706,977.72 from July to October of 1990. Ross Service failed to keep up with its weekly payments. Of the $706,977.72 owed under the contract, Ross Service did not pay $194,204.40. It claimed, among other things, that it had not received all the wire that KG & E's records indicated.

As a result of Ross Service's failure to pay the amount owed, KG & E sued Ross Service and Jeff Ross. KG & E later settled its dispute with Ross Service, but sought to recover from Jeff Ross individually by piercing the corporate veil.

Ross Service was incorporated in March of 1979 by John and Edith Ross. John Ross is president and Edith Ross is vice president and secretary of the corporation. They are the parents of Jeff Ross. It is undisputed that Jeff Ross was employed by the corporation from 1979 to July of 1991. Rodney Ross, Jeff's brother, was the treasurer of the corporation until his death in 1984.

At the time of incorporation, an initial subscription of 640 shares of stock was issued by John Ross. He then kept 319 shares for himself, gave 319 shares to Edith Ross and the remaining two shares to Rodney Ross.

Although Jeff Ross never received any of the original subscription shares, there is a dispute of fact regarding Jeff Ross's status as a shareholder. Edith Ross testified that after Rodney's death in 1984, his two shares were given to Jeff Ross. This testimony is the only evidence that Jeff Ross was ever a shareholder in Ross Service. Jeff Ross denies that he has ever been a shareholder in the company. Even when we view this factual issue in favor of KG & E and assume that the transfer was made to Jeff Ross, his ownership interest amounts to only .3125 percent of the outstanding stock.

The facts are also in dispute whether Jeff Ross served as an officer and/or director of Ross Service. The corporation's annual reports for 1989 and 1990 list Jeff Ross as a director for Ross Service. These reports were prepared entirely by Edith Ross. Jeff Ross denies that he was ever informed or consented to serving as a director of Ross Service. The annual report for 1991, which was filed on March 25, 1990, does not list Jeff Ross as a director even though he did not leave the employment of Ross Service until July of 1991.

Jeff Ross admits that two corporate notes bear his signature as treasurer of Ross Service. However, he claims to have no recollection of having signed these notes and states that he most likely did so at the direction of his parents or the bank.

The evidence also reveals that Ross Service's tax returns for 1989 and 1990 show all the officers who were compensated by the corporation and list only John and Edith Ross as officers of Ross Service. Jeff Ross is not listed as an officer.

In addition to his employment with Ross Service, Jeff Ross operated his own trucking company. The trucking company maintained a checking account at Norwest Bank in Dell Rapids, South Dakota. Ross Service maintained its corporate account with Dakota State Bank in Colman, South Dakota.

Ross Service experienced financial difficulties in the spring of 1990. As a result, Dakota State Bank began to apply all deposits made to the corporate account to existing loan balances Ross Service owed to the bank. To avoid this, Edith Ross asked Jeff Ross whether the corporation could use Jeff's trucking business account. Jeff agreed.

From April of 1990 to January of 1991, both Ross Service and Jeff Ross used the trucking company's account. Different size checks were used in an effort to distinguish Jeff Ross's personal expenses from Ross Services's corporate expenses.

In October of 1990, Ross Service issued two checks drawn on the trucking company's account in the amount of $7,500 for the purchase of a 1976 Ford truck and $2,200 for the purchase of a trailer. Jeff Ross kept the truck and trailer for his own personal use. The record shows that he reimbursed the account for these items by depositing $10,000 into the trucking company account in October of 1990 from a loan he received from Norwest Bank. The record also shows that the truck and trailer were listed on the loan documents as the items being purchased and as the items in which a security interest was being granted to Norwest Bank.

At the close of discovery, Jeff Ross moved for summary judgment. A hearing was held by the trial court on December 21, 1992, where the motion was granted. The court concluded that even though Jeff Ross may have had some control over the corporation as a manager, he was such a minor shareholder that the court could not say that he was operating the business as his alter ego. KG & E appeals the judgment.

The only issue raised on appeal is whether the trial court erred in granting summary judgment to Jeff Ross. KG & E argues that summary judgment is improper because there are genuine issues of material fact to be determined in this case.

DECISION . . .

II. PIERCING THE CORPORATE VEIL

A firmly entrenched doctrine of American law is the concept that a corporation is considered a legal entity separate and distinct from its officers, directors and shareholders until there is sufficient reason to the contrary.

We have long recognized this doctrine as well.

This concept of "limited liability" is considered the central purpose for choosing the corporate form because it permits corporate shareholders to limit their personal liability to the extent of their investment.

Incorporation for the purpose of achieving limited liability is one of the principal objectives of incorporation. Limited liability is enjoyed even by a controlling shareholder. Under corporate contracts, ordinarily the corporation, and not the shareholders, suffers the liabilities. Shareholders, directors and officers who cause their corporation to breach its contract with a third party are usually not liable for inducing breach of contract.

The principal exception to the limited liability rule is the doctrine of "piercing the corporate veil." This doctrine is equitable in nature and is used by the courts to disregard the distinction between a corporation and its shareholders to prevent fraud or injustice. The general rule which has emerged is that a corporation will be looked upon as a legal entity separate and distinct from its shareholders, officers and directors unless and until sufficient reason to the contrary appears, but when the notion of a legal entity is used to defeat public convenience, justify wrong, protect fraud, or defend crime, then sufficient reason will exist to pierce the corporate veil.

"In deciding whether the corporate veil will be pierced, we recognize that 'each case is sui generis and must be decided in accordance with its own underlying facts.'" *Mobridge Community Industries v. Toure*, 273 N.W.2d 128, 132 (S.D. 1978) (quoting *Brown Brothers Equipment Co. v. State*, 51 Mich. App. 448, 215 N.W.2d 591, 593 (1974)).

In our past decisions, we have discussed a number of factors[18] that might justify "piercing the corporate veil." After review of those decisions and the factors discussed therein, it is apparent that in making this determination, we have applied a two-part test: (1) was there such unity of interest and ownership that the separate personalities of the corporation and its shareholders, officers or directors are indistinct or non-existent; and (2) would adherence to the fiction of separate corporate existence sanction fraud, promote injustice or inequitable consequences or lead to an evasion of legal obligations?

As to the first part of the test, the "separate corporate identity" prong, we note:

> The "separate corporate identity" prong is meant to determine whether the stockholder and the corporation have maintained separate identities. There are strong public policy reasons for upholding the corporate fiction. Where stockholders follow the technical rules that govern the corporate structure, they are entitled to rely on the protections of limited liability that the corporation affords. In determining whether the personalities and assets of the corporation and the stockholders have been blurred we consider (i) the degree to which the corporate legal formalities have been maintained, and (ii) the degree to which individual and corporate assets and affairs have been commingled.

N.L.R.B. v. Greater Kansas City Roofing, 2 F.3d 1047, 1052 (10th Cir. 1993).

Of the six specific factors which we have considered in the past, four are used in determining whether the first prong is met: (1) undercapitalization; (2) failure to observe corporate formalities; (3) absence of corporate records; and (4) payment by the corporation of individual obligations. If these factors are present in sufficient number and/or degree, the first prong is met and the court will then consider the second prong.[19]

---

18. [FN 6] These factors include:
   (1) fraudulent misrepresentation by corporation directors;
   (2) undercapitalization;
   (3) failure to observe corporate formalities;
   (4) absence of corporate records;
   (5) payment by the corporation of individual obligations; and
   (6) use of the corporation to promote fraud, injustice or illegality.

19. [FN 9] We have held that a court should pierce the corporate veil only upon the strongest evidence of these factors. *Ethan Dairy Products v. Austin*, 448 N.W.2d 226, 230 (S.D. 1989) and *Farmers Feed & Seed*, 344 N.W.2d at 702.

As to the second part of the test, the "fraud or inequitable consequences" prong, we note:

> Under the fraud, injustice, or evasion of obligations prong of the test we ask whether there is adequate justification to invoke the equitable power of the court. We require an element of unfairness, injustice, fraud, or other inequitable conduct as a prerequisite to piercing the corporate veil.
>
> . . .
>
> [T]he showing of inequity necessary to satisfy the second prong must flow from the misuse of the corporate form. The mere fact that a corporation . . . breaches a contract . . . does not mean that the individual shareholders of the corporation should personally be liable. To the contrary, the corporate form of doing business is typically selected precisely so that the individual shareholders will not be liable. It is only when the shareholders disregard the separateness of the corporate identity *and when that act of disregard causes the injustice or inequity or constitutes the fraud* that the corporate veil may be pierced. . . . In most cases the mere fact that a corporation is incapable of paying all of its debts is insufficient for a finding of injustice. . . . That condition will exist in virtually all cases in which there is an attempt to pierce the corporate veil.

Greater Kansas City Roofing, 2 F.3d at 1052-53 (citations omitted) (emphasis original).

The two factors which we have considered in the past to satisfy the second prong include: (1) fraudulent misrepresentation by corporation directors; and (2) use of the corporation to promote fraud, injustice, or illegalities.

If both the "separate corporate identity" prong and the "fraud or inequitable consequence" prong of the test are met and "the court deems it appropriate to pierce the corporate veil, the corporation and its stockholders will be treated identically." *Baatz v. Arrow Bar*, 452 N.W.2d 138, 141 (S.D. 1990).

We will next apply this two-part test to the instant facts.

III. APPLICATION OF THE TWO-PART TEST

Implicit in the first prong of the test is the idea that the person or persons whom the plaintiff wishes to hold individually liable must have exercised such control over the corporation that the notion of separate legal entity no longer exists. The corporation must have been used as the mere alter ego or instrumentality through which the defendant was conducting his or her personal business.

The control which is necessary to satisfy the first prong is that which is normally exercised by the shareholders, officers or directors of a corporation and must be distinguished from the type of control which may be exercised by a corporate manager or employee who merely acts as an agent of the corporation.

Thus, a threshold requirement for the first prong of the test is that the plaintiff must establish that the person which he or she seeks to hold individually liable was in fact a corporate shareholder, officer, director or similar corporate representative, such that this person could exercise the type of control over the corporation necessary to satisfy the first prong of the test.

Our standard of review for summary judgments requires that the evidence be viewed most favorably to the nonmoving party, KG & E in this case. Although the evidence in the settled record tends to show that any control Jeff Ross may have had over Ross Service was in his capacity as a corporate manager or employee rather than as a shareholder, officer or director, this fact is in dispute.

We noted earlier that Jeff Ross may own .3125 percent of the outstanding corporate stock; that he signed two promissory notes to Dakota State Bank as "treasurer" of Ross Service; and that he was listed as a corporate director on the corporation's annual reports for 1989 and 1990. He also signed the bid submitted to KG & E as the "owner" of Ross Service company. We will therefore view this evidence most favorably to KG & E and treat Jeff Ross as a shareholder, officer and/or director of Ross Service for purposes of applying the two-part test.

A. THE SEPARATE CORPORATE IDENTITY PRONG

KG & E has advanced four factors it contends justify disregard of the corporate entity: (1) undercapitalization; (2) failure to observe corporate formalities; (3) commingling of Jeff Ross's personal funds with corporate funds; and (4) Jeff Ross's appropriation of corporate property for his personal use. We will now review the evidence in light of these factors to determine whether the first prong of the test has been met.

1. Undercapitalization

"Shareholders must equip a corporation with a reasonable amount of capital for the nature of the business involved." *Baatz, supra.*

KG & E argues that because Ross Service was experiencing financial troubles at the time the agreement was entered into, the corporation was undercapitalized. KG & E relies on *Mobridge, supra* as authority for this assertion.[20] That case, however, is clearly distinguishable from the instant case.

First, KG & E has made no assertion, and the record is devoid of any evidence tending to show that Jeff Ross or Ross Service made any representations as to the corporation's financial ability to perform the contract. There is no evidence in the record that KG & E even investigated Ross Service's financial ability to perform.

Second, in April of 1990, Jeff Ross and Edith Ross individually borrowed $20,000 on behalf of the corporation and placed it in Jeff Ross's trucking company account which was also being used as Ross Service's corporate account. The record also shows that prior to entering into the contract with KG & E, Ross Service had over $200,000 in corporate equity. It still had well over $100,000 in corporate equity after entering into the contract.

---

20. [FN 11] In *Mobridge*, the directors of the defendant corporation made various misrepresentations as to the corporation's financial ability to perform a contract which required it to pay $250,000 for plant and equipment in five equal annual installments as well as insurance on the property and payments on a rental building. At the time these misrepresentations were made, the defendant corporation had only $62.08 in its corporate account. We also noted that the legal corporation had only existed for two and one-half years, and was never used for any purpose except the personal immunity of the board members.

Third, we note that whether or not Ross Service was experiencing financial difficulties, it is undisputed that Ross Service paid over $500,000 of the $700,000 contract price. Unlike the defendant corporation in *Mobridge*, Ross Service had been in existence for eleven years when it entered into the contract with KG & E. There is no evidence that it was formed solely to provide personal immunity to the board members.

"Inadequate capitalization means capitalization very small in relation to the nature of the business of the corporation and the risks the business entails measured at the time of formation." *Global Credit Services v. AMISUB*, 508 N.W.2d 836, 843 (Neb. 1993). A corporation which was sufficiently capitalized at formation but which has suffered losses is not necessarily undercapitalized, *Southern Lumber v. M.P. Olson Real Est.*, 426 N.W.2d 504, 509 (Neb. 1988), and a mere assertion that the corporation is undercapitalized does not make it so. *Baatz*, 452 N.W.2d at 142.

Finally, "[s]imply identifying evidence of financial problems is insufficient to show that [Ross Service] was undercapitalized." *Bollwerk v. Susquehanna Corp.*, 811 F. Supp. 472, 478 (D.S.D. 1993).

There is simply no evidence that Ross Service's capital in whatever amount was inadequate for the operation of business. *Baatz, supra*. "Without some evidence of the inadequacy of the capital, [KG & E] fails to present specific facts demonstrating a genuine issue of material fact." Id.

2. Failure to Observe Corporate Formalities

KG & E contends that Ross Service failed to maintain corporate formalities because corporate meetings were discontinued after 1983. Corporate minutes are also unavailable after that time. When corporate owners, by their own acts, show that they have ignored the corporate entity, the courts may do likewise. *Ethan Dairy Products*, 448 N.W.2d 226, 230 (S.D. 1989) (citing Annot. *Disregarding Corporate Entity*, 46 A.L.R.3d 428 (1972)).

The evidence in the settled record shows that KG & E was clearly aware that it was dealing with the corporation and not Jeff Ross individually.[21] Despite a lack of certain corporate formalities, the trial court found, and the record shows that Ross Service was operated and conducted business as a separate corporation, that corporate tax returns and annual reports were filed, and that the corporation borrowed money and entered into contracts in its own name.

" 'Genuine corporate organization, even when adopted for the express purpose of avoiding personal liability, is not to be lightly disregarded, and mere failure upon occasion to follow all the forms prescribed by law for the conduct of corporate activities will not justify such disregard.' " *Larson v. Western Underwriters, Inc.*, 77 S.D. 157, 164, 87 N.W.2d 883, 887 (1958) (quoting *P.S. & A. Realties, Inc. v.*

---

21. [FN 12] Jeff Ross did sign the bid as "Jeff Ross, Owner, Ross Service Company." However in accepting the bid, KG & E responded to Ross Service Company, not Jeff Ross personally. In addition, statements of account were sent to Ross Service Company, not to Jeff Ross.

Lodge Gate Forest, Inc., 205 Misc. 245, 127 N.Y.S.2d 315, 324 (1954)). KG & E fails to present a genuine issue of material fact regarding this factor.

3. Commingling of Personal Funds with Corporate Funds

KG & E's third contention is that because Jeff Ross commingled his personal funds with those of Ross Service in the trucking company account, Jeff Ross and Ross Service failed to maintain separate identities.

Both sides agree that Ross Service used Jeff Ross's trucking company account at Norwest Bank in Dell Rapids as a depository for Ross Service's corporate funds between April 1990 and January of 1991. They also agree that this commingling was done for the corporation's benefit because Ross Service's regular bank in Colman, South Dakota would have automatically applied any deposits in that account to Ross Service's outstanding loans.

KG & E's argument focuses on Jeff Ross's personal deposits and withdrawals from his trucking company account during the contract period between KG & E and Ross Service. In its argument to the circuit court, KG & E specifically alleged that because Jeff Ross's personal withdrawals exceeded his personal deposits in this account between July 1990 and January 1991 by approximately $14,000, he had in effect stolen this money from Ross Service. KG & E claimed that this alleged theft justified piercing the corporate veil of Ross Service to hold Jeff Ross individually liable for the unpaid contract price of about $194,000.

However, Jeff Ross effectively rebutted this argument and demonstrated that there was no issue of material fact by showing: (1) that KG & E was conveniently looking only at the months of July 1990 through January 1991 to establish this $14,000 deficit; and (2) that KG & E had overlooked the fact that he had deposited $14,715.59 into this account on May 29, 1990.

On appeal, KG & E has fashioned a new argument in an effort to show that Jeff Ross's personal withdrawals exceeded his personal deposits. KG & E now claims that by including the $9,700 spent on a Ford truck and trailer, Jeff Ross's withdrawals exceed his deposits in the trucking company account by $9,032.40. We will not consider an argument raised for the first time on appeal.

Even if we were to accept KG & E's argument as true, this in and of itself would not justify piercing the corporate veil. At most, these facts (1) demonstrate that Jeff Ross may have taken money or property from Ross Service and (2) may give Ross Service a cause of action against Jeff Ross for the amount of the account deficit. These facts, however, do not demonstrate that Jeff Ross and Ross Service failed to maintain separate identities or that Ross Service was merely the alter ego of Jeff Ross. As to this factor then, KG & E fails to present a genuine issue of material fact which would justify piercing the corporate veil.

4. Misappropriation of Corporate Assets for Personal Use

KG & E's final contention is that Jeff Ross misappropriated corporate property for his personal use. It argues that because Jeff Ross acquired a 1976 Ford truck and trailer through the trucking company account in October of 1990, he took corporate property.

The record clearly shows, however, that (1) Jeff Ross reimbursed Ross Service for these items by depositing $10,000 into the account from a loan he received from Norwest Bank, (2) that the 1976 Ford truck and the trailer were listed on the loan documents as the property being purchased, and (3) that Jeff Ross gave a security interest in this property to Norwest Bank. The claim that Jeff Ross took corporate property for his own use does not appear to be sufficiently supported in the evidence to create a genuine issue of material fact.

Even if we accept these allegations as true, however, these facts do not prove that there was such a unity of interest and ownership that the separate personalities of Jeff Ross and Ross Service were indistinct or non-existent.

Ross Service shareholders, other than Jeff Ross, owned 99.7 percent of the corporation. If Jeff Ross did, in fact, take the truck and trailer, he took it, ultimately, from the value of the corporation owned by those shareholders. But neither Ross Service, in being wronged, nor Jeff Ross in committing that wrong, engaged in conduct demonstrating a unity of interest and ownership that rendered non-existent the difference between Jeff Ross and Ross Service.

At all times the interests of Jeff Ross and Ross Service remained separate and distinct. Committing a wrong against the corporation neither changed that fact nor justifies disregard of the corporate entity. As to this factor, then, KG & E fails to present a genuine issue of material fact which would justify piercing the corporate veil.

In summary, KG & E has not satisfied the first prong of the test because it has not presented any genuine issue of material fact showing that Jeff Ross disregarded Ross Service's corporate identity or treated it as his alter ego. Even so, we will briefly analyze the facts as they apply to the second prong of the test.

B. THE FRAUD, INJUSTICE, OR INEQUITABLE CONSEQUENCES PRONG

As we have stated, the piercing doctrine is an equitable remedy. Therefore, the party seeking to pierce the corporate veil must demonstrate that there has been a substantial disregard for the separate corporate identity, and that there is some material equitable reason for the court to hold the shareholder, officer or director personally liable. Such material equitable reason might include fraud, injustice or other inequitable consequences which result from the disregard of the separate corporate identity.

Further, the individual who is sought to be charged personally with corporate liability must have shared in the moral culpability or injustice that is found to satisfy the second prong of the test. It has been stated that:

> The alter ego doctrine is not applied to eliminate the consequences of corporate operations, but to avoid inequitable results; a necessary element of the theory is that the fraud or inequity sought to be eliminated must be that

of the party against whom the doctrine is invoked, and such party must have been an actor in the course of conduct constituting the abuse of corporate privilege — the doctrine cannot be applied to prejudice the rights of an innocent third party.

Charles R.P. Keating & Gail O'Gradney, *Fletcher Cyclopedia of the Law of Private Corporations* §41.20 at 639 (perm. ed. 1990).

KG & E contends that Jeff Ross shared in the moral culpability or injustice complained of in that corporate funds were commingled with Jeff Ross's personal funds and Jeff Ross misappropriated corporate funds and took corporate property as his own. To this extent, then, Jeff Ross is not an innocent third party but an actor whose course of conduct constitutes the claimed abuse of corporate privilege.

Even if we accept these allegations as true, however, a genuine issue of material fact still does not exist. The conduct of Jeff Ross would only amount to fraud or injustice perpetrated on the corporation, not on KG & E, a third party corporate creditor.

> The doctrine of alter ego fastens liability on the individual who uses a corporation merely as an instrumentality to conduct his or her own personal business, and *such liability arises from fraud or injustice perpetrated not on the corporation but on third persons dealing with the corporation.* The corporate form may be disregarded only where equity requires the action to assist a third party.

Keating & O'Gradney, supra, §41.10 at 615 (emphasis added). We will not disregard the corporate entity for the benefit of KG & E, a third party corporate creditor, when the only fraud or injustice which may be present was perpetrated on the corporation itself.

KG & E has failed to present any specific genuine issues of material fact which would justify disregarding the corporate entity to hold Jeff Ross individually liable for the corporate debt. Accordingly, the judgment is affirmed.

Questions

1. What is the South Dakota test for piercing the corporate veil?
2. Why didn't the court pierce in this case?
3. Why do you think KG & E pursued Jeff Ross instead of John or Edith Ross?
4. In hindsight, what should KG & E have done differently?
5. In light of the case, what would you advice a corporation to do to minimize piercing risk?

Piercing the corporate veil is a long-established doctrine. The same is not true for piercing the LLC veil, given the relative newness of LLCs. A few states specifically provide for piercing in their LLC statutes. For example, Minn. Stat. §322B.303(2) provides, "The case law that states the conditions and circumstances under which the corporate veil of a corporation may be pierced under Minnesota law also applies to limited liability companies." Outside of these states, every court that has addressed the issue has adopted veil piercing for LLCs, and therefore its application to LLCs appears settled.

Many courts simply apply corporate veil piercing factors to LLCs. Some courts, however, have fine-tuned some of the factors for the LLC context. Here's a take on the issue from a New Jersey court:

> [P]ersuasive authorities indicate that corporate veil-piercing doctrine should not be mechanically applied to cases involving limited liability companies. In particular, a court should view in a different light the factors of adherence to corporate formalities, and scrutiny of owners' dominion and control.
>
> [A]dherence to formalities is one factor that should weigh differently in the case of a limited liability company. . . . First, a small-business owner's failure to adhere to formalities may simply reflect disregard of formalities "irrelevant to their actual operation," and lack of funds to hire lawyers and others to keep track of statutory obligations. None of that may evidence misuse of the statute. Second, "LLC's have relatively few statutorily mandated formalities and have a considerable amount of freedom and flexibility as to the management structure of the entity." This informality, encouraged by statute, should not then be a basis to avoid statutory limited liability.
>
> Reliance on dominance and control of the L.L.C. form also conflicts with the underlying policy of flexibility within the L.L.C. statute.
>
>> LLC's are more often than not managed by the LLC members. In addition, generally speaking, members are normally authorized agents and/or managers of LLC's for the purpose of conducting its affairs. As such, it could be argued that the later ego factor is usually satisfied for LLC's. As one commentator noted, given the statutory authorization of flexible LLC management structures, domination of LLC management by members of the LLC, absent other equitable issues, would appear to be an "inappropriate" factor for the courts to use to pierce the veil to the detriment of the interest holders. Thus, application of the alter ego factor to LLC's will often lead to "illogical" results.
>
> Jeffrey K. Vandervoort, *Piercing the Veil of Limited Liability Companies: The Need for a Better Standard*, 3 DePaul Bus. & Com. L.J. 51 (2004).

D.R. Horton Inc.-New Jersey v. Dynastar Development, L.L.C., 2005 WL 1939778 (N.J. Super. Ct. Law Div. 2005). Thus, an LLC organized in New Jersey or other state with case law similar to *D.R. Horton Inc.* arguably has a stronger inside liability shield than a corporation or an LLC organized in a state that simply applies corporate veil piercing factors in the LLC context. Furthermore, because there are fewer statutory formalities required of LLCs, it is perhaps less likely that an

LLC will be found to have failed to observe LLC formalities. In other words, it may be more difficult for a plaintiff to convince a court to pierce the veil of an LLC as compared to a corporation.

c. Direct Liability

A liability shield does not protect a business owner from liability arising from the business owner's own actions or inactions. For example, say you own a bike rickshaw business that you operate in the LLC form. While transporting some clients, you negligently make a turn too fast and flip the rickshaw. If the clients are seriously hurt, they are likely to sue you personally for negligence. (They will probably sue your LLC as well.) Because you are being sued in your individual capacity and not in your capacity as a member of the LLC, the LLC's liability shield does not protect you. You committed a tort and are therefore personally liable. The fact that you committed the tort while working for an LLC is not relevant to your personal liability. Now, if it was not you but one of your employees who flipped the rickshaw, the LLC's shield would protect you from personal liability from the accident (assuming the plaintiff has no negligent hiring or similar claim on which to sue you directly). In this later scenario, the LLC is likely to get sued, too, but even if the LLC is unable to cover the judgment, the plaintiffs will not be able to recover against your personal assets (unless they can convince the court to pierce the veil).

2. Outside Liability Exposure

a. Overview

Outside liability exposure refers to the extent to which the creditors of the individual owners of a business operated in a particular legal form can recover against the business's assets. When it comes to outside liability exposure, unincorporated entities are generally superior to corporations as shown through the following example.

Say you own 90 percent of a bike rickshaw business, with the other 10 percent owned by your aunt. The business operates as a corporation. You are out with some friends one Friday night and have a few too many drinks. As a result, while driving home you blow through a red light and plow into an oncoming car, severely injuring the driver. You get sued personally for negligence and the driver wins a $2 million verdict. Unfortunately for you, your auto liability insurance has a $500,000 cap, so after your insurance company pays this amount to the plaintiff, you still owe him $1.5 million. The plaintiff then gets a writ of execution from a court and seizes your assets to satisfy the claim. Your assets include the stock of your rickshaw business, so 90 percent of the business is now owned by the plaintiff, and he therefore now controls your business. Hence, the plaintiff liquidates the business and pays out 90 percent of the proceeds to himself (your aunt would get the other 10 percent). In effect, the plaintiff has reached your business's assets to satisfy a claim against you, notwithstanding the fact that the assets were owned by the corporation and not you personally.

The outcome would likely be different if the business were instead an LLC. Under the LLC statute of most states, the plaintiff would not be able to seize your ownership interest in the business. Instead, the plaintiff will get a "charging order," which entitles him to any distributions made by the LLC until the judgment is paid off. For example, §18-703 of the Delaware Limited Liability Company Act (DLLCA) provides as follows:

> (a) On application by a judgment creditor of a member or of a member's assignee, a court having jurisdiction may charge the limited liability company interest of the judgment debtor to satisfy the judgment. To the extent so charged, the judgment creditor has only the right to receive any distribution or distributions to which the judgment debtor would otherwise have been entitled in respect of such limited liability company interest.
>
> (b) A charging order constitutes a lien on the judgment debtor's limited liability company interest. . . .
>
> (d) The entry of a charging order is the exclusive remedy by which a judgment creditor of a member or of a member's assignee may satisfy a judgment out of the judgment debtor's limited liability company interest.
>
> (e) No creditor of a member or of a member's assignee shall have any right to obtain possession of, or otherwise exercise legal or equitable remedies with respect to, the property of the limited liability company. . . .

As you can see, the above provision does not transfer management rights to the plaintiff, so he cannot force the LLC to liquidate, make distributions or anything else. You retain management control of the LLC, so the business's assets are protected from the plaintiff.

UPA, RUPA, RULPA (1976), and RULPA (2006) contain provisions similar to DLLCA §18-703,[22] so the analysis would be essentially the same if your bike rickshaw business was instead organized as a general partnership, LLP, or LP.

Many states permit a creditor to pursue judicial foreclosure of a charging order, in other words, a court order directing a judicial sale of the ownership interest to which the charging order relates. For example, §503 of the ULLCA (2006) provides as follows:

> . . .
>
> (c) Upon a showing that distributions under a charging order will not pay the judgment debt within a reasonable time, the court may foreclose the lien and order the sale of the transferable interest. The purchaser at the foreclosure sale obtains only the transferable interest, and does not thereby become a member . . . .

---

22. *See* UPA §28; RUPA §504 RULPA (1976) §703; RULPA (2001) §703.

(d) At any time before foreclosure, the member or transferee whose transferable interest is subject to a charging order under subsection (a) may extinguish the charging order by satisfying the judgment and filing a certified copy of the satisfaction with the court that issued the charging order.

(e) At any time before foreclosure, a limited liability company or one or more members whose transferable interests are not subject to the charging order may pay to the judgment creditor the full amount due under the judgment and thereby succeed to the rights of the judgment creditor, including the charging order.

Note that under subsection (c), the purchaser at the foreclosure sale does not become a member of the LLC, which means he or she acquires no management rights. Thus, even if a creditor forecloses on a charging order, the LLC's assets are still protected. There is, however, an additional wrinkle. Some states allow a transferee of an LLC interest who has not become a member to seek a court order dissolving the LLC. A court would then determine if it would be equitable to do so.

b. Single-Member LLCs

There is a big caveat to the above analysis. Figure out what it is by reading the next case.

In re Albright
291 B.R. 538 (Bankr. D. Colo. 2003)

CAMPBELL, B.J.

This matter is before the Court on the (1) Motion to Allow Trustee to Take Any and All Necessary Actions to Liquidate Property Owned by Western Blue Sky LLC ("Motion to Liquidate"); (2) Motion to Appoint and Compensate Bob Karls as Real Estate Broker to the Trustee; and (3) Debtor's Response to Trustee's Motion to Retain Realtor and Liquidate LLC Property. Following a hearing on February 4, 2003, the parties agreed to submit the matter on briefs.

Ashley Albright, the debtor in this Chapter 7 case ("Debtor"), is the sole member and manager of a Colorado limited liability company named Western Blue Sky LLC. The LLC owns certain real property located in Saguache County, Colorado (the "Real Property"). The LLC is not a debtor in bankruptcy.

The Chapter 7 Trustee contends that because the Debtor was the sole member and manager of the LLC at the time she filed bankruptcy, he now controls the LLC and he may cause the LLC to sell the Real Property and distribute the net sales proceeds to his bankruptcy estate. The Debtor maintains that, at best, the Trustee is entitled to a charging order and cannot assume management of the LLC or cause the LLC to sell the Real Property.

Pursuant to the Colorado limited liability company statute, the Debtor's membership interest constitutes the personal property of the member. Upon the Debtor's bankruptcy filing, she effectively transferred her membership interest to the estate. Because there are no other members in the LLC, the entire membership interest passed to the bankruptcy estate, and the Trustee has become a "substituted member."

Section 7-80-702 of the Limited Liability Company Act requires the unanimous consent of "other members" in order to allow a transferee to participate in the management of the LLC. Because there are no other members in the LLC, no written unanimous approval of the transfer was necessary. Consequently, the Debtor's bankruptcy filing effectively assigned her entire membership interest in the LLC to the bankruptcy estate, and the Trustee obtained all her rights, including the right to control the management of the LLC.

The Debtor argues that the Trustee acts merely for her creditors and is only entitled to a charging order against distributions made on account of her LLC member interest. However, the charging order, as set forth in Section 703 of the Colorado Limited Liability Company Act, exists to protect other members of an LLC from having involuntarily to share governance responsibilities with someone they did not choose, or from having to accept a creditor of another member as a co-manager. A charging order protects the autonomy of the original members, and their ability to manage their own enterprise. In a single-member entity, there are no non-debtor members to protect. The charging order limitation serves no purpose in a single member limited liability company, because there are no other parties' interests affected.[23]

The Colorado limited liability company statute provides that the members, including the sole member of a single member limited liability company, have the power to elect and change managers. Because the Trustee became the sole member of Western Blue Sky LLC upon the Debtor's bankruptcy filing, the Trustee now controls, directly or indirectly, all governance of that entity, including decisions regarding liquidation of the entity's assets. . . .

Based on the foregoing, it is hereby:

ORDERED that the Trustee, as sole member, controls the Western Blue Sky LLC and may cause the LLC to sell its property and distribute net proceeds to his estate. Alternatively, the Trustee may elect to distribute the LLC's property to the bankruptcy estate, and, in turn, liquidate that property himself . . . .

---

23. [FN 9] The harder question would involve an LLC where one member effectively controls and dominates the membership and management of an LLC that also involves a passive member with a minimal interest. If the dominant member files bankruptcy, would a trustee obtain the right to govern the LLC? Pursuant to Colo. Rev. Stat. §7-80-702, if the non-debtor member did not consent, even if she held only an infinitesimal interest, the answer would be no. The Trustee would only be entitled to a share of distributions, and would have no role in the voting or governance of the company. Notwithstanding this limitation, 7-80-702 does not create an asset shelter for clever debtors. To the extent a debtor intends to hinder, delay or defraud creditors through a multi-member LLC with "peppercorn" co-members, bankruptcy avoidance provisions and fraudulent transfer law would provide creditors or a bankruptcy trustee with recourse. 11 U.S.C. §§544(b)(1) and 548(a).

Questions

1. What is a charging order?
2. What is the big caveat regarding the outside liability shield of an LLC?
3. What was the court's reasoning for imposing the caveat?
4. Is there any way around the caveat?

It is unclear whether courts applying the LLC law of other jurisdictions (or even other courts applying the LLC law of Colorado) will follow *In re Albright,* as the effect of a charging order limitation on single member LLCs is unsettled. Recently, the Florida Supreme Court in *Olmstead v. F.T.C.*[24] reached a similar conclusion as the court in *In re Albright* although under slightly different reasoning. This spurred the Florida legislature to add to the Florida LLC statute provisions specifically addressing foreclosing on a single member LLC interest.[25]

c. *Reverse Veil Piercing*

Creditors of a business owner may also be able to reach the assets of a business under the doctrine of reverse veil piercing, which applies to all limited liability entities (corporation, LLC, LLP, etc.). The next case discusses reverse veil piercing in the context of a limited partnership.

C.F. Trust, Inc. v. First Flight Limited Partnership
580 S.E.2d 806 (Va. 2003)

HASSELL, SR., C.J.

I.

Pursuant to Rule 5:42, the United States Court of Appeals for the Fourth Circuit certified to this Court the following questions of law, which we agreed to consider:

"(1) Would Virginia recognize a claim for outsider reverse veil-piercing under the facts of this case?

"(2) If the answer to (1) is yes, what standards must be met before Virginia would allow reverse veil-piercing of the limited partnership here?"

---

24. 44 So. 3d 76 (Fla. 2010).
25. See FLA. STAT. §608.433(6)-(8).

II.

A.

C.F. Trust, Inc., a Florida corporation, and Atlantic Funding Corporation, a Nevada corporation, filed an action in the United States District Court for the Eastern District of Virginia and sought a declaration that First Flight Limited Partnership, a Virginia limited partnership, is the alter ego of Barrie M. Peterson, who had endorsed and guaranteed certain promissory notes. C.F. Trust and Atlantic Funding obtained judgments against Peterson for the principal and interest on the notes and sought to satisfy their judgments against Peterson with assets held by First Flight. The federal district court concluded that this Court would permit reverse veil piercing and that court entered a judgment requiring First Flight to use its assets to satisfy the judgments of C.F. Trust and Atlantic Funding.

B.

The United States Court of Appeals' certification order contained the following facts which are relevant to our disposition of this proceeding.

"C.F. Trust and Atlantic Funding each hold commercial promissory notes endorsed and guaranteed by Peterson. As the district court noted, this case constitutes just one chapter in a prolonged tale involving C.F. Trust's and Atlantic Funding's efforts to collect a combined total of more than $8 million on their notes, and Peterson's equally determined efforts to avoid paying anything to them.

"C.F. Trust . . . holds two notes, dated November 1, 1993, in the total principal amount of $6,064,903.57. Not only Barrie Peterson, individually and as trustee, but also his wife, Nancy Peterson, endorsed and guaranteed both notes. C.F. Trust formally notified the Petersons of their default on the notes on August 31, 1995. . . . On February 1, 1996, a [circuit court in Virginia] entered judgment in favor of C.F. Trust and against the Petersons, jointly and severally, for the amount of the notes, plus interest. . . . In September 1998, when the Petersons still had not paid on the judgment, C.F. Trust sought and obtained a charging order from the [circuit] court that charged the Peterson[s'] interests in various partnerships, including First Flight, with paying the judgment on the notes. Then, on March 18, 1999, the [federal] district court issued garnishment orders against various Peterson corporations, including Birchwood Holdings Group, Inc., to C.F. Trust.

"Atlantic Funding . . . holds a single note, endorsed and guaranteed by Peterson, individually and as trustee, in the principal amount of $1,000,000. Atlantic Funding purchased its note along with the right to enforce a corresponding and preexisting judgment, entered on November 15, 1991, against Peterson for the principal amount of that note, plus interest. On March 1, 1996, a Virginia [circuit] court granted Atlantic Funding a charging order charging Peterson's interest in First Flight with paying the judgment on the Atlantic Funding note, and, on March 15, 1996, issued a second charging order charging another Peterson entity with paying the same judgment.

"On November 18, 1999, having still received no payment on the judgments, C.F. Trust and Atlantic Funding initiated this diversity action against Peterson, Mrs. Peterson, and Peterson's son, Scott Peterson, as well as against various Peterson entities, including First Flight. . . . C.F. Trust and Atlantic Funding alleged that Peterson still owed on the judgments and sought a declaration that each of the other defendants was Peterson's alter ego and, therefore, liable on the judgments. . . .

"A four-day bench trial began on August 28, 2000. The evidence presented at trial showed that Peterson had engaged in two different practices in order to avoid paying C.F. Trust's and Atlantic Funding's judgments.

"First, Peterson directed transfers from various Peterson entities to Birchwood Holdings Group, Inc. (BHG), a corporation wholly owned by Peterson. BHG provided managerial and administrative support to other Peterson entities for a fee, which was calculated according to a cost allocation method. During the relevant period, however, Peterson directed transfers of approximately $1.9 million in overpayments to BHG — excess payments beyond those to which BHG was entitled based on the applicable cost allocation and then directed BHG to pay more than $2 million of Peterson's personal expenses.

"Through this method, Peterson maintained a lifestyle that, he estimated, cost 'between 10 and 15 thousand dollars a month.' The expenses paid by BHG included: mortgage and repair payments on a Peterson residence in Fairfax, Virginia; mortgage payments on a Peterson residence in Nantucket, Massachusetts; Peterson's country club membership fees; car payments for Peterson's Mercedes [Benz]; the Petersons' credit card bills; Peterson's ATM fees; college tuition for Peterson's younger son, Christopher Peterson; and payments to Mrs. Peterson. BHG even paid the substantial legal fees incurred by Peterson and Mrs. Peterson, as well as by various Peterson entities, to defend the suits brought by C.F. Trust and Atlantic Funding to collect on their notes.

"Yet, Peterson contended that he derived no salary and had no income subject to the judgments entered in favor of C.F. Trust and Atlantic Funding. Peterson instead testified that the BHG payments toward his personal expenses constituted repayments of prior loans that he had made to his corporations before the dates of the judgments. However, BHG's accountant testified — and the ledgers reflected — that many of BHG's payments toward Peterson's personal expenses were 'distributions,' not loan repayments. Moreover, no underlying documentation supported Peterson's explanation for the disbursements or the companies' asserted obligations to Peterson, other than the checks and distributions themselves. Only in 1999 did Peterson generate 'promissory notes,' purportedly representing monies owed to him by his companies as repayment for the asserted loans.

"First Flight provided the bulk of the transfers to BHG during this time period. First Flight, the primary source of outside revenue for the Peterson entities, owned and operated a large commercial and industrial rental property called Top Flight Airpark. Beginning in 1992 and continuing through March 15, 1996, Barrie Peterson held a 98 percent limited partnership interest in First Flight, including a 2 percent interest held by Top Flight Airpark, Incorporated, a corporation wholly owned by him. Upland Group, an entity wholly owned by Peterson's elder son, Scott Peterson, held the remaining 2 percent general partnership interest.

"However, on March 15, 1996 — six weeks after C.F. Trust obtained a judgment against Peterson and two weeks after Atlantic Funding obtained its first charging order[—]Top Flight withdrew as 2 percent partner of First Flight, and Peterson transferred half of his resulting 98 percent partnership interest in First Flight to Scott Peterson. Upland Group, however, retained its 2 percent general partnership interest. Through this transfer, Peterson purportedly surrendered legal control of First Flight to Scott Peterson, although Peterson himself continued to manage First Flight's day-to-day affairs.

"This transfer provided Peterson a second means of siphoning money from First Flight, other than through intercompany transfers to BHG, to pay his personal expenses. Peterson directed Scott Peterson to distribute First Flight's funds to himself, and then pay those distributions to Mrs. Peterson or to BHG, or use the distributions to pay the personal expenses of Peterson and Mrs. Peterson. Thus, between March 15, 1996, and December 31, 1999, although First Flight did not directly distribute funds to Barrie Peterson, [First Flight] distributed more than $4.3 million to Scott Peterson.

"To justify these distributions, Peterson and Scott Peterson amended First Flight's partnership agreement to allow Scott Peterson, as the general partner, 'to approve any distributions to the limited partners' and 'to determine whether any part of the profits of the Partnership should be distributed to the limited partners.' At trial, Peterson and Scott Peterson contended that this amendment to the partnership agreement extinguished the agreement's requirement of pro rata distributions to partners, although the amendment did not expressly alter its pro rata payout requirement. Peterson also argued that money used by his son to pay Peterson's own personal expenses were repayments of loans Peterson had made to his respective companies."

C.

The federal district court held that C.F. Trust and Atlantic Funding had "conclusively established the grounds necessary to support piercing the corporate veil in reverse." The federal district court applied this Court's precedent for traditional veil piercing and required that C.F. Trust and Atlantic Funding prove (i) a "unity of interest and ownership" between Peterson and First Flight, and (ii) that Peterson "used the corporation to evade a personal obligation, to perpetrate fraud or a crime, to commit an injustice, or to gain an unfair advantage." The federal district court concluded that First Flight was the alter ego of Barrie Peterson and "that the 'separate personalities of [First Flight and Barrie Peterson] no longer exist[ed].'"

III.

A.

First Flight argues that this Court should not permit outsider reverse piercing of a limited partnership by a creditor of a limited partner. Responding, C.F. Trust and Atlantic Funding assert that this Court has permitted traditional veil piercing and that the same principles this Court applied in those instances would also permit reverse veil piercing in the present case.

We have stated that "[t]he proposition is elementary that a corporation is a legal entity entirely separate and distinct from the shareholders or members who compose it. This immunity of stockholders is a basic provision of statutory and common law and supports a vital economic policy underlying the whole corporate concept." The decision to ignore the separate existence of a corporate entity and impose personal liability upon shareholders for debts of the corporation is an extraordinary act to be taken only when necessary to promote justice.

We have stated that "no single rule or criterion . . . can be applied to determine whether piercing the corporate veil is justified," and that the corporate entity will be disregarded and the veil pierced only if:

"[T]he shareholder sought to be held personally liable has controlled or used the corporation to evade a personal obligation, to perpetrate fraud or a crime, to commit an injustice, or to gain an unfair advantage. . . . Piercing the corporate veil is justified when the unity of interest and ownership is such that the separate personalities of the corporation and the individual no longer exist and to adhere to that separateness would work an injustice."

The decision to disregard a corporate structure to impose personal liability is a fact-specific determination, and the factual circumstances surrounding the corporation and the questioned act must be closely scrutinized in each case.

This Court has been very reluctant to permit veil piercing. We have consistently held, and we do not depart from our precedent, that only "an extraordinary exception" justifies disregarding the corporate entity and piercing the veil.

Traditionally, a litigant who seeks to pierce a veil requests that a court disregard the existence of a corporate entity so that the litigant can reach the assets of a corporate insider, usually a majority shareholder. In a reverse piercing action, however, the claimant seeks to reach the assets of a corporation or some other business entity, as in this instance the assets of a limited partnership, to satisfy claims or a judgment obtained against a corporate insider. This proceeding, often referred to as "outsider reverse piercing," is designed to achieve goals similar to those served by traditional corporate piercing proceedings.

We conclude that there is no logical basis upon which to distinguish between a traditional veil piercing action and an outsider reverse piercing action. In both instances, a claimant requests that a court disregard the normal protections accorded a corporate structure to prevent abuses of that structure. Therefore,

· 105 ·

we hold that Virginia does recognize the concept of outsider reverse piercing and that this concept can be applied to a Virginia limited partnership. Indeed, limited partnerships, like corporations, have a legal existence separate from the partners in the limited partnership, and the structure of the statutorily-created limited partnership limits the potential liability of each limited partner. . . .

B.

Virginia has adopted the Revised Uniform Limited Partnership Act, Code §50-73.1, et seq. First Flight argues that the Act "specifies whether and when a limited partner may be held liable for the debts of the partnership, and thereby provides a statutory remedy analogous to the judicially-created remedy of piercing the corporate veil. . . . More importantly, the Act *also* provides a remedy for creditors of a limited partner by specifying the manner in which the assets of a limited partnership may be subjected to a creditor's claims." Continuing, First Flight claims that the Virginia Revised Uniform Limited Partnership Act prescribes the only methods that creditors may utilize to reach assets of a limited partnership.

We agree with First Flight that the Virginia Revised Uniform Limited Partnership Act prescribes certain statutory remedies for creditors of a limited partnership. For example, Code §50-73.46, which is a part of the Act, permits a court to charge the partnership interest of a limited partner against whom a judgment has been entered. However, there is simply no language in the Act that prohibits a court from piercing the veil of a limited partnership.

IV.

When determining whether *reverse* piercing of a limited partnership is appropriate, a court must consider the same factors summarized in Part III.A. of this opinion that this Court considers when determining whether *traditional* veil piercing should be permitted. Also, as we have stated in Part III.A. of this opinion, even though no single rule or criterion is dispositive, the litigant who seeks to disregard a limited partnership entity must show that the limited partnership sought to be pierced has been controlled or used by the debtor to evade a personal obligation, to perpetrate a fraud or a crime, to commit an injustice, or to gain an unfair advantage.

In Virginia, unlike in some states, the standards for veil piercing are very stringent, and piercing is an extraordinary measure that is permitted only in the most egregious circumstances, such as under the facts before this Court. The piercing of a veil is justified when the unity of interest and ownership is such that the separate personalities of the corporation and/or limited partnership and the individual no longer exist, and adherence to that separateness would create an injustice.

Additionally, a court considering reverse veil piercing must weigh the impact of such action upon innocent investors, in this instance, innocent limited partners or innocent general partners. A court considering reverse veil piercing must also consider the impact of such an act upon innocent secured and unsecured creditors. The court must also consider the availability of other remedies the creditor may pursue. And, a litigant who seeks reverse veil piercing must prove the necessary standards by clear and convincing evidence.

V.

In view of the foregoing, we answer the first certified question in the affirmative, and we answer the second certified question by referring the United States Court of Appeals for the Fourth Circuit to Parts III.A. and IV. of this opinion. *Certified question answered in the affirmative.*

Questions

1. What entity is C.F. Trust asking the court to reverse pierce? Why?
2. What is the Virginia test for reverse piercing? How does it differ from traditional veil piercing? How does it differ from the South Dakota test for traditional piercing?
3. As the court mentions, C.F. Trust obtained a charging order "that charged the Peterson[s'] interests in various partnerships, including First Flight, with paying the judgment on the notes. Then, on March 18, 1999, the [federal] district court issued garnishment orders against various Peterson corporations, including Birchwood Holdings Group, Inc., to C.F. Trust." Why did C.F. Trust nonetheless pursue reverse veil piercing of First Flight?

As the court notes, *C.F. Trust* involves an "outsider" as opposed to "insider" reverse veil piercing claim—a third-party creditor is seeking to reach the assets of a business entity to satisfy a claim it has against one of the entity's owners. Insider reverse piercing involves an entity owner seeking to have the entity disregarded so that, for example, the owner can pursue entity claims against third parties, or to assert defenses available only to individuals to protect entity assets from third-party claims. Thus, the key distinction between insider and outsider reverse veil piercing is the status (insider or outsider) of the person pursuing the piercing.

3. Prevalence of Sole Proprietorships

As you probably noticed in the business forms table in Chapter 1, sole proprietorships are by far the most common form of business in the United States. Why is this, given the form provides no liability protection for its owner? I suspect it is mostly because the large majority of businesses are owned by a single individual and, as you know, a sole proprietorship is the default form for a single-owner business. Oftentimes a business owner is focused on launching and growing a business and it may not occur to him or her to consult a lawyer about possible forms, or he or she may not want to spend the time or money to do so. Either way, the business ends up as a sole proprietorship. Even if a business owner talks about choice of form with a lawyer, the owner may decide that the costs of forming and maintaining a limited liability entity outweigh the benefits. This may be because the business does not engage in particularly risky activities, the owner is not very risk adverse or misjudges the risk, or the owner carries considerable liability insurance for the business.

In fact, liability insurance and not a liability shield is typically the first line of defense for a business, at least with respect to tort liability. For example, assume you operate your bike rickshaw business as a sole proprietorship and carry $1 million of liability insurance for the business. The insurer will be obligated to pay for an attorney to represent the business and your employee when they get sued for flipping the bike. The insurer will also have to cover any resulting settlement or judgment, so long as it does not exceed $1 million. Your personal assets would come into play only if the settlement or judgment exceeded the limits of your liability insurance and the business's assets. Thus, one way to think about the costs of forming and maintaining a limited liability entity is in terms of excess insurance. Specifically, these costs are equivalent to premiums for insurance that protects you from personal liability when the business's assets and primary insurance are exhausted.

C. ATTRACTIVENESS TO INVESTORS

Emerging growth companies, such as businesses pursuing research and development of new technologies, need to raise a significant amount of capital from outside investors. Thus, for these companies the primary consideration when it comes to choice of form is the form's attractiveness to outside investors, specifically venture capitalists and angel investors.

Venture capitalists (VCs) specialize in investing in emerging growth and other development-stage companies with great potential but high risk. Specifically, a VC raises money from institutional investors (pension funds, endowments, insurance companies, etc.) and wealthy individuals by selling them interests in an investment fund formed and managed by the VC. The fund then makes large investments (usually in the millions of dollars) in a handful of companies (called portfolio companies) that the VC views as promising. The hope is that at least a few of the portfolio companies will be successful and either go public or be acquired at a favorable valuation. The VC makes money by charging the fund a management fee of 1 to 3 percent of assets and a performance fee of 20 percent of the fund's profits. At the end of some predetermined timeframe (usually ten years), the VC liquidates the fund and distributes the cash to the fund's investors.

Angel investors are wealthy individuals who directly invest in emerging growth companies (as opposed to investing through a VC fund), typically prior to a VC investment. Oftentimes an angel's wealth comes from his or her own success in starting, growing, and then cashing out of an emerging growth company.

A startup business often loses money for a number of years while it works on developing and commercializing its products or services. It will therefore need a significant amount of capital during this timeframe to fund its operations. The business's founders will usually not be able to provide all of the required funding out of their own pockets or through debt financing such as bank loans. Thus, they will need to raise the balance by selling ownership interests to investors. This type of financing is referred to as equity financing.

As a general rule, VCs only invest in businesses organized as corporations and taxed under Sub-C for the following reasons, among others:

- VCs insist on preferred stock in exchange for their investments, and only a C-corp can issue preferred stock.
- VCs want to avoid the extra accounting and tax complications associated with passing through portfolio company profits or losses to fund investors if a portfolio company is taxed under Sub-S or Sub-K.[26]
- A gain on the sale of stock in a C-corporation may qualify for favorable tax treatment under IRC §1202, a treatment not available for the sale of S-corporation stock or an ownership interest in an unincorporated entity.

A VC fund could never invest in a corporation taxed under Sub-S because an S-corp cannot have an entity as an investor (VC funds are organized as LLCs or limited partnerships). Furthermore, an S-corp cannot issue preferred stock, because it would then have two classes of stock outstanding (common and preferred) and would therefore no longer qualify to be taxed under Sub-S. As for LLCs or LLPs, the statutes are flexible enough to allow operating/partnership agreement provisions to replicate the features of preferred stock. However, even if a VC was open to investing in a pass-through taxation entity or the LLC/LLP elected to be taxed under Sub-C, the VC would have to rework its standard investment documents, all of which are geared towards C-corp investments. It would also have to sacrifice the comfort of investing in a security (preferred stock) the terms of which have been tested and refined over decades. Additionally, the VC would forfeit the possibility of favorable tax treatment under IRC §1202.

Angel investors are typically individuals and therefore can invest in S-corps. They are also likely more open than VCs to investing in a pass-through taxation entity because resulting tax issues are often not as complicated for them, and

---

26. For example, many VC funds have both tax-exempt and foreign entities as investors. Pass-through taxation can raise unrelated business taxable income issues for a tax-exempt investor or cause a foreign investor to be deemed "doing business" in the United States, obligating it to file a U.S. tax return.

many angels have passive income against which they could offset passive losses. However, angel investors typically invest in a business with the expectation that venture capital funds will provide later rounds of financing, and they know that VCs generally only invest in C-corporations. This reality combined with the fact that favorable tax treatment under IRC §1202 is only available for C-corp stock leads most angels to have a strong preference for investing in C-corps.

The bottom line is that a business needing to raise money from angel investors and VCs should probably organize as a corporation and stick with Sub-C taxation, because this is the form most attractive to these investors. The founders will not be able to benefit from passed-through losses, but for many founders, this is an acceptable tradeoff for the business being in the best position from a choice of form standpoint to attract VC and angel financing.

Exercise 3.3

1. You have three clients coming to see you today to figure out what legal form they should use for a new business they are starting. Make a list of questions to ask them.

2. Amin, Basu, and Cano are planning to open a flight training school in Tucson, Arizona, which they will own equally. Amin is the instructor and will largely run the operation. Amin intends to provide all his time, but no initial cash, to the venture. Amin's incentive is to use the flight time he accumulates to qualify for a commercial pilot's license. Basu is the technical engineer whose function will be to provide all the necessary aircraft maintenance. Basu intends to work only part time as she is currently taking classes at the University of Arizona. Both Amin and Basu will receive a salary. Cano will be a passive investor in the venture and does not intend to participate in the management or day-to-day operations unless things do not go well.

   Cano is a very wealthy individual and, accordingly, has substantial passive income that she would like to eliminate or reduce with passive losses. Consequently, Cano has agreed to provide all funds necessary to purchase the aircraft and to defray the working capital needs of this venture provided that all losses generated by this venture be specially allocated to her. Additionally, Cano requires that no funds be distributed to Amin or Basu until she has recouped all of the money she has invested in the venture.

   Under which legal form should the business operate?

3. Xu is a spine surgeon who has developed a prototype vertebrate replacement device. Xu is involved in many projects and does not have the time to further develop the device, although it has shown promise. Yazzie is a recently retired CEO of a major medical device company and is already bored. Thus, she is planning to launch a startup to complete development of and hopefully commercialize Xu's device. Xu will contribute the device

to the business, and Yazzie will contribute $500,000. Yazzie would like Xu to be involved with the development of the device, but not with the overall direction of the business. Yazzie estimates that development costs (including obtaining FDA approval) will run at least $50 million. Fortunately, Yazzie has many contacts with venture capitalists and angel investors. Xu and Yazzie are both wealthy and have various investments that generate passive income.

Under which legal form should the business operate?

4. Doyle is the owner of 18 laundromats, all of which are located in the Tucson, Arizona area. She started the business 20 years ago with one laundromat and has grown it steadily over the ensuing years. She has always operated the business as a sole proprietorship, and the business has been quite profitable. Doyle has recently considered adding one or more partners to her business so that she'd have the capital to expand into the Phoenix area. These plans are currently on hold, but Doyle may pursue them again in the future.

Doyle's nephew, is a second-year law student at the University of Arizona. He recently told Doyle about his Business Organizations class at which he learned, among other things, that from a legal perspective a sole proprietorship is not a good form in which to operate a business (although he can't remember why that is). Hence, Doyle has come to see you about changing the legal form of her business. Doyle's priorities, in order, are minimizing taxes, protecting personal wealth, minimizing legal and filing fees, and being attractive to potential future partners.

Under which legal form should Doyle operate her business?

5. Flores owns ten different apartment buildings in the Dinkytown area of Minneapolis, Minnesota. She rents the apartments almost exclusively to University of Minnesota undergraduate students. She does not invest much money in upkeep, because she figures the students will trash the apartments anyway. She is, however, concerned about liability exposure. In particular, she is worried that a catastrophic occurrence at one building (such as a fire) will cost her all of her buildings. The ten buildings are currently owned by Flores Apartments, Inc., a Minnesota corporation. Flores is the sole shareholder of the corporation, and it is taxed under Sub-S.

How could Flores reorganize her business to decrease liability exposure?

6. Cheapskate is starting a website design business that he will run out of his apartment. He will do all the work himself. He has come to you for advice on choice of form for his business. (He is a childhood friend of yours, so you have agreed to provide some initial advice for free.) He is cheap, so he does not want to pay any filing fees or legal fees related to the form. He also wants to minimize taxes.

Under which legal form should Cheapskate operate his business?

D. OTHER CONSIDERATIONS

While liability exposure, taxation, and attractiveness to investors are the primary drivers of entity selection, there are some other considerations that occasionally come into play or are at least sometimes mentioned as factors. These considerations are briefly discussed below.

1. Formalities

The amount of legal formalities involved for formation and maintenance varies across business forms. For example, a sole proprietorship involves very few legal formalities because no filings are required to form or maintain the proprietorship. Conversely, forming a corporation requires, among other things, filing a charter, adopting bylaws, electing directors, appointing officers, and issuing stock. Maintaining a corporation generally requires annual secretary of state filings, board and shareholder meetings, and the preparation of meeting minutes. The unincorporated entities fall in between the two, with all them requiring or necessitating a written agreement among owners. LLCs, LLPs, and limited partnerships also require initial and annual filings with the applicable secretary of state. These entities do not, however, have the same meeting and other operation requirements as corporations, unless otherwise specified in the entity's partnership or operating agreement.

2. Expense

Expense is related to formalities. The more formalities associated with a business form, the more expensive it is to form and maintain. Expenses include filing fees, legal fees, and franchise taxes. Additionally, in some states fees vary depending on entity. For example, Delaware imposes on LLPs a $200 annual fee per partner (not to exceed $120,000), but has no analogous fee for other business forms.

3. Continuity of Existence

A corporation can exist perpetually, regardless if all of its founders die or sell their shares. An LLC can likewise exist perpetually, although a few states impose a maximum duration. Conversely, a sole proprietorship terminates upon the death of the sole proprietor. Additionally, the withdrawal of a partner may terminate the existence of a general partnership, LLP, or limited partnership, depending on the state of formation and/or partnership agreement.

4. Fiduciary Duty Waivers

Business entity law generally imposes fiduciary duties on owners and managers of a business, regardless of form. These duties are owed by an owner to his or her co-owners and to the business entity. Managers also owe fiduciary duties to the owners and to the business entity. The LLC statute of a number of states allows an LLC to waive these duties in its operating agreement. Similarly, most partnership and limited partnership statutes afford partners wide latitude to narrow these duties. Conversely, fiduciary duties generally cannot be waived in the corporate context.

5. Form Eligibility

Some types of businesses are prohibited by licensing requirements or ethical rules to operate in particular forms. For example, many states prohibit law firms from operating as LLCs or corporations.

Additionally, a single-owner business cannot operate as a general partnership, LLP, or limited partnership because state statutes require these entities to have at least two owners. All states allow single-shareholder corporations and all states but Wyoming allow single-member LLCs.

6. Management Default Rules

LLC and partnership default rules assume that all owners will participate equally in management. Conversely, corporate law default rules provide for centralized management by a board of directors and complete control by a shareholder owning a majority of the corporation's outstanding stock. Most LLC and partnership rules, however, can be varied by agreement of the owners, as can most corporate law rules either through a shareholders' agreement or provisions in the corporation's charter or bylaws (at least with respect to a closely held corporation). Thus, it is possible to structure an LLC or partnership so that it has a corporate-type management structure or a corporation so that it has a partnership-type management structure.

7. Buyout Rights

Partnership and many LLC statutes include a default rule requiring the entity to buy out a departing owner. Corporate law statutes do not provide an analogous right, but at least in closely held corporations, it is common for shareholders to address buyout and similar rights in a shareholders' agreement or the corporation's bylaws.

8. Newness

LLCs and LLPs are relatively new forms and therefore have a much shallower body of case law, less developed customs and form documents, less name recognition, and a lower comfort level associated with them than corporations, partnerships, and limited partnerships. These factors explain in part why private investment funds (venture capital funds, hedge funds, and private equity funds) are still typically organized as limited partnerships even though the LLC form appears superior.

E. CONVERSION

A business is not locked in to the form it initially chooses. It can always change forms later if warranted. Historically, a business changed forms through a merger. For example, a limited partnership that wanted to become a corporation would form a new corporation and merge the limited partnership into it. More recently, many states have amended their business entity statutes to add provisions that allow one type of entity to change to another type of entity simply by adopting a plan of conversion and then making a filing with the secretary of state.[27]

Conversion from one type of unincorporated entity to another type of unincorporated entity can normally be done without any adverse tax consequences for the entity's owners. Conversely, converting from an unincorporated entity to a corporation or vice versa, may result in adverse tax consequences, depending on how the conversion is structured and other factors. Thus, the owners will need to consult a tax professional.

Conversion also involves legal fees, filing fees, and other transaction costs. For example, a business that converts from an LLP to an LLC will have to have a lawyer essentially convert its partnership agreement to an operating agreement. Conversion may also require approval of a business's lender(s) or trigger contract termination rights. All these factors need to be weighed by the business against the anticipated benefits of converting.

---

27. *See, e.g.,* DGCL §265; MBCA Ch. 9, Subch. E.

· PART II ·

UNINCORPORATED ENTITIES

· CHAPTER FOUR ·

PARTNERSHIPS AND LIMITED LIABILITY PARTNERSHIPS

This chapter elaborates a bit on the basic characteristics of partnerships and limited liability partnerships touched on in Chapter 1 and covers some additional related topics.

A. PARTNERSHIPS

1. Governing Law

A partnership is governed by the partnership statute of the state in which it is organized. Usually, partners will agree upfront under which state's partnership laws they are forming the partnership, and this state statute will be specified in the partnership agreement. This is what is meant by the state of organization, that is, the state of the partnership statute specified in the partnership agreement as governing the partnership. As discussed in the next subsection, however, sometimes people do not realize they are forming a partnership and therefore obviously do not know to agree on a state of formation. In this situation, the common law rule is that the partnership law of the jurisdiction where the partnership agreement was made governs. (Note that this agreement does not have to be in writing.) RUPA, however, includes a governing law provision that provides that "the law of the jurisdiction in which a partnership has its chief executive office governs relations among the partners and between the partners and the partnership." RUPA §106(a).

As mentioned in Chapter 1, each state has its own partnership statute based either on UPA or RUPA, with the exception of the Louisiana statute. Here is the UPA/RUPA breakdown by state as of 2012:

UPA States	RUPA States	
Georgia	Alabama	Mississippi
Indiana	Alaska	Montana
Massachusetts	Arizona	Nebraska
Michigan	Arkansas	Nevada
Missouri	California	New Jersey
New Hampshire	Colorado	New Mexico
New York	Connecticut	North Dakota
North Carolina	Delaware	Ohio
Pennsylvania	Florida	Oklahoma
Rhode Island	Hawaii	Oregon
South Carolina	Idaho	South Dakota
Wisconsin	Illinois	Tennessee
	Iowa	Texas
	Kansas	Utah
	Kentucky	Vermont
	Maine	Virginia
	Maryland	Washington
	Minnesota	West Virginia
		Wyoming

Given this breakdown (12 UPA states versus 37 RUPA states), we will focus primarily on RUPA.

As stated in Chapter 1 (but it bears repeating), you should not assume that a state has adopted UPA or RUPA verbatim. States are free to make changes or not adopt uniform act amendments. Thus, in practice, when a partnership issue comes up, you should consult the applicable state partnership statute and not the UPA or RUPA.

2. Formation

No formalities are required to form a partnership. A partnership is formed when (1) two or more people associate to carry on as co-owners a business for profit, and (2) they do not file the paperwork (e.g., articles of incorporation/organization) to operate the business in some other form.[1] If these elements are met, the people involved have created a partnership even if they had no idea they were doing so. This situation is called an inadvertent partnership.

People that intend to form a partnership typically express their intentions in a written partnership agreement, so there is no issue as to formation. However, formation issues come up with some frequency when two or more people have some sort of business relationship, but it is unclear whether they intended to

---

1. *See* UPA §6; RUPA §202.

create a partnership. RUPA provides guidance on the issue. Specifially, RUPA §202(c) states that, with certain exceptions, "[a] person who receives a share of the profits of a business is presumed to be a partner in the business . . . ." Exceptions include profits paid on a debt or as compensation.

While this guidance is helpful, in many cases it is not definitive, and thus the formation issue is frequently resolved by a court as exemplified by the following case.

Holmes v. Lerner
74 Cal. App. 4th 442 (1999)

MARCHIANO, J.

This case involves an oral partnership agreement to start a cosmetics company known as "Urban Decay." Patricia Holmes prevailed on her claim that Sandra Kruger Lerner breached her partnership agreement and that David Soward interfered with the Holmes-Lerner contract, resulting in Holmes' ouster from the business. Lerner and Soward appeal from the judgment finding them liable to Holmes for compensatory and punitive damages of over $1 million. . . .

We affirm the judgment against Lerner, primarily because we determine that an express agreement to divide profits is not a prerequisite to prove the existence of a partnership. We also determine that the oral partnership agreement between Lerner and Holmes was sufficiently definite to allow enforcement. . . .

BACKGROUND . . .

Sandra Lerner is a successful entrepreneur and an experienced business person. She and her husband were the original founders of Cisco Systems. When she sold her interest in that company, she received a substantial amount of money, which she invested, in part, in a venture capital limited partnership called "& Capital Partners." By the time of trial in this matter, Lerner was extremely wealthy. Patricia Holmes met Lerner in late 1993, when Lerner visited Holmes' horse training facility to arrange for training and boarding of two horses that Lerner was importing from England. Holmes and Lerner became friends, and after an initial six-month training contract expired, Holmes continued to train Lerner's horses without a contract and without cost.

In 1995, Lerner and Holmes traveled to England to a horse show and to make arrangements to ship the horses that Lerner had purchased. On this trip, Lerner decided that she wanted to celebrate her 40th birthday by going pub crawling in Dublin. Lerner was wearing what Holmes termed "alternative clothes" and black nail polish, and encouraged Holmes to do the same.[2] Holmes, however,

---

2. [FN 1] There were references throughout the trial to Lerner's "alternative" look and to "alternative" culture. Lerner, who referred to herself as an "edgy cosmetics queen," described "alternative culture" as "not really mainstream," "edgy," and "fashion forward." As an example, she noted her own purple hair. She defined "edgy" as not trying to be cute, and being unconventional.

did not like black nail polish, and was unable to find a suitable color in the English stores. At Lerner's mansion outside of London, Lerner gave Holmes a manicuring kit, telling her to see if she could find a color she would wear. Holmes looked through the kit, tried different colors, and eventually developed her own color by layering a raspberry color over black nail polish. This produced a purple color that Holmes liked. Holmes showed the new color to Lerner, who also liked it.

On July 31, 1995, the two women returned from England and stayed at Lerner's West Hollywood condominium while they waited for the horses to clear quarantine. While sitting at the kitchen table, they discussed nail polish, and colors. Len Bosack, Lerner's husband, was in and out of the room during the conversations. For approximately an hour and a half, Lerner and Holmes worked with the colors in a nail kit to try to recreate the purple color Holmes had made in England so they could have the color in a liquid form, rather than layering two colors. Lerner made a different shade of purple, and Holmes commented that it looked just like a bruise. Holmes then said that she wanted to call the purple color she had made "Plague." Holmes had been reading about 16th century England, and how people with the plague developed purple sores, and she thought the color looked like the plague sores. Lerner and Holmes discussed the fact that the names they were creating had an urban theme, and tried to think of other names to fit the theme. Starting with "Bruise" and "Plague," they also discussed the names "Mildew," "Smog," "Uzi," and "Oil Slick." Len Bosack walked into the kitchen at that point, heard the conversation about the urban theme, and said "What about decay?" The two women liked the idea, and decided that "Urban Decay" was a good name for their concept.

Lerner said to Holmes: "This seems like a good [thing], it's something that we both like, and isn't out there. Do you think we should start a company?" Holmes responded: "Yes, I think it's a great idea." Lerner told Holmes that they would have to do market research and determine how to have the polishes produced, and that there were many things they would have to do. Lerner said: "We will hire people to work for us. We will do everything we can to get the company going, and then we'll be creative, and other people will do the work, so we'll have time to continue riding the horses." Holmes agreed that they would do those things. They did not separate out which tasks each of them would do, but planned to do it all together.

Lerner went to the telephone and called David Soward, the general partner of & Capital, and her business consultant. Holmes heard her say "Please check Urban, for the name, Urban Decay, to see if it's available and if it is, get it for us." Holmes knew that Lerner did not joke about business, and was certain, from the tone of her voice, that Lerner was serious about the new business. The telephone call to secure the trademark for Urban Decay confirmed in Holmes' mind that they were forming a business based on the concepts they had originated in England and at the kitchen table that day. Holmes knew that she would be taking the risk of sharing in losses as well as potential success, but the two friends did not discuss the details at that time. Lerner's housekeeper heard Lerner tell Holmes: "It's going to be our baby, and we're going to work on it together." After Holmes left, the housekeeper asked what gave Lerner the idea to go into the cosmetics business, since her background was computers. Lerner replied: "It was all Pat's idea over in England, but I've got the money to make it work." Lerner told her housekeeper that she hoped to sell Urban Decay to Estee Lauder for $50 million.

Although neither of the two women had any experience in the cosmetics business, they began work on their idea immediately. Holmes and Lerner did market research by going to stores, talking with people about nail polish, seeing what nail polishes were available, and buying samples to bring back to discuss with each other. They met frequently in August and September at Lerner's home, and experimented with nail colors. They took pictures of various color mixing sessions. In early August, they met with graphic artist Andrea Kelly and discussed putting together a logo and future advertising work for Urban Decay.

Prior to the first scheduled August meeting, Holmes told Lerner she was concerned about financing the venture. Lerner told her not to worry about it because Lerner thought they could convince Soward that the nail polish business would be a good investment. She told Holmes that Soward took care of Lerner's investment money. Holmes and Lerner discussed their plans for the company, and agreed that they would attempt to build it up and then sell it. Lerner and Holmes discussed the need to visit chemical companies and hire people to handle the daily operations of the company. However, the creative aspect, ideas, inspiration, and impetus for the company came from Holmes and Lerner.

Lerner, Holmes, Soward, and Kelly attended the first scheduled meeting. The participants in these meetings referred to them as "board meetings," even though there was no formal organizational structure, and technically, no board. They discussed financing, and Soward reluctantly agreed to commit $500,000 towards the project. Urban Decay was financed entirely by & Capital, the venture capital partnership composed of Soward as general partner, and Lerner and her husband as the only limited partners. Neither Lerner nor Holmes invested any of their individual funds.

Lerner and Soward went to Kirker Chemical Company later in August of 1995 and learned about mixing and manufacturing nail polish colors. Lerner discouraged Holmes from accompanying them. Although Lerner returned to Kirker, she never took Holmes with her. At the second board meeting, in late August, Soward introduced Wendy Zomnir, a friend of Soward's former fiancée, as an advertising and marketing specialist. After Zomnir and Kelly left the meeting, Holmes, Lerner and Soward discussed her presentation. Holmes was enthusiastic about Zomnir and they decided to hire her. At the conclusion of the September board meeting, after Holmes had left, Lerner and Soward secretly made Zomnir an offer of employment, which included a percentage ownership interest in Urban Decay. It wasn't until a couple of meetings later, when Lerner or Soward referred to Zomnir as the "Chief Operating Officer" of Urban Decay, that Holmes learned of the terms of the offer.

In early October, after Holmes learned of the secret offer to Zomnir, she asked Lerner to define her role at Urban Decay. Lerner responded: "Your role is anything you want it to be." When Holmes asked to discuss the issue in more detail, Lerner turned and walked away. Holmes believed that Lerner was nervous about an upcoming photo session, and decided to discuss it with Lerner at a later date. At their regular board meetings, Holmes participated with Soward, Lerner, Zomnir, Kelly and another person in discussing new colors, and deciding which ones they wanted to sell, and which names would be used.

In September of 1995, Soward signed an application for trademark registration as President of Urban Decay. In December of 1995, Urban Decay was incorporated. Holmes asked for a copy of the articles of incorporation, but was given only two pages showing the name and address of the company. On December 31, Holmes sent a fax to Lerner stating that it had been difficult to discuss her position in Urban Decay with Lerner. Holmes asked Lerner: "What are my responsibilities and obligations, and what are my rights or entitlements?" Holmes also asked: "What are my current and potential liabilities and assets?" She requested that Lerner provide the information in writing. At this point, Holmes wanted to memorialize the agreement she and Lerner had made on July 31.

Soward intercepted the fax and called Holmes, asking: "What's going on?" Holmes explained that she wanted a written agreement, and Soward apologized, telling her that Lerner had asked him to get "something . . . in writing" to Holmes. Soward told Holmes that no one in the company had a written statement of their percentage interest in the company yet. Soward asked: "What do you want, one percent, two percent?" When Holmes did not respond, he told her that five percent was high for an idea. Holmes told him: "I'm not selling an idea. I'm a founder of this company." Soward exclaimed: "Surely you don't think you have fifty percent of this company?" Holmes told him that it was a matter between herself and Lerner, and that Soward should speak to Lerner. Soward agreed to talk to Lerner.

On January 11, 1996, Lerner and Holmes met at a coffee shop to discuss the fax. Holmes explained that she wanted "something in writing" and an explanation of her interest and position in the company. Lerner responded that a startup business is "like a freight train . . . you can either run and catch up, and get on, and take a piece of this company and make it your own, or get out of the way." As a result of this conversation, Holmes decided to double her efforts on behalf of Urban Decay. Because she was most comfortable working at the warehouse, she focused on that aspect of the business.[3] Holmes was reimbursed for mileage, but received no pay for her work.

---

3. [FN 4] Holmes testified that her work at the warehouse included responding to requests for brochures, developing a system for handling increased telephone inquiries, and negotiating a contract with a skills center to assist with the mail order business. She had authority to hire and fire employees and to sign

During January and February, Urban Decay was launching its new nail polish product. Publicity included press releases, brochures, and newspaper interviews with Lerner. An early press release stated: "The idea for Urban Decay was born after Lerner and her horse trainer, Pat Holmes, were sitting around in the English countryside." Lerner approved the press release. In February of 1996, an article was printed in the San Francisco Examiner containing the following quotes from Lerner. "Since we couldn't find good nail polish, in cool colors there must be a business opportunity here. Pat had the original idea. Urban Decay was my spin." The Examiner reporter testified at trial that the quote attributed to Lerner was accurate. Lerner was also interviewed in April by CNN. In that interview she told the story of herself and Holmes looking for unusual colors, mixing their own colors at the kitchen table, and that "we came up with the colors, and it just sort of suggested the urban thing."[4]

Lerner had always notified Holmes whenever there was a board meeting, and she sent Holmes an agenda for the February 20, 1996 meeting. Lerner also sent a memo stating that she thought they should have an "operations meeting" with the warehouse supervisor first. Lerner's memo continued: "and then have a regular board meeting, including [Zomnir], me, David, and Pat, and no one else." Holmes understood that the regular board meeting would be for the purpose of discussing general Urban Decay business. At the operations meeting, Holmes made a presentation regarding the warehouse operations. The financial report showed $205,000 in revenues and $431,000 in expenses. The "directors" thought this early sales figure was "terrific." Soward handed out an organizational chart, which showed Lerner, with the title "CEO" at the top; Soward, as "President" beneath her; and Zomnir, as "COO" beneath Soward. Holmes asked "Where am I?" Lerner responded by pointing to the top of the chart and telling Holmes that she was a director, and was at the top of the chart, above all the other names.[5]

In March of 1996, Holmes received a document from Soward offering her a 1 percent ownership interest in Urban Decay. Soward explained that Urban Decay had been formed as a limited liability company, which was owned by its members. For the first time, Holmes realized that Lerner and Soward had produced an organizational document that did not include her, and she was now being asked to become a minor partner. When she studied the document, she discovered that it referred to an Exhibit A, which was purported to show the distribution of ownership interests in Urban Decay. Soward had given Zomnir a copy of Exhibit A when he offered her an ownership interest in Urban Decay.

---

checks on the Urban Decay account. Only Holmes, Soward, Lerner, Zomnir and the warehouse manager were authorized to sign on the account. Only the manager's authority was limited to $1500. Holmes was spending four to five days a week at the warehouse. Urban Decay accountant Sharon Land testified that Holmes "contributed a great deal" to Urban Decay and directed the retail business. Soward, Lerner and Zomnir seldom came to the office. Soward told Land that Holmes was on the board of directors.

4. [FN 5] When asked at trial why she used the word "we," Lerner responded that she was stressed. Lerner testified that almost every statement she made in the CNN interview was false and a result of stress.

5. [FN 8] An organization chart which was presented at a board meeting in June of 1996 showed a box labeled "Board of Directors" at the top, and did not specifically name Lerner or Holmes.

However, when Holmes asked Soward for a copy of Exhibit A, he told her it did not exist.[6] By this time, Holmes was planning to consult an attorney about the document.

Despite the deterioration of her friendship with Lerner, and her strained relationship with Soward, Holmes continued to attend the scheduled board meetings, hoping that her differences with Lerner could be resolved. She also continued to work at the warehouse on various administrative projects and on direct mail order sales. As late as the April board meeting, Holmes was still actively engaged in Urban Decay business. She made a presentation on a direct mail project she had been asked to undertake. As a result of Holmes' attendance at a sales presentation when she referred to herself as a co-founder of Urban Decay, Lerner instructed Zomnir to draft a dress code and an official history of Urban Decay. Lerner told Zomnir that it was a "real error in judgment" to allow Holmes to attend the sales presentation because she did not project the appropriate image. The official history, proposed in the memo, omitted any reference to Holmes. Finally, matters deteriorated to the point that Soward told Holmes not to attend the July board meeting because she was no longer welcome at Urban Decay.

On August 27, 1996, Holmes filed a complaint against Lerner and Soward, alleging ten causes of action, including breach of an oral contract, intentional interference with contractual relations, fraud, breach of fiduciary duty, and constructive fraud. Holmes eventually dismissed some of her claims and the court dismissed others, sending the case to the jury on the causes of action noted above. At the trial, cosmetics industry expert Gabriella Zuckerman testified that Urban Decay was not just a fad. In her opinion, Urban Decay had discovered and capitalized on a trend that was just beginning. She reviewed projected sales figures of $19.9 million in 1997, going up to $52 million in 2003, and found them definitely obtainable. Arthur Clark, Holmes' expert at valuing start-up businesses, valued Urban Decay under different risk scenarios. In Clark's opinion, the value of Urban Decay to a potential buyer was between $4,672,000 and $6,270,000. Lerner's expert, who had never valued a cosmetics company, testified that Urban Decay had $2.7 million in sales in 1996. He estimated the value of Urban Decay as approximately $2 million, but concluded that it was not marketable.

Lerner and Soward claimed that Holmes was never a director, officer, or even an employee of Urban Decay. According to Lerner, she was just being nice to Holmes by letting her be present during Urban Decay business. Lerner denied Holmes had any role in creating the colors, names, or concepts for Urban Decay. When Holmes asked Lerner about her assets and liabilities in Urban Decay, Lerner thought she was asking for a job. She explained her statements to the

---

6. [FN 10] Holmes was never given Exhibit A, and did not see it until trial. It showed & Capital Partners, L.P. with a 92 percent interest, having contributed $489,900. It also showed Lerner and her husband with contributions of $5050 each, and 1 percent apiece. Zomnir's contribution was listed as $5050, but she had a 5 percent interest. None of the individuals actually paid in the listed contributions.

press regarding Urban Decay being Holmes' idea as misquotes or the product of her stress.

The jury found in favor of Holmes on every cause of action. The jury assessed $480,000 in damages against Lerner, and $320,000 against Soward. Following presentation of evidence as to net worth, the jury awarded punitive damages of $500,000 against Lerner and $130,000 against Soward. . . .

DISCUSSION

Lerner and Soward argue that there was no partnership agreement as a matter of law . . . .

I. There Was No Error in the Determination That a Partnership Was Formed

Holmes testified that she and Lerner did not discuss sharing profits of the business during the July 31, "kitchen table" conversation. Throughout the case, Lerner and Soward have contended that without an agreement to share profits, there can be no partnership. Lerner and Soward begin their argument on appeal by quoting a statement from *Westcott v. Gilman* (1915) 170 Cal. 562, 568, 150 P. 777, that profit sharing is "an essential element of every partnership. . . ." They argue that nothing has changed since the "ancient truth" regarding profit sharing was expressed in *Westcott*. However, an important element supporting the *Westcott* decision has changed, because Westcott relied on the language of former section 2395 of the Civil Code. That statutory predecessor of the Uniform Partnership Act (UPA) defined a partnership as: ". . . the association of two or more persons, for the purpose of carrying on business together, and dividing its profits between them." Civil Code former section 2395 was repealed and replaced with the UPA in 1949.

The applicable version of the UPA . . . omitted the language regarding division of profits and defined a partnership as: "an association of two or more persons to carry on as co-owners a business for profit." When the legislature enacts a new statute, replacing an existing one, and omits express language, it indicates an intent to change the original act. We can only conclude that the omission of the language regarding dividing profits from the definition of a partnership was an intentional change in the law. The UPA relocated the provision regarding profits to former section 15007, subdivision (4), which provided that in determining whether a partnership exists, "[t]he receipt by a person of a share of the profits of a business is prima facie evidence that he is a partner. . . ." This relocation of the element of sharing the profits indicates that the Legislature intends profit sharing to be evidence of a partnership, rather than a required element of the definition of a partnership. The presence or absence of any of the various elements set forth in former section 15007, including sharing of profits and losses, is not necessarily dispositive. As explained in *Cochran v. Board of Supervisors* (1978) 85 Cal. App. 3d 75, 80, 149 Cal. Rptr. 304, the rules to establish the existence of a partnership in former section 15007 should be viewed in the light of the crucial factor of the intent of the parties revealed in the terms of their agreement, conduct, and the surrounding circumstances when determining whether a partnership exists.

The UPA provides for the situation in which the partners have not expressly stated an agreement regarding sharing of profits. Section 15018 provides in relevant part: "The rights and duties of the partners in relation to the partnership shall be determined, subject to any agreement between them, by the following rules: (a) Each partner shall . . . share equally in the profits and surplus remaining after all liabilities, including those to partners, are satisfied." This provision states, subject to an agreement between the parties, partners "shall" share equally in the profits. Lerner and Soward argue that using section 15018 to supply a missing term regarding profit sharing ignores the provision of section 15007, subdivision (2). That section, headed "rules for determining existence of partnership," provides that mere joint ownership of common property "does not of itself establish a partnership, whether such co-owners do or do not share any profits made by the use of the property." Lerner and Soward are mistaken. The definition in section 15006 provides that the association with the intent to carry on a business for profit is the essential requirement for a partnership. Following that definition does not transform mere joint ownership into the essence of a partnership. . . .

The trial court in this case refused to add additional elements to the statutory definition and properly instructed the jury in the language of section 15006. We agree with the trial court's interpretation of the law. The actual sharing of profits (with exceptions which do not apply here) is prima facie evidence, which is to be considered, in light of any other evidence, when determining if a partnership exists. In this case, there were no profits to share at the time Holmes was expelled from the business, so the evidentiary provision of section 15007, subdivision (4) is not applicable. According to section 15006, parties who expressly agree to associate as co-owners with the intent to carry on a business for profit, have established a partnership. Once the elements of that definition are established, other provisions of the UPA and the conduct of the parties supply the details of the agreement. Certainly implicit in the Holmes-Lerner agreement to operate Urban Decay together was an understanding to share in profits and losses as any business owners would. The evidence supported the jury's implicit finding that Holmes birthed an idea which was incubated jointly by Lerner and Holmes, from which they intended to profit once it was fully matured in their company.

II. The Agreement Was Sufficiently Definite

Lerner and Soward argue that the agreement between Lerner and Holmes was too indefinite to be enforced. . . .

The agreement between Holmes and Lerner was to take Holmes' idea and reduce it to concrete form. They decided to do it together, to form a company, to hire employees, and to engage in the entire process together. The agreement here, as presented to the jury, was that Holmes and Lerner would start a cosmetics company based on the unusual colors developed by Holmes, identified by the urban theme and the exotic names. The agreement is evidenced by Lerner's statements: "We will do . . . everything," "it's going to be our baby, and we're going to work on it together." Their agreement is reflected in Lerner's words: "We will hire people to work for us." "We will do . . . everything we can to get the company going, and then we'll be creative, and other people will do the work, so we'll have time to continue riding the horses." The additional terms were filled in as the two women immediately began work on the multitude of details necessary to bring their idea to fruition. The fact that Holmes worked for almost a year, without expectation of pay, is further confirmation of the agreement. Lerner and Soward never objected to her work, her participation in board meetings and decision making, or her exercise of authority over the retail warehouse operation. Even as late as the trial in this matter, when Lerner was claiming that everything Holmes said was a lie, Lerner admitted: "It was not only my intention to give Pat every opportunity to be a part of this, but I had hoped that she would." In the words of the court in *Weddington*, the parties agreed on the "same thing in the same sense." (*Weddington Productions, Inc. v. Flick*, supra, 60 Cal. App. 4th at p. 811, 71 Cal. Rptr. 2d 265.) Holmes was not seeking specific enforcement of a single vague term of the agreement. She was frozen out of the business altogether, and her agreement with Lerner was completely renounced. The agreement that was made and the subsequent acts of the parties supply sufficient certainty to determine the existence of a breach and a remedy. . . .

DISPOSITION . . .

[T]he judgment and postjudgment order are affirmed. The parties are to bear their own costs on appeal.

Questions

1. Why was Holmes arguing that her relationship with Lerner constituted a partnership?
2. What did the defendants argue as to why there was no partnerships?
3. What facts in this case point to there being a partnership?
4. In hindsight, what should Lerner have done differently?
5. Early in the opinion the court writes, "In December of 1995, Urban Decay was incorporated." Later it writes, "Urban Decay had been formed as a limited liability company." I thought this was a partnership case. What is going on?

The *Holmes* case illustrates a common fact pattern for partnership formation issues—one of the people in a business relationship argues that the relationship constituted a partnership so that he or she can claim a violation of the partnership statute, for example, breach of fiduciary duty. Another common fact pattern is where a creditor of a sole proprietorship argues that the business was actually an inadvertent partnership in an effort to reach additional pockets. For example, say that Clare operated Clare's Conery from Chapter 3 as a sole proprietorship. Maria, Clare's sister and a successful hedge fund manager, loaned Clare money to get the business up and running and occasionally provided Clare with business advice. If Clare's Conery later fails, leaving various unpaid debts and Clare declaring personal bankruptcy, a debtor may argue that Clare's Conery was in fact an inadvertent partnership with two partners—Clare and Maria—so that it can recover from the deep-pocketed Maria.

Exercise 4.1

1. You and three classmates agree to form a study group for this course. Does the study group constitute a partnership?
2. Same facts as Question 1, but you also agree to market and sell the outline the group develops to other students, with the money to be used to buy snacks for consuming during the group study sessions. Now is it a partnership?
3. Same facts as Question 2, but instead the group agrees that the money will be divvied up among its members. Now is it a partnership?
4. Same facts as Question 3, but you all sign a document stating as follows: "This study group is not formed with the intent to carry on a business for profit and therefore is not a partnership." Now is it a partnership?

---

3. Management

The default statutory rule under RUPA is that "[e]ach partner has equal rights in the management and conduct of the partnership business."[7] This default rule generally translates into partners voting on a proposed course of action, with each partner getting one vote. It does not, however, mean that every partnership decision is put to a vote of the partners. Instead, a matter is normally put to a vote only if there is disagreement among the partners as to how to proceed, the matter is outside the ordinary course of the partnership's business, or a third party is requiring formal partner approval as a condition of entering into a transaction with the partnership. Under the statutory default rule, an ordinary course of business matter put to a partnership vote is approved if a majority of partners votes in favor of it.[8] Under this rule, each partner gets one vote regardless of how much capital or time the partner has contributed to the partnership. The statutory default rule for approval of a matter outside

---

7. *See* RUPA §401(f).
8. *See id.* §401(j).

the partnership's ordinary course of business requires unanimous partner approval.[9]

It is fairly common for a partnership to vary RUPA's default management rules. Variations include the following:

- Allocating votes proportionally based on the amount of capital each partner has contributed to the partnership. In other words, a partner who has contributed 65 percent of the partnership's capital would get 65 percent of the total voting power.
- Delegating decision-making authority with respect to partnership business to one partner (typically called the managing partner) or a committee of partners (typically called the management committee).
- Requiring supermajority votes for specified decisions. For example, the partners could agree that any expenditure by the partnership in excess of $X requires the approval of at least 75 percent of the partners or voting power.
- Changing the approval requirement for matters outside the partnership's ordinary course of business to something less than unanimous partner approval.

Exercise 4.2

1. Continuing with the study group hypo from Exercise 4.1, assume the group is a partnership governed by RUPA. If there is disagreement as to whether to give a non-study group member student the outline for free, how is the disagreement resolved?
2. All of the members of the study group except you want to expand by purchasing the right to sell outlines for other courses prepared by other study groups. Can the partnership do this without your approval?
3. De Silva wants to join the study group and everyone is in favor of her doing so except you. Can De Silva be admitted against your wishes?

---

4. Partnership Agreement

As mentioned in Chapter 1, most partnerships have a written partnership agreement signed by each partner. These agreements typically address, among other things, management structure, allocation of profits and losses among the partners, partner taxation, admission and withdrawal of partners, and dissolution. It is through the partnership agreement that partners alter or opt out of default partnership statutory rules that do not meet the partners' needs or preferences. This is spelled out in RUPA §103, which provides:

---

9. *See id.*

(a) Except as otherwise provided in subsection (b), relations among the partners and between the partners and the partnership are governed by the partnership agreement. To the extent the partnership agreement does not otherwise provide, this [Act] governs relations among the partners and between the partners and the partnership.

Thus, under RUPA, partners are free to alter or opt out of any statutory provision unless the provision is listed in RUPA §103(b). This section lists ten items that are essentially mandatory partnership rules, meaning they apply even if the partnership agreement says otherwise. You should read subsection (b) now to familiarize yourself with this list.

Notice that per RUPA §103(a), a default statutory rule applies to a partnership with a partnership agreement if the partnership agreement does not provide a contrary rule. In other words, if the partnership agreement is silent on a particular issue addressed by a default statutory rule, the default statutory rule applies.

Exercise 4.3

Read the Anderson, Barrera, and Choi L.L.P. (AB&C) partnership agreement located at the end of this chapter and answer the following questions. Make sure you note any applicable partnership agreement and/or statutory provision that supports your answer. In that regard, assume that Florida has adopted RUPA verbatim.

1. Anderson wants to paint the exterior of the Property beige; Barrera and Choi want to paint it pink. Whose preference will prevail? Why?
2. What would be the answer to Question 1 if Section 6 was not included in the partnership agreement?
3. Anderson wants to mortgage the Property in connection with a $100,000 loan from a bank to the partnership. What approval is required for this transaction?
4. Anderson wants to demolish the house located on the Property and replace it with a miniature golf course. What approval is required for this transaction?
5. What changes to the partnership agreement would you suggest if you represented Choi in negotiations of it?
6. Are any provisions of the partnership agreement invalid under RUPA?

---

5. Fiduciary Duties

Partners owe each other and the partnership fiduciary duties. Historically, these duties were pursuant to common law, but RUPA has codified them. In that regard, RUPA §404 provides as follows: "(a) The only fiduciary duties a partner owes to the partnership and the other partners are the duty of loyalty and the duty of care set forth in subsections (b) and (c). . . ." Under RUPA §404(b), the duty of loyalty is comprised of a duty "to account to the partnership and hold as trustee for it any property, profit, or benefit . . . derived from a use by the partner of partnership property" and prohibitions against self-dealing and competing against the partnership. Under RUPA §404(c), the duty of care is comprised of a duty to refrain "from engaging in grossly negligent or reckless conduct, intentional misconduct, or a knowing violation of law" in connection with partnership business.

Next up is undoubtedly the most famous case regarding partnership fiduciary duties. Last I checked, the case had been cited in over one thousand judicial opinions.

Meinhard v. Salmon
164 N.E. 545 (N.Y. 1928)

CARDOZO, C.J.

On April 10, 1902, Louisa M. Gerry leased to the defendant Walter J. Salmon the premises known as the Hotel Bristol at the northwest corner of Forty-Second Street and Fifth Avenue in the city of New York. The lease was for a term of 20 years, commencing May 1, 1902, and ending April 30, 1922. The lessee undertook to change the hotel building for use as shops and offices at a cost of $200,000. Alterations and additions were to be accretions to the land.

Salmon, while in course of treaty with the lessor as to the execution of the lease, was in course of treaty with Meinhard, the plaintiff, for the necessary funds. The result was a joint venture with terms embodied in a writing. Meinhard was to pay to Salmon half of the moneys requisite to reconstruct, alter, manage, and operate the property. Salmon was to pay to Meinhard 40 percent of the net profits for the first five years of the lease and 50 percent for the years thereafter. If there were losses, each party was to bear them equally. Salmon, however, was to have sole power to "manage, lease, underlet and operate" the building. There were to be certain pre-emptive rights for each in the contingency of death.

The two were coadventurers, subject to fiduciary duties akin to those of partners. As to this we are all agreed. The heavier weight of duty rested, however, upon Salmon. He was a coadventurer with Meinhard, but he was manager as well. During the early years of the enterprise, the building, reconstructed, was operated at a loss. If the relation had then ended, Meinhard as well as Salmon would have carried a heavy burden. Later the profits became large with the result that for each of the investors there came a rich return. For each the venture had its phases of fair weather and of foul. The two were in it jointly, for better or for worse.

When the lease was near its end, Elbridge T. Gerry had become the owner of the reversion. He owned much other property in the neighborhood, one lot adjoining the Bristol building on Fifth Avenue and four lots on Forty-Second Street. He had a plan to lease the entire tract for a long term to someone who would destroy the buildings then existing and put up another in their place. In the latter part of 1921, he submitted such a project to several capitalists and dealers. He was unable to carry it through with any of them. Then, in January, 1922, with less than four months of the lease to run, he approached the defendant Salmon. The result was a new lease to the Midpoint Realty Company, which is owned and controlled by Salmon, a lease covering the whole tract, and involving a huge outlay. The term is to be 20 years, but successive covenants for renewal will extend it to a maximum of 80 years at the will of either party. The existing buildings may remain unchanged for seven years. They are then to be torn down, and a new building to cost $3,000,000 is to be placed upon the site. The rental, which under the Bristol lease was only $55,000, is to be from $350,000 to $475,000 for the properties so combined. Salmon personally guaranteed the performance by the lessee of the covenants of the new lease until such time as the new building had been completed and fully paid for.

The lease between Gerry and the Midpoint Realty Company was signed and delivered on January 25, 1922. Salmon had not told Meinhard anything about it. Whatever his motive may have been, he had kept the negotiations to himself. Meinhard was not informed even of the bare existence of a project. The first that he knew of it was in February, when the lease was an accomplished fact. He then made demand on the defendants that the lease be held in trust as an asset of the venture, making offer upon the trial to share the personal obligations incidental to the guaranty. The demand was followed by refusal, and later by this suit. A referee gave judgment for the plaintiff, limiting the plaintiff's interest in the lease, however, to 25 percent. The limitation was on the theory that the plaintiff's equity was to be restricted to one-half of so much of the value of the lease as was contributed or represented by the occupation of the Bristol site. Upon cross-appeals to the Appellate Division, the judgment was modified so as to enlarge the equitable interest to one-half of the whole lease. With this enlargement of plaintiff's interest, there went, of course, a corresponding enlargement of his attendant obligations. The case is now here on an appeal by the defendants.

Joint adventurers, like copartners, owe to one another, while the enterprise continues, the duty of the finest loyalty. Many forms of conduct permissible in a workaday world for those acting at arm's length, are forbidden to those bound by fiduciary ties. A trustee is held to something stricter than the morals of the market place. Not honesty alone, but the punctilio of an honor the most sensitive, is then the standard of behavior. As to this there has developed a tradition that is unbending and inveterate. Uncompromising rigidity has been the attitude of courts of equity when petitioned to undermine the rule of undivided loyalty by the "disintegrating erosion" of particular exceptions. Only thus has the level of conduct for fiduciaries been kept at a level higher than that trodden by the crowd. It will not consciously be lowered by any judgment of this court.

The owner of the reversion, Mr. Gerry, had vainly striven to find a tenant who would favor his ambitious scheme of demolition and construction. Baffled in the search, he turned to the defendant Salmon in possession of the Bristol, the keystone of the project. He figured to himself beyond a doubt that the man in possession would prove a likely customer. To the eye of an observer, Salmon held the lease as owner in his own right, for himself and no one else. In fact he held it as a fiduciary, for himself and another, sharers in a common venture. If this fact had been proclaimed, if the lease by its terms had run in favor of a partnership, Mr. Gerry, we may fairly assume, would have laid before the partners, and not merely before one of them, his plan of reconstruction. The pre-emptive privilege, or, better, the pre-emptive opportunity, that was thus an incident of the enterprise, Salmon appropriate to himself in secrecy and silence. He might have warned Meinhard that the plan had been submitted, and that either would be free to compete for the award. If he had done this, we do not need to say whether he would have been under a duty, if successful in the competition, to hold the lease so acquired for the benefit of a venture then about to end, and thus prolong by indirection its responsibilities and duties. The trouble about his conduct is that he excluded his coadventurer from any chance to compete, from any chance to enjoy the opportunity for benefit that had come to him alone by virtue of his agency. This chance, if nothing more, he was under a duty to concede. The price of its denial is an extension of the trust at the option and for the benefit of the one whom he excluded.

No answer is it to say that the chance would have been of little value even if seasonably offered. Such a calculus of probabilities is beyond the science of the chancery. Salmon, the real estate operator, might have been preferred to Meinhard, the woolen merchant. On the other hand, Meinhard might have offered better terms, or reinforced his offer by alliance with the wealth of others. Perhaps he might even have persuaded the lessor to renew the Bristol lease alone, postponing for a time, in return for higher rentals, the improvement of adjoining lots. We know that even under the lease as made the time for the enlargement of the building was delayed for seven years. All these opportunities were cut away from him through another's intervention. He knew that Salmon was the manager. As the time drew near for the expiration of the lease, he would naturally assume from silence, if from nothing else, that the lessor was willing to extend it for a term of years, or at least to let it stand as a lease from year to year. Not impossibly the lessor would have done so, whatever his protestations of unwillingness, if Salmon had not given assent to a project more attractive. At all events, notice of termination, even if not necessary, might seem, not unreasonably, to be something to be looked for, if the business was over the another tenant was to enter. In the absence of such notice, the matter of an extension was one that would naturally be attended to by the manager of the enterprise, and not neglected altogether. At least, there was nothing in the situation to give warning to any one that while the lease was still in being, there had come to the manager an offer of extension which he had locked within his breast to be utilized by himself alone. The very fact that Salmon was in control with exclusive powers of direction charged him the more obviously with the duty of disclosure, since only through disclosure could opportunity be equalized. If he might cut off renewal by a purchase for his own benefit when four months were to pass before the lease would have an end, he might do so with equal right while there remained as many years. He might steal a march on his comrade under cover of the darkness, and then hold the captured ground. Loyalty and comradeship are not so easily abjured. . . .

We have no thought to hold that Salmon was guilty of a conscious purpose to defraud. Very likely he assumed in all good faith that with the approaching end of the venture he might ignore his coadventurer and take the extension for himself. He had given to the enterprise time and labor as well as money. He had made it a success. Meinhard, who had given money, but neither time nor labor, had already been richly paid. There might seem to be something grasping in his insistence upon more. Such recriminations are not unusual when coadventurers fall out. They are not without their force if conduct is to be judged by the common standards of competitors. That is not to say that they have pertinency here. Salmon had put himself in a position in which thought of self was to be renounced, however hard the abnegation. He was much more than a coadventurer. He was a managing coadventurer. For him and for those like him the rule of undivided loyalty is relentless and supreme. A different question would be here if there were lacking any nexus of relation between the business conducted by the manager and the opportunity brought to him as an incident of management. For this problem, as for most, there are distinctions of degree. If Salmon had received from Gerry a proposition to lease a building at a location far removed, he might have held for himself the privilege thus acquired, or so we shall assume. Here the subject-matter of the new lease was an extension and enlargement of the subject-matter of the old one. A managing coadventurer appropriating the benefit of such a lease without warning to his partner might fairly expect to be reproached with conduct that was underhand, or lacking, to say the least, in reasonable candor, if the partner were to surprise him in the act of signing the new instrument. Conduct subject to that reproach does not receive from equity a healing benediction.

A question remains as to the form and extent of the equitable interest to be allotted to the plaintiff. The trust as declared has been held to attach to the lease which was in the name of the defendant corporation. We think it ought to attach at the option of the defendant Salmon to the shares of stock which were owned by him or were under his control. The difference may be important if the lessee shall wish to execute an assignment of the lease, as it ought to be free to do with the consent of the lessor. On the other hand, an equal division of the shares might lead to other hardships. It might take away from Salmon the power of control and management which under the plan of the joint venture he was to have from first to last. The number of shares to be allotted to the plaintiff should, therefore, be reduced to such an extent as may be necessary to preserve to the defendant Salmon the expected measure of dominion. To that end an extra share should be added to his half. . . .

The judgment should be modified by providing that at the option of the defendant Salmon there may be substituted for a trust attaching to the lease a trust attaching to the shares of stock, with the result that one-half of such shares together with one additional share will in that event be allotted to the defendant Salmon and the other shares to the plaintiff, and as so modified the judgment should be affirmed with costs.

The opinion characterizes the relationship of Meinhard and Salmon not as a partnership but as a joint venture (or joint adventure). As mentioned in Chapter 1, a joint venture is when two or more businesses or individuals combine resources to pursue a discrete business opportunity or venture such as reconstructing, managing, and operating the Bristol Hotel for 20 years. Many courts have simply analogized joint ventures to partnerships and applied partnership law to the relationship, as was done in *Meinhard v. Salmon*. However, as the comments to RUPA indicate, "[r]elationships that are called 'joint ventures' are partnerships if they otherwise fit the definition of a partnership." The Meinhard/Salmon relationship appears to fit squarely within the RUPA definition of partnership we discussed in Section A.2 above. Technically, the relationship would likely be considered a "partnership for a definite term," that is, one that ends after a specified time period, in this case, 20 years.[10]

Questions

1. According to *Meinhard*, what is the standard of behavior imposed on partners by the duty of loyalty?
2. How might the *Meinhard* opinion have differed if RUPA existed during the relevant timeframe and applied to the Meinhard/Salmon relationship?
3. Would the case have come out differently if Gerry had approached Salmon about the new lease six months later than he did?
4. Salmon comes to you for advice prior to entering into the new deal with Gerry. What do you tell him?
5. Would the case have come out differently if the agreement between Meinhard and Salmon included the provison below?

---

10. Under RUPA, a partnership falls under one of three categories: (1) a partnership for a definite term; (2) a partnership for a particular undertaking (partnership agreement provides that the partnership ends upon the completion of a specified task); and (3) a partnership at will ("a partnership in which the partners have not agreed to remain partners until the expiration of a definite term or the completion of a particular undertaking." RUPA §101(8)).

> Either Meinhard or Salmon may engage in or possess an interest in other business ventures of every nature and description, independently or with others, including, but not limited to, the ownership, financing, leasing, operation, management, syndication, brokerage, and development of any property, including properties in direct competition with the Bristol Hotel, and neither Meinhard nor Salmon shall have, or have the right to acquire, any right by virtue of this Agreement in and to such independent venture or to the income or profits derived therefrom.

As you probably noted from reading RUPA §103(b), a partnership agreement cannot eliminate the duty of loyalty or care. Specifically, RUPA §103 states:

> (b) The partnership agreement may not:
> . . .
> (3) eliminate the duty of loyalty under Section 404(b) . . . , but:
> (i) the partnership agreement may identify specific types or categories of activities that do not violate the duty of loyalty, if not manifestly unreasonable; or
> (ii) all of the partners or a number or percentage specified in the partnership agreement may authorize or ratify, after full disclosure of all material facts, a specific act or transaction that otherwise would violate the duty of loyalty;
> (4) unreasonably reduce the duty of care under Section 404(c). . . .

The Official Comment provides the following with respect to RUPA §103(b)(3):

> There has always been a tension regarding the extent to which a partner's fiduciary duty of loyalty can be varied by agreement, as contrasted with the other partners' consent to a particular and known breach of duty. On the one hand, courts have been loathe to enforce agreements broadly "waiving" in advance a partner's fiduciary duty of loyalty, especially where there is unequal bargaining power, information, or sophistication. For this reason, a very broad provision in a partnership agreement in effect negating any duty of loyalty, such as a provision giving a managing partner complete discretion to manage the business with no liability except for acts and omissions that constitute willful misconduct, will not likely be enforced. See, e.g., *Labovitz v. Dolan*, 189 Ill. App. 3d 403, 136 Ill. Dec. 780, 545 N.E.2d 304 (1989). On the other hand, it is clear that the remaining partners can "consent" to a particular conflicting interest transaction or other breach of duty, after the fact, provided there is full disclosure.
>
> RUPA attempts to provide a standard that partners can rely upon in drafting exculpatory agreements. It is not necessary that the agreement be restricted to a particular transaction. That would require bargaining over every transaction or opportunity, which would be excessively burdensome. The agreement may be

drafted in terms of types or categories of activities or transactions, but it should be reasonably specific.

A provision in a real estate partnership agreement authorizing a partner who is a real estate agent to retain commissions on partnership property bought and sold by that partner would be an example of a "type or category" of activity that is not manifestly unreasonable and thus should be enforceable under the Act. Likewise, a provision authorizing that partner to buy or sell real property for his own account without prior disclosure to the other partners or without first offering it to the partnership would be enforceable as a valid category of partnership activity.

Ultimately, the courts must decide the outer limits of validity of such agreements, and context may be significant. It is intended that the risk of judicial refusal to enforce manifestly unreasonable exculpatory clauses will discourage sharp practices while accommodating the legitimate needs of the parties in structuring their relationship. . . .

Subsection (b)(3)(ii) is intended to clarify the right of partners, recognized under general law, to consent to a known past or anticipated violation of duty and to waive their legal remedies for redress of that violation. This is intended to cover situations where the conduct in question is not specifically authorized by the partnership agreement. It can also be used to validate conduct that might otherwise not satisfy the "manifestly unreasonable" standard.

As for the duty of care, the Official Comment states as follows:

Under subsection (b)(4), the partners' duty of care may not be unreasonably reduced below the statutory standard set forth in Section 404(d), that is, to refrain from engaging in grossly negligent or reckless conduct, intentional misconduct, or a knowing violation of law.

For example, partnership agreements frequently contain provisions releasing a partner from liability for actions taken in good faith and in the honest belief that the actions are in the best interests of the partnership and indemnifying the partner against any liability incurred in connection with the business of the partnership if the partner acts in a good faith belief that he has authority to act. Many partnership agreements reach this same result by listing various activities and stating that the performance of these activities is deemed not to constitute gross negligence or willful misconduct. These types of provisions are intended to come within the modifications authorized by subsection (b)(4). On the other hand, absolving partners of intentional misconduct is probably unreasonable. As with contractual standards of loyalty, determining the outer limit in reducing the standard of care is left to the courts.

The standard may, of course, be increased by agreement to one of ordinary care or an even higher standard of care.

6. Obligation of Good Faith and Fair Dealing

RUPA §404(d) provides, "A partner shall discharge the duties to the partnership and the other partners under this [Act] or under the partnership agreement and exercise any rights consistently with the obligation of good faith and fair dealing."

The Official Comment to RUPA §404 elaborates on the obligation:

> The obligation of good faith and fair dealing is a contract concept, imposed on the partners because of the consensual nature of a partnership. It is not characterized, in RUPA, as a fiduciary duty arising out of the partners' special relationship. Nor is it a separate and independent obligation. It is an ancillary obligation that applies whenever a partner discharges a duty or exercises a right under the partnership agreement or the Act. The meaning of "good faith and fair dealing" is not firmly fixed under present law. "Good faith" clearly suggests a subjective element, while "fair dealing" implies an objective component. It was decided to leave the terms undefined in the Act and allow the courts to develop their meaning based on the experience of real cases. . . .
>
> The UCC definition of "good faith" is honesty in fact and, in the case of a merchant, the observance of reasonable commercial standards of fair dealing in the trade. See UCC §§1-201(19), 2-103(b). Those definitions were rejected as too narrow or not applicable.

As with the duties of care and loyalty, a partnership agreement cannot eliminate the obligation of good faith and fair dealing. Specifically, RUPA §103 provides:

> (b) The partnership agreement may not:
> . . .
> (5) eliminate the obligation of good faith and fair dealing under Section 404(d), but the partnership agreement may prescribe the standards by which the performance of the obligation is to be measured, if the standards are not manifestly unreasonable. . . .

Here is sample language from a partnership agreement defining good faith and fair dealing:

> In order for a determination or other action to be in "good faith and fair dealing" for purposes of this Agreement, the Person or Persons making such determination or taking or declining to take such other action must believe that the determination or other action is in the best interests of the Partnership.

7. Liability Exposure

Each partner is personally liable for the obligations of the partnership. Under RUPA §306(a), this liability is joint and several. This means that a judgment creditor of the partnership can recover the entire amount owed to it by the partnership from any partner or partners of its choosing. Note, however, that pursuant to RUPA §307(d), a judgment creditor generally must first seek to recover against the partnership itself. In other words, the creditor has to try to get the money from the partnership before the creditor can levy execution against the assets of a partner to satisfy the judgment. This is known as the "exhaustion rule."

A partner who has to pay a judgment creditor of the partnership out of his or her pocket will have the right to recover some of this money from the other partners. Specifically, the partner will be entitled to indemnification, or repayment, by the partnership pursuant to RUPA §401(c). The partnership will obviously not be able to cover this indemnification obligation if its assets are exhausted (which is normally the case if a partner had to cover a judgment against the partnership). The other partners, however, are essentially obligated to cover part of this indemnification obligation based on the partnership's applicable rule for sharing losses.[11] For example, say you and I were the only partners in a partnership and our partnership agreement provided that we would share profits and losses 50/50. Our business fails and, after coming up empty against the partnership, a judgment creditor pursues me for the $10,000 owed to it by the partnership. A court orders me to pay the creditor the $10,000, so I do so. Because our partnership agreement says we split losses 50/50, you would owe me $5,000, all else being equal.

8. Transfer of Partnership Interests

The default rule is that an ownership interest in a partnership (what RUPA calls a "partnership interest") is not freely transferable in its entirety. Specifically, RUPA §502 provides that "[t]he only transferable interest of a partner in the partnership is the partner's share of the profits and losses of the partnership and the partner's right to receive distributions." In other words, the default rule is that a partner can transfer his or her economic but not management rights. RUPA §503 then elaborates:

> A transfer . . . of a partner's transferable interest in the partnership . . . is permissible [but] does not, as against the other partners or partnership, entitle the transferee, during the continuance of the partnership, to participate in the management or conduct of the partnership business, to require access to information concerning partnership transactions, or to inspect or copy the partnership books or records.

These provisions reflect the "pick your partner" principle, that is, partners get to choose with whom they share management rights for the business. The principle is also reflected in RUPA §401(i), which provides that "[a] person may become a partner only with the consent of all of the partners."

---

11. The applicable rule would either be specified in the partnership agreement or by RUPA §401(b) if the partnership agreement is silent on sharing losses.

Neither RUPA §502, §503, nor §401(i) is on the §103(b) mandatory rule list, which means that the "pick your partner" principle can be modified or eliminated by a partnership agreement.

Exercise 4.4

Refer again to the AB&C partnership agreement at the end of this chapter and answer the following questions. Make sure you note any applicable partnership agreement and/or statutory provision that supports your answer. In that regard, assume that Florida has adopted RUPA verbatim.

1. Barrera wants to sell his transferable interest in AB&C to Dixon. Whose consent is needed for him to do so?
2. Choi wants to pledge his transferable interest to Bank to secure an $800,000 loan Bank made to Choi. Whose consent is needed for him to do so?
3. Anderson has become seriously ill and is on the verge of death. Anderson's will leaves everything to her husband. Will Anderson's partnership interest in AB&C pass to her husband following her death?

Exercise 4.5

Anderson has prepared the following amendment to the AB&C partnership agreement. What changes would you make to it? What approval is required to amend the agreement?

Section 9 of the partnership agreement is hereby amended as follows:

A partner may transfer his economic rights in his partnership interest without the consent of the other partners. A partner may transfer his management rights only with the consent of the other partners. A partner may encumber his economic rights only with the written consent of a majority.

---

9. Allocation of Profits and Losses

RUPA §401(b) provides the default rule for the allocation of partnership profits and losses among the partners: "Each partner is entitled to an equal share of the partnership profits and is chargeable with a share of the partnership losses in proportion to the partner's share of the profits." This per capita allocation may make sense if each partner contributed the same amount of capital to the partnership but oftentimes this is not the case. Furthermore, as discussed in Chapter 3, it often makes sense from a tax perspective to allocate losses in a manner other than per capita. As a result, partnership agreements very often provide for a different allocation rule, for example, pro rata based on the amount of capital contributed to the partnership by each partner.

Note that partnership law makes a distinction between the allocation of profits and the distribution of profits. An allocation of profits refers to the amount of partnership profits a partner has to include as income on his or her individual income tax return. A distribution of profits refers to the amount of partnership profits that are actually paid out to a partner. For example, say you and I are the only partners in a partnership and our partnership agreement provides that we share profits and losses 50/50. The partnership generates a profit of $50,000 for the latest year. We decide (1) that $30,000 of the $50,000 will be paid out to us ($15,000 each), and (2) to use the remaining $20,000 to buy new office equipment for the business. Because our partnership agreement specifies that we split profits 50/50, each of us is allocated $25,000 in partnership profits, which we will have to include on our respective individual income tax returns, even though each of us only received a $15,000 distribution from the partnership. This probably is not a big deal for either of us, because the $15,000 is more than enough to cover the taxes we have to pay on our respective $25,000 allocation, that is, $7,000 assuming our applicable individual marginal tax rates are 28 percent. However, it may be a big deal for one or both of us if our partnership did not distribute any of the profits to us (perhaps because we could not agree on the amount), because we would still each owe the extra $7,000 in tax, even though we got no money from the partnership.

In light of this possibility, it is common for a partnership agreement to include a provision requiring the partnership to distribute to each partner sufficient funds to cover the partners' tax liabilities resulting from the allocation of the partnership's earnings to the partners. Here is sample language:

Tax Burden Distributions. As soon as practicable following the end of each year, the Partnership shall distribute to each Partner an amount sufficient for the Partner to pay the taxes owed by the Partner from income of the Partnership allocated to the Partner for that year.

If our partnership agreement included the above provision, the partnership would be required to distribute at least $7,000 to each of us (again, assuming our applicable individual marginal tax rates are 28 percent).

Note that there is no specific RUPA default rule requiring a partnership to distribute profits to its partners. Thus, in the absence of a partnership agreement provision to the contrary, the decision of whether to make a distribution is governed by the management provisions of the partnership agreement or, if the agreement contains none, the default management rules under RUPA.

Exercise 4.6

Refer again to the AB&C partnership agreement at the end of this chapter and answer the following questions. Make sure you note any applicable partnership agreement and/or statutory provision that supports your answer.

1. How does AB&C allocate profits? Why do you think the partnership went with this allocation?
2. AB&C had $20,000 in profits for its latest fiscal year. How much of this is allocated to Barrera? How much is distributed to Barrera?
3. How much would AB&C distribute to Barrera if the partnership agreement included the tax burden distribution provision from above?

---

10. Dissociation

Dissociation is the term used by RUPA for when a partner departs a partnership. RUPA §601 provides the default rule for dissociation. Under this rule, a partner can dissociate at any time by notifying the partnership of his or her express will to withdraw. The rule also provides for automatic dissociation upon a partner's (1) expulsion from the partnership pursuant to the partnership agreement, (2) bankruptcy, or (3) death. Additionally, the rule allows the other partners to cause a partner's dissociation through a unanimous vote if, subject to limited exceptions, "there has been a transfer of all or substantially all of that partner's transferable interest in the partnership. . . ." Upon dissociation, a partner's right to participate in partnership management terminates (subject to a limited exception).

The default rule under RUPA §701 is that, unless a partner's dissociation triggers a dissolution of the partnership's business (see the next subsection), the partnership is required to cause the dissociated partner to be bought out of his or her partnership interest for cash. In other words, the partnership has to facilitate the buyout by the partnership, one or more partners, or a third party. RUPA §§701(b) and (c) specify the default formula for determining the buyout price. RUPA §§701(e) and (h) dictate the timing of the buyout, that is, when the dissociated partner gets his or her cash.

11. Dissolution

Partnership dissolution is triggered by various events specified in RUPA §801. Once triggered, the partnership's business must be wound up. In other words, as used in RUPA, "dissolution" is the point at which the partnership begins the winding-up phase of its existence. As explained in Official Comment 2 to RUPA §801, following dissolution:

[t]he partnership continues for the limited purpose of winding up the business. In effect, that means the scope of the partnership business contracts to completing work in process and taking such other actions as may be necessary to wind up the business. Winding up the partnership business entails selling its assets, paying its debts, and distributing the net balance, if any, to the partners in cash according to their interests. The partnership entity continues, and the partners are associated in the winding up of the business until winding up is completed. When the winding up is completed, the partnership entity terminates.

Unless the partnership agreement provides otherwise, per RUPA §801, dissolution is triggered in a partnership at will whenever a partner notifies the partnership of his or her express will to withdraw as a partner. In a partnership for a definite term or particular undertaking, the RUPA default rule is that dissolution is triggered by "the expiration of the term or completion of the undertaking"[12] or "the express will of all the partners to wind up the business" before the expiration or completion.[13] (Recall the distinction between partnerships at will, for a definite term, and for a particular undertaking is discussed in footnote 10 above.)

Regardless of the type of partnership, dissolution is triggered by "an event that makes it unlawful for all or substantially all of the business of the partnership to be continued, but a cure of illegality within 90 days after notice to the partnership of the event is effective retroactively to the date of the event for purposes of this section."[14] Furthermore, dissolution may be ordered by a court on application by a partner if the court determines that "(i) the economic purpose of the partnership is likely to be unreasonably frustrated; (ii) another partner has engaged in conduct relating to the partnership business which makes it not reasonably practicable to carry on the business in partnership with that partner; or (iii) it is not otherwise reasonably practicable to carry on the partnership business in conformity with the partnership agreement. . . ."[15] Dissolution may also be ordered by a court on application by a transferee of a partner's transferable interest if the court determines that "it is equitable to wind up the partnership business: (i) after the expiration of the term or completion of the undertaking, if the partnership was for a definite term or particular undertaking at the time of the transfer or entry of the charging order that gave rise to the transfer; or (ii) at any time, if the partnership was a partnership at will at the time of the transfer or entry of the charging order that gave rise to the transfer."[16] The court-ordered dissolution rules are mandatory rules and thus cannot be altered by a partnership agreement. In other words, they appear on the RUPA §103(b) list.[17]

---

12. RUPA §801(2)(iii).
13. *Id.* §801(2)(ii).
14. *Id.* §801(4).
15. *Id.* §801(5).
16. *Id.* §801(6).
17. *See id.* §103(b)(8).

As mentioned above, part of the winding-up process involves the settlements of accounts among partners. RUPA §807 provides the default rule. Specifically, any amounts remaining after the partnership liquidates its assets and pays its creditors (RUPA refers to this as "surplus") are divvied up among the partners based on each partner's capital account balance and, if any money remains, each partner's profit sharing percentage. A partner's capital account consists of (1) contributions made to the partnership by the partner (e.g., cash or other property transferred by a partner to the partnership in exchange for his or her partnership interest) and the partner's share of partnership profits, minus (2) amounts distributed by the partnership to the partner and the partner's share of partnership losses.[18] The partnership then pays each partner an amount equal to his or her capital account balance, and the remaining surplus, if any, is divided among the partners based on their profit sharing percentages.

For example, say you and I are the only partners in a partnership, our partnership agreement provides that we share profits and losses 50/50, and the following events occurred:

- We each contributed $5,000 to the partnership upon its founding.
- In year 1, the partnership made $20,000 in profits and distributed $3,000 to each of us.
- In year 2, the partnership made $30,000 in profits and distributed $4,000 to me and $14,000 to you (you needed the extra money to help cover your law school tuition).

Following year 2, my capital account balance would be $23,000[19] and yours would be $13,000[20] with the difference coming from the $10,000 extra distributed to you by the partnership in year 2. Say we then decide to dissolve the partnership. The partnership sells off all of its assets, pays off all of its liabilities, and has $50,000 remaining, in other words, a $50,000 surplus. The partnership would then pay me my capital account balance of $23,000 and you your capital account balance of $13,000. The remaining $14,000 ($50,000 – $23,000 – $13,000) would be split equally between us, because our partnership agreement specifies that we split profits 50/50. In other words, we would each get $7,000 of the $14,000 surplus.

If the surplus is less than the aggregate of the partners' capital accounts, the shortfall is allocated to the partners' capital accounts based on their loss sharing percentage. The partnership then pays each partner an amount equal to his or her capital account balance. Thus, continuing with the example from above,

---

18. *See* RUPA §401(1)(a) & (b).

19. The calculation is as follows: $5,000 capital contribution + $10,000 share of year 1 profits – $3,000 year 1 distribution to me + $15,000 share of year 2 profits – $4,000 year 2 distribution to me.

20. The calculation is as follows: $5,000 capital contribution + $10,000 share of year 1 profits – $3,000 year 1 distribution to you + $15,000 share of year 2 profits – $14,000 year 2 distribution to you.

assume the partnership had $20,000 instead of a $50,000 surplus after liquidating and paying off creditors. The aggregate of our capital accounts is $36,000 ($23,000 + $13,000) so there is a $16,000 surplus shortfall. Hence, because our partnership agreement states that we share losses 50/50, each of our capital accounts will be reduced by $8,000 to account for this shortfall, reducing my capital account to $15,000 and yours to $5,000. As a result, I will get $15,000 and you will get $5,000 of the $20,000 surplus.

Exercise 4.7

Refer again to the AB&C partnership agreement at the end of this chapter and answer the following questions. Make sure you note any applicable partnership agreement and/or statutory provision that supports your answer. Assume the facts given in each question only apply to that question.

1. Barrera is going through a midlife crisis and, as a result, informs Anderson that he no longer wants to be a partner in AB&C. Barrera asks Anderson and Choi to buy him out. Are they required to do so? Assuming Barrera does dissociate from AB&C, does he get a say in its business going forward? Does AB&C have to dissolve? Would it have to dissolve if Section 15 was not included in the partnership agreement?
2. Barrera runs into financial trouble and is forced to declare bankruptcy. Does AB&C have to dissolve? Is Barrera's bankruptcy trustee required to sell Barrera's partnership interest to Anderson? To Choi?
3. What is the initial balance of each of the AB&C partners' capital accounts?
4. Assume the following occurred:
   - In year 1, AB&C made $30,000 in profits.
   - In year 2, AB&C made $35,000 in profits and distributed $10,000 to Choi.
   - At the beginning of year 3, Anderson, Barrera, and Choi decided to dissolve their partnership, so AB&C liquidated its assets for $755,000 and paid the $5,000 it owed to its creditors.

How much surplus does AB&C have following these events? How much money does it pay out to each of Anderson, Barrera, and Choi to settle their accounts?

B. LIMITED LIABILITY PARTNERSHIPS

1. Formation

As mentioned in Chapter 1, a limited liability partnership, or LLP for short, is simply a partnership that has elected LLP status under the applicable provisions of its partnership statute. Under RUPA, that provision is §1001, and it requires a partnership to file a "statement of qualification" with the applicable secretary of state to become an LLP. As you can see by reading §1001(c), the contents of a statement of qualification are pretty minimal. It includes the name of the partnership, the street address of the partnership's chief executive office, and a statement that the partnership elects to be a limited liability partnership.

Note that under RUPA §1002, the name of an LLP "must end with 'Registered Limited Liability Partnership,' 'Limited Liability Partnership,' 'R.L.L.P.,' 'L.L.P.,' 'RLLP,' or 'LLP.'" As the Official Comment to that section explains, "[t]he name provisions are intended to alert persons dealing with a limited liability partnership of the presence of the liability shield."

RUPA §1001(b) requires a partnership vote approving the partnership becoming an LLP. This vote is typically done in connection with approving revisions to the partnership agreement. While partners are not required to revise their agreement when the partnership becomes an LLP, doing so is advisable because, among other things, partner contribution and indemnification provisions will likely need to be revised. A new business that chooses to operate as an LLP will simply include a provision in the initial partnership agreement stating that the partnership shall be a limited liability partnership (see, e.g., Section 1.a of the AB&C partnership agreement) with necessary consent of each partner indicated by him or her signing the partnership agreement. The attorney handling the LLP's formation typically drafts the partnership agreement.

2. Liability Exposure

As stated in Chapter 1, the same statute governs partnerships and LLPs, with a handful of provisions of the statute applying only to a partnership that has elected to become an LLP. The most important of these provisions under RUPA is §306(c), which provides:

> An obligation of a partnership incurred while the partnership is a limited liability partnership, whether arising in contract, tort, or otherwise, is solely the obligation of the partnership. A partner is not personally liable, directly or indirectly, by way of contribution or otherwise, for such an obligation solely by reason of being or so acting as a partner. This subsection applies notwithstanding anything inconsistent in the partnership agreement that existed immediately before the vote required to become a limited liability partnership under Section 1001(b).

Thus, unlike partners in a general partnership, partners in an LLP are *not* personally liable for the obligations of the LLP just because they are partners.

Exercise 4.8

Payne and Fear are the two partners of Payne & Fear (P&F) law firm, which they founded ten years ago as a partnership. P&F filed a statement of qualification to become an LLP one year ago. In answering the following questions, assume that P&F has no formal partnership agreement and that RUPA applies.

1. Fear's former legal assistant won a tort judgment last week against P&F as a result of Fear slandering her two years ago. Can she recover against Payne? Can she recover against Fear?
2. Payne and Fear have a falling out and decide to cease operations of P&F. As a result, P&F purposely defaults on the rent it owes on the office lease it signed three years ago. Can the lessor recover amounts owed under the lease from Payne or Fear? How does the lessor go about it?
3. Continuing with the facts from Question 2, P&F also purposely defaults on the copy machine lease it signed six months ago. Can the lessor recover amounts owed under the lease from Payne or Fear?
4. Would your answers to any of the above questions change if P&F was organized as an LLP when it was originally founded? What about if P&F has been a South Carolina LLP since its inception?

LIMITED LIABILITY PARTNERSHIP
AGREEMENT

This Limited Liability Partnership Agreement (this "**Agreement**") is dated March 11, 2011, between Shirley K. Anderson, Diego W. Barrera III, and Zhu H. Choi (each a "**Partner**" and collectively, the "**Partners**"). The Partners agree as follows:

1. **Formation, Name, and Purpose.**

   a. The Partners hereby form a partnership (the "**Partnership**") under the Florida Partnership Laws, as amended from time to time. The Partnership shall be a limited liability partnership and shall promptly file a statement of qualification to that effect with the Florida Department of State.

   b. The name of the Partnership is Anderson, Barrera & Choi L.L.P. and all business of the Partnership shall be conducted in such name.

   c. The purposes of the Partnership are (i) to own, renovate, improve, sell, lease, and maintain the premises described in Schedule A (the "**Property**") and (ii) to carry on any and all activities related to the Property.

2. **Office.** The chief executive office of the Partnership shall be located at 25 Bluebill Avenue, Apartment 203, Naples, FL 34108, or at such other location as determined from time to time by a vote of the Partners.

3. **Term.** The term of the Partnership shall commence on the date hereof and shall continue until terminated as provided in this Agreement.

4. **Percentage Interests.** Each Partner's percentage interest in the Partnership ("**Percentage Interest**") is as follows:

Anderson: 65%
Barrera: 25%
Choi: 10%

5. **Capital Accounts and Contributions.**

   a.   An individual capital account shall be maintained for each Partner. The capital account of each Partner shall consist of the Partner's original contribution of capital, increased by (1) additional capital contributions and (2) his share of Partnership profits, and decreased by (a) distributions and (b) his share of Partnership losses.

   b.   The Partners are this date contributing the Property to the Partnership and other amounts as specified on Schedule A as their original capital contributions.

   c.   Additional capital contributions shall be made by the Partners from time to time whenever the Partners determine by vote that such additional capital contributions are necessary or desirable to accomplish the purposes and objectives of the Partnership. Such additional capital contributions shall be made in proportion to the Percentage Interest then held by each of the Partners.

6. **Management, Duties, and Restrictions.**

   a.   Except as otherwise provided in this Agreement, each Partner shall have a weighted vote in the management of the business of the Partnership that is equal to the Partner's respective Percentage Interest, and the vote of a Partner or Partners owning a majority of Percentage Interest shall control.

   b.   Anything to the contrary contained herein notwithstanding, no Partner or the Partnership shall, without the prior written consent of all Partners, (i) borrow or loan money on behalf of the Partnership; (ii) lease, rent, purchase, sell, mortgage, or otherwise create a lien upon any Partnership real estate (including the Property) or any interest therein, or enter into any contract for any such purpose; or (iii) make or incur any expenditure on behalf of the Partnership in excess of $50,000.

   c.   No Partner shall receive any salary or other compensation for services rendered to the Partnership as a Partner or otherwise, except as otherwise agreed upon by the Partners.

   d.   No Partner shall owe any other Partner or the Partnership the duty of loyalty or the duty of care.

7. **Allocation of Profits and Losses.** Profits and losses in respect of each fiscal year of the Partnership shall be credited or charged, as the case may be, to the Partners in proportion to their Percentage Interests.

8. **Distributions.** The Partnership shall make cash distributions to the Partners in proportion to their Percentage Interests at such times as voted on by the Partners.

9. **Transfer of Partnership Interest.** Except as is otherwise expressly provided herein, no Partner shall voluntarily or involuntarily transfer any part of his interest in the Partnership without the written consent of a majority of Percentage Interest of the other Partners nor shall any Partner cause or allow his interest in the Partnership or its property to be liened, attached, or otherwise encumbered.

10. **Bankruptcy or Insolvency.** In the event of the bankruptcy, insolvency, assignment for the benefit of creditors, legally adjudged incompetency or insanity, total and permanent disability or dissolution of a Partner (the "**Affected Partner**"), such Affected Partner or his trustee, committee, or other legal representative ("**Representative**") shall offer to sell to the Partnership or its designee the Affected Partner's interest in the Partnership upon the terms and conditions as hereinafter stated. The purchase price of the Affected Partner's interest in the Partnership, in the event that the parties fail to agree on a price, shall be determined as follows: Within 30 days of the date of the offer to sell, the Affected Partner or his Representative shall choose one real estate broker licensed in Florida and the remaining Partnership shall choose a second broker. These brokers shall determine the fair market value of the Affected Partner's interest in the Partnership. In the event that the brokers fail within 30 days of their appointment to determine the value of such interest, a real estate appraiser shall be appointed by the two brokers within 10 days after the expiration of such 30-day period and a majority of the three appointees shall reach a decision within 30 days after the appointment of the appraiser. The cost of such appraisal shall be borne equally by the Affected Partner and the Partnership. Within 7 days after the value of the Affected Partner's interest in the Partnership is determined either by agreement of the parties or by such appraisal procedure, the Affected Partner or his Representative shall offer to sell the Affected Partner's interest in the Partnership to the Partnership or its designee, at such price. Should the Partnership or its designee elect to purchase the Affected Partner's interest in the Partnership, the conveyance shall be made to the Partnership within 60 days after acceptance of such offer, and the Purchase Price shall, at the option of the Partnership or its designee, be paid, in cash at the time of closing of title, or 20 percent upon closing of title and the balance within 10 years in equal quarterly installments, together with interest at the prime rate published in *The Wall Street Journal* (U.S. edition) (the "**Prime Rate**") in effect at the time of the involuntary transfer, such

balance to be secured by a mortgage on the Property. Failure to elect to purchase the interest offered as provided in this section shall operate as approval and agreement to the conveyance of the interest of the Affected Partner in the Partnership without restriction; provided, however, that any such transferee shall become a party to this Agreement with respect to such interest by executing a duplicate of this Agreement.

11. **Death of a Partner.**

a.   Upon the death of any Partner, the Partnership or its designee shall have the option, upon 30 days' notice to the Executor or Administrator of the deceased Partner's estate after the determination of the purchase price, to purchase all but not less than all of the deceased Partner's interest in the Partnership. The purchase price of such deceased Partner's interest in the Partnership shall be determined in accordance with the appraisal procedure set forth in Section 10, provided, however, that the appraising brokers shall be chosen within 30 days of a Partner's death. Within 10 days after the value of the deceased Partner's interest in the Partnership is determined as aforesaid, the Executor or Administrator shall offer to sell the deceased Partner's interest to the Partnership or its designee at such price.

b.   If the Partnership or its designee elects to purchase the Partnership interest of a deceased Partner, the conveyance of the deceased Partner's interest in the Partnership shall be made to such party within 30 days after the date of determination of the purchase price, and the purchase price shall, at the option of the Partnership or its designee, be paid in cash at the time of closing of title, or 20 percent upon closing of title and the balance within 10 years in equal quarterly installments, together with interest at the Prime Rate, in effect at the time of the closing.

c.   If the Partnership or its designee does not elect to purchase the deceased Partner's interest as provided in this Section, the deceased Partner's interest shall pass to his heirs at law or the beneficiaries designated in his last will and testament.

12. **No Buyout Rights.** No Partner or the Partnership shall have any obligation to purchase or cause to be purchased a dissociated Partner's interest in the Partnership.

13. **Banking.** All funds of the Partnership shall be deposited and kept in its name in such Partnership bank account or accounts as shall be designated by the Partners. The Partners are hereby jointly authorized to sign all checks, withdrawal slips, or other orders in respect of such accounts and to endorse all checks payable to the Partnership for deposit in such accounts.

14. **Books.** The Partnership shall maintain full and accurate books and records at its principal office and all Partners shall have the right to inspect and examine the same at reasonable times. The books shall be

kept on an accrual basis and the fiscal year of the Partnership shall be the calendar year. If such records and books are to be kept at any place other than at the principal office of the Partnership, each Partner shall be immediately notified thereof in writing. The books shall be closed and balanced at the end of each fiscal year at the expense of the Partnership by an independent certified public accountant designated by the Partners.

15. **Dissolution of Partnership.** The bankruptcy, death, dissolution, removal, dissociation, withdrawal of, or assignment for the benefit of creditors by a Partner shall not require a dissolution of the Partnership.

16. **Liquidation of Partnership.** Upon any dissolution or termination of the Partnership, the assets of the Partnership shall be liquidated as promptly as possible, but in an orderly and businesslike manner so as not to involve undue sacrifice, and the Partners shall cause to be prepared by the firm of certified public accountants then retained by the Partnership a statement setting forth the assets and liabilities of the Partnership as of the date of dissolution, which statement shall be furnished to all of the Partners.

17. **Miscellaneous.**

   a. **Entire Agreement.** This Agreement is the final, complete, and exclusive statement of the parties' agreement on the matters contained in this Agreement and supersedes all prior communications, understandings, and agreements between the parties related thereto.

   b. **Counterparts.** This Agreement may be executed in one or more counterparts, each of which shall be deemed an original, but all of which taken together constitute only one agreement.

   c. **Pronouns.** All pronouns and any variations thereof shall be deemed to refer to the masculine, feminine, neuter, singular or plural, as the identity of the person may require.

   d. **Governing Law.** This Agreement shall be interpreted and the rights and liabilities of the parties to this Agreement, determined in accordance with, the laws of the State of Florida, without regard to conflicts of law principles.

To evidence the Partners' agreement to this Agreement's provisions, they have executed and delivered this Agreement on the date set forth in the preamble.

/s/ Shirley K. Anderson
_____
Shirley K. Anderson

/s/ Diego W. Barrera III
_____
Diego W. Barrera III

/s/ Zhu H. Choi
_____
Zhu H. Choi

Schedule A

"**Property**": Premises known as 10028 Gulf View Drive, Naples, Florida Section: 53 Block: 107 Lot: 1511, 1512 & 1513.

The Partners agree that the value of the Property on the date of contribution to the Partnership is $1,000,000.

Prior to the contribution to the Partnership, the Property was owned by Anderson and Barrera as joint tenants. In that regard, the table below specifies the percentage of the Property contribution attributable to each Partner. It also specifies the cash contribution made by each Partner as part of his or her original contribution to the partnership.

Partner	Property Percentage	Cash Contribution
Anderson	65%	$30,000
Barrera	35%	$10,000
Choi	0%	$1,000

Choi will provide all labor with respect to the Partnership as part of his contribution.

· CHAPTER FIVE ·

LIMITED PARTNERSHIPS AND LIMITED LIABILITY LIMITED PARTNERSHIPS

A. LIMITED PARTNERSHIPS

As we learned in Chapter 1, limited partnerships are of decreasing importance today, in large part because of the rise of LLPs and LLCs. I nonetheless cover them in a bit more depth here (focusing on where they differ from general partnerships), in part because private investment funds (venture capital funds, hedge funds, and private equity funds) are still typically organized as limited partnerships and estate planners continue to use "family" limited partnerships as a means to reduce a client's federal gift tax burden.[1]

1. Formation

You form a limited partnership by filing a "certificate of limited partnership" with the secretary of state of the state in which the client wants the limited partnership organized. The state's limited partnership statute will specify the short list of information that must be included in the certificate (i.e., the name of the limited partnership, its office address, and the name(s) and address(es) of its general partners). Per every state's limited partnership statute, the name of

---

1. With a family limited partnership, or FLiP for short, the parents of a wealthy family set up a limited partnership and serve as general partners. They then transfer various family assets to the limited partnership and gift limited partnership interests to their children and other family members over time. The structure can save on gift tax because the aggregate fair market value of the limited partnership interests is much less than the aggregate fair market value of the assets transferred by the parents to the limited partnership. Other estate planning aspects of FLiPs are beyond the scope of this book.

a limited partnership must contain the phrase "limited partnership" or the abbreviation "L.P." or "LP." Recall from Chapter 1 that a limited partnership must have one or more general partners and one or more limited partners.

2. Governing Law

A limited partnership is governed by the limited partnership statute of the state in which it filed its certificate of limited partnership. Each state has its own limited partnership statute based on some version of the Uniform Limited Partnership Act, with the exception of the Louisiana statute.

The National Conference of Commissioners on Uniform State Laws (NCCUSL) adopted the Uniform Limited Partnership Act in 1916, revised it in 1976, amended it in 1985, and again revised it 2001. The limited partnership statute in a majority of states is currently based on the 1976 version (ULPA-1976 for short) with many, but not all, of these states also adopting the 1985 amendments (RULPA for short). As of 2012, 18 states (Alabama, Arkansas, California, Florida, Hawaii, Idaho, Illinois, Iowa, Kentucky, Maine, Minnesota, Montana, Nevada, New Mexico, North Dakota, Oklahoma, Utah, and Washington) have adopted the 2001 version (ULPA-2001 for short). We will focus primarily on ULPA-2001, but will examine some RULPA provisions too.

Note that RULPA is not a standalone statute; it incorporates, or is linked to, the Uniform Partnership Act. Specifically, RULPA §1105 provides, "In any case not provided for in this [Act] the provisions of the Uniform Partnership Act govern."[2] Basically, RULPA provides different or additional rules for various aspects of limited partnerships but leaves in place the UPA rules that more or less work for limited partnerships. Conversely, ULPA-2001 is a standalone act. As the Prefatory Note to ULPA-2001 explains:

> The [Drafting] Committee saw several substantial advantages to de-linking. A stand alone statute would:
>
> - be more convenient, providing a single, self-contained source of statutory authority for issues pertaining to limited partnerships;
> - eliminate confusion as to which issues were solely subject to the limited partnership act and which required reference (i.e., linkage) to the general partnership act; and
> - rationalize future case law, by ending the automatic link between the cases concerning partners in a general partnership and issues pertaining to general partners in a limited partnership.

Just like general partnership statutes, limited partnership statutes are composed mostly of default rules that the partners can alter or opt out of through a

---

2. The reference to the Uniform Partnership Act is to the 1914 version (what we've been calling UPA) because the NCCUSL did not adopt RUPA until 1994.

partnership agreement. ULPA-2001 follows the same approach as RUPA — §110 basically provides that all ULPA-2001 rules are default rules except those that are listed in §110(b).

Conversely, RULPA uses a provision-by-provision approach. In other words, each provision will specify whether it can be altered in a partnership agreement. For example, RULPA §107 provides, "*Except as provided in the partnership agreement*, a partner may lend money to and transact other business with the limited partnership. . . ." (emphasis added). The italicized language indicates that §107 is a default rule. As we'll see, this is the same approach to designating default rules used under corporate statutes.

3. Management

Under the default rule, a limited partnership is managed by its general partner(s), and the limited partners have no rights to participate in the control of the business. For example, UPLA-2001 §406(a) provides:

> Each general partner has equal rights in the management and conduct of the limited partnership's activities. Except as expressly provided in this [Act], any matter relating to the activities of the limited partnership may be exclusively decided by the general partner or, if there is more than one general partner, by a majority of the general partners.

The default rule under ULPA-2001 does, however, require the consent of the limited partners to amend the partnership agreement or to sell, lease, or otherwise dispose of all, or substantially all, of the limited partnership's property, other than in the normal course of business.[3]

Exercise 5.1

Read the Wildcat Capital Partners Fund IV, L.P. (Fund IV) limited partnership agreement located at the end of this chapter and answer the following questions. Make sure you note any applicable partnership agreement and/or statutory provision that supports your answer. In that regard, the Nevada Limited Partnership Act is available at http://www.leg.state.nv.us/nrs/NRS-088.html.

1. The General Partner wants to move the partnership's office from Tucson, Arizona, to La Jolla, California. Is limited partner approval required? If so, what vote is necessary for approval?
2. The General Partner wants the partnership to open and operate a Hyundai dealership. Is limited partner approval required? If so, what vote is necessary for approval?

---

3. *See* ULPA-2001 §406(b).

3. The General Partner wants to extend the partnership agreement's term to December 31, 2021. Is limited partner approval required? If so, what vote is necessary for approval? What about if the General Partner wants to extend the term until December 31, 2024?

4. A member of the General Partner wants to make an investment in a promising startup company alongside the partnership (i.e., both the partnership and the member would invest in the startup). Is this allowed under the limited partnership agreement?

5. The General Partner wants to serve as general partner of a new limited partnership that will have the same business purpose as Fund IV. Is this allowed under the limited partnership agreement?

4. Liability Exposure

As mentioned in Chapter 1, general partners of limited partnerships are personally liable for the debts and obligations of the limited partnership,[4] while limited partners are not.[5] RULPA, however, recognizes an exception to the limited liability of a limited partner known as the "control rule." Specifically, a limited partner that participates in the control of the limited partnership's business will be personally liable for the obligations of the limited partnership to persons who transact business with the limited partnership while reasonably believing, based on the limited partner's conduct, that such limited partner is a general partner.[6] There is no specific definition of what constitutes "participating in the control of the business," but the limited partnership statute of a control rule state will list activities that do not. Among items typically on the exclusion list are (1) working for the limited partnership or its general partner; (2) guaranteeing limited partnership obligations; (3) attending partner meetings; or (4) voting on dissolving or selling the partnership, changing the nature of its business, admitting or removing a general or limited partner, or an amendment to the partnership agreement.[7] It is left to the courts to decide whether limited partner activities that are not on the exclusion list constitute "participating in the control of the business."

The drafters of ULPA-2001 decided to drop the control rule. Specifically, RUPLA §303 provides, "A limited partner is not personally liable, directly or indirectly, by way of contribution or otherwise, for an obligation of the limited partnership solely by reason of being a limited partner, even if the limited partner participates in the management and control of the limited partnership." The Official Comment to §303 explains:

---

4. *See* RULPA §403(b); ULPA-2001 §404(a).
5. *See* RULPA §303(a); ULPA-2001 §303.
6. RULPA §303(a).
7. *Id.* §303(b).

This section provides a full, status-based liability shield for each limited partner, "even if the limited partner participates in the management and control of the limited partnership." The section thus eliminates the so-called "control rule" with respect to personal liability for entity obligations and brings limited partners into parity with LLC members, LLP partners and corporate shareholders.

The "control rule" first appeared in a uniform act in 1916, although the concept is much older. Section 7 of the original Uniform Limited Partnership Act provided that "A limited partner shall not become liable as a general partner [i.e., for the obligations of the limited partnership] unless . . . he takes part in the control of the business." The 1976 Uniform Limited Partnership Act (ULPA-1976) "carrie[d] over the basic test from former Section 7," but recognized "the difficulty of determining when the 'control' line has been overstepped." Comment to ULPA-1976, Section 303. Accordingly, ULPA-1976 tried to buttress the limited partner's shield by (i) providing a safe harbor for a lengthy list of activities deemed not to constitute participating in control, ULPA-1976, Section 303(b), and (ii) limiting a limited partner's "control rule" liability "only to persons who transact business with the limited partnership with actual knowledge of [the limited partner's] participation in control." ULPA-1976, Section 303(a). However, these protections were complicated by a countervailing rule which made a limited partner generally liable for the limited partnership's obligations "if the limited partner's participation in the control of the business is . . . substantially the same as the exercise of the powers of a general partner." ULPA-1976, Section 303(a).

The 1985 amendments to ULPA-1976 (i.e., RULPA) further buttressed the limited partner's shield, removing the "substantially the same" rule, expanding the list of safe harbor activities and limiting "control rule" liability "only to persons who transact business with the limited partnership reasonably believing, based upon the limited partner's conduct, that the limited partner is a general partner."

In a world with LLPs, LLCs and, most importantly, LLLPs, the control rule has become an anachronism. This Act therefore takes the next logical step in the evolution of the limited partner's liability shield and renders the control rule extinct.

5. Fiduciary Duties and the Obligation of Good Faith and Fair Dealing

General partners of limited partnerships owe the limited partnership and its limited partners the duty of loyalty and care.[8] As with a general partnership, under ULPA-2001, a partnership agreement cannot eliminate the duty of loyalty but can "identify specific types or categories of activities that do not violate . . . [it], if not manifestly unreasonable."[9] Likewise, a limited partnership agreement may not "unreasonably reduce the duty of care."[10] Furthermore, a general

---

8. *See, e.g.,* ULPA-2001 §408(a).
9. *Id.* §110(6)(5)(A).
10. *Id.* §110(b)(6).

partner owes the limited partnership and its limited partners an obligation of good faith and fair dealing.[11] Under ULPA-2001, a partnership agreement may not eliminate this obligation but "may prescribe the standards by which the performance of the obligation is to be measured, if the standards are not manifestly unreasonable."[12]

The default rule is that a limited partner does *not* owe fiduciary duties to the limited partnership or any other partner solely by reason of being a limited partner.[13] In that regard, ULPA-2001 §305(c) provides, "A limited partner does not violate a duty or obligation under this [Act] or under the partnership agreement merely because the limited partner's conduct furthers the limited partner's own interest." Per ULPA-2001 §305(b), a limited partner does owe the limited partnership and partners an obligation of good faith and fair dealing, and this obligation cannot be eliminated in the partnership agreement.[14] The Official Comment to §305 explains the different treatment of limited partners when it comes to fiduciary duties:

> Fiduciary duty typically attaches to a person whose status or role creates significant power for that person over the interests of another person. Under this Act, limited partners have very limited power of any sort in the regular activities of the limited partnership and no power whatsoever justifying the imposition of fiduciary duties either to the limited partnership or fellow partners. It is possible for a partnership agreement to allocate significant managerial authority and power to a limited partner, but in that case the power exists not as a matter of status or role but rather as a matter of contract. The proper limit on such contract based power is the obligation of good faith and fair dealing, not fiduciary duty, unless the partnership agreement itself expressly imposes a fiduciary duty or creates a role for a limited partner which, as a matter of other law, gives rise to a fiduciary duty. For example, if the partnership agreement makes a limited partner an agent for the limited partnership as to particular matters, the law of agency will impose fiduciary duties on the limited partner with respect to the limited partner's role as agent.

Exercise 5.2

1. Notably, the limited partnership agreement of a Delaware limited partnership can eliminate general partner liability to a limited partnership and its limited partners for breach of fiduciary duty. What is the statutory support for this statement? (See http://delcode.delaware.gov/title6/c017/index. shtml for the Delaware Limited Partnerships Act.)
2. Is Section 7(e) of Fund IV's limited partnership agreement valid?

---

11. *See, e.g., id.* §408(c).
12. *Id.* §110(a)(7).
13. *See, e.g., id.* §305(a).
14. *See id.* §110(b)(7).

6. Transfer of Partnership Interests

As was the case for general partnerships, the default rule is that a partnership interest of a limited partnership is not freely transferable in its entirety. Specifically, ULPA-2001 §701 provides that "[t]he only interest of a partner which is transferable is the partner's transferable interest." ULPA-2001 §102(22) defines "transferable interest" as "a partner's right to receive distributions." It is fairly common, however, for a limited partnership agreement to override this default rule, given that limited partners generally have no say in management, so there is less concern by the other partners as to who becomes a limited partner.

Exercise 5.3

Refer again to the Fund IV limited partnership agreement at the end of this chapter and answer the following questions. Make sure you note any applicable partnership agreement and/or statutory provision that supports your answer.

1. Sean Elliot wants to sell his Fund IV interest to Luke Walton. Is this allowed by the Agreement? If so, what formalities are involved?
2. Steve Kerr wants to gift 50 percent of his Fund IV interest to his niece. Is this allowed by the Agreement? If so, what formalities are involved?
3. Wildcat Capital Management, LLC wants to sell its Fund IV interest to Oprah Winfrey. Is this allowed by the Agreement? If so, what formalities are involved?

---

7. Allocation of Profits and Losses

UPLA-2001 does not contain a default provision for the allocation of profits and losses. It does, however, provide a default rule for distributions. Specifically, §503 provides, "A distribution by a limited partnership must be shared among the partners on the basis of the value, as stated in the required records when the limited partnership decides to make the distribution, of the contributions the limited partnership has received from each partner." The Official Comment to that section explains the omission of an allocation provision: "Nearly all limited partnerships will choose to allocate profits and losses in order to comply with applicable tax, accounting and other regulatory requirements. Those requirements, rather than this Act, are the proper source of guidance for that profit and loss allocation."

Exercise 5.4

Refer again to the Fund IV limited partnership agreement at the end of this chapter and answer the following questions. Make sure you note any applicable partnership agreement and/or statutory provision that supports your answer.

1. Fund IV earned $10 million for the latest fiscal year. How much of this amount is allocated to Larry Fitzgerald? How much is allocated to Wildcat Capital Management, LLC?
2. How much of this $10 million is Fund IV required to distribute to its limited partners?

---

8. No Default Buyout Right

Recall from the last chapter that under the default RUPA rule, a partner's dissociation, with certain exceptions, triggered the right to be bought out of his or her partnership interest for cash. This is not the case under UPLA-2001. Per §602(a)(3), the limited partnership interest of a limited partner who dissociates before the termination of the limited partnership is essentially converted to a transferable interest owned by the dissociated limited partner.

B. LIMITED LIABILITY LIMITED PARTNERSHIPS

1. Formation

In some states, mainly those that have adopted UPLA-2001 (with the exception of California), a limited liability limited partnership, or LLLP for short, is simply a limited partnership that has elected LLLP status under the applicable provisions of its limited partnership statute. Under UPLA-2001, a limited partnership can elect to be an LLLP by including a line in its certificate of limited partnership along the lines of "this limited partnership is a limited liability limited partnership" (an existing limited partnership can amend its certificate of limited partnership to so state).[15] Per UPLA-2001 §108(c), "[t]he name of a limited liability limited partnership must contain the phrase "limited liability limited partnership" or the abbreviation "LLLP" or "L.L.L.P." and must not contain the abbreviation "L.P." or "LP."

In other states, a limited partnership becomes an LLLP by registering the limited partnership as an LLP under the state's partnership statute.[16] As of 2012, the business organizations statutes of the following states do not provide for

---

15. *See id.* §201(a)(4).
16. *See, e.g.,* Del. Code Ann. ch. 17, tit. 6, §17-214.

LLLPs: Alaska, California, Connecticut, Indiana, Kansas, Louisiana, Massachusetts, Michigan, Mississippi, Nebraska, New Hampshire, New Jersey, New York, Ohio, Oregon, Rhode Island, South Carolina, Vermont, West Virginia, Wisconsin, and Wyoming. As mentioned in Chapter 3, the fact that a good number of states do not provide for LLLPs is a major disadvantage of operating a business in the LLLP form, because it gives rise to the risk of interstate non-recognition of the liability shield.

2. Liability Exposure

The primary distinction between a limited partnership and an LLLP is that the latter provides a full liability shield for all partners. In other words, a general partner of an LLLP is not personally liable for the obligations of the LLLP just because he or she is a general partner. For example, UPLA-201 §404(c) provides:

> An obligation of a limited partnership incurred while the limited partnership is a limited liability limited partnership, whether arising in contract, tort, or otherwise, is solely the obligation of the limited partnership. A general partner is not personally liable, directly or indirectly, by way of contribution or otherwise, for such an obligation solely by reason of being or acting as a general partner.

Exercise 5.5

Refer once again to the Fund IV limited partnership agreement at the end of this chapter and answer the following questions. Make sure you note any applicable partnership agreement and/or statutory provision that supports your answer.

1. What does Fund IV need to do to become an LLLP?
2. Do you think it makes sense for Fund IV to become one?
3. If Fund IV does become an LLLP, what changes would need to be made to its limited partnership agreement?

LIMITED PARTNERSHIP AGREEMENT
OF WILDCAT CAPITAL PARTNERS FUND IV, L.P.

THIS LIMITED PARTNERSHIP AGREEMENT (this "**Agreement**") is dated April 25, 2011 between Wildcat Capital Management, LLC, a Delaware limited liability company (the "**General Partner**") and the persons listed as limited partners on Schedule A of this Agreement (the "**Limited Partners**").

The Partners agree as follows:

1. **Definitions.** Terms defined in the preamble and elsewhere in this Agreement have their assigned meanings, and the following terms have the meanings assigned to them:

(a) "**Accounting Period**" means any period fixed from time to time by the General Partner for the determination of profits and losses of the Partnership (it being expected that the normal accounting period will be a calendar quarter).

(b) "**Bankruptcy**" means with respect to any person that a petition shall have been filed by or against such person as a "debtor" and the adjudication of such person as a bankrupt under the provisions of the bankruptcy laws of the United States of America shall have commenced, or that such person shall have made an assignment for the benefit of its creditors generally or a receiver shall have been appointed for substantially all of the property and assets of such person.

(c) "**Capital Account**" of a Partner means the individual Capital Account maintained in accordance with Section 5(a).

(d) "**Capital Contribution**" of a Partner means that amount of capital actually contributed by the Partner to the Partnership pursuant to Section 4.

(e) "**Capital Interest**" of a Limited Partner means that portion of the profit or loss of the Partnership allocated to Limited Partners as a group or of distributions made to Limited Partners as a group which is equal to the ratio of the Capital Contribution of that Limited Partner to the Capital Contributions of all Limited Partners.

(f) "**Dissolution**" of a Partner which is not a natural person means that such Partner has terminated its existence, whether partnership or corporate, wound up its affairs, and dissolved.

(g) "**Incompetency**" of a person means that such person shall have been judged incompetent or insane by a decree of a court of appropriate jurisdiction.

(h) "**Majority Interest of Limited Partners**" means Limited Partners whose Capital Contributions constitute a majority of the Capital Contributions of all Limited Partners.

(i) "**Partners**" means the General Partner and the Limited Partners.

(j) "**Value**" means that valuation of an investment determined in accordance with Section 5(e).

2. **Formation, Name, and Business.**

(a) **Formation.** The parties hereby form a limited partnership (the "**Partnership**") under the Nevada Uniform Partnership Act, as amended from time to time (the "**Act**"). The General Partner shall promptly execute a Certificate of Limited Partnership pursuant to the provisions of the Act and file it with the Nevada Secretary of State.

(b) **Name and Principal Place of Business.** The name of the Partnership is Wildcat Capital Partners Fund IV, L.P., and its office and principal place of business shall be in Tucson, Arizona and thereafter at such other place or places as the General Partner may from time to time determine.

(c) **Business.** The Partnership shall engage in the investment business as a private business development company, with emphasis on venture capital type investments and with the objective of seeking capital appreciation by investing in both marketable and nonmarketable securities. The Partnership, either itself or through others with whom it co-invests or through subsequent venture capital investors, may make available significant managerial assistance to companies in which it invests. In the course of its operations, the Partnership may invest its capital in securities and other lawful business interests of any and all types.

3. **Term; Termination.** The Partnership shall commence upon the filing and recording of its Certificate of Limited, and shall continue for a period ending the earlier of: (i) December 31, 2020; provided, however, that the General Partner may elect to extend such date for up to three additional one-year periods; or (ii) the election by the General Partner, with the consent of a Majority Interest of Limited Partners, to terminate the Partnership.

4. **Capital Contributions.** No Capital Contributions shall be required of the General Partner. Each Limited Partner shall contribute capital to the Partnership in the amount set forth opposite such Limited Partner's name on Schedule A of this Agreement.

5. **Financial Accounting.**

(a) **Capital Accounts.** An individual capital account shall be maintained for each Partner consisting of the Partner's original capital contribution, increased by (1) additional capital contributions and (2) his share of Partnership profits, and decreased by (a) distributions in reduction of Partnership capital and (b) his share of Partnership losses, if charged to the capital account of the Partners.

(b) **Financial and Tax Reporting.** The Partnership shall prepare its financial statements in accordance with generally accepted accounting principles as from time to time in effect using the accrual method of accounting on a calendar year basis, and shall prepare its income tax information returns using the cash method of accounting on a calendar year basis.

(c) **Allocation of Profits or Losses.** Profits and losses in respect of each Accounting Period shall be credited or charged, as the case may be, to the Partners as follows: (i) 80% shall be allocated to the Limited Partners and shall be divided among them in proportion to their respective Capital Contributions; and (ii) 20% shall be allocated to the General Partner.

(d) **Time of Allocations.** The profit or loss of the Partnership for each Accounting Period shall be allocated to the Partners' Capital Accounts at the end of the Accounting Period in accordance with the provisions of Section 5(c).

(e) **Valuation of Investments Owned by Partnership.** Subject to the specific standards set forth below, the Value of investments hereunder shall be at estimated fair value as determined by the General Partner and shall be determined not less than once per calendar quarter. In determining the value of the interest of any Partner in the Partnership, or in any accounting among the Partners or any of them, no value shall be placed on the goodwill or name of the Partnership. No tax reserves shall be set up for unrealized gains or profits unless the tax obligations of the Partnership are established by law. As of the end of each calendar quarter, the Limited Partners shall be advised in writing of the valuation so made. The Limited Partners shall have thirty (30) days after receipt of such valuation to notify the General Partner in writing of any objections to the valuation. If a Majority Interest of Limited Partners so notifies the General Partner of any such objections, and if the General Partner and a Majority Interest of Limited Partners are unable to agree upon a valuation, the Value shall be determined by a mutually acceptable, independent securities expert (who may engage an expert appraiser or other expert, if necessary, to determine the Value of the property other than cash and securities which are actively traded on a securities exchange or over the counter), whose determination shall be final and binding on all Partners.

(f) **Limitation of Liability.** Notwithstanding anything to the contrary contained in this Agreement, no Limited Partner shall be liable for any debts, expenses, liabilities, or obligations of the Partnership except as provided in the Act. No Limited Partner shall be required or obligated to make further contributions or payments of any kind to or with respect to the Partnership, but to the extent required by law or by Section 6(c) any capital distributed to a Limited Partner shall be restored to the Partnership as necessary to meet such Limited Partner's share of any Partnership liability or loss which may have accrued prior to such distribution. It is expressly understood and agreed that the Limited Partners shall not participate in the management or control of the business of the Partnership.

(g) **Supervision, Inspection of Books.** Proper and complete books of account and records of the business of the Partnership shall be kept under the supervision of the General Partner at the principal place of business of the Partnership or such other place as designated by the General Partner. Such books and records shall be open to inspection, audit, and copying by any Partner, or his designated representative, upon reasonable notice at any time during business hours, but any information so obtained or copied shall be kept and maintained in strictest confidence.

(h) **Quarterly Reports.** The General Partner shall transmit to the Limited Partners within 45 days after the close of each calendar quarter a report on the affairs of the Partnership during such quarter, including a statement containing pertinent information regarding the receipts, expenditures, and investment transactions of the Partnership during that quarter.

(i) **Annual Reports.** The annual financial statements of the Partnership shall be audited and reported on as of the end of each calendar year by PricewaterhouseCoopers LLP or another firm of independent certified public accountants of comparable national standing selected by the General Partner. The Value of investments held by the Partnership shall be reviewed by the accounting firm but shall not be subject to an opinion by them. A copy of the audit report from such accountants shall be transmitted to the Limited Partners within 90 days after the end of each calendar year.

(j) **Tax Return.** The General Partner shall, within 90 days after the end of each calendar year, file a Federal income tax information return and transmit to each Partner a copy of such return and a schedule (Schedule K-1 or successor schedule) showing such Partner's distributive share of the Partnership's income, deductions and credits. Upon request, the General Partner will provide a Limited Partner with any additional information required to prepare its Federal income tax return.

6. **Distributions**

(a) **Distributions in Cash.**

(1) In order to permit the Partners to pay taxes as incurred, the General Partner shall distribute at least annually to the Partners up to an amount in cash which, at the time of such distribution, when added to all prior distributions pursuant to this Section 6(a)(1), equals the increase in the cumulative maximum tax payable by an individual taxpayer at the highest marginal tax rates under Federal tax laws on the net realized ordinary income plus the net realized capital gains of the Partnership, as determined for Federal income tax reporting purposes, for all prior Accounting Periods of the Partnership.

(2) The General Partner may in its discretion during any Accounting Period distribute cash ratably to the Partners up to the amount of the net credit balances in their Capital Accounts.

(3) No Limited Partner shall have the right to make withdrawals or receive disproportionate distributions from the Partnership, except as provided by this Agreement.

(b) **Distributions in Kind.**

(1) The General Partner may in its sole discretion elect to distribute any investment held by the Partnership in kind to the Partners.

(2) In the event of such distribution in kind, the Value of the investment shall be determined in accordance with Section 5(e), the difference between such Value and the cost of the investment shall be allocated among the Partners as provided in Section 5(c), and each Partner receiving the distribution shall have his Capital Account debited with the Value of the investment distributed to him.

(c) **Obligation to Repay.** If, on final dissolution and winding up of the Partnership, the Partnership property is insufficient to satisfy its liabilities and return the remaining credit balance of the Limited Partners' Capital Accounts, each Partner shall return such part or all of distributions made to it pursuant to Section 6(a) and Section 6(b), valued pursuant to Section 5(e), as of the date the General Partner sends written notice to the Partners that such return is required, as may be required to make up such insufficiency, each in proportion to its share in each such distribution. Such returns may be in cash or, at each Partner's option, in the investments received in the distributions, valued as aforesaid. No Partner shall be obligated at any time to repay or restore to the Partnership all or any part of any distributions to it from the Partnership, except as is specifically provided in this Section 6(c) and the Act.

(d) **Insolvency.** No distribution shall be made which would render the Partnership insolvent.

7. **Management and Restrictions.**

(a) **General Partner.**

(1) Except as hereinafter specified, the right to manage, control, and conduct the business of the Partnership shall be vested exclusively in the General Partner, and all decisions affecting the Partnership, its policy, and management, shall be made by the General Partner, and all Partners agree to abide by any such decision.

(2) The General Partner may, on behalf of the Partnership, borrow money or guarantee the obligations of one or more portfolio companies (and secure payment of any such borrowing or guarantee by hypothecation or pledge of Partnership properties or otherwise).

(3) Except as otherwise specifically provided herein, the General Partner shall have and exercise all of the powers of a general partner in a partnership without limited partners and is authorized and empowered to carry out and implement any and all purposes and objects of the Partnership.

(4) The General Partner may offer the right to participate in investment opportunities of the Partnership to other private investors, groups, partnerships, corporations, or Partners or employees of the Partnership whenever the General Partner, in its discretion, determines that such would be in the best interests of the Partnership; provided, however, that neither the General Partner nor the members of the General Partner shall directly participate in any investment opportunity which, at the time such investment is entered into by it or any of them, meets the then applicable investment criteria for the Partnership without the prior written consent of a Majority Interest of Limited Partners; but nothing herein shall prevent the General Partner or any member of the General Partner from continuing or holding an investment which subsequently becomes an investment opportunity meeting the investment criteria of the Partnership.

(b) **Duties and Activities of the General Partner.**

(1) The General Partner shall, so long as it remains the General Partner, devote such of its time as is reasonably necessary to the conduct of the business of the Partnership in good faith.

(2) Various members of the General Partner currently act as general partners in existing venture capital partnerships. Except for such existing partnerships, the General Partner and the managers of the General Partner may not act as general partner or in a similar management capacity for an entity having business objectives substantially similar to the Partnership until the satisfaction of one of the following conditions: (i) the consent of a Majority Interest of Limited Partners to such action is obtained, or (ii) an amount equal to 75 percent of the Capital Contributions shall have been initially invested in venture capital type investments.

(3) Except as provided in Section 7(b)(2), the General Partner and its members may be engaged in one or more businesses other than the business of the Partnership, but only to the extent that this activity does not materially interfere with the business of the Partnership and does not conflict with the obligations of that General Partner under this Agreement. Neither the Partnership nor any other Partner shall have any right to any income or profit derived by the General Partner and its members from any employment or business activity permitted under this Section 7(b)(3).

(c) **Management Services and Fees; Organizational Expenses.**

(1) The General Partner shall provide (either directly or by contract with related or unrelated entities), and shall pay for out of the management fee specified in Section 7(c)(2), all personnel, office space, office equipment, supplies, and other necessary operating, administrative, and clerical services to the Partnership,

and shall pay the compensation and fringe benefits of its members, consultants, and employees, all of its own operating expenses, and normal legal and accounting fees associated with the acquisition of investments in portfolio companies. The Partnership will be and remain obligated to pay for all other legal, auditing, and accounting fees and all other expenses of the Partnership, including without limitation custodian fees, taxes, interest on borrowed moneys, brokerage fees and commissions and any other finder's fees or other fees and expenses not payable by the General Partner as provided above.

(2) There shall be payable by the Partnership to the General Partner, in advance on the first day of each month, a management fee equal to one-sixth of one percent of the then net Value determined for all of the Partnership's assets. For purposes of determining the management fee, the General Partner shall determine such Value in accordance with Section 5(e) once each month.

(3) The Partnership shall reimburse the General Partner for all paid or accrued organizational and start-up expenses of the Partnership including, without limitation, legal and accounting fees, printing expenses, and travel expenses.

(d) **Limited Partner Participation.** The Limited Partners shall take no part in the control or management of the Partnership business nor shall the Limited Partners have any power or authority to act for or on behalf of the Partnership, except as is specifically permitted by this Agreement and by law.

(e) **Standard of Care.** It is understood that the business of the Partnership involves the investment of its funds in ventures involving a high degree of risk. The General Partner shall not have any liability to the Partnership or any Limited Partner except by reason of willful misconduct or reckless disregard of duties by the General Partner in the performance of its duties under this Agreement.

(f) **Interest and Capital Withdrawals.**

(1) No interest shall be paid to any Partner on account of his Capital Contribution.

(2) Except as specifically provided in Section 6, no Partner shall have the right to withdraw or receive a disproportionate distribution of any part of his contribution to the capital of the Partnership. No Limited Partner shall have the right to demand and receive property other than cash in return for his Capital Contribution.

8. **Transfer of Partnership Interests.**

(a) **Transfer of General Partner's Interest.** The General Partner shall not transfer, sell, encumber, mortgage, assign, or otherwise dispose of any portion of its interest as General Partner in the Partnership. Any purported transfer, sale, encumbrance, mortgage, assignment, or disposition of the General Partner's interest shall be void and of no effect against the Partnership, any other Partner, any creditor of the Partnership, or any claimant against the Partnership.

(b) **Death, Etc. of Limited Partner.** In the event of the death, Incompetency, or Bankruptcy of a Limited Partner, the interest of such Limited Partner shall continue at the risk of the Partnership business until termination of the Partnership, at which time the legal representative of such Limited Partner shall be entitled to receive such amount as the Limited Partner would have been entitled to receive if such event had not occurred.

(c) **Transfer of Limited Partner's Interest.**

(1) No Limited Partner shall transfer, sell, encumber, assign, or otherwise dispose of any portion of its interest in the Partnership without the written consent of the General Partner, except that the General Partner agrees to consent to the following transfers, sales, and assignments upon compliance with Section 8(c)(3):

(aa) Transfer to another Partner of the Partnership or to any person who is then a member of the General Partner;

(bb) A gift to a parent, spouse, lineal descendant, brother, or sister of a Limited Partner, or in trust for any such person or for himself;

(cc) Succession or testamentary disposition upon the death of a Limited Partner or to a successor trustee or fiduciary;

(dd) Transfer to a spouse or former spouse pursuant to an agreement or decree for division of community property upon marital dissolution or legal separation;

(ee) In the case of a Limited Partner which is itself a partnership, transfer to the former partners upon its dissolution, or to any other entity or persons which are the successors in interest to such partnership;

(ff) In the case of a Limited Partner which is a retirement, pension, or profit sharing trust, transfer to any successor trust or trusts, including, without limitation, any one or more trusts, funds, fiduciaries, or other entities which are derived from, or evolve or devolve, directly or indirectly, out of such Limited Partner or any pension trust which has an interest therein, or reversion to the entity which created such trust;

(gg) In the case of a corporate Limited Partner, transfer to any parent, subsidiary or corporation, the stockholders of which are substantially the same as the Limited Partner, or to any partnership in which such Limited Partner is a partner;

(hh) In the case of a Limited Partner which is a trust, transfer to other trusts or to beneficiaries in accordance with the terms of such trusts, as amended from time to time, or to the grantor of such trust by way of reversion; and

(2) If at any time a Limited Partner wishes to transfer its interest in the Partnership, in whole or in part, and such transfer does not fall within clauses (aa) through (hh) of Section 8(c)(1), such Limited Partner may nonetheless transfer such interest after first extending to the Partnership and the other Partners a right of first refusal in conformity with the following procedure: Such Limited Partner shall give written notice to the General Partner indicating its wish to sell, the price and terms at which it is willing to make such sale, and the identity, if known, of the proposed buyer or buyers. Upon receipt of such notice the General Partner shall promptly give notice of the same to the other Limited Partners. At any time within 60 days after the giving of such notice by the Limited Partner proposing to sell, the General Partner, with the consent of a Majority Interest of Limited Partners, may cause the Partnership to agree to redeem such interest at the price and terms stipulated in such notice, or, if the Partnership does not decide to effect such redemption, the other Partners may agree to purchase such Partnership interest at the price and terms stipulated in such notice. If such purchase is made by the other Partners, and the purchasing Partners offer to purchase in the aggregate more than the interest being offered, such interest shall be prorated among such Partners in proportion to the amount which each offered to purchase. If the Partnership does not agree to redeem such Partnership interest and the Partners do not agree to so purchase the entire interest being offered by such Limited Partner, such Limited Partner may, within the four months immediately following the date of the original giving of notice, sell such interest to any financial institution within the United States having total assets in excess of $100 million (as shown on its audited financial statements) on terms which are economically no more favorable to such buyer than the stipulated offering price and terms. An assignee of a Limited Partner's interest pursuant to this Section 8(c) shall become a substituted Limited Partner, subject to Sections 8(c)(3).

(3) No transfer or other disposition of the interest of a Limited Partner shall be permitted until the transferee shall have agreed in writing to assume all of the obligations of the transferor, to the extent of the interest transferred, and the General Partner shall have concluded (which conclusion may be based upon an opinion of counsel satisfactory to it) that such transfer or disposition would not:

(aa) Result in a violation of the Securities Act of 1933;

(bb) Require the Partnership to register as an investment company under the Investment Company Act of 1940;

(cc) Require the Partnership or the General Partner to register as an investment adviser under the Investment Advisers Act of 1940;

(dd) Result in a termination of the Partnership for Federal or state income tax purposes or result in the Partnership being taxed as a corporation for Federal income tax purposes; or

(ee) Result in a violation of any law, rule, or regulation by the Limited Partner, the Partnership, or the General Partner.

9. **Procedure on Termination.**

(a) **Termination Procedures.** Upon termination of the Partnership at the expiration of the Partnership term or for any other cause:

(1) The affairs of the Partnership shall be wound up and the Partnership liquidated by the General Partner. All items of income, gain, and loss (including any gain or loss from liquidation of the Partnership) for the Accounting Period in which the Partnership is finally liquidated shall be allocated among the Partners as provided in Section 5.

(2) The net proceeds of liquidation shall be distributed in payment of liabilities of the Partnership in the following order:

(aa) to creditors of the Partnership other than the General Partner in the order of priority provided by law;

(bb) to the General Partner for any amount the Partnership owes it, other than in respect of the net credit balances of its Capital Account;

(cc) to the Limited Partners in respect of the net credit balances of their Capital Accounts;

(dd) to the General Partner in respect of the net credit balance of its Capital Account:

(ee) 80% of any balance to the Limited Partners to be divided among them in accordance with their respective Capital Interests; and

(ff) 20% of any balance to the General Partner.

(3) Distributions in liquidation may be made in cash or kind or partly in cash and partly in kind at the discretion of the General Partner. Distributions in kind shall be made as provided in Section 6(b).

(4) The General Partner shall use its best judgment as to the most advantageous time for the Partnership to sell investments or to make distributions in kind.

10. **Meetings and Voting.**

(a) **Meetings of Partners.**

(1) Meetings of Partners shall be held at such time and place as the General Partner may designate.

(2) Meetings shall be held only when called by the General Partner at its discretion or, for any matters on which the Limited Partners are entitled to vote pursuant to Section 10(b), at the request of Limited Partners representing more than 20% of the total Capital Contributions.

(3) Notice of a meeting called pursuant to Section 10(a)(2) shall be given not less than 10, nor more than 60, days before the date of the meeting to each Partner entitled to vote at the meeting. The notice shall state the place, date, and hour of the meeting and the general nature of the business to be transacted, and no other business may be transacted. The Limited Partners shall call a meeting by delivering to the General Partner one or more calls in writing stating that the signing Limited Partners wish to call a meeting and indicating the general or specific purposes for which the meeting is to be called. Within 15 days after receipt of such a call from Limited Partners, the General Partner shall send a notice of the meeting to the Limited Partners. The General Partner may solicit proxies with respect to any matter proposed to be considered at a meeting of the Partners. Partners may vote either in person or by proxy at any meeting. Any Partner approval at a meeting, other than unanimous approval by those entitled to vote, shall be valid only if the general nature of the proposal was stated in the notice of meeting or in any written waiver of notice.

(4) Notice of a meeting called pursuant to Section 10(a)(2) shall be given either personally or by mail or other means of written communication, addressed to the Partner at the address of the Partner appearing on the books of the Partnership or given by the Partner to the Partnership for the purpose of notice. The notice shall be deemed to have been given at the time when delivered personally or deposited in the mail or sent by other means of written communication. An affidavit of mailing of any notice in accordance with the provisions of this Section 10(a), executed by the General Partner, shall be prima facie evidence of the giving of notice. If any notice addressed to the Partner at the address of the Partner appearing on the books of the Partnership is returned to the Partnership by the United States Postal Service marked to indicate that the United States Postal Service is unable to deliver it, the notice and any subsequent notices shall be deemed to have been duly given without further mailing if they are available for the Partner at the principal executive office of the Partnership for a period of one year from the date of the giving of the notice to all other Partners.

(5) A Majority Interest of Limited Partners, represented either in person or by proxy, shall constitute a quorum at such a meeting.

(6) The General Partner shall have full power and authority concerning the manner of conducting any meeting of Partners, including, without limitation, the determination of Partners entitled to vote at the meeting, the existence of a quorum, the conduct of voting, the validity and effect of any proxies, and the determination of any controversies, votes, or challenges arising in connection with or during the meeting. The General Partner shall designate a person to serve as chairman of the meeting and shall further designate a person to take the minutes of the meeting in either case including, without limitation, a member, manager, or officer of the General Partner. All minutes shall be kept with the records of the Partnership maintained by the General Partner.

(7) Any action that may be taken at a meeting of the Partners may be taken without a meeting if a consent in writing setting forth the action so taken is signed by Partners owning not less than the minimum percentage of interests that would be necessary to authorize or take such action at a meeting at which all the Partners were present and voted. The General Partner may specify that any written ballot submitted to Partners for the purpose of taking any action without a meeting shall be returned to the Partnership within the time, not less than 10 days, specified by the General Partner. If Partners are requested to consent on a matter without a meeting, each Partner shall be given notice of the matter to be voted upon in the same manner as described in this Section 10(a). If any General Partner, or Limited Partners representing more than 20 percent of the total Capital Contributions, requests a meeting for the purpose of discussion or voting upon the matter, the notice of a meeting shall be given in accordance with this Section 10(a) and no action shall be taken until the meeting is held. Unless delayed in accordance with the provisions of the preceding sentence, any action taken without a meeting will be effective 10 days after the required minimum number of voters has signed the consent; however, the action will be effective immediately if Partners representing at least 80 percent of total Capital Contributions have signed the consent.

(b) **Voting.** Limited Partners shall have the right, by vote or written consent of a Majority Interest of Limited Partners to approve or disapprove the following matters:

(1) Election of an additional general partner;

(2) Termination and dissolution of the Partnership;

(3) Change in the nature of the business of the Partnership; and

(4) Amendment of this Agreement pursuant to Section 11(a).

Approval of any of the above items shall also require the written consent of the General Partner.

(c) **Waiver.** The Limited Partners shall only have the voting rights expressly granted in Section 10(b). The Limited Partners waive the right to vote on all other matters.

(d) **Proxy Representation.** Every Limited Partner may authorize another person or persons to act as his proxy at a meeting or by written action. No proxy shall be valid after the expiration of eleven months from the date of its execution unless otherwise provided in the proxy. Every proxy shall be revocable at the pleasure of the person executing it prior to the vote or written action pursuant thereto. As used herein, a "proxy" shall be deemed to mean a written authorization signed by a Limited Partner or a Limited Partner's attorney-in-fact giving another person or persons power to vote or consent in writing with respect to the interests in the Partnership of such Limited Partner, and "Signed" as used herein shall be deemed to mean the placing of such Limited Partner's name on the proxy, whether by manual signature, typewriting, telegraphic transmission, or otherwise by such Limited Partner or such Limited Partner's attorney-in-fact.

11. **Miscellaneous.**

(a) **Amendments.** This Agreement may be amended with the written consent of the General Partner and of a Majority Interest of Limited Partners; provided however, that the following provisions of this Agreement may be amended in a manner adverse to the interest of the Limited Partners only with the consent of Limited Partners holding 75% of the Capital Contributions made by all Limited Partners: Section 3, Section 4, Section 5(c), Section 5(f), Section 8(c), Section 9(a), and this Section 11(a). Amendments to Sections 5(c), 5(f), and 8(c)(2) and to this sentence will not be effective against any Partner adversely affected thereby who has not consented thereto.

(b) **Entire Agreement.** This Agreement is the final, complete, and exclusive statement of the parties' agreement on the matters contained in this Agreement and supersedes all prior communications, understandings and agreements between the parties related thereto.

(c) **Governing Law.** This Agreement shall be interpreted and the rights and liabilities of the parties to this Agreement, determined in accordance with, the laws of the State of Nevada, without regard to conflicts of law principles.

(d) **Notices.** All notices and requests to the General Partner under this Agreement shall be in writing and shall be effective upon personal delivery or, if sent by registered or certified mail, postage prepaid, addressed to Wildcat Capital Management, LLC at 1721 E. Enke Drive, Tucson, AZ, 85721 (or such other address as the General Partner shall have notified the Limited Partners), upon the deposit of such notice in the United States mail. Notices of assignment, sale, pledge or transfer of a Limited Partner's interest in the Partnership shall be effective upon timely receipt by the General Partner. Except as otherwise provided herein, all reports and notices under this Agreement shall be in writing and shall be sent by first-class mail to the last known address of the Limited Partner.

(e) **Pronouns.** All pronouns and any variations thereof shall be deemed to refer to the masculine, feminine, neuter, singular or plural, as the identity of the person or entity may require.

(f) **Counterparts.** This Agreement may be executed in several counterparts, each of which shall be deemed an original but all of which shall constitute one and the same instrument.

(g) **Severability.** In the event that any provision of this Agreement shall be declared invalid or unenforceable, such invalidity or unenforceability shall not affect the validity or enforceability of the other provisions of this Agreement, it being hereby agreed that such provisions are severable and that this Agreement shall be construed in all respects as if such invalid or unenforceable provision were omitted.

(h) **No Third Party Beneficiaries**. This Agreement is not intended and shall not convey any rights to persons not party to this Agreement.

(i) **Definitional Provisions**.

(1) The words "hereof," "herein," and "hereunder" and words of similar import, when used in this Agreement, shall refer to this Agreement as a whole and not to any particular provisions of this Agreement.

(2) The terms defined in the singular shall have a comparable meaning when used in the plural, and vice versa.

(3) References to a "Section" are, unless otherwise specified, to one entire whole numbered section (including all subsections thereof) of this Agreement.

(j) **Headings**. The headings contained in this Agreement are for convenience of reference only and shall not affect the meaning or interpretation of this Agreement.

To evidence the Partners' agreement to this Agreement's provisions, they have executed and delivered this Agreement on the date set forth in the preamble.

General Partner:
Wildcat Capital Management, LLC

By: /s/ Robert L. Olson
_____
President

Limited Partners:

/s/ Gilbert J. Arenas
_____
Gilbert J. Arenas

Arizona State Retirement System

By /s/ Maria Y. Delgado
_____
Its Trustee
_____

Arizona State University Foundation

By /s/ Jeremy S. Linsanity
_____
Its Trustee
_____

/s/ Michael Bibby
_____
Michael Bibby

/s/ Sean Elliott
_____
Sean M. Elliott

/s/ Larry D. Fitzgerald, Jr.
_____
Larry D. Fitzgerald, Jr.

/s/ Channing T. Frye
_____
Channing T. Frye

/s/ Stephen D. Kerr
_____
Stephen D. Kerr

Sjostrom Family Trust

By /s/ William K. Sjostrom, Jr.
_____
Its Trustee
_____

Tempest Investments LLLP

By: Tempest Asset Advisers, Inc.
Its: General Partner

By /s/ Napoleon Dynamite
_____
Its Vice President
_____

/s/ Jason E. Terry
_____
Jason E. Terry

/s/ Luke T. Walton
_____
Luke T. Walton

/s/ Kurt E. Warner
_____
Kurt E. Warner

University of Arizona Foundation

By /s/ Sergio Garcia
_____
Its Trustee
_____

Winding Road Fund, LP

By: Honey Badger, LLC
Its: General Partner

By /s/ Nancy G. Beckman
_____
Its President
_____

/s/ Derrick L. Williams
_____
Derrick L. Williams

B. Limited Liability Limited Partnerships

Schedule A

Limited Partner	Capital Contribution
Gilbert J. Arenas	$5,000,000
University of Arizona Foundation	$20,000,000
Arizona State University Foundation	$10,000,000
Sean M. Elliott	$5,000,000
Channing T. Frye	$5,000,000
Sjostrom Family Trust	$15,000,000
Jason E. Terry	$5,000,000
Kurt E. Warner	$8,000,000
Windsor Fund, LP	$12,000,000
Arizona State Retirement System	$5,000,000
Michael Bibby	$5,000,000
Larry D. Fitzgerald, Jr.	$10,000,000
Stephen D. Kerr	$5,000,000
Tempest Investments LLLP	$14,000,000
Luke T. Walton	$6,000,000
Derrick L. Williams	$5,000,000
Total	$135,000,000

· CHAPTER SIX ·

LIMITED LIABILITY COMPANIES

This chapter elaborates a bit on the basic characteristics of limited liability companies (LLCs) touched on in Chapter 1, and covers some additional related topics.

A. FORMATION

You form an LLC by filing a "certificate of formation" (or other similarly named document) with the secretary of state of the state in which the client wants the LLC organized. The state's LLC statute will specify the short list of information that must be included in the certificate. Under the Delaware statute, the list of required items consists of the name of the LLC, the address of the LLC's office in Delaware, and the name and address of the LLC's agent in Delaware for service of process.[1] Per Delaware Limited Liability Company Act (DLLCA) §18-102, an LLC's name must "contain the words 'Limited Liability Company' or the abbreviation 'L.L.C.' or the designation 'LLC.'"

Here is a sample certificate of formation for a Delaware LLC using the form available on the Delaware Division of Corporations website:

---

1. DLLCA §18-201.

STATE *of* DELAWARE
LIMITED LIABILITY COMPANY
CERTIFICATE *of* FORMATION

First: The name of the limited liability company is ___AAA Pool Services,___
___LLC___

Second: The address of its registered office in the State of Delaware is ___1209___
___Orange Street___ in the City of ___Wilmington___.

Zip code ___19801___. The name of its Registered agent at such address is
___The Corporation Trust Company___

Third: (Use this paragraph only if the company is to have a specific effective date of
dissolution: "The latest date on which the limited liability company is to dissolve is
_____.")

Fourth: (Insert any other matters the members determine to include herein.)

In Witness Whereof, the undersigned have executed this Certificate of Formation this
___24th___ day of ___April___, ___2009___.

By: _____
               Authorized Person (s)

Name: ___George W. Smith___

B. GOVERNING LAW

A limited liability company is governed by the limited liability company statute of the state in which it filed its certificate of organization. Each state has its own limited liability company statute. Although the NCCUSL adopted the Uniform Limited Liability Company Act (ULLCA) in 1995 and revised it in 2006, neither the original nor revised versions have been widely adopted by the states. As of 2012, five states (Alabama, Hawaii, Illinois, Montana, and South Dakota) have adopted the 1996 version, and five states (Idaho, Iowa, Nebraska, Utah, and Wyoming) have adopted the 2006 version. Thus, unlike with other business entity statutes, there is not a lot of uniformity across states. As a result, in this chapter we focus on the DLLCA as opposed to one of the versions of the uniform act. This is because Delaware attracts 80 percent of LLCs formed outside of their home states. (We touch on why Delaware is successful in attracting out-of-state businesses in Chapter 7.)

C. OPERATING AGREEMENT

Most LLCs have a written operating agreement that tailors the applicable LLC statute's default rules to the specific needs and preferences of the LLC's members and managers. Thus, as stated before, the starting point for providing advice to an LLC on LLC law issues is usually a review of this agreement and not the applicable statute. The statute does, however, remain relevant, because it contains some rules that the parties cannot contract around. Note that the DLLCA uses the phrase "limited liability company agreement" (often referred to as an LLC agreement for short) instead of "operating agreement"; but the definition of LLC agreement states that it includes an agreement referred to as an "operating agreement," so it is not uncommon for a Delaware LLC to title its LLC agreement "operating agreement."[2]

An LLC/operating agreement is analogous to a partnership agreement if the LLC is to be member managed, or a combination of a corporate charter and bylaws if the LLC is to be manager managed. An LLC/operating agreement typically addresses, among other things, management structure, allocation of profits and losses among the members, member taxation, transfer of membership interests, and dissolution. An operating agreement can be oral or even implied, but as we discussed with partnership agreements, going with an oral agreement is inadvisable. A written agreement will lessen the likelihood of future disputes between the members and managers as to what was agreed. It will also allow the members to tailor the rules in much greater depth than is realistic with an oral agreement.

D. MANAGEMENT

As mentioned in Chapter 1, LLC statutes contemplate an LLC being either member managed or manager managed. Member management (recall that LLC owners are referred to as members) is similar to partnership or decentralized management—the statute vests the members with the authority to manage the LLC. Manager management is similar to corporate or centralized management—the statute vests management authority in a board of managers elected by the LLC members.

---

2. *See* DLLCA §18-101(7).

The default rule under the DLLCA is member management. Specifically, DLLCA §18-402 provides:

> Unless otherwise provided in a limited liability company agreement, the management of a limited liability company shall be vested in its members in proportion to the then current percentage or other interest of members in the profits of the limited liability company owned by all of the members, the decision of members owning more than 50 percent of the said percentage or other interest in the profits controlling. . . .

Notice that the provision provides for voting based on percentage ownership in the LLC as opposed to on a per capita basis as is the default management rule under RUPA.

A Delaware LLC can instead opt for manager management by providing so in its limited liability company agreement. In such an event, the limited liability company agreement should also provide how the manager or managers of the LLC are to be chosen. Typically, it is by member voting based on percentage ownership in the LLC. LLCs that opt for manager management often choose to duplicate the corporate governance structure of having ultimate authority vested in a board of managers elected annually by the LLC's members.

Exercise 6.1

Read the AAA Pool Services, LLC (APS) Limited Liability Company Agreement located at the end of this chapter and answer the following questions. Make sure you note any applicable partnership agreement and/or statutory provision that supports your answer. In that regard, the Delaware Limited Liability Company Act is available at http://delcode.delaware.gov/title6/c018/index.shtml.

1. Is APS member managed or manager managed?
2. Smith and Watson want to expand the business to include landscaping. Gray is opposed to expansion. Can APS expand against Gray's wishes?
3. Smith no longer wants Gray to be an APS manager. Can he remove him from the board? What about if Smith gets Watson to go along?
4. Watson signs a contract on behalf of APS for the purchase of pool chemicals. Neither Smith nor Gray authorized him to sign it. Is APS bound to the contract?

E. FIDUCIARY DUTIES

Unlike the ULLCA (and, for that matter, RUPA and ULPA-2002), the DLLCA does not have a provision specifying the fiduciary duties owed by managers and members of a Delaware LLC.[3] Defining these duties is instead left to the applicable

---

3. *See* ULLCA-2006 §409 Standards of Conduct for Members and Managers.

LLC agreement and the courts. (Note that Delaware takes the same approach in the corporate context.) The next case discusses LLC fiduciary duties.

William Penn Partnership v. Saliba
13 A.3d 749 (Del. 2011)

STEELE, Chief Justice.

. . . I. FACTS AND PROCEDURAL HISTORY

The Parties

Anis K. Saliba, M.D., is a retired surgeon who lives in Lewes, Delaware. Saliba, in his capacity as trustee of the Revocable Trust Agreement of Anis K. Saliba, owned a one-sixth interest in Del Bay [Associates, LLC].

Rosa Ksebe lives in Lewes, Delaware and is a trustee of the Revocable Trust Agreement of Kamal Ksebe, her deceased husband. In her capacity as trustee of the Ksebe Trust, Ksebe also owned a one-sixth interest in Del Bay.

Robert Hoyt, as trustee of the Revocable Trust of Robert M. Hoyt, also owned a one-sixth interest in Del Bay. Hoyt resides in Maryland.

The William Penn Partnership owned the remaining one-half interest in Del Bay. William Penn is a partnership organized and existing under the laws of the State of Delaware with its principal place of business in Rehoboth Beach, Delaware. T. William (Bill) Lingo, Bryce Lingo, and their mother, Margaret Lingo, each own a one third interest in William Penn. Bryce and Bill are its managing partners.

Jack Lingo, Inc. Realtor, a real-estate agency in Sussex County employs the Lingos. Bill and Bryce are both Vice Presidents of Jack Lingo and are brokers of record.

J.G. Townsend Jr. & Co. is a Delaware Subchapter S corporation with its principal place of business in Georgetown, Delaware. JGT is a landholdings and agricultural company. The Lingos, together with their two younger brothers, collectively own 40 percent of JGT and form a majority of its board of directors. The Lingos serve on the JGT board of directors, and Bryce is the Chairman.

Beacon Revex, LLC is a Delaware limited liability company that was formed on or about June 12, 2003 to serve as the exchange accommodation titleholder for JGT in connection with the purchase of the Beacon Motel. Bill Lingo is the sole manager of Beacon Revex.

Background to Del Bay

Del Bay was originally formed in 1986 to construct a motel on land owned and contributed to Del Bay by Ksebe's now deceased husband. Del Bay also received capital contributions from the William Penn Partnership, Hoyt, and Saliba. The parties divided Del Bay ownership interests as described above.

They built the Beacon Motel in 1987 on a four acre site in Lewes, Delaware. It is a three-story structure, housing 66 guest units. It is located adjacent to the shops of downtown Lewes. The first floor of the Motel houses small commercial tenants typical of a beach community. It operates on a seasonal basis from May through September. For the three years predating the challenged sale, the Beacon Motel generated a net income stream of approximately $250,000 for Del Bay.

Del Bay converted to a Delaware LLC pursuant to an Operating Agreement dated December 23, 1994. The ownership interests of the members of the LLC remained the same as the interest of each partner in the partnership. Under the LLC Operating Agreement, "all decisions and approvals of the members" required a vote of two thirds of the interests held by the members. The Operating Agreement does not expressly eliminate any fiduciary duties. The Lingos were the initial managers, and the Lingos in fact remained the managers of Del Bay at all times relevant to this case. Under Article VII, the Operating Agreement provided a mechanism for members to dispose of their interest in Del Bay. A member who wished to dispose of his interest could first offer it to Del Bay, and then, if not accepted by Del Bay within 45 days, to the other members, at a price "determined by the accountant regularly employed by the Company." A non-selling member would have 30 days to purchase the disposing member's interest if Del Bay's option lapsed unexercised. If a member's offer to the Company or the other members lapsed or was waived, that member could then sell his interest to a third party.

Hoyt initially called periodic meetings of the members of Del Bay, but around 1998, Saliba and Ksebe had a falling out with the Lingos with respect to a real estate venture unrelated to this litigation. After the falling out, the Del Bay members ceased meeting together, and in July 2000, Hoyt contacted attorney James Griffin requesting an opinion concerning the disposition and or partition options for his ownership interest under the Operating Agreement. Hoyt indicated to Griffin that he was interested in selling his membership interest to Saliba and he asked whether two thirds of the members could force the sale of the Motel. Griffin "did not provide a clear answer" to the question of whether two thirds of the members could force a sale, but he did advise that under Article VII, any member who desired to dispose of their interest could do so by offering it to the Company and to the other members at the value determined by the Company's accountant. Hoyt, disappointed with Griffin's opinion, took no action. As of July 2000, neither Ksebe nor Saliba had any interest in selling the Motel.

Two offers to purchase the Motel property were presented to Del Bay before the Lingos decided to sell the entire property. In 2001, the Lingos declined an offer for $2 million, and in 2003, they declined an offer for $4 million. They never communicated either offer to Saliba or Ksebe.

Lingos Decide to Sell

The Lingos eventually decided to end their business relationship with Saliba and Ksebe. In May 2003, they sought the advice of attorney Bob Thomas, who responded that the Motel property could be sold with the approval of two-thirds of the members. Thomas also informed the Lingos that Article VII of the agreement provided a mechanism for members to sell their respective interests in Del Bay. The Lingos decided they could sell the property using the two thirds vote provision after obtaining Hoyt's approval.

To that end, the Lingos offered to sell the Motel to JGT, recognizing the benefit to JGT because the Motel produced cash and the sale would allow JGT to take advantage of a Section 1031 tax free exchange under the Internal Revenue Code. To take advantage of a tax deferral from a previously sold piece of property, JGT needed to purchase a replacement property by April 2004. The Lingos told the JGT board that they had decided to pay $6 million for the property. They provided JGT's controller with financial information so that he could prepare a valuation for the JGT board. JGT's controller prepared the business valuation for Del Bay on May 23, 2003. At no time did anyone send this information to Saliba or Ksebe.

Contemporaneously, the Lingos called Hoyt and told him that they had decided to sell the Motel and that their attorney had advised them that they could sell the property with the vote of two-thirds of the memberships' interests. The Lingos also told Hoyt they were working on a deal with JGT. On May 17, 2003, Hoyt received a prepared sales contract listing the Lingos and or their assignees as purchasers.

On May 19, Ksebe found a sales contract for the Motel in her mailbox. After Ksebe telephoned Saliba, he discovered a copy of the same sales contract in his mailbox. Attached to the contract was a note that read, "Mr. Hoyt has received a copy of the contract. Please call with questions." The contract listed the Lingos and or their "assigns" as purchasers, and indicated a purchase price of $6 million. The contract indicated that settlement "shall be completed" on or before June 30, 2003.

The timing of the sale particularly disconcerted Saliba and Hoyt because they were scheduled to be out of town the week after they received the Lingos' proposal and it came near the peak earning season for the Motel. However, on May 27, Saliba and Ksebe met with Griffin to discuss their options and gave him the signed Articles of Partnership (which had been superseded by the LLC Operating Agreement) because they could not locate a copy of the Operating Agreement. During the meeting, they advised Griffin that they did not want the property sold and also expressed their desire to purchase the property in the event they could not stop its sale. Accordingly, that same day, Griffin faxed a letter to Hoyt and the Lingos indicating Saliba and Ksebe's desire to purchase Hoyt's interest for $1 million and the Lingos' combined interest for $3 million. Ksebe and Saliba understood their offer to include assumption of the outstanding $625,000 mortgage on the property, although the faxed offer letter did not expressly state so.

On or about the same time on May 27, the JGT board was evaluating the Business Valuation prepared by its controller while considering purchasing the property. Two days later, the Lingos telephoned Griffin to express a willingness to accept Saliba and Ksebe's offer, but added the condition that the settlement must occur by June 30 for tax reasons related to a Section 1031 exchange. However, during this call, the Lingos did not advise Griffin that the Operating Agreement had superseded the Articles of Partnership referred to in his letter, that they had received the advice of counsel regarding the legal requirements to sell the property, or that JGT was considering purchasing the property. Furthermore, stating that June 30 was the operative date for a Section 1031 tax exchange was a direct misrepresentation as in fact JGT had until April 2004 to benefit from the exchange.

After hearing from Griffin on May 29 about the Lingos' willingness to accept the offer, Saliba contacted Wilmington Trust and received adequate assurance of loan approval from a loan officer. Saliba then contacted Hoyt to inform him that Saliba and Ksebe would be willing to purchase Hoyt's interest in Del Bay. June 2 and 3, Saliba and Hoyt both went out of town. The Lingos contacted Griffin on June 3, asked when a contract would be ready, and again misrepresented the significance of the June 30 date. Meanwhile, Saliba and Ksebe contacted Laurence Moynihan, an appraiser, to obtain a valuation of Del Bay to assure that the price was reasonable. Saliba explained to Hoyt that he was working to arrange financing and asked Hoyt to wait until June 11 before taking any action on the Lingos' proposal.

Hoyt informed the Lingos that Saliba and Ksebe's offer was superior because it included an assumption of the mortgage on the property. The Lingos then agreed to assume the mortgage. However, neither the Lingos nor Hoyt ever communicated this information to Saliba and Ksebe or their attorney, Griffin.

On June 10, 2003, the Lingos convinced Hoyt to sign the contract immediately so they could present it to the JGT board. The Lingos told Hoyt that if he did not sign the contract, JGT might back off. Hoyt signed the contract and faxed it to the Lingos. Neither Hoyt nor the Lingos contacted Saliba and Ksebe at that time to give them the opportunity to match or exceed the Lingo offer. On the same day, Moynihan gave Saliba and Ksebe a fairness opinion that valued the property at approximately $5.7 million. They believed this valuation to be low, but the appraisal did not dissuade them from pursuing the purchase.

The next day, Saliba tried to contact Hoyt to reconfirm his interest in purchasing Del Bay, but was unable to reach him. Saliba then contacted Del Bay's accountant to obtain valuation information. Only then did he learn that Hoyt had already signed the sales contract with the Lingos. Two days later, on June 12, the JGT board formally approved the purchase of the Beacon Motel. The Lingos assigned their rights to purchase the property to JGT.

Around June 23, JGT informed Griffin that the closing date was to be June 30, 2003. Four days later, Griffin contacted JGT's attorney, Dennis Schrader, to object to the sale and renew his clients' interest in negotiating a resolution to the dispute. Griffin also requested signed copies of the real estate sales contract and the Operating Agreement. The closing occurred on June 30, 2003. Saliba and Ksebe were not at the closing and no attorney was present to represent Del Bay's interests. At the closing, Bill Lingo signed a Del Bay resolution, falsely stating that at a special June 30 meeting the members of Del Bay "unanimously" authorized the sale of the Beacon Motel.

JGT financed the purchase of the Motel through a Wilmington Trust loan. Wilmington Trust requested an appraisal, which Hospitality Appraisals, Inc. conducted, and concluded the fair market value of the property as is was $5,060,000. This appraisal also noted that the highest and best use of the property was as a commercial development, but it did not value the property on that basis.

Because JGT purchased the Beacon Motel as an exchange property, they received a $1.6 million tax refund in 2004 pursuant to Section 1031 of the Internal Revenue Code. The Lingos' share was approximately $434,000 in total.

PROCEDURAL HISTORY

Appellees Saliba and Ksebe filed an action for breach of fiduciary duty against the managers of Del Bay Associates, LLC, on December 12, 2003. . . . [T]he Chancellor issued a telephonic ruling holding that defendants [breached their fiduciary duties to the members of Del Bay].

II. ANALYSIS

A. *William Penn Partnership Failed to Establish Its Burden of Entire Fairness.* . . .

The parties here agree that managers of a Delaware limited liability company owe traditional fiduciary duties of loyalty and care to the members of the LLC, unless the parties expressly modify or eliminate those duties in the operating agreement. The Del Bay Operating Agreement did not purport to modify or eliminate fiduciary duties and it named the Lingos as the managers of the LLC. Therefore, as fiduciaries the parties here agree that the Lingos owe fiduciary duties of loyalty and care to the members of Del Bay. The Lingos here acted in their own self interest by orchestrating the sale of Del Bay's sole asset, the Beacon Motel, on terms that were favorable to them. By standing on both sides of the transaction — as the seller, through their interest in and status as managers of Del Bay, and the buyer, through their interest in JGT — they bear the burden of demonstrating the entire fairness of the transaction.

The concept of entire fairness consists of two blended elements: fair dealing and fair price. Fair dealing involves analyzing how the transaction was structured, the timing, disclosures, and approvals. Fair price relates to the economic and financial considerations of the transaction. We examine the transaction as a whole and both aspects of the test must be satisfied; a party does not meet the entire fairness standard simply by showing that the price fell within a reasonable range that would be considered fair.

Here, the Chancellor appropriately lacked confidence in the process. Because the Lingos procured the sale of the Beacon Motel without full disclosure to the other members of Del Bay, it is impossible to demonstrate that the sale was entirely fair, no matter what the price. The Lingos manipulated the sales process through misrepresentations and repeated material omissions such as (1) imposing an artificial deadline justified by "tax purposes"; (2) failing to inform Saliba and Ksebe that they were matching their offer by assuming the existing mortgage; (3) failing to inform Saliba and Ksebe that they had already committed to selling the property to JGT, an entity the Lingos controlled; (4) failing to inform Saliba and Ksebe that Hoyt signed the contract on June 10th and that the JGT board approved the purchase of the Beacon Motel on June 13th; (5) failing to inform Saliba, Ksebe and their counsel that the partnership agreement had been superseded and the Lingos had been advised by counsel of the requirements to sell the Beacon Motel under the LLC Agreement; and (6) failing to hold a vote on the transaction as required by the Operating Agreement, while falsely stating that the Del Bay members unanimously authorized the sale at a special meeting. Because the Lingos acted in their own self interest and contrary to the interests of other members of Del Bay, their actions precluded the possibility that the property would be sold pursuant to an open and fair process. Therefore, the Lingos failed to meet their burden of establishing fair dealing.

While fair dealing and fair price are distinct concepts, the burden to establish them is not bifurcated. Rather, this Court must evaluate a transaction as a whole to determine if the interested party has met his burden of establishing entire fairness.

The Lingos argue here that the deal was entirely fair because the purchase price was a premium to the appraisal price. JGT paid $6,625,000 for the Beacon Motel, which the Lingos contend was within the range of fairness based on numerous property valuations. First, Saliba and Ksebe requested a valuation report from Larry Moynihan. Moynihan valued the property between $5,176,000-$5,681,000 in June 2003. Next, Robert White performed a valuation at the request of Wilmington Trust, the mortgage lender for JGT. White valued the property "as is" at $5,060,000 as of August 2003. However, White concluded that the highest and best use of the improved portion of the property was not as a hotel or motel, but rather as a commercial development with mixed dwellings. Despite this assertion, White did not provide a valuation of the property as a commercial development. Also, Joe Melson, Jr. performed a valuation, at the request of Saliba and Ksebe, with an effective date of June 2006. Melson completed his valuation from the standpoint that the property's highest and best use included demolition of the existing improvements and redevelopment of the site with a mixed use building of commercial space and residential condominiums. Melson valued the property under those conditions in 2006 at $8,000,000. After trial, the Chancellor appointed independent experts to determine the value at which the property would likely have sold as a result of a fair bidding process in the open market in which all participants had the benefit of full and accurate disclosure. The Court retained appraisal valued the property at $5,480,000. Merely showing that the sale price was in the range of fairness, however, does not necessarily satisfy the entire fairness burden when fiduciaries stand on both sides of a transaction and manipulate the sales process. Here, the Lingos' manipulation of the sales process denied Saliba and Ksebe the benefit of knowing the price a fair bidding process might have brought.

The Court of Chancery had ample evidence on which to base its conclusion that the Lingos prevented a fair and open process by withholding full information, providing misleading information, and imposing an artificial deadline on the transaction. The Lingos' self-interest in the transaction and their domination of the sales process tainted the entire transaction. Therefore, we hold that the record supports the Chancellor's factual findings and the Chancellor's conclusions are not clearly wrong. . . .

Questions

1. What fiduciary duties do the managers of Del Bay Associates, LLC owe to its members?
2. What fiduciary duty are the plaintiffs claiming the Lingos breached? What is the factual basis for the claim?
3. What test did the court apply to determine the breach? What facts did the court point to for finding a breach?
4. In hindsight, what could the Lingos have done differently to avoid the litigation? What about Saliba and Ksebe?
5. Why do you think the Delaware legislature chose not to include in the DLLCA a provision specifying the fiduciary duties owed by managers and members of a Delaware LLC?

As the above case indicates, the fiduciary duties of care and loyalty owed under the DLLCA can be modified or even entirely eliminated in an LLC's limited liability company agreement. Specifically, DLLCA §18-1101(c) provides:

> To the extent that, at law or in equity, a member or manager or other person has duties (including fiduciary duties) to a limited liability company or to another member or manager or to another person that is a party to or is otherwise bound by a limited liability company agreement, the member's or manager's or other person's duties may be expanded or restricted or eliminated by provisions in the limited liability company agreement; provided, that the limited liability company agreement may not eliminate the implied contractual covenant of good faith and fair dealing.[4]

---

4. The current version of §18-1101(c) was adopted by the legislature in 2004 in response to *Gotham Partners, L.P. v. Hallwood Realty Partners, L.P.*, 817 A.2d 160 (Del. 2002). Prior to 2004, the section provided that fiduciary duties could only be "expanded or restricted" by the LLC agreement. In *Gotham Partners*, the Delaware Supreme Court called into question lower court dictum that stated a Delaware Revised Uniform Partnership Act provision analogous to the pre-2004 version of §18-1101(c) allowed a limited partnership agreement to

This is in contrast to the ULLCA, which allows an operating agreement to modify but not eliminate these duties.[5]

As the above case also indicates, the default rule appears to be that managers of a Delaware LLC owe the LLC the duty of care and loyalty. I mention this point and include the "appears to be" modifier for two reasons. First, Delaware Supreme Court Chief Justice Myron Steele wrote in a 2009 law journal article that "the costs of default fiduciary duties outweigh the minimal benefits they provide,"[6] suggesting that he thinks there should be no default fiduciary duties. Second, the *William Penn* opinion states that "[t]he parties here agree that managers of a Delaware limited liability company owe traditional fiduciary duties . . ." as opposed to something along of the lines of "the court holds that managers owe fiduciary duties. . . ."

With that said, Chancellor Strine addressed the issue of whether default fiduciary duties exist in the LLC context in *Auriga Capital Corp. v. Gatz Properties, LLC*[7] and concluded that the answer is yes. As Chancellor Strine explains under the heading "Default Fiduciary Duties Do Exist in the LLC Context":

> The Delaware LLC Act does not plainly state that the traditional fiduciary duties of loyalty and care apply by default as to managers or members of a limited liability company. In that respect, of course, the LLC Act is not different than the DGCL, which does not do that either. In fact, the absence of explicitness in the DGCL inspired the case of *Schnell v. Chris-Craft.*[8] Arguing that the then newly-revised DGCL was a domain unto itself, and that compliance with its terms was sufficient to discharge any obligation owed by the directors to the stockholders, the defendant corporation in that case won on that theory at the Court of Chancery level. But our Supreme Court reversed and made emphatic that the new DGCL was to be read in concert with equitable fiduciary duties just as had always been the case, stating famously that "inequitable action does not become legally permissible simply because it is legally possible."[9]
>
> The LLC Act is more explicit than the DGCL in making the equitable overlay mandatory. Specifically, §18-1104 of the LLC Act provides that "[i]n any case not provided for in this chapter, *the rules of law and equity . . . shall govern.*" In this way, the LLC Act provides for a construct similar to that which is used in the corporate context. But unlike in the corporate context, the rules of equity apply in the LLC context *by statutory mandate,* creating an even stronger justification for application of fiduciary duties grounded in equity to managers of LLCs to the extent that such duties have not been altered or eliminated under the relevant LLC agreement.[10]

eliminate fiduciary duties. The legislature thus amended the provision referenced in *Gotham Partners* and DLLCA §18-1101(c) to make clear that operative agreements could eliminate these duties.

5. *See* ULLCA-2006 §110(c)(5).

6. Myron T. Steele, *Freedom of Contract and Default Contractual Duties in the Delaware Limited Partnerships and Limited Liability Companies,* 46 Am. Bus. L.J. 221, 224 (2009).

7. 40 A.3d 839 (Del. Ch. 2012).

8. [FN 30] *Schnell v. Chris-Craft Indus., Inc.,* 285 A.2d 437 (Del. 1971).

9. [FN 32] *Schnell,* 285 A.2d at 439 (Del. 1971).

10. [FN 34] Section 18-1101(c) of the LLC Act provides: *"To the extent that, at law or in equity, a member or manager or other person has duties (including fiduciary duties)* to a limited liability company or to another member

It seems obvious that, under traditional principles of equity, a manager of an LLC would qualify as a fiduciary of that LLC and its members. Under Delaware law, "[a] fiduciary relationship is a situation where one person reposes special trust in and reliance on the judgment of another or where a special duty exists on the part of one person to protect the interests of another."[11] Corporate directors, general partners and trustees are analogous examples of those who Delaware law has determined owe a "special duty." Equity distinguishes fiduciary relationships from straightforward commercial arrangements where there is no expectation that one party will act in the interests of the other.

The manager of an LLC—which is in plain words a limited liability "company" having many of the features of a corporation—easily fits the definition of a fiduciary. The manager of an LLC has more than an arms-length, contractual relationship with the members of the LLC. Rather, the manager is vested with discretionary power to manage the business of the LLC.

Thus, because the LLC Act provides for principles of equity to apply, because LLC managers are clearly fiduciaries, and because fiduciaries owe the fiduciary duties of loyalty and care, the LLC Act starts with the default that managers of LLCs owe enforceable fiduciary duties.[12]

On appeal, the Delaware Supreme Court ruled that "it was improvident and unnecessary for the trial court to reach out and decide, *sua sponte*, the default fiduciary duty issue as a matter of statutory construction."[13] It further stated that "we decline to express any view regarding whether default fiduciary duties apply as a matter of statutory construction. The Court of Chancery likewise should have so refrained."[14] Hence, whether default fiduciary duties exist in the Delaware LLC context is unsettled.

---

or manager or to another person that is a party to or is otherwise bound by a[n] [LLC] agreement, *the member's or manager's or other person's duties may be expanded or restricted or eliminated by provisions in the [LLC] agreement;* provided, that the [LLC] agreement may not eliminate the implied covenant of good faith and fair dealing." 6 Del. C. §18-1101(c) (emphasis added). Although §18-1101(c) allows parties to an LLC agreement to contract out of owing fiduciary duties to one another, the fact that these duties can be contractually avoided suggests that they exist by default in the first place. When read together, the most logical reading of §18-1104 and §18-1101(c) that results is that if, *i.e.,* "to the extent that," equity would traditionally make a manager or member a fiduciary owing fiduciary duties, then that manager or member *is* a fiduciary, subject to the express right of the parties to contract out of those duties. By contrast, if a member or manager would not be considered a fiduciary owing circumstantially-relevant duties under traditional equitable principles, then the member or manager is immune from fiduciary liability, not because of the statute, but because equity itself would not consider the member or manager to have case-relevant fiduciary duties. The "to the extent that" language makes clear that the statute does not itself impose some broader scope of fiduciary coverage than traditional principles of equity.

11. [FN 35] *Metro Ambulance, Inc. v. E. Med. Billing, Inc.,* 1995 WL 409015, at *2 (Del. Ch. July 5, 1995) (citing *Cheese Shop Int'l, Inc. v. Steele,* 303 A.2d 689, 690 (Del. Ch. 1973), *rev'd on other grounds,* 311 A.2d 870 (Del. 1973)).

12. *Auriga,* 40 A.3d at 849-51.

13. Gatz Properties, LLC v. Auriga Capital, __ A.3d __, 2012 WL 5425227, at *9 (Del. 2012).

14. *Id.* at *10.

Exercise 6.2

Refer again to the APS LLC Agreement at the end of this chapter and answer the following questions. Make sure you note any applicable LLC agreement and/or statutory provision that supports your answer.

1. What fiduciary duties do the members of APS owe each other?
2. What fiduciary duties do the managers of APS owe to APS?
3. When is an APS member or manager liable for breach of fiduciary duty?

F. OBLIGATION OF GOOD FAITH AND FAIR DEALING

You probably noticed that a proviso at the end of DLLCA §18-1101(c) does not allow an LLC agreement to "eliminate the implied contractual covenant of good faith and fair dealing." In *Airborne Health, Inc. v. Squid Soap, LP*, the court elaborated on this covenant as follows:

> The implied covenant of good faith and fair dealing inheres in every contract governed by Delaware law and "requires a party in a contractual relationship to refrain from arbitrary or unreasonable conduct which has the effect of preventing the other party to the contract from receiving the fruits of the bargain." *Dunlap v. State Farm Fire & Cas. Co.*, 878 A.2d 434, 442 (Del. 2005) (internal quotation omitted). The implied covenant does not apply when "the subject at issue is expressly covered by the contract." *Dave Greytak Enters., Inc. v. Mazda Motors of Am., Inc.*, 622 A.2d 14, 23 (Del. Ch.1992), *aff'd*, 609 A.2d 668 (Del. 1992). At the same time, the covenant exists to fulfill the reasonable expectations of the parties, and thus the implied obligation must be consistent with the terms of the agreement as a whole. *See Alliance Data Sys. Corp. v. Blackstone Capital Partners V L.P.*, 963 A.2d 746, 770 (Del. Ch. 2009) ("[T]he implied covenant only applies where a contract lacks specific language governing an issue and the obligation the court is asked to imply advances, and does not contradict, the purposes reflected in the express language of the contract."), *aff'd*, 976 A.2d 170 (Del. 2009). The doctrine thus operates only in that narrow band of cases where the contract as a whole speaks sufficiently to suggest an obligation and point to a result, but does not speak directly enough to provide an explicit answer. In the Venn diagram of contract cases, the area of overlap is quite small.
>
> The test for the implied covenant depends on whether it is "clear from what was expressly agreed upon that the parties who negotiated the express terms of the contract would have agreed to proscribe the act later complained of as a breach of the implied covenant of good faith-had they thought to negotiate with respect to that matter." *Katz v. Oak Indus., Inc.*, 508 A.2d 873, 880 (Del. Ch. 1986) (Allen, C.). "[I]mplying obligations based on the covenant of good faith and fair dealing is a cautious enterprise." *Cincinnati SMSA Ltd. v. Cincinnati Bell*

Cellular Sys. Co., 708 A.2d 989, 992 (Del. 1998). "[C]ourts should be most chary about implying a contractual protection when the contract easily could have been drafted to expressly provide for it." *Allied Capital Corp. v. GC-Sun Holdings, L.P.,* 910 A.2d 1020, 1035 (Del. Ch. 2006).[15]

[handwritten: policy re. implying protection]

G. LIABILITY SHIELD

As mentioned in Chapters 1 and 3, an LLC affords its members a full liability shield. Under the DLLCA, this is pursuant to §18-303(a), the scope of which is addressed in the next case.

Pepsi-Cola Bottling Co. of Salisbury, Md. v. Handy
2000 WL 364199 (Del. Ct. Ch. 2000)

JACOBS, Vice Chancellor.

This case arises out of the purchase by the plaintiff, The Pepsi-Cola Bottling Company of Salisbury, Maryland ("Pepsi"), from the defendants, of a 66.19 acre parcel of undeveloped real property in Delmar, Delaware. Certain defendants (the "moving defendants") have moved to dismiss all five counts of the complaint. . . .

For the reasons stated below, both motions will be denied.

I. BACKGROUND

The plaintiff, Pepsi, is a Maryland corporation that bottles soft-drink beverages. Pepsi's principal place of business is in Salisbury, Maryland.

The five named defendants are: (i) Handy Realty, Inc. ("Handy Realty"), which is a Delaware corporation engaged in the development, sale, and brokering of real property in Delaware; (ii) Willow Creek Estates, LLC ("Willow Creek"), which is a Delaware limited liability company created on August 18, 1997 to develop and sell real property in Delaware; (iii) Randall C. Handy, Jr. ("Handy"), who at all relevant times was an officer, director, and shareholder of Handy Realty and was also a member and the manager of Willow Creek; and (iv) Michael Ginsburg ("Ginsburg") and (v) C. Larry McKinley ("McKinley"), both of whom were members of Willow Creek.

On April 5, 1997, Handy, acting on his own behalf and the behalf of Ginsburg and McKinley, contracted to purchase a 66.13 acre parcel of undeveloped real property (the "Property") for development into a residential subdivision called "Willow Creek Estates." Before settling on the contract to purchase, Handy began taking steps to develop the Property into a residential subdivision. Shortly after he began development planning, Handy learned, from a study by Coastal & Estuarine Research, Inc. ("Coastal"), that the Property contained wetlands—a fact that adversely affected the Property's value and development potential.

---

15. *Airborne Health, Inc. v. Squid Soap, LP,* 984 A.2d 126 (Del. Ch. 2009).

Handy had retained Coastal to perform a wetlands jurisdictional determination on the Property. From and after April 21, 1997, Coastal performed site tests that revealed field evidence of wetlands. A later report by Coastal (the "Coastal Wetlands Report") detailed Coastal's examination of the Property, including its determination that a portion of the land contained federally protected wetlands or waters. The Coastal Wetlands Report established preliminary wetlands boundary lines on the Property. It also included photographs that showed various specific wetlands areas on the Property, and a map that showed where the preliminary wetlands boundary lines had been established.

After learning that the Property contained wetlands, the defendants abandoned their plans to develop the Property, and instead opted to sell it. To advertise and promote that sale, a Handy Realty sign was placed on the Property. The sign announced that the Property had "Excellent Development Potential," and remained on the Property at all relevant times.

In June, 1997, Pepsi became interested in the Property as a possible site to construct a new soft-drink bottling facility. Unaware of the existence of wetlands, Pepsi acquired an option to purchase the Property from Handy on August 5, 1997. At that time, Willow Creek had not yet been formed and Handy had not yet purchased the Property. Handy, Ginsburg, and McKinley formed the LLC, Willow Creek, on August 18, 1997.

During the option period, Pepsi hired soil engineering consultant John D. Hynes & Associates, Inc. to conduct a Phase I environmental investigation of the Property. As part of its investigation the Hynes firm interviewed Handy and sent him an "Owner/Operator Questionnaire." In his written answers to specific questions about the Property, Handy did not disclose on that questionnaire that the Property contained wetlands or that Coastal had already performed a written preliminary wetlands determination the month before. Moreover, in his response to the question whether any analytical tests or inspections had previously been performed on the Property, Handy falsely represented that no "analytical tests or inspections [had] been conducted on the groundwater, surface water, or soil of the Property." By that point Willow Creek had been formed, and Handy was acting as the agent on behalf of all defendants in their efforts to sell the Property.

On September 4, 1997, the defendants, through Willow Creek, settled on and took title to the Property for a purchase price of $174,000. Four months later, the Defendants, again through Willow Creek, sold the Property to Pepsi for $455,000. Willow Creek's members — Handy, Ginsberg, and McKinley — realized a profit of $281,000 on the sale.

After Pepsi learned that the Property contained wetlands, it brought this action for rescission and damages.

II. THE CONTENTIONS

Pepsi's complaint asserts five counts. Those counts allege: (1) violation of the Consumer Fraud Act, (2) common law fraud, (3) equitable fraud, (4) breach of express warranty, and (5) unjust enrichment. Although the counts plead different legal theories, all are grounded upon the same essential pleaded facts, namely that (i) neither Handy nor any other defendant told Pepsi that the Property contained wetlands, and (ii) the defendants knew that if Pepsi had been told about the wetlands, Pepsi would not have paid $455,000 for the Property. . . .

The defendants have moved to dismiss all five. . . . The motion to dismiss does not attack the sufficiency of the claims. Rather, it is grounded upon the argument that even if the claims are legally sufficient, no relief can be granted because there can be no recovery against individual members of the LLC in this particular case. . . .

III. ANALYSIS . . .

The essence of the moving defendants' argument is that the plaintiff cannot recover directly against the movants as LLC members, because none of the movants ever directly held legal or equitable title to the Property. The defendants argue that a plaintiff can recover distributions made to members of an LLC only if (i) the plaintiff pierces the LLC's corporate veil, or (ii) 6 Del. C. §18-607 is applicable. Section 18-607(b) provides that if an LLC member receives a distribution that results in the LLC becoming insolvent, and knew at that time that the LLC would become insolvent as a result of the distribution, the LLC member is liable to the LLC for the amount of the distribution. The defendants argue that because neither of these two circumstances is alleged, the complaint must be dismissed as against Ginsburg, McKinley, and Handy, who are being sued in their capacity as members of Willow Creek.

Any analysis of the defendants' position begins with 6 Del. C. §18-303(a), which codifies the liability of LLC members to third parties. That statute provides:

> Except as otherwise provided by this chapter, the debts, obligations, and liabilities of a limited liability company, whether arising in contract, tort or otherwise, shall be solely the debts, obligations and liabilities of the limited liability company, *and no member or manager of a limited liability company shall be obligated personally for any such debt, obligation or liability of the limited liability company solely by reason of being a member or acting as a manager of the limited liability company.*[16]

Section 18-303(a) protects members and managers of an LLC against liability for any obligations of the LLC solely by reason of being or acting as LLC members or managers. But its phrase, "solely by reason of being a member . . ." does imply that there are situations where LLC members and managers would not be shielded by this provision. As two leading Delaware corporation law treatise commentators have observed:

---

16. [FN 8] 6 Del. C. §18-303(a) (emphasis added). Section 18-202(b) permits an LLC member or manager to agree, in the LLC agreement or other contract, to become obligated personally for any debt, obligation, or liability of the LLC.

The word "solely," which is used in Section 18-303, indicates that a member or manager will not be liable for the debts, obligations, or liabilities of a Delaware LLC only by reason of being a member or manager; however, other acts or events could result in the imposition of liability upon or assumption of liability by a member or manager.[17]

The issue presented is whether the defendants here are being sued "solely by reason of being a member" of Willow Creek (the LLC) where the claim is based upon fraudulent acts committed by the LLC members before the LLC was formed and took title to the Property. To express it in terms of the facts at bar, if a person makes material misrepresentations to induce a purchaser to purchase a parcel of land at a price far above fair market value, and thereafter forms an LLC to purchase and hold the land, can that person later claim that his status as an LLC member protects him from liability to the purchaser under §18-303? I think not.

In this case the complaint alleges that the sequence of relevant events is as follows:

- *April 5, 1997* — Handy contracts to purchase the Property with intent of forming an LLC with Ginsburg and McKinley for the purpose of building a residential community on the Property.
- *April 21, 1997* — Coastal provides conclusive evidence that the Property contains wetlands. Handy, Ginsburg, and McKinley abandon construction plans and instead decide to sell the Property.
- *August 5, 1997* — Pepsi and Handy negotiate an option to purchase the Property. Pepsi discloses its intent to build a bottling facility on the Property and Handy has not disclosed the existence of wetlands.
- *August 18, 1997* — Defendants Handy, Ginsburg, and McKinley form Willow Creek Estates, LLC.
- *During option period* — Pepsi hires Hynes to do Phase I, during which time Hynes specifically asks Handy about the existence of wetlands, to which Handy responds in the negative.
- *September 4, 1997* — The defendants, through Willow Creek, settle and take title to the Property.
- *Four months later* — The defendants, through Willow Creek, sell the unimproved Property to Pepsi for over twice the amount of their purchase price, and do not disclose the existence of wetlands.

Because the facts alleged in the complaint establish that the LLC was not formed (and the Property was not acquired by the LLC) until after the allegedly critical wrongful acts had been committed, it follows that the defendants could

---

17. [FN 9] R. Franklin Balotti and Jesse A. Finkelstein, *The Delaware Law of Corporations & Business Organizations* 20-6 (3rd ed. 1998).

not have been acting "*solely* as members of the LLC when they committed those acts." Therefore, the defendants are not protected by §18-303.

The defendants next argue that they are protected by 6 Del. C. §18-607(a), which provides:

> A limited liability company shall not make a distribution to a member to the extent that at the time of the distribution, after giving effect to the distribution, all liabilities of the limited liability company, other than liabilities to members on account of their limited liability company interests and liabilities for which the recourse of creditors is limited to specified property of the limited liability company, exceed the fair value of the assets of the limited liability company, except that the fair value of property that is subject to a liability for which the recourse of creditors is limited shall be included in the assets of the limited liability company only to the extent that the fair value of that property exceeds that liability.

The movants interpret this language as limiting the right of third parties to bring direct claims against LLC members to cases where the LLC makes a distribution to LLC members who know, at the time, that the distribution would leave the LLC insolvent. Section 12-607(b) provides, in that circumstance, that an LLC member who knew of that fact at the time it received the distribution is liable to the LLC for the amount of the distribution. Here, the defendants contend that (i) §18-607 is the only provision that allows a third party to recover from an LLC member without piercing the LLC's corporate veil, and (ii) because the complaint does not allege a claim under §18-607, they cannot be held liable.

Section 18-607 prohibits the stripping of corporate assets so as to render an LLC insolvent, and creates a corporate cause of action against LLC members who improperly receive a distribution of those assets. The defendants, however, give a far more expansive reading to §18-607 than its language warrants. They claim that the statute shields LLC members against *any* other claims against them; *i.e.,* against *all* claims except those that arise under §18-607. Nothing in §18-607 so provides. Moreover, and as previously discussed, under §18-303, a third party may recover from an LLC member on claims that do not arise "*solely* by reason of being a member or acting as a manager of the limited liability company."

Because all five counts of the complaint are based on conduct that occurred before the LLC was formed, those claims are not barred by §18-303. Under the Limited Liability Company Act, no protection against liability is afforded to LLC members who (as here) are sued in capacities other than as members of the LLC. Accordingly, there is no reason to address the alternative argument that the corporate veil of the LLC must be pierced in order to state a cognizable claim.

For the above reasons, the motion to dismiss Pepsi's claims will be denied. . . .

Questions

1. What is the defendants' argument for why the court should dismiss Pepsi's claims?
2. Why did the court reject this argument?
3. Would the case have come out differently if the alleged fraudulent acts of the defendants occurred (1) after the LLC was formed and took title to the property, and (2) its LLC agreement disclaimed all liability?

H. TRANSFER OF LLC INTERESTS

Similar to the default rule for partnerships and limited partnerships, the default rule under the DLLCA is that an LLC interest is freely transferable but, per DLLCA §18-702(a), "[t]he assignee of a member's limited liability company interest shall have no right to participate in the management of the business and affairs of a limited liability company except as provided in a limited liability company agreement or, unless otherwise provided in the limited liability company agreement, upon the affirmative vote or written consent of all of the members of the limited liability company." DLLCA §18-702(b) further provides:

> Unless otherwise provided in a limited liability company agreement:
> (1) An assignment of a limited liability company interest does not entitle the assignee to become or to exercise any rights or powers of a member; [and]
> (2) An assignment of a limited liability company interest entitles the assignee to share in such profits and losses, to receive such distribution or distributions, and to receive such allocation of income, gain, loss, deduction, or credit or similar item to which the assignor was entitled, to the extent assigned. . . .

Exercise 6.3

Refer again to the APS LLC Agreement at the end of this chapter and answer the following questions. Make sure you note any applicable LLC agreement and/or statutory provision that supports your answer.

1. Watson wants to sell his APS Units to Alan Greenspan. Is this allowed under the LLC Agreement? If so, what formalities are involved?
2. Assuming the sale occurred, does Greenspan have any management rights? Does Watson retain any management rights?
3. Does your answer to Question 2 change if Watson sold his Units to Gray?
4. What additional provisions regarding transfer should perhaps have been included in the LLC Agreement?

I. ALLOCATION OF PROFITS AND LOSSES; DISTRIBUTIONS

Per DLLCA §18-503, the default rule for the allocation of LLC profits and losses is "on the basis of the agreed value (as stated in the records of the limited liability company) of the contributions made by each member to the extent they have been received by the limited liability company and have not been returned." DLLCA §18-504 provides a similar default rule for distributions: "[D]istributions shall be made on the basis of the agreed value (as stated in the records of the limited liability company) of the contributions made by each member to the extent they have been received by the limited liability company and have not been returned." DLLCA §18-101(3) defines "contribution" as "any cash, property, services rendered or a promissory note or other obligation to contribute cash or property or to perform services, which a person contributes to a limited liability company in the person's capacity as a member."

Typically, an LLC agreement will tie ownership interests in an LLC to contributions. In other words, if you contribute cash to an LLC equal to 60 percent of total contributions received by the LLC, you will get a 60 percent ownership interest. Thus, as a general matter, you can think of the default allocation and distribution rules as being based on the ownership interests (or percentages) of an LLC's members.

Exercise 6.4

Refer again to the APS LLC Agreement at the end of this chapter and answer the following questions. Make sure you note any applicable LLC agreement and/or statutory provision that supports your answer. Assume that Watson did not sell his Units.

1. APS earned $200,000 for its latest fiscal year. How are these profits allocated among the Members?
2. How much of this $200,000 is APS required to distribute to the Members?
3. APS decides to distribute $100,000 to its Members. How much of this amount does each Member get?
4. How much does APS owe in federal income tax on the $200,000?

J. DISSOLUTION

DLLCA Subchapter VIII provides for both voluntary and judicial dissolution of an LLC. The next case discusses judicial dissolution. Voluntary dissolution is addressed in DCLLA §18-801. Per that section, the default rule is that an LLC is dissolved and must be wound up at the time specified in the LLC Agreement (if a time is so specified), upon the happening of an event (if any) specified in the LLC Agreement as triggering dissolution, or upon an affirmative vote of members holding more than two-thirds of the LLC's ownership interests.

Haley v. Talcott
864 A.2d 86 (Del. Ch. 2004)

STRINE, Vice Chancellor.

. . . I. FACTUAL BACKGROUND

Haley and Talcott each have a 50 percent interest in Matt & Greg Real Estate, LLC, a Delaware limited liability company they formed in 2003. The creation of the company, however, is only a recent event in the history between the parties.

Haley and Talcott have known each other since the 1980s. In 2001 Haley was the manager of the Rehoboth location of The Third Edition, a restaurant owned by Talcott that also had a location in Washington, D.C. In 2001, Haley found the location for what would become the Redfin Grill. Talcott contributed substantial start-up money and Haley managed the Redfin Grill without drawing a salary for the first year.

The structure of the agreements between the parties forming the Redfin Grill is complex and the subject of additional litigation before this court. For reasons that are not relevant, Haley and Talcott chose to create and operate the Redfin Grill as an entity solely owned by Talcott, with Haley's rights and obligations being defined by a series of contracts. Those agreements, all dated November 30, 2001, included an Employment Agreement, a Retention Bonus Agreement, and a Side Letter Agreement (together, the "Employment Contract"), as well as an Agreement regarding an option to purchase real estate (the "Real Estate Agreement"). . . .

From late 2001 into 2003, under Haley's supervision, the Redfin Grill grew into a successful business. By the second year of its existence, the start-up money had been repaid to Talcott with interest, both parties were drawing salaries (Talcott's substantially smaller since he was not participating in day-to-day management), and the parties each received approximately $150,000 in profit sharing.

In 2003, the parties formed Matt & Greg Real Estate, LLC to take advantage of the option to purchase the Property that was the subject of the Real Estate Agreement. The option price was $720,000 and the new LLC took out a mortgage from County Bank in Rehoboth Beach, Delaware, for that amount, exercised the option, and obtained the deed to the Property on or about May 23, 2003. Importantly, both Haley and Talcott, individually, signed personal guaranties for the entire amount of the mortgage in order to secure the loan. The Redfin Grill continued to operate at the site, paying the LLC $6,000 per month in rent, a payment sufficient to cover the LLC's monthly obligation under the mortgage. Thus by mid-2003, the parties appeared poised to reap the fruits of their labors; unfortunately, at that point their personal relationship began to deteriorate.

Haley, having managed the restaurant from the time it opened in May 2001, and having formalized his management position in the Employment Contract, apparently believed that the relationship would be reformulated to provide him a direct stock ownership interest in the Redfin Grill at some point. The reasons underlying that belief are not important here, but in late October they caused a rift to develop between the parties. On or about October 27, 2003, the conflict that had been brewing between the parties led to some kind of confrontation. As a result, Talcott sent a letter of understanding to Haley dated October 27, 2003, purporting to accept his resignation and forbidding him to enter the premises of the Redfin Grill.

Haley responded on November 3, 2003 with two separate letters from his counsel to Talcott. In the first, Haley asserts that he did not resign, and that he regarded Talcott's October 27, 2003 letter of understanding as terminating him without cause in breach of the Employment Contract. Haley goes on to express his intent to pursue legal remedies, an intent that he acted upon in the related case in this court.

In his second November 3, 2003 letter, Haley purported to take several positions expressly as a 50 percent member in the LLC including: 1) rejecting the new lease proposed by Talcott for the Redfin Grill; 2) voting to revoke any consent to possession by the Redfin Grill and terminating any lease by which the Redfin Grill asserts the right to possession; and 3) voting that the Property be put up for sale on the open market.

Of course, as a 50 percent member, Haley could not force the LLC to take action on these proposals because Talcott opposed them. As a result, the pre-existing status quo continued by virtue of the stalemate — a result that Talcott favored. The Redfin Grill's lease has expired and, as a consequence, the Redfin Grill continues to pay $6,000 per month to the LLC in a month-to-month arrangement. The $6,000 rent exceeds the LLC's required mortgage payment by $800 per month, so the situation remains stable. With only a 50 percent ownership interest, Haley cannot force the termination of the Redfin Grill's lease and evict the Redfin Grill as a tenant; neither can he force the sale of the Property, land that was appraised as of June 14, 2004 at $1.8 million. In short, absent intervention by this court, Haley is stuck, unless he chooses to avail himself of the exit mechanism provided in the LLC Agreement.

That exit mechanism, like judicial dissolution, would provide Haley with his share of the fair market value of the LLC, including the Property. Section 18 of the LLC Agreement provides that upon written notice of election to "quit" the company, the remaining member may elect, in writing, to purchase the departing member's interest for fair market value. If the remaining member elects to purchase the departing member's interest, the parties may agree on fair value, or have the fair value determined by three arbitrators, one chosen by each member and a third chosen by the first two arbitrators. The departing member pays the reasonable expenses of the three arbitrators. Once a fair price is determined, it may be paid in cash, or over a term if secured by: 1) a note signed by the company and personally by the remaining member; 2) a security agreement; and 3) a recorded UCC lien. Only if the remaining member fails to elect to purchase the departing member's interest is the company to be liquidated. . . .

Rather than use the exit mechanism, Haley has simultaneously sought: 1) dissolution of the LLC; and 2) relief in an employment litigation filed against Talcott and Redfin Grill, a case also pending in this court. Haley does not view himself as being obligated by the LLC Agreement to be the one who exits; moreover, he would bear the cost of the exit mechanism and that mechanism, as will be discussed, would not release him from the guaranty.

As a tactical move, Talcott—on the same day as this suit was filed—putatively reinstated Haley as a manager of the Redfin Grill, but with no duties and only $1.00 per year in pay. Talcott claims, however, to recognize Haley's right to 50 percent of the Redfin Grill profits. It appears that Talcott took this step as a method to preempt relief being granted to Haley by a court in lawsuits that Talcott knew were likely to be imminently filed by Haley. Despite the so-called "reinstatement," Talcott and Haley have not had any direct business contact since October 2003.

Haley has moved on since leaving the Redfin Grill in an active capacity, and now operates another restaurant in Lewes, Delaware. Despite his shift in focus, Haley continues to be interested in the Redfin Grill, and has expressed his desire to buy Talcott out of both the LLC and the Redfin Grill itself if given the opportunity. Talcott, by urging the exit remedy provided in the LLC Agreement, has expressed his desire to buy Haley out of the LLC and has no interest in selling the Redfin Grill. Haley continues to refuse to use the exit mechanism.

Pragmatically, the current impasse arises because we have two willing buyers and no willing sellers. Haley alleges that, given this practical dilemma, and his evident inability to effect his desired direction for the LLC, judicial dissolution is his only practicable remedy. . . .

III. LEGAL ANALYSIS

A. *Procedural Framework*

Haley alleges that pursuant to 6 Del. C. §18-802 the court should exercise its discretion and dissolve the LLC because it is not reasonably practicable for it to continue the business of the company in conformity with the LLC Agreement. Section 18-802 provides in its entirety:

> On application by or for a member or manager the Court of Chancery may decree dissolution of a limited liability company whenever it is not reasonably practicable to carry on the business in conformity with a limited liability company agreement.

Haley argues that dissolution is required because the two 50 percent managers cannot agree how to best utilize the sole asset of the LLC, the Property, because no provision exists for breaking a tie in the voting interests, and because the LLC cannot take any actions, such as entering contracts, borrowing or lending money, or buying or selling property, absent a majority vote of its members. Because this circumstance resembles corporate deadlock, Haley urges that 8 Del. C. §273 provides a relevant parallel for analysis. . . .

B. *Case Law Under §273 of the Delaware General Corporate Law ("DGCL") Provides an Appropriate Framework for Analysis*

Section 18-802 of the Delaware LLC Act is a relatively recent addition to our law, and, as a result, there have been few decisions interpreting it. Nevertheless, §18-802 has the obvious purpose of providing an avenue of relief when an LLC cannot continue to function in accordance with its chartering agreement. Thus §18-802 plays a role for LLCs similar to the role that §273 of the DGCL plays for joint venture corporations with only two stockholders. When a limited liability agreement provides for the company to be governed by its members, when there are only two members, and when those members are at permanent odds, §273 provides relevant insight into what should happen. . . .

Section 273 essentially sets forth three pre-requisites for a judicial order of dissolution: 1) the corporation must have two 50 percent stockholders, 2) those stockholders must be engaged in a joint venture, and 3) they must be unable to agree upon whether to discontinue the business or how to dispose of its assets. Here, by analogy, each of the three provisions is indisputably met.

First, there is no dispute that the parties are 50 percent members of the LLC. The LLC agreement provided that both Haley and Talcott would have an initial 50 percent interest in the LLC. . . .

Second, there is no rational doubt that the parties intended to be and are engaged in a joint venture. While the standard for establishing a joint venture has evolved over time, it has always included the circumstances presented here, where two parties "agree[d] for their mutual benefit to combine their skills, property and knowledge, actively managing the business." The relationship between Haley and Talcott indicates active involvement by both parties in creating a restaurant for their mutual benefit and profit, and the Employment Contract shows that Haley was to be the "Operations Director" of the Redfin Grill; a position that, according to the Side Letter Agreement, would only be terminated if the restaurant was sold. Haley was also entitled to a 50 percent share of the Redfin Grill's profits. In short, Haley and Talcott were in it together for as long as they owned the restaurant, equally sharing the profits as provided in the Employment Contract.

Most importantly, Haley never agreed to be a passive investor in the LLC who would be subject to Talcott's unilateral dominion. Instead, the LLC agreement provided that: "no member/managers may, *without the agreement of a majority vote of the managers' interest,* act on behalf of the company." Acts of the company expressly include: borrowing money in the company name; using company property as collateral; binding the company to any obligation such as a guarantor or surety; selling, mortgaging or encumbering any personal or real property of the company except for business purposes for proper consideration; lending company funds; contracting for any debt except for a proper company purpose; and drawing checks on the company account in excess of $5,000. Under these terms, as a 50 percent member/manager, no major action of the LLC could be taken without Haley's approval. Thus, Haley is entitled to a continuing say in the operation of the LLC.

Finally, the evidence clearly supports a finding of deadlock between the parties about the business strategy and future of the LLC. Haley's second letter of November 3, 2003 expresses his desire to end the lease of the Redfin Grill and sell the Property at fair market value. The very fact that dissolution has not occurred, combined with Talcott's opposition in this lawsuit, leads inevitably to the conclusion that Talcott opposes such a disposition of the assets. Neither is Talcott's opposition surprising given his economic interest in the continued success of the Redfin Grill, success that one must assume relies, in part, on a continuing favorable lease arrangement with the LLC.

Talcott suggests that Haley has merely voluntarily removed himself from the management process and that no express disagreement has arisen. This court, however, may consider the totality of the circumstances in determining whether the parties disagree, and only a rational dispute of fact will preclude the entry of summary judgment. Contrary to Talcott's assertion, it is not, at least in a §273 suit, necessary that the parties formally attempt to reach an agreement before coming to court. In any event, it is clear that, through counsel, the parties have made efforts to resolve this impasse.

Moreover, there is no evidentiary support for Talcott's suggestion that the parties are not at an impasse. The parties have not interacted since their falling out in October, 2003. Clearly, Talcott understands that the end of Haley's managerial role from the Redfin Grill profoundly altered their relationship as co-members of the LLC. After all, it has left Haley on the outside, looking in, with no power. Of course, Talcott insists that the LLC can and does continue to function for its intended purpose and in conformity with the agreement, receiving payments from the Redfin Grill and writing checks to meet its obligations under the mortgage on Talcott's authority. But that reality does not mean that the LLC is operating in accordance with the LLC Agreement. Although the LLC is technically functioning at this point, this operation is purely a residual, inertial status quo that just happens to exclusively benefit one of the 50 percent members, Talcott, as illustrated by the hands-tied continuation of the expired lease with the Redfin Grill. With strident disagreement between the parties regarding the appropriate deployment of the asset of the LLC, and open hostility as evidenced by the related suit in this matter, it is not credible that the LLC could, if necessary, take any important action that required a vote of the members. Abundant, uncontradicted documents in the record demonstrate the inability of the parties to function together.

For all these reasons, if the LLC were a corporation, there would be no question that Haley's request to dissolve the entity would be granted. But this case regards an LLC, not a corporation, and more importantly, an LLC with a detailed exit provision. That distinguishing factor must and is considered next.

C. Even Given the Contractual Emphasis of the Delaware LLC Act, the Exit Remedy Provided in the LLC Agreement Is An Insufficient Alternative to Dissolution

The Delaware LLC Act is grounded on principles of freedom of contract. For that reason, the presence of a reasonable exit mechanism bears on the propriety of ordering dissolution under 6 Del. C. §18-802. When the agreement itself provides a fair opportunity for the dissenting member who disfavors the inertial status quo to exit and receive the fair market value of her interest, it is at least arguable that the limited liability company may still proceed to operate practicably under its contractual charter because the charter itself provides an equitable way to break the impasse.

Here, that reasoning might be thought apt because Haley has already "voted" as an LLC member to sell the LLC's only asset, the Property, presumably because he knew he could not secure sole control of both the LLC and the Redfin Grill. Given that reality, so long as Haley can actually extract himself fairly, it arguably makes sense for this court to stay its hand in an LLC case and allow the contract itself to solve the problem.

Notably, reasoning of this nature has been applied in the §273 context. Even under §273, this court's authority to order dissolution remains discretionary and may be influenced by the particular circumstances. Talcott rightly argues that the situation here is somewhat analogous to that in *In re Delaware Bay Surgical Services* where this court declined to dissolve a corporation under §273 in part because a mechanism existed for the repurchase of the complaining member's 50 percent interest.[18]

But, this matter differs from *Surgical Services* in two important respects. First, in *Surgical Services,* the respondent doctor had owned the company before admitting the petitioner to his practice as a 50 percent stakeholder. The court found that both parties clearly intended, upon entering the contract, that if the parties ended their contractual relationship, the respondent would be the one permitted to keep the company. By contrast, no such obvious priority of interest exists here. Haley and Talcott created the LLC together and while the detailed exit provision provided in the formative LLC Agreement allows either party to leave voluntarily, it provides no insight on who should retain the LLC if both parties would prefer to buy the other out, and neither party desires to leave. In and of itself, however, this lack of priority might not be found sufficient to require dissolution, because of a case-specific fact; namely, that Haley has proposed — as a member of the LLC — that the LLC's sole asset be sold. But I need not — and do not — determine how truly distinguishing that fact is, because forcing Haley to ⌐ ✳

---

18. [FN 32] *In re Delaware Bay Surgical Services,* C.A. No. 2121-S (Del. Ch. Jan. 28, 2002) (resolving cross summary judgment motions).

exercise the contractual exit mechanism would not permit the LLC to proceed in a practicable way that accords with the LLC Agreement, but would instead permit Talcott to penalize Haley without express contractual authorization.

Why? Because the parties agree that exit mechanism in the LLC Agreement would not relieve Haley of his obligation under the personal guaranty that he signed to secure the mortgage from County Bank. If Haley is forced to use the exit mechanism, Talcott and he both believe that Haley would still be left holding the bag on the guaranty. It is therefore not equitable to force Haley to use the exit mechanism in this circumstance. While the exit mechanism may be workable in a friendly departure when both parties cooperate to reach an adequate alternative agreement with the bank, the bank cannot be compelled to accept the removal of Haley as a personal guarantor. Thus, the exit mechanism fails as an adequate remedy for Haley because it does not equitably effect the separation of the parties. Rather, it would leave Haley with no upside potential, and no protection over the considerable downside risk that he would have to make good on any future default by the LLC (over whose operations he would have no control) to its mortgage lender. Thus here, unlike in *Surgical Services,* the parties do not, in fact, "have at their disposal a far less drastic means to resolve their personal disagreement."

IV. CONCLUSION

For the reasons discussed above, I find that it is not reasonably practicable for the LLC to continue to carry on business in conformity with the LLC Agreement. The parties shall confer and, within four weeks, submit a plan for the dissolution of the LLC. The plan shall include a procedure to sell the Property owned by the LLC within a commercially reasonable time frame. Either party may, of course, bid on the Property.

IT IS SO ORDERED.

Questions

1. Why is Haley seeking judicial dissolution of the LLC?
2. What is the standard under the applicable statutory provision for when a court can order dissolution?
3. What is Talcott's argument for why judicial dissolution is inappropriate? Why does the court reject this argument?
4. In hindsight, what could Talcott have done differently to avoid this litigation?
5. Does the APS LLC Agreement have an exit mechanism? If not, should it?

Oftentimes the owners of an LLC that is operating a successful business but facing judicial dissolution will work something out to avoid the death of the business. Such was not the case for Haley and Talcott. The LLC was dissolved, and consequently the real estate was sold at auction. Haley was the high bidder at the auction and bought the real estate. He then opened a new restaurant at the location called Bluecoast Seafood Grill.

AAA POOL SERVICES, LLC
LIMITED LIABILITY COMPANY AGREEMENT

THIS LIMITED LIABILITY COMPANY AGREEMENT of AAA Pool Services, LLC is entered into April 24, 2009, by and among the persons named on <u>Schedule 1</u> attached to this Agreement.

Agreement:

The parties agree as follows:

ARTICLE 1

GENERAL

1.1. **Definitions.** Unless the context otherwise specifies or requires, the terms defined in this Article shall, for the purposes of this Agreement, have the following meanings. Certain other capitalized terms used in this Agreement are defined elsewhere in the Agreement.

(a) "**Agreement**" means this Limited Liability Company Agreement of the Company as it may be amended, restated, or supplemented from time to time.

(b) "**Capital Accounts**" means the capital accounts maintained by the Company for each Member in respect of such Member's Units.

(c) "**Capital Contribution**" means the amount of money or the fair market value of any property or services (as agreed by such contributing Member and the Board of Managers) contributed to the Company by any Member.

(d) "**Code**" means the Internal Revenue Code of 1986, as amended, and the Treasury Regulations promulgated thereunder. All references in this Agreement to a section of the Code or the Treasury Regulations shall be considered also to include any subsequent amendment or replacement of that section.

(e) "**Company**" means AAA Pool Services, LLC, a Delaware limited liability company.

(f) "**Manager**" means a natural person elected or appointed to serve on the Board of Managers of the Company.

(g) "**Member**" means any Person who has been admitted to the Company as a member of the Company in accordance with this Agreement and includes any Person admitted as an additional or substituted member of the Company pursuant to the provisions of this Agreement, and "Members" means two (2) or more of such Persons when acting in their capacities as members of the Company.

(h) "**Person**" means any natural person, partnership (whether general or limited), limited liability company, trust, estate, association, corporation, joint venture, proprietorship, governmental agency, custodian, nominee, or any other individual or entity, whether acting in an individual, fiduciary, representative, or other capacity.

(i) "**Total Units**" means the aggregate outstanding Units issued to all Members as of a given date, which Units represent the aggregate ownership interest in the Company as of a given date.

(j) "**Unit**" means the designation which the Company has established to represent the limited liability company interests of its Members in the Company and to represent each Member's share of the profits and losses of the Company and each Member's right to receive distributions of the Company's assets all in accordance with the provisions of this Agreement and the LLC Act.

1.2. **Agreement.** This Agreement is the only agreement which constitutes the "limited liability company agreement" of the Company within the meaning of Section 18-101(7) of the Delaware Limited Liability Company Act, 6 Del. C. §18-101, et seq., as amended from time to time (the "**LLC Act**"). The Members agree to form the Company as a limited liability company under and pursuant to the provisions of the LLC Act and this Agreement and agree that the LLC Act shall govern the rights, duties, and obligations of the Members, except as otherwise expressly stated in this Agreement.

1.3. **Name.** The name of the Company shall be, and the business of the Company shall be conducted under the name of, "AAA Pool Services, LLC."

1.4. **Principal Place of Business.** The location of the principal place of business of the Company shall be 5503 Chula Vista, Tucson, Arizona, 85718, or such other place as the Board of Managers may from time to time determine.

1.5. **Names of Initial Members.** The names of the initial Members are as set forth in Schedule 1.

1.6. **Term of Existence.** The term of the Company commenced as of the time of the filing of the initial certificate of formation of the Company (the "**Certificate**") in the Office of the Secretary of State of Delaware and shall continue until dissolved in accordance with the provisions of this Agreement or the Act.

1.7. **Registered Agent.** The name and address of the Company's registered agent for service of process in the State of Delaware is, until changed by the Board of Managers in its sole discretion, as set forth in the Certificate of Formation.

1.8. **Purposes.** The Company is formed for the object and purpose of, and the nature of the business to be conducted by the Company is, engaging in any lawful act or activity for which limited liability companies may be formed under the LLC Act and engaging in any and all activities necessary, convenient, desirable, or incidental to the foregoing.

ARTICLE 2

CAPITAL; VOTING; ALLOCATIONS; DISTRIBUTIONS

2.1. **Authorized Units.** The Total Units in the Company shall be divided into authorized 1,000 Units. From such authorized number of Units, the Board of Managers may issue some or all of such Units in accordance with the terms of Section 3.1 and any Units so issued shall be reflected in Schedule 1 as updated from time to time.

2.2. **Voting Power.** Each Unit shall entitle the Member owner thereof to one vote on all matters submitted to the vote of the Members.

2.3. **Distributions.**

(a) Sharing. Subject to any restrictions imposed by the LLC Act and the other provisions of this Agreement, all distributions made by the Company shall be made to each Member pro rata based on the number of Units owned by such Member. However, in the event of any changes in Total Units outstanding during a fiscal year, the Board of Managers, in its discretion, may make distributions to Members to reflect such changes in the Total Units outstanding.

(b) As Declared. Distributions may be declared and paid from funds lawfully available therefor as and when determined by the Board of Managers, in its discretion, subject to distributions required to be made under Section 2.3(c).

(c) Tax Burden Distributions. The Company shall distribute to the Members each year an amount sufficient for the Members to pay the taxes owing by the Members from income of the Company allocated to the Members. To the maximum extent practicable, the Company shall make each calendar quarter, at least five days before the due date for the Members to file estimated tax returns for such quarter, the amount required to permit the Members to pay income taxes, including estimated income taxes, on their respective distributive shares of the estimated taxable income of the Company.

2.4. **Allocation of Income, Profits, Gains, Losses, and Credits.** It is the intent of the Members that income, profits, gains, losses, and tax credits of the Company shall be allocated for tax and financial purposes to the maximum extent possible in the same manner in which the Members have the right to receive distributions under Section 2.3 and in the same year in which the Members receive distributions thereunder. Accordingly, the Members agree as follows:

(a) Allocations. Except as required by Section 2.4(b), all income, profits, gains, losses, and tax credits of the Company shall be allocated to each Member pro rata based on the number of Units owned by the Member.

(b) Other Allocations of Taxable Income and Loss.

(i) Discretion of the Board of Managers; Required Tax Allocations. Notwithstanding Section 2.4(a), the Board of Managers, in its discretion and based on consultation with the Company's tax advisors, may allocate any taxable income and loss in any manner other than that expressly set forth in this Agreement if required in order to comply with the Code, including, without limitation, Code Sections 704(b) and 704(c).

(ii) Changes in Total Units. In the event of any changes in Total Units outstanding during a fiscal year, all income, profits, gains, losses, and tax credits from operations of the Company during such fiscal year, using such methods of accounting for depreciation and other items as the Board of Managers determines to use for federal income tax purposes, shall be allocated to each Member owning a Unit in accordance with Section 706 of the Code. The Board of Managers, in its sole discretion, shall determine in accordance with Section 706 of the Code whether to prorate items of income and deduction according to the portion of the year for which a Member owned a Unit or whether to close the books on an interim basis and divide such operating year into two or more segments.

ARTICLE 3

ISSUANCE OF UNITS; ADMISSION OF MEMBERS; CAPITAL ACCOUNTS

3.1. **Issuance of Units.**

(a) Issuance of Units. The Company's initial issuance of Units is as specified on the initial Schedule 1. The Board of Managers is authorized from time to time to accept subscriptions for, issue, sell, and deliver additional Units at such times and upon such terms and conditions as the Board of Managers shall determine. In connection therewith, the Board of Managers shall value all nonmonetary consideration and establish a price in money or other consideration, or a minimum price, or a general formula or method by which the price will be determined.

(b) <u>Price per Unit</u>. Units shall be issued at such price per Unit as determined by the Board of Managers, in its discretion.

(c) <u>Unit Dividends and Splits</u>. The Board of Managers shall have the authority to declare and effect any Unit dividend or Unit split in which the number of issued and outstanding Units are increased or decreased on a ratable basis.

(d) <u>Preemptive Rights</u>. Each Member shall have the right to purchase such Member's pro rata share (determined based on the number of Units held by the Member and the total number of Units outstanding) of any additional Units or rights to acquire Units proposed to be issued by the Company, on the same terms and conditions as that offered by the Company to a third party. A Member shall have ten days after notice of any proposed offering of additional Units or rights to acquire Units, or, if less, ten days after the Board of Managers approved the offering if the Member serves on the Board to exercise such preemptive right by providing written notice thereof to the Company. If the Member does not exercise such right within such time period, the Company may issue such Units or rights to acquire Units to such persons as the Board deems appropriate. Subject to compliance with the foregoing, a Member shall not have any preemptive rights to acquire Units issued upon exercise of rights to acquire Units.

3.2. **Admission of Members Upon Issuance of Units.**

(a) <u>Issuance or Assignment of Units</u>. A Person not a Member purchasing newly issued Units shall be issued the Units and admitted as a Member only upon making or agreeing to make the required contributions for the Units issued to such Person pursuant to <u>Section 3.1</u>, effective when such Person executes or otherwise evidences an intent to be bound by this Agreement. Notwithstanding the foregoing, an assignee of a Member's Units may be admitted as a Member only following approval of the Board of Managers.

(b) <u>Schedule 1</u>. The Board of Managers is authorized from time to time to update <u>Schedule 1</u> attached hereto to reflect the identity of all Members, the Capital Contributions made or agreed to be made and the Units which are issued and outstanding.

3.3. **Registration of Units.**

(a) <u>Register</u>. The Company shall keep at its principal office a register in which shall be entered the names and addresses of the owners of the outstanding Units and all transfers of outstanding Units. References to the owner of a Unit shall mean the Person shown as the owner thereof in such register, and the ownership of a Unit shall be proved by such register. Except as otherwise specifically provided in this Agreement, the registered owner of a Unit shall be deemed to be the owner of such Unit for all purposes of this Agreement.

(b) <u>Certificates</u>. Certificates evidencing the Units owned by a Member may, but need not, be issued by the Company. Such certificates shall serve only as evidence of ownership of the Units identified therein and shall not be assignable.

(c) <u>Registration of a Transfer</u>. Each Unit issued hereunder, whether originally or in substitution for, or upon transfer, exchange or other issuance of a limited liability company interest represented by such Unit, shall be registered on the effective date of the Transfer, exchange, or other issuance as determined in good faith by the Board of Managers on behalf of the Company.

3.4. **Capital Accounts.**

(a) <u>Maintenance of Capital Accounts</u>. A separate Capital Account shall be maintained for each owner of Units. Except as set forth below, the Capital Account of each such owner shall consist of such owner's Capital Contribution, increased by each such owner's respective share of net income (including exempt income) and additional capital contributions, if any, and decreased by each such owner's respective share of net losses (including nondeductible losses and expenses) and distributions from the Company. The Board of Managers, in its discretion and based on consultation with the Company's tax advisors, may maintain and adjust the Capital Accounts in accordance and adjusted in accordance with Treasury Regulation promulgated under Code Section 704(b).

(b) <u>Assignees</u>. If any assignment of a Unit in the Company is permitted hereunder, such permitted assignee shall succeed to the assignor's Capital Account balance effective as of the date of the assignment. Capital Account balances shall not bear interest. A debit or negative balance in a Capital Account balance shall not constitute a liability to the Company by the Member whose Capital Account has a debit or negative balance.

ARTICLE 4

MANAGEMENT AND OPERATION OF THE COMPANY

4.1. **Designation of the Board of Managers as the Managers of the Company.** In accordance with Section 18-402 of the LLC Act and the Company's Certificate, management of the business and affairs of the Company is hereby vested in managers who shall be referred to in this Agreement as Managers. The Managers shall act collectively as the Board of Managers. The individuals serving as Managers shall be elected or designated by the Members as provided in this Agreement, and such Board shall serve as the "Manager" or "Managers" of the Company within the meaning of the LLC Act. Except as otherwise specifically required by the LLC Act or this Agreement, no Member shall have any authority in such

Person's capacity as a Member to manage or control the business and affairs of the Company or otherwise to act for, or to assume any obligations or responsibility on behalf of, or to bind the Company or any other Member of the Company.

4.2. **The Board of Managers.**

(a) <u>Rights and Powers</u>. The Board of Managers shall have the sole right and power to manage the business and affairs of the Company, except as otherwise specifically required by the LLC Act or this Agreement.

(b) <u>Delegation</u>. The Board of Managers shall be entitled to delegate such part of its duties as it may deem reasonable or necessary in the conduct of the business of the Company to one or more officers, employees, or agents of the Company, who shall each have such duties and authority as shall be determined from time to time by the Board of Managers or as may be set forth in this Agreement or any agreement between such Person and the Company.

(c) <u>Number and Election</u>. The Board of Managers shall consist of one or more natural persons. Managers shall be elected by majority of Units outstanding.

(d) <u>Qualification and Term of Office</u>. Managers need not be Members or employees of the Company. A Manager shall hold office until such person's successor shall have been appointed, or until the earlier death, resignation, removal, or disqualification of such Manager.

(e) <u>Initial Board</u>. The persons serving on the Company's initial Board of Managers are as follows:

Thomas J. Gray

George W. Smith

Michael B. Watson

(f) <u>Voting Power</u>. Each Manager shall have one vote on any matters submitted to the vote of the Board of Managers.

(g) <u>Acts of the Board</u>. The Board of Managers shall take action by the affirmative vote of a majority of Managers present at a duly held meeting at the time the action is taken. The Board may also take action without a meeting pursuant to a written document signed by all of the Managers.

(h) <u>Fiduciary Duties</u>. The only fiduciary duty a Manager shall have in connection with serving on the Board of Managers is the duty of loyalty.

4.3. **Officers.** The Company shall have one or more natural persons exercising the functions of the offices, however designated, of Chief Executive Officer and/or President, and Chief Financial Officer or Treasurer. The Board of Managers may elect or appoint such other officers or agents as it deems necessary for the operation and management.

4.4. **Limitation of Liability.**

(a) <u>In General</u>. No Member or Manager or other employee or agent of the Company (each a "**Covered Person**" and collectively, the "**Covered Persons**") shall be liable, responsible, or accountable in damages or otherwise to the Company, or to any Member, for any failure to act or for any acts performed, unless such failure or action constitutes gross negligence or willful misconduct. Except as expressly provided in the LLC Act, no Covered Person shall be obligated personally for any debts, obligations, or liabilities of the Company (whether arising in contract, tort, or otherwise) solely by reason of being a Member or the Manager or agent thereof.

(b) <u>Reliance</u>. To the extent that, at law or in equity, a Covered Person has duties (including fiduciary duties) and liabilities relating thereto to the Company or to any other Covered Person, a Covered Person acting under this Agreement shall not be liable to the Company or to any other Covered Person for its good faith reliance on the provisions of this Agreement. The provisions of this Agreement, to the extent that they restrict the duties and liabilities of a Covered Person otherwise existing in law or in equity, are agreed by the parties hereto to replace such other duties and liabilities of such Covered Person.

4.5. **Indemnification.** To the fullest extent permitted by law, the Company shall indemnify such Covered Persons, for such expenses and liabilities, in the same manner, under the same circumstances, and to the same extent, as such indemnification would be permitted pursuant to Section 145 of the Delaware General Corporation Law (as now enacted or hereafter amended), as fully as if the Company were a corporation subject to such law. For the purposes of applying the provisions of such law, the term "director" shall include Members and the Board of Managers of the Company, and the terms "officer, employee, or agent" shall mean an officer, employee, or agent of the Company, and all references to a "corporation" therein shall be deemed to mean the Company. The adoption after the date hereof of any limitation, prohibition, or restriction in any indemnification provisions of this Agreement shall not affect the right of any Person entitled to indemnification with respect to any acts or omissions of the Person occurring prior to the effective date of the adoption of the limitation, prohibition, or restriction.

ARTICLE 5

MEMBERS

5.1. **Limited Liability of Members.**

(a) <u>Liability Limited</u>. The personal liability of Members is limited as set forth in Section 18-303 of the LLC Act and Section 4.4 of this Agreement.

(b) <u>Nonassessable Units</u>. Each Unit, on issuance, shall be fully paid, and to the fullest extent permitted by the LLC Act, no Member shall be subject to assessment for additional Capital Contributions. No Member shall be required to lend any funds to the Company as a condition to admission or continued membership of such Member in the Company.

(c) <u>Improper Distributions</u>. It is the intent of the Members that no distribution to any Member shall be deemed a return of any money or other property in violation of the LLC Act. The payment of any such money or distribution of any such property to a Member shall be deemed to be a compromise within the meaning of Section 18-502(b) of the LLC Act, and the Member receiving any such money or property shall not be required to return any such money or property to any Person, the Company or any creditor of the Company. However, if any court of competent jurisdiction holds that, notwithstanding the provisions of this Agreement, any Member is obligated to return such money or property, such obligation shall be the obligation of such Member and not of the Board of Managers or any other Member.

5.2. **No Right to Return of Contribution.** Except as provided in this Agreement, no Member shall have the right to withdraw or receive any return of its initial Capital Contribution or any additional Capital Contribution. Under circumstances requiring a return of any Capital Contribution, no Member shall have the right to receive any of the Company's assets other than cash.

5.3. **Loans to the Company.** The Members may, but are not obligated to, make loans to the Company from time to time, as authorized by the Board of Managers. Any such loans shall not be treated as Capital Contributions to the Company for any purpose hereunder nor entitle such Member to any increase in its share of the profits and losses and cash distributions of the Company.

ARTICLE 6

BOOKS OF ACCOUNT; REPORTS AND FISCAL MATTERS

6.1. **Books; Place; Access.** The Company shall maintain books of account on behalf of the Company at the office of the principal executive offices of the Company. Each Member shall at all reasonable times, as determined by the Board of Managers, for any purpose reasonably related to its interest in the Company, have access to and the right to inspect the same at any time during ordinary business hours, subject to reasonable confidentiality obligations with respect thereto, and the Company's right to keep confidential from Members (for such period of time as the Board of Managers deems reasonable) trade secrets, confidential information, proprietary information, personnel records, and subscriber financial information.

6.2. **Fiscal Year.** The fiscal year of the Company shall end on December 31 of each year.

6.3. **Tax Information.** Within 90 days after the close of each fiscal year, all necessary tax information shall be transmitted to all Members.

6.4. **Method of Accounting.** Unless otherwise determined by the Board of Managers, the books and records of the Company shall be in accordance with generally accepted accounting principles.

6.5. **Certain Tax Matters.** The Board of Managers, in its discretion, may cause the Company to make an election under Code Section 754 to adjust basis of Company assets pursuant to either Code Section 734 or Code Section 743, and if any such election is made, taxable income and losses shall be computed and allocated in accordance with the requirements thereof. The Board of Managers shall have the right to designate a member to serve as the "tax matters partner" of the Company.

ARTICLE 7

DISSOLUTION AND LIQUIDATION

7.1. **Events Causing Dissolution.** The Company shall be dissolved and its affairs wound up only upon the occurrence of any of the following events:

(a) _Consent of Members._ The written consent of the Board of Managers and of Members owning a majority of the issued and outstanding Units.

(b) _Termination of Continued Membership of a Member._ The death, insanity, bankruptcy, resignation, retirement, expulsion, or dissolution of a Member or the occurrence of any other event which terminates the continued membership of a Member in the Company, unless the business of the Company is continued by the consent of the remaining Members within 90 days of the termination of the continued membership; provided that such consent is given by Members who own a majority of the Total Units (other than the Units of the terminated Member). However, the Board of Managers may in its discretion, reduce the percentage of Members requiring such consent or waive entirely the requirement for such consent from such Members.

(c) _Sale of Assets._ The sale, transfer, or other disposition of all or substantially all of the assets of the Company.

7.2 **Continued Membership of a Member.** The assignment of all of a Member's Units, the bankruptcy or dissolution of a Member or the occurrence of any other event which terminates the continued membership of a Member in the Company shall not dissolve the Company. Further, no Member shall have the right to resign or retire, nor shall one Member have the right to expel the other Member.

7.3. <u>Liquidation and Winding Up</u>. If dissolution of the Company occurs pursuant to <u>Section 7.1</u>, then the Company shall be liquidated and the Board of Managers (or other Person or Persons designated by a decree of court) shall wind up the affairs of the Company. Unless the business of the Company is continued in a successor entity, the Board of Managers or other Persons winding up the affairs of the Company shall promptly proceed to the liquidation of the Company and, in settling the accounts of the Company, the Company's assets shall be distributed in the following order of priority:

(a) <u>Creditors</u>. To creditors (including any Member and the Managers if they are creditors), to the extent otherwise permitted by law, in satisfaction of liabilities of the Company (whether by payment or the making of reasonable provision for payment thereof), other than liabilities for which reasonable provision for payment has been made and liabilities for distributions to Members;

(b) <u>Remainder</u>. The balance, if any, to the Members pursuant to <u>Section 2.3</u>.

ARTICLE 8

MISCELLANEOUS PROVISIONS

8.1. <u>Additional Actions and Documents</u>. Each of the Members shall take or cause to be taken such further actions and shall execute, acknowledge, deliver, and file, or cause to be executed, acknowledged, delivered, and filed, such further documents and instruments, and to use all reasonable efforts to obtain such consents, as may be necessary or as may be reasonably requested in order to fully effectuate the purposes, terms, and conditions of this Agreement.

8.2. <u>Notice</u>. Any notice, demand, consent, authorization, or other communication which any Member is required or may desire to give to or make hereunder shall be in writing and shall be deemed to be valid and duly given for all purposes when hand-delivered or five (5) business days after it is deposited in the mail if mailed by registered or certified mail, return receipt requested and postage prepaid; if to the Company or any person serving as a Manager thereof, to the principal office of the Company set forth in Section 1.3 or to such other address as the Company shall notify the Members in writing; and if to a Member, to the address set forth in Schedule 1 hereto or in the register maintained by the Company pursuant to Section 3.3(a), or to such other address as any such Member may hereafter designate by notice in writing to the Company.

8.3. <u>Severability</u>. The invalidity of any one or more provisions of this Agreement or of any other agreement or instrument given pursuant to or in connection with this Agreement shall not affect the remaining portions of this Agreement or any such other agreement or instrument or any part thereof; and in the event that one or more of the provisions contained in this Agreement or therein should be invalid, or should operate to render this Agreement or any such other agreement or instrument invalid, this Agreement and such other agreements and instruments shall be construed as if such invalid provisions had not been inserted.

8.4. **Survival.** It is the express intention and agreement of the Members that all covenants, agreements, statements, representations, warranties, and indemnities made in this Agreement shall survive the execution and delivery of this Agreement.

8.5. **Waivers.** Neither the waiver by a Member of a breach of or a default under any of the provisions of this Agreement, nor the failure of a Member, on one or more occasions, to enforce any of the provisions of this Agreement or to exercise any right, remedy, or privilege hereunder shall thereafter be construed as a waiver of any such provisions, rights, remedies, or privileges hereunder.

8.6. **Amendment.** The Board of Managers or any Member or Members owning more than 20 percent of the Total Units issued and outstanding may at any time propose an amendment to this Agreement and shall notify the Members thereof in writing, together with a statement of the purpose(s) of the amendment and such other matters as the Board of Managers or such Member or Members deem material to the consideration of such amendment. Such proposal shall be adopted and this Agreement shall be deemed amended with the written approval of the Board of Managers and the approval of Members owning a majority of the Total Units then outstanding. Any such amendment so adopted shall be binding on all of the Members.

8.7. **Exercise of Rights.** No failure or delay on the part of a Member or the Company in exercising any right, power, or privilege hereunder and no course of dealing between the Members or between a Member and the Company shall operate as a waiver thereof, nor shall any single or partial exercise of any right, power, or privilege hereunder preclude any other or further exercise thereof or the exercise of any other right, power, or privilege. The rights and remedies in this Agreement expressly provided are cumulative and not exclusive of any other rights or remedies which a Member or the Company would otherwise have at law or in equity or otherwise.

8.8. **Binding Effect.** Subject to any provisions of this Agreement restricting assignment, this Agreement shall be binding upon and shall inure to the benefit of the Members and their respective successors and permitted assigns.

8.9. **Limitation on Benefits of this Agreement.** It is the explicit intention of the Members that no person or entity other than the

Members and the Company is or shall be entitled to bring any action to enforce any provision of this Agreement against any Member or the Company, and that the covenants, undertakings, and agreements set forth in this Agreement shall be solely for the benefit of, and shall be enforceable only by, the Members (or their respective heirs, legal representatives, successors, and assigns as permitted hereunder) and the Company; provided, however, that a Covered Person under Section 4.4 or Section 4.5 shall be entitled to enforce the provisions thereof, but only as insofar as the obligations sought to be enforced thereunder are those of the Company.

8.10. **Waiver of Partition.** The Members agree that the Company's assets are not and will not be suitable for partition. The Members hereby waive any right of partition or any right to take any action that otherwise might be available to them for the purpose of severing their relationship with the Company or interest in assets held by the Company from the interest of the other Members.

8.11. **Pronouns.** All pronouns and any variations thereof shall be deemed to refer to the masculine, feminine, neuter, singular or plural, as the identity of the Person may require.

8.12. **Headings.** Article and Section headings contained in this Agreement are inserted for convenience of reference only, shall not be deemed to be a part of this Agreement for any purpose, and shall not in any way define or affect the meaning, construction, or scope of any of the provisions of this Agreement.

8.13. **Governing Law.** This Agreement, the rights and obligations of the parties hereto, and any claims or disputes relating thereto, shall be governed by and construed in accordance with the laws of the State of Delaware.

8.14. **Execution in Counterparts.** To facilitate execution, this Agreement may be executed in as many counterparts as may be required; and it shall not be necessary that the signatures of, or on behalf of, each party, or that the signatures of all Persons required to bind any party, appear on each counterpart; but it shall be sufficient that the signature of, or on behalf of, each party, or that the signatures of the Persons required to bind any party, appear on one or more of the counterparts. All counterparts shall collectively constitute a single agreement. It shall not be necessary in making proof of this Agreement to produce or account for more than a number of counterparts containing the respective signatures of, or on behalf of, all of the parties hereto.

8.15. **Section References.** References to a "Section" are, unless otherwise specified, to one entire whole numbered section (including all subsections thereof) of this Agreement.

To evidence the parties' agreement to this Agreement's provisions, they have executed and delivered this Agreement on the date set forth in the preamble.

The Company: **AAA POOL SERVICES, LLC**

By: /s/ George W. Smith _____

Its: _____ President _____

The Members:

/s/ Thomas J. Gray _____
Thomas J. Gray

/s/ George W. Smith _____
George W. Smith

/s/ Michael B. Watson _____
Michael B. Watson

Schedule 1

AAA POOL SERVICES, LLC

Initial Schedule 1 as of April 24, 1999

Members	Total Capital Contribution	Units Owned	Percentage
Thomas J. Gray 308 4th Street Tucson AZ 85722	$90,000	45	45%
George W. Smith 5899 Main Street Oro Valley AZ 85793	$90,000	45	45%
Michael B. Watson 7 Main Street Tucson AZ 85703	$20,000	10	10%
TOTAL	$200,000	100	100%

· PART III ·

CORPORATIONS

· CHAPTER SEVEN ·

THE INCORPORATION PROCESS

This chapter covers various legal issues relating to the incorporation of a business, including pre-incorporation activities, jurisdiction choice, incorporation mechanics, defective incorporation, and ethical issues.

A. PRE-INCORPORATION ACTIVITIES

A business starts with an idea — a new restaurant concept, smartphone app, bike rickshaw service, medical device, etc. — not with a corporation or other legal entity. A corporation comes into the picture only after the founders have developed the idea into a business plan, decided there is enough potential to warrant moving forward, and that the best legal form for their startup business is a corporation. However, when founders come to you to get a corporation incorporated, oftentimes one or more of them will have already lined up office space, hired a receptionist, ordered supplies, and otherwise entered into contracts.

A person who engages in these sorts of pre-incorporation activities is commonly referred to as a promoter. In this section, we discuss two legal issues related to promoter contracts: (1) whether the promoter is personally liable on a pre-incorporation contract, and (2) whether the corporation is liable on the contract following incorporation.

1. Promoter Liability on Contracts

If things go as planned, the business will get up and running and honor the pre-incorporation contracts signed by a promoter. For example, the corporation will make the rental payments due under the office lease agreement signed by the promoter, and therefore the issue of promoter liability on the lease agreement will never come up.

If, however, the business never gets off the ground or is not interested in the contract and therefore does not make the rental payments, the landlord is likely to look to the promoter to pay out of his or her own pocket. The general rule is that a promoter is personally liable on pre-incorporation contracts even after the corporation is formed. However, the analysis varies depending on how the promoter signed the contract. Specifically, if a promoter signs a contract in his or her own name, the promoter is personally liable under basic principles of contract law—by signing the contract the promoter has manifested an intent to be bound. If instead a promoter signs a contract in the name of a yet-to-be-formed corporation knowing the corporation has not been formed and the other party is unaware that the corporation has not been formed, the promoter is personally liable under the agency law rule that an agent who acts on behalf of a nonexistent principal is personally liable.

The analysis is a bit more complicated if the promoter signs the contract along the lines of the following:

To evidence the parties' agreement to this Lease Agreement, they have signed it on the date stated in the preamble.

Apex Advisers, Inc.
A corporation to be formed

Office Space, LLC

By: __/s/ Edward L. Ford__

By: ___/s/ Alberto Lopez_____

Its: ___Promoter_____

Its: ____Vice President_____

This is because courts have held that a promoter is not liable on a contract if he or she can prove that the other party agreed to look solely to the corporation on the contract. Courts look to the facts and circumstances surrounding the making of the contract at issue to determine whether there was such an agreement. Signing a contract as Ford did above is evidence that there was such an agreement.

Note that §2.04 of the MBCA provides as follows:

> All persons purporting to act as or on behalf of a corporation, knowing there was no incorporation under this Act, are jointly and severally liable for all liabilities created while so acting.

As you can see, this language tracks the general rule for promoter liability, but does not include the exception just discussed. However, the Official Comment to the section states that "the section does not foreclose the possibility that persons who urge defendants to execute contracts in the corporate name knowing that no steps to incorporate have been taken may be estopped to impose personal liability on individual defendants."

2. Corporation Liability on Promoter Contracts

The general rule is that a corporation is not liable on a pre-incorporation contract unless the corporation adopts it. A corporation adopts a contract by manifesting assent to be bound by it. Adoption can only occur after the corporation is formed and is valid only if at the time of adoption the corporation has knowledge of all material facts concerning the contract.

Adoption can either be by express action or implied through conduct. Implied adoption may occur when a corporation receives the benefits of the contract or accepts goods or services under the contract with knowledge of the contract. It can also occur if the corporation makes payments under the contract or attempts to modify or enforce the contact. This is sometimes called adoption through acquiescence.

Some courts also cite ratification as a means by which a corporation can become bound to a pre-incorporation contract. Ratification is similar to adoption in that it involves the corporation manifesting assent to be bound. The distinction between the two is that a corporation is deemed to have been bound to a ratified contract as of the date the contract was executed, whereas a corporation becomes bound to an adopted contract on the date it adopts it. There is some disagreement as to whether a corporation can ratify a contract that was executed before the corporation existed, because under agency law, a purported principal cannot ratify a contract executed before the principal existed.

Adoption does not relieve a promoter from liability on a contract unless the other party agrees to substitute the corporation for the promoter on the contract. This is called novation. Absent a novation, both the corporation and the promoter will be liable on an adopted contract, although the promoter would likely be entitled to indemnification by the corporation if he has to pay out on the contract. A well-informed promoter will include novation language in the pre-incorporation contract, that is, a provision that states the corporation is automatically substituted for the promoter upon incorporation.

B. JURISDICTION OF INCORPORATION

Once a business settles on the corporate form, it then needs to decide in which jurisdiction to incorporate. A business is generally free to choose any of the 50 states or even a non-U.S. jurisdiction. For a business planning to operate in a single state, it usually makes the most sense to incorporate in that state unless the business will need VC funding or plans to go public. For a business that plans to operate in multiple states, that will need VC funding, or that plans on going public, the choice is typically between the state in which the business will be headquartered and Delaware.

Delaware has been the leading non-home state in which to incorporate a business for decades. Hundreds of thousands of businesses are incorporated in Delaware, including more than 50 percent of U.S. publicly traded companies and 63 percent of Fortune 500 companies. Lewis S. Black, Jr., a renowned Delaware corporate lawyer, offers the following explanation for Delaware's preeminence:

> Why do corporations choose Delaware? I think the answer is not one thing but a number of things. It includes the Delaware General Corporation Law, which is one of the most advanced and flexible corporation statutes in the nation. It includes the Delaware courts and, in particular, Delaware's highly respected corporations court, the Court of Chancery. It includes the state legislature, which takes seriously its role in keeping the corporation statute and other business laws current. It includes the Secretary of State's Office, which thinks and acts more like one of the corporations it administers than a government bureaucracy.
>
> There are other, less tangible, factors that go into the mix that make Delaware appealing to corporations and other business forms. There is the fact that Delaware is a small state whose populace is generally pro-business. The people of Delaware are aware that the income received from corporation franchise taxes is an important part of the state budget and that Delaware law firms that specialize in business law matters employ significant numbers of people. As a result, the Delaware citizenry supports the legislature in keeping Delaware's business laws state-of-the-art. There is the fact that lawyers all over the country feel comfortable with Delaware corporation law. Many lawyers have learned Delaware corporation law in law school. Delaware cases are studied in almost every corporations course; hence, American lawyers generally are knowledgeable about Delaware business law. It provides a *lingua franca* for lawyers and an instant credibility that facilitates business transactions. Perhaps the most important element is also the most difficult to articulate. It is the history and tradition that surrounds the Delaware corporation law and, in particular, the Court of Chancery, that invests the law with a predictability and respect that cannot be matched. A law school professor friend of mine was once asked about the merits of creating a national corporation law. He replied: "We already have a national corporation law. It's called the Delaware corporation law." He meant, of course, not just the statute but the case by case development of a common law of corporations that is widely accepted as America corporation law.[1]

Given Black's gushing about Delaware, why would any corporation not incorporate there? Well, a business that operates in a single state will likely save money by incorporating in that state. If it incorporated in Delaware, it would need to pay Delaware filing and other fees for the privilege. It would also need to have a registered office and registered agent in Delaware, which will entail additional expense. Furthermore, it will need to "qualify to do business" in its

---

1. Lewis S. Black, Jr., Why Corporations Choose Delaware, at 1-2 (2007).

home state, which requires paying filing and other fees that are typically higher than the fees for incorporating in the state. If the business instead went with its home state, it would not have to pay Delaware anything or maintain an office there. Nor would it have to qualify to do business in its home state and pay the related fees. It would only have to pay its home state the filing and other fees that state charges for incorporating in the state, fees that are often lower than those charged by Delaware. Additionally, incorporating in Delaware exposes the business to being sued in Delaware. Defending an out-of-state suit is often more expensive and certainly less convenient than litigating in your home state, and the business loses its home court advantage. The bottom line is that incorporating in Delaware has both advantages and disadvantages and for many non-Delaware businesses, the disadvantages outweigh the advantages.

The calculus is slightly more complicated for businesses that will be seeking VC financing and/or are planning on going public. VCs have a bias toward investing in Delaware corporations because of the certainty provided by its deep body of corporate law, a preference for resolving disputes in the Delaware Court of Chancery, and their familiarity and experience with Delaware corporate law. Thus, for example, a South Dakota business that needs to attract VC financing is probably better off incorporating in Delaware, even though it entails additional expenses over a South Dakota incorporation. Otherwise, VCs may pass on investing in the company or require the company to reincorporate[2] in Delaware as a funding condition. Likewise, investment banking firms (firms that take companies public) are biased toward Delaware corporations, because the cachet of a Delaware incorporation makes it easier for them to sell the deal to the public and may result in a higher valuation for the company. Investment bankers have also been known to require a company to reincorporate in Delaware as part of the IPO process.

C. INCORPORATION MECHANICS

You incorporate a corporation by filing "articles of incorporation" or a similarly named document (e.g., Delaware and New York use the term "certificate of incorporation") with the secretary of state of the state in which the client wants the corporation incorporated. The state's corporate law statute will specify what must be included in the articles/certificate of incorporation (this document is often called a "charter" for short, regardless of the term used by the applicable state). The following is a certificate of incorporation form available on the Delaware Secretary of State website:

---

2. "Reincorporate" means change the state of incorporation. A corporation would do so through a merger. For example, say a South Dakota company wanted to reincorporate in Delaware. It would form a Delaware corporation and then merge the South Dakota company into it. Under the merger statute, all of the assets and liabilities of the South Dakota corporation would be transferred to the Delaware corporation by operation of the law, all the outstanding shares of the South Dakota corporation would be automatically converted to shares of the Delaware corporation, and the South Dakota corporation would no longer exist.

STATE *of* DELAWARE
CERTIFICATE *of* INCORPORATION
A STOCK CORPORATION

- **First:** The name of this Corporation is _____
  _____.

- **Second:** Its registered office in the State of Delaware is to be located at _____
  _____ Street, in the City of _____
  County of _____ Zip Code _____. The registered agent in
  charge thereof is _____
  _____.

  Third: The purpose of the corporation is to engage in any lawful act or activity for
  which corporations may be organized under the General Corporation Law of
  Delaware.
- **Fourth:** The amount of the total stock of this corporation is authorized to issue is
  _____ shares (number of authorized shares) with a par value of
  _____ per share.
- **Fifth:** The name and mailing address of the incorporator are as follows:
  Name _____
  Mailing Address_____
  _____ Zip Code _____

- **I, The Undersigned,** for the purpose of forming a corporation under the laws of the
  State of Delaware, do make, file and record this Certificate, and do certify that the
  facts herein stated are true, and I have accordingly hereunto set my hand this
  _____ day of _____, A.D. 20 _____.

BY:_____
(Incorporator)

NAME:[_____]
(type or print)

The form corresponds to Delaware General Corporation Law (DGCL) §102, which specifies the information required to be in a Delaware corporation's certificate of incorporation. As you can see, not a lot of information is required, as is the case under all states' corporate law statutes.

1. Name Selection

As the "First" line indicates, forming a corporation requires picking a name. States typically require that the name be distinguishable from all existing names on record with the secretary of state. The principal justification for this requirement is to prevent confusion within the secretary of state's office, state tax authority, and litigants desiring to name and serve a corporation. Names of record include the names of all entities incorporated in the state and all foreign entities qualified to do business in the state as well as trade names registered in the state. Arizona provides the following guidance on the meaning of "distinguishable":

> A "distinguishable" name is one that is different in any way except for differences in (a) corporation designation (Inc, LLC, Corporation, etc.), (b) spaces between words ("roll out now co." vs. "rollout now co."), (c) specific punctuation ("Great Expectations" vs. "Great Expectations!"), (d) the case of the letters contained in the name ("TOO COOL" vs. "Too Cool"), (e) the use of ampersand (&) versus "and" ("U & I Inc." vs. "U AND I Inc."), (f) the use of Arabic numerals (1, 2, 3, etc.) and words representing these numerals ("One Stop LLC" vs. "1 Stop LLC") and (g) the use of the articles "a," "an" and "the" (A Birdcage vs. The Birdcage).

Upon receipt of a charter, a secretary of state clerk will check the name you have listed for the corporation against the names on record. If the clerk determines that the name you listed is not distinguishable, he or she will reject your filing. Most states allow you to check name availability online and reserve an available name in advance of filing to ensure it is still available when you file your document.

The fact that a secretary of state search indicates a particular name is available says nothing about whether the name has been registered as a trademark with the U.S. Patent and Trademark Office (PTO). A trademark is a word, phrase, symbol, or design (or combination of any of the foregoing) that identifies and distinguishes the source of one good from another. For example, the trademark "Coke" distinguishes the cola drink made by The Coca-Cola Company from the cola drink made by Pepsi Co, Inc. Registering a trademark with the PTO generally provides the trademark owner with the exclusive right to use the mark nationwide on or in connection with the goods/services listed in the registration.

Thus, say you want to name your rickshaw business "Kona Rickshaw Services Inc." You do a name availability search on the applicable secretary of state website and determine that the name is available. Thus, you prepare articles of incorporation listing this name, and the articles are accepted by the secretary of state. You may nonetheless get a cease and desist letter from Kona USA Inc., the owner of the trademark "Kona" for use on bikes, essentially telling you to change your business's name or get sued for trademark infringement. A small business in this situation usually opts for changing its name instead of hiring a trademark attorney to do battle. This means redoing signage, letterhead, business cards, etc. The best way to keep this from happening is to make sure a proposed name is not already trademarked for use on goods/services similar to what your business provides. You can do a trademark search yourself on the

PTO's website[3] or hire a professional to do it for you. You may then want to register the name as a trademark with the PTO so you can send out some of your own cease and desist letters.

In addition to a distinguishable requirement, most states require that a corporation's name contain a designation alerting those doing business with the company that they are dealing with a corporation. For example, MBCA §4.01(a) provides, "A corporate name . . . must contain the word 'corporation,' 'incorporated,' 'company,' or 'limited,' or the abbreviation 'corp.,' 'inc.,' 'co.,' or 'ltd.,' or words or abbreviations of like import in another language. . . ."

2. Authorized Shares

Probably, the only issue of substance you would discuss with the client in filling out the form is what numbers to put in the blanks in the "Fourth" line. You use the first blank to indicate the number of shares of stock the corporation will be authorized to issue. This number is referred to as the corporation's "authorized shares" and represents the maximum number of shares the corporation has the authority to issue. A corporation issues shares when, for example, it sells stock to an investor.

You use the second blank to set the par value of the corporation's shares. Par value is the *minimum* amount of consideration the corporation must receive when issuing a share. It is not the price at which the corporation has to sell shares. For example, say a corporation sets its par value at $10.00 per share. (If it is using the above form, it would do this by writing $10.00 in the second blank of the fourth bullet point.) This would mean it must receive at least $10.00 worth of consideration for each share it issues. If it issues you 100 shares, it must receive at least $1,000.00 in consideration. Typically, the consideration is money, but a corporation may issue shares in exchange for property or services. The corporation, however, is free to charge more than $10.00 per share. Additionally, par value only sets the minimum price for the corporation. It has no impact on the price at which you could sell your 100 shares to someone else. For example, if the corporation's business has faltered, $5.00 per share may be the most someone is willing to pay you for your shares.

Historically, par value was used to assure early investors that the corporation would not later sell shares for less than they paid. For example, if the initial investors were to buy shares at $8.00 per share, they may insist that the par value of the shares be set at $8.00. The problem with doing this is that it hinders a corporation's ability to raise money if the business's prospects have diminished, and therefore no one is willing to pay $8.00 per share for its shares any longer. Hence, to avoid this type of problem, today it is customary to set par value at

---

3. Note that a PTO trademark search only covers names that applicants have registered, or applied for registration, with the PTO. Common law trademark rights may accrue to a business simply by using a name in commerce. A professional search is designed to pick up uses that have not been registered with the PTO.

a nominal amount, such as one cent or even one-tenth of a cent per share. In fact, Delaware allows a corporation to have shares without par value by saying so in its certificate (see DGCL §102(a)(4)). The MBCA does not require shares to have par value or par value to even be mentioned in a corporation's articles. As a result, par value has little relevance today.

You can set authorized shares at any number, but in some states, including Delaware, the amount the corporation has to pay to file its charter and annual fee is based on the number of authorized shares it has. As a result, in a state like Delaware, if feasible, you want to set authorized shares at the highest possible number that still allows the corporation to pay the minimum filing fee and annual fee. In Delaware, this number is 5,000. In other words, if you were using the above form, you would insert "5,000" in the first blank of bullet point four. The resulting filing fee would be $89.00 and franchise tax (the Delaware term of annual fee) would be $75.00. If you expect that the corporation will need to issue more than 5,000 shares, you will obviously have to set the number higher, and the corporation will then have to pay a higher filing fee and/or franchise tax. For example, the filing fee for a Delaware corporation with 1 million authorized shares with a par value of $0.01 would still be only $89.00 but its franchise tax would jump to $7,575.00.[4] The maximum Delaware franchise tax is $180,000.00, which a corporation will be required to pay if it has 23,990,000 authorized shares or more.

Many states simply charge a corporation a flat filing and annual fee. For example, Arizona charges $60.00 for filing articles of incorporation and a $45.00 annual fee, regardless of how many authorized shares a corporation has. Delaware is able to charge more because a Delaware incorporation is a premium product.

Notice that the Delaware form includes a purpose provision (see the third bullet point) as such a provision is required by DGCL §102(a)(3). Most corporations go with a purpose provision that is as broad as possible, and thus Delaware builds as broad as a purpose possible into the form. A corporation is free to specify a narrower purpose, but doing so raises the issue of *ultra vires*, and is therefore typically avoided unless required by applicable regulations. (For example, some states' bank regulations require a corporation engaged in banking to include a purpose clause limiting the corporation's purpose to banking and related activities.) *Ultra vires* means "beyond the powers" in Latin and prohibits a corporation from acting beyond its purpose. Under the doctrine, a corporate act that exceeds its purpose is invalid. The MBCA allows, but does not require, articles of incorporation to include a purpose, so most corporations incorporated in MBCA states do not include one.

While the above form meets the requirements of the DGCL, it is rarely used in practice. This is in part because lawyers routinely want to include in a certificate optional provisions that go beyond the form. For example, the form only

---

4. *See* http://corp.delaware.gov/fee.shtml for links to a "New Company Filing Fee Calculator," and a "Franchise Tax Calculator."

provides for a single class of stock (typically referred to as common stock), but oftentimes a corporation will want the ability to issue both common and preferred stock. Thus, its certificate will need to set forth the number of shares of common stock, and the number of shares of preferred stock the corporation is authorized to issue as well as the rights and preferences of the preferred stock. The characteristics of common and preferred stock are discussed in Chapter 8.

As a general rule, you only include in the charter required provisions and desired optional provisions that the statute requires to be set forth in the charter. Everything else you put in the bylaws. This is because a corporation's charter is a public document and is more difficult and costly to amend than its bylaws.

All states require the charter to list the name (and usually the address) of the incorporator and to be signed by the incorporator. An incorporator is simply the person listed in the charter as such and can be anyone. It is common for the attorney who drafted the charter to list him- or herself as incorporator.

Once the charter is finalized, you send it to the secretary of state office along with the required filing fee. A clerk at the office reviews the charter to make sure it meets the statutory requirements. If everything appears to be in order, the clerk accepts the filing, at which point the corporation comes into existence. (Most states date stamp the filing so that the date of incorporation is clear.)

3. Organization of the Corporation

After incorporation, the incorporator needs to elect the corporation's board of directors.[5] This is normally done by the incorporator signing a "written consent," which is simply a document along the lines of the following:[6]

**WRITTEN CONSENT
OF
SOLE INCORPORATOR
OF
CLARE'S CONERY, INC.**

The undersigned sole incorporator of Clare's Conery, Inc., an Arizona corporation, hereby consents to the adoption of the following resolution as and for the action of the sole incorporator without a meeting thereof:

RESOLVED, that Clare T. Holmes and Maria R. Holmes are hereby elected directors of the corporation to serve until the first regular meeting of stockholders or until their successors shall be elected and qualified, subject to their earlier death, disqualification, resignation, or removal.

---

5. This step is not taken if the names of initial directors are included in the charter. Most corporations, however, do not include them.
6. *See* DGCL §108; MBCA §2.05.

The undersigned has executed this consent effective as of August 10, 2012.

/s/ William K. Sjostrom, Jr.
William K. Sjostrom, Jr.
Sole Incorporator

Once the directors are elected, the board needs to complete the organization of the corporation by, at a minimum, adopting bylaws, appointing officers, and approving stock issuances. This can be done at the first official board meeting, but is more commonly done by having all the directors sign a written consent covering these matters.[7] If it is done at a meeting, someone will need to prepare minutes for the meeting that specify any resolutions voted on by the board and whether they passed. The attorney handling the incorporation typically prepares the bylaws, board resolutions or written consent, and a shareholder agreement if one is desired. (We discuss shareholder agreements in Chapter 12.) At least for closely held corporations, the corporation's charter, bylaws, written consents, meeting minutes, stock ledger, and copies of issued stock certificates are normally maintained by the corporation's corporate attorney in a three-ring binder called a corporate record book.

Here is a sample written consent for the organization of Clare's Conery, Inc.

UNANIMOUS CONSENT OF
THE BOARD OF DIRECTORS OF
CLARE'S CONERY, INC.

The undersigned, being all of the directors of Clare's Conery, Inc., an Arizona corporation, hereby consent to the adoption of the following resolutions as and for the action of the Board of Directors without a meeting thereof, in accordance with Section 8.21 of the Model Business Corporation Act:

ACTIONS OF INCORPORATOR

RESOLVED that all actions of the incorporator as disclosed by the written Consent of Sole Incorporator or upon the public records be, and the same hereby are, in all things ratified, confirmed, and adopted as the acts and deeds of the corporation.

---

7. *See* DGCL §141(f); MBCA §8.21.

BYLAWS

RESOLVED that the bylaws presented to and reviewed by the Directors and incorporated herein by reference be, and the same hereby are, adopted as the bylaws of the corporation, and the secretary is hereby directed to file them in the minute books of the corporation and to authenticate them by certificate.

OFFICERS

RESOLVED that Clare T. Holmes be and hereby is elected to the offices of President, Treasurer, and Secretary, subject to her earlier disqualification, resignation, or removal.

STOCK SUBSCRIPTIONS

RESOLVED that the stock subscription of Clare T. Holmes annexed hereto be, and it hereby is, accepted, and upon receipt by the corporation of the consideration set forth therein, the secretary of the corporation is hereby authorized and directed to issue the corporation's shares to the subscriber in accordance with such subscription, which shares, when so issued, shall be fully paid and non-assessable.

ORGANIZATIONAL EXPENSES

RESOLVED that any officer of the corporation hereby is authorized and directed to pay all fees and expenses incidental to and necessary for the organization of the corporation. Pursuant to Section 248 of the Internal Revenue Code of 1986, as amended, and the regulations thereunder, the corporation hereby elects to deduct its organization expenditures ratably over a period of 60 months commencing in the month in which it begins doing business; and the proper officers of the corporation hereby are authorized and directed to do and perform any and all acts and deeds necessary to make the foregoing election effective.

STOCK CERTIFICATE

RESOLVED that the form of stock certificate annexed hereto be, and it hereby is, approved and adopted.

FOREIGN QUALIFICATION

RESOLVED that for the purpose of authorizing the corporation to do business in any state, territory, or dependency of the United States or any foreign country in which it is necessary or expedient for the corporation to transact business, the proper officers of this corporation are hereby authorized to appoint and substitute all necessary agents or attorneys for service of process, to designate and change the location of all necessary statutory offices and to make and file all necessary applications, certificates, reports, powers of attorney, and other instruments as may be required by the laws of such state, territory, dependency, or country to authorize the corporation to transact business therein; and whenever it is expedient for the corporation to cease doing business therein and withdraw therefrom, to revoke any appointment of agent or attorney for service of process, and to file such certificates, reports, revocation of appointment, or surrender of authority as may be necessary to terminate the authority of the corporation to do business in any such state, territory, dependency, or country.

IN WITNESS WHEREOF, the undersigned have executed these resolutions effective as of August 10, 2012.

_____

Clare T. Holmes

_____

Maria R. Holmes

All of the above can be accomplished in a matter of hours, if not less. In other words, a corporation can be formed and organized rapidly, if need be. In that regard, many states offer expedited processing of a charter filing for a fee. For example, Delaware will process a certificate of incorporation the same day for an extra $100.00, within two hours for an extra $500.00, and within one hour for an extra $1,000.00.

Exercise 7.1

1. Below are draft articles of incorporation to be filed in Arizona. What changes would you make to the draft? Assume that Arizona has adopted the current version of the MBCA verbatim.

ARTICLES OF INCORPORATION
OF
CLARE'S CONERY

1. The name of the corporation is Clare's Conery.
2. The corporation is authorized to issue 10 billion shares of common stock and preferred stock.
3. The street address of the corporation's registered office is 100 Waffle Cone Way, Globe, Arizona 85501.
4. The purpose of the corporation is to operate an ice cream parlor in Globe Arizona.
5. No shareholder shall be personally liable for the debts or obligations of the corporation.
6. The number of directors of the Corporation shall be one.
7. No director or officer of the company shall be liable to the corporation or any of its stockholders for money damages for any action taken, or any failure to take any action, as a director or officer.
8. These articles may be amended, altered, or modified at any time by the board of directors.

_____
Clare Holmes, Incorporator

[handwritten margin notes: agent name, par value $, purpose provision, common/preferred stock]

2. What additional changes would you need to make so that the above document meets the requirements for filing in Delaware?
3. You have a meeting tomorrow with Clare about incorporating her business. Make a list of questions to ask her.

4. Doing Business in Other States

A corporation operating in its state of incorporation is referred to in that state as a "domestic" corporation. A corporation operating in a state other than its state of incorporation is referred to in that state as a "foreign" corporation. Most states require any foreign corporation transacting business in the state to obtain a certificate of authority from the secretary of state. This is often referred to as "qualifying to do business" in a state. To obtain a certificate of authority, the corporation needs to fill out a form and pay a filing fee. Here's a sample form for qualifying in Kentucky:

C. Incorporation Mechanics

COMMONWEALTH OF KENTUCKY
ELAINE N. WALKER, SECRETARY OF STATE

Division of Corporations **Business Filings** PO Box 718 Frankfort, KY 40602 (502) 564-3490 www.sos.ky.gov	Certificate of Authority (Foreign Business Entity)	**FBE**

Pursuant to the provisions of KRS 14A and KRS 271B, 273, 274,275, 362 and 386 the undersigned hereby applies for authority to transact business in Kentucky on behalf of the entity named below and, for that purpose, submits the following statements:

1. The entity is a :   ☐ profit corporation (KRS 271B). ☐ nonprofit corporation (KRS 273). ☐ professional service corporation (KRS 274).
☐ business trust (KRS 386). ☐ limited liability company (KRS 275). ☐ professional limited liability company (KRS 275).
☐ limited partnership (KRS 362).

2. The name of the entity is _____
(The name must be identical to the name on record with the Secretary of State.)

3. The name of the entity to be used in Kentucky is (if applicable): _____
(Only provide if "real name" is unavailable for use; otherwise, leave blank.)

4. The state or country under whose law the entity is organized is _____

5. The date of organization is _____ and the period of duration is _____
(If left blank, the period of duration
is considered perpetual.)

6. The mailing address of the entity's principal office is

_____
Street Address   **City**   **State**   **Zip Code**

7. The street address of the entity's registered office in Kentucky is

_____
Street Address (No P.O. Box Numbers)   **City**   **State**   **Zip Code**

and the name of the registered agent at that office is _____

8. The names and business addresses of the entity's representatives (secretary, officers and directors, managers, trustees or general partners):

Name	**Street or P.O. Box**	**City**	**State**	**Zip Code**
Name	**Street or P.O. Box**	**City**	**State**	**Zip Code**
Name	**Street or P.O. Box**	**City**	**State**	**Zip Code**

9. If a professional service corporation, all the individual shareholders, not less than one half (1/2) of the directors, and all of the officers other than the secretary and treasurer are licensed in one or more states or territories of the United States or District of Columbia to render a professional service described in the statement of purposes of the corporation.

10. I certify that, as of the date of filing this application, the above-named entity validly exists under the laws of the jurisdiction of its formation.

11. If a limited partnership, it elects to be a limited liability limited partnership.   Check the box if applicable: ☐

12. This application will be effective upon filing, unless a delayed effective date and/or time is provided.
The effective date or the delayed effective date cannot be prior to the date the application is filed. The date and/or time is _____
(Delayed effective date and/or time)

_____
Signature of Authorized Representative   **Printed Name & Title**   **Date**

I, _____ , consent to serve as the registered agent on behalf of the business entity.
Type/Print Name of Registered Agent

_____
Signature of Registered Agent   **Printed Name**   **Title**   **Date**

(01/11)

As is standard, the form requires the corporation (or other type of entity) to specify a registered office in Kentucky and a registered agent at that office (see item 7). Many companies that transact business in a state do not have a location in the state or do not want qualification-related paperwork to be sent to their location in the state (e.g., a manufacturing plant) for fear of the paperwork being mishandled. Hence, a number of business services companies have offices and agents in every state (typically located in the state's capital) that will serve as a corporation's registered office and registered agent for a fee.

Additionally, states typically require the foreign corporation's name to be distinguishable from all existing names on record with the secretary of state. If a foreign corporation's name is not distinguishable, it can still qualify in the state, but it will have to operate under a different name. This is contemplated by item 3 of the Kentucky form.

Qualifying to do business in a state has several consequences. First, the foreign corporation will have to pay the annual fee/franchise tax charged by the state. Second, the foreign corporation will be subject to service of process in the state. Third, the foreign corporation will have to file an annual report with the state.

As a result, it is common for a corporation to take the position that it is not transacting business in a particular state so that it can avoid these consequences. It is also common for a state to send a letter to a foreign corporation with activities in the state informing the corporation that it has to qualify in the state. This corporation is likely to respond by arguing that its activities do not constitute "transacting business." Because state statutes do not define the phrase precisely, its meaning periodically comes up in litigation, as exemplified by the following case.

Harold Lang Jewelers, Inc. v. Johnson
576 S.E.2d 360 (N.C. App. 2002)

HUDSON, Judge.

Appellant Harold Lang Jewelers, Inc. ("Lang"), a Florida corporation, filed suit against the appellees ("Johnson"). As one of its affirmative defenses, Johnson argued that Lang could not sue in a North Carolina court because Lang was transacting business in the state without a certificate of authority to do so. The trial court agreed and dismissed the suit prior to trial. Lang appealed. For the reasons set forth below, we affirm the decision of the trial court.

Lang filed suit in April 1999, alleging that Johnson owed it $160,322.90 plus interest for jewelry sold or consigned. Johnson answered in May 1999, asserting as one of its eight affirmative defenses that Lang could not sue in a North Carolina court because Lang had failed to obtain a certificate of authority to transact business in the state. On January 7, 2002, the case was called for trial. At that time, Johnson orally raised the defense of Lang's failure to obtain a certificate of authority and requested a hearing on that issue. After hearing evidence and argument, the district court granted the motion and dismissed Lang's action. Lang now appeals. . . .

Lang argues that the trial court did not find sufficient facts to support its conclusion that Lang was, in fact, transacting business in the state of North Carolina. Again, we disagree.

To "transact business" is defined by statute and common law. Specifically, N.C. Gen. Stat. §55-15-01 sets forth examples of when a foreign corporation is NOT transacting business:

(1) Maintaining or defending any action or suit or any administrative or arbitration proceeding, or effecting the settlement thereof or the settlement of claims or disputes;

(2) Holding meetings of its directors or shareholders or carrying on other activities concerning its internal affairs;

(3) Maintaining bank accounts or borrowing money in this State, with or without security, even if such borrowings are repeated and continuous transactions;

(4) Maintaining offices or agencies for the transfer, exchange, and registration of its securities, or appointing and maintaining trustees or depositories with relation to its securities;

(5) Soliciting or procuring orders, whether by mail or through employees or agents or otherwise, where such orders require acceptance without this State before becoming binding contracts;

(6) Making or investing in loans with or without security including servicing of mortgages or deeds of trust through independent agencies within the State, the conducting of foreclosure proceedings and sale, the acquiring of property at foreclosure sale and the management and rental of such property for a reasonable time while liquidating its investment, provided no office or agency therefor is maintained in this State;

(7) Taking security for or collecting debts due to it or enforcing any rights in property securing the same;

(8) Transacting business in interstate commerce;

(9) Conducting an isolated transaction completed within a period of six months and not in the course of a number of repeated transactions of like nature;

(10) Selling through independent contractors;

(11) Owning, without more, real or personal property.

N.C. Gen. Stat. §55-15-01(b). Our courts have interpreted transacting business in the state to "require the engaging in, carrying on or exercising, in North Carolina, some of the functions for which the corporation was created." The business done by the corporation must be of such nature and character "as to warrant the inference that the corporation has subjected itself to the local jurisdiction and is, by its duly authorized officers and agents, present within the State." *Spartan Equip. Co. v. Air Placement Equip. Co.*, 263 N.C. 549, 556, 140 S.E.2d 3, 9 (1965). In other words, the activities carried on by the corporation in North Carolina must be substantial, continuous, systematic, and regular.

Here, the trial court concluded that Lang's business activity in North Carolina was regular, continuous, and substantial such that it was transacting business in the state. We uphold this conclusion only if it is supported by the findings of fact, and, contrary to Lang's assertion, we hold that it is.

Specifically, the court found that Lang, through its single employee, had sold and consigned merchandise to jewelry stores in Franklin, Asheville and Highlands, North Carolina, since 1970. The court also found that Lang's employee came to North Carolina at least twice every six weeks during the year and at least twice every four weeks during the summer months for the purpose of transacting business. Sometimes he came to North Carolina to transact business as often as three times a month. The court found that when the employee came to North Carolina, he always brought jewelry with him for delivery. When he visited jewelry stores in the state, he would either (1) make a direct sale on the spot without any confirmation from any other person or corporation in any other place or (2) consign the jewelry, also without any further confirmation or approval from any other person or corporation anywhere. When the employee took orders, he either shipped the ordered items to the business in North Carolina or personally delivered the merchandise. He also took returns of merchandise from customers in the state. The court further found that the business that Lang conducted in North Carolina did not require it to communicate with any other person or seek any authority from any other person.

In sum, we conclude that the trial court's conclusions of law are adequately supported by the facts found in this case. There is ample evidence that Lang's business in this state has been regular, systematic, and extensive. Lang has been coming to North Carolina since about 1970 to sell and consign merchandise to several jewelry stores. In fact, Lang routinely came to North Carolina as frequently as twice every four weeks during some parts of the year, and each time he brought with him merchandise to deliver. Moreover, the orders did not require "acceptance without this State before becoming binding contracts" (N.C. Gen. Stat. §55-15-01(b)(5)); instead, Lang's employee finalized the sales in North Carolina. Accordingly, Lang's assignments of error on this ground are overruled.

Finally, Lang contends that the trial court erred when it dismissed the action, arguing that the court should have continued the case to permit Lang to obtain the requisite certificate of authority. The applicable statute, N.C. Gen. Stat. §55-15-02, does not specify the procedure in the event of failure to obtain a certificate of authority. The statute simply indicates that an action cannot be maintained unless the certificate is obtained prior to trial. N.C. Gen. Stat. §55-15-02(a). Lang has not cited, nor have we found, a case where a continuance has been granted by a court in these circumstances. Moreover, Lang was aware that Johnson's motion was pending and could have obtained the certificate in the year and a half that passed between the filing of the motion and the court's dismissal of the case. In the absence of statutory or other authority dictating a continuance, we hold that the trial court acted within its discretion in dismissing the action.

For the reasons set forth above, we affirm the decision of the trial court. Affirmed.

Questions

1. What test does the court provide for what constitutes "transacting business"?
2. What facts does the court point to for upholding the trial court's decision that Lang was transacting business in North Carolina?
3. What could Lang have done differently to still sell in North Carolina, but not be "transacting business" in North Carolina?

N.C. Gen. Stat. §55-15-01 reflects a common approach among states of defining what constitutes "transacting business" in the negative. Note that the list goes only to whether a corporation does not have to qualify in the state notwithstanding various contacts. The list is not applicable to whether a corporation is subject to personal jurisdiction or taxation in the state, as these questions are addressed under different statutes. It is common for a corporation to be subject to one or the other or both and yet not be "transacting business" in the state.

The *Lang* case mentions one of the consequences for a corporation that transacts business in a state but does not qualify—the corporation will not be allowed to maintain an action in any court of the state. A corporation is, however, free to qualify in anticipation of bringing a suit, so this consequence is somewhat insignificant. Another consequence is that the state may impose a monetary penalty on the corporation. For example, §2203(a) of the California Corporation Code provides, "Any foreign corporation which does not hold a valid certificate from the Secretary of State may be subject to a penalty of twenty dollars ($20) for each day that unauthorized intrastate business is transacted. . . ." A few state statutes go as far as voiding the contracts of an unqualified corporation. For example, §10-2B-15.02(a) of the Alabama Corporations statute provides, "All contracts or agreements made or entered into in this state by foreign corporations prior to obtaining a certificate of authority to transact business in this state shall be held void at the action of the foreign corporation or by any person claiming through or under the foreign corporation by virtue of the contract or agreement; but nothing in this section shall abrogate the equitable rule that he who seeks equity must do equity."

D. DEFECTIVE INCORPORATION

Occasionally, a business decides to go with the corporate form, gets up and running, but because of an unknown foul-up with its secretary of state paperwork (someone forgets to mail it, it gets lost in the mail, it gets rejected, etc.), the corporation does not actually get incorporated. Once the mishap is discovered, it is easy enough to fix. The paperwork is redone and perhaps this time hand-delivered to the secretary of state office. The corporation then formally adopts any contracts someone entered into on its behalf before it existed and everyone goes about their business.

Sometimes, however, a dispute arises concerning a contract signed by the business in the name of the corporation when, because of the foul-up, the corporation did not actually exist. The other side then discovers the defective incorporation and thus argues that the person signing on behalf of the nonexistent corporation is personally liable. It will likely also argue that the business is by default a partnership and thus the non-signing owners are personally liable, too.

Under agency law and partnership law, the other side should win.[8] However, courts have recognized that, in many cases, this would be a rather harsh result. The other side entered into the contract thinking it had no recourse against the signer or owners, yet because of a technicality, these people are now unexpectedly personally liable. Thus, courts have developed two doctrines — de facto corporation and corporation by estoppel — that may save the signer or owners from this unexpected liability. Both of these doctrines are outlined in the case below.

Pharmaceutical Sales and Consulting Corp. v. J.W.S. Delavau Co.
59 F. Supp. 2d 398 (D.N.J. 1999)

COOPER, J.

This matter comes before the Court on the motion by defendant J.W.S. Delavau, Co., Inc. ("Delavau") to dismiss plaintiff's Complaint pursuant to Federal Rules of Civil Procedure 17(b) and 12(b)(1). For the reasons expressed herein, defendant's motion is denied.

BACKGROUND

Plaintiff Pharmaceutical Sales and Consulting Corporation ("PSCC") filed this action in the New Jersey Superior Court on October 16, 1995. Defendant subsequently removed the action to this Court. Plaintiff and defendant entered into a Sales, Consulting and Confidential Disclosure Agreement ("the Agreement") whereby Delavau was to pay PSCC a commission for sales PSCC brought to Delavau from Lederle Laboratories, Inc. The Agreement was executed on July 1, 1992. PSCC alleges that defendant Delavau failed to pay commissions due

---

8. The other side should win because under agency law an agent who acts on behalf of a nonexistent principal is personally liable. Additionally, a business that thinks it's a corporation but is not because it never actually filed its charter is a partnership by default. As you know, partners are personally liable for partnership obligations.

and owing to PSCC pursuant to the Agreement. The Agreement was signed by John Sadlon, as president and on behalf of PSCC.

The case proceeded through discovery. . . . Throughout discovery, PSCC represented that it was a corporation organized under the laws of New Jersey. In November 1998, as part of its preparation for trial in this matter, counsel for Delavau contacted the New Jersey Department of Treasury, Commercial Recording Division, to determine whether PSCC remained a corporation in good standing with the state of New Jersey. Defendant's counsel represents that they were informed for the first time that PSCC was not a New Jersey corporation, nor had it ever been registered as a New Jersey corporation.

Counsel for defendant brought the matter to the Court's attention in a telephone conference on November 16, 1998. Plaintiff's counsel verified at that time that no certificate of incorporation had been filed. This Court raised the issue of whether PSCC had legal capacity to sue under the Agreement. Consequently, we referred this matter to Judge Wolfson so that the parties could conduct limited discovery on the issue of plaintiff's corporate status. Plaintiff provided additional materials on or about December 16, 1998.

Defendant filed the instant motion pursuant to Federal Rule of Civil Procedure 17(b) and 12(b)(1). Delavau argues that plaintiff lacks capacity to sue defendant on the parties' July 1992 contract because PSCC should not be considered a de facto corporation as of that date. Defendant further maintains in this connection that plaintiff's lack of corporate status as of the date of the parties' contract renders the Agreement invalid and unenforceable. Defendant relies upon the absence of several documents which, in its view, are essential to any claim that PSCC has attained status as a de facto corporation. Defendant also points out that the only documents produced which tend to support plaintiff's de facto corporate status are the following: (1) plaintiff's handwritten certificate of incorporation which bears the notation "mailed 8-14-92"; (2) plaintiff's federal and state tax returns for years 1993 through 1997; (3) checks for payment of those taxes; and (4) certain correspondence with the Internal Revenue Service (advising of change of corporation's address). Defendant maintains, however, that the notation on the certificate of incorporation is "self-serving," and the documents produced do not demonstrate a bona fide attempt to incorporate. Defendant points out that there are inconsistencies in the information supplied in the documents which in fact support defendant's argument in support of dismissal.

Plaintiff maintains that this Court should afford PSCC de facto corporate status. John Sadlon, president of PSCC, submitted a certification with exhibits in opposition to defendant's motion to dismiss. Sadlon claims that on or about August 14, 1992, he prepared and mailed to the state of New Jersey a certificate of incorporation for PSCC. He claims that he "assumed that the Certificate of Incorporation was filed, as [he] never received notice of the Secretary of State to the contrary." Sadlon states further that in light of his belief that his attempts at incorporation were successful, he prepared an application with the Internal

Revenue Service ("IRS") for an employer identification number, sent notice to the IRS of a change of corporate address, obtained a corporate book and seal for PSCC (but never filled them out), filed corporate tax returns for tax years 1993 through 1997, and paid taxes with PSCC checks.

π Plaintiff argues in the alternative that even if a de facto corporation is not established, defendant should be estopped from relying upon plaintiff's failure to effectuate incorporation prior to the effective date of the parties' contract based upon the doctrine of corporation by estoppel. Defendant counters that under general principles of estoppel, plaintiff should not have the benefit of the doctrine of corporation by estoppel because John Sadlon actively misled defendant by signing the Agreement on behalf of PSCC on July 1, 1992 when it was clear that Sadlon had not taken any steps towards incorporating PSCC until August 14, 1992, at the earliest. Defendant maintains that throughout the parties' business dealings and this litigation, Delavau was under the mistaken impression that PSCC was a New Jersey corporation. We will address each argument in turn.

DISCUSSION . . .

A. De Facto Corporate Status Under New Jersey Law

There exists authority for the proposition that a corporation must qualify as "either de jure or de facto or it has no legal capacity to sue or be sued." *St. John the Baptist Greek Catholic Church v. Gengor,* 118 N.J. Eq. 467, 473, 180 A. 379, 383 (N.J. Super. Ct. Chan. Div. 1935). Plaintiff does not contest this general proposition; nor does it dispute that PSCC does not qualify as a de jure corporation. Rather, the parties' positions diverge on the issue of whether plaintiff qualifies as a de facto corporation.

Our research reveals that prior to the codification of the modern New Jersey Business Corporation Act in 1968, (hereinafter "the Act"), several New Jersey cases recognized the concept of a de facto corporation. Those cases found that a de facto corporation exists if the following three elements are present: (1) there is a law under which a corporation with the power assumed might be incorporated; (2) there has been a bona fide attempt to organize a corporation in the manner prescribed by the statute; and (3) there has been an actual exercise of corporate powers. The burden of establishing de facto corporate status is on the party seeking to rely upon it.

While not raised by the parties, we begin our analysis with the preliminary question of whether the codification of the Act in 1968 had any effect upon the continued viability of the doctrine of de facto corporate status. We have found no New Jersey case authority expressly on point. However, the following provision in the Act raises the issue:

14A:2-7. Certificate of Incorporation
(2) The certificate of incorporation shall be filed in the office of the Secretary of State. The corporate existence shall begin upon the effective date of the

certificate, which shall be the date of the filing or such later time, not to exceed 90 days from the date of filing, as may be set forth in the certificate. *Such filing shall be conclusive evidence that all conditions precedent required to be performed by the incorporators have been complied with and, after the corporate existence has begun, that the corporation has been incorporated under this act.* . . .

N.J. Stat. Ann. ("N.J.S.A.") §14A:2-7(2) (emphasis added). Adopted from the Model Business Corporations Act §50 (the "Model Act"), the Commissioner's Comments accompanying this subsection provide the following explanation of the highlighted passage:

> The last sentence of subsection 14A:2-7(2) has no counterpart in Title 14 [New Jersey's prior Business Corporations Law]. It is adapted from section 50 of the Model Act. Such a provision, which virtually eliminates the distinction between *de jure* and *de facto* corporations, has been enacted in about half the states. . . .

Id. Commissioners' Comment — 1968 (emphasis in original).

Several commentators have noted that the drafters of the Model Act intended to eliminate the common law doctrines of de facto corporation and corporation by estoppel by the enactment of §50. While we have found at least one state Supreme Court case which abolished the de facto corporation concept based upon its statute's similar language, we note that at least two New Jersey Appellate Division cases discussed and applied the de facto corporate concept after the enactment of the Act in 1968 without addressing the effect of N.J.S.A. §14A:2-7(2) or its commentary. Yet, it appears from the commentary appended to §14A:2-7(2) that the drafters sought to eliminate the de facto corporation concept.

While it appears that the effect of similar versions of the Model Act's §50 has produced divergent views and significant debate among commentators and courts from other jurisdictions, we need not decide whether §14A:2-7(2) has abolished the de facto corporate concept in New Jersey at this juncture. Assuming *arguendo* that a would-be corporation could in fact prove its corporate existence by demonstrating that it qualifies as a de facto corporation, the facts of this case demonstrate that PSCC cannot qualify as a de facto corporation because it made no "bona fide" attempt to incorporate. Our research has confirmed that there has not been much development in the relevant case law concerning the requirement of a "bona fide" attempt to organize a corporation in the manner prescribed by the statute. However, we have uncovered two New Jersey cases where the courts found de facto corporate status which are instructive. The differences between the facts presented in those cases and this case lead us to conclude that plaintiff has not provided sufficient evidence of a bona fide attempt to organize a corporation in the manner prescribed by the statute.

We begin our analysis with the more recent case, *Cantor v. Sunshine Greenery, Inc.*, 398 A.2d 571 (App. Div. 1979). There the plaintiffs, lessors of property formerly occupied by the corporate defendant, brought suit against Sunshine

Greenery, Inc. and its incorporator William Brunetti for breach of the parties' lease agreement. It was undisputed that Brunetti intended to act on behalf of the corporation in entering into the lease with plaintiffs. After entering default judgment against the defunct corporation, the Law Division also found Brunetti personally liable on the lease. The primary question on appeal was whether there was a de facto corporation in existence at the time of the execution of the lease. The evidence revealed that on December 3, 1974, prior to entering into the lease agreement, Brunetti signed a certificate of incorporation and forwarded the certificate and check for filing to the Secretary of State. The parties executed the lease on December 16, 1974 with all parties under the impression that Sunshine Greenery was a corporation existing under New Jersey law. However, for some unexplained reason, the certificate was not officially filed until December 18, 1974, two days after the agreement was signed. The trial court held that no de facto corporation existed, and that as a consequence, Brunetti was individually liable for the breach of the lease.

The Appellate Division reversed, holding that there "was ample evidence of the fact that [Sunshine Greenery] was a de facto corporation and that there was a bona fide attempt to incorporate sometime before the consummation of the contract." *Cantor,* 398 A.2d at 573. The court explained:

> The act of executing the certificate of incorporation, the bona fide effort to file it and the dealings with plaintiffs [lessors] in the name of that corporation fully satisfy the requisite proof of the existence of a de facto corporation. To deny such existence because of a mere technicality caused by administrative delay in filing runs counter to the purpose of the de facto concept, and would accomplish an unjust and inequitable result in favor of plaintiffs contrary to their own expectations.

Id. Thus in *Cantor,* the undisputed evidence demonstrated that Brunetti had taken steps towards incorporation prior to the execution of the lease at issue.

Similarly, in *Paragon Distributing Corp. v. Paragon Laboratories, Inc.,* 129 A. 404 (N.J. Super. Ct. Chan. Div. 1925), the plaintiff filed an injunctive application against the defendants, arguing that defendants' conduct breached the contract between the parties. Defendants argued, *inter alia,* that the contract lacked mutuality because the plaintiff had not been incorporated at the time the parties executed the agreement. The Chancery Court rejected defendants' argument, explaining that the plaintiff had attempted to file a certificate of incorporation prior to the date the contract was executed. The fact that certain final steps were not taken prior to the parties' contract was deemed immaterial. *Id.* at 405.

The critical difference between the cases cited above and the present case lies in the undisputed fact that prior to the Agreement dated July 1, 1992, plaintiff, through its agent John Sadlon, did not make a bona fide attempt to incorporate PSCC. Sadlon certifies that he prepared and mailed the certificate of incorporation on August 14, 1992. However, the parties' "Sales, Consulting and Confidential Disclosure Agreement" provides the following: "THIS AGREEMENT effective as of July 1, 1992, by and between J.W.S. DELAVAU CO., INC . . . and PHARMACEUTICAL SALES AND CONSULTING CORPORATION." Therefore, it is clear that there was no bona fide attempt to incorporate prior to the execution of the contract. Rather, by his own testimony, Sadlon did not attempt to file a certificate of incorporation until 1½ months had elapsed from the date of the contract. Under these circumstances, we need not decide the more troubling question of whether Sadlon's mailing of a completed certificate, without proof of payment of the filing fee or proof of receipt by the Secretary of State of New Jersey, amounted to a "bona fide" attempt to incorporate. Put simply, assuming that Sadlon did in fact execute and mail the completed certificate on August 14, 1992, any such conduct came too late. Accordingly, we find that plaintiff may not rely on the doctrine of de facto incorporation to demonstrate that it may sue defendant for breach of the parties' Agreement.

Reasoning [handwritten marginalia]

Holding re: De facto filing [handwritten marginalia]

B. Corporation by Estoppel Under New Jersey Law

Plaintiff argues in the alternative that the doctrine of corporation by estoppel saves its claim against defendant. Plaintiff seeks recognition as a corporation by estoppel as a means of validating the contract with Delavau and maintaining this action, contending that Delavau should be estopped from asserting plaintiff's lack of corporate status where Delavau had intended from the outset to deal with plaintiff as a corporate entity.

Defendant counters that plaintiff should not benefit from the corporation by estoppel concept because John Sadlon entered into the Agreement with the knowledge that PSCC had not yet been incorporated. Defendant maintains that estoppel is premised upon a lack of fraud in the dealings between the parties. Thus, defendant argues that it would be inequitable to apply the doctrine of corporation by estoppel in this instance because Sadlon knew at the time of the parties' Agreement that PSCC did not yet exist as a corporation.

The doctrines of de facto incorporation and corporation by estoppel are two related but distinct concepts. Thus, the fact that §14A:2-7(2) of the Act could be construed to have abolished the de facto corporation concept has no bearing upon the continued vitality of the corporation by estoppel construct under New Jersey law. Nevertheless, there appears to be a dearth of modern New Jersey case law applying or interpreting the contours of the doctrine of corporation by estoppel.

The doctrine of corporation by estoppel may be summarized in general as follows: one who contracts and deals with an entity as a corporation thereby admits that the entity is a corporation and is estopped to deny its incorporation in an action arising out of the contract or course of dealing. However, one of the stated limitations to that general rule is stated succinctly in the Fletcher treatise [Cyc. Corp. (Perm. Ed. 1992)] §3916:

Doctrine of corporation by Estoppel [handwritten marginalia]

> Inasmuch as the rule [of corporation by estoppel] originates in equitable principles, it does not apply when it would be inequitable to apply it, or where equitable principles do not require its application, as in case of fraud.

We concur with the Oregon Supreme Court's observation that "courts and writers have 'gone all over the lot' in attempting to define and apply the doctrine [of corporation by estoppel]." *Timberline Equip. Co. v. Davenport*, 514 P.2d 1109, 1111-12 (Or. 1973). We also agree that, in order to apply the doctrine correctly, the cases must be classified according to the nature of the claim at issue and the party being charged with estoppel. *See id.* This approach is particularly necessary in light of the various contexts in which the estoppel issue may arise.[9]

Specifically in this case, plaintiff has sued defendant for breach of contract; in defense, Delavau seeks to avoid liability upon the contract by contending that plaintiff was not a lawful corporation at the time of the contract. Delavau concludes from that analysis that the parties' contract is invalid and unenforceable.

The parties have not cited, nor could this Court find, any cases from the New Jersey Supreme Court applying the doctrine of corporation by estoppel in this factual and procedural circumstance.

It appears that the weight of authority holds that in this context, where a defendant seeks to avoid potential liability to a would-be corporate plaintiff by contending that the plaintiff was or is not a lawful corporate entity, the doctrine of corporation by estoppel applies such that plaintiff may pursue the contract claim against the defendant despite plaintiff's noncorporate status. *See* Wayne N. Bradley, Comment, *An Empirical Study of Defective Incorporation*, 29 Emory L.J. 523, 560 (1990) and notes accompanying text. The rationale underlying this approach in this factual circumstance is premised upon the courts' desire to effectuate the parties' intent in entering into the contractual arrangement at issue. Bradley, *supra* at 560 (citing cases) ("If the defendant thought it was dealing with a corporation, and later discovered it was in fact dealing with a defective corporation, absent prejudice to the defendant, there is no reason to let the defendant escape liability" based upon a technicality such as defective incorporation). In essence, these cases recognize that permitting the defendant (person or entity) to deny the fact of plaintiff's corporate existence so as to escape potential liability under a contractual arrangement would result in a windfall to defendant beyond that which was expected at the time of the execution of the contract. *Id.*

We find this line of cases persuasive in this instance. . . .

---

9. [FN 5] Courts and commentators have outlined the three most common categories of cases wherein the concept of corporation by estoppel may be implicated. The first is the case in which an association, or its owners, having claimed corporate status in an earlier transaction with a third party, later denies that status in a suit brought by the third party. The third party would seek the benefit of the doctrine of corporation by estoppel, such that the association could not deny its existence in a suit by the third party. The second situation is the case where the question of corporate status is raised by a defendant in a suit brought by the would-be corporation. The defendant in this situation may seek to raise the defense that the plaintiff is not really a corporation, and therefore cannot sue in the corporate name. The final category of cases is where a third party has dealt with a business as a corporation and seeks to impose personal liability on would-be shareholders who in turn raise estoppel as a defense. *See* Carey and Eisenberg, Note on Estoppel, *Cases and Materials on Corporations* at 159 (7th ed. 1995). Obviously, the instant case falls in the second category of cases.

We have considered defendant's argument that plaintiff should not be entitled to invoke the doctrine of corporation by estoppel because John Sadlon affirmatively misrepresented the fact of PSCC's corporate existence at the time of the parties' contract by signing the contract as president on behalf of the corporation, and continued to misrepresent that material fact until defendant actually uncovered the plaintiff's true corporate status. While not cited by either party, the Court has found minimal support for defendant's argument in this context, namely, where the defendant is attempting to avoid potential contractual liability by asserting that plaintiff, as other party to the contract, lacked corporate status and thus the capacity to contract.

At first blush, defendant's argument has some appeal. However, we find it ultimately unpersuasive when considered in light of three important countervailing considerations which exist in this case. First, permitting defendant to avoid liability under the contract based upon a technicality such as plaintiff's defective incorporation appears contrary to general principles of New Jersey law. While not directly on point, we have uncovered cases which indicate in general a reluctance to permit avoidance of potential contractual liability based upon a technical defense such as lack of corporate status of the other party at the time of contracting. Second, accepting defendant's argument would be contrary to the parties' intent at the time of the Agreement and would thus present a windfall to defendant. Finally, permitting defendant to escape liability would be particularly inequitable in this instance in light of the fact that defendant has provided no evidence that it has relied on plaintiff's misrepresentations regarding its alleged corporate status to its detriment. In balance, these three countervailing considerations must prevail in the particular posture of this case. Accordingly, we find that defendant is estopped from relying upon plaintiff's lack of corporate status at the time of the parties' contract in order to avoid suit on the July 1992 Agreement.

Reasoning

Holding Re: Estoppel

The Court will deny defendant's motion to dismiss. . . .

Questions

1. How did Delavau discover that PSCC was never incorporated?
2. What is a de jure corporation? What is a de facto corporation?
3. Why is PSCC arguing it is a de facto corporation? Why does the court conclude it is not?
4. What is the doctrine of corporation by estoppel?
5. What was Delavau's argument for why corporation by estoppel should not apply to PSCC? Why did the court reject the argument?

E. ETHICAL ISSUES

In this section, we discuss three ethical issues that come up in the incorporation context: who is the client, investing in a client, and practicing the law of other states.

1. Who Is the Client?

The client issue comes up when a new business has multiple founders who jointly meet with the same lawyer to discuss choice of form considerations and decide on the appropriate legal form for the business. A single lawyer can and typically does represent all founders at this point, but such a joint representation implicates state ethical rules on conflicts of interest. Most states have adopted some form of the American Bar Association (ABA) Model Rules of Professional Conduct (MRPC) for their ethical rules. MRPC Rule 1.7 provides as follows:

> (a) Except as provided in paragraph (b), a lawyer shall not represent a client if the representation involves a concurrent conflict of interest. A concurrent conflict of interest exists if:
> (1) the representation of one client will be directly adverse to another client; or
> (2) there is a significant risk that the representation of one or more clients will be materially limited by the lawyer's responsibilities to another client, a former client or a third person or by a personal interest of the lawyer.
> (b) Notwithstanding the existence of a concurrent conflict of interest under paragraph (a), a lawyer may represent a client if:
> (1) the lawyer reasonably believes that the lawyer will be able to provide competent and diligent representation to each affected client;
> (2) the representation is not prohibited by law;
> (3) the representation does not involve the assertion of a claim by one client against another client represented by the lawyer in the same litigation or other proceeding before a tribunal; and
> (4) each affected client gives informed consent, confirmed in writing.

In light of this Rule (in particular, (b)(4)), the standard practice is for a lawyer to get informed consent from each founder and have each sign a conflict waiver. Comment [18] to the Rule provides the following guidance on the meaning of informed consent in this context:

> Informed consent requires that each affected client be aware of the relevant circumstances and of the material and reasonably foreseeable ways that the conflict could have adverse effects on the interests of that client. . . . The information required depends on the nature of the conflict and the nature of the risks involved. When representation of multiple clients in a single matter is undertaken,

the information must include the implications of the common representation, including possible effects on loyalty, confidentiality and the attorney-client privilege and the advantages and risks involved.

Thus, a lawyer will typically discuss the various issues related to multiple representation at the initial meeting with the founders and, if the lawyer is well prepared, have conflict waivers prepared for them to sign on the spot.

Once the corporation is formed, the standard practice is for the lawyer to then represent the corporation and not the individual founders. Here is the body of a letter dealing with this transition:

I want to thank you and your co-founders for retaining me to form your new corporation, Braintune Inc. (the "Company"), and authorizing it to retain me as corporate counsel going forward. Now that the Company has been incorporated, I will be preparing and discussing with you and your co-founders bylaws, a shareholders' agreement, and other similar documents for the Company. As we discussed, my client in this matter and related matters will be the Company itself and not any of its shareholders, including you.

While I intend to prepare the bylaws, shareholders' agreement, and other documents relating to the Company in a fair and equitable manner, you are advised to have them reviewed by your own legal counsel prior to signing. I can provide you with a list of attorneys you may want to consider to represent you. If you choose not to retain your own legal counsel, you acknowledge that I have advised you to do so in order to protect your interests.

You should also be aware of the possibility that your relationship with the Company and/or your co-founders could at some point turn adversarial. Thus, you hereby consent to my representation of the Company and to my continued representation of the Company even if such representation is directly adverse to you.

If the above is acceptable, please so indicate by signing in the space below and returning this letter to me. Feel free to contact me with any questions.

---

2. Investing in a Client

Startup businesses are typically strapped for cash, and thus sometimes ask or even insist that their corporate attorneys accept stock or stock options in lieu of legal fees. While frowned on by some, accepting such a deal is allowed by ethical rules. The ABA issued a formal opinion on the issue in July 2000. The opinion provides as follows:

> The Model Rules of Professional Conduct do not prohibit a lawyer from acquiring an ownership interest in a client, either in lieu of a cash fee for providing legal services or as an investment opportunity in connection with such services, as long as the lawyer complies with Rule 1.8(a) governing business transactions

with clients, and, when applicable, with Rule 1.5 requiring that a fee for legal services be reasonable. To comply with Rule 1.8(a), the transaction by which the lawyer acquires the interest and its terms must be fair and reasonable to the client, and fully disclosed and transmitted in writing in a manner that can be reasonably understood by the client. The client also must be given a reasonable opportunity to seek the advice of independent counsel in the transaction and must consent to the transaction in writing. In providing legal services to the client's business while owning its stock, the lawyer must take care to avoid conflicts between the client's interests and the lawyer's personal economic interests as an owner, as required by Rule 1.7(b), and must exercise independent professional judgment in advising the client concerning legal matters as required by Rule 2.1.[10]

Question

What are some advantages and disadvantages of investing in a client?

3. Practicing the Law of Other States

Corporate lawyers routinely provide legal advice to clients concerning the laws of states in which they are not licensed to practice. For example, a lawyer practicing in Chicago and licensed only in Illinois may advise an entrepreneur about incorporating in Delaware a business operating in Kenosha, Wisconsin. The attorney then prepares and files a certificate of incorporation for the business with the Delaware Secretary of State, drafts bylaws and resolutions in compliance with Delaware law, and fills out and files the paperwork to qualify the corporation to do business in Wisconsin, and registers it with the Wisconsin Department of Revenue. The attorney is certainly practicing Delaware law and arguably Wisconsin law as well.

All states prohibit a lawyer from practicing law in the state unless he or she is licensed in the state (see, e.g., MRPC Rule 5.1). Normally, these rules do not pose a problem for lawyers like our Chicago attorney, as he may be practicing Delaware and Wisconsin law, but he is likely not doing so in Delaware or Wisconsin. I say "likely" because the professional responsibility rules of most states do not define the phrase "in the state," so it is left to the courts to define, and courts in different states have defined the phrase differently.

The most well-known (and perhaps notorious) case on the issue is probably *Birbrower, Montalbano, Condon & Frank, P.C. v. Superior Court*, 949 P.2d 1 (Cal. 1998), *cert. denied*, 525 U.S. 920 (1998). In that case, Birbrower, Montalbano, Condon & Frank, P.C., a New York law firm, represented ESQ Business Services, Inc., a California corporation based in Santa Clara County, California, in

---

10. American Bar Association, Acquiring ownership in a client in connection with performing legal services, ABA Formal op. 00-418 (July 7, 2000).

a contract dispute with Tandem Computers Incorporated, which was also based in Santa Clara County. Lawyers from Birbrower traveled to California on several occasions to work on the matter, and the dispute was ultimately settled. ESQ later sued Birbrower for malpractice, and Birbrower counterclaimed, seeking its legal fees on the Tandem matter, which ESQ had never paid. In response to this counterclaim, ESQ argued that its fee agreement with Birbrower was invalid because Birbrower had practiced law in California without a license in violation of California Business and Professions Code §6125 which states, "No person shall practice law in California unless the person is an active member of the State Bar," and thus ESQ did not have to pay. The case was eventually heard by the California Supreme Court, which gave it occasion to address the meaning of "practice law in California" as used in §6125. The court held that "practice law" means representing clients in court or "legal advice and legal instrument and contract preparation, whether or not these subjects were rendered in the course of litigation." The court then addressed the meaning of "in California" and stated as follows:

> Section 6125 has generated numerous opinions on the meaning of "practice law" but none on the meaning of "in California." In our view, the practice of law "in California" entails sufficient contact with the California client to render the nature of the legal service a clear legal representation. In addition to a quantitative analysis, we must consider the nature of the unlicensed lawyer's activities in the state. Mere fortuitous or attenuated contacts will not sustain a finding that the unlicensed lawyer practiced law "in California." The primary inquiry is whether the unlicensed lawyer engaged in sufficient activities in the state, or created a continuing relationship with the California client that included legal duties and obligations.
>
> Our definition does not necessarily depend on or require the unlicensed lawyer's physical presence in the state. Physical presence here is one factor we may consider in deciding whether the unlicensed lawyer has violated section 6125, but it is by no means exclusive. For example, one may practice law in the state in violation of section 6125 although not physically present here by advising a California client on California law in connection with a California legal dispute by telephone, fax, computer, or other modern technological means. Conversely, although we decline to provide a comprehensive list of what activities constitute sufficient contact with the state, we do reject the notion that a person *automatically* practices law "in California" whenever that person practices California law anywhere, or "virtually" enters the state by telephone, fax, e-mail, or satellite.

The court held that Birbrower had violated §6125 given Birbrower attorneys were physically in the state rendering legal advice to ESQ on a number of occasions. Thus, it invalidated the fee agreement with respect to fees for the practice of law by Birbrower in California. The court, however, found that Birbrower was entitled to fees for any of the work it did in New York, and therefore remanded the case to the trial court to allow Birbrower to present evidence in that regard.

The disallowance of compensation is a common consequence imposed by states for the unauthorized practice of law. In some states, the unauthorized practice of law is a criminal misdemeanor or is punishable by injunction or contempt of court. Additionally, an attorney may face a disciplinary action by the bar of the state in which he or she is licensed. The issue comes up most often as it did *Birbrower*—in the context of a fee dispute with a client.

Birbrower caused a stir in the legal community and in part motivated the ABA to revisit MRPC Rule 5.5, its model rule on the unauthorized practice of law. In 2002, it adopted a new version of the Rule that also addresses the multi-jurisdictional practice of law. The Rule provides as follows:

> (a) A lawyer shall not practice law in a jurisdiction in violation of the regulation of the legal profession in that jurisdiction, or assist another in doing so.
> (b) A lawyer who is not admitted to practice in this jurisdiction shall not:
> (1) except as authorized by these Rules or other law, establish an office or other systematic and continuous presence in this jurisdiction for the practice of law; or
> (2) hold out to the public or otherwise represent that the lawyer is admitted to practice law in this jurisdiction.
> (c) A lawyer admitted in another United States jurisdiction, and not disbarred or suspended from practice in any jurisdiction, may provide legal services on a temporary basis in this jurisdiction that:
> (1) are undertaken in association with a lawyer who is admitted to practice in this jurisdiction and who actively participates in the matter;
> (2) are in or reasonably related to a pending or potential proceeding before a tribunal in this or another jurisdiction, if the lawyer, or a person the lawyer is assisting, is authorized by law or order to appear in such proceeding or reasonably expects to be so authorized;
> (3) are in or reasonably related to a pending or potential arbitration, mediation, or other alternative dispute resolution proceeding in this or another jurisdiction, if the services arise out of or are reasonably related to the lawyer's practice in a jurisdiction in which the lawyer is admitted to practice and are not services for which the forum requires pro hac vice admission; or
> (4) are not within paragraphs (c)(2) or (c)(3) and arise out of or are reasonably related to the lawyer's practice in a jurisdiction in which the lawyer is admitted to practice. . . .

The large majority of states have adopted Rule 5.5, including Delaware and Wisconsin.

The key provision for lawyers such as our Chicago attorney is Rule 5.5(c)(4), which allows a lawyer admitted in one state to provide legal services on a "temporary basis" in a state in which he or she is not admitted provided the services "arise out of or are reasonably related to the lawyer's practice" in his or her home state. Comment [6] to the Rule provides the following guidance on the meaning of "temporary basis": "There is no single test to determine whether a lawyer's services are provided on a 'temporary basis' in this jurisdiction, and may therefore be permissible under paragraph (c). Services may be 'temporary' even though the lawyer provides services in this jurisdiction on a recurring basis, or for an extended period of time, as when the lawyer is representing a client in a single lengthy negotiation or litigation." Comment [14] to the Rule provides the following guidance on the meaning of "arise out of or are reasonably related to the lawyer's practice":

> A variety of factors evidence such a relationship. The lawyer's client may have been previously represented by the lawyer, or may be resident in or have substantial contacts with the jurisdiction in which the lawyer is admitted. The matter, although involving other jurisdictions, may have a significant connection with that jurisdiction. In other cases, significant aspects of the lawyer's work might be conducted in that jurisdiction or a significant aspect of the matter may involve the law of that jurisdiction. The necessary relationship might arise when the client's activities or the legal issues involve multiple jurisdictions, such as when the officers of a multinational corporation survey potential business sites and seek the services of their lawyer in assessing the relative merits of each. In addition, the services may draw on the lawyer's recognized expertise developed through the regular practice of law on behalf of clients in matters involving a particular body of federal, nationally-uniform, foreign, or international law.

Thus, the services provided by our Chicago attorney to the Delaware corporation located in Wisconsin seem to fall under Rule 5.5(c)(4), which both Delaware and Wisconsin have adopted, and hence, he should be fine even if he meets with his client in one of those states.

California has not adopted the MRPC, nor does it recognize an exception to §6125 similar to Rule 5.5(c)(3) or (c)(4). Thus, *Birbrower* would likely come out the same today.

Exercise 7.2

Assume you are a corporate lawyer at a Chicago law firm and you are licensed only in Illinois. A corporation headquartered in California has just hired you to serve as its outside corporate counsel. It is a large corporation and you suspect it will become your biggest client. How should you proceed in light of *Birbrower*?

· CHAPTER EIGHT ·

CORPORATE FINANCE

Every corporation needs money to run its operations. In this chapter, we discuss the three broad categories of financing: debt, equity, and internally generated funds. We then discuss capital structure and introduce federal securities laws.

A. DEBT

1. Overview

Debt is synonymous with a loan. It is borrowed money that the business has to pay back to the lender with interest. The terms of the debt are set through negotiations between the business and the lender, and include the following:

- Loan amount: This is the amount of money the lender will be loaning to the borrower. It is also referred to as the principal amount.
- Interest rate: This is the rate at which a borrower pays interest to the lender on the loan, and is usually expressed as an annual percentage of the principal amount of the loan. For example, if a business borrows $10,000 at a simple interest rate of 10 percent per year, it would owe the lender $1,000 per year in interest, in addition to paying back the $10,000 principal amount. Interest is compensation to the lender for letting the borrower use the lender's money, and it is how lenders make money on loans.
- Repayment schedule: This specifies when the borrower has to make principal and interest payments to the lender. It usually provides for payments due monthly, quarterly, or annually.

Below is a sample promissory note, a document typically drafted by a lawyer to evidence a loan.

PROMISSORY NOTE

$500,000   Tucson, Arizona   April 1, 2011

Sjostrom Brothers Corp. ("**Borrower**"), a Hawaii corporation, promises to pay to the order of Distressed Lending LP ("**Lender**"), a Delaware limited partnership, its assigns or successors, at 3570 Las Vegas Blvd, South, Las Vegas, NV, or other place as Lender may designate in writing, the principal sum of $500,000 together with interest on the unpaid balance thereof at the rate of 10 percent per annum compounded monthly from April 1, 2011 until paid, payable in equal monthly installments of $10,623.52 each, including interest at the rate provided above, with the first installment due on May 1, 2011, and a like installment due on the first day of each calendar month thereafter until the unpaid balance and all accrued interest has been paid in full. All payments will be applied first to accrued interest to the date of payment and then to principal.

In case of default in the payment of any installment when due, all principal and interest will become immediately due and collectible at the option of the holder of this note. Failure to exercise this option in the event of a default will not constitute a waiver of the right to exercise it in the event of any subsequent default.

If this note is placed in the hands of an attorney for collection, the maker promises to pay the holder's reasonable collection costs, including reasonable attorney's fees, even though no legal proceeding is filed on this note. But if a legal proceeding is filed for the purpose of interpreting or enforcing this note, the holder will be entitled to recover reasonable attorney's fees in the proceeding, or any appeal thereof, to be set by the court without the necessity of hearing testimony or receiving evidence, in addition to the costs and disbursements allowed by law. Borrower waives presentment for payment, notice of dishonor, protest, notice of protest, and diligence in collection, and consents that the time of payment of any amount due under this note may be extended by the holder without otherwise modifying, altering, releasing, affecting, or limiting the liability of Borrower.

Sjostrom Brothers Corp.

By /s/ William K. Sjostrom, Jr.
William K. Sjostrom, Jr.
President

The note reflects a loan made by Distressed Lending LP to Sjostrom Brothers Corp. on April 1, 2011 in the principal amount of $500,000. The interest rate on the loan is 10 percent per annum (a lawyerly word for year) and repayment is to be made in installments of $10,623.52 per month, which works out to the loan being paid back over five years with Borrower having paid $137,411.34 in interest. A lender calculates the monthly payment using a loan amortization calculator where it inputs the principal amount, term of the loan (the date by when it wants all of the money paid back), the interest rate, and how often interest is compounded. The calculator then generates the monthly payment accordingly.

The last two paragraphs of the note are standard provisions to protect the holder of the note in the event Sjostrom Brothers misses a payment. Note that the holder could be someone different than Distressed Lending LP, because it is common for a lender to sell a note to someone else. (This is contemplated by the language in the first paragraph of the note defining "Lender" as Distressed Lending, LP, its *assigns* and successors.)

2. Credit Risk

A lender generally does not lend money to a business unless it believes the business will be able to pay the money back. Hence, before making a loan, a lender will have the business furnish its financial and other information so that the lender can assess the credit risk associated with the proposed loan. Credit risk is the risk that a borrower will not be able to repay a loan. Depending on this assessment, the lender may or may not choose to go forward with the loan. The higher a borrower's credit risk, the higher the interest rate a lender will require on a loan. The additional interest as compared to a lower credit risk borrower is to compensate the lender for taking on greater credit risk.

If you have ever applied for a mortgage loan to buy a home, you are probably familiar with these concepts. In that setting, the mortgage broker, bank or other lender will assess the credit risk you pose by checking your credit score with one or more national credit reporting agencies (TransUnion, Equifax, Experian). Your credit score is based on your credit history (e.g., history of borrowings and repayments), with a lower score indicating more credit risk. If your score is on the high end and you have a steady job, there is a good chance the broker or lender will offer you a loan at its best, or prime, rate. If not, you will be offered a loan at a higher rate (a non-prime, or sub-prime loan) or none at all.

There are firms that provide credit scores for businesses that a lender can use in assessing a business's credit risk. For example, Dun and Bradstreet maintains a PAYDEX score for many businesses, which it describes as follows:

> The PAYDEX Score is D&B's unique dollar-weighted numerical indicator of how a firm paid its bills over the past year, based on trade experiences reported to D&B by various vendors. The D&B PAYDEX Score ranges from 1 to 100, with higher scores indicating better payment performance.[1]

---

1. Dun and Bradstreet, PAYDEX® Score Business Definition, *available at* http://smallbusiness.dnb.com/glossaries/paydex-score/11815414-1.html.

Frequent lenders such as commercial banks have their own models into which they input data obtained from a potential borrower to assess credit risk.

A business that is borrowing money by issuing publicly traded debt such as bonds (see the discussion of bonds below) will have the debt "rated" by a credit rating agency. To have its debt rated, a business furnishes a credit rating agency the same type of information a bank would require to make a loan. The credit rating agency evaluates the information and the terms of the debt the borrower plans to issue and assigns the debt a rating. There are three major credit rating agencies in the United States: Standard & Poor's (S&P), Moody's Investor Service, and Fitch Ratings. S&P describes its credit ratings as follows:

> Credit ratings are forward-looking opinions about credit risk. Standard & Poor's credit ratings express the agency's opinion about the ability and willingness of an issuer, such as a corporation or state or city government, to meet its financial obligations in full and on time.
>
> Credit ratings can also speak to the credit quality of an individual debt issue, such as a corporate note, a municipal bond or a mortgage-backed security, and the relative likelihood that the issue may default.[2]

Each of the "Big Three" uses a similar rating scale to communicate the agency's opinion of the relative level of credit risk concerning a debt instrument. Below is a summary of S&P's scale:

> "AAA"—Extremely strong capacity to meet financial commitments. Highest Rating.
> "AA"—Very strong capacity to meet financial commitments.
> "A"—Strong capacity to meet financial commitments, but somewhat susceptible to adverse economic conditions and changes in circumstances.
> "BBB"—Adequate capacity to meet financial commitments, but more subject to adverse economic conditions.
> "BBB-"—Considered lowest investment grade by market participants.
> "BB+"—Considered highest speculative grade by market participants.
> "BB"—Less vulnerable in the near-term but faces major ongoing uncertainties to adverse business, financial and economic conditions.
> "B"—More vulnerable to adverse business, financial and economic conditions but currently has the capacity to meet financial commitments.
> "CCC"—Currently vulnerable and dependent on favorable business, financial and economic conditions to meet financial commitments.
> "CC"—Currently highly vulnerable.
> "C"—Currently highly vulnerable obligations and other defined circumstances.
> "D"—Payment default on financial commitments.

> Note: Ratings from "AA" to "CCC" may be modified by the addition of a plus (+) or minus (–) sign to show relative standing within the major rating categories.[3]

---

2. Standard & Poor's, Credit Ratings Definitions and FAQs, *available at* http://www.standardandpoors.com/ratings/definitions-and-faqs/en/us.
3. *Id.*

A credit rating agency monitors each company for whom it has provided a rating and adjusts the rating as its opinion on a company's credit risk changes. Here is what S&P says about changes to credit ratings:

> The reasons for ratings adjustments vary, and may be broadly related to overall shifts in the economy or business environment or more narrowly focused on circumstances affecting a specific industry, entity, or individual debt issue.
>
> In some cases, changes in the business climate can affect the credit risk of a wide array of issuers and securities. For instance, new competition or technology, beyond what might have been expected and factored into the ratings, may hurt a company's expected earnings performance, which could lead to one or more rating downgrades over time. Growing or shrinking debt burdens, hefty capital spending requirements, and regulatory changes may also trigger ratings changes.[4]

Questions

1. Which would carry a higher interest rate: debt issued by a business rated BBB by S&P or a business rated BB+, all else being equal? Why?
2. To which business would you rather lend money: one rated BBB or BB+, all else being equal? Why?
3. Which business would you rather have as a client, one rated BBB or BB+ by S&P? Why?
4. What are some consequences to a business resulting from its credit rating being downgraded?

3. Loan Agreements

Most loans involve a loan agreement in addition to a promissory note like the one above. A loan agreement is a contract between the borrower and lender(s) and includes, among other things, representations and warranties and covenants of the borrower. The greater the principal amount of the loan, the more likely it will involve a loan agreement. If it does, the promissory note will include a provision making reference to the loan agreement. Here is an example of such a provision:

> This Note is the Note referred to in the Loan Agreement, which, among other things, contains provisions for the acceleration of the maturity hereof upon the happening of certain events and for optional prepayment of the principal.

---

4. *Id.*

a. Representations and Warranties

Loan agreements typically include representations and warranties (commonly called "reps" for short). A rep is an assertion of fact by a contracting party. As mentioned above, a lender analyzes financial and other information furnished by a potential borrower in deciding whether to extend a loan and, if so, how much to lend and what interest rate to charge. Reps are designed to provide a lender with recourse in the event that this information turns out to be erroneous or incomplete. Here are some sample reps from a loan agreement:

SECTION 5.5. FINANCIAL STATEMENTS; FINANCIAL CONDITION; ETC. The internally prepared financial statements of the Borrower dated as of August 31, 2011 (the "**Internal Financials**") delivered to the Lender in connection with this Agreement were prepared in accordance with GAAP consistently applied and fairly present the financial condition and the results of operations of the Lender covered thereby on the dates and for the periods covered thereby and subject to normally recurring year-end adjustments. The Lender does not have any material liability (contingent or otherwise) other than those reflected on the Internal Financials or as set forth on Schedule 5.5.

SECTION 5.6. PROJECTIONS. The projections delivered to the Lender in connection with this Agreement have been prepared on the basis of the assumptions accompanying them, and such projections and assumptions, as of the date of preparation thereof, are reasonable and represent the Borrower's good faith estimate of its future financial performance, it being understood that nothing contained in this Section shall constitute a representation or warranty that such future financial performance or results of operations will in fact be achieved.

SECTION 5.7. MATERIAL ADVERSE EFFECT. Since the date of the most recent audited consolidated financial statements of the Borrower dated June 30, 2011, there has occurred no event, act, or condition which has or could have resulted in a Material Adverse Effect.

Note that with the exception of "Internal Financials," the capitalized terms that appear in the above reps (e.g., "Borrower," "Lender," "Material Adverse Effect") were defined elsewhere in the loan agreement from which the provisions were lifted. The use of defined terms is a standard contract drafting technique to avoid having to repeat long definitions every time the concept is addressed in an agreement. For example, the definition section of the loan agreement provides that "Material Adverse Effect" "shall mean a material adverse effect upon the business, operations, properties, assets, prospects, or condition (financial or otherwise) of the Borrower and its subsidiaries, taken as a whole."

If it turns out a rep made by a borrower in a loan agreement was false, the lender will have a breach of contract claim against the borrower, and, more importantly, under a different provision of the agreement, the lender will likely be able to accelerate the loan, that is, require the borrower to immediately pay back the principal amount plus interest.

b. Covenants

Covenants are promises by the borrower to do something (affirmative covenants) or not to do something (negative covenants). They are included in loan agreements to allow a lender to closely monitor how the business is doing and protect against a business taking actions that may negatively impact the business's ability to repay the loan. For example, a standard affirmative covenant requires the borrower to furnish the lender various monthly, quarterly, and annual financial reports. Here are some sample affirmative covenants from a loan agreement:

> SECTION 6.3. MAINTENANCE OF INSURANCE. The Borrower shall, and shall cause each of its Subsidiaries to, maintain with financially sound and reputable insurance companies insurance on itself and its properties in at least such amounts and against at least such risks as are customarily insured against in the same general area by companies engaged in the same or a similar business, which insurance shall in any event not provide for materially less coverage than the insurance in effect on the Original Effective Date.
>
> SECTION 6.4. TAXES. (a) The Borrower shall pay or cause to be paid, and shall cause each of its Subsidiaries to pay or cause to be paid, prior to becoming past due, all taxes, charges, and assessments and all other lawful claims required to be paid by the Borrower or such Subsidiaries, except as contested in good faith and by appropriate proceedings diligently conducted, if adequate reserves have been established with respect thereto in accordance with GAAP.

Obviously, a business will maintain insurance and pay its taxes even if it is not required to do so under a loan agreement. A lender nonetheless insists on these types of covenants, because a borrower's failure to meet them serves as a red flag of underlying problems at the business, and hence the lender will want to be able to take action under the loan agreement. Typically, the loan agreement provides that breach of a covenant (in some instances, subject to a cure period) constitutes an "event of default" under the loan agreement allowing the lender to cancel the loan and declare all outstanding principal and interest immediately due and payable.

Negative covenants are designed, among other things, to prevent a business from squandering the loan proceeds or other business assets or otherwise engaging in a transaction that would negatively impact the business's ability to repay the loan. Standard negative covenants include prohibitions on distributions, bonuses, acquisitions, capital expenditures, and incurring additional indebtedness. Below is some sample language.

SECTION 7.1. DIVIDENDS. The Borrower shall not, and shall not permit any of its Subsidiaries to, declare or pay any dividends (other than dividends payable solely in common stock), or return any capital to, its stockholders or authorize or make any other distribution, payment, or delivery of property or cash to its stockholders as such, or redeem, retire, purchase, or otherwise acquire, directly or indirectly, any shares of any class of its Capital Stock now or hereafter outstanding (or any options or warrants issued with respect to its Capital Stock), or set aside any funds for any of the foregoing purposes.

SECTION 7.2. CAPITAL EXPENDITURES. The Borrower shall not make or incur and shall not permit any of its Subsidiaries to make or incur any Capital Expenditures in an amount exceeding $10,000,000 in the aggregate during any fiscal year of the Borrower.

SECTION 7.3. INDEBTEDNESS. The Borrower shall not, and shall not permit any of its Subsidiaries to, create, incur, assume, suffer to exist or otherwise become or remain directly or indirectly liable with respect to, any Indebtedness, other than Indebtedness hereunder and Indebtedness outstanding on the Effective Date and set forth on Schedule 7.3 hereto and any extension, refinancing or refunding thereof, PROVIDED that the principal amount of the Indebtedness so extended, refinanced or refunded shall not be increased above the principal amount thereof outstanding immediately prior to such extension, refinancing, or refunding, the final maturity of the Indebtedness so extended, refinanced, or refunded shall not be changed to an earlier date, nor shall the amortization schedule be changed in a manner which results in a shorter average life to maturity, nor shall the terms (financial and otherwise) of such extension, refinancing or refunding be less favorable to the Borrower or its Subsidiary, as the case may be.

Generally, the intent of negative covenants is not to prevent a borrower from taking a particular action but to prevent it from doing so without the consent of the lender. Hence, for example, if a business subject to the above negative covenants determines it is in the business's best interest to make a $15 million capital expenditure, it will request a waiver of Section 7.2 from the lender. The lender will grant the waiver, unless it thinks doing so will negatively impact the business's ability to meet its obligations under the loan.

Most loan agreements also include financial covenants that stipulate specific financial ratios a borrower is required to maintain. Common financial covenants include debt-to-earnings, cash flow-to-interest expense, and earnings-to-interest expense. Here is sample language for a cash flow-to-interest expense financial covenant:

(a) INTEREST COVERAGE RATIO. The Borrower shall not permit the ratio of Consolidated Cash Flow to Consolidated Interest Expense to be less than 2.50 to 1.00 at any time.

A lender does not necessarily expect a borrower to always remain in compliance with financial covenants. These covenants are designed to serve as an early warning system. Once triggered, a lender may more carefully monitor a borrower or renegotiate terms of the loan. (The lender will be in a strong negotiating position because the non-compliance will be an "event of default.")

As a general rule, the lower the creditworthiness of the borrower, the more covenants the lender will insist on including in the loan agreement. High-quality borrowers are sometimes able to negotiate so-called cov-lite loans, that is, loans that do not include financial covenants.

Exercise 8.1

1. The Borrower referenced in the "SECTION 7.1. DIVIDENDS" covenant above wants to repurchase all the shares of its commons stock owned by its former head of marketing who has quit to take a job at a competitor. Can the Borrower do the repurchase? Why would the lender care one way or the other?

2. The Borrower referenced in the "SECTION 7.2. CAPITAL EXPENDITURES" covenant above wants to do a $13 million upgrade to its plant. Assuming the money to be spent on the upgrade falls under the definition of "Capital Expenditures," can the Borrower do the upgrade? Why would the lender care one way or the other?

3. The Borrower referenced in the "SECTION 7.3. INDEBTEDNESS" covenant above currently has another loan with a different lender in the principal amount of $30 million that bears interest at 10 percent per annum. The lender has offered to reduce the interest rate on the loan to 8 percent provided that the Borrower agrees to extend the maturity of the loan by one year and delete from the loan agreement the Borrower's right to prepay the loan. Can the Borrower do the extension?

4. What would be the consequence to a Borrower who went forward with any of the actions mentioned above that you concluded are not allowed under the loan agreement?

---

4. Liens

Oftentimes a lender will not be willing to loan a business money or will insist on a much higher interest rate unless the borrower grants it a lien on some or all of the borrower's property to secure the loan. It is not uncommon for a lender to insist on two types of liens—a mortgage on all of a borrower's real property and a security interest on all of a borrower's personal property. The basic idea is that if the business defaults on the loan, the lender can foreclose on this collateral and then sell it to satisfy all or part of the loan. This makes the loan less risky from the lender's perspective, and thus it is willing to charge a reduced interest rate. The details of any liens will be specified in a mortgage agreement and/or security agreement executed by the borrower in addition to a promissory note and a loan agreement. We will leave the mechanics and other issues related to mortgages, security interests, and other liens to other classes such as Secured Transactions and Real Estate.

5. Guaranties

As you know, corporate law affords shareholders limited liability, meaning they are not personally liable for debts incurred or torts committed by the business as a result of being shareholders. Thus, as a general rule, if a bank lends a corporation money, and the business fails to repay the loan, it can look only to assets held in the name of the corporation and not to the personal assets of the corporation's shareholders for repayment, even if the shareholders have funneled large amounts of money out of the business through distributions and salaries and therefore could easily repay the loan. Lenders often require shareholders to contractually opt out of this general rule through guaranties. A guaranty is simply a contract under which one party agrees to pay the debt of another. The following is sample language from a personal guaranty:

> This guaranty is given by William K. Sjostrom, Jr. ("**Guarantor**") to Distressed Lenders LP, its assigns and successors ("**Lender**"), in order to induce Lender to loan money to Sjostrom Brothers Corp. ("**Borrower**") pursuant to the Promissory Note in the principal amount of $500,000 dated April 1, 2011 (the "**Note**").
>
> Guarantor guaranties to Lender the prompt payment of all amounts due under the Note. This is a continuing guaranty and shall remain in force until revoked by the written consent of Lender. Guarantor shall pay to Lender all costs incurred by Lender in enforcing its rights under this Guaranty, including, without limitation, attorneys' fees and court costs.

A lender will typically require a guarantor to furnish it financial information so that it can assess the guarantor's creditworthiness and thus the strength of the guaranty. A guaranty by a deep-pocketed guarantor is likely to result in the bank charging a lower interest rate to the borrower.

Questions

1. What possible motivation would Sjostrom have to sign the above guaranty?
2. Why would a bank be willing to charge a borrower a lower interest rate on a loan if a deep-pocketed person signs a guaranty?

6. Types of Debt

All debt shares the same basic characteristic: it is borrowed money that has to be paid back with interest. Debt, however, goes by many different names, with the name often related to some secondary characteristic of the specific type. This section describes some of the more common debt types, in no particular order.

Term loan. A term loan is a loan made to a business, typically by a bank, that calls for regular periodic payments of interest and principal, usually over a period of one to ten years. The loan reflected in the above note would likely be called a term loan.

Line of credit. A line of credit is a loan that a business can draw down when needed. For example, say Sjostrom Brothers Corp. (SBC) arranges a $250,000 line of credit with its bank. This means the bank stands ready to lend SBC up to $250,000 upon request. Thus, if SBC is running $100,000 short of cash in a particular month, it could "draw down" $100,000 on its line of credit to cover the shortfall. If the next month it is running $150,000 short of cash, it can draw down another $150,000 on the line, at which point the line will be maxed out. When business picks up, SBC can pay back some or all of the $250,000 outstanding on the line and then re-borrow it again in the future. SBC will owe interest on the amounts it draws down based on how long they are outstanding, and the lender may also charge SBC a "commitment fee" for making the line available. This type of loan is also called a revolving loan or revolver.

Equipment loan. An equipment loan is a loan made to a business to buy capital equipment. Capital equipment is an accounting term that generally means equipment a business uses to produce products or provide services that has a lifespan of years. Examples include computers, vehicles, machinery, and furniture. A loan secured by capital equipment is also called an equipment loan. Lenders are generally willing to lend a business from 50 percent to 80 percent of the value of capital equipment securing the loan, depending on the lender's assessment of how easy it would be to resell the equipment.

Equipment lease. An equipment lease is a financing transaction where a finance company buys a piece of equipment selected by a business and leases it to the business. Lease payments are set at a slight premium to the equivalent of what the business's loan payment would have been if it instead borrowed the money to buy the equipment. The lease often runs for the useful life of the equipment and may grant the business the option to buy the equipment at the end of the lease. Depending on how the lease is structured, this type of financing may not be considered debt for accounting purposes, which is an important feature for a company concerned about its debt to equity ratio.

Inventory loan. An inventory loan is a loan secured by a business's inventory of finished goods. Banks are generally willing to lend a business 50 percent of the value of the inventory securing the loan.

Mortgage loan. A mortgage loan is a loan secured by a mortgage on the business's real estate. A business can normally get a loan for up to 85 percent of the value of the real estate securing it.

Subordinated debt. Subordinated (also called junior) debt is a loan or debt instrument that ranks below other debt (called unsubordinated or senior debt) in payment priority. For example, a borrower may take out a loan from a bank and then later take out another loan from a different bank, with the loan agreement for the second loan stating that repayment is subordinated to the first loan. The initial lender may require subordination as a condition to allowing the borrower to take out the second loan. Most loan agreements contain a negative covenant prohibiting the borrower from borrowing more money without the lender's approval (see Section 7.3 of the sample covenants above). A borrower is obligated to make payments due on its senior debt before it pays anything on its junior debt. Thus, if a borrower is in financial distress, it may have enough money to pay its senior debt, but not its junior debt. As a result, junior debt is more risky and therefore will carry a higher interest rate than senior debt.

Accounts receivable loan. An accounts receivable loan is a loan secured by a business's accounts receivable. A business may be able to finance up to 85 percent of the value of its accounts receivable depending on the creditworthiness of its customers. Typically, loan payments are due as the business collects on the accounts.

Syndicated loan. A syndicated loan is a loan funded by a group, or syndicate, of lenders. Typically, a bank serves as lead lender (also called agent or arranger) and lines up other lenders (banks, pension funds, hedge funds, etc.) to join the syndicate. The lead lender negotiates the terms of the loan and the loan agreement with the borrower, monitors the borrower's compliance with the loan agreement, and collects the loan payments on behalf of the syndicate. A syndicate is used to spread the risk of borrower default on a large loan across multiple lenders.

Corporate bond financing. Corporate bond financing is debt raised by a business through the sale of bonds to investors (mutual funds, pension funds, insurance companies, etc.). A bond is a debt instrument issued by a company in exchange for money. Bonds are normally secured by business assets, issued in denominations of $1,000, and entitle their holders to interest payments at a specified rate (called the coupon). The company pays its bondholders interest typically every six months and the principal amount on maturity, which ranges from three to ten years from the date of issuance.

For example, if a corporation wanted to raise $10 million in long-term debt financing, it could do so by selling 10,000 bonds that matured in ten years. It would have the bonds rated by a credit rating agency and set the coupon rate accordingly. Say it set the coupon rate at 8 percent. It would then make semi-annual interest payments of $40 per bond, or $800,000 total per year. In ten years, it would repay its bondholders the $10 million of principal.

Bonds are issued pursuant to an indenture which resembles a loan agreement, but is between the company and an indenture trustee. (The indenture trustee is normally a bank and is willing to serve in such capacity for a fee.) The indenture trustee monitors the company's compliance with the indenture on behalf of the bondholders.

Bonds issued by businesses are referred to as corporate bonds to distinguish them from bonds issued by governments, but that does not mean they can only be issued by a corporation. Any type of business entity can issue corporate bonds so the name is a bit of a misnomer.

Debenture financing. Debenture financing is debt raised by a business through the sale of debentures. A debenture is basically the same as a bond, but is unsecured, that is, it is not backed by any collateral. Many people use the terms "debentures" and "bonds" interchangeably.

Junk bond financing. Junk bond financing is debt raised by a business through the sale of bonds with a credit rating below "investment grade." This would be a rating of BB+ or lower under S&P's rating scale (see above). Junk bonds carry higher interest rates than investment grade debt to compensate investors for the greater credit risk. They are also called high-yield bonds and non-investment grade bonds.

Commercial paper. Commercial paper is short-term, unsecured loans to companies with high credit ratings the proceeds of which will be used to fund "current transactions" (e.g., operating expenses, receivables, and inventory). Maturities range from two to 270 days. The "current transactions" and 270 days come from federal securities regulations that allow debt with a maturity of nine months or less to be used for "current transactions" to be issued with much less regulatory oversight and therefore lower transaction costs. Money market mutual funds are big investors in commercial paper.

Trade debt. Trade debt (also called accounts payable) is money owed to a supplier or other creditor of a business (called a "trade creditor") for goods or services sold by the trade creditor to the business on credit, that is, it provided the business with the goods or services, but did not require the business to pay until a later date. A trade creditor is willing to implicitly lend money to its customers to facilitate more sales. If a trade creditor becomes wary of a business paying late or concerned about a business's creditworthiness, it may shift the business to "cash-on-delivery" (or C.O.D.) status, meaning payment is due by the business at the time of delivery or start of services.

Questions

1. Of the above types of debt, where would money owed by a business on a corporate credit card best fit? What about money owed by Monet from Chapter 2 on his paint store account?
2. Why do lenders typically lend only up to 85 percent of the value of accounts receivables as opposed to 100 percent?
3. If a company issued bonds and debentures at the same time, which would carry a higher interest rate?
4. Why do bonds involve an indenture instead of a loan agreement?
5. Are junk bonds a bad investment?

7. Lawyer Roles

To give you a flavor for a typical bank financing transaction and the roles played by lawyers on such a deal, what follows is a fictional commercial loan deal by New York Bank (NYB) to Bluecast Corp. (Bluecast). NYB is represented by Max Martinez and Tracy Clark, a partner and associate in the banking and finance group of Sjostrom & Sjostrom LLP, a law firm that NYB uses frequently on its commercial loans. Bluecast is represented by Lara Sandhu and Liam Lang, a partner and associate in the banking and finance group of Babel & Brooks PLLP, the firm Bluecast uses as corporate counsel. Below is the initial draft of the term sheet for the loan. A term sheet is a non-binding enumeration of the basic terms of a deal agreed to by the parties. Its purpose is to facilitate drafting of the deal documents (in this case, a loan agreement, security agreement, promissory notes, etc.).

Loan Term Sheet

Borrower:	Bluecast Corp., a Delaware corporation.
Loans:	• $60 million term loan. • $15 million working capital revolver.
Use of Proceeds:	Bluecast will use the term loan proceeds to refinance a portion of its existing long-term debt and the working capital revolver proceeds for working capital and general corporate purposes.
Collateral:	First priority perfected liens on and security interest in all assets of Bluecast, including all accounts receivable, machinery and equipment, inventory and real estate (including leasehold interests), except as NYB, in its discretion, may otherwise designate.

Amortization and Final Maturity:	The term loan will be amortized over seven years, and the working capital revolver will mature seven years from the Closing Date.
Interest Rate:	All loans will bear interest at a rate of 1.5% per annum (360-day basis) over NYB's Prime Rate, as defined and announced from time to time by NYB as its prime rate.
Representations and Warranties:	Representations and warranties customarily found in credit facilities of this nature, including a representation as to the absence of material adverse change.
Conditions Precedent to Closing:	Those customarily found in credit facilities of this nature including closing documentation in form and substance satisfactory to NYB, including legal opinions.
Conditions to Borrowing:	Those customarily found in credit facilities of this nature including absence of default and accuracy of representations and warranties.
Covenants:	Those standard negative, affirmative, and financial covenants customarily found in credit facilities of this nature including the following with respect to Bluecast: (a) restrictions on investments; (b) restrictions on debt and guarantees; (c) restrictions on mergers, acquisition, joint ventures, partnerships, and changes of business or conduct of business; (d) restrictions on disposition of assets other than in the ordinary course of business-asset sale proceeds used to prepay bank debt; (e) transactions with affiliates on arm's-length basis; (f) prohibition on any significant change in accounting treatment or reporting practices except as permitted or required by generally accepted accounting principles consistently applied; (g) restrictions on liens; (h) prohibition on the granting of negative pledges to any person if the effect thereof would be to inhibit the taking of collateral by NYB; (i) maintenance of insurance satisfactory to NYB; (j) prohibition on the use or disposition of hazardous materials or hazardous waste as those terms are defined in federal environmental laws on any real property owned by Bluecast; and (k) financial covenants on Bluecast's ratio of operating cash flow to total debt, fixed charge coverage ratio and tangible net at levels to be determined by NYB.

Expenses:	Bluecast will pay legal and other reasonable out-of-pocket expenses of NYB, including the fees and expenses of counsel regardless of whether the proposed loans actually close.
Governing Law:	State of New York.
Non-binding:	This term sheet does not constitute a commitment on the part of NYB to make the proposed loans. This term sheet is intended as an outline only and does not purport to summarize all of the terms, conditions, covenants, representations, warranties, and other provisions which would be contained in definitive legal documentation for this transaction. The actual commitment of NYB to make the loans is subject to the negotiation, to the satisfaction of NYB and its counsel, of all open issues outlined in this term sheet.

The term sheet was drafted by Raghav Gupta, the NYB loan officer assigned to the deal, with assistance from Martinez. The first that Sandhu heard of the deal was when she received an email from Steve Simmons, Bluecast's chief financial officer (CFO) with a draft of the term sheet attached. She forwarded the email to Lang with instructions to review the term sheet and get back to her with any comments. NYB's term sheet was fairly generic, so neither Sandhu nor Lang had any major comments. Sandhu and Lang then called Simmons, and Sandhu walked him through the term sheet with particular emphasis on the Covenants section. Simmons pointed out that Bluecast was in the process of acquiring a small company that would likely close after the closing on this deal. He noted that the NYB loan officer was aware of this. Lang reminded Simmons that Bluecast had granted a security interest in some of its equipment in connection with an equipment financing that Lang worked on for Bluecast last year. Simmons told Lang to mention this to NYB's counsel and did not think it would be a big deal. Sandhu also mentioned that closing on this deal would require the consent of Bluecast's existing lender. Simmons indicated that he had talked to them, and they were on board.

After the call with Simmons, Sandhu had Lang call Clark to give her the few comments they had, including carving out (1) the acquisition Simmons mentioned from the language of clause (c) of the covenants description, and (2) the security interest on the equipment Lang mentioned from the collateral description. Clark conferred with Gupta and then made the changes requested by Lang. Clark sent out the revised term sheet by email to the "working group" (Gupta, Simmons, Martinez, Sandhu, Lang, and Bluecast's CEO) and the parties signed off on it.

In accordance with the custom that lender's counsel drafts the documents, Clark cranked out the first draft of the loan agreement for the deal. She started with an early draft of a loan agreement she did for a similar NYB deal a few months ago and tailored it to this deal. Martinez reviewed the draft and gave Clark a few comments, which she incorporated and then emailed the draft to Gupta. Gupta gave the draft a quick once-over and gave Clark the go-ahead to circulate it. Clark then emailed the draft (about 40 pages long) to the members of the working group.

Sandhu and Lang spent a good part of the next two days carefully reading and commenting on the draft. They then called Simmons and discussed their comments with him and got his comments. Lang then consolidated Sandhu's, Simmons's, and his own comments in a "mark-up," meaning he took Clark's draft and on it hand-wrote comments, questions, corrections, and additions. Sandhu gave Lang's mark-up a quick once-over, and then Lang scanned it and emailed it to the working group. The mark-up, among other things, flagged discrepancies between the draft and the term sheet, corrected some drafting errors, fleshed out some ambiguous language, and added some qualifiers (knowledge, materiality, etc.) to the reps, covenants, and closing conditions. Simmons had instructed Sandhu and Lang not to be too aggressive on comments, because Bluecast wanted to close the deal fairly quickly.

Martinez and Clark accepted many of the changes on Lang's mark-up in consultation with NYB. Clark revised the draft accordingly and circulated it to the working group. For several days, Bluecast and NYB haggled over a number of the requested qualifiers to the reps, covenants, and closing conditions, but were able to resolve their differences. Clark turned another draft reflecting the resolution. She then cranked out the security agreement, promissory notes, and related documents and circulated them to the working group. Sandhu and Lang had a few more comments on the loan agreement and some relatively minor comments on the other documents, which they passed on to Clark.

While the drafting and revising was going on, Lang sent Oliver Bond, a junior associate at his firm, to Bluecast's corporate headquarters to review various corporate records and contracts. This is known as a "due diligence investigation" and is necessary to (1) ensure that the various disclosure schedules to the loan agreement are accurate and complete, and (2) allow Babel & Brooks to render a legal opinion on the deal.

As for disclosure schedules, a number of reps made by the borrower in the loan agreement reference a schedule that either contains additional information supplementing the particular rep or a list of exceptions to the rep. Here is language that Clark included in the Bluecast loan agreement.

SECTION 5.21. OWNERSHIP OF PROPERTY.

(a) Schedule 5.21(a) sets forth all the real property owned or leased by the Borrower and used or held for use in connection with the business of the Borrower and identifies the street address (or a legal description of such property), the

---

current owner (and current record owner, if different) and whether such property is leased or owned.

(b) Except as set forth on Schedule 5.21(b), all buildings, structures, heating and air conditioning equipment, plumbing, electrical, and other mechanical systems and equipment and the roofs, walls, and other structural components included in the Properties are in good operating condition and repair (normal wear and tear excepted), do not require any material repairs and are adequate for the uses for which they are currently utilized and comply in all material respects with all applicable laws, building, fire, health and safety codes, ordinances, and zoning rules and zoning ordinances.

Thus, as part of his due diligence investigation, Bond reviewed Bluecast's real property records and compiled Schedule 5.21(a). He also met with Bluecast's property manager who informed him of some issues Bluecast has with some of its properties. Bond wrote these up for Schedule 5.21(b).

As for legal opinions, for a commercial loan of any significance, the lender will require borrower's counsel to furnish it a legal opinion providing, among other things, that

- The borrower validly exists and is in good standing in its jurisdiction of organization;
- The person signing on behalf of the borrower has the power and authority to execute the loan agreement and related documents; and
- The execution, delivery, and performance of the loan agreement by the borrower has been duly authorized and will not conflict with any provision of the borrower's organizational documents or material agreements.

Because of bullet point three, Bond reviewed all of Bluecast's material contracts as part of his due diligence investigation to determine whether any of them restrict Bluecast's ability to incur additional indebtedness. He discovered that its existing loan agreement does, as Sandhu had flagged earlier, but did not find any other agreements that do. He notified Lang of his findings. As for bullet point one, B&B will order a certificate of good standing and certified certificate of incorporation for Bluecast from the Delaware Secretary of State as backup for giving that opinion. As for bullet point two, Lang will have Bluecast's board adopt resolutions he has drafted authorizing Simmons to execute the loan agreement and related documents on behalf of Bluecast.

A legal opinion is written in letter form, so here it would be a letter from B&B to NYB. It will contain a number of qualifiers and limitations in an effort by the opinion giver to limit exposure. Here is qualifying language B&B included in its legal opinion to NYB:

> In rendering this opinion we have assumed the legal capacity of all natural persons, the genuineness of all signatures, the authenticity of all documents submitted to us as originals, the conformity to original documents of all documents submitted to us as certified, conformed, or photostatic copies and the authenticity of the originals of such latter documents. As to all questions of fact material to this opinion that have not been independently established, we have relied upon certificates or comparable documents of officers and representatives of the Borrower and upon the representations and warranties of the Borrower contained in the Loan Agreement.

After spending two days at Bluecast, Bond returned to his office and prepared the schedules for the loan agreement. In the meantime, Clark had circulated to the working group the latest drafts of all the documents. The next day, everyone in the working group signed off on the documents, and the parties closed on the loan two days later. Simmons executed the various documents on behalf of Bluecast, B&B signed its legal opinion, and NYB wired the money to Bluecast's account.

Question

While at Bluecast corporate headquarters doing due diligence, Bond noticed that the men's bathroom on the third floor was out of order. Does Bond need to include something about this in Schedule 5.21(b)?

B. EQUITY

Equity is an ownership stake in a business. When you make an equity investment in a company, instead of getting a contractual right to your money back plus interest like you would with a loan, you get a slice of the company. This slice goes by a different name depending on the entity type. Equity investors in corporations get shares of stock, or just shares for short.

A corporation gets to pick the number and type of shares it is authorized to issue through provisions in its charter. For example, if a corporation decides it wants to have 2 million authorized shares of common stock, it would include in its charter a provision such as the following:

> The aggregate number of shares that the corporation is authorized to issue is 2,000,000 shares of common stock having no par value.

There are basically two types of stock—common stock and preferred stock. The standard approach is for a corporation to initially only have common stock and then add preferred stock if necessary to raise additional equity capital.

1. Common Stock

Corporate law statutes generally do not actually use the term "common stock," but it has a commonly understood meaning. The term means stock that is entitled (1) to full voting rights, and (2) to receive the net assets of the corporation upon dissolution (this is called the "residual claim"). As discussed in Chapter 9, full voting rights include the right to elect directors and the right to vote on certain fundamental changes to the corporation. Common stock is entitled to one vote per share unless the charter says otherwise, that is, if you own 100 shares, you get to cast 100 votes on all matters put to a vote of the common shareholders.[5]

The residual claim component of common stock is what makes a share of it fluctuate in value. As a corporation's performance and prospects rise and fall, investor assessments of the value of the residual claim, and therefore the value of a share, rise and fall.

The single sentence in the box above is sufficient for authorizing common stock, because if a corporation's charter only provides for one class of stock or labels a class of stock "common," the class is deemed to have full voting rights and a residual claim, that is, the charter provision does not have to state this. Note that owning common stock does not entitle you to pre-dissolution pay-outs from the corporation, even if it is making money hand over fist. Corporations can and do distribute cash to shareholders, typically in the form of dividends, but doing so is entirely within the discretion of the board of directors.

Some corporations have more than one class of common stock, typically with different votes per share. For example, the charter of Google Inc. authorizes it to issue both Class A Common Stock and Class B Common Stock. The only difference of substance between the two classes is that pursuant to the charter Class A is entitled to one vote per share and Class B is entitled to ten votes per share. Having two classes of common stock entitled to a different number of votes is referred to as "dual class capitalization" and allows founders of a company to maintain majority voting power without owning a majority of outstanding shares. In Google's case, over 90 percent of its Class B Common Stock is owned by its two founders and board chairman.

The issuance of common stock requires board approval.[6] If a corporation has already issued all of the common stock it has authorized, it will need to get shareholder approval to amend its charter to increase its authorized shares.

---

5. *See* DGCL §212(a); MBCA §7.21(a).
6. *See* DGCL §153; MBCA §6.21.

2. Preferred Stock

Corporate law statutes generally do not use the term "preferred stock" but, as with common stock, it has a commonly understood meaning. Preferred stock generally means stock that has a preference over common stock in either the payment of dividends (a dividend preference) or the distribution of assets upon dissolution (a liquidation preference), or both. Here is sample charter language that authorizes the corporation to issue preferred stock in addition to common stock:

The total number of shares of capital stock which the Corporation shall have authority to issue is 10,000,000, comprised of 5,000,000 shares of common stock having a par value of $0.01 per share and 5,000,000 shares of Series A Preferred Stock having a par value of $0.01 per share (the "Series A Preferred"). Each share of Series A Preferred has the following preferences:

(a) Dividend preference. The holders of the Series A Preferred are entitled to receive dividends in the amount of $5.00 per share annually before any dividends shall be payable on the common stock. Dividends on the Series A Preferred shall be cumulative (regardless of whether they were declared or whether the Corporation was legally allowed to pay any dividends).

(b) Liquidation preference. Upon any voluntary or involuntary liquidation, dissolution or other winding up of the affairs of the Corporation, before any distribution or payment shall be made to the holders of Common Stock, the holders of the Series A Preferred shall be entitled to be paid, to the extent possible in cash, $10.00 per share.

As you can see, the above Series A Preferred includes both a dividend preference and a liquidation preference. These and other common features of preferred stock are discussed below.

Corporations typically do multiple rounds of preferred stock financing. For example, a corporation may raise $10 million from the sale of preferred stock in year 1, $20 million in year 2, and $30 million in year 3. Investors in each of these rounds will require stock with different terms. Thus, after year 3 the corporation will have three different types of preferred stock outstanding. Lawyers refer to each type as a "series," and the convention is to label series sequentially with capital letters. Hence, a corporation will designate the preferred it created and issued in round one as "Series A," the preferred it created and issued in round two as "Series B," etc.

Note that the terms of a corporation's preferred stock are generally the product of negotiations between the corporation and the investors who will be buying it from the corporation. A corporation's preferred stock may, but will not necessarily, include all of the features discussed below, and the specific wording of the features that are included will almost assuredly differ from the wording below.

a. Dividend Preference

A dividend preference specifies a per share amount (usually a fixed dollar amount, but sometimes a formula for determining the amount) the holders of the particular shares are entitled to receive before any dividends are payable on the common stock. In the above sample language, that amount is $5.00, meaning in any particular year at least $5.00 per share has to be paid to the holders of Series A Preferred before any dividends can be paid by the Corporation to holders of common stock.

Dividends are either non-cumulative or cumulative, depending on what is specified in the charter. Non-cumulative means if the specified dividend per share is not paid in a particular year, for example, because the board of directors, in its discretion, decides not to pay it, the shareholders are not entitled to it in a subsequent year. Cumulative means that a missed dividend is carried forward and will have to be paid before the corporation can pay any dividends on its common stock. (Such missed dividends are referred to as "in arrears.") In the example above, the Series A Preferred dividends are cumulative per sentence two of subsection (a). Hence, if the corporation wants to pay a dividend on its common stock in year 3 but it failed to pay dividends on its Series A Preferred in both of year 1 and year 2, it will have to first pay holders of Series A Preferred $15.00 per share ($5.00 for each of years 1, 2, and 3) before it can pay any dividends on its common stock. If a charter provides for preferred dividends, but is silent on the issue of cumulative versus non-cumulative, the default rule under case law is that the dividends are impliedly cumulative.

*Default:
impliedly
cumulative
(preferred
dividends)*

Additionally, dividends are non-participating unless the charter says they are participating. Hence, in our example above the Series A Preferred dividends are non-participating. Participating means the holders of the preferred first get their dividend preference and then if the corporation decides to pay dividends on its common stock they participate in that dividend as well. Non-participating means they do not participate in dividends paid on common stock. Here is sample participating dividend language:

> In the event that the corporation declares or pays any dividends upon the common stock (whether payable in cash, securities, or other property) other than dividends payable solely in shares of common stock, the Corporation shall also declare and pay to the holders of the Series A Preferred at the same time that it declares and pays such dividends to the holders of the common stock, the dividends which would have been declared and paid with respect to the Series A Preferred if each outstanding share of Series A Preferred were reclassified as common stock immediately prior to the record date for such dividend, or if no record date is fixed, the date as of which the record holders of common stock entitled to such dividends are to be determined.

Let's look at an example. Assume that Shoe Corp. has the language from the last two boxes in its charter. Shoe Corp. has 100,000 shares of common stock outstanding and 100,000 shares of Series A Preferred outstanding. It is up to date on its Series A Preferred dividends, so this year it only has to pay $5.00 per share before paying dividends on its common stock. Shoe Corp. has $2 million it wants to pay in dividends. Pursuant to its charter, it would pay the dividends as follows: $5.00 per each outstanding share of Series A Preferred ($500,000 in total) and $7.50 ($1,500,000/200,000) to each outstanding share of common stock and Series A Preferred. Thus, the Series A Preferred would end up getting $12.50 per share. If instead the Series A Preferred was non-participating, it would get its dividend preference of $5.00 per share and that is it. The remaining $1.5 million would be paid to the common stock, meaning they would get $15.00 per share ($1,500,000/100,000).

!
Example

b. Liquidation Preference

A liquidation preference specifies a per share amount, either a fixed dollar amount or a formula for determining the amount, the holders of the particular shares are entitled to receive before any amounts are payable on the common stock following liquidation of the corporation. A liquidation is when a corporation ceases operations and sells off all of its assets. Usually, this is because the business has failed and thus there likely will not be any money left to distribute to shareholders. Regardless, investors routinely insist on preferred stock that includes a liquidation preference and sometimes they insist that a sale of the company be deemed a liquidation, a concept that makes a liquidation preference much more likely to come into play. In the sample language above, the liquidation preference is $10.00 per share and a sale of the company is not deemed a liquidation because the language does not so provide.

As with dividends, a liquidation preference can be participating or non-participating. Here is sample participating language:

Upon voluntary or involuntary liquidation, dissolution, or other winding up of the affairs of the Corporation, immediately after the holders of Series A Preferred shall have been paid in full in cash $10.00 per share, the remaining assets of the Corporation available for distribution shall be distributed in the following order and priority:

(i) First, to the holders of outstanding Common Stock, an aggregate amount equal to $5,000,000 pro rata based on the number of shares of Common Stock held by each such holder.

(ii) Second, the remaining assets of the Corporation available for distribution shall be distributed ratably among the holders of Common Stock and Series A Preferred on an as converted basis.

This language adds a wrinkle to participation. As you can see, the Series A Preferred first gets its $10.00 per share, then $5 million is divvied up among the holders of common stock, and then any remaining funds are divvied up among the holders of common stock and Series A Preferred. The existence of such a wrinkle is the product of negotiations between the corporation and investors in the preferred stock. It highlights the fact that while oftentimes corporations' preferred stock contain the same types of provision (e.g., dividend and liquidation preferences), there is no standard practice regarding the details of these provisions. Thus, you cannot make assumptions based on labels.

There is no such thing as a cumulative liquidation preference, because a liquidation is a one-time event. Sometimes, however, the terms of preferred stock provide that any dividends in arrears on the preferred stock at the time of liquidation are added to the liquidation preference. The sample language above does not so provide.

c. Conversion

Oftentimes preferred stock is convertible into common stock at the option of the holder. Here is sample language:

---

5. Subject to and in compliance with the provisions of this paragraph 5, each share of Preferred Stock may, at the option of the holder thereof, be converted at any time and from time to time, and without the payment of additional consideration by the holder thereof, into fully-paid and non-assessable shares of Common Stock. The number of shares of Common Stock which a holder shall be entitled to receive upon conversion shall be equal to the product obtained by multiplying (a) the number of shares of Preferred Stock being converted at any time by (b) the Conversion Rate then in effect. The "**Conversion Rate**" in effect at any time shall be the quotient obtained by dividing (a) $100.00 by (b) the Conversion Price then in effect. The initial "**Conversion Price**," subject to adjustment in accordance with this paragraph 5, shall be equal to $2.50.

Upon the happening of an Extraordinary Common Stock Event (as hereinafter defined), the Conversion Price of each share of Preferred Stock shall, simultaneously with the happening of such Extraordinary Common Stock Event, be adjusted by multiplying such Conversion Price by a fraction, the numerator of which shall be the number of shares of Common Stock outstanding immediately prior to such Extraordinary Common Stock Event and the denominator of which shall be the number of shares of Common Stock outstanding immediately after such Extraordinary Common Stock Event and the product so obtained shall thereafter be the Conversion Price, which, as so adjusted, shall be readjusted in the same manner upon the happening of any successive Extraordinary Common Stock Event or Events. An "**Extraordinary Common Stock Event**" shall mean (a) the issuance

---

of additional shares of Common Stock as a dividend or other distribution on outstanding shares of Common Stock, (b) a subdivision of outstanding shares of Common Stock, or (c) a combination or reverse stock split of outstanding shares of Common Stock into a smaller number of shares of Common Stock.

Conversion language gets complicated in a hurry. The above language is actually simplified and incomplete so as to not overwhelm you.

The $100.00 and $2.50 amounts in the language could be set at anything but likely mean that the corporation issued the preferred for $100.00 per share and at the time of such issuance the value of its common stock was $2.50. The basic idea is for the preferred to be convertible into the number of shares of common stock the investor would have gotten for its money if it bought common stock instead of preferred. For example, say you invested $1 million at $100 per share in preferred stock with the above conversion language. The corporation thus issued you 10,000 shares of preferred. These shares would be convertible into 400,000 shares of common stock calculated as follows: $10,000 \times (100.00/2.50) = 400,000$.

The second paragraph of the sample language (and it is the part that is incomplete) is to address situations where a corporation's number of outstanding shares of common stock change without a change to the shares' overall economics. For example, corporations sometimes subdivide or split their shares for reasons we discuss later. Say a corporation has 1 million shares of common stock outstanding and it decides to effect a 2-for-1 split. As part of the split, the corporation would issue an additional share for each share it has outstanding, but would receive no additional consideration. Thus, its outstanding common stock would increase from 1 million to 2 million shares and the value per share of common stock would be cut in half. Under the language above, the conversion price of the preferred stock would adjust to $1.25 per share upon the happening of the split, calculated as follows: $(1,000,000/2,000,000) \times \$2.50 = \$1.25$. Thus, the preferred stock will now be convertible into 800,000 shares of common stock $[10,000 \times (100.00/1.25)]$.

Note that holders of preferred stock generally do not convert it into common stock unless (1) the corporation has agreed to be acquired and converting as part of the acquisition would result in a bigger payout, or (2) there is a public market for the common stock but not the preferred stock and a holder of preferred wants to cash out of its investment. In this second situation, the holder would convert the preferred into common stock and then immediately sell these shares in the public market.

Additionally, it is standard for preferred stock to automatically convert into common stock upon an initial public offering (IPO) of common stock by the corporation meeting certain criteria. Here is sample language:

> Upon the closing of the sale of shares of Common Stock to the public at a price of at least $15.00 per share (subject to appropriate adjustment in the event of any stock dividend, stock split, combination or other similar recapitalization with respect to the Common Stock), in a firm-commitment underwritten public offering pursuant to an effective registration statement under the Securities Act of 1933, as amended, resulting in at least $50,000,000 of gross proceeds to the Corporation all outstanding shares of Series A Preferred Stock shall automatically be converted into shares of Common Stock, at the then effective conversion rate.

This type of provision cleans up a corporation's capital structure by eliminating all of its outstanding preferred stock. This in turn simplifies its IPO registration statement making the IPO easier to sell to investors. Investors in preferred stock are typically agreeable to such a provision, because they are hoping for an IPO so they can exit the investment at a nice profit.

d. Anti-Dilution

A conversion feature is normally coupled with anti-dilution provisions. Dilution refers to a decrease in the percentage interests of existing shareholders with respect to earnings, book value, voting power, etc. For example, say a corporation has 200 shares of stock outstanding, you and I each own 100 of the shares, and the corporation's book value is $100,000. Thus, we each hold 50 percent of the voting power and the book value per share is $500 ($100,000/200). The corporation then issues an additional 100 shares to a new investor for $20,000. As a result, the book value of its shares has been diluted down from $500 to $400 ($120,000/300), and the voting power of each of us has been diluted down from 50 percent to 33.33 percent. The dilution to book value occurred because the investor paid less than the then existing book value per share for her shares. The dilution to our voting power occurred because voting power is based on the number of shares a shareholder owns divided by the number of outstanding shares, and the number of shares we own (the numerator) remained the same while the number of shares outstanding (the denominator) increased.

Anti-dilution provisions furnish some level of protection against dilution, depending on the language. Here is sample language:

> 4.1 Adjustment of Series A Conversion Price Upon Issuance of Additional Shares of Common Stock. In the event the Corporation shall at any time after the Series A Preferred original issue date issue any additional shares of common stock, without consideration or for a consideration per share less than the Series A Conversion Price in effect immediately prior to such issue, then the Series A Conver-

sion Price shall be reduced, concurrently with such issue, to a price (calculated to the nearest one-hundredth of a cent) determined in accordance with the following formula:

$$CP2 = CP1 \times (A + B) \div (A + C).$$

For purposes of the foregoing formula, the following definitions shall apply:

(a) "CP2" shall mean the Series A Conversion Price in effect immediately after such issue of additional shares of Common Stock;

(b) "CP1" shall mean the Series A Conversion Price in effect immediately prior to such issue of additional shares of Common Stock;

(c) "A" shall mean the number of shares of Common Stock outstanding immediately prior to such issue of additional shares of Common Stock;

(d) "B" shall mean the number of shares of Common Stock that would have been issued if such additional shares of Common Stock had been issued at a price per share equal to CP1 (determined by dividing the aggregate consideration received by the Corporation in respect of such issue by CP1); and

(e) "C" shall mean the number of such additional shares of Common Stock issued in such transaction.

Attorneys refer to the above language as a "weighted average" anti-dilution provision because the formula takes into account the number of shares issued at a price lower than the then effective Series A Conversion Price with the more shares issued the greater the reduction to the conversion price.

Let's look at an example. Assume the corporation currently has 1 million shares of common stock outstanding and that the Series A Conversion Price is $10.00 per share. The corporation then issues 500,000 shares of common stock at $5.00 per share. Thus, CP1 equals $10.00; A equals 1,000,000; B equals 250,000 (500,000 × 5.00/10.00); and C equals 500,000. Hence CP2 equals 10.00 × (1,000,000 + 250,000) ÷ (1,000,000 + 500,000) or $8.3333, that is, the anti-dilution formula has adjusted the conversion price down by $1.6667. If the corporation instead issued 1,000,000 shares at $5.00 per share, CP1 would still equal $10.00; A would still equal 1,000,000; B would instead equal 500,000 (1,000,000 × 5.00/10.00); and C would instead equal 1,000,000. Hence, CP2 would equal 10.00 × (1,000,000 + 500,000) ÷ (1,000,000 + 1,000,000) or $7.50, that is, the conversion price would have dropped by $2.50 because under this second scenario the corporation issued more shares at the lower price.

In any event, adjusting the conversion price down means a share of preferred stock will be convertible into more shares of common stock. This negates, at least in part, the dilution holders of preferred stock would otherwise suffer from the common stock issuance.

An alternative type of anti-dilution provision is called "full-ratchet." Here is sample language:

> 4.1 <u>Adjustment of Series A Conversion Price Upon Issuance of Additional Shares of Common Stock</u>. In the event the Corporation shall at any time after the Series A Preferred original issue date issue any additional shares of common stock, without consideration or for a consideration per share less than the Series A Conversion Price in effect immediately prior to such issue, then the Series A Conversion Price shall be reduced, concurrently with such issue, to the consideration per share received by the Corporation for such issue or deemed issue of the Additional Shares of Common Stock; <u>provided that</u> if such issuance or deemed issuance was without consideration, then the Corporation shall be deemed to have received an aggregate of $.001 of consideration for all such Additional Shares of Common Stock issued or deemed to be issued.

Full-ratchet anti-dilution is more favorable to a holder of preferred (and easier to apply) than weighted-average. The conversion price is simply ratcheted down to whatever lower price at which the corporation issued additional shares. Thus, in both of our examples above, a full-ratchet anti-dilution provision would have adjusted the conversion price down to $5.00 instead of $8.3333 and $7.50.

e. *Protective Provisions*

Protective provisions are another common feature of preferred stock. These provisions prevent a corporation from taking specified actions that may harm the holders of preferred stock without their approval. Here is some sample language:

> 7. <u>Protective Provisions</u>. So long as any shares of Series A Preferred remain outstanding, the Corporation shall not, without the vote or written consent by the holders of at least a majority of the then outstanding shares of Series A Preferred:
>
> (a) Authorize or issue, or obligate itself to issue, any other equity security senior or equal to the Series A Preferred as to dividend rights, redemption rights, liquidation preferences, voting rights, election of directors, or conversion rights;
>
> (b) Declare, pay, or otherwise set aside a dividend payable on the Common Stock;
>
> (c) Effect any voluntary liquidation or dissolution of the Corporation or permit any of its subsidiaries to voluntarily liquidate or dissolve;
>
> (d) Effect any sale, lease, assignment, transfer, or other conveyance of all or substantially all of the assets of the Corporation or any of its subsidiaries, or any consolidation or merger involving the Corporation or any of its subsidiaries, or any reclassification or other change of any stock, or any recapitalization of the Corporation; or
>
> (e) Alter or change the powers, preferences, or special rights of the Series A Preferred or Common Stock.

You may have noticed that preferred stock protective provisions resemble loan agreement negative covenants. This is because investors in preferred stock have some of the same concerns as lenders.

f. Voting Rights

Preferred stock provisions typically address the number of votes to which each share is entitled. Here is some sample language:

> On any matter presented to the stockholders of the Corporation for their action or consideration at any meeting of stockholders of the Corporation (or by written consent of stockholders in lieu of meeting), each holder of outstanding shares of Series A Preferred Stock shall be entitled to cast the number of votes equal to the number of whole shares of Common Stock into which the shares of Series A Preferred Stock held by such holder are convertible as of the record date for determining stockholders entitled to vote on such matter.

Lawyers refer to the above as voting on an "as-converted basis," because the preferred gets one vote for each share of common stock into which it is convertible. If the terms of the preferred stock do not address voting, under corporate law statute default rules, each share gets one vote.[7]

g. Electing Directors

Oftentimes preferred stock provides its holders with the right to elect a specified number of directors to a corporation's board. Here is some sample language:

> The holders of record of the shares of Series A Preferred Stock, exclusively and as a separate class, shall be entitled to elect three directors of the Corporation. Any director elected as provided in the preceding sentence may be removed without cause by, and only by, the affirmative vote of the holders of the Series A Preferred Stock, given either at a special meeting of such stockholders duly called for that purpose or pursuant to a written consent of stockholders.

---

7. *See* DGCL §212(a); MBCA §7.21(a).

h. Redemption

A redemption provision enables the holders of preferred stock to require the corporation to buy the stock back. (It is also known as a "put" right.) Here is some sample language.

Shares of Series A Preferred Stock shall be redeemed by the Corporation out of funds lawfully available therefor at a price of $10.00 per share (the "Redemption Price"), in three annual installments commencing not more than 60 days after receipt by the Corporation at any time on or after July 1, 2015, from the holders of at least a majority of the then outstanding shares of Series A Preferred Stock, of written notice requesting redemption of all shares of Series A Preferred Stock (the "Redemption Request"). The date of each such installment shall be referred to as a "Redemption Date." On each Redemption Date, the Corporation shall redeem, on a pro rata basis in accordance with the number of shares of Series A Preferred Stock owned by each holder, that number of outstanding shares of Series A Preferred Stock determined by dividing (i) the total number of shares of Series A Preferred Stock outstanding immediately prior to such Redemption Date by (ii) the number of remaining Redemption Dates (including the Redemption Date to which such calculation applies). If the Corporation does not have sufficient funds legally available to redeem on any Redemption Date all shares of Series A Preferred Stock to be redeemed on such Redemption Date, the Corporation shall redeem a pro rata portion of each holder's redeemable shares of such capital stock out of funds legally available therefor, based on the respective amounts which would otherwise be payable in respect of the shares to be redeemed if the legally available funds were sufficient to redeem all such shares, and shall redeem the remaining shares to have been redeemed as soon as practicable after the Corporation has funds legally available therefor.

The redemption price is normally set at the price the investors paid the corporation for the preferred stock (here, it is set at $10.00 per share). The sample language provides for a "staggered redemption" over a period of three years. The idea here is to perhaps make it possible for a corporation to survive a redemption, because it will not have to immediately come up with all the funds.

A redemption provision could also give the corporation the right to buy back the preferred stock at a specified price (known as a "call" right). In the private corporation context, call rights are rarely agreed to by investors, and if they are, the redemption price is usually set at some multiple of the original investment price.

B. Equity

Exercise 8.2

Review the certificate of designation below and then answer the following questions. Assume these events occurred:

- On February 28, 2011, Riffpad issued 10,000 shares of Series A preferred.
- On March 1, 2011, Riffpad paid a dividend on the Series A preferred of $20 per share.
- On June 1, 2011, Riffpad issued as a stock dividend one share of common stock per every one share of common stock it had outstanding.
- On July 1, 2011, Riffpad issued 50,000 shares of common stock to a consultant in exchange for $200,000 of services.
- On September 1, 2011, Riffpad issued 200,000 shares of common stock to an investor for $6.00 per share.

1. What was the dollar amount per share of the Series A preferred dividend preference on February 28, 2011? Is the preference cumulative? Is it participating?
2. What was the dollar amount per share of the Series A preferred liquidation preference on June 2, 2011? Is the preference participating?
3. What was the Series A preferred conversion price on February 28, 2011? On June 2, 2011?
4. Into how many shares of common stock was a share of Series A preferred convertible on February 28, 2011? On March 2, 2011? On June 2, 2011? On July 2, 2011? On September 2, 2011?
5. Assume that A owns 7,000 and B owns 3,000 shares of Series A preferred, respectively. Both A and B decide to convert their shares and at that time the conversion price was $15.00 per share. What are they entitled to from Riffpad upon conversion?
6. What provision of the certificate of designation provides anti-dilution protection? What type of protection is it (i.e., weighted average, full-ratchet, other)?
7. Does Series A preferred have put rights?
8. In addition to the events from the bullet point list above, assume that Riffpad paid the Series A preferred a $10 dividend per share on March 1, 2012. What would be the Redemption Price on June 15, 2012? When would it make sense for Riffpad to exercise its redemption rights?

**CERTIFICATE OF DESIGNATION OF
SERIES A 3% CONVERTIBLE PREFERRED STOCK
OF RIFFPAD, INC.**

RESOLVED, that pursuant to the authority vested in the Board of Directors of Riffpad, Inc. (the "Corporation"), a Delaware corporation, in

· 287 ·

accordance with the provisions of its Amended and Restated Certificate of Incorporation, a series of 14,900 shares of Preferred Stock, par value $0.01 per share, designated as Series A 3% Convertible Preferred Stock (the "Preferred Stock") be, and it hereby is created, and that the designation and amount and relative rights, limitations, and preferences thereof are as follows:

1. Certain Definitions. Unless the context otherwise requires, the terms defined in this paragraph 1 shall have, for all purposes of this resolution, the meanings herein specified.

"*Affiliate*" means, with respect to any Person, any other Person directly or indirectly controlling or controlled by or under direct or indirect common control with such Person. For purposes of this definition, "control" when used with respect to any Person means the power to direct the management and policies of such Person, directly or indirectly, whether through the ownership of voting securities, by contract or otherwise; and the terms "controlling" and "controlled" have meanings correlative to the foregoing.

"*Business Day*" means any day other than a Saturday, a Sunday or a day when commercial banks in the City of New York are authorized by law, rule, or regulation to be closed.

"*Board of Directors*" means the Board of Directors of the Corporation.

"*Capital Stock*" means, with respect to any Person, any and all shares, interests, participations or other equivalents (however designated) of corporate stock or other equity participations, including partnership interests, whether general or limited, of such Person.

"*Common Stock*" means, with respect to any Person, Capital Stock of such Person that does not rank prior, as to the payment of dividends or as to the distribution of assets upon any voluntary or involuntary liquidation, dissolution or winding up of such Person, to any other shares of Capital Stock of such Person. Except as otherwise expressly provided or unless the context otherwise requires, references to "Common Stock" shall mean the Common Stock, $0.01 par value, of the Corporation.

"*Conversion Date*" shall have the meaning set forth in subparagraph 5(d) below.

"*Conversion Price*" means the price per share of Common Stock used to determine the number of shares of Common Stock deliverable upon conversion of a share of the Preferred Stock, which price shall initially be $15.00 per share, subject to adjustment in accordance with the provisions of paragraph 5 below.

"*Current Market Price*" at any date, means (in each case as adjusted for any stock dividend, split, combination, or reclassification that took effect during the Measurement Period);

   (a) if the Common Stock (or other security for which the Current Market Price is to be calculated) is publicly traded on any national securities exchange or the Nasdaq Stock Market ("Nasdaq"), the average of the daily closing prices per share of Common Stock (or of such other security) during the Measurement Period (as reported (absent manifest error) in *The Wall Street Journal*);

(b) if the Common Stock (or other security for which the Current Market Price is to be calculated) is not publicly traded on any national securities exchange or Nasdaq, but traded over-the-counter, the average of the daily closing reported bid and asked prices of the Common Stock (or of such other security) during the Measurement Period, as reported by Nasdaq or any comparable system (or if not so reported by Nasdaq or any comparable system, as furnished by two members of the National Association of Securities Dealers, Inc. selected from time to time by the Corporation for that purpose which, in the case of a security other than the Common Stock, shall be those market makers who post the two highest average asked prices for the applicable Measurement Period); or

(c) if the Common Stock (or other security for which the Current Market Price is to be calculated) is not traded in such manner that the quotations referred to above are available for the Measurement Period, Current Market Price shall be deemed to be the fair market value as determined in good faith by the Board of Directors.

"*Dividend Payment Date*" means March 1 of each year, commencing March 1, 2011.

"*Dividend Period*" means (a) with respect to the first dividend period, the period beginning on and including the Issue Date and ending on and excluding the first Dividend Payment Date and (b) thereafter, each annual period beginning on and including a Dividend Payment Date and ending on and excluding the next succeeding Dividend Payment Date.

"*Exchange Act*" means the Securities Exchange Act of 1934 (or any successor statute), as it may be amended from time to time.

"*Excluded Stock*" means shares of Common Stock issued or reserved for issuance by the Corporation (a) as a stock dividend payable in shares of Common Stock, (b) upon any subdivision or split-up of the outstanding shares of Common Stock, (c) upon conversion of shares of Preferred Stock, (d) pursuant to the Company's 2009 Stock Incentive Plan or other bona fide employee benefit plan, (e) pursuant to the Company's 2009 Stock Option Plan for Non-Employee Directors, (f) options outstanding on the date hereof, (g) up to 100,000 shares of Common Stock issued in exchange for services rendered to the Corporation or a Subsidiary of the Corporation, or (h) in a transaction that is addressed in subparagraph 5(f) (other than clauses (i), (ii), and (iii) of subparagraph 5(f)).

"*Issue Date*" means the date that shares of Preferred Stock are first issued by the Corporation.

"Junior Stock" means any class or series of stock of the Corporation not entitled to receive any dividends and/or any assets upon the liquidation, dissolution, or winding up of the affairs of the Corporation until the Preferred Stock shall have received the entire amount to which such stock is entitled.

"Liquidation Preference" means, on any date, the sum of (a) $1,000 per share of Preferred Stock, plus (b) accrued and unpaid dividends that were added to the Liquidation Preference prior to such date in accordance with subparagraph 2(c) below.

"Measurement Period" means, as of any date, the five consecutive trading days immediately preceding such date.

"Parity Stock" means any other class or series of stock of the Corporation entitled to receive payment of dividends and/or assets upon the liquidation, dissolution, or winding up of the affairs of the Corporation, in either case on a parity with the Preferred Stock.

"Person" means any individual, corporation, limited liability company, partnership, joint venture, trust, unincorporated organization, or government or any agency or political subdivision thereof and, shall include any successor (by merger or otherwise) of such entity.

"Purchase Agreement" shall mean the Purchase Agreement, dated as of February 28, 2011, by and between the Corporation and the Purchaser named therein, as it may be amended from time to time, a copy of which is on file at the principal office of the Company.

"Qualified IPO" means a sale of the Corporation's Common Stock pursuant to an initial public offering (the "IPO") of the Corporation's Common Stock on Form S-1 (or any equivalent general registration form) under the Securities Act of 1933, as amended, the gross proceeds from which aggregate not less than $50,000,000.

"Record Date" means, with respect to the dividend payable on March 1 of each year, the preceding February 15.

"Redemption Date" means the date fixed for redemption of the Preferred Stock pursuant to subparagraph 4(b) below or, if the Corporation shall default in the payment of the Redemption Price on such date, the date the Corporation actually makes such payment.

"Redemption Price" means the Liquidation Preference on the Redemption Date.

"Senior Stock" means any class or series of stock of the Corporation ranking senior to the Preferred Stock in respect of the right to receive dividends and/or assets upon the liquidation, dissolution, or winding up of the affairs of the Corporation.

"Subsidiary" of any Person means any corporation or other entity of which a majority of the voting power or the voting equity securities or equity interest is owned, directly or indirectly, by such Person.

2. Dividends. The holders of Preferred Stock shall be entitled to receive cash out of funds legally available for that purpose, in the amounts set forth below before any dividends shall be payable on the Common Stock. Such Preferred Stock dividends shall be payable when, as, and if declared by the Board of Directors, on each Dividend Payment Date, commencing on the first Dividend Payment Date following the Issue Date; *provided*, that if any such payment date is not a Business Day then such dividend shall be payable on the next Business Day.

(a) Dividends for a given Dividend Period shall be payable annually on each Dividend Payment Date at an annual rate equal to 3% of the Liquidation Preference of each share of Preferred Stock.

(b) Dividends shall be paid to the holders of record of the Preferred Stock as their names appear on the share register of the Corporation on the corresponding Record Date. Dividends on account of arrears for any particular Dividend Period in which dividends were not paid in cash on the Dividend Payment Date applicable to such Dividend Period shall be added to the Liquidation Preference on the relevant Dividend Payment Date and may no longer be declared or paid as dividends in cash.

(c) If full cash dividends are not paid or made available to the holders of all outstanding shares of Preferred Stock on the applicable Dividend Payment Date, and funds available shall be insufficient to permit payment in full in cash to all such holders of the preferential amounts to which they are then entitled, the entire amount available for payment of cash dividends shall be distributed among the holders of the Preferred Stock ratably in proportion to the full amount to which they would otherwise be respectively entitled, and any remainder not paid in cash to the holders of the Preferred Stock shall be added to the Liquidation Preference as provided in subparagraph 2(b) above.

(d) If the Corporation is required by a "determination" (as defined below) to pay any United States federal income tax (a "Tax Payment") in respect of any addition to the Liquidation Preference as a result of subparagraph 2(c) with respect to a record holder of the Preferred Stock, the Corporation may withhold such Tax Payment (but not any interest factor, penalty, or addition thereto) from a subsequent cash dividend to such record holder (in addition to any required withholdings of United States federal income tax on such cash dividend). For avoidance of doubt, the Corporation shall not be entitled to withhold any Tax Payment if the record holder of the Preferred Stock at the time of any required Tax Payment is not the record holder at the time of any subsequent cash dividend. A "determination" shall mean a decision, judgment, decree, or other order by any court of competent jurisdiction, which decision, judgment, decree, or other order has become final, a closing agreement entered into under Section 7121 (or any successor to such Section) of the Internal Revenue Code of 1986, as amended, or any other settlement agreement entered into in connection with an administrative or judicial proceeding.

3. Distributions Upon Liquidation, Dissolution, or Winding Up. Upon any voluntary or involuntary liquidation, dissolution, or other winding up of the affairs of the Corporation, before any distribution or payment shall be made to the holders of Junior Stock, the holders of the Preferred Stock shall be entitled to be paid, to the extent possible in cash, the greater of (a) the Liquidation Preference, and (b) the amount that would be payable to the holders of the Preferred Stock if such holders had converted all outstanding shares of Preferred Stock into shares of Common Stock immediately prior to such liquidation, dissolution, or other winding up. If such payment shall have been made in full to the holders of the Preferred Stock, the remaining assets and funds of the Corporation shall be distributed among the holders of Junior Stock, according to their respective shares and priorities. If, upon any such liquidation, dissolution, or other winding up of the affairs of the Corporation, the net assets of the Corporation distributable among the holders of all outstanding shares of the Preferred Stock shall be insufficient to permit the payment in full to such holders of the preferential amounts to which they are entitled, then the entire net assets of the Corporation shall be distributed among the holders of the Preferred Stock ratably in proportion to the full amounts to which they would otherwise be respectively entitled. The consolidation or merger of the Corporation into or with another corporation or corporations, shall not be deemed a liquidation, dissolution, or winding up of the affairs of the Corporation within the meaning of this paragraph 3. The sale of all or substantially all of the assets of the Corporation to another corporation or corporations shall be deemed a liquidation, dissolution, or winding up of the affairs of the Corporation within the meaning of this paragraph 3.

4. Redemption by the Corporation. The Corporation shall not have the right to redeem the Preferred Stock prior to the first anniversary of the Issue Date. Thereafter, the Corporation shall have the right, at any time or from time to time, to redeem the Preferred Stock, in whole or in part, at the Redemption Price.

(a) A Redemption Notice shall be sent by the Corporation, by first class mail, postage prepaid, to the holders of record of the Preferred Stock at their respective addresses as they shall appear on the records of the Corporation, not less than thirty days nor more than sixty days prior to the Redemption Date (i) notifying such holders of the election of the Corporation to redeem such shares and of the date of redemption, (ii) stating the date on which the shares cease to be convertible and the Conversion Price, (iii) stating the place or places at which the shares called for redemption shall, upon presentation and surrender of the certificates evidencing such shares, be redeemed, and the

Redemption Price to be paid therefor, and (iv) stating the name and address of the Corporation's transfer agent for the Preferred Stock. Neither failure to mail any such Redemption Notice to one or more such holders nor any defect in any Redemption Notice shall affect the sufficiency of the proceedings for redemption as to other holders.

(b) If a Redemption Notice shall have been given as hereinbefore provided, then each holder of Preferred Stock shall be entitled to all preferences and relative and other rights accorded by this resolution until and including the Redemption Date. From and after the Redemption Date, Preferred Stock shall no longer be deemed to be outstanding, and all rights of the holders of such shares shall cease and terminate, except the right of the holders of such shares, upon surrender of certificates therefor, to receive amounts to be paid hereunder.

5. Conversion Rights. The Preferred Stock shall be convertible as follows:

(a) *Optional Conversion.* Subject to and upon compliance with the provisions of this paragraph 5, each share of Preferred Stock shall be convertible in whole but not in part at the request of a majority of the holders of the Preferred Stock and at any time and from time to time from and after the Issue Date, into fully paid and non-assessable shares of Common Stock, in each case, at the Conversion Price in effect on the Conversion Date. If the Preferred Stock has been called for redemption, such right of conversion shall terminate at the close of business on the business day prior to the Redemption Date.

(b) *Mandatory Conversion.* Subject to and upon compliance with the provisions of this paragraph 5, the Corporation shall have the right to require the conversion of all but not less than all of the shares of Preferred Stock into Common Stock at any time and from time to time after the earlier to occur of (i) the third anniversary of the Issue Date and (ii) any merger, consolidation, or other business combination transaction of the Corporation.

(c) *Conversion Price.* Each share of Preferred Stock shall be converted into a number of shares of Common Stock determined by dividing the Liquidation Preference on the Conversion Date by the Conversion Price in effect on the Conversion Date, *provided, however,* that in no event will a share of Preferred Stock be converted into more than 90.909 shares of Common Stock, which number shall be adjusted proportionately in the same manner as the Conversion Price in the event of any adjustment in the Conversion Price pursuant to subparagraph 5(f)(iii) or (iv) hereof.

(d) *Mechanics of Conversion.* The holder of any shares of Preferred Stock may exercise the conversion right specified in subparagraph 5(a) by surrendering to the Corporation or any transfer agent of the Corporation the certificate or certificates for the shares to be converted, accompanied by written notice specifying the number of shares to be converted. Conversion shall be deemed to have been effected on the date when delivery of notice of an election to convert and certificates for shares is received by the Corporation, and such date is referred to herein as the "Conversion Date." Subject to the provisions of subparagraph 5(f)(v), as promptly as practicable thereafter, the Corporation shall issue and deliver to or upon the written order of such holder a certificate or certificates for the number of full shares of Common Stock to which such holder is entitled and a check or cash with respect to any fractional interest in a share of Common Stock as provided in subparagraph 5(e).

Subject to the provisions of subparagraph 5(f)(vi), the person in whose name the certificate or certificates for Common Stock are to be issued shall be deemed to have become a holder of record of such Common Stock immediately prior to the close of business on the Conversion Date.

(e) *Fractional Shares.* No fractional shares of Common Stock shall be issued upon conversion of shares of Preferred Stock. If more than one share of Preferred Stock shall be surrendered for conversion at any one time by the same holder, the number of full shares of Common Stock issuable upon conversion thereof shall be computed on the basis of the aggregate number of shares of Preferred Stock so surrendered. Instead of any fractional shares of Common Stock that would otherwise be issuable upon conversion of any shares of Preferred Stock, the Corporation shall pay a cash adjustment in respect of such fractional interest in an amount equal to that fractional interest of a share multiplied by the then Current Market Price. In lieu of paying cash on account of any fractional interests, the Corporation may, at its option, cause an agent to aggregate all fractional share interests and sell such aggregated number of shares on the open market in regular way brokerage transactions and cause the aggregate net proceeds (with all costs of sale and brokerage commissions deducted from the gross proceeds) to be paid pro rata to each Person who otherwise would be entitled to receive cash in lieu of a fractional share interest.

(f) *Conversion Price Adjustments.* The Conversion Price shall be subject to adjustment from time to time as follows:

(i) *Adjustment Upon Occurrence of Certain Events.* If, prior to the consummation of a Qualified IPO, the Corporation shall issue any Common Stock, other than Excluded Stock, without consideration or for a consideration per share less than the current Conversion Price immediately prior to such issuance, or the Corporation shall consummate a Qualified IPO at a public offering price per share of less than the Conversion Price in effect immediately prior to such Qualified IPO, the Conversion Price in effect immediately prior to any such issuance or Qualified IPO shall immediately (except as provided below) be reduced to the value of the consideration per share received in such transaction; <u>provided</u> that in no event shall the Conversion Price be reduced pursuant to this clause below $11.00 per share, which amount shall be adjusted proportionately in the same manner as the Conversion Price in the event of any adjustment in the Conversion Price pursuant to subparagraph 5(f)(iii) or (iv) hereof.

(ii) *No Qualified IPO Within 36 Months of the Issue Date.* If the Corporation shall have failed to consummate a Qualified IPO within the first 36 months of the Issue Date, the Conversion Price shall be reduced pursuant to this clause to $11.00 per share, which amount shall be adjusted proportionately in the same manner as the Conversion Price in the event of any adjustment in the Conversion Price pursuant to subparagraph 5(f)(iii) or (iv) hereof.

For the purposes of any adjustment of the Conversion Price pursuant to this clause (f), the following provisions shall be applicable:

(A) *Cash.* In the case of the issuance of Common Stock for cash, the amount of the consideration received by the Corporation shall be deemed to be the amount of the cash proceeds received by the Corporation for such Common Stock before deducting therefrom any discounts, commissions, taxes, or other expenses allowed, paid, or incurred by the Corporation for any underwriting or otherwise in connection with the issuance and sale thereof.

(B) *Consideration Other Than Cash.* In the case of the issuance of Common Stock (otherwise than upon the conversion of shares of capital stock or other securities of the Corporation) for a consideration in whole or in part other than cash, including securities acquired in exchange therefor (other than securities by their terms so exchangeable), the consideration other than cash shall be deemed to be the fair market value thereof determined in good faith by the Board of Directors, irrespective of any accounting treatment, provided that if any such consideration consists of publicly traded securities, the fair market value of such securities shall be the Current Market Price of such securities.

(C) *Options and Convertible Securities.* In the case of the issuance of (1) options, warrants, or other rights to purchase or acquire Common Stock (whether or not at the time exercisable), (2) securities by their terms convertible into or exchangeable for Common Stock (whether or not at the time so convertible or exchangeable) or options, warrants, or rights to purchase such convertible or exchangeable securities (whether or not at the time exercisable):

(1) the shares of Common Stock deliverable upon exercise of such options, warrants, or other rights to purchase or acquire Common Stock shall be deemed to have been issued for a consideration equal to the consideration (determined in the manner provided in subclauses (A) and (B) above), if any, received by the Corporation upon the issuance of such options, warrants, or rights plus the minimum purchase price provided in such options, warrants, or rights for the shares of Common Stock covered thereby; and

(2) if the Conversion Price shall have been adjusted upon the issuance of any such options, warrants, rights, or convertible or exchangeable securities, no further adjustment of the Conversion Price shall be made for the actual issuance of Common Stock upon the exercise, conversion, or exchange thereof.

(iii) *Stock Dividends Subdivisions, Reclassifications or Combinations.* If the Corporation shall (A) declare a dividend or make a distribution on its Common Stock in shares of its Common Stock, (B) subdivide or reclassify the outstanding shares of Common Stock into a greater number of shares, or (C) combine or reclassify the outstanding Common Stock into a smaller number of shares, the Conversion Price in effect at the time of the record date for such dividend or distribution or the effective date of such subdivision, combination, or reclassification shall be proportionately adjusted so that the holder of any shares of Preferred Stock surrendered for conversion after such date shall be entitled to receive the number of shares of Common Stock that such holder would have owned or been entitled to receive had such Preferred Stock been converted immediately prior to such date. Successive adjustments in the Conversion Price shall be made whenever any event specified above in this clause (iii) shall occur.

(iv) *Consolidation, Merger, Sale, Lease or Conveyance.* In case of any consolidation with or merger of the Corporation with or into another corporation or entity, or in case of any sale, lease, or conveyance to another corporation of the assets of the Corporation as an entirety or substantially as an entirety, each share of Preferred Stock shall after the date of such consolidation, merger, sale, lease, or conveyance be convertible into the number of shares of stock or other securities or property (including cash) to which the Common Stock issuable (immediately prior to the time of such consolidation, merger, sale, lease, or conveyance) upon conversion of such share of Preferred Stock would have been entitled upon such consolidation, merger, sale, lease, or conveyance; and in any such case, if necessary, the provisions set forth herein with respect to the rights and interests thereafter of the holders of the shares of Preferred Stock shall be appropriately adjusted so as to be applicable, as nearly as may reasonably be, to any shares of stock or other securities or property thereafter deliverable on the conversion of the shares of Preferred Stock.

(v) *Rounding of Calculations.* All calculations under this subparagraph (f) shall be made to the nearest cent or to the nearest one ten thousandth of a share, as the case may be.

(vi) *Timing of Issuance of Additional Common Stock Upon Certain Adjustments.* In any case in which the provisions of this subparagraph (f) shall require that an adjustment shall become effective immediately after a record date for an event, the Corporation may defer until the occurrence of such event (A) issuing to the holder of any share of Preferred Stock converted after such record date and before the occurrence of such event the additional shares of Common Stock issuable upon such conversion by reason of the adjustment required by such event over and above the shares of Common Stock issuable upon such conversion before giving effect to such adjustment and (B) paying to such holder any amount of cash in lieu of a fractional share of Common Stock pursuant to subparagraph 5(e); *provided* that the Corporation, upon request, shall deliver to such holder a due bill or other appropriate instrument evidencing such holder's right to receive such additional shares and such cash, upon the occurrence of the event requiring such adjustment.

(g) *Notice to Holders.* In the event the Corporation shall propose to take any action of the type described in clause (i) and (ii) (but only if the action of the type described in clause (i) would result in an adjustment in the Conversion Price), (iii), (iv), or (v) of subparagraph 5(f), the Corporation shall give notice to each holder of shares of Preferred Stock, sent by mail, first class postage prepaid, to each holder of shares of Preferred Stock at its address appearing on the Corporation's records, which notice shall specify the record date, if any, with respect to any such action and the approximate date on which such action is to take place. Such notice shall also set forth such facts with respect thereto as shall be reasonably necessary to indicate the effect of such action (to the extent such effect may be known at the date of such notice) on the Conversion Price and the number, kind, or class of shares or other securities or property which shall be deliverable upon conversion of shares of Preferred Stock. In the case of any action which would require the fixing of a record date, such notice shall be given at least ten days prior to the date so fixed, and in case of all other action, such notice shall be given at least fifteen days prior to the taking of such proposed action. Failure to give such notice, or any defect therein, shall not affect the legality or validity of any such action. Any such notice shall be deemed given upon receipt.

(h) *Treasury Stock.* For the purposes of this paragraph 5, the sale or other disposition of any Common Stock theretofore held in the Corporation's treasury shall be deemed to be an issuance thereof.

(i) *Costs.* The Corporation shall pay all documentary, stamp, transfer or other transactional taxes attributable to the issuance or delivery of shares of Common Stock upon conversion of any shares of Preferred Stock; *provided* that the Corporation shall not be required to pay any taxes which may be payable in respect of any transfer involved in the issuance or delivery of any certificate for such shares in a name other than that of the holder of the shares of Preferred Stock in respect of which such shares are being issued.

(j) *Reservation of Shares.* The Corporation shall reserve at all times so long as any shares of Preferred Stock remain outstanding, free from preemptive rights, out of its treasury stock (if applicable) or its authorized but unissued shares, or both, solely for the purpose of effecting the conversion of the shares of Preferred Stock, sufficient shares of Common Stock to provide for the conversion of all outstanding shares of Preferred Stock.

(k) *Approvals.* If any shares of Common Stock to be reserved for the purpose of conversion of shares of Preferred Stock require registration with or approval of any governmental authority under any Federal or state law before such shares may be validly issued or delivered upon conversion, then the Corporation will in good faith and as expeditiously as possible endeavor to secure such registration or approval, as the case may be. If, and so long as, any Common Stock into which the shares of Preferred Stock are then convertible is then listed on any national securities exchange, the Corporation will, if permitted by the rules of such exchange, list and keep listed on such exchange, upon official notice of issuance, all shares of such Common Stock issuable upon conversion.

(l) *Valid Issuance.* All shares of Common Stock which may be issued upon conversion of the shares of Preferred Stock will upon issuance by the Corporation be duly and validly issued, fully paid and non-assessable, not issued in violation of any preemptive rights arising under law or contract and free from all taxes, liens, and charges with respect to the issuance thereof, and the Corporation shall take no action which will cause a contrary result (including without limitation, any action which would cause the Conversion Price to be less than the par value, if any, of the Common Stock).

6. Voting Rights

(a) Except as required by applicable law or as provided herein, holders of shares of Preferred Stock shall not have the right to vote on any matters.

(b) Without the consent of the holders of at least a majority of the shares of Preferred Stock then outstanding, given in writing or by vote at a meeting of stockholders called for such purpose, the Corporation will not:

(i) declare, pay, or otherwise set aside a dividend payable on the Common Stock;

(ii) create or issue any Parity Stock or Senior Stock, increase the authorized amount of any such class, or reclassify any class or series of any Junior Stock into Parity Stock or Senior Stock; or

(iii) amend, alter, or repeal any provision of, or add any provision to, the Corporation's Amended and Restated Certificate of Incorporation or Amended and Restated By-Laws (by merger or otherwise), if such action would alter or change the powers, preferences, or special rights of the shares of the Preferred Stock so as to affect them adversely, or increase or decrease below the number then outstanding the number of shares of Preferred Stock authorized hereby.

7. Capital. On any redemption of Preferred Stock, the Corporation's capital shall be reduced by an amount equal to the Liquidation Preference multiplied by the number of shares of Preferred Stock redeemed on such date. The provisions of this paragraph 7 shall apply to all certificates representing Preferred Stock whether or not all such certificates have been surrendered to the Corporation.

8. Exclusion of Other Rights. Except as may otherwise be required by law, the shares of Preferred Stock shall not have any preferences or relative, participating, optional, or other special rights, other than those specifically set forth in this resolution (as such resolution may be amended from time to time) and in the Corporation's certificate of incorporation. The shares of Preferred Stock shall have no preemptive or subscription rights.

9. Headings of Subdivisions. The headings of the various subdivisions hereof are for convenience of reference only and shall not affect the interpretation of any of the provisions hereof.

10. Severability of Provisions. If any right, preference, or limitation of the Preferred Stock set forth in this resolution (as such resolution may be amended from time to time) is invalid, unlawful, or incapable of being enforced by reason of any rule of law or public policy, all other rights, preferences, and limitations set forth in this resolution (as so amended) which can be given effect without the invalid, unlawful, or unenforceable right, preference, or limitation shall, nevertheless, remain in full force and effect, and no right, preference, or limitation herein set forth shall be deemed dependent upon any other such right, preference, or limitation unless so expressed herein.

11. Status of Reacquired Shares. Shares of Preferred Stock which have been issued and reacquired in any manner shall (upon compliance with any applicable provisions of the laws of the State of Delaware) have the status of authorized and unissued shares of preferred stock undesignated as to series and may, subject to subparagraph 6(b)(i), be redesignated and reissued.

IN WITNESS WHEREOF, the undersigned has executed this Certificate of Designation as the act and deed of the Corporation and acknowledges the foregoing as true this 28th day of February, 2011.

RIFFPAD, INC.

By: <u>Sandra K. Martinez</u>
Name: Sandra K. Martinez
Title: Chief Financial Officer

---

i. Careful Drafting Required

Preferred stock provisions are typically drafted by investors' counsel. As the next case illustrates, this drafting needs to be done with great care, because the provisions are likely to be scrutinized for holes in connection with future financings and will be strictly construed by the courts. While reading the case, focus in on the hole exploited by CIBC and see if you can come up with language to close the hole.

Benchmark Capital Partners IV, L.P. v. Vague
2002 WL 1732423 (Del. Ch. 2002)

NOBLE, Vice Chancellor.

I. INTRODUCTION

This is another one of those cases in which sophisticated investors have negotiated protective provisions in a corporate charter to define the balance of power or certain economic rights as between the holders of junior preferred stock and senior preferred stock. These provisions tend to come in to play when additional financing becomes necessary. One side cannot or will not put up more money; the other side is willing to put up more money, but will not do so without obtaining additional control or other diminution of the rights of the other side. In short, these cases focus on the tension between minority rights established through the corporate charter and the corporation's need for additional capital.

In this case, Plaintiff Benchmark Capital Partners IV, L.P. ("Benchmark") invested in the first two series of the Defendant Juniper Financial Corp.'s ("Juniper") preferred stock. When additional capital was required, Defendant Canadian Imperial Bank of Commerce ("CIBC") was an able and somewhat willing investor. As a result of that investment, Benchmark's holdings were relegated to the status of junior preferred stock and CIBC acquired a controlling interest in Juniper by virtue of ownership of senior preferred stock. The lot of a holder of junior preferred stock is not always a happy one. Juniper's Fifth Amendment and Restated Certificate of Incorporation (the "Certificate") contains several provisions to protect the holders of junior preferred stock from abuse by the holder of senior preferred stock. . . . [Among other things,] [t]he Certificate grants the junior preferred stockholders a series vote on corporate actions that would "[m]aterially adversely change the rights, preferences and privileges of the [series of junior preferred stock]."

Juniper now must seek more capital in order to satisfy regulators and business requirements, and CIBC, and apparently only CIBC, is willing to provide the necessary funds. Juniper initially considered amending its charter to allow for the issuance of another series of senior preferred stock. When it recognized that the protective provisions of the Certificate could be invoked to thwart that strategy, it elected to structure a more complicated transaction that now consists principally of a merger and a sale of Series D Preferred Stock to CIBC. The merger is scheduled to occur on July 16, 2002 with a subsidiary merging with and into Juniper that will leave Juniper as the surviving corporation, but with a restated certificate of incorporation that will authorize the issuance of a new series of senior preferred stock and new junior preferred stock with a reduced liquidation preference and will cause a number of other adverse consequences or limitations to be suffered by the holders of the junior preferred. As part of this overall financing transaction, Juniper, after the merger, intends to issue a new series of preferred, the Series D Preferred Stock, to CIBC in exchange for a $50 million capital contribution. As the result of this sequence of events, the equity holdings of the junior preferred stockholders will be reduced from approximately 29% to 7%. Juniper will not obtain approval for these actions from the holders of the junior preferred stock. It contends that the protective provisions do not give the junior preferred stockholders a vote on these plans. . . .

Benchmark, on the other hand, asserts that the protective provisions preclude Juniper's and CIBC's heavy-handed conduct and brings this action to prevent the violation of the junior preferred stockholder's fundamental right to vote on these corporate actions as provided in the Certificate and to obtain interim protection from the planned evisceration of its equity interest in Juniper.

Because of the imminence of the merger and the issuance of the new senior preferred stock, Benchmark has moved for a preliminary injunction to stop the proposed transaction. This is the Court's decision on that motion.

II. THE PARTIES

Benchmark, a Delaware limited partnership based in Menlow Park, California, is a venture capital firm specializing in preferred stock investments. It manages more than $2 billion and has made approximately 50 preferred stock investments in the preceding 5 years.

Juniper is a Delaware corporation with its principal place of business in Wilmington, Delaware, where it has more than 300 employees. It is a financial services enterprise with the issuance of credit cards as its core business. Juniper Bank is Juniper's wholly-owned state-chartered banking subsidiary.

CIBC is a Canadian bank based in Toronto and controls Juniper through a subsidiary as the result of a $145 million investment in 2001.

The individual defendants are directors of Juniper. Defendants Richard Vague and James Stewart are founders and officers of Juniper. Defendant John Tolleson is a member of the special committee appointed by the board of Juniper to review the Series D Preferred financing.

III. FACTUAL BACKGROUND

A. Benchmark and CIBC Invest in Juniper

Benchmark became the initial investor in Juniper when in June 2000, it invested $20 million and, in exchange, was issued Series A Preferred Shares. Juniper raised an additional $95.5 million in August 2000 by issuing its Series B Preferred Shares. Benchmark contributed $5 million in this effort. It soon became necessary for Juniper to obtain even more capital. Efforts to raise additional funds from existing investors and efforts to find new potential investors were unavailing until June 2001 when CIBC and Juniper agreed that CIBC would invest $27 million in Juniper through a mandatory convertible note while CIBC evaluated Juniper to assess whether it was interested in acquiring the company. CIBC also agreed to provide additional capital through a Series C financing in the event that it chose not to acquire Juniper and if Juniper's efforts to find other sources for the needed funding were unsuccessful.

In July 2001, CIBC advised Juniper that it would not seek to acquire Juniper. After reviewing its options for other financing, Juniper called upon CIBC to invest the additional capital. The terms of the Series C financing were negotiated during the latter half of the summer of 2001. A representative of Benchmark, J. William Gurley, and its attorney were active participants in these negotiations. Through the Series C Transaction, which closed on September 18, 2001, CIBC invested $145 million (including the $27 million already delivered to Juniper). With its resulting Series C Preferred holdings, CIBC obtained a majority of the voting power in Juniper on an as-converted basis and a majority of the voting power of Juniper's preferred stock. CIBC also acquired the right to select six of the eleven members of Juniper's board. As required by Juniper's then existing certificate of incorporation, the approval of the holders of Series A Preferred and Series B Preferred Stock, including Benchmark, was obtained in order to close the Series C Transaction.

B. The Certificate's Protective Provisions . . .

Another protection afforded the holders of both the Series A Preferred and Series B Preferred Stock was set forth in Sections C.6.c(ii) & C.6.d(ii) of the Certificate. Those provisions require a vote of the holders of each series . . . if that corporate action would "[m]aterially adversely change the rights, preferences and privileges of the Series A Preferred [and Series B] Preferred Stock."

C. Additional Financing Becomes Necessary

By early 2002, Juniper was advising its investors that even more capital would be necessary to sustain the venture. Because Juniper is in the banking business, the consequences of a capital shortage are not merely those of the typical business. Capital shortfall for a banking entity may carry the potential for significant and adverse regulatory action. Regulated not only by the Federal Reserve Board and the Federal Deposit Insurance Corporation but also by the Delaware Banking Commissioner, Juniper is required to maintain a "well-capitalized" status. Failure to maintain that standard (or to effect a prompt cure) may result in, among other things, regulatory action, conversion of the preferred stock into a "senior common stock" which could than be subjected to the imposition of additional security through the regulatory authorities, and the loss of the right to issue Visa cards and to have its customers serviced through the Visa card processing system.

Juniper, with the assistance of an investment banking firm, sought additional investors. The holders of the Series A Preferred and Series B Preferred Stock, including Benchmark, were also solicited. Those efforts failed, thus leaving CIBC as the only identified and viable participant available for the next round of financing, now known as the Series D Transaction.

D. The Series D Preferred Transaction

Thus, Juniper turned to consideration of CIBC's proposal, first submitted through a term sheet on March 15, 2002, to finance $50 million through the issuance of Series D Preferred Stock that would grant CIBC an additional 23% of Juniper on a fully-diluted basis and reduce the equity interests of the Series A Preferred and Series B Preferred holders from approximately 29% to 7%.

The board, in early April 2002, appointed a special committee to consider the CIBC proposal. As the result of the negotiations among Juniper, the special committee, and CIBC, the special committee was able to recommend the Series D Transaction with CIBC. The terms of the Series D Transaction are set forth in the "Juniper Financial Corp. Series D Preferred Stock Purchase Agreement" and the "Agreement and Plan of Merger and Reorganization by and Between Juniper Financial Corp. and Juniper Merger Corp."

In general terms, the Series D Transaction consists of the following three steps:

1. Juniper will carry out a 100-1 reverse stock split of its common stock.

2. Juniper Merger Corp., a subsidiary of Juniper established for these purposes, will be merged with and into Juniper which will be the surviving corporation. The certificate of incorporation will be revised as part of the merger.

3. Series D Preferred Stock will be issued to CIBC (and, at least in theory, those other holders of Series A, B and C Preferred who may exercise preemptive rights) for $50 million.

Each share of existing Series A Preferred and each share of existing Series B Preferred will be converted into one share of new Series A Preferred or Series B Preferred, respectively, and the holders of the existing junior preferred will also receive, for each share, a warrant to purchase a small fraction of a share of common stock in Juniper and a smaller fraction of a share of common stock in Juniper. A small amount of cash will also be paid. Juniper will receive no capital infusion as a direct result of the merger. Although the existing Series A Preferred and Series B Preferred shares will cease to exist and the differences between the new and distinct Series A Preferred and Series B Preferred shares will be significant,[8] the resulting modification of Juniper's certificate of incorporation will not alter the class and series votes required by Section C.6. The changes to Juniper's charter as the result of the merger include, *inter alia,* authorization of the issuance of Series D Preferred Shares, which will be senior to the newly created Series A Preferred and Series B Preferred Stock with respect to, for example, liquidation preferences, dividends, and as applicable, redemption rights. Also the Series D Stock will be convertible into common stock at a higher ratio than the existing or newly created Series A Preferred and Series B Preferred Stock, thereby providing for a currently greater voting power. In general terms, the equity of the existing Series A Preferred and Series B Preferred holders will be reduced from approximately 29% before the merger to approximately 7% after the Series D financing, and CIBC will hold more than 90% of Juniper's voting power.

Juniper intends to proceed with the merger on July 16, 2002 and to promptly thereafter consummate the Series D financing. It projects that, without the $50 million infusion from CIBC, it will not be able to satisfy the "well-capitalized" standard as of July 31, 2002. That will trigger, or so Juniper posits, the regulatory problems previously identified and business problems, such as the risk

---

8. [FN 20] For example, the holders of the newly created Series A Preferred and Series B Preferred Stock will have an aggregate liquidation preference of $15 million as compared to the liquidation preference of the existing Series A Preferred and Series B Preferred holders of approximately $115 million. *See* Juniper Financial Corp.'s June 26, 2002 Proxy Statement, at 2. Moreover, "[t]he dividend payable . . . to the holders of the New Series A Stock will be reduced from $0.1068 per share to $0.020766 per share and the dividend payable . . . to the holders of the New Series B Preferred Stock will be reduced from $0.23 per share to $0.030268 per share." *Id.* at 46. The redemption rights and other preferences of the existing Series A Preferred and Series B Preferred holders will similarly be compromised by the conversion to the New Series A Preferred and New Series B Preferred Stock as a result of the merger. *See id.* at 47-48. Finally, the New Series A Preferred and New Series B Preferred Stock will be subordinate to another series of preferred stock, the Series D Preferred Stock.

of losing key personnel and important business relationships. Indeed, Juniper predicts that liquidation would ensue and, in that event (and Benchmark does not seriously contest this), that the holders of Series A Preferred and Series B Preferred Stock would receive nothing (or essentially nothing) from such liquidation.

IV. CONTENTIONS OF THE PARTIES

Benchmark begins its effort to earn a preliminary injunction by arguing that the junior preferred stockholders are entitled to a vote on the merger on a series basis under Sections C.6.c(ii) & C.6.d(ii) because the merger adversely affects, *inter alia,* their liquidation preference and dividend rights. . . .

In response, Juniper and CIBC argue that the junior preferred stockholders are not entitled to a class or series vote on any aspect of the Series D financing, particularly the merger. The adverse effects of the transaction arise from the merger and not from any separate amendment of the certificate of incorporation, which would have required the exercise of the junior preferred stockholders' voting rights.[9] Juniper and CIBC emphasize that none of the junior preferred stock protective provisions expressly applies to mergers. . . .

V. ANALYSIS . . .

1. General Principles of Construction

Certificates of incorporation define contractual relationships not only among the corporation and its stockholders but also among the stockholders. Thus, the Certificate defines, as a matter of contract, both the relationship between Benchmark and Juniper and the relative relationship between Benchmark, as a holder of junior preferred stock, and CIBC, as the holder of senior preferred stock. For these reasons, courts look to general principles of contract construction in construing certificates of incorporation.[10]

---

9. [FN 24] Juniper focuses on the separate statutory regimes for amendments of certificates of incorporation and for mergers. A corporation may amend its certificate of incorporation to reclassify its authorized stock, 8 Del. C. §242(a)(3), or to create a new class of stock with rights and preferences superior to other classes of stock, 8 Del. C. §242(a)(5). By 8 Del. C. §242(b)(2), "[t]he holders of the outstanding shares of a class shall be entitled to vote as a class upon a proposed amendment, whether or not entitled to vote thereon by the certificate of incorporation, if the amendment would increase or decrease the aggregate number of authorized shares of such class, increase or decrease the par value of the shares of such class, or alter or change the powers, preferences, or special rights of the shares of such class so as to affect them adversely." Mergers, by contrast, are accomplished in accordance with 8 Del. C. §251. A merger agreement, in accordance with 8 Del. C. §251(b)(3), and a certificate of merger, in accordance with 8 Del. C. §253(c)(4), shall state: "[I]n the case of a merger, such amendments or changes in the certificate of incorporation of the surviving corporation as are desired to be effected by the merger. . . ."

10. [FN 28] These principles, of course, include: the Court must first determine if the intent of the parties can be ascertained from the words chosen by the parties; unless the contract is ambiguous, extrinsic evidence may not be considered; and the document should be construed "as a whole" to reconcile, if possible, all of its provisions. *See generally id.* at 15-16. I note in passing that the record before me does not allow application of the principle that any ambiguity should be construed against the drafter of the document, because it appears that Benchmark, Juniper and CIBC all actively participated in negotiation of the Certificate's protective provisions resulting from the authorization of the Series C Preferred Stock. *See Kaiser Aluminum Corp. v. Matheson,* 681 A.2d 392 (Del. 1996).

[A court's function in ascertaining the rights of preferred stockholders] is essentially one of contract interpretation against the background of Delaware precedent. These precedential parameters are simply stated: Any rights, preferences and limitations of preferred stock that distinguish that stock from common stock must be expressly and clearly stated, as provided by statute. Therefore, these rights, preferences and liquidations will not be presumed or implied.[11]

These principles also apply in construing the relative rights of holders of different series of preferred stock.

2. Challenges to the Merger

Benchmark . . . argues that Section C.6.c(ii), which protects the rights of the holders of Series A Preferred, and Section C.6.d(ii), which protects the rights of the holders of Series B Preferred, preclude the merger without a series vote because the merger "[m]aterially adversely changes the rights, preferences and privileges" of those classes of preferred stock. . . .

a. Merger as Changing the Rights, Preferences and Privileges

Benchmark looks at the Series D Preferred financing and the merger that is integral to that transaction and concludes that the authorization of the Series D Preferred Stock and the other revisions to the Juniper certificate of incorporation accomplished as part of the merger will materially adversely affect the rights, preferences, and privileges of the junior preferred shares. Among the adverse affects to be suffered by Benchmark are a significant reduction in its right to a liquidation preference, the authorization of a new series of senior preferred stock that will further subordinate its interests in Juniper, and a reduction in other rights such as dividend priority. These adverse consequences will all be the product of the merger. Benchmark's existing Series A Preferred and Series B Preferred shares will cease to exist as of the merger and will be replaced with new Series A Preferred Stock, new Series B Preferred Stock, warrants, common stock, and a small amount of cash. One of the terms governing the new junior preferred stock will specify that those new junior preferred shares are not merely subordinate to Series C Preferred Stock, but they also will be subordinate to the new Series D Preferred Stock. Thus, the harm to Benchmark is directly attributable to the differences between the new junior preferred stock, authorized through the merger, and the old junior preferred stock as evidenced by the planned post-merger capital structure of Juniper.

Benchmark's challenge is confronted by a long line of Delaware cases which, in general terms, hold that protective provisions drafted to provide a class of preferred stock with a class vote before those shares' rights, preferences and privileges may be altered or modified do not fulfill their apparent purpose of assuring a class vote if adverse consequences flow from a merger and the

---

11. [FN 29] *Elliot Assocs., L.P. v. Avatex Corp.,* 715 A.2d 843, 852-53 (Del. 1998) (footnotes omitted). *See* 8 Del. C. §151. The Supreme Court in *Avatex* further noted that "strict construction" as an analytical methodology is "problematic" in interpreting such provisions in corporate charters. *See id.* at 853 n.46.

protective provisions do not expressly afford protection against a merger. This result traces back to the language of 8 Del. C. §242(b)(2), which deals with the rights of various classes of stock to vote on amendments to the certificate of incorporation that would "alter or change the powers, preferences, or special rights of the shares of such class so as to affect them adversely." That language is substantially the same as the language ("rights, preferences and privileges") of Sections C.6.c(ii) & C.6.d(ii). Where the drafters have tracked the statutory language relating to charter amendments in 8 Del. C. §242(b), courts have been reluctant to expand those restrictions to encompass the separate process of merger as set forth in 8 Del. C. §251, unless the drafters have made clear the intention to grant a class vote in the context of a merger.

For example, in *Warner Communications Inc. v. Chris-Craft Industries, Inc.,* where Warner stock through merger was converted into Time stock, this Court was confronted with a provision in the certificate that accorded preferred stock-holders a class vote on corporate action to "'amend, alter or repeal any of the provisions of the Certificate of Incorporation or By-laws of the Corporation so as to affect adversely any of the preferences, rights, powers or privileges of the Series B Stock or the holders thereof. . . .'"[12] The Court, nonetheless, determined that the merger was not subject to a class vote by the preferred stock holders.

> The draftsmen of this language — the negotiators to the extent it has actually been negotiated — must be deemed to have understood, and no doubt did understand, that under Delaware law (and generally) the securities whose characteristics were being defined in the certificate of designation could be converted by merger into "shares or other securities of the corporation surviving or resulting from [a] merger or consolidation" or into "cash, property, rights or securities of any other corporation." 8 Del. C. §251(b); *Federal United Corporation v. Havender,* Del. Supr., 11 A.2d 331 (1940). . . .
>
> I can only conclude that it is extraordinarily unlikely that the drafters of Section 3.3(i), who obviously were familiar with and probably expert in our corporation law, would have chosen language so closely similar to that of Section 242(b)(2) [providing for a class vote where a charter would "alter or change" the powers, preferences or special rights" of a class or series of stock] had they intended a merger to trigger the class vote mechanism of that section.[13]

The range of Sections C.6.c(ii) and C.6.d(ii) is not expressly limited to changes in the Certificate. However, given the well established case law construing the provisions of certificates of incorporations and the voting rights of classes of preferred stockholders, I am satisfied that the language chosen by the drafters (*i.e.,* the "rights, preferences, and privileges") must be understood as those rights, preferences and privileges which are subject to change through

---

12. [FN 33] *Warner,* 583 A.2d at 965 (quoting the pertinent charter provision).
13. [FN 34] *Id.* at 969-70.

a certificate of incorporation amendment under the standards of 8 Del. C. §242(b) and not the standards of 8 Del. C. §251.[14]

In *Starkman v. United Parcel Service of America, Inc.*, this Court concluded that a supermajority vote was not necessary to accomplish a merger in part because the existing company became a wholly-owned subsidiary of the new primary company and the old company's charter had not been amended. However, the Court went on to observe that the supermajority vote would not have been required *"even if* the charter of the surviving corporation in the merger amended or deleted the right of first refusal [at issue]."[15] It explained its reasoning as follows:

> I reach this conclusion because the Supreme Court in *Avatex* rested its holding on the presence of language in the *Avatex* certificate of incorporation, specifically referring to the possibility of an amendment, alteration or repeal by merger, consolidation or otherwise. The critical language, referring to merger, consolidation or otherwise, was not found in *Warner* and is not found here. Thus, *Warner*, which was reaffirmed by the Supreme Court, requires that I read [the supermajority provision] to pertain only to charter amendments proposed in accordance with section 242 of the Delaware General Corporation Law. Because the transaction at issue is a merger proposed under the authority of Section 251 of the Delaware General Corporation Law, *Warner* requires a finding that [the supermajority provision] has no application.[16]

Finally, the corporate charter of Juniper was adopted after our Supreme Court's decision in *Avatex* and the drafters of the Certificate are charged with knowledge of its holding and the following:

> The path for future drafters to follow in articulating class vote provisions is clear. Where a certificate (like the Warner certificate or the Series A provisions here) grants only the right to vote on an amendment, alteration or repeal, the preferred have no class vote in a merger. When a certificate (like the First Series Preferred certificate here) adds the terms "whether by merger, consolidation or otherwise" and a merger results in an amendment, alteration or repeal that causes an adverse effect on the preferred, there would be a class vote.[17]

In short, to the extent that the merger adversely affects the rights, preferences and privileges of either the Series A Preferred or Series B Preferred Stock,

---

14. [FN 35] "In *Warner*, the Chancellor found that the provision that conferred a class-vote right did not encompass mergers, *in part* because the language of the *Warner* provision tracked §242(b)(2) of the General Corporation Law, which mandates a class vote for classes of stock that would be adversely affected by amendments to a certificate of incorporation, but does not create a class voting right in the event of merger." *Sullivan Money Mgmt.*, mem. op. at 6 (emphasis added).

15. [FN 36] *Starkman*, tr. at 19 (emphasis added).

16. [FN 37] *Id.* at 19-20.

17. [FN 38] *Avatex*, 715 A.2d at 855; *see also* Sullivan Money Mgmt., mem. op. at 9 ("Unarguably had the Certificate's drafters intended to expressly entitle the Series A Preferred Stockholders to a class vote on a merger, they knew fully well how to do so.").

those consequences are the product of a merger, a corporate event which the drafters of the protective provision could have addressed, but did not.

Accordingly, I am satisfied that Benchmark has not demonstrated a reasonable probability of success on the merits of its claim that Sections C.6.c(ii) and C.6.d(ii) require a series vote on the merger contemplated as part of the Series D Transaction. . . .

[handwritten margin note: language could have been included but wasn't. π does not prevail.]

Questions

1. What hole in the Series A and B protective provisions did CIBC exploit?
2. What language would you suggest to close the hole?
3. Is the same hole present in the protective provisions of Riffpad's Series A preferred?

j. *Public Company Preferred Stock*

Public companies also issue preferred stock, although with few of the features discussed above. The terms of public company preferred stock are normally set in consultation with the investment banking firm that will be leading the sale of the stock to investors. In this setting, the key provision is the dividend rate because the stock is pitched to investors as a debt-like security with the dividend rate the equivalent of interest. Here is a description of Series D Preferred Stock issued by Bank of America Corporation in 2006.

Preferential Rights. The Series D Preferred Stock ranks senior to our common stock and ranks equally with our Series B Preferred Stock as to dividends and distributions on our liquidation, dissolution, or winding up. Series D Preferred Stock is not convertible into or exchangeable for any shares of our common stock or any other class of our capital stock. Holders of the Series D Preferred Stock do not have any preemptive rights. We may issue stock with preferences superior or equal to the Series D Preferred Stock without the consent of the holders of the Series D Preferred Stock.

Dividends. Holders of the Series D Preferred Stock are entitled to receive dividends, when, as, and if declared by our board of directors or a duly authorized committee of our board, at an annual dividend rate per share of 6.204 percent on the liquidation amount of $25,000 per share. Dividends on the Series D Preferred Stock are non-cumulative and are payable quarterly in arrears. As long as shares of Series D Preferred Stock remain outstanding, we cannot declare or pay cash dividends on any shares of our common stock or other capital stock ranking junior to the Series D Preferred Stock unless full dividends on all outstanding shares of Series D Preferred Stock for the then current dividend period have been paid in full or declared and a sum sufficient for the payment thereof set aside. We cannot declare or pay cash dividends on capital stock ranking equally with the Series D Preferred Stock for any period unless full dividends on all outstanding shares of Series D Preferred Stock for the then-current dividend period have been paid in full or declared and a sum sufficient for the payment thereof set aside. If we declare dividends on the Series D Preferred Stock and on any capital stock ranking equally with the Series D Preferred Stock but cannot make full payment of those declared dividends, we will allocate the dividend payments on a pro rata basis among the holders of the shares of Series D Preferred Stock and the holders of any capital stock ranking equally with the Series D Preferred Stock.

Voting Rights. Holders of Series D Preferred Stock do not have voting rights, except as specifically required by Delaware law and in the case of certain dividend arrearages in relation to the Series D Preferred Stock. If any quarterly dividend payable on the Series D Preferred Stock is in arrears for six or more quarterly dividend periods, whether or not for consecutive dividend periods, the holders of the Series D Preferred Stock will be entitled to vote as a class, together with the holders of all series of our preferred stock ranking equally with the Series D Preferred Stock, for the election of two Preferred Stock Directors. When we have paid full dividends on the Series D Preferred Stock for at least four quarterly dividend periods following a dividend arrearage described above, these voting rights will terminate.

Distributions. In the event of our voluntary or involuntary liquidation, dissolution or winding up, holders of Series D Preferred Stock are entitled to receive, out of assets legally available for distribution to stockholders, before any distribution or payment out of our assets may be made to or set aside for the holders of our capital stock ranking junior to the Series D Preferred Stock as to distributions, a liquidating distribution of $25,000 per share, plus any declared and unpaid dividends, without accumulation of any undeclared dividends, to the date of liquidation. Shares of Series D Preferred Stock are not subject to a sinking fund.

Redemption. We may redeem the Series D Preferred Stock, in whole or in part, at our option, on any dividend payment date for the Series D Preferred Stock on or after September 14, 2011, at the redemption price equal to $25,000 per share, plus any accrued and unpaid dividends.

k. Corporate Law Requirements

The terms of preferred stock have to be set forth in a corporation's charter.[18] Because a corporation will not know in advance what terms investors in a particular round of preferred stock financing will require, the corporation will have to amend its charter to specify the terms once they have been finalized. Such an amendment generally requires shareholder approval. However, if a corporation's charter contains a "blank check preferred" provision, the board

---

18. *See* DGCL §151(a); MBCA §6.01(a).

can amend the corporation's charter to create a new series of preferred stock without obtaining shareholder approval.[19] Here is sample charter language that includes a "blank check preferred" provision:

> The Corporation is authorized to issue two classes of stock to be designated, respectively, "Common Stock" and "Preferred Stock." The total number of shares which the Corporation is authorized to issue is 6,000,000 shares, each with a par value of $0.001 per share. Of these shares, 5,000,000 shall be Common Stock and 1,000,000 shall be Preferred Stock. The Preferred Stock may be issued from time to time in one or more series. The Board of Directors is hereby authorized, within the limitations and restrictions stated in this Certificate of Incorporation, to determine or alter the rights, preferences, privileges, and restrictions granted to or imposed upon any wholly unissued series of Preferred Stock and the number of shares constituting any such series and the designation thereof, or any of them; and to increase or decrease the number of shares of any series subsequent to the issuance of shares of that series, but not below the number of shares of such series then outstanding. In case the number of shares of any series shall be so decreased, the shares constituting such decrease shall resume the status which they had prior to the adoption of the resolution originally fixing the number of shares of such series.

Under the above language, if, for example, the corporation reached an agreement to sell 50,000 shares of Series A Preferred Stock to an investor, the board would adopt a resolution designating 50,000 of the 1 million shares of Preferred Stock as Series A Preferred Stock and setting forth the terms of the Series A Preferred Stock that the corporation negotiated with the investor. The corporation would then file with the secretary of state a "certificate of designation" specifying the terms of the Series A Preferred Stock approved by the board. Such certificate becomes part of the corporation's charter upon filing.[20]

Once the particular series of preferred stock is created, the board must adopt a resolution approving its issuance.[21] If the preferred stock is convertible into common stock, it is customary for the board to also adopt a resolution reserving sufficient authorized but unissued shares of common stock for issuance upon conversion of the preferred stock.

Exercise 8.3

You represent a corporation that is seeking to amend its charter to include a blank check preferred provision. A group of minority shareholders has expressed trepidation about the amendment. You have been charged with the task of explaining to them why the amendment is beneficial to the corporation. What do you tell them? What concerns do you anticipate them having?

---

19. *See* DGCL §151(g); MBCA §6.02(a).
20. *See* DGCL §104; MBCA §6.02(c).
21. *See* DGCL §153; MBCA §6.21.

3. Warrants and Options

Warrants and options issued by a corporation share the same fundamental characteristic: they entitle the holder to buy common stock (or some other security) from the corporation at a specified price (called the strike price or exercise price) on or before a specified date (called the expiration date). Thus, they do not confer to their holders an ownership stake, so strictly speaking, they are not equity. We nonetheless cover them here because they confer the right to buy equity.

A holder of a warrant or option can profit to the extent the value of the corporation's stock exceeds the warrant or option exercise price. For example, suppose a company grants an employee the option to buy 100 shares of stock at $15.00 per share. A year later, the company's stock is trading at $20.00 per share. At that time, the employee could exercise her option and buy 100 shares at $15.00 per share and immediately resell them at the market price of $20.00 per share, making a pre-tax profit of $5.00 per share or $500.00 in the aggregate.

a. Warrants

A corporation typically issues warrants in connection with an equity or debt financing. For example, a lender may initially insist on a certain interest rate but agree to lower it in exchange for the company issuing the lender a warrant in connection with the loan. Such a warrant is referred to as a "sweetener." Below is a sample term sheet for a warrant:

Number of shares:	500,000 shares of common stock
Exercise price:	$10.00 per share; method of exercise to include net issuance rights
Expiration:	Three years
Adjustments:	Customary adjustments to the exercise price and number of shares subject to the warrant for stock splits, stock, dividends, and the like.

The terms would be reflected in a warrant agreement (sometimes the document is simply titled "warrant") executed by the corporation. As per the above terms, the agreement would provide the other party with the right to buy 500,000 shares of the corporation's common stock for $10.00 per share on or before the three-year anniversary of the date of the agreement. The "Adjustments" term denotes a concept similar to what was discussed above concerning adjustments to the conversion price of preferred stock, that is, where a corporation's number of outstanding shares of common stock change without a change to the shares' overall economics. Here is some sample language:

9. <u>Adjustment Provisions</u>. Subject to the provisions of this Section 9, the exercise price and the number of shares issuable upon exercise of the Warrant (the "**Warrant Shares**") in effect from time to time shall be subject to adjustment, as follows:

(a) <u>Stock Dividends</u>. If at any time after the date hereof (i) the Company shall declare or pay a stock dividend payable in shares of Common Stock or (ii) the number of shares of Common Stock shall have been increased by a subdivision or split-up of shares of Common Stock, then the number of Warrant Shares to be delivered upon exercise of the Warrant shall be increased so that the Holder will be entitled to receive the number of Warrant Shares that the Holder would have owned had the Warrant been exercised immediately prior to such dividend payment, subdivision or split-up, and the exercise price shall be adjusted as provided for in subsection (c) of this Section 9.

(b) <u>Combination of Stock</u>. If the number of shares of Common Stock outstanding at any time after the date of the issuance of the Warrant shall have been decreased by a combination or reverse split of the outstanding shares of Common Stock, then the number of Warrant Shares to be delivered upon exercise of the Warrant will be decreased so that the Holder thereafter shall be entitled to receive the number of Warrant Shares that the Holder would have owned had the Warrant been exercised immediately prior to such combination or reverse split, and the exercise price shall be adjusted as provided for in subsection (c) of this Section 9.

(c) <u>Exercise Price Adjustment</u>. Whenever the number of Warrant Shares purchasable upon the exercise of the Warrant is adjusted as provided pursuant to this Section 9, the exercise price payable upon the exercise of the Warrant shall be adjusted by multiplying such exercise price immediately prior to such adjustment by a fraction, of which the numerator shall be the number of Warrant Shares purchasable upon the exercise of the Warrant immediately prior to such adjustment, and of which the denominator shall be the number of Warrant Shares purchasable immediately thereafter; <u>provided</u>, <u>however</u>, that the exercise price for each Warrant Share shall in no event be less than the par value of such Warrant Share.

Let's look at an example involving this language. Say a corporation has 1 million shares of common stock outstanding and it decides to effect a 1-for-4 share combination (also called a reverse split). In such an event, every four shares of the corporation are combined into one share. For example, if you owned 400 shares before the combination, you would own 100 shares after the combination. Overall, the corporation's outstanding shares would drop from 1 million to 250,000. Under section 9(b) of the above language, the number of shares issuable upon exercise of the Warrant would drop to 125,000 (500,000/4). Under section 9(c) the warrant exercise price would increase to $40 ($10.00 \times 500,000/125,000$). This makes sense because prior to the combination, the warrant entitled the holder to buy a number of shares equal to 50 percent of the corporation's then outstanding shares for $5 million—the holder could buy

500,000 shares (50 percent of 1,000,000) at $10.00 per share or $5 million in total. After the combination, the warrant still entitles the holder to buy a number of shares equal to 50 percent of the corporation's then outstanding shares for $5 million—the holder could buy 125,000 shares (50 percent of 250,000) at $40.00 per share or $5 million in total.

The reference to "net issuance rights" in the Exercise Price term means that the warrant agreement will provide for what is often called "cashless exercise." Cashless exercise, as the name indicates, allows a holder to exercise a warrant without having to come up with the cash to pay the exercise price. Instead, the holder forfeits shares equal to the exercise price. For example, suppose you hold a Sjostrom Co. warrant for the purchase of 100,000 shares of common stock at $10.00 per share. You would like to exercise the warrant because Sjostrom Co. shares are currently trading at $25.00 per share, but you do not have the cash to pay the $1 million exercise price. Instead, if the warrant so provides, you can elect cashless exercise, which means that when you exercise the warrant, you do not pay anything to Sjostrom Co. and Sjostrom Co. issues you 60,000 shares instead of 100,000. Basically, you forfeit 40,000 shares to cover the $1 million exercise price (40,000 x $25.00 = $1,000,000).

Exercise 8.4

Review the warrant below and then answer the following questions.

1. What is the initial exercise price of the warrant? How many Warrant Shares does the warrant initially entitle Lopez to purchase? When would it make sense for Lopez to exercise the warrant?
2. Assume Snapbuzz effects a 1-for-10 reverse stock split. What is the Purchase Price and number of Warrant Shares issuable upon exercise of the warrant following the split?
   Note that a reverse stock split is when a corporation combines its outstanding shares into fewer shares. Thus, if Snapbuzz had 1 million shares of common stock outstanding prior to the reverse split, after the split it would have 100,000.
3. Can Lopez do a cashless exercise of the warrant?
4. What procedures does Lopez have to follow to transfer the warrant?
5. Can Lopez do a partial exercise of the warrant?

NEITHER THIS WARRANT NOR THE SECURITIES ISSUABLE UPON EXERCISE HAS BEEN REGISTERED UNDER EITHER THE SECURITIES ACT OF 1933, AS AMENDED (THE "ACT"), OR APPLICABLE

BLUE SKY LAWS, AND IS SUBJECT TO CERTAIN INVESTMENT REP-
RESENTATIONS. NEITHER THIS WARRANT NOR THE SECURITIES
ISSUABLE UNPON EXERCISE MAY BE SOLD, OFFERED FOR SALE
OR TRANSFERRED IN THE ABSENCE OF AN EFFECTIVE REGISTRA-
TION UNDER THE ACT AND APPLICABLE BLUE SKY LAWS, OR AN
OPINION OF COUNSEL SATISFACTORY TO THE COMPANY THAT
SUCH REGISTRATION IS NOT REQUIRED.

WARRANT TO PURCHASE COMMON STOCK

This certifies that, for value received, Jennifer Lopez, or her successors
or assigns ("**Holder**"), is entitled during the Exercise Period (as defined
below), subject to the terms set forth below, to purchase from Snapbuzz
Incorporated, a Delaware corporation (the "**Company**"), up to 1,000,000
shares of Common Stock, par value $.001 per share, of the Company
("**Common Stock**") at the price of $8.00 per share, subject to adjustment
as set forth below (the "**Purchase Price**"), upon surrender of this Warrant
at the principal office of the Company referred to below, with the subscription form attached hereto (the "**Subscription Form**") duly executed,
and simultaneous payment therefor in the manner specified in Section 1.
The Purchase Price and the number of shares of Common Stock purchasable hereunder are subject to adjustment as provided in Section 3.

As used herein, "**Exercise Date**" means the particular date (or dates)
on which this Warrant is exercised. "**Exercise Period**" means the period
during which this Warrant is exercisable; such period shall begin on the
date hereof and shall end at 6:00 P.M., Central Daylight Time, on June 11,
2016. "**Issue Date**" means the date hereof, June 12, 2011. "**Warrant**" includes this Warrant and any warrant delivered in substitution or exchange
therefor as provided herein. "**Warrant Shares**" means any shares of Common Stock acquired by Holder upon exercise of this Warrant.

1. **Exercise.**

(a) This Warrant may be exercised, in whole or in part, at any time
or from time to time, on any business day during the Exercise Period,
by surrendering it at the principal office of the Company at 100 East
7th Street, Saint Paul, MN 55101, together with an executed Subscription Form and a check in an amount equal to (i) the number of Warrant Shares being purchased, multiplied by (ii) the Purchase Price.

(b) This Warrant may be exercised for less than the full number of
Warrant Shares as of the Exercise Date. Upon such partial exercise,
this Warrant shall be surrendered, and a new Warrant of the same
tenor and for the purchase of the Warrant Shares not purchased upon
such exercise shall be issued to Holder by the Company.

(c) A Warrant shall be deemed to have been exercised immediately prior to the close of business on the date of its surrender for exercise as provided above, and the person entitled to receive the Warrant Shares issuable upon such exercise shall be treated for all purposes as the holder of such shares of record as of the close of business on such date. As soon as practicable on or after such date, and in any event within ten business days thereafter, the Company shall issue and deliver to the person or persons entitled to receive the same a certificate or certificates for the number of shares of Common Stock issuable upon such exercise.

(d) Notwithstanding the foregoing, the Company shall not be required to deliver any certificate for Warrant Shares upon exercise of this Warrant except in accordance with exemptions from the applicable securities registration requirements or registrations under applicable securities laws. Nothing herein shall obligate the Company to effect registrations under federal or state securities laws. If registrations are not in effect and if exemptions are not available when the Holder seeks to exercise the Warrant, the Warrant exercise period will be extended, if need be, to prevent the Warrant from expiring, until such time as either registrations become effective or exemptions are available, and the Warrant shall then remain exercisable for a period of at least 30 calendar days from the date the Company delivers to the Holder written notice of the availability of such registrations or exemptions. The Holder agrees to execute such documents and make such representations, warranties, and agreements as may be required solely to comply with the exemptions relied upon by the Company, or the registrations made, for the issuance of the Warrant Shares.

2. Payment of Taxes. All shares of Common Stock issued upon the exercise of this Warrant shall be validly issued, fully paid and non-assessable and the Company shall pay all taxes and other governmental charges that may be imposed in respect of the issue or delivery thereof, other than any tax or other charge imposed in connection with any transfer involved in the issue of any certificate for shares of Common Stock in any name other than that of the registered Holder of this Warrant, and in such case the Company shall not be required to issue or deliver any stock certificate until such tax or other charge has been paid or it has been established to the Company's satisfaction that no tax or other charge is due.

3. Certain Adjustments.

(a) Adjustment for Reorganization, Consolidation, Merger. In case of any reclassification or change of outstanding Company securities, or of any reorganization of the Company (or any other entity, the stock or securities of which are at the time receivable upon the exercise of this Warrant) or any similar corporate reorganization on or after the date hereof, then and in each such case Holder, upon the exercise hereof at any time after the consummation of such reclassification, change, reorganization, merger or conveyance, shall be entitled to receive, in lieu of the stock or other securities and property receivable upon the exercise hereof prior to such consummation, the stock or other securities or property to which Holder would have been entitled upon such consummation if Holder had exercised this Warrant immediately prior thereto, the terms of this Section 3 shall be applicable to the Company securities properly receivable upon the exercise of this Warrant after such consummation.

(b) Adjustments for Dividends in Common Stock. If the Company at any time or from time to time after the Issue Date declares any dividend on the Common Stock which is payable in shares of Common Stock, the number of Warrant Shares issuable upon exercise of this Warrant shall be proportionately increased and the Purchase Price shall be proportionately decreased.

(c) Stock Split and Reverse Stock Split. If the Company at any time or from time to time after the Issue Date effects a subdivision of the Common Stock, the Purchase Price shall be proportionately decreased and the number of Warrant Shares issuable upon exercise of this Warrant shall be proportionately increased. If the Company at any time or from time to time after the Issue Date combines the outstanding shares of Common Stock into a smaller number of shares, the Purchase Price shall be proportionately increased and the number of Warrant Shares issuable upon exercise of this Warrant shall be proportionately decreased. Each adjustment under this Section 3(c) shall become effective at the close of business on the date the subdivision or combination becomes effective.

(d) Accountants' Certificate as to Adjustment. In each case of an adjustment in the shares of Common Stock receivable on the exercise of this Warrant, if Holder so requests in writing, the Company at its expense shall cause its independent public accountants to compute such adjustment in accordance with the terms of this Warrant and prepare a certificate setting forth such adjustment and showing the facts upon which such adjustment is based. The Company will mail a copy of each such certificate to each holder of a Warrant at the time outstanding.

(e) Rights Under Warrant Agreement. The Company will not, by amendment of its Certificate of Incorporation, as amended, or through reorganization, consolidation, merger, dissolution, issue or sale of securities, sale of assets or any other voluntary action, avoid or seek to avoid the observance or performance of any of the terms of this Warrant, but will at all times in good faith assist in the carrying out of all such terms and in the taking of all such action as may be necessary or appropriate in order to protect the rights of the holders of the Warrants under this Warrant Agreement.

4. <u>Notices of Record Date.</u> If either (a) the Company shall take a record of the holders of its Common Stock for the purpose of entitling them to receive any dividend or other distribution, or any right to subscribe for or purchase any shares of stock of any class or any other securities, or to receive any other right; or (b) the Company undertakes a voluntary dissolution, liquidation, or winding up of the Company, then, and in each such case, the Company shall mail or cause to be mailed to each holder of a Warrant at the time outstanding a notice specifying, as the case may be, (1) the date on which a record is to be taken for the purpose of such dividend, distribution, or right, and stating the amount and character of such dividend, distribution, or right, or (2) the date on which such reorganization, reclassification, consolidation, merger, conveyance, dissolution, liquidation, or winding up is to take place, and the time, if any is to be fixed, as of which the holders of record of Common Stock shall be entitled to exchange their shares of Common Stock for securities or other property deliverable upon such reorganization, reclassification, consolidation, merger, conveyance, dissolution, liquidation, or winding up.

5. <u>No Rights as Shareholder.</u> Prior to the exercise of this Warrant, Holder shall not be entitled to any rights of a shareholder with respect to the Warrant Shares, including without limitation the right to vote such Warrant Shares, receive dividends or other distributions thereon or be notified of shareholder meetings, and Holder shall not be entitled to any notice or other communication concerning the business or affairs of the Company. However, nothing in this Section 5 shall limit the right of Holder to be provided the notices required under this Warrant. In addition, nothing contained in this Warrant shall be construed as imposing any liabilities on Holder to purchase any securities (upon exercise of this Warrant or otherwise) or as a shareholder of the Company, whether such liabilities are asserted by the Company or by creditors of the Company.

6. <u>Notice of Transfer of Warrant or Resale of the Warrant Shares.</u>

(a) The Holder, by acceptance hereof, agrees to give written notice to the Company before transferring this Warrant or transferring any Warrant Shares of such Holder's intention to do so, describing briefly the manner of any proposed transfer. Promptly upon receiving such written notice, the Company shall present copies thereof to the Company's counsel. If in the opinion of such counsel the proposed transfer may be effected without registration or qualification under any federal or state securities laws, the Company, as promptly as practicable, shall notify the Holder of such opinion, whereupon the Holder shall be entitled to transfer this Warrant or the Warrant Shares received upon the exercise of this Warrant, all in accordance with the terms of the notice delivered by the Holder to the Company.

(b) If, in the opinion of the Company's counsel, the proposed transfer or disposition of this Warrant or such Warrant Shares described in the written notice given pursuant to this Section 6 may not be effected without registration or qualification of this Warrant or such Warrant Shares, the Company shall promptly give written notice thereof to the Holder, and the Holder will limit its activities in respect to such transfer or disposition as, in the opinion of such counsel, are permitted by law.

7. Investment Intent. Holder, by acceptance hereof, agrees that this Warrant and the Warrant Shares to be issued upon exercise hereof are being acquired for investment and not with a view toward resale and that it will not offer, sell, or otherwise dispose of this Warrant or any Warrant Shares to be issued upon exercise hereof except under circumstances which will not result in a violation of the Securities Act. Upon exercise of this Warrant, Holder shall confirm in writing, in the form of Exhibit A, that the Warrant Shares so purchased are being acquired for investment and not with a view toward distribution or resale. This Warrant and all shares of Warrant Shares issued upon exercise of this Warrant (unless registered under the Securities Act) shall be stamped or imprinted with a similar legend indicated on the first page of this Warrant.

8. Loss or Mutilation. Upon receipt by the Company of evidence satisfactory to it (in the exercise of reasonable discretion) of the ownership of and the loss, theft, destruction, or mutilation of any Warrant and, in the case of loss, theft, or destruction, of indemnity satisfactory to it (in the exercise of reasonable discretion), and in the case of mutilation, upon surrender and cancellation thereof, the Company will execute and deliver in lieu thereof a new Warrant of like tenor.

9. Notices. All notices, requests, consents, and other communications given hereunder to any party shall be deemed to be sufficient if contained in a written instrument: (a) delivered in person, (b) sent by confirmed facsimile transmission to the number provided by the receiving party, or (c) duly sent by first class registered or certified mail, return receipt requested, postage prepaid, or overnight delivery service (e.g., Federal Express), addressed to such party at the address designated in writing by receiving party, as may be revised by the receiving party. All such notices and communications shall be deemed to have been received (i) in the case of personal delivery, on the date of such delivery, (ii) in the case of facsimile transmission, on the date of transmission, and (iii) in the case of mailing or delivery by service, on the date of delivery as shown on the return receipt or delivery service statement.

10. Change; Waiver. Neither this Warrant nor any term hereof may be changed, waived, discharged or terminated orally, but only by an instrument in writing signed by the Company and the Holder.

11. Headings. The headings in this Warrant are for purposes of convenience in reference only, and shall not be deemed to constitute a part hereof.

12. Governing Law. This Warrant is delivered in Minnesota and shall be construed and enforced in accordance with and governed by the internal laws, and not the law of conflicts thereof.

IN WITNESS WHEREOF, the Company has caused its duly authorized officer to execute this Warrant as of the date first above written.

> SNAPBUZZ INCORPORATED
> By: /s/ Ricki Lake
> Ricki Lake, President

Exhibit A

SUBSCRIPTION FORM
(To be executed only upon exercise of Warrant)

The undersigned registered owner of this Warrant irrevocably exercises this Warrant and purchases _____ of the number of shares of Common Stock of SNAPBUZZ INCORPORATED, a Delaware corporation, purchasable with this Warrant, and makes payment therefore in the amount of $_____.

The undersigned hereby represents and warrants that the undersigned is acquiring such shares of Common Stock for the undersigned's own account for investment purposes only, and not for resale or with a view to distribution of such shares or any part thereof.

_____
(Signature of Registered Owner)   Date

_____
(Street Address)

_____
(City), (State), (Zip)

b. Options

A corporation typically issues options to employees pursuant to a stock option or incentive compensation plan that sets forth terms that apply to all options granted under the plan. The company then enters into a separate option agreement with each person to whom it issues options. The option agreement incorporates the provisions of the plan and specifies the number of shares, exercise price, expiration date, etc., applicable for the issuance to the particular person. The theory behind issuing options to employees is to better align their interests with those of the company's shareholders.

Corporations often include options as part of the compensation package they offer to employees. Here is sample language from an offer letter to a prospective employee:

> In addition, if you decide to join the Company, it will be recommended at the first meeting of the Company's Board of Directors following your start date that the Company grant you an option to purchase 10,000 shares of the Company's Common Stock at a price per share equal to the fair market value per share of the Common Stock on the date of grant, as determined by the Company's Board of Directors. Twenty percent of the shares subject to the option shall vest 12 months after the date your employment begins subject to your continuing employment with the Company, and no shares shall vest before such date. The remaining shares shall vest monthly over the next 40 months in equal monthly amounts subject to your continuing employment with the Company. This option grant shall be subject to the terms and conditions of the Company's Stock Option Plan and Stock Option Agreement, including vesting requirements. No right to any stock is earned or accrued until such time that vesting occurs, nor does the grant confer any right to continue vesting or employment.

For tax reasons, the standard practice is to set the exercise price at the fair market value on the date of grant, as reflected in the above language.

Note that the language provides for vesting. In this context, vesting means that the employee must be employed by the company for a specified period of time before the employee is entitled to buy shares under the option. Under the above language, 2,000 shares ($10,000 \times 0.20$) vest after one year and an additional 200 shares ($8,000/40$) vest each of the next 40 months thereafter. Vesting serves as an employee retention tool. If a company's stock price has steadily risen, a lot of employees will be "in-the-money" on their options, that is, they hold options with exercise prices below the company's stock price. Thus, these employees have an economic incentive to remain with the company at least until all their options are fully vested. In that regard, it is common for companies to issue additional options to their good employees in connection with an annual performance review or promotion. That way, these employees continually have unvested option shares and therefore incentive to stay with the company.

If you are lucky enough to work for and be issued options by a successful startup that later goes public, your options may become extremely valuable. For example, before it went public, Google Inc. issued its employees options to purchase over 6 million shares at a weighted average price of $9.62 per share. In October of 2012, Google's shares were trading at around $750.00 per share. Hence, if in 2004 you were issued options to purchase just 10,000 shares at

$9.62 per share, exercised them, and sold the shares at $750.00 per share, you would end up with $7,403,800 in your pocket pre-tax.

Unlike warrants, which are typically freely transferable, options are not generally transferable except by will or the laws of descent or distribution.

Note that options of many larger public companies trade on exchanges such as the Chicago Board Options Exchange. These options are *not* issued by the companies. Instead they are standardized option contracts with standardized exercise prices and expiration dates written by market making firms and other traders.

Exercise 8.5

Say you own an option to purchase 10,000 shares of Riffpad common stock at $5.00 per share, the option provides for cashless exercise, and Riffpad's common stock is currently worth $15.00 per share. You elect to do a cashless exercise of the option. How many shares will Riffpad issue you? Will the issuance trigger an adjustment to the conversion price of Riffpad's Series A preferred?

---

c. Corporate Law Requirements

The issuance of warrants and options requires board approval.[22] Additionally, it is customary for the board to adopt a resolution reserving sufficient authorized but unissued shares of common stock for issuance upon exercise of the approved warrant or option.

4. Terminology

Before we leave the subject of corporate equity, make sure you understand the terminology we used or touched on above:

Authorized shares. Number and type (e.g., common and preferred) of shares a corporation's charter states it has the authority to issue.

Issued shares. Number of shares the corporation has sold to shareholders.

Outstanding shares. Number of shares held by a corporation's shareholders.

Treasury shares. Number of shares repurchased by a corporation from its shareholders.

For example, assume the authorized stock provision of a Delaware corporation's charter provides as follows:

---

22. DGCL §157; MBCA §6.24.

> The aggregate number of shares that the corporation is authorized to issue is 1,000,000 shares of common stock having no par value.

Of these 1 million shares, the corporation issues 15,000 shares to Smith and 5,000 shares to Gray. We would say the corporation has 1 million authorized shares, 20,000 issued shares, and 20,000 outstanding shares or 20,000 shares issued and outstanding. Assume the corporation buys back 5,000 shares from Smith. The corporation would still have 1 million authorized shares and 20,000 issued shares but would now have 15,000 outstanding shares and 5,000 treasury shares. In both of these scenarios, we could also say that the corporation has 980,000 authorized but unissued shares.

Note that the MBCA does not recognize the concept of treasury shares. Thus, in the second scenario (where the corporation buys back 5,000 shares from Smith), under the MBCA the corporation would have 1 million authorized shares, 15,000 issued shares, and 15,000 outstanding shares.[23] The 5,000 shares it repurchased from Smith revert to authorized but unissued status (unless the corporation's charter prohibits the reissue of acquired shares),[24] so after the buyback, the corporation has 985,000 authorized but unissued shares.

From a shareholder's perspective, the key number is outstanding shares. This is because only outstanding shares are entitled to vote and to distributions upon liquidation. Thus, the actual number of shares owned by a shareholder is not what is important. What is important is the percentage of outstanding shares the number represents. For example, if you own 80 shares of a corporation that only has 100 shares outstanding, you control 80 percent of the voting power and are entitled to 80 percent of the residual claim. We would call you the majority or controlling shareholder, because you control a majority of voting power. If instead the corporation had 1 million shares outstanding, your 80 shares would represent only 0.008 percent of the voting power and residual claim. We would call you a minority or non-controlling shareholder because of your minimal voting power. Note that treasury shares (if we're talking a non-MBCA state) are not relevant when calculating voting power and residual claim percentages, because they do not vote or have a residual claim.

5. Lawyer Roles

To give you a flavor for an equity financing transaction and the roles played by lawyers, below is a fictional angel financing deal by the Angel Group (AG)

---

23. *See* MBCA §6.31(a).
24. *See id.* §6.31(b).

to Zazu Corp. AG is essentially an investment club composed of wealthy individuals who enjoy investing in startup companies (i.e., angel investors). AG holds monthly meetings where promising startups are invited to pitch their companies to the group. If a critical mass of AG members want to invest in a company, they form an LLC to pool their money, and the LLC makes the investment. Zazu Corp. is a startup company that is developing a new battery technology, made a pitch at the last AG meeting, and convinced ten angels to invest. Below is the term sheet for the deal.

Equity Investment Term Sheet

Investment:	AG ZC Investment Vehicle LLC (the "Fund") will purchase 1,000,000 shares of Zazu Corp. (the "Company") common stock at a price of $1.00 per share (the "Shares"). So long as the Fund holds a majority of the Shares and until a liquidity event, it shall have the right to exchange them for the same kind and class of securities issued by the Company (the "New Securities") in any follow on financings should such New Securities have rights superior to the Shares.
Vesting:	To align the interests of the company's founders with those of the Fund, the founders agree that all of their previously issued shares will vest as follows: • 50% of the shares will vest monthly and linearly over a three year period; and • the other 50% will not vest unless and until the Company completes a firm-commitment initial public offering of its common stock or is sold. All share and option vesting will accelerate on a sale of the Company. An Escrow Agreement will be entered into to provide for the vesting.
Right of First Offer:	The Fund will have a right of first offer, subject to certain limitations, to purchase its pro rata portion of any new equity securities offered by the Company.
Board of Directors:	The Company's Board will be comprised of five directors, being the Company's CEO, one nominee of the Fund, and three nominees independent of management that the Company and the Fund agree on. Each director shall have a meaningful investment in the Company.

Information Rights:	The Company will provide the Fund with audited annual financial statements no later than 90 days after the end of each fiscal year, unaudited quarterly financial statements no later than 45 days after the end of each quarter, unaudited monthly financial statements no later than 30 days after the end of each month, and an annual budget for the upcoming fiscal year promptly following approval by the Board.
Protective Provisions:	So long as the Fund holds a majority of the Shares and until a liquidity event, the Company shall not amend its articles of incorporation, declare or pay any dividends, issue any equity securities, or sell the Company without the written consent of the Fund.
Documentation and Expenses:	Counsel to the Fund will draft an Investment Agreement and related agreements to document the terms of the Fund's investment. The Company will pay up to $10,000 of legal fees incurred by the Fund in connection with this investment.
Non-binding:	This is a non-binding Term Sheet and neither the Fund nor the Company will have any legal obligation in respect of this Term Sheet, except each party's obligations under the next paragraph (Confidentiality), unless the Agreement is executed by the parties.
Confidentiality:	The terms hereof are made in strict confidence, and may not be disclosed to third parties other than advisors to the parties hereto who agree to likewise keep them confidential.

The above term sheet was drafted by Jim Johnson, the lead angel on the deal. Johnson has been an active member of AG for eight years and has negotiated and invested in five startups over that timeframe. Zazu is anxious for the funding and short on cash, and so did not have the term sheet reviewed by counsel prior to signing off on it. Johnson forwarded the term sheet to Rob Smith, a partner at Davis & Wilson, who has represented AG on a number of other investments. Given the $10,000 cap on legal fees specified in the term sheet, Johnson handed the deal off to Beth Hall, a mid-level associate at Davis & Wilson, specializing in corporate and securities law.

In accordance with the custom that investors' counsel drafts the documents, Hall cranked out the first draft of the investment agreement for the deal. She started with a draft of an investment agreement Smith used on the last AG deal he worked on, and tailored it to this deal. Hall asked Smith for clarification on a couple of points, changed her draft accordingly, and then emailed it to Johnson. Johnson had a couple of minor comments, which Hall incorporated. She then emailed the draft to Tim Green, Zazu's corporate counsel.

Zazu instructed Green to turn the draft around quickly and to try to minimize comments. The draft matched the term sheet and Clark was an excellent drafter so Green had very few comments. (He asked for a couple of materiality and knowledge qualifiers in the reps and closing conditions and reworded a few of the provisions specifying the legal opinion Green's firm would need to render at closing.) Hall accepted all of Green's comments and revised the draft accordingly.

During the same timeframe, Hall had Kevin Vold, a legal assistant at Davis & Wilson, prepare articles of organization and related documents to organize AG ZC Investment Vehicle LLC. Vold also prepared a due diligence request letter for Hall's signature to send to Green. The request asked for copies of Zazu's organizational documents and material contracts, among other things. Green's firm sent over the documents a few days later. Vold reviewed them and found nothing surprising.

Hall circulated a draft of the escrow agreement (mentioned in the vesting section of the term sheet). Green emailed Hall a draft of the legal opinion for the deal. Hall and Green exchanged a few comments on these documents and finalized them. They both then informed their clients that the documents were ready, and the deal closed the next day.

C. INTERNALLY GENERATED FUNDS

The final category of financing is internally generated funds. A profitable business may be able to finance its operations from internally generated funds. These funds include proceeds from the sale of the goods and services the business provides. Many profitable businesses nonetheless carry some debt because their sales and therefore cash flow vary by season. For example, a recreational powerboat manufacturer will generate the bulk of its sales in early spring as dealers restock their inventories for the upcoming boat season, but will incur the bulk of its expenses in late fall and winter as it ramps up manufacturing for the new model year. As a result, even if the manufacturer is profitable, it will likely have to carry some debt because of the mismatch in timing of revenues and expenses.

Other profitable companies may take on additional debt or sell equity, because their internally generated funds are insufficient to finance expansion plans. For example, it is common for a company to borrow money or sell equity to complete an acquisition.

Finally, a business can sell some of its assets to generate funds. For example, a struggling business may decide to downsize and sell off a plant, store, or product line. Businesses can even sell their accounts receivable. Finance companies called factors will buy them at a discount of 1 percent to 5 percent of face value, depending on the creditworthiness of the account debtors.

D. CAPITAL STRUCTURE

Capital structure refers to the mix of debt and equity a company uses to finance its business. For example, a corporation that has financed its operations by selling $6 million of common stock and borrowing $4 million would have a capital structure of $6 million in equity and $4 million in debt. A company's capital structure changes over time as it borrows money, repays loans, and sells more equity. Hence, it is shaped largely by a company's choice between debt and equity financing when raising additional capital.

Capital structure is a complicated topic that involves mostly business and finance as opposed to legal considerations. Thus, an in-depth study is beyond the scope of this book. Nonetheless, to give you a flavor for the topic, below we discuss some key differences between debt and equity financing, some of which were touched on above.

1. Ownership Dilution

A company raises equity financing by selling additional ownership stakes in itself. As a result, the percentage ownership of the company's existing owners is diluted down by an equity financing. For example, say you own 100 shares of a corporation that has 1,000 shares issued and outstanding. Thus, your ownership percentage is currently 10 percent (100/1,000). The company decides to raise capital by selling an additional 200 shares to a new investor. Following this transaction, your ownership percentage in the corporation decreases from 10 percent to 8.33 percent because you now own 100 out of 1,200 shares instead of 100 out of 1,000 shares. Hence, your proportionate right to distributions by the corporation and residual claim on the corporation's assets has decreased accordingly.

example

Conversely, if the corporation raised capital by borrowing money instead of selling shares, your percentage ownership would be unchanged. This is because a loan does not represent an ownership stake in a corporation. All a lender gets is the right to its money back plus interest. Put differently, debt financing does not dilute down the percentage ownership of a company's existing owners.

2. Leverage

Debt financing creates leverage. In this context, leverage refers to the fact that a borrower retains returns earned on borrowed money in excess of the interest a lender charges. The following examples illustrate the concept.

Example 1.

You have decided that the housing market has bottomed out, so you buy a house for $200,000 paying cash. A year later, you sell the house for $220,000. Thus, you turned your $200,000 investment in the house into $220,000, a $20,000 return or 10 percent.

Example 2.

Instead of paying cash, you put 20 percent down on the house ($40,000) and borrow the balance ($160,000) at 5 percent interest. A year later you sell the house for $220,000, using part of the proceeds to repay the loan and interest. You have $52,000 left after paying off the loan ($220,000 sale proceeds – $160,000 principal amount of loan – $8,000 interest on the loan). Hence, you turned your $40,000 investment (the down payment) into $52,000 through the use of debt (the $160,000 loan), a $12,000 return (or 30 percent).

Example 3.

You put 5 percent down on the house instead of 20 percent and borrow the balance ($190,000) at 5 percent interest. A year later you sell the house for $220,000, using part of the proceeds to repay the loan and interest. You have $20,500 ($220,000 sale proceeds – $190,000 principal amount of loan – $9,500 interest on the loan). Hence, you turned your $10,000 investment (the down payment) into $20,500, an $11,500 return (or 115 percent).

leverage effect →

As the above examples illustrate, the more debt you use to buy the house, the greater the percentage return on the money invested by you (115 percent > 30 percent > 10 percent). This is the leverage effect. It reflects the fact that all a lender is entitled to is a return of principal plus interest regardless of how much money the borrower made on the money it borrowed.

Now, you may be thinking to yourself that you would rather have the $20,000 from Example 1 as opposed to the $12,000 from Example 2 or $11,500 from Example 3. However, keep in mind that you can deploy the money you did not invest in the house because of borrowings into other houses (or some other investment) to increase the total dollar amount of your returns as illustrated in the following example:

Example 4.

You buy five houses for $200,000 each putting $40,000 down ($200,000 in total) on each house and borrowing the balance ($160,000 per house) at 5 percent interest. A year later, you sell each house for $220,000 using part of the proceeds to repay the loan and interest. You have $52,500 left per house after paying off the loan ($220,000 sale proceeds – $160,000 principal amount of loan – $8,000 interest on the loan). Thus, you made $12,000 on each house for a total of $60,000, which is three times what you made in Example 1 where you did not borrow any money and instead invested your entire $200,000 in a single house.

In the business context, substitute houses for widgets. For example, a business could deploy $200,000 dollars to make 20,000 widgets that it sells for $220,000 earning $20,000. Alternatively, it could borrow $800,000 at 5 percent interest (like you did in Example 4), add it to the $200,000 it already has and make 100,000 widgets that it sells for $1.1 million. In this scenario, it would earn $60,000 on the $200,000 investment ($1,100,000 widget proceeds – $800,000 loan repayment – $40,000 interest payment on the loan – $200,000 investment).

Note that while leverage allows you to increase your returns, it also exposes you to greater losses if things do not work out as planned. For instance, if in Example 4 each house decreased in value by $10,000 so you sold them for $190,000 instead of $220,000, you would be left with $22,000 per house ($190,000 sale proceeds – 160,000 principal repayment – $8,000 interest), meaning you lost $18,000 of your $40,000 investment per house or $90,000 in total (5 houses × $18,000). If, instead, you had gone with Example 1, you would only have lost $10,000 ($200,000 invested – $190,000 in sale proceeds). Hence, leverage magnifies both gains and losses.

The sale of common equity does not create leverage. For example, if you and four friends each contribute $40,000 in exchange for a 20 percent equity interest in a company that buys a house for $200,000 and then flips it a year later for $220,000, you each have a claim to 20 percent of the $20,000 profit or $4,000. Compare this outcome to Example 2 above where instead of having your friends contribute $160,000 in equity, you borrowed $160,000 and ended up with $12,000 in your pocket.

3. Repayment Obligations

Debt contractually obligates a company to repay principal plus interest, usually through periodic payments. If a company hits tough times, these payments can drain it of cash, crippling its business. If it misses payments, it may end up in bankruptcy. Basically, lenders have to be paid whether the company is making money or not. This fixed obligation may limit management flexibility, but it may also cause it to be more cost-conscious.

Equity is permanent capital that a company never has to pay back. Even if a company has historically made regular cash distributions to its equity holders, in tough times it can cut or eliminate these distributions to preserve cash. Thus, equity capital can be viewed as a cushion protecting a company when it is struggling.

4. Priority

Debt claims have priority over equity claims upon the liquidation or bankruptcy of a company. This means a debt holder is entitled to be paid in full before anything is paid to equity holders (whether preferred or common). This priority is a big part of why a lender is willing to provide capital to a business even though the lender's return is fixed, meaning the lender does not participate in any upside.

5. Taxation

Interest payments on debt are deductible by a borrower for tax purposes. This deductibility reduces the effective interest rate paid by a borrower. For example, a C-corporation that borrows money at 10 percent and is subject to a marginal tax rate of 34 percent will essentially be paying interest at an after-tax rate of 6.6 percent. Note that if a C-corporation does not generate taxable income in a particular year, it will not benefit from the deduction that year, but the deduction will increase the loss the corporation can carry forward to offset against income in future years.

Conversely, a business does not get to deduct cash distributions it makes to its equity holders. This includes dividends paid by a corporation on preferred stock.

6. Bottom Line

Companies generally prefer debt financing over equity financing because of the lack of ownership dilution, leverage effect, and tax deductibility of interest. Thus, many companies will borrow money up until the point they can no longer do so on reasonable terms or are no longer allowed to do so by their existing lenders (pursuant to a negative covenant in the loan agreement regarding incurring additional debt) and only then turn to equity for additional financing. As a company takes on more and more debt, its default risk increases, because it will have to devote more and more of its cash resources to servicing the debt, that is, to make periodic principal and interest payments. Thus, later lenders will charge higher interest rates as compensation for increased default risk. Hence, at some point the costs of additional debt will exceed the benefits. As for existing lenders, they may be fine with the company incurring additional debt so long as the new debt is subordinated to their loans. However, at some point, existing lenders will become uncomfortable with a borrower incurring any more debt, because of increasing default risk and will therefore not allow it.

Note that many emerging companies are almost entirely equity financed. This is not because they prefer equity over debt, but because they do not have the hard assets or cash flow to secure debt on reasonable terms. If they do take on some debt, it will normally be personally guaranteed by one or more founders, because the lender will require this as a condition to the loan or will be convertible into equity at the option of the lender.

E. INTRODUCTION TO FEDERAL SECURITIES REGULATION

Sales of securities are regulated by federal law under the Securities Act of 1933 (Securities Act) and the Securities Exchange Act of 1934 (Exchange Act), which Congress enacted in the wake of the stock market crash of 1929. Section 5 of the Securities Act makes it unlawful to sell a security unless the sale is registered with the Securities and Exchange Commission (SEC) or is exempt from registration. Additionally, both the Securities Act and the Exchange Act include antifraud provisions making it unlawful for anyone to misstate or withhold material facts in connection with the sale of a security. This subsection, provides an overview of the definition of security, registered offerings, and exempt offerings. We cover Rule 10b-5, the principal antifraud provision under the Exchange Act, in Chapter 13.

1. Definition of Security

Section 2(a)(1) of the Securities Act defines security as follows:

> The term "security" means any note, stock, . . . bond, debenture, evidence of indebtedness, . . . transferable share, investment contract, voting-trust certificate, . . . put, call, straddle, option, . . . any interest or instrument commonly known as a "security," . . . or warrant or right to subscribe to or purchase, any of the foregoing.

Section 3(a)(10) of the Exchange Act includes a virtually identical definition.

As you can see, the definition of security is quite broad and appears to encompass all of the debt and equity instruments we discussed above, because it either lists them specifically or picks them up through broad language such as "evidence of indebtedness" or "investment contract." The analysis, however, is more complicated than the statutory language suggests, as illustrated by the next case. When reading the case, focus on the test the Court articulates for determining whether a "note" is a security and what the Court says about stock as a security.

Reves v. Ernst & Young
494 U.S. 56 (1990)

MARSHALL, J.

This case presents the question whether certain demand notes issued by the Farmers Cooperative of Arkansas and Oklahoma (Co-Op) are "securities" within the meaning of §3(a)(10) of the Securities Exchange Act of 1934. We conclude that they are.

I

The Co-Op is an agricultural cooperative that, at the time relevant here, had approximately 23,000 members. In order to raise money to support its general business operations, the Co-Op sold promissory notes payable on demand by the holder. Although the notes were uncollateralized and uninsured, they paid a variable rate of interest that was adjusted monthly to keep it higher than the rate paid by local financial institutions. The Co-Op offered the notes to both members and nonmembers, marketing the scheme as an "Investment Program." Advertisements for the notes, which appeared in each Co-Op newsletter, read in part: "YOUR CO-OP has more than $11,000,000 in assets to stand behind your investments. The Investment is not Federal [*sic*] insured but it is . . . Safe . . . Secure . . . and available when you need it." (ellipses in original). Despite these assurances, the Co-Op filed for bankruptcy in 1984. At the time of the filing, over 1,600 people held notes worth a total of $10 million.

After the Co-Op filed for bankruptcy, petitioners, a class of holders of the notes, filed suit against Arthur Young & Co., the firm that had audited the Co-Op's financial statements (and the predecessor to respondent Ernst & Young). . . . Petitioners maintained that, had Arthur Young properly treated the plant in its audits, they would not have purchased demand notes because the Co-Op's insolvency would have been apparent. On the basis of these allegations, petitioners claimed that Arthur Young had violated the antifraud provisions of the 1934 Act as well as Arkansas' securities laws.

Petitioners prevailed at trial on both their federal and state claims, receiving a $6.1 million judgment. Arthur Young appealed, claiming that the demand notes were not "securities" under either the 1934 Act or Arkansas law, and that the statutes' antifraud provisions therefore did not apply. A panel of the Eighth Circuit, agreeing with Arthur Young on both the state and federal issues, reversed. We granted certiorari to address the federal issue, and now reverse the judgment of the Court of Appeals.

II

A

This case requires us to decide whether the note issued by the Co-Op is a "security" within the meaning of the 1934 Act. . . .

The fundamental purpose undergirding the Securities Acts is "to eliminate serious abuses in a largely unregulated securities market." In defining the scope of the market that it wished to regulate, Congress painted with a broad brush. It recognized the virtually limitless scope of human ingenuity, especially in the creation of "countless and variable schemes devised by those who seek the use of the money of others on the promise of profits," and determined that the best way to achieve its goal of protecting investors was "to define 'the term "security" in sufficiently broad and general terms so as to include within that definition the many types of instruments that in our commercial world fall within the ordinary concept of a security.'" Congress therefore did not attempt precisely to cabin the scope of the Securities Acts. Rather, it enacted a definition of "security" sufficiently broad to encompass virtually any instrument that might be sold as an investment.

Congress did not, however, "intend to provide a broad federal remedy for all fraud." Accordingly, "[t]he task has fallen to the Securities and Exchange Commission (SEC), the body charged with administering the Securities Acts, and ultimately to the federal courts to decide which of the myriad financial transactions in our society come within the coverage of these statutes." In discharging our duty, we are not bound by legal formalisms, but instead take account of the economics of the transaction under investigation. Congress' purpose in enacting the securities laws was to regulate *investments*, in whatever form they are made and by whatever name they are called.

A commitment to an examination of the economic realities of a transaction does not necessarily entail a case-by-case analysis of every instrument, however. Some instruments are obviously within the class Congress intended to regulate because they are by their nature investments. In *Landreth Timber Co. v. Landreth*, 471 U.S. 681 (1985), we held that an instrument bearing the name "stock" that, among other things, is negotiable, offers the possibility of capital appreciation, and carries the right to dividends contingent on the profits of a business enterprise is plainly within the class of instruments Congress intended the securities laws to cover. *Landreth Timber* does not signify a lack of concern with economic reality; rather, it signals a recognition that stock is, as a practical matter, always an investment if it has the economic characteristics traditionally associated with stock. Even if sparse exceptions to this generalization can be found, the public perception of common stock as the paradigm of a security suggests that stock, in whatever context it is sold, should be treated as within the ambit of the Acts.

We made clear in *Landreth Timber* that stock was a special case, explicitly limiting our holding to that sort of instrument. Although we refused finally to rule out a similar *per se* rule for notes, we intimated that such a rule would be unjustified. Unlike "stock," we said, "'note' may now be viewed as a relatively broad term that encompasses instruments with widely varying characteristics, depending on whether issued in a consumer context, as commercial paper, or in some other investment context." *Ibid.* While common stock is the quintessence of a security, and investors therefore justifiably assume that a sale of stock is covered by the Securities Acts, the same simply cannot be said of notes, which are used in a variety of settings, not all of which involve investments. Thus, the phrase "any note" should not be interpreted to mean literally "any note," but must be understood against the backdrop of what Congress was attempting to accomplish in enacting the Securities Acts.

Because the *Landreth Timber* formula cannot sensibly be applied to notes, some other principle must be developed to define the term "note." A majority of the Courts of Appeals that have considered the issue have adopted, in varying forms, "investment versus commercial" approaches that distinguish, on the basis of all of the circumstances surrounding the transactions, notes issued in an investment context (which are "securities") from notes issued in a commercial or consumer context (which are not).

The Second Circuit's "family resemblance" approach begins with a presumption that *any* note with a term of more than nine months is a "security." See, e.g., *Exchange Nat. Bank of Chicago v. Touche Ross & Co.*, 544 F.2d 1126, 1137 (CA2 1976). Recognizing that not all notes are securities, however, the Second Circuit has also devised a list of notes that it has decided are obviously not securities. Accordingly, the "family resemblance" test permits an issuer to rebut the presumption that a note is a security if it can show that the note in question "bear[s] a strong family resemblance" to an item on the judicially crafted list of exceptions, *id.*, at 1137-1138, or convinces the court to add a new instrument to the list, see, e.g., *Chemical Bank v. Arthur Andersen & Co.*, 726 F.2d 930, 939 (CA2 1984).

The . . . "family resemblance" and "investment versus commercial" tests are really two ways of formulating the same general approach. Because we think the "family resemblance" test provides a more promising framework for analysis, however, we adopt it. The test begins with the language of the statute; because the Securities Acts define "security" to include "any note," we begin with a presumption that every note is a security. We nonetheless recognize that this presumption cannot be irrebuttable. . . . Congress was concerned with regulating the investment market, not with creating a general federal cause of action for fraud. In an attempt to give more content to that dividing line, the Second Circuit has identified a list of instruments commonly denominated "notes" that nonetheless fall without the "security" category. See *Exchange Nat. Bank, supra,* at 1138 (types of notes that are not "securities" include "the note delivered in consumer financing, the note secured by a mortgage on a home, the short-term note secured by a lien on a small business or some of its assets, the note evidencing a 'character' loan to a bank customer, short-term notes secured by an assignment of accounts receivable, or a note which simply formalizes an open-account debt incurred in the ordinary course of business (particularly if, as in the case of the customer of a broker, it is collateralized)"); *Chemical Bank, supra,* at 939 (adding to list "notes evidencing loans by commercial banks for current operations").

We agree that the items identified by the Second Circuit are not properly viewed as "securities." More guidance, though, is needed. It is impossible to make any meaningful inquiry into whether an instrument bears a "resemblance" to one of the instruments identified by the Second Circuit without specifying what it is about *those* instruments that makes *them* non-"securities." Moreover, as the Second Circuit itself has noted, its list is "not graven in stone," 726 F.2d, at 939, and is therefore capable of expansion. Thus, some standards must be developed for determining when an item should be added to the list.

An examination of the list itself makes clear what those standards should be. In creating its list, the Second Circuit was applying the same factors that this Court has held apply in deciding whether a transaction involves a "security." First, we examine the transaction to assess the motivations that would prompt a reasonable seller and buyer to enter into it. If the seller's purpose is to raise money for the general use of a business enterprise or to finance substantial investments and the buyer is interested primarily in the profit the note is expected to generate, the instrument is likely to be a "security." If the note is exchanged to facilitate the purchase and sale of a minor asset or consumer good, to correct for the seller's cash-flow difficulties, or to advance some other commercial or consumer purpose, on the other hand, the note is less sensibly described as a "security." *See, e.g., Forman,* 421 U.S., at 851 (share of "stock" carrying a right to subsidized housing not a security because "the inducement to purchase was solely to acquire subsidized low-cost living space; it was not to invest for profit"). Second, we examine the "plan of distribution" of the instrument, *SEC v. C.M. Joiner Leasing Corp.,* 320 U.S. 344, 353 (1943), to determine whether it is an instrument in which there is "common trading for speculation or investment," *id.,* at 351. Third, we examine the reasonable expectations of the investing public: The Court will consider instruments to be "securities" on the basis of such public expectations, even where an economic analysis of the circumstances of the particular transaction might suggest that the instruments are not "securities" as used in that transaction. . . . Finally, we examine whether some factor such as the existence of another regulatory scheme significantly reduces the risk of the instrument, thereby rendering application of the Securities Acts unnecessary.

We conclude, then, that in determining whether an instrument denominated a "note" is a "security," courts are to apply the version of the "family resemblance" test that we have articulated here: A note is presumed to be a "security," and that presumption may be rebutted only by a showing that the note bears a strong resemblance (in terms of the four factors we have identified) to one of the enumerated categories of instrument. If an instrument is not sufficiently similar to an item on the list, the decision whether another category should be added is to be made by examining the same factors.

B

Applying the family resemblance approach to this case, we have little difficulty in concluding that the notes at issue here are "securities." Ernst & Young admits that "a demand note does not closely resemble any of the Second Circuit's family resemblance examples." Brief for Respondent 43. Nor does an examination of the four factors we have identified as being relevant to our inquiry suggest that the demand notes here are not "securities" despite their lack of similarity to any of the enumerated categories. The Co-Op sold the notes in an effort to raise capital for its general business operations, and purchasers bought them in order to earn a profit in the form of interest. Indeed, one of the primary inducements offered purchasers was an interest rate constantly revised to keep it slightly above the rate paid by local banks and savings and loans. From both sides, then, the transaction is most naturally conceived as an investment in a business enterprise rather than as a purely commercial or consumer transaction.

As to the plan of distribution, the Co-Op offered the notes over an extended period to its 23,000 members, as well as to nonmembers, and more than 1,600 people held notes when the Co-Op filed for bankruptcy. To be sure, the notes were not traded on an exchange. They were, however, offered and sold to a broad segment of the public, and that is all we have held to be necessary to establish the requisite "common trading" in an instrument.

The third factor — the public's reasonable perceptions — also supports a finding that the notes in this case are "securities." We have consistently identified the fundamental essence of a "security" to be its character as an "investment." The advertisements for the notes here characterized them as "investments," and there were no countervailing factors that would have led a reasonable person to question this characterization. In these circumstances, it would be reasonable for a prospective purchaser to take the Co-Op at its word.

Finally, we find no risk-reducing factor to suggest that these instruments are not in fact securities. The notes are uncollateralized and uninsured. Moreover, unlike the certificates of deposit in *Marine Bank, supra,* at 557-558, which were insured by the Federal Deposit Insurance Corporation and subject to substantial regulation under the federal banking laws, and unlike the pension plan in *Teamsters v. Daniel,* 439 U.S. 551, 569-570 (1979), which was comprehensively regulated under the Employee Retirement Income Security Act of 1974, the notes here would escape federal regulation entirely if the Acts were held not to apply.

The court below found that "[t]he demand nature of the notes is very uncharacteristic of a security," 856 F.2d, at 54, on the theory that the virtually instant liquidity associated with demand notes is inconsistent with the risk ordinarily associated with "securities." This argument is unpersuasive. Common stock traded on a national exchange is the paradigm of a security, and it is as readily convertible into cash as is a demand note. The same is true of publicly traded corporate bonds, debentures, and any number of other instruments that are plainly within the purview of the Acts. The demand feature of a note does permit a holder to eliminate risk quickly by making a demand, but just as with publicly traded stock, the liquidity of the instrument does not eliminate risk altogether. Indeed, publicly traded stock is even more readily liquid than are demand notes, in that a demand only eliminates risk when, and if, payment is made, whereas the sale of a share of stock through a national exchange and the receipt of the proceeds usually occur simultaneously.

We therefore hold that the notes at issue here are within the term "note" in §3(a)(10). . . .

IV

For the foregoing reasons, we conclude that the demand notes at issue here fall under the "note" category of instruments that are "securities" under the 1933 and 1934 Acts. . . .

So ordered.

Questions

1. What is the test for determining whether a note is a security?
2. Monet gets behind on paying his account with the paint store. As a result, the paint store has Monet sign a promissory note with the following terms:

Principal amount: $2,350 (the amount Monet owes the paint store on his account)

Interest rate: 10% per annum

Maturity: One year

Is this note a security? Why or why not? Why does it matter?

The bottom line is that the issuance of stock will almost always involve a security and therefore must be done in compliance with federal securities laws. Oftentimes, however, the incurrence of debt does not involve a security because it "resembles" one of the family resemblance examples of *Reves*. If it is unclear whether a particular debt transaction has the requisite resemblance, prudence dictates operating under the assumption that the transaction involves the sale of a security.

Whether an ownership interest in a partnership or LLC constitutes a security is analyzed under the definition of "investment contract" as used in §2(a)(1) of the Securities Act and §(a)(10) of the Exchange Act. Neither Act defines the term, but the Supreme Court did in *Securities and Exchange Commission v. W.J. Howey Co.*, 328 U.S. 293 (1946). The Court held that "investment contract" means "a contract, transaction or scheme whereby a person invests his money in a common enterprise and is led to expect profits solely from the efforts of [others]." When it comes to partnership and LLC interests, the investment contract analysis normally turns on the "solely from the efforts of others" element. Specifically, courts look at the level of participation a partner or member has in the management and operation of a business. If participation is minimal, courts are likely to conclude that the "solely from the efforts of others" element is met, and assuming the other elements are also met (which is normally the case), the interests will thus fall under the definition of security.

Note that the plaintiffs in *Reves* were not suing the Co-Op, presumably because the Co-Op was bankrupt and therefore judgment proof, but Ernst & Young, the Co-Op's accounting firm. Such a suit is possible even though Ernst & Young did not issue the notes because of the broad reach of the federal securities regulation antifraud provisions, in particular, Rule 10b-5 under the Exchange Act, which is covered in Chapter 13.

Additionally, as the Court mentioned, the plaintiffs also sued Ernst & Young under Arkansas's securities laws. All 50 states have their own securities laws (also known as blue-sky laws). Like federal securities laws, these laws (1) prohibit the sale of a security in the state unless the sale is registered with the state or is exempt from registration, and (2) make it unlawful for anyone to misstate or withhold material facts in connection with the sale of a security. As a result, a business must comply with federal securities laws and the securities laws of each state in which it is offering securities. Additionally, as illustrated by *Reves*, in a securities fraud case it is typical for the plaintiff to sue under both federal and state securities laws.

2. Registering an Offering

A company registers a securities offering with the SEC by preparing and filing a registration statement. Under SEC regulations, the registration statement must contain detailed and voluminous disclosures about the issuer and the offering. These disclosures include audited financial statements, comparative selected financial information, and management's discussion and analysis (MD&A) of the issuer's financial condition and results of operation. They also include a detailed description of the issuer's business, properties, transactions with management, legal proceedings, and executive compensation.

The SEC reviews the registration statement and provides the issuer comments. The company then revises the registration statement in light of SEC comments, and at some point the SEC declares the registration statement "effective," which means the issuer can then sell the securities covered by the registration statement. The policy behind the registration requirement is to provide investors with sufficient information concerning an offering so that they can make informed investment decisions. In that regard, the issuer is required to make a "prospectus" available to each investor in a registered offering. A prospectus is a subpart of the registration statement that contains the bulk of the required disclosures about the issuer and the offering.

Registering a sale of securities with the SEC for the first time is time-consuming and expensive. It takes at least three months to draft, revise, and have the registration statement declared effective by the SEC. The registration statement is drafted by the company's outside securities counsel with extensive input from the company's senior management and accounting firm. Hence, the company incurs significant legal and accounting fees and management opportunity costs in connection with the registration process.

A registered offering is synonymous with a public offering. The first time a company registers stock for sale to the public is called an initial public offering or IPO.

3. Exempt Offerings

In passing the Securities Act, Congress recognized that it was inefficient to require the registration of all securities offerings and therefore included a number of registration exemptions in the Act. Because of time, cost, and other concerns, the overwhelming majority of securities transactions are conducted in compliance with a registration exemption. Below we discuss the most common exemptions relied on by businesses when issuing securities. Issuance by a business in compliance with an exemption is referred to as an exempt offering.

a. Section 4(a)(2)/Rule 506

Section 4(a)(2) of the Securities Act exempts from the registration requirement "transactions by an issuer not involving any public offering." This means that, as a general matter, public offerings must be registered with the SEC, and non-public or private offerings (also called private placements) do not. The Securities Act, however, is silent on what does and does not constitute a public offering, but this gap has been filled in by the courts. Below is the seminal opinion on the distinction.

SEC v. Ralston Purina Co.
346 U.S. 119 (1953)

Mr. Justice CLARK delivered the opinion of the Court.

Section 4[(a)(2)] of the Securities Act of 1933 exempts "transactions by an issuer not involving any public offering" from the registration requirements of §5. We must decide whether Ralston Purina's offerings of treasury stock to its "key employees" are within this exemption. . . .

Ralston Purina manufactures and distributes various feed and cereal products. Its processing and distribution facilities are scattered throughout the United States and Canada, staffed by some 7,000 employees. At least since 1911 the company has had a policy of encouraging stock ownership among its employees; more particularly, since 1942 it has made authorized but unissued common shares available to some of them. Between 1947 and 1951, the period covered by the record in this case, Ralston Purina sold nearly $2,000,000 of stock to employees without registration and in so doing made use of the mails.

In each of these years, a corporate resolution authorized the sale of common stock "to employees . . . who shall, without any solicitation by the Company or its officers or employees, inquire of any of them as to how to purchase common stock of Ralston Purina Company." A memorandum sent to branch and store managers after the resolution was adopted, advised that "The only employees to whom this stock will be available will be those who take the initiative and are interested in buying stock at present market prices." Among those responding to these offers were employees with the duties of artist, bakeshop foreman, chow loading foreman, clerical assistant, copywriter, electrician, stock clerk, mill office clerk, order credit trainee, production trainee, stenographer, and veterinarian. The buyers lived in over fifty widely separated communities scattered from Garland, Texas, to Nashua, New Hampshire and Visalia, California. The lowest salary bracket of those purchasing was $2,700 in 1949, $2,435 in 1950 and $3,107 in 1951. The record shows that in 1947, 243 employees bought stock, 20 in 1948, 414 in 1949, 411 in 1950, and the 1951 offer, interrupted by this litigation, produced 165 applications to purchase. No records were kept of those to whom the offers were made; the estimated number in 1951 was 500.

The company bottoms its exemption claim on the classification of all offerees as "key employees" in its organization. Its position on trial was that "A key employee . . . is not confined to an organization chart. It would include an individual who is eligible for promotion, an individual who especially influences others or who advises others, a person whom the employees look to in some special way, an individual, of course, who carries some special responsibility, who is sympathetic to management and who is ambitious and who the management feels is likely to be promoted to a greater responsibility." That an offering to all of its employees would be public is conceded.

The Securities Act nowhere defines the scope of §4[(a)(2)]'s private offering exemption. Nor is the legislative history of much help in staking out its boundaries. The problem was first dealt with in §4(1) of the House Bill, H.R. 5480, 73d Cong., 1st Sess., which exempted "transactions by an issuer not with or through an underwriter; . . . " The bill, as reported by the House Committee, added "and not involving any public offering." H.R. Rep. No. 85, 73d Cong., 1st Sess. 1. This was thought to be one of those transactions "where there is no practical need for . . . (the bill's) application or where the public benefits are too remote." Id., at 5. The exemption as thus delimited became law. It assumed its present shape with the deletion of "not with or through an underwriter" by §203(a) of the Securities Exchange Act of 1934, 48 Stat. 906, a change regarded as the elimination of superfluous language. H.R. Rep. No. 1838, 73d Cong., 2d Sess. 41. . . .

Decisions under comparable exemptions in the English Companies Acts and state "blue sky" laws, the statutory antecedents of federal securities legislation have made one thing clear — to be public, an offer need not be open to the whole world. . . .

Exemption from the registration requirements of the Securities Act is the question. The design of the statute is to protect investors by promoting full disclosure of information thought necessary to informed investment decisions. The natural way to interpret the private offering exemption is in light of the statutory purpose. Since exempt transactions are those as to which "there is no practical need for . . . (the bill's) application," the applicability of §4[(a)(2)] should turn on whether the particular class of persons affected need the protection of the Act. An offering to those who are shown to be able to fend for themselves is a transaction "not involving any public offering."

The Commission would have us go one step further and hold that "an offering to a substantial number of the public" is not exempt under §4[(a)(2)]. We are advised that "whatever the special circumstances, the Commission has consistently interpreted the exemption as being inapplicable when a large number of offerees is involved." But the statute would seem to apply to a "public offering" whether to few or many. It may well be that offerings to a substantial number of persons would rarely be exempt. Indeed nothing prevents the commission, in enforcing the statute, from using some kind of numerical test in deciding when to investigate particular exemption claims. But there is no warrant for superimposing a quantity limit on private offerings as a matter of statutory interpretation.

The exemption, as we construe it, does not deprive corporate employees, as a class, of the safeguards of the Act. We agree that some employee offerings may come within §4[(a)(2)], e.g., one made to executive personnel who because of their position have access to the same kind of information that the act would make available in the form of a registration statement. Absent such a showing of special circumstances, employees are just as much members of the investing "public" as any of their neighbors in the community. . . .

Keeping in mind the broadly remedial purposes of federal securities legislation, imposition of the burden of proof on an issuer who would plead the exemption seems to us fair and reasonable. Agreeing, the court below thought the burden met primarily because of the respondent's purpose in singling out its key employees for stock offerings. But once it is seen that the exemption question turns on the knowledge of the offerees, the issuer's motives, laudable though they may be, fade into irrelevance. The focus of inquiry should be on the need of the offerees for the protections afforded by registration. The employees here were not shown to have access to the kind of information which registration would disclose. The obvious opportunities for pressure and imposition make it advisable that they be entitled to compliance with §5.

Reversed.

Questions

1. What is the test for determining whether a sale of securities involves a public offering?
2. What is the significance of a sale constituting a public as opposed to private offering?

It was, of course, left to the lower courts to flesh out how to determine which offerees can fend for themselves and/or have the requisite access to information, among other things. Approaches to applying *Ralston Purina* varied. Some courts emphasized the relationship between the issuer and the purchaser, some focused on the sophistication of the purchasers, and some stressed the type of disclosure made to purchasers and the number of offerees. One attorney categorized the resulting §4(a)(2) jurisprudence as "a kind of mishmash. The issuer is now told that all of these factors have something to do with whether he has an exemption under Section 4(a)(2), but he is never given a hint as to the proper proportions in the brew. The saving recipe is kept secret, a moving target which he can never be sure he has hit."[25]

---

25. Ray Garrett, Jr., The Private Offering Exemption Today, in Fourth Ann. Inst. on Sec. Reg. 3, 10-11 (Robert H. Mundheim et al. eds., 1973).

Fortunately, the SEC has largely cleaned up the "mishmash" by adopting, revising, and reconfiguring various rules, culminating with the adoption of Rule 506 of Regulation D in 1982. Rule 506 serves as a "safe harbor" for §4(a)(2); that is, if an offering complies with the conditions specified in Rule 506, the offering will be deemed exempt under §4(a)(2). To fall within the safe harbor, the offering must be limited to accredited investors and no more than 35 non-accredited investors. Rule 501(a) defines "accredited investor." The definition includes banks, insurance companies, mutual funds, and certain other specified institutional investors; individuals with net worth in excess of $1 million (not including the value of the person's primary residence[26]), annual incomes in excess of $200,000, or joint annual incomes in excess of $300,000; and executive officers and directors of the issuer. The safe harbor also requires that all non-accredited investors in the offering have to be sophisticated, or the issuer has to reasonably believe that they are sophisticated. Sophistication in this context means that the investor "has such knowledge and experience in financial and business matters that he is capable of evaluating the merits and risks of the prospective investment," either in his own right or with the aid of one or more purchaser representatives.

The accredited investor concept is central in cleaning up the mishmash. If an issuer excludes non-accredited investors from its private placement, as many issuers do, it does not have to make a subjective sophistication determination that could later be disavowed by the SEC or by a court. As the SEC explained:

> [The accredited investor] approach is based on the presumption that accredited investors can fend for themselves without the protections afforded by registration and thereby satisfy the requirements of proposed Rule 506(b)(1) without a separate subjective determination by the issuer. The majority of commentators believed accredited investors as defined in proposed Rule 501(a) have the ability to fend for themselves in larger offerings contemplated under a Section 4(a)(2) exemptive rule. The Commission agrees with these commentators. . . .[27]

As for access to information, Rule 506 requires the issuer to furnish any non-accredited investors that purchase securities in the offering with certain specified information about the issuer and the offering within a reasonable time prior to the purchase. The rule contains no specific requirement that the issuer furnish accredited investors with information, but it does essentially instruct an issuer to provide to accredited investors any information that it furnished to non-accredited investors. Further, the issuer is required to afford all investors, whether or not accredited, "the opportunity to ask questions and receive answers concerning the terms and conditions of the offering. . . ."

---

26. The primary residence exclusion from the net worth calculation was added by Congress as part of the Dodd-Frank Wall Street Reform and Consumer Protection Act (*see* §413(a)).

27. Proposed Revision of Certain Exemptions from the Registration Provisions of the Securities Act of 1933 for Transactions Involving Limited Offers and Sales, Securities Act Release No. 6339, 46 Fed. Reg. 41,791, 41,802 (Aug. 18, 1981).

Additionally, Rule 506 prohibits the issuer and anyone acting on its behalf from soliciting investors through "any form of general solicitation or general advertising. . . ." unless the offering is limited to accredited investors. The SEC has interpreted this prohibition broadly. Specifically, the SEC commonly considers as general solicitation the solicitation of anyone with whom the company or someone acting on its behalf does not have a pre-existing, substantive relationship. The SEC considers a relationship pre-existing if it is established prior to the solicitation for the particular offering. The SEC considers a relationship substantive if it "would enable the issuer (or a person acting on its behalf) to be aware of the financial circumstances or sophistication of the persons with whom the relationship exists or that otherwise are of some substance and duration."[28] Up until 2012, general solicitation and advertising was prohibited for all Rule 506 offerings, even those limited to accredited investors. However, as part of Jumpstart Our Business Startups Act (commonly referred to as the JOBS Act), Congress required the SEC to revise Rule 506 to allow general solicitation and advertising in Rule 506 offerings limited to accredited investors.[29]

Section 4(a)(2) remains relevant even with the adoption of Rule 506, because companies still do frequently rely on it in the following settings:

- Offerings to a small number of sophisticated investors such as banks or venture capital funds who have performed significant due diligence on the company, so there is no question that they had the requisite access to information. Here, the §4(a)(2) reliance is often because the parties want to keep all details of the transaction confidential and thus do not want to file a Form D with the SEC or, in the case of a loan, do not want to essentially admit that it is a security by filing a Form D.
- Issuances of securities to company founders in connection with the organization of the company, especially when one or more of the founders does not fall under the definition of accredited investor.
- Issuances of securities to investors by a company without consulting legal counsel and therefore not in compliance with all the requirements of Rule 506.

b. Rules 504 and 505

Regulation D contains two additional exemptions, Rules 504 and 505, which the SEC promulgated under §3(b) of the Securities Act. Section 3(b) empowers the SEC to exempt offerings of up to $5 million if a small amount is involved or if the offering is of limited character. Under Rule 504, a company may offer and sell securities to an unlimited number of persons. The total dollar amount

---

28. Mineral Lands Research & Mktg. Corp., SEC No-Action Letter, 1985 SEC No-Act. LEXIS 2811, at *2 (Dec. 4, 1985)

29. *See* Jumpstart Our Business Startups Act, Pub. L. 112-106, 126 Stat. 306 §201(a)(1) (2012).

of the offering, however, cannot exceed $1 million. Unlike Rule 506, Rule 504 has no specific information requirements or limit on the number of "non-accredited" investors that may participate in the offering. Rule 505 is identical to Rule 506 except that the total dollar amount of the offering cannot exceed $5 million, and Rule 505 does not impose a sophistication requirement for non-accredited investors.

Although Rule 504 and Rule 505 offer some advantages over Rule 506, Rule 506 is the preferred Regulation D exemption because a security sold under it falls within the definition of "covered security" and is, therefore, exempt from state registration and qualification requirements. Conversely, a security sold under Rule 504 or 505 is not a covered security. As a result, an offering under either of these exemptions would need to be registered or exempt under the securities laws of each state in which offers were made, adding to the transaction costs associated with the offering. Rule 506 has the additional advantages of (1) having no monetary cap on the size of the offering, and (2) allowing general solicitation so long as the offering is limited to accredited investors.

c. Private Placement Memorandum

Companies typically solicit investors for exempt offerings through a "private placement memorandum" or PPM for short. A PPM contains the same sort of information found in a prospectus but is not reviewed by the SEC. A company will normally prepare a PPM even if it is doing a Rule 506 offering limited to accredited investors (meaning it is not required to furnish investors any information) in light of the antifraud provisions of the Securities Act and the Exchange Act.

· CHAPTER NINE ·

CORPORATE GOVERNANCE

The corporate governance structure involves three groups: shareholders, directors, and officers. Specifically, shareholders elect a board of directors, the board elects officers, and officers manage the day-to-day affairs of the corporation. In this chapter, we explore the state corporate law rules applicable to each of these groups. Although corporate law statutes draw a sharp distinction between the three groups, recall that in the closely held corporation it is common for all shareholders to be on the board of directors and to serve as officers, somewhat blurring the lines between the groups. The chapter closes by taking a closer look at bylaws and the charter amendment process.

A. SHAREHOLDERS

Shareholders[1] are regarded as the owners of a corporation but, reflecting the centralized management structure of corporate law, get a say in only a limited number of matters, a say they express through voting. In that regard, corporate law statutes provide shareholders a vote on the following matters only:

(1) election and removal of directors,
(2) amendments to the corporation's charter,
(3) shareholder (as opposed to board) initiated amendments to the corporation's bylaws,
(4) dissolution of the corporation,

---

1. The MBCA uses the term "shareholder" while the DGCL uses the term "stockholder." The terms are synonymous, but I've decided to go with "shareholder" even when referring to the DGCL. Some attorneys, however, make a point to use the term "shareholder" when talking about a corporation incorporated in an MBCA state and the term "stockholder" when talking about a Delaware corporation, and will call others on it who do not do the same. You can do it, too, if you want, but I think it is kind of silly.

(5) a merger of the corporation, and

(6) a sale of all (or substantially all) of the corporation's assets.

The board may choose to put additional matters to a shareholder vote (e.g., approval of a conflict of interest transaction) even though it is not required to under state corporate law. Furthermore, a corporation's charter or bylaws may specify additional matters on which shareholders get to vote, but expanding the list is fairly uncommon except with respect to voting by holders of preferred stock. Finally, as discussed in Chapter 13, in the public company context, it is fairly common for a shareholder to put a non-binding proposal to a vote of fellow shareholders, and federal law and exchange listing standards require public companies to put a few other matters to a shareholder vote. The bottom line is that there are a lot of important decisions made by a corporation on which shareholders get no vote. This generally includes such things as whether the corporation should fire its chief executive officer, issue additional shares of stock, go public, borrow money, build a new manufacturing plant, and relocate overseas. These decisions are made by the corporation's board of directors and executive officers.

1. Shareholder Meetings

Shareholder voting is done through the mechanism of a shareholders' meeting. There are two types of shareholders' meetings, annual and special. An annual meeting is a regularly scheduled meeting held by a corporation each year so that shareholders can vote on the election of directors. Corporate law statutes require corporations to hold annual meetings, unless the corporation's directors are elected by written consent (discussed below).[2] Shareholders may also be asked to vote on other matters at the annual meeting, for example, a proposed amendment to the corporation's charter.

A special meeting is one held between annual meetings to have shareholders vote on a matter or matters that cannot wait until the next annual meeting.[3] For example, say the board has approved the sale of all of the corporation's assets, and the buyer wants to close the transaction as soon as possible. As noted above, the sale of all of a corporation's assets is one of the few matters that requires shareholder approval. Assume the corporation had held its annual meeting the previous month. Instead of waiting the eleven months until its next annual meeting, the corporation can call and hold a special meeting on fairly short notice so that shareholders can vote on the proposed sale of assets.

---

2. *See* MBCA §7.01(a); DGCL §211(b).
3. *See* MBCA §7.02; DGCL §251(d).

Corporate law statutes specify who can call a special meeting with the rules normally supplemented by the corporation's bylaws.[4] Here is a sample provision from a Delaware corporation's bylaws addressing the issue:

> A special meeting of the stockholders may be called at any time only by the Board of Directors, or by the chairman of the board, or by the chief executive officer.

For a vote at a meeting to be valid, (1) a corporation must provide its shareholders with notice of the meeting (subject to waiver[5]), and (2) a quorum of shares must be present at the meeting. As for notice, both the MBCA and the DGCL require a corporation to notify its shareholders of the date, time, and place of the meeting at least 10 but not more than 60 days prior to the meeting.[6] For a special meeting, the notice must include a description of the purpose or purposes for which the meeting is called.[7] Below is a sample special meeting notice.

SNAPBUZZ INCORPORATED
NOTICE OF SPECIAL SHAREHOLDERS' MEETING

PLEASE TAKE NOTICE that a Special Meeting of the shareholders of Snapbuzz Incorporated (the "Corporation") will be held on September 1, 2012, at 10:00 A.M. local time at the offices of the Corporation, 100 Fifth Avenue, Austin, Texas, for the purpose of amending the Corporation's Articles of Incorporation to increase its authorized capital stock from 10,000,000 shares of common stock to 20,000,000 shares of common stock. Specifically, shareholders will vote on amending Article 2 of the Corporation's Articles of Incorporation to read as follows:

"2. The corporation is authorized to issue 20,000,000 shares of common stock."

Your vote is important. We encourage you to attend the meeting and vote on the items listed above. However, if you are unable to attend the meeting, please complete, date, and sign the enclosed proxy form and fax it to the Corporation at 512-337-1950 or, if you are unable to fax it, return it in the enclosed envelope.

BY ORDER OF THE BOARD OF DIRECTORS

Grant Heisenberg, Chairman of the Board

Dated: August 1, 2012
          Austin, Texas

---

4. *See id.*
5. *See* MBCA §7.06; DGCL §229.
6. *See* MBCA §7.05; DGCL §222.
7. *See id.*

In the shareholder voting context, a quorum is the minimum number of shares that must be present at a shareholders' meeting. It is *not* the number of shareholders that must be present, because shareholder voting is based on shares not headcount. The default rule under both the MBCA and DGCL is that a quorum is a majority of the corporation's outstanding shares.[8] Thus, if a corporation has 10,000 shares outstanding and you own 5,001 of these shares, the quorum requirement will be met if you show up at the corporation's shareholders' meeting even if no other shareholders attend. Note that the MBCA allows a corporation to have a greater quorum requirement through a provision in its charter.[9] The DGCL allows a corporation to have a lower (but no less than one-third of outstanding shares) or greater quorum requirement through a provision in its charter or bylaws.[10]

2. Proxies

A shareholder does not have to physically attend a shareholders' meeting for his or her shares to be considered present for purposes of a quorum and voted. Instead, the shareholder can appoint a person who will be attending the meeting to serve as the shareholder's "proxy" at the meeting. In this context, a proxy is an agent appointed by a shareholder to whom the shareholder gives express actual authority to vote the shareholder's shares at a shareholders' meeting. Corporate law statutes specify the rules for a valid appointment of a proxy.[11] Among other things, the appointment must be reflected in a written or electronic transmission.

The term "proxy" is sometimes used to refer to the grant of authority to vote, sometimes to the document granting the authority, and sometimes to the person to whom authority is granted. If you want to be precise, refer to the grant of authority as a proxy appointment, the document as a proxy form, and the person as the proxy.

Any corporation with more than a handful of shareholders routinely solicits its shareholders to appoint the proxy chosen by the corporation for a particular shareholders' meeting. The corporation does this to ensure that enough shares are present at the meeting in person or by proxy to meet the quorum requirement. Below is a sample appointment form that Snapbuzz Incorporated would send with the above sample shareholders' meeting notice (the "proxy form" referenced in the last sentence of the notice).

---

8. *See* MBCA §7.25(a); DGCL §216.
9. *See* MBCA §7.27.
10. *See* DGCL §216.
11. *See* MBCA §7.22; DGCL §212.

SNAPBUZZ INCORPORATED
PROXY FORM FOR SPECIAL MEETING OF STOCKHOLDERS

The undersigned hereby appoints Michael Jordan and Mia Hamm, and each of them, with full power of substitution, as proxies to represent and vote, as designated below, all shares of stock of Snapbuzz Incorporated (the "Corporation") registered in the name of the undersigned at the Special Shareholders' Meeting of Corporation to be held at 10:00 A.M. local time at the Corporation's offices at 100 Fifth Avenue, Austin, Texas on September 1, 2012, and at any adjournment thereof.

The Board of Directors recommends that you empower the proxies to vote FOR the below proposal below.

Amend the Corporation's Articles of Incorporation to increase its authorized shares from 10 million to 20 million shares of common stock.

[] FOR   [] AGAINST   [] ABSTAIN

THIS PROXY WHEN PROPERLY EXECUTED WILL BE VOTED AS DIRECTED OR, IF NO DIRECTION IS GIVEN WITH RESPECT TO THE PROPOSAL, WILL BE VOTED FOR THE PROPOSAL.

This proxy appointment is solicited on behalf of the Corporation's Board of Directors.

Date: _____, 2012   _____
                                     PLEASE DATE AND SIGN ABOVE

PLEASE MAIL THIS PROXY IN THE
ENCLOSED RETURN ENVELOPE OR
FAX IT TO SNAPBUZZ AT 512-337-1950.

Jordan and Hamm are presumably Snapbuzz officers. The form lists both of their names as proxies in case one of them cannot make the meeting.

As you can see, a proxy form resembles an absentee ballot in that it lists the item(s) up for a vote followed by check-off boxes. It is not, however, a ballot because technically the shareholder is not casting his or her votes by filling out the proxy form. Instead, he or she is authorizing the proxy (in this case, Jordan and Hamm) to vote the shareholder's shares at the meeting as directed in the proxy form. At the meeting, the proxy (in the Snapbuzz example, this would be Jordan or Hamm) will fill out a ballot indicating how he or she votes all of the shares for which the proxy has been granted authority to vote pursuant to proxy forms signed and sent in by a corporation's shareholders. It is pursuant to this ballot that a shareholder who votes by proxy is actually voting.

As touched on in Chapter 13 when discussing director elections at public companies, a shareholder can appoint someone other than the company-selected person or persons to serve as the shareholder's proxy for a shareholders' meeting, but this does not come up very often. In the Snapbuzz example, a shareholder against increasing Snapbuzz's authorized common stock would obviously just check the "against" box. In other words, there is no need for the shareholder to line up someone else to serve as a proxy so that the shareholder's votes could be cast against the proposal.

As discussed in Chapter 13, the proxy solicitation process with respect to public companies is also governed by the federal proxy rules. These rules are much more elaborate than those under state corporate law.

3. Written Consents

A vote at a formal shareholders' meeting is not the only way a corporation can obtain shareholder approval of a matter. Corporate law statutes also provide for shareholder approval through written consent.[12] For example, MBCA §7.04(a) provides:

> Action required or permitted by this Act to be taken at a shareholders' meeting may be taken without a meeting if the action is taken by all the shareholders entitled to vote on the action. The action must be evidenced by one or more written consents bearing the date of signature and describing the action taken, signed by all the shareholders entitled to vote on the action, and delivered to the corporation for inclusion in the minutes or filing with the corporate records.

Basically, instead of holding a shareholders' meeting, a corporation can secure shareholder approval by having its shareholders sign a piece of paper indicating their approval. The above language requires a written consent to be signed by all shareholders. However, §7.04(b) allows this unanimity requirement to be reduced through a charter provision to signatures by shareholders owning "not less than the minimum number of votes that would be required to authorize or take the action at a meeting at which all shares entitled to vote on the action were present and voted." The DGCL goes with the same minimum number of votes standard as MBCA §7.04(b) for its default rule as opposed to the unanimity requirement of MBCA §7.04(a).[13] We discuss voting requirements, or minimum number of votes required for an action to pass, below.

Here is a sample written action that Snapbuzz Incorporated could send to its shareholders to get their approval of the articles amendment increasing its authorized common stock instead of holding a shareholders' meeting.

---

12. *See* MBCA §7.04; DGCL §228.
13. *See* DGCL §228(a).

**WRITTEN CONSENT
OF THE SHAREHOLDERS OF
SNAPBUZZ INCORPORATED**

The undersigned shareholders of Snapbuzz Incorporated (the "Corporation"), hereby adopt the following resolution as and for the action of the shareholders without a meeting:

Articles Amendment

RESOLVED, that Article 2 of the Corporation's Articles of Incorporation is amended in its entirety to read as follows:

"2. The corporation is authorized to issue 20,000,000 shares of common stock."

The above document would then have a signature page or pages attached to it with lines for each Snapbuzz shareholder to sign and date.

The advantage to a corporation of using a written consent instead of holding a meeting is that no notice period is required for a written consent, so the *advantage* shareholder approval can potentially be obtained much faster and without dealing with the logistics of holding a meeting. In other words, as soon as a corporation's board approves a matter requiring shareholder approval, its counsel can draft and send out a written consent to obtain such approval. This means the approval can potentially be secured in a matter of days depending on how many shareholders the corporation has and how many of them need to sign. With a meeting, as discussed above, approval would be delayed because the corporation would have to provide, at a minimum, ten days' advance notice to its shareholders. With that said, the more shareholders a corporation has, the less *disadvantage* likely that it will be possible for the corporation to secure the necessary signatures for its shareholders to approve an item by written consent. Thus, corporations with large numbers of shareholders will not view the written consent route as a viable option and will therefore always hold a shareholders' meeting when they need shareholder approval. In other words, shareholder action by written consent is frequently utilized by closely held corporations but rarely, if ever, utilized by public corporations.

4. Voting Requirements

As mentioned above, a voting requirement refers to the minimum number of votes a matter must receive to pass. The default MBCA shareholder voting requirement for matters other than the election of directors is what I call a "more votes for than against" requirement. Specifically, §7.25(c) provides that "unless the articles of incorporation or this Act require a greater number of affirmative votes," a matter passes if "the votes cast . . . favoring the action exceed the votes cast opposing the action." The default DGCL shareholder voting requirement is higher. It is what I call a "majority of a quorum" requirement. Specifically, §216 provides that unless a different requirement is set forth in another section of the DGCL or the corporation's charter or bylaws, "the affirmative vote of the majority of shares present in person or represented by proxy at the meeting and entitled to vote on the subject matter shall be the act of the stockholders."[14]

Note that earlier versions of the MBCA set the default shareholder voting requirement at a majority of a quorum, and several MBCA states have retained this requirement. The Official Comment to §7.25 gives the following explanation for the change to more votes for than against:

> . . . The traditional rule [majority of a quorum] in effect treated abstentions as negative votes; the revised Model Act treats them truly as abstentions. The rule set forth in section 7.25(c) is considered desirable in part because it permits action to be taken by the shareholders when considered appropriate by a majority of those with views on the matter in question. Potential concern about the effect of abstentions in public corporations has also been increased by changes in the SEC proxy regulations that permit shareholders of such companies to abstain on issues.
>
> The treatment of abstaining votes under the traditional rule gave rise to anomalous results in some situations. For example, if a corporation has 1,000 shares of a single class outstanding, all entitled to cast one vote each, a quorum consists of 501 shares; if 600 shares are represented and the vote on a proposed action is 280 in favor, 225 opposed, and 95 abstaining, the action is not approved since fewer than a majority of the 600 shares attending voted in favor of the action. This is anomalous since if the shares abstaining had not been present at the meeting at all a quorum would have been present and the action would have been approved. Under section 7.25(c) the action would not be defeated by the 95 abstaining votes.

A number of provisions of the DGCL, including those addressing mergers, the sale of all (or substantially all) of a corporation's assets, and amendments to the corporation's charter, set the voting requirement at a majority of outstanding shares. In contrast, the analogous provisions in the MBCA governing these matters do not replace the default "more votes for than against" requirement. Thus, the DGCL not only has a higher default voting requirement than the MBCA but, unlike the MBCA, it goes with an even higher requirement for many of the matters shareholders get to vote on.

When it comes to the election of directors, the default voting standard is plurality.[15] In this context, plurality means that the director candidates who receive the largest number of votes are elected, up to the maximum number of

---

14. DGCL §216.
15. *See* MBCA §7.28(a); DGCL §216(3).

director slots up for election. For example, if five individuals are running for three slots, the top three vote-getters would win. The reason for a non-majority standard for elections is presumably to avoid failed elections. If more candidates are running than seats up for election, it is possible that an insufficient number of nominees would receive a majority of votes cast, especially if there were more than two candidates for each seat. In such an event, if a majority standard applied, only those nominees receiving a majority of votes would be elected. The election would thus fail in the sense that shareholders were unable to elect the entire board. Because under a plurality standard, the candidates receiving the most votes win, regardless if fewer than a majority, there will be no failed elections even if the number of nominees greatly exceeds the number of seats up for election. As we discuss in Chapter 13, in recent years, a number of public companies have implemented a majority vote standard for their board elections.

5. Class Voting

The issue of class voting arises when a corporation has more than one class or series of stock outstanding. For instance, a corporation may have common stock and multiple series of preferred stock outstanding. This sort of capital structure raises the issue of whether all shares vote together as a single class or whether one or more types of shares gets to vote as a separate class. For example, say Janga, Inc., a Delaware corporation, has the following shares of stock outstanding:

Type of Stock	Shares Outstanding
Common Stock	1,000,000
Series A Preferred Stock	200,000
Series B Preferred Stock	100,000

Figuring out whether all 1,300,000 shares vote together as a single class and whether common, Series A, or Series B gets a separate vote depends on (1) what the corporation's charter says with respect to voting, and (2) the particular matter up for vote, because for some matters the DGCL requires one or more types of shares to vote as a separate class.

To exemplify situation (1), let's assume Janga's charter is silent on voting rights with respect to the Common Stock (thus by default Common gets one vote per share), states that Series A gets one vote per share and votes with Common as a single class, and states that Series B gets one vote per share and votes as a separate class. Now let's say Janga is putting the sale of all of its assets to a vote of its shareholders. Under DGCL §271 (the section that governs the sale of all of a corporation's assets), approval of the sale requires an affirmative vote "by holders of a majority of the outstanding stock of the corporation entitled to vote thereon. . . ."[16] This means that the Common, Series A, and Series B would vote as a single class on the sale and of those 1,300,000 shares, at least 650,001 would have to vote in favor of the sale. But that is not the end of the story. A class consisting of Common and Series A would also have to approve the sale, because Janga's charter says Common and Series A get a separate class vote. Thus, a majority of a quorum of the shares of Common and Series A combined would have to vote in favor of the sale.[17] Finally, Series B would also have to approve the sale, because Janga's charter says Series B votes as a separate class. Thus, a majority of a quorum of shares of Series B would have to vote in favor of the sale.[18] In other words, there would be three separate votes on the matter and it would have to carry all three votes to be approved. The need for three votes comes from the language of Janga's charter. If it had instead said that Common, Series A, and Series B vote together on all matters as a single class, only one vote (the first one I mentioned) would have been required.

As for situation (2), the most commonly encountered circumstances of a corporate law statutory provision requiring a separate class vote is when the board has proposed a charter amendment that would alter the rights or preferences of a class of shares so as to affect them adversely. For example, say Janga's board has approved a charter amendment to reduce the dividend preference of its Series A Preferred from $1.00 per share to $0.50 per share. This obviously adversely affects the Series A Preferred given that $0.50 is less than $1.00. As a result, the Series A Preferred would get to vote on the amendment as a separate class per DGCL §242(b)(2), and per DGCL §242(b)(1), the voting requirement for approval is the affirmative vote of a majority of outstanding shares of Series A Preferred, in addition to the requisite votes by Common and Series B. Analogous MBCA provisions are found in §10.04. Note that even if a corporation's charter provides that a class of stock is nonvoting, corporate law statutes afford the class a class vote on a charter amendment in a limited number of circumstances, including on an amendment that would adversely affect the rights or preferences of the nonvoting shares.[19]

Note that the MBCA refers to what I've been calling, and most lawyers call, "class voting" as "voting by a voting group."[20] MBCA §1.40(26) defines "voting group" as "all shares of one or more classes or series that under the articles of incorporation or this Act are entitled to vote and be counted together collectively on a matter at a meeting of shareholders."

---

16. DGCL §271(a).
17. *See* DGCL §216(4).
18. *See id.*
19. *See* MBCA §10.04(a) & (d); DGCL §242(b)(2).
20. *See* MBCA §§7.25 & 7.26.

B. DIRECTORS

The default corporate law rule is that ultimate managerial authority resides in a corporation's board of directors. In that regard, MBCA §8.01(b) provides:

> All corporate powers shall be exercised by or under the authority of the board of directors of the corporation, and the business and affairs of the corporation shall be managed by or under the direction, and subject to the oversight, of its board of directors. . . .

The analogous provision under the DGCL is §141(a). Typically, a board of directors does not make day-to-day decisions with respect to a corporation's business. Instead, it elects officers to run the business, subject to board oversight. This arrangement is contemplated by the "by or under" phraseology used in the above provision. As the Official Comment to §8.01 explains:

> The phrase "by or under the direction, and subject to the oversight, of," encompasses the varying functions of boards of directors of different corporations. In some closely held corporations, the board of directors may be involved in the day-to-day business and affairs and it may be reasonable to describe management as being "by" the board of directors. But in many other corporations, the business and affairs are managed "under the direction, and subject to the

oversight, of" the board of directors, since operational management is delegated to executive officers and other professional managers.

While section 8.01(b), in providing for corporate powers to be exercised under the authority of the board of directors, allows the board of directors to delegate to appropriate officers, employees or agents of the corporation authority to exercise powers and perform functions not required by law to be exercised or performed by the board of directors itself, responsibility to oversee the exercise of that delegated authority nonetheless remains with the board of directors.[21]

Note that a corporation can limit the authority of its board or, in some situations (mainly, the closely held context), dispense with a board entirely and go with a shareholder-managed structure. We discuss this more in Chapter 12.

1. Number and Qualifications

Typically, a corporation's bylaws dictate the size of the corporation's board or means for setting the size.[22] Here are some sample bylaw provisions addressing board size:

Sample 1:

The Board of Directors of the Corporation shall consist of nine directors.

Sample 2:

The Board of Directors of the Corporation shall consist of nine directors or such other number of directors, but not less than three, as shall from time to time be fixed exclusively by resolution of the Board of Directors.

Sample 3:

The number of directors constituting the entire Board of Directors shall be determined, from time to time, by a resolution of the Board of Directors.

Both the MBCA and DGCL allow for boards consisting of a single director.[23]

Neither the MBCA nor DGCL dictate any qualifications for directors, although a corporation is free to impose them in its charter or bylaws. Most corporations do not do so, with the exception of those in regulated industries such

---

21. *See* MBCA §8.01 Offic. Cmt.

22. *See* MBCA §8.03(a); DGCL §141(b). These provisions also contemplate a corporation's charter specifying board size but most corporations opt to address the issue in their bylaws, because bylaw provisions addressing board size can normally be amended by board action alone, while such a provision in a charter would require shareholder approval.

23. *See* MBCA §8.03(a); DGCL §141(b). At one time, the MBCA required a corporation's board to have at least three directors, but this was changed in 1969 (the following six states still have this requirement: California, Massachusetts, Missouri, Ohio, Utah, and Vermont).

as banking where regulatory authorities essentially require it. Note that as discussed in Chapter 13, exchange listing standards have rules relating to director qualifications applicable to companies with shares listed on the exchange.

2. Board Action

Similar to shareholders, boards take action by voting at a board meeting. There are two types of meetings—regular and special. The dates for regular meetings are specified in a corporation's bylaws. Special meetings are those held between regular meetings. The default rule under the MBCA is that directors must be provided at least two days' notice of a special meeting, but this period can be, and normally is, reduced by a bylaw provision. The DGCL does not have a default provision for board meeting notice, so Delaware corporations normally specify a notice period in their bylaws.

There must be a quorum present at a meeting for a board to act. Under the default rule, the presence of a majority of directors constitutes a quorum (a director participating by phone or similar means is considered present).[24] Both the MBCA and DGCL allow a corporation to lower the board meeting quorum requirement through a bylaws provision to as little as one-third of directors.[25] An item must receive the affirmative vote of a majority of directors present at the meeting to pass.[26]

A board can also act through written consent. For example, MBCA §8.21(a) provides:

> Except to the extent that the articles of incorporation or bylaws require that action by the board of directors be taken at a meeting, action required or permitted by this Act to be taken by the board of directors may be taken without a meeting if each director signs a consent describing the action to be taken and delivers it to the corporation.

Basically, instead of holding a board meeting, a corporation can secure board approval by having all of its directors sign a piece of paper indicating their approval. Section 141(f) is the analogous DGCL provision. Here is a sample written consent:

UNANIMOUS WRITTEN CONSENT OF THE BOARD OF DIRECTORS OF SNAPBUZZ INCORPORATED

The undersigned, being all of the members of the Board of Directors of Snapbuzz Incorporated (the "Corporation") do hereby unanimously consent to the

---

24. *See* MBCA §§8.20(b) & 8.24(a); DGCL §141(b) & (i).
25. *See* MBCA §8.24(b); DGCL §141(b).
26. *See* MBCA §8.24(c); DGCL §141(b).

adoption of the following resolutions in lieu of a formal meeting of the Board of Directors of the Corporation.

Election of Officer

RESOLVED, that David H. Victorino is hereby elected as a Vice President of the Corporation to serve until his successor is elected and qualified, subject to his earlier disqualification, resignation, or removal.

IN WITNESS WHEREOF, the undersigned have executed this Written Consent as of October 15, 2011.

_____

Grant E. Heisenberg

_____

Roger R. Carlson

_____

Ricki Lake

The Official Comment to MBCA §8.21 explains the thinking behind the rule:

The power of the board of directors to act unanimously without a meeting is based on the pragmatic consideration that in many situations a formal meeting is a waste of time. For example, in a closely held corporation, there will often be informal discussion by the manager-owners of the venture before a decision is made. And, of course, if there is only a single director (as is permitted by section 8.03), a written consent is the natural method of signifying director action. Consent may be signified on one or more documents if desirable. . . .

In publicly held corporations, formal meetings of the board of directors may be appropriate for many actions. But there will always be situations where prompt action is necessary and the decision noncontroversial, so that approval without a formal meeting may be appropriate.

Under section 8.21 the requirement of unanimous consent precludes the possibility of stifling or ignoring opposing argument. A director opposed to an action that is proposed to be taken by unanimous written consent, or uncertain about the desirability of that action, may compel the holding of a directors' meeting to discuss the matter simply by withholding consent.

3. Elections

The default rule under the MBCA and DGCL is that shareholders elect directors using straight voting.[27] Under straight voting, each shareholder can cast

---

27. *See* MBCA §7.28(a); DGCL §216(3).

the number of votes he or she has (assuming one vote per share, this would correspond to the number of shares the shareholder owns) on her preferred candidates for the board seats up for election. For example, say Banana Pants Inc. (BPI) has 1,000 shares of common stock outstanding, you own 400 of these shares, and I own 600 of these shares. BPI's bylaws set the size of the BPI board of directors at three, and all three slots are up for election. Your preferred candidates are yourself, your sister, and your roommate. Thus, you cast 400 votes for yourself, 400 votes for your sister, and 400 votes for your roommate. My preferred candidates are me, my wife, and my son. Thus, I cast 600 votes for myself, 600 votes for my wife, and 600 votes for my son. Remember, the voting standard for the election of directors is plurality, meaning that the top three vote getters win. (It's the top three in this example, because there are three slots up for election.) Here, the top three vote getters are myself, my wife, and my son.

As the above example demonstrates, under straight voting, he or she who controls a majority of votes (in this case, that would be me) selects the entire board. In other words, a minority shareholder or shareholders do not get to pick any of the board members. This is where cumulative voting comes in, a topic covered in detail in Chapter 12, but with a quick overview provided here. Under cumulative voting

> each shareholder may multiply the number of votes he is entitled to cast (based on the number of shares held by him) by the number of directors to be elected by the voting group at the meeting and may cast the product for a single candidate or distribute the product among two or more candidates. By casting all his votes for a single candidate or a limited number of candidates, a minority shareholder increases his voting power and may be able to elect one or more directors.[28]

Thus, in the above example, you would have 1,200 votes (400 × 3) and could place all of your 1,200 votes on a single candidate (presumably yourself). I would have 1,800 votes (3 x 600) and regardless of how I spread them among my preferred candidates, would only be able to elect two of the members of the board. Under this example, cumulative voting afforded you the ability to elect one member of the board instead of zero as was the case under straight voting. Under both the MBCA and DGCL, a corporation opts into cumulative voting by including a provision to that effect in its charter.[29] Here is a sample of such a provision:

Shareholders of the Corporation are entitled to cumulate their votes when electing directors.

---

28. *See* MBCA §7.28 Offic. Cmt.
29. *See* MBCA §7.28(b) & (c); DGCL §214.

4. Terms

Under the default rule, a director's term is generally one year. I say generally because a director's term technically lasts until the next election, which is normally a year later, but could be sooner or later than that.[30]

A corporation can instead choose to stagger, or classify, its board, meaning the terms of only a portion of its directors expire in a particular year. For example, DGCL §141(d) provides:

> The directors of any corporation organized under this chapter may, by the certificate of incorporation or by an initial bylaw, or by a bylaw adopted by a vote of the stockholders, be divided into 1, 2 or 3 classes; the term of office of those of the first class to expire at the first annual meeting held after such classification becomes effective; of the second class 1 year thereafter; of the third class 2 years thereafter; and at each annual election held after such classification becomes effective, directors shall be chosen for a full term, as the case may be, to succeed those whose terms expire. The certificate of incorporation or bylaw provision dividing the directors into classes may authorize the board of directors to assign members of the board already in office to such classes at the time such classification becomes effective.[31]

Here is a sample provision staggering a board into three classes:

> The Board of Directors shall be divided into three classes. Initially, the Board of Directors shall designate by resolution, from among its members, directors to serve as class I directors, class II directors, and class III directors. To the extent possible, the classes shall have the same number of directors. The term of office of the class I directors shall continue until the first annual meeting of stockholders after the date on which the corporation establishes the classified board and until their successors are elected and qualify. The term of office of the class II directors shall continue until the second annual meeting of stockholders after the date on which the corporation establishes the classified board and until their successors are elected and qualify. The term of office of the class III directors shall continue until the third annual meeting of stockholders following the date on which the corporation establishes the classified board and until their successors are elected and qualify. At each annual meeting of the stockholders of a corporation, the successors to the class of directors whose term expires at that meeting shall be elected to hold office for a term continuing until: (i) the annual meeting of stockholders held in the third year following the year of their election; and (ii) their successors are elected and qualified.

---

30. *See* MBCA §8.05(b); DGCL §141(b).
31. The analogous MBCA provision is §8.06.

The effect of the above language is that each director term runs three years with one-third of the board coming up for election each year. The traditional policy justification for staggering a board is to "assure the continuity and stability of the corporation's business strategies and policies as determined by the board" because it prevents the entire board from turning over at once. A staggered board also reduces the impact of cumulative voting, because a minority shareholder will then need a greater number of votes to elect a director than if the entire board were up for election. For instance, continuing with the BPI example from above, assume BPI's charter provides for cumulative voting and a board staggered into three classes. Thus, only one director comes up for election each year. Thus, each year you would have 400 votes (400 x 1) to cast on a nominee for the open seat, and I would have 600 votes (600 x 1), so whomever I vote for would win every year.

As discussed in Chapter 14, in the public company context, a staggered board also serves as an anti-takeover device.

5. Removal

Corporate law statutes give the shareholders the right to remove directors at any time. Under the default rule, they can do so with or without cause.[32] It is fairly common, however, for a corporation to impose a "for cause" requirement in its charter, as allowed by statute.[33] Here is sample charter language to that effect:

> Any director or the entire Board of Directors may be removed by the shareholders only for cause.

"Cause" generally includes fraudulent or criminal conduct and gross abuse of office amounting to a breach of trust.[34] Note that Delaware flips the default rule for corporations with staggered boards. Specifically, under the DGCL, a director on a staggered board may only be removed for cause unless the corporation's charter otherwise provides.[35]

To remove a director, shareholders generally need to call a special shareholders' meeting or secure the requisite signatures for action by written consent. The voting requirement for removal under the MBCA is more votes for removal than against removal.[36] Under the DGCL, the requirement is a major-

---

32. *See* MBCA §8.08(a); DGCL §141(k).
33. *See id.*
34. *See* MBCA §8.08 Offic. Cmt.
35. *See* DGCL §141(k)(1).
36. *See* MBCA §8.08(b).

ity of outstanding votes in favor of removal.[37] The voting requirements are slightly different for a corporation that has opted in to cumulative voting. In that case, the MBCA provides "a director may not be removed if the number of votes sufficient to elect him under cumulative voting is voted against his removal."[38] The rule under the DGCL is that "no director may be removed without cause if the votes cast against such director's removal would be sufficient to elect such director if then cumulatively voted at an election of the entire board of directors. . . ."[39] Note that under both the MBCA and DGCL only the shareholders have the power to remove directors. In other words, a director cannot be removed by board vote.

6. Filling Vacancies

A vacancy can occur on a board because of death, removal, or resignation of a director. A vacancy can also result from an increase in the size of the board. A board size increase can normally be effected by the existing board of directors by resolution or amendment to the corporation's bylaws, depending on what the bylaws say regarding the size of the board.

Vacancies may be filled by the remaining directors or by the shareholders.[40] In other words, both the board and shareholders share the power to fill vacancies. Normally, vacancies are filled by the board because it is able to call and hold a meeting to do so, or secure the requisite signatures to act by written consent, much quicker than the shareholders are able to do the same. It is possible, though, for a shareholder to combine the removal of a director and election of someone to fill the resulting vacancy in a single shareholders' meeting.

7. Committees

Corporate law statutes allow the board to delegate power to committees comprised of one or more directors.[41] Action by a properly formed board committee is deemed to be action of the entire board. Both the MBCA and DGCL, however, prohibit committees from taking certain actions such as amending the corporation's bylaws or approving a matter that requires shareholder approval.[42]

Whether a private company has standing (i.e., permanent) board committees typically depends on the size of the corporation's board. Basically, the larger the

---

37. *See* DGCL §144(k).
38. *See* MBCA §8.08(c).
39. DGCL §144(k)(2).
40. *See* MBCA §8.10(a); DGCL §223(a)(1).
41. *See* MBCA §8.25(a); DGCL §141(c).
42. *See* MBCA §8.25(e); DGCL §141(c).

board, the more likely a corporation is to have standing committees, because the more difficult it is to schedule a board meeting or secure the necessary signatures for action by written consent. Pretty much all public companies have a number of standing committees (e.g., nominating, audit, and compensation committees) to meet exchange listing requirements (discussed in Chapter 13) and/or market expectations.

A board will also create ad hoc committees on occasion. For example, as we discuss in Chapter 10, a board may create a negotiating committee to handle a transaction between the corporation and one or more of its directors or a special litigation committee to deal with a derivative suit brought against members of the board.

As with the full board, committees can act through a committee meeting or by written consent. The same rules regarding notice, quorum, and required vote that apply to board meetings also apply to committee meetings.

Exercise 9.2

Refer again to the Articles of Incorporation and Bylaws of Snapbuzz and answer the following questions. Make sure you note any applicable articles, bylaws, and/or statutory provision that support your answer.

1. How many directors are on Snapbuzz's board?
2. How much notice is Snapbuzz required to provide for a board meeting?
3. How many directors constitute a quorum for a board meeting?
4. How many directors need to sign a written consent for it to be valid?
5. Can the Snapbuzz board create a board committee comprised of Ricki Lake and delegate to the committee the authority to choose a replacement for any director who resigns?
6. Snapbuzz shareholders want to remove Heisenberg from the board. Do they need cause? How do they go about removing him?
7. Assume Snapbuzz has outstanding 6,000,000 shares of common stock, 100,000 shares of Series A Preferred, and 100,000 shares of Series B Preferred, and that the shareholders have called a shareholders' meeting to remove a director. How many shares need to be represented at the meeting to meet the quorum requirement? What is the minimum vote required for Snapbuzz shareholders to remove a director assuming no abstentions?
8. Does Snapbuzz have a staggered board?
9. The Snapbuzz board has adopted an amendment to Snapbuzz's Bylaws to increase the size of the board to five directors. How are the new seats filled?
10. What is the minimum number of votes an individual could receive and still be elected to Snapbuzz's board of directors?

C. OFFICERS

Officers oversee the day-to-day management of the corporation and are elected by the board or appointed by more senior officers. Corporate law statutes have few specifics regarding them, leaving it to a corporation to specify the titles and duties of its officers in its bylaws or through a board resolution.[43] One of the only statutory requirements with respect to officers under both the MBCA and DGCL is that the corporation must designate an officer to prepare and maintain board and shareholder meeting minutes and authenticate the corporate records.[44] Such an officer is normally given the title of secretary. At one time, the MBCA required a corporation to have certain specified officers (president, treasurer, and secretary) and this is still the case under a number of states' corporate law statutes.

Below are sample bylaw provisions regarding officers:

5.1 Officers.

The officers of the Corporation shall consist of a chief executive officer, a president, one or more vice presidents, a secretary, and a chief financial officer, and such other officers as the Board of Directors may deem expedient. Any number of offices may be held by the same person unless otherwise prohibited by applicable law, the Certificate of Incorporation, or these Bylaws.

5.2 Appointment of Officers.

The officers of the Corporation, except such officers as may be appointed in accordance with the provisions of Section 5.3 of these Bylaws, shall be appointed by the Board of Directors, subject to the rights, if any, of an officer under any contract of employment. Such officers shall exercise such powers, perform such duties, and hold office for such terms as shall be determined from time to time by the Board of Directors, until such officer's successor is elected and qualified, or until such officer's earlier death, resignation, or removal.

5.3 Subordinate Officers.

In addition to the officers appointed by the Board of Directors in accordance with the provisions of Section 5.1 of these Bylaws, the Corporation may have a treasurer and one or more appointed vice presidents, assistant secretaries, assistant treasurers or other officers who shall also be officers of the Corporation (each an "Appointed Officer"). The chief executive officer shall have the power to appoint and remove any Appointed Officer and/or agents as the business of the Corporation may require, each of whom shall perform such duties and have such authority as the chief executive officer may from time to time determine.

---

43. *See* MBCA §8.40(a); DGCL §142(a).
44. *See id.*

5.4 Chief Executive Officer.

Subject to such supervisory powers, if any, as may be given by the Board of Directors to the chairman of the board, if any, the chief executive officer of the Corporation shall, subject to the control of the Board of Directors, have general supervision, direction, and control of the business and the officers of the Corporation. He or she, or his or her designee, shall preside at all meetings of the stockholders and, in the absence or nonexistence of a chairman of the board, at all meetings of the Board of Directors and shall have the general powers and duties of management usually vested in the office of chief executive officer of a corporation and shall have such other powers and duties as may be prescribed by the Board of Directors or these Bylaws.

5.5 President.

Subject to such supervisory powers, if any, as may be given by the Board of Directors to the chairman of the board, if any, or the chief executive officer, the president shall have general supervision, direction, and control of the business and other officers of the Corporation. He or she shall have the general powers and duties of management usually vested in the office of president of a corporation and such other powers and duties as may be prescribed by the Board of Directors or these Bylaws.

5.6 Vice Presidents.

In the absence or disability of the chief executive officer and president, the vice presidents, if any, in order of their rank as fixed by the Board of Directors or, if not ranked, a vice president designated by the Board of Directors, shall perform all the duties of the chief executive officer and, when so acting, shall have all the powers of, and be subject to all the restrictions upon, the chief executive officer. The vice presidents shall have such other powers and perform such other duties as from time to time may be prescribed for them respectively by the Board of Directors, these Bylaws, the chief executive officer or the chairman of the board.

5.7 Secretary.

The secretary shall keep, or cause to be kept, at the principal executive office of the Corporation or such other place as the Board of Directors may direct, a book of minutes of all meetings and actions of directors, committees of directors, and stockholders. The minutes shall show the time and place of each meeting, the names of those present at directors' meetings or committee meetings, the number of shares present or represented at stockholders' meetings, and the proceedings thereof.

The secretary shall keep, or cause to be kept, at the principal executive office of the Corporation or at the office of the Corporation's transfer agent or registrar, as determined by resolution of the Board of Directors, a share register, or a duplicate share register, showing the names of all stockholders and their addresses, the number and classes of shares held by each, the number and date of certificates (if any) evidencing such shares, and the number and date of cancellation of every such certificate surrendered for cancellation.

The secretary shall give, or cause to be given, notice of all meetings of the stockholders and of the Board of Directors required to be given by law or by these Bylaws. He or she shall keep the seal of the Corporation, if one be adopted, in safe custody, and shall have such other powers and perform such other duties as may be prescribed by the Board of Directors or these Bylaws.

5.8 Chief Financial Officer.

The chief financial officer shall keep and maintain, or cause to be kept and maintained, adequate and correct books and records of accounts of the properties and business transactions of the Corporation, including accounts of its assets, liabilities, receipts, disbursements, gains, losses, capital retained earnings, and shares. The books of account shall at all reasonable times be open to inspection by any director.

The chief financial officer shall deposit or direct the treasurer to deposit all moneys and other valuables in the name and to the credit of the Corporation with such depositories as may be designated by the Board of Directors. He or she shall disburse, or direct the treasurer to disburse, the funds of the Corporation as may be ordered by the Board of Directors, shall render to the president, the chief executive officer, or the directors, upon request, an account of all his or her transactions as chief financial officer and of the financial condition of the Corporation, and shall have other powers and perform such other duties as may be prescribed by the Board of Directors or these Bylaws.

D. BYLAWS

As you probably picked up from the above reading, a lot of the formalities applicable to both shareholder and board action are specified in a corporation's bylaws, so we need to focus on them a bit.

1. Overview

A corporation's bylaws specify rules regarding the governance of the corporation. These rules address, among other things, notice and quorum requirements for board and shareholder meetings, number and qualifications of directors, voting standards, proxy voting, appointment of officers, and stock certificates. Bylaws are normally drafted by the attorney retained to handle the incorporation of a business. The standard approach is to draft them as a self-contained document that can be read and understood by business people unfamiliar with the applicable corporate statute. Thus, the bylaws will recite a default rule even though it would still apply if omitted. With that said, as an attorney reviewing a corporation's bylaws, you should consult the applicable corporate law statute and the corporation's charter, because on more than one occasion I've come across bylaw provisions that conflict with the statute or the corporation's charter. In terms of hierarchy, the statute trumps the charter which trumps the bylaws.[45] In other words, if a bylaw provision is inconsistent with the statute or the charter, the statute or the charter controls. For that matter, if a charter provision is inconsistent with the statute, the statute controls.

A common mistake is to include something in the bylaws that the statute provides is only effective if included in the charter. For example, as mentioned above, under the MBCA, a corporation can raise the quorum requirement for a shareholders' meeting but only pursuant to a provision in its articles. Thus, a provision in its bylaws purporting to do so would be invalid.[46] However, such a provision would be valid in the bylaws of a Delaware corporation, because the DGCL allows the shareholder quorum requirement to be altered via a charter or bylaws provision.[47] In other words, you need to pay attention to whether a particular statutory provision can be altered in a corporation's bylaws. The tricky thing is that, as the above example demonstrates, the answer varies by state (even among states that have adopted the MBCA because they are free to alter it), and I suspect this variance is at the root of a lot of erroneous bylaw provisions.

2. Amendments

It is fairly common for a corporation to amend its bylaws from time to time. The default rule under the MBCA is that both the board and shareholders have the power to unilaterally amend or repeal the bylaws.[48] This power can be limited or eliminated with respect to the board (but not the shareholders) through a charter provision.[49] The standard practice is not to include such a limitation so that the board has the flexibility to quickly change the corporation's bylaws if need be.

The default rule is slightly different under the DGCL. Here, shareholders have the power to unilaterally amend or repeal the bylaws but the board does not. However, a corporation may confer such power to its board through a charter provision. Below is a sample provision to that effect:

> The Board of Directors of the Corporation is expressly authorized to make, alter, or repeal the Bylaws of the Corporation.

---

45. *See, e.g., Gaskill v. Gladys Belle Oil Co.*, 146 A. 337, 340 (Del. Ch. 1929) ("[W]ith respect to corporations, the law of their being is characterized by gradation of authority. That which is superior over-rides all below it in rank. The by-laws must succumb to the superior authority of the charter; the charter if it conflicts with the statute must give way; and the statute, if it conflicts with the Constitution, is void.").
46. *See* MBCA §7.27(a).
47. *See* DGCL §216.
48. *See* MBCA §10.20.
49. *See id.*

It is standard practice to include this sort of language in a Delaware corporation's charter. In other words, the boards of most Delaware corporations have the power to unilaterally amend the corporation's bylaws notwithstanding that the default rule provides they do not.

The board exercises its power to amend the bylaws as it would any other power, either by adopting a resolution reflecting the amendment at a board meeting or having each director sign a written consent setting forth the proposed amendment. Here is a sample board resolution reflecting a bylaw amendment:

RESOLVED, that Article III, Section 3.2 of the Corporation's Restated Bylaws is amended in its entirety to read as follows:

"The Board of Directors of the Corporation shall consist of nine directors."

Assuming proper notice (or waivers of notice) and a quorum of directors, the above resolution would pass if it received the affirmative vote of a majority of directors present at the board meeting. The corporation's secretary (perhaps with the assistance of counsel) would then draft minutes for the meeting reflecting the outcome of the vote (setting forth the resolution and specifying how many for and against votes it received, as well as abstentions), and, if the resolution passed, a document to be included with the bylaws setting forth the amendment.

As mentioned above, under both the MBCA and DGCL, shareholders have the power to unilaterally amend or repeal a corporation's bylaws, and this power cannot be taken away. By unilaterally, I mean shareholders can themselves initiate and adopt a bylaw change with no involvement of the board. Most everything else shareholders get to vote on (charter amendments, mergers, dissolution, etc.) requires board approval followed by shareholder approval. Thus, shareholder power to amend bylaws enjoys a unique status under corporate law. It is essentially the only corporate governance power shareholders possess that is proactive rather than reactive to the board.

This power seemingly gives shareholders wide latitude to exert control over corporate affairs because of the broad statutory language specifying what can be addressed in a corporation's bylaws. For example, DGCL §109(b) provides, "The bylaws may contain any provision, not inconsistent with law or with the certificate of incorporation, relating to the business of the corporation, the conduct of its affairs, and its rights or powers or the rights or powers of its stockholders, directors, officers or employees."[50] The next case examines the scope of permissible shareholder amendments to the bylaws under Delaware law.

---

50. The analogous provision under the MBCA is §2.06(b), which provides, "The bylaws of a corporation may contain any provision for managing the business and regulating the affairs of the corporation that is not inconsistent with law or the articles of incorporation."

CA, Inc. v. AFSCME Employees Pension Plan
953 A.2d 227 (Del. 2008)

[AFSCME Employees Pension Plan (AFSCME) was a shareholder of CA, Inc. (CA or the Company), a Delaware corporation. AFSCME proposed and sought shareholder approval of the following amendment to CA's bylaws:

> RESOLVED, that pursuant to section 109 of the Delaware General Corporation Law and Article IX of the bylaws of CA, Inc., stockholders of CA hereby amend the bylaws to add the following Section 14 to Article II:
>
> The board of directors shall cause the corporation to reimburse a stockholder or group of stockholders (together, the "Nominator") for reasonable expenses ("Expenses") incurred in connection with nominating one or more candidates in a contested election of directors to the corporation's board of directors, including, without limitation, printing, mailing, legal, solicitation, travel, advertising and public relations expenses, so long as (a) the election of fewer than 50 percent of the directors to be elected is contested in the election, (b) one or more candidates nominated by the Nominator are elected to the corporation's board of directors, (c) stockholders are not permitted to cumulate their votes for directors, and (d) the election occurred, and the Expenses were incurred, after this bylaw's adoption. The amount paid to a Nominator under this bylaw in respect of a contested election shall not exceed the amount expended by the corporation in connection with such election.

In the opinion below, the court addresses two questions: (1) whether the above proposal is a proper subject for action by shareholders as a matter of Delaware law, and (2) whether the above proposal, if adopted, would cause CA to violate any Delaware law to which it is subject.]

III. THE FIRST QUESTION

A. Preliminary Comments

The first question presented is whether the Bylaw is a proper subject for shareholder action, more precisely, whether the Bylaw may be proposed and enacted by shareholders without the concurrence of the Company's board of directors. Before proceeding further, we make some preliminary comments in an effort to delineate a framework within which to begin our analysis.

First, the DGCL empowers both the board of directors and the shareholders of a Delaware corporation to adopt, amend or repeal the corporation's bylaws. 8 Del. C. §109(a) relevantly provides that:

> After a corporation has received any payment for any of its stock, the power to adopt, amend or repeal bylaws shall be in the stockholders entitled to vote . . . ; provided, however, any corporation may, in its certificate of incorporation, confer the power to adopt, amend or repeal bylaws upon the directors. . . . The fact that such power has been so conferred upon the directors . . . shall not divest the

stockholders . . . of the power, nor limit their power to adopt, amend or repeal bylaws.

Pursuant to Section 109(a), CA's Certificate of Incorporation confers the power to adopt, amend or repeal the bylaws upon the Company's board of directors. Because the statute commands that that conferral "shall not divest the stockholders . . . of . . . nor limit" their power, both the board and the shareholders of CA, independently and concurrently, possess the power to adopt, amend and repeal the bylaws.

Second, the vesting of that concurrent power in both the board and the shareholders raises the issue of whether the stockholders' power is coextensive with that of the board, and vice versa. As a purely theoretical matter that is possible, and were that the case, then the first . . . question would be easily answered. That is, under such a regime any proposal to adopt, amend or repeal a bylaw would be a proper subject for either shareholder or board action, without distinction. But the DGCL has not allocated to the board and the shareholders the identical, coextensive power to adopt, amend and repeal the bylaws. Therefore, how that power is allocated between those two decision-making bodies requires an analysis that is more complex.

Moving from the theoretical to this case, by its terms Section 109(a) vests in the shareholders a power to adopt, amend or repeal bylaws that is legally sacrosanct, *i.e.,* the power cannot be non-consensually eliminated or limited by anyone other than the legislature itself. If viewed in isolation, Section 109(a) could be read to make the board's and the shareholders' power to adopt, amend or repeal bylaws identical and coextensive, but Section 109(a) does not exist in a vacuum. It must be read together with 8 Del. C. §141(a), which pertinently provides that:

> The business and affairs of every corporation organized under this chapter shall be managed by or under the direction of a board of directors, except as may be otherwise provided in this chapter or in its certificate of incorporation.

No such broad management power is statutorily allocated to the shareholders. Indeed, it is well-established that stockholders of a corporation subject to the DGCL may not directly manage the business and affairs of the corporation, at least without specific authorization in either the statute or the certificate of incorporation. Therefore, the shareholders' statutory power to adopt, amend or repeal bylaws is not coextensive with the board's concurrent power and is limited by the board's management prerogatives under Section 141(a).

Third, it follows that, to decide whether the Bylaw proposed by AFSCME is a proper subject for shareholder action under Delaware law, we must first determine: (1) the scope or reach of the shareholders' power to adopt, alter or repeal the bylaws of a Delaware corporation, and then (2) whether the Bylaw at issue here falls within that permissible scope. Where, as here, the proposed bylaw is one that limits director authority, that is an elusively difficult task. As one noted scholar has put it, "the efforts to distinguish by-laws that permissibly limit director authority from by-laws that impermissibly do so have failed to provide a coherent analytical structure, and the pertinent statutes provide no guidelines for distinction at all."[51] The tools that are available to this Court to answer those questions are other provisions of the DGCL and Delaware judicial decisions that can be brought to bear on this question.

B. *Analysis*

1.

Two other provisions of the DGCL, 8 Del. C. §§109(b) and 102(b)(1), bear importantly on the first question and form the basis of contentions advanced by each side. Section 109(b), which deals generally with bylaws and what they must or may contain, provides that:

> The bylaws may contain any provision, not inconsistent with law or with the certificate of incorporation, relating to the business of the corporation, the conduct of its affairs, and its rights or powers or the rights or powers of its stockholders, directors, officers or employees.

And Section 102(b)(1), which is part of a broader provision that addresses what the certificate of incorporation must or may contain, relevantly states that:

> (b) In addition to the matters required to be set forth in the certificate of incorporation by subsection (a) of this section, the certificate of incorporation may also contain any or all of the following matters:
>
> (1) Any provision for the management of the business and for the conduct of the affairs of the corporation, and any provision creating, defining, limiting and regulating the powers of the corporation, the directors and the stockholders, or any class of the stockholders . . . ; if such provisions are not contrary to the laws of this State. Any provision which is required or permitted by any section of this chapter to be stated in the bylaws may instead be stated in the certificate of incorporation.

AFSCME relies heavily upon the language of Section 109(b), which permits the bylaws of a corporation to contain "any provision . . . relating to the . . . rights or powers of its stockholders [and] directors. . . ." The Bylaw, AFSCME argues, "relates to" the right of the stockholders meaningfully to participate in the process of electing directors, a right that necessarily "includes the right to nominate an opposing slate."

CA argues, in response, that Section 109(b) is not dispositive, because it cannot be read in isolation from, and without regard to, Section 102(b)(1). CA's

---

51. [FN 8] Lawrence A. Hamermesh, *Corporate Democracy and Stockholder-Adopted By-Laws: Taking Back the Street?*, 73 Tul. L. Rev. 409, 444 (1998); *Id.* at 416 (noting that "neither the courts, the legislators, the SEC, nor legal scholars have clearly articulated the means of . . . determining whether a stockholder-adopted by-law provision that constrains director managerial authority is legally effective.").

argument runs as follows: the Bylaw would limit the substantive decision-making authority of CA's board to decide whether or not to expend corporate funds for a particular purpose, here, reimbursing director election expenses. Section 102(b)(1) contemplates that any provision that limits the broad statutory power of the directors must be contained in the certificate of incorporation. Therefore, the proposed Bylaw can only be in CA's Certificate of Incorporation, as distinguished from its bylaws. Accordingly, the proposed bylaw falls outside the universe of permissible bylaws authorized by Section 109(b).

Implicit in CA's argument is the premise that *any* bylaw that in *any* respect might be viewed as limiting or restricting the power of the board of directors automatically falls outside the scope of permissible bylaws. That simply cannot be. That reasoning, taken to its logical extreme, would result in eliminating altogether the shareholders' statutory right to adopt, amend or repeal bylaws. Bylaws, by their very nature, set down rules and procedures that bind a corporation's board and its shareholders. In that sense, most, if not all, bylaws could be said to limit the otherwise unlimited discretionary power of the board. Yet Section 109(a) carves out an area of shareholder power to adopt, amend or repeal bylaws that is expressly inviolate. Therefore, to argue that the Bylaw at issue here limits the board's power to manage the business and affairs of the Company only begins, but cannot end, the analysis needed to decide whether the Bylaw is a proper subject for shareholder action. The question left unanswered is what is the scope of shareholder action that Section 109(b) permits yet does not improperly intrude upon the directors' power to manage corporation's business and affairs under Section 141(a).

It is at this juncture that the statutory language becomes only marginally helpful in determining what the Delaware legislature intended to be the lawful scope of the shareholders' power to adopt, amend and repeal bylaws. To resolve that issue, the Court must resort to different tools, namely, decisions of this Court and of the Court of Chancery that bear on this question. Those tools do not enable us to articulate with doctrinal exactitude a bright line that divides those bylaws that shareholders may unilaterally adopt under Section 109(b) from those which they may not under Section 141(a). They do, however, enable us to decide the issue presented in this specific case.

2.

It is well-established Delaware law that a proper function of bylaws is not to mandate how the board should decide specific substantive business decisions, but rather, to define the process and procedures by which those decisions are made. As the Court of Chancery has noted:

> Traditionally, the bylaws have been the corporate instrument used to set forth the rules by which the corporate board conducts its business. To this end, the DGCL is replete with specific provisions authorizing the bylaws to establish the procedures through which board and committee action is taken. . . . [T]here is a general consensus that bylaws that regulate the process by which the board acts are statutorily authorized.

* * *

. . . I reject International's argument that that provision in the Bylaw Amendments impermissibly interferes with the board's authority under §141(a) to manage the business and affairs of the corporation. Sections 109 and 141, taken in totality, . . . make clear that bylaws may pervasively and strictly regulate the process by which boards act, subject to the constraints of equity.

Examples of the procedural, process-oriented nature of bylaws are found in both the DGCL and the case law. For example, 8 Del. C. §141(b) authorizes bylaws that fix the number of directors on the board, the number of directors required for a quorum (with certain limitations), and the vote requirements for board action. 8 Del. C. §141(f) authorizes bylaws that preclude board action without a meeting. And, almost three decades ago this Court upheld a shareholder-enacted bylaw requiring unanimous board attendance and board approval for any board action, and unanimous ratification of any committee action. Such purely procedural bylaws do not improperly encroach upon the board's managerial authority under Section 141(a).

The process-creating function of bylaws provides a starting point to address the Bylaw at issue. It enables us to frame the issue in terms of whether the Bylaw is one that establishes or regulates a process for substantive director decision-making, or one that mandates the decision itself. Not surprisingly, the parties sharply divide on that question. We conclude that the Bylaw, even though infelicitously couched as a substantive-sounding mandate to expend corporate funds, has both the intent and the effect of regulating the process for electing directors of CA. Therefore, we determine that the Bylaw is a proper subject for shareholder action, and set forth our reasoning below.

Although CA concedes that "restrictive procedural bylaws (such as those requiring the presence of all directors and unanimous board consent to take action) are acceptable," it points out that even facially procedural bylaws can unduly intrude upon board authority. The Bylaw being proposed here is unduly intrusive, CA claims, because, by mandating reimbursement of a stockholder's proxy expenses, it limits the board's broad discretionary authority to decide whether to grant reimbursement at all. CA further claims that because (in defined circumstances) the Bylaw mandates the expenditure of corporate funds, its subject matter is necessarily substantive, not process-oriented, and, therefore falls outside the scope of what Section 109(b) permits.

Because the Bylaw is couched as a command to reimburse ("The board of directors shall cause the corporation to reimburse a stockholder"), it lends itself to CA's criticism. But the Bylaw's wording, although relevant, is not dispositive of whether or not it is process-related. The Bylaw could easily have been worded differently, to emphasize its process, as distinguished from its mandatory payment, component. By saying this we do not mean to suggest that this Bylaw's reimbursement component can be ignored. What we do suggest is that a bylaw that requires the expenditure of corporate funds does not, for that reason alone, become automatically deprived of its process-related character. A hypothetical example illustrates the point. Suppose that the directors of a corporation live in different states and at a considerable distance from the corporation's headquarters. Suppose also that the shareholders enact a bylaw that requires all meetings of directors to take place in person at the corporation's headquarters. Such a bylaw would be clearly process-related, yet it cannot be supposed that the shareholders would lack the power to adopt the bylaw because it would require the corporation to expend its funds to reimburse the directors' travel expenses. Whether or not a bylaw is process-related must necessarily be determined in light of its context and purpose.

The context of the Bylaw at issue here is the process for electing directors — a subject in which shareholders of Delaware corporations have a legitimate and protected interest. The purpose of the Bylaw is to promote the integrity of that electoral process by facilitating the nomination of director candidates by stockholders or groups of stockholders. Generally, and under the current framework for electing directors in contested elections, only board-sponsored nominees for election are reimbursed for their election expenses. Dissident candidates are not, unless they succeed in replacing at least a majority of the entire board. The Bylaw would encourage the nomination of non-management board candidates by promising reimbursement of the nominating stockholders' proxy expenses if one or more of its candidates are elected. In that the shareholders also have a legitimate interest, because the Bylaw would facilitate the exercise of their right to participate in selecting the contestants. The Court of Chancery has so recognized:

> [T]he unadorned right to cast a ballot in a contest for [corporate] office . . . is meaningless without the right to participate in selecting the contestants. As the nominating process circumscribes the range of choice to be made, it is a fundamental and outcome-determinative step in the election of officeholders. To allow for voting while maintaining a closed selection process thus renders the former an empty exercise. . . . [52]

The shareholders of a Delaware corporation have the right "to participate in selecting the contestants" for election to the board. The shareholders are entitled to facilitate the exercise of that right by proposing a bylaw that would encourage candidates other than board-sponsored nominees to stand for election. The Bylaw would accomplish that by committing the corporation to reimburse the election expenses of shareholders whose candidates are successfully elected. That the implementation of that proposal would require the expenditure of corporate funds will not, in and of itself, make such a bylaw an improper subject matter for shareholder action. Accordingly, we answer the first question certified to us in the affirmative.

---

52. [FN 22] *Harrah's Entm't v. JCC Holding Co.*, 802 A.2d 294, 311 (Del. Ch. 2002) (quoting *Durkin v. Nat'l Bank of Olyphant*, 772 F.2d 55, 59 (3d Cir. 1985)).

That, however, concludes only part of the analysis. The DGCL also requires that the Bylaw be "not inconsistent with law."[53] Accordingly, we turn to the second certified question, which is whether the proposed Bylaw, if adopted, would cause CA to violate any Delaware law to which it is subject.

IV. THE SECOND QUESTION

In answering the first question, we have already determined that the Bylaw does not facially violate any provision of the DGCL or of CA's Certificate of Incorporation. The question thus becomes whether the Bylaw would violate any common law rule or precept. . . .

This Court has previously invalidated contracts that would require a board to act or not act in such a fashion that would limit the exercise of their fiduciary duties. In *Paramount Communications, Inc. v. QVC Network, Inc.*,[54] we invalidated a "no shop" provision of a merger agreement with a favored bidder (Viacom) that prevented the directors of the target company (Paramount) from communicating with a competing bidder (QVC) the terms of its competing bid in an effort to obtain the highest available value for shareholders. We held that:

> The No-Shop Provision could not validly define or limit the fiduciary duties of the Paramount directors. To the extent that a contract, or a provision thereof, purports to require a board to act or not act in such a fashion as to limit the exercise of fiduciary duties, it is invalid and unenforceable. [. . .] [T]he Paramount directors could not contract away their fiduciary obligations. Since the No-Shop Provision was invalid, Viacom never had any vested contract rights in the provision.[55]

Similarly, in *Quickturn Design Systems, Inc. v. Shapiro*,[56] the directors of the target company (Quickturn) adopted a "poison pill" rights plan that contained a so-called "delayed redemption provision" as a defense against a hostile takeover bid, as part of which the bidder (Mentor Graphics) intended to wage a proxy contest to replace the target company board. The delayed redemption provision was intended to deter that effort, by preventing any newly elected board from redeeming the poison pill for six months. This Court invalidated that provision, because it would "impermissibly deprive any newly elected board of both its statutory authority to manage the corporation under 8 Del. C. §141(a) and its concomitant fiduciary duty pursuant to that statutory mandate."[57] We held that:

> One of the most basic tenets of Delaware corporate law is that the board of directors has the ultimate responsibility for managing the business and affairs of a corporation. [. . .] The Quickturn certificate of incorporation contains no

---

53. [FN 23] 8 Del. C. §109(b).
54. [FN 27] 637 A.2d 34 (Del. 1994).
55. [FN 28] *Paramount v. QVC*, 637 A.2d at 51.
56. [FN 29] 721 A.2d 1281 (Del. 1998).
57. [FN 30] *Quickturn*, 721 A.2d at 1291.

provision purporting to limit the authority of the board in any way. The Delayed Redemption Provision, however, would prevent a newly elected board of directors from *completely* discharging its fundamental management duties to the corporation and its stockholders for six months. While the Delayed Redemption Provision limits the board of directors' authority in only one respect, the suspension of the Rights Plan, it nonetheless restricts the board's power in an area of fundamental importance to the shareholders—negotiating a possible sale of the corporation. Therefore, we hold that the Delayed Redemption Provision is invalid under Section 141(a), which confers upon any newly elected board of directors *full* power to manage and direct the business and affairs of a Delaware corporation.[58]

Both *QVC* and *Quickturn* involved binding contractual arrangements that the board of directors had voluntarily imposed upon themselves. This case involves a binding bylaw that the shareholders seek to impose involuntarily on the directors in the specific area of election expense reimbursement. Although this case is distinguishable in that respect, the distinction is one without a difference. The reason is that the internal governance contract—which here takes the form of a bylaw—is one that would also prevent the directors from exercising their full managerial power in circumstances where their fiduciary duties would otherwise require them to deny reimbursement to a dissident slate. That this limitation would be imposed by a majority vote of the shareholders rather than by the directors themselves, does not, in our view, legally matter.

AFSCME contends that it is improper to use the doctrine articulated in *QVC* and *Quickturn* as the measure of the validity of the Bylaw. Because the Bylaw would remove the subject of election expense reimbursement (in circumstances as defined by the Bylaw) entirely from the CA's board's discretion (AFSCME argues), it cannot fairly be claimed that the directors would be precluded from discharging their fiduciary duty. Stated differently, AFSCME argues that it is unfair to claim that the Bylaw prevents the CA board from discharging its fiduciary duty where the effect of the Bylaw is to relieve the board entirely of those duties in this specific area.

That response, in our view, is more semantical than substantive. No matter how artfully it may be phrased, the argument concedes the very proposition that renders the Bylaw, as written, invalid: the Bylaw mandates reimbursement of election expenses in circumstances that a proper application of fiduciary principles could preclude. That such circumstances could arise is not far fetched. Under Delaware law, a board may expend corporate funds to reimburse proxy expenses "[w]here the controversy is concerned with a question of policy as distinguished from personnel o[r] management."[59] But in a situation where the proxy contest is motivated by personal or petty concerns, or to promote

---

58. [FN 31] *Id.* at 1291-92 (italics in original, internal footnotes omitted).
59. [FN 33] *Hall v. Trans-Lux Daylight Picture Screen Corp.,* 171 A. 226, 227 (Del. Ch. 1934); *See also Hibbert v. Hollywood Park, Inc.,* 457 A.2d 339, 345 (Del. 1983) (reimbursement of "reasonable expenses" permitted where the proxy contest "was actually one involving substantive differences about corporation policy.").

interests that do not further, or are adverse to, those of the corporation, the board's fiduciary duty could compel that reimbursement be denied altogether.

It is in this respect that the proposed Bylaw, as written, would violate Delaware law if enacted by CA's shareholders. As presently drafted, the Bylaw would afford CA's directors full discretion to determine what *amount* of reimbursement is appropriate, because the directors would be obligated to grant only the "reasonable" expenses of a successful short slate. Unfortunately, that does not go far enough, because the Bylaw contains no language or provision that would reserve to CA's directors their full power to exercise their fiduciary duty to decide whether or not it would be appropriate, in a specific case, to award reimbursement at all.

In arriving at this conclusion, we express no view on whether the Bylaw as currently drafted, would create a better governance scheme from a policy standpoint. We decide only what is, and is not, legally permitted under the DGCL. That statute, as currently drafted, is the expression of policy as decreed by the Delaware legislature. Those who believe that CA's shareholders should be permitted to make the proposed Bylaw as drafted part of CA's governance scheme, have two alternatives. They may seek to amend the Certificate of Incorporation to include the substance of the Bylaw; *or* they may seek recourse from the Delaware General Assembly.

Questions

1. What is the purpose of AFSCME's proposed bylaw?
2. What is the test for determining whether a bylaw is a proper subject for shareholder action? Was the proposed bylaw proper here?
3. How would the bylaw, if adopted, cause CA to violate Delaware law?
4. How could the bylaw be revised so that it wouldn't cause CA to violate Delaware law?

Exercise 9.3

1. Snapbuzz shareholders adopt the following amendment to Snapbuzz's bylaws:

   "Each director shall be at least 40 years of age and a resident of Utopia."

   Is this a valid bylaw?

   At its next meeting, the Snapbuzz board unanimously approves a resolution deleting the age and residency requirement from Snapbuzz's Bylaws. Can the board do this? What should the shareholders have done differently?
2. Redo Question 1 assuming Snapbuzz is a Delaware corporation.

E. CHARTER AMENDMENT PROCESS

It is fairly common for a corporation to amend its charter from time to time. To give you a sense for the formalities involved, let's review an articles of incorporation amendment for the fictional corporation Utz Incorporated (UI), a corporation incorporated in an MBCA state. The following is the current provision of UI's articles with respect to capital stock:

Article III.

The aggregate number of shares that the corporation is authorized to issue is 10,000,000 shares of Common Stock, without par value.

UI is a private company and currently has four million shares of common stock issued and outstanding owned by an aggregate of 20 shareholders. UI's articles and bylaws simply track the default provisions of the MBCA. UI is seeking venture capital financing and thus wants to amend Article III to add a blank check preferred provision so that it can act quickly when it secures an investor. Hence, UI's CFO, Don Draper, calls and tells you to put together the paperwork for the amendment. You inform Draper that an articles amendment requires board and shareholder approval. Board approval is a non-issue and can be accomplished through written consent, but UI will need to hold a special shareholders' meeting because (1) it just held its regular meeting two months ago, and (2) a couple of shareholders have not been happy with UI's management and are therefore unlikely to sign a written shareholders' consent.

To get the ball rolling, you draft the following written consent, have Draper sign off on it, and then circulate it to the UI directors with a cover letter explaining the purpose of the amendment, offering to answer any questions they may have, and asking them to sign the consent and return it to you.

UNANIMOUS WRITTEN CONSENT OF THE BOARD OF DIRECTORS OF UTZ INCORPORATED

The undersigned, being all of the members of the Board of Directors of Utz Incorporated (the "Corporation") do hereby unanimously consent to the adoption of the following resolutions in lieu of a formal meeting of the Board of Directors of the Corporation.

Amendment to Articles of Incorporation

The Corporation is seeking venture capital financing and thus the Board of Directors deems it advisable to amend the Corporation's Articles of Incorporation to provide for blank check preferred stock. In that regard:

RESOLVED, that subject to shareholder approval, Article III of the Corporation's Articles of Incorporation is amended to read in its entirety as follows:

"The aggregate number of shares that the corporation is authorized to issue is 10,000,000 shares of Common Stock, without par value and 1,000,000 shares of Preferred Stock. The board of directors is authorized to issue Preferred Stock from time to time in one or more classes or series and to fix the number of shares, par value, and the relative dividend rights, conversion rights, voting rights, and special rights and qualification of any such class or series."

Special Meeting of Shareholders

RESOLVED, that a Special Meeting of the Corporation's shareholders be held at 10:00 A.M. on April 2, 2012 at the Corporation's offices for the purpose of submitting to the shareholders for approval the above amendment to the Corporation's Articles of Incorporation.

RESOLVED, that the record date for determining shareholders entitled to vote at the Special Meeting is set at the close of business on March 10, 2012.

RESOLVED, that Donald Draper and Peggy Olson be and they hereby are designated as proxies who may be appointed by the shareholders in connection with the voting of shares of the Corporation's stock at the Special Meeting.

RESOLVED, that the officers be and hereby are directed to take all action which they shall deem necessary or desirable in connection with the holding of the Special Meeting, including the preparation and mailing of a Notice of Special Meeting and the solicitation of proxies.

IN WITNESS WHEREOF, the undersigned have executed this Written Consent as of March 5, 2012.

_____
Joan Harris

_____
Roger Sterling

_____
Peter Campbell

_____
Robert Cooper

_____
Salvatore Romano

_____
Bethany Francis

Notice that the above resolution sets the "record date" at March 10, 2012. A record date is the date set by a corporation for determining the holders of its shares for various purposes such as voting and dividend rights.[60] In this context, it means that the UI shareholders who, according to UI's records, own shares on March 10, 2012 are entitled to receive notice of and vote at the special shareholders' meeting. A record date is typically not of much significance for a private company whose shares change hands infrequently. It is, however, critical in the public company context because shares potentially change hands every day. Thus, a cut-off date is needed so the corporation knows who to send notice to. Note that if you were to buy UI shares after March 10, 2012 but before April 2, 2012 (the date of the special shareholders' meeting), you would be the record holder but would not get to vote the shares at the meeting because you were not the record holder on the record date. Instead, the person you bought the shares from would be entitled to vote them. If this was a concern for you, you could require that he or she give you a proxy to vote the shares at the upcoming meeting as a condition to you buying them.

While waiting for the signatures to come in, you draft the following cover letter, notice, and proxy form for the special shareholders' meeting.

March ___, 2012
[shareholder's address]

Re: Special Meeting of Shareholders

Dear Utz shareholder:

As you may be aware, Utz is pursuing venture capital financing to fund the continued development of our products. In that regard, we need to amend our articles of incorporation to create blank check preferred stock in order to facilitate a possible venture capital investment. Hence, enclosed is a Notice of Special Shareholders' Meeting to be held on April 2, 2012, at 10:00 A.M. at our offices, 10 North Avenue, Chicago, Illinois. While your vote is important, you do not need to attend the meeting to vote. All you need to do is complete, date, and sign the enclosed proxy form and fax it to us at 312-555-2833 or return it in the enclosed envelope.

If you have any questions regarding the enclosed, please call our CFO, Don Draper, at 312-555-2828.

Sincerely,

Roger Sterling
Chairman of the Board

---

60. *See* MBCA §7.08; DGCL §213.

UTZ INCORPORATED
NOTICE OF SPECIAL SHAREHOLDERS' MEETING

PLEASE TAKE NOTICE that Utz Incorporated (the "Corporation") is holding a Special Shareholders' Meeting on April 2, 2012 at 10:00 A.M. CST at the offices of the Corporation, 10 North Avenue, Chicago, Illinois, for the following purpose:

Articles Amendment Adding Blank Check Preferred Stock

The Corporation's Board of Directors proposes that the shareholders amend Article III of the Corporation's Articles of Incorporation to read in its entirety as follows:

"The aggregate number of shares that the corporation is authorized to issue is 10,000,000 shares of Common Stock, without par value and 1,000,000 shares of Preferred Stock. The board of directors is authorized to issue Preferred Stock from time to time in one or more classes or series and to fix the number of shares, par value, and the relative dividend rights, conversion rights, voting rights, and special rights and qualification of any such class or series."

BY ORDER OF THE BOARD OF DIRECTORS

Roger Sterling, Chairman of the Board

Dated: March __, 2012
            Chicago, Illinois

UTZ INCORPORATED PROXY FORM
FOR SPECIAL SHAREHOLDERS' MEETING

The undersigned hereby appoints Donald Draper and Peggy Olson, and each of them, with full power of substitution, as proxies to represent and vote, as designated below, all shares of stock of Utz Incorporated (the "Corporation") registered in the name of the undersigned at the Special Shareholders' Meeting of the Corporation to be held at 10:00 A.M. local time at the Corporation's offices at 10 North Avenue, Chicago, Illinois on April 2, 2012, and at any adjournment thereof.

The Board of Directors recommends that you empower the proxies to vote FOR the proposal below.

Amend Article III of the Corporation's Articles of Incorporation to provide for blank check preferred stock.

[ ] For   [ ] Against   [ ] Abstain

THIS PROXY WHEN PROPERLY EXECUTED WILL BE VOTED AS DIRECTED OR, IF NO DIRECTION IS GIVEN WITH RESPECT TO THE PROPOSAL, WILL BE VOTED FOR THE PROPOSAL.

This proxy appointment is solicited on behalf of the Corporation's Board of Directors.

Date: _____, 2012   _____

PLEASE DATE AND SIGN ABOVE

Please mail this proxy in the enclosed return envelope or fax it to Utz at 312-555-2833.

After haranguing two of the directors, you secure all of the directors' signatures on the board written consent. You then fill in the blanks on the above documents, Draper signs off on them, and your assistant mails them out.

You check with Draper a week later to see how many proxy forms have been sent in. He tells you that he's received forms for about 1 million shares. You tell him to give it a few days and then start calling the larger shareholders who have not returned their forms to get them to do so. You point out that at least 2,000,001 shares need to be represented at the meeting. A few days later, Draper emails you saying he has received proxy forms for about 2,500,000 shares.

At 9:00 A.M. on April 2, you stroll over to Utz's offices. While you do not expect anyone to actually attend the meeting, Draper's assistant has reserved Utz's largest conference room in case some shareholders do show up. As it turns out, no one attends in person. Draper calls the meeting to order promptly at 10:00 A.M., votes the 2,500,000 plus shares for which he serves as proxy in favor of the articles amendment and adjourns the meeting at 10:03 A.M. You return to your office and prepare the following documents:

UTZ INCORPORATED
MINUTES OF SHAREHOLDERS' SPECIAL MEETING

Utz Incorporated (the "Corporation") held a Special Shareholders' Meeting at the offices of the Corporation on April 2, 2012, pursuant to due notice. Donald Draper, Chief Financial Officer, called the meeting to order at 10:00 A.M. and appointed [you] to act as secretary and inspector of the meeting.

Mr. Draper reported that 2,583,400 shares of stock were present either in person or by proxy and that, since legal notice of the meeting has been given and a quorum was present, the meeting was regularly and lawfully convened and ready to transact business.

The following resolution was adopted by a vote of 2,583,400 shares in favor, zero shares against, and zero shares abstaining:

RESOLVED, that Article III of the Corporation's Articles of Incorporation is amended to read in its entirety as follows:

"The aggregate number of shares that the corporation is authorized to issue is 10,000,000 shares of Common Stock, without par value and 1,000,000 shares of Preferred Stock. The board of directors is authorized to issue Preferred Stock from time to time in one or more classes or series and to fix the number of shares, par value, and the relative dividend rights, conversion rights, voting rights, and special rights and qualification of any such class or series."

There being no further business to come before the meeting it was adjourned.

Respectfully submitted,

_____

[You], Secretary of the Meeting

UTZ INCORPORATED
ARTICLES OF AMENDMENT[61]

1. The name of the corporation is Utz Incorporated (the "Corporation").
2. The Corporation amended Article III of its Articles of Incorporation to read in its entirety as follows:

"The aggregate number of shares that the corporation is authorized to issue is 10,000,000 shares of Common Stock, without par value and 1,000,000 shares of Preferred Stock. The board of directors is authorized to issue Preferred Stock from time to time in one or more classes or series and to fix the number of shares, par value, and the relative dividend rights, conversion rights, voting rights, and special rights and qualification of any such class or series."

3. The amendment was adopted on April 2, 2012.
4. The amendment was duly approved by the Corporation's shareholders in the manner required by the Model Business Corporation Act and by the Corporation's Articles of Incorporation.

Submitted by:

_____

Donald Draper, Chief Financial Officer

---

61. The contents of this document is dictated by MBCA §10.06.

You forward these documents to Draper. He signs the Articles of Amendment, returns it to you, and your assistant sends it by FedEx to the Secretary of State along with the applicable filing fee. A clerk in the Secretary of State's office accepts the Articles of Amendment for filing the next day, at which point it becomes effective.[62]

Exercise 9.4

Assume Snapbuzz has the following shares outstanding:

Type of Stock	Shares Outstanding
Common Stock	6,000,000
Series A Preferred Stock	100,000
Series B Preferred Stock	100,000

1. What is the minimum number of affirmative votes required for each type of stock for the following actions to pass (see MBCA Chapter 10, Subchapter A for provisions governing charter amendments):
   (a) An articles amendment to change the par value of Snapbuzz's common stock to $0.001.
   (b) An articles amendment to change Snapbuzz's name from Snapbuzz Incorporated to Snapbuzz Inc.
   (c) An articles amendment to lower the dividend rate on the Series B Preferred from $3.00 to $1.00.
2. Redo Questions 1(a)-(c) assuming Snapbuzz is a Delaware corporation (see DGCL Subchapter VIII for provisions governing charter amendments).

ARTICLES OF INCORPORATION
OF SNAPBUZZ INCORPORATED

The undersigned, desiring to form a corporation for profit under the Model Business Corporation Act (the "Act"), does hereby certify:

1. The name of the corporation is Snapbuzz Incorporated.

2. The total number of shares of capital stock which the corporation shall have authority to issue is 10,200,000, comprised of 10,000,000

---

shares of common stock having a par value of $0.01 per share, 100,000 shares of Series A Preferred Stock having a par value of $0.01 per share (the "Series A Preferred"), and 100,000 shares of Series B Preferred Stock having a par value of $0.01 per share (the "Series B Preferred").

(a) Each share of Series A Preferred has the following preferences and rights:

(i) <u>Dividends</u>. The holders of outstanding Series A Preferred shall be entitled to receive in each year cumulative dividends in cash at a rate per share of $1.00.

(ii) <u>Liquidation Preference</u>. Upon any voluntary or involuntary liquidation, dissolution, or other winding up of the affairs of the corporation, before any distribution or payment shall be made to the holders of Common Stock, the holders of the Series A Preferred shall be entitled to be paid, to the extent possible in cash, $10.00 per share.

(iii) <u>Voting</u>. The holders of outstanding Series A Preferred shall be entitled to vote with the Common Stock as a single voting group upon any matter submitted to the shareholders for a vote. Each share of Series A Preferred shall be entitled to 10 votes.

(b) Each share of Series B Preferred has the following preferences and rights:

(i) <u>Dividends</u>. The holders of outstanding Series B Preferred shall be entitled to receive in each year cumulative dividends in cash at a rate per share of $3.00.

(ii) <u>Voting</u>. The holders of outstanding Series B Preferred shall have no voting rights except as required by the Act.

3. The street address of the corporation's initial registered office is 742 Evergreen Terrace, Springfield, Utopia 41099. The name of its initial registered agent at that office is Homer J. Simpson.

4. The mailing address of the corporation's principal office is 742 Evergreen Terrace, Springfield, Utopia 41099.

5. The name and mailing address of the incorporator is Homer J. Simpson, 742 Evergreen Terrace, Springfield, Utopia 41099.

6. The liability of a director to the corporation or its shareholders for money damages for any action taken, or failure to take any action as a director shall be eliminated or limited to the maximum extent permitted by law; provided, however, that this provision shall not eliminate or limit the liability of a director regarding (a) the amount of a financial benefit received by a director to which the director is not entitled; (b) an intentional infliction of harm on the corporation or its shareholders; (c) a violation of §8.33 of the Act; or (d) an intentional violation of criminal law.

7. The holders of two-thirds of the voting shares present and entitled to vote, in person or by proxy, shall constitute a quorum at any and all meetings of shareholders.

8. Any action required or permitted by the Act to be taken at a shareholders' meeting may be taken without a meeting, and without prior notice, if consents in writing setting forth the action so taken are signed by the holders of outstanding shares having not less than the minimum number of votes that would be required to authorize or take the action at a meeting at which all shares entitled to vote on the action were present and voted.

9. Directors may be removed only for cause.

The undersigned has duly executed these Articles of Incorporation on October 3, 2003.

/s/ Homer J. Simpson
Incorporator

SNAPBUZZ INCORPORATED
BYLAWS

Article I.
Shareholders Meetings

(a) <u>Annual Meetings</u>. The annual meeting of the shareholders shall be held at the principal office of the corporation or at such other place as may be designated by the Board of Directors, on the 15th day of June of each year, at 10 A.M., if not a legal holiday, but if a legal holiday, then on the day following which is not a legal holiday, at the same hour. The first annual meeting shall be held in a place to be designated by the then acting Board of Directors.

(b) <u>Special Meetings</u>. Special meetings of the shareholders shall be called upon the written request of the president, or in the case of the president's absence, death or, disability, the vice president authorized to exercise the authority of the president, the directors by action at a meeting, or a majority of the directors acting without a meeting, or of shareholders representing at least 15 percent of all shares entitled to vote. Calls for such meetings shall specify the time, place, and objects thereof. No business other than that specified in the call shall be considered at any special meeting.

(c) <u>Notice of Meetings</u>. A written or printed notice of the annual meeting shall be given to each shareholder of record entitled to vote at such meeting, as the same appears on the books of the corporation, by personal delivery or by mail to his or her or its address as the same may appear on the records of the corporation, no less than 7 days nor more than 60 days before the date of meeting, unless waived in writing.

(d) Quorum. The holders of a majority of the voting shares present and entitled to vote, in person or by proxy, shall constitute a quorum at any and all meetings of shareholders, but in absence of a quorum, a majority of voting shares present in person or by proxy may adjourn any meeting from time to time.

(e) Proxies. Any shareholder entitled to vote at a meeting of shareholders may be represented and vote thereat, by proxy appointed by an instrument in writing subscribed by the shareholder or his duly authorized agent, and submitted to the secretary of the corporation or the secretary of the meeting at or before said meeting.

(f) Place of Meetings. Meetings of shareholders shall be held at the principal office of the corporation unless the Board of Directors decides that a meeting shall be held some other place within or without the Commonwealth of Utopia and causes the notice thereof to so state.

Article II.
Certificates

(a) Certificates. Certificates evidencing the ownership of shares of the corporation shall be issued to those entitled to them by transfer or otherwise. Each certificate for shares shall bear a distinguishing letter and/or number, the signature of the chairman of the Board of Directors, the president or vice president, and/or the secretary or an assistant secretary, or the treasurer or an assistant treasurer, the seal of the corporation (but failure to affix the seal shall not invalidate the certificate if properly signed) and such recitals as may be required by law.

(b) Lost Certificate. The Board of Directors may order a new certificate or certificates of stock to be issued in place of any certificate or certificates alleged to be lost, stolen, or destroyed, on proof to its satisfaction of its loss, theft, or destruction, and if lost or stolen that it was not endorsed by the shareholder; but in every such case the owner of the lost certificate or certificates shall first cause to be given to the corporation a bond with surety or sureties satisfactory to the corporation in such sum and on such terms as the Board of Directors in its discretion may determine proper.

Article III.
Directors

(a) Number; Election. The Board of Directors shall consist of a minimum of one and a maximum of three directors as shall from time to time be fixed exclusively by resolution of the Board of Directors. The election of directors shall be at the annual meeting of the shareholders, or in default thereof, at a special meeting called for that purpose, and shall be by ballot if there are more nominees than the number of directors to be elected.

Directors shall hold office until the expiration of the term for which they were elected and shall continue in office until their respective successors have been duly elected and qualified. The directors elected at the first meeting of shareholders, or any adjournment thereof, shall hold office until the first annual meeting.

(b) <u>Vacancies</u>. In case of any vacancy in the Board of Directors, the remaining directors, by a majority vote, shall elect a successor who shall hold office for the unexpired term. If the membership of the Board of Directors should at any time fall below the number necessary to constitute a quorum, or the remaining directors fail to agree promptly on a successor, then, in either such case, a special meeting of the shareholders shall be called as provided in Article I and such number of directors shall be elected thereat as may be necessary to bring the Board of Directors to its full membership. The shareholders may remove any or all of the directors at any time in such manner as is provided by law.

(c) <u>Meetings</u>. After each annual election of directors, the newly elected directors may meet, without notice, for the purpose of organization, the election of officers, and the transaction of other business. The place and time of such first meeting may be fixed by the shareholders at the meeting at which the directors are elected, and if a majority of the directors be present at such place and time, no prior notice of such meeting shall be required to be given to the directors. The place and time of such first meeting may also be fixed by written consent of the directors or by the Bylaws. Regular meetings may be held at such times and places within or without the Commonwealth of Utopia as may be determined by the Board. Special meetings of the Board of Directors may be held at any time and place within or without the state upon written call of the president, vice president, or of any two (2) of the directors.

(d) <u>Notice of Meetings; Matters to Be Considered</u>. The secretary shall give notice of all meetings of the Board of Directors, other than annual meetings, to each member of the Board at least 24 hours before the time of such meeting. Such notice shall be deemed to be given at the time when it is mailed or delivered personally to the director, as the case may be. Any matter may be considered by the directors at a regular or special meeting, whether stated in the notice for such meeting or not. When all the directors shall be present at any meeting, however called or wherever held, or shall waive notice of the meeting in writing either before or after such meeting, or after the meeting shall sign a written assent thereto, the acts of such meeting shall be valid as if such meeting had been regularly called.

(e) <u>Quorum</u>. A majority of the number of the Board of Directors fixed at the previous shareholders' meeting shall constitute a quorum at all meetings thereof (except that a majority of the directors in office shall constitute a quorum for filling a vacancy in the Board).

(f) <u>Compensation; Expenses</u>. Each director shall receive such compensation for his attendance at any regular or special meeting of the Board of Directors or any committee thereof as may be fixed from time to time by the Board of Directors. He may also be reimbursed for his reasonable expenses incurred in attending meetings of the Board of Directors or any committee thereof.

(g) <u>Action by Written Consent</u>. Any action required or permitted to be taken at any meeting of the Board may be taken without a meeting if at least 75 percent of directors consent thereto in writing, and the writing or writings are filed with the minutes of proceedings of the Board.

Article IV.
Officers

(a) <u>Authority of Board</u>. At the first annual meeting of the Board of Directors in each year held next after the annual meeting of the shareholders, or at any special meeting as hereinabove provided, the Board of Directors shall elect officers of the corporation and designate and appoint such subordinate officers and employees as it shall determine.

(b) <u>Offices</u>. The Board of Directors shall elect a president, such number of vice presidents as the Board may from time to time determine, a secretary and treasurer (or secretary/treasurer) and, in its discretion, a chairman of the Board of Directors. The Board of Directors may, from time to time, create such offices and appoint such other officers, subordinate officers, and assistant officers as it may determine. The president, any vice president who succeeds to his office, and the chairman of the Board shall be, but the other officers need not be, chosen from among the members of the Board of Directors. Any two or more of such offices may be held by the same person.

(c) <u>Term of Office; Compensation</u>. The officers of the corporation shall hold office until their successors are chosen and qualified at the next annual or special meeting at which officers are elected, as provided in paragraph (a) hereof, or for such shorter period as may be designated by the Board of Directors; but any officer may be removed at any time, with or without cause, by the Board of Directors. Compensation of officers shall be fixed by the directors or any committee or officer or officers to whom such authority is delegated by the directors.

(d) <u>Vacancies</u>. A vacancy in any office, however created, shall be filled by the Board of Directors at a regular or special meeting.

Article V.
Transfers of Securities

All endorsements, assignments, transfers, stock powers, or other instruments of transfer of securities standing in the name of the corporation shall be executed for and in the name of the corporation by the president or a vice president and also by the treasurer or secretary or an assistant treasurer or assistant secretary.

Article VI.
Indemnity of Officers and Directors

Each present and future director and officer shall be indemnified by the corporation against expenses reasonably incurred by him (including, but not limited to, counsel fees and settlements out of court in amounts approved by the Board of Directors but not including any case wherein, in the opinion of disinterested reputable counsel selected by the corporation, the directors and officers affected are guilty of negligence or misconduct) and against judgments against him in favor of the corporation or other persons in connection with any action, suit, or proceeding to which he may be made a party by reason of his being or having been a director or officer of the corporation (whether or not he continues to be a director or officer at the time of incurring such expenses), except in relation to matters as to which he shall be adjudged in such action, suit, or proceeding to be liable because of negligence or misconduct. The foregoing right of indemnification shall not be exclusive of other rights to which any director or officer may be entitled as a matter of law.

Article VII.
Commitees

The Board of Directors shall have power to create from time to time such committees, standing or special, and to give them such powers and authority, as it shall deem best, and to revoke their appointment or restrict or modify their powers. It may appoint an executive committee and delegate to such committee any of its powers to be exercised in intervals between meetings of the Board.

Article VIII.
Closing Stock Transfer Books

The Board of Directors may fix a date, which shall not be a past date, not exceeding sixty (60) days preceding the date of any meeting of shareholders or any dividend or distribution payment date or any date for the allotment of rights or other matters provided by law, as a record date for the determination of the shareholders entitled to notice of such meeting or to vote thereat or to receive such dividends, distributions, or rights as the case may be and/or the Board of Directors may close the books of the corporation against transfer of shares during the whole or any part of such period.

Article IX.
Order of Business

At all shareholders' meetings, the order of business shall generally be as follows:

(a) call to order by the presiding officer;
(b) proof of notice of meeting, if necessary;
(c) presentation and examination of any proxies;
(d) reading of minutes of previous meeting;
(e) reports of officers and committees;
(f) election of directors, if necessary;
(g) unfinished business;
(h) new business; and
(i) adjournment.

This order may be changed by affirmative vote of a majority of the voting shares present.

Article X.
Amendment

These Bylaws may be added to, amended, or repealed at any time by the Board of Directors.

· CHAPTER TEN ·

CORPORATE FIDUCIARY DUTIES

In this chapter we cover fiduciary duties imposed on directors, officers, and controlling shareholders of corporations.

A. FIDUCIARY DUTIES OF DIRECTORS

As you know by now, the default corporate governance structure is centralized management with ultimate authority vested in a corporation's board of directors. This structure has its advantages. In particular, it allows a small collaborative body with business expertise and full access to corporate information to advise and monitor the corporation's senior executives, set corporate policy, and occasionally make important business decisions. In any corporation with more than a handful or two of shareholders, it simply is not desirable, practical, or wise for the shareholders to serve this role.

But centralized management has its disadvantages. Specifically, it gives rise to the principal-agent problem. This is because shareholders are essentially delegating authority to the board of directors to make decisions on their behalf, and the interests of directors and shareholders will sometimes diverge. Thus, there is a risk that directors might take actions that benefit themselves rather than shareholders. For example, directors may allocate themselves excessive compensation or other perquisites, sell property to the corporation at inflated prices, take business opportunities for themselves that should go to the corporation, or shirk responsibility. In light of this risk, corporate law imposes two broad fiduciary duties on directors: the duty of care and the duty of loyalty. These duties are judge-made under Delaware law, which we will discuss first, in large part because Delaware law is the most developed and influential in this area. We then examine some aspects of the MBCA's statutory approach.

1. The Business Judgment Rule: No Liability for Bad Decisions

Before we dive into the intricacies of corporate fiduciary duties, it is important to understand upfront that a director is not liable for a breach of fiduciary duty solely on the grounds that he or she made a bad business decision, even if the decision resulted in the demise of the corporation. This concept is embodied in the business judgment rule. Under Delaware law, the business judgment rule is a "presumption that in making a business decision the directors of a corporation acted on an informed basis, in good faith and in the honest belief that the action taken was in the best interests of the company."[1] As demonstrated by the next case, the rule prevents a plaintiff from prevailing on a breach of fiduciary duty claim against a board of directors for a bad business decision unless the plaintiff can prove that the board's decision-making process was inadequate or tainted. In other words, a plaintiff needs to prove more than just a board decision turned out poorly for the corporation.

Gagliardi v. Trifoods International, Inc.
683 A.2d 1049 (Del. Ch. 1996)

ALLEN, Chancellor.

Currently before the Court is a motion to dismiss a shareholders action against the directors of TriFoods International, Inc. and certain partnerships and individuals that own stock in TriFoods. In broadest terms the motion raises the question, what must a shareholder plead in order to state a derivative claim to recover corporate losses allegedly sustained by reason of "mismanagement" unaffected by directly conflicting financial interests?

Plaintiff, Eugene Gagliardi, is the founder of the TriFoods, Inc. and in 1990 he induced certain persons to invest in the company by buying its stock. In 1993 he was removed as Chairman of the board and his employment with the company terminated. He continues to own approximately 13% of the company's common stock. The business of the company has, according to the allegations of the complaint, deteriorated very badly since Mr. Gagliardi's ouster.

The suit asserts that defendants are liable to the corporation and to plaintiff individually on a host of theories, most importantly for mismanagement. . . .

COUNT IV: NEGLIGENT MISMANAGEMENT

This count, which is asserted against all defendants, alleges that "implementation of their grandiose scheme for TriFoods' future growth . . . in only eighteen months destroyed TriFoods." Plaintiff asserts that the facts alleged, which sketch that "scheme" and those results, constitute mismanagement and waste.

---

1. *Aronson v. Lewis*, 473 A.2d 805, 812 (Del. 1984).

The allegations of Count IV are detailed. They assert most centrally that prior to his dismissal Gagliardi disagreed with Hart [TriFoods' former president] concerning the wisdom of TriFoods manufacturing its products itself and disagreed strongly that the company should buy a plant in Pomfret, Connecticut and move its operations to that state. Plaintiff thought it foolish (and he alleges that it was negligent judgment) to borrow funds . . . for that purpose.

Plaintiff also alleges that Hart caused the company to acquire and fit-out a research or new product facility in Chadds Ford, Pennsylvania, which "duplicated one already available and under lease to Designer Foods [the predecessor name of TriFoods], and which was therefore, a further waste of corporate assets."

Next, it is alleged that "defendants either acquiesced in or approved a reckless or grossly negligent sales commission to build volume."

Next, it is alleged that "Hart and the other defendants caused TriFoods to purchase [the exclusive rights to produce and sell a food product known as] Steak-umms from Heinz in April 1994." The price paid compared unfavorably with a transaction in 1980 in which this product had been sold and which earlier terms are detailed. "Defendants recklessly caused TriFoods to pay $15 million for Steak-umms alone (no plant, no equipment, etc) which was then doing annual sales of only $28 million."

Next, it is alleged that "Hart caused TriFoods . . . to pay $125,000 to a consultant for its new name, logo and packaging."

Next, it is alleged that Hart destroyed customer relationships by supplying inferior products.

Next, it is alleged that "Hart refused to pay key manufacturers and suppliers . . . thus injuring TriFoods' trade relations."

Next, it is alleged that "defendants entered into a transaction whereby TriFoods was to acquire "Lloyd's Ribs" at a grossly excessive price, knowing (or recklessly not knowing) that the Company could not afford the transaction." . . .

Do these allegations of Count IV state a claim upon which relief may be granted? In addressing that question, I start with what I take to be an elementary precept of corporation law: in the absence of facts showing self-dealing or improper motive, a corporate officer or director is not legally responsible to the corporation for losses that may be suffered as a result of a decision that an officer made or that directors authorized in good faith. There is a theoretical exception to this general statement that holds that some decisions may be so "egregious" that liability for losses they cause may follow even in the absence of proof of conflict of interest or improper motivation. The exception, however, has resulted in no awards of money judgments against corporate officers or directors in this jurisdiction and, to my knowledge only the dubious holding in this Court of *Gimbel v. Signal Companies, Inc.*, (Del. Ch.) 316 A.2d 599 *aff'd* (Del. Supr.) 316 A.2d 619 (1974), seems to grant equitable relief in the absence of a claimed conflict or improper motivation. Thus, to allege that a corporation has suffered a loss as a result of a lawful transaction, within the corporation's powers, authorized by a corporate fiduciary *acting in a good faith pursuit of corporate purposes,* does not state a claim for relief against that fiduciary no matter how foolish the investment may appear in retrospect.

The rule could rationally be no different. Shareholders can diversify the risks of their corporate investments. Thus, it is in their economic interest for the corporation to accept in rank order all positive net present value investment projects available to the corporation, starting with the *highest risk adjusted rate of return first.* Shareholders don't want (or shouldn't rationally want) directors to be risk averse. Shareholders' investment interests, across the full range of their diversifiable equity investments, will be maximized if corporate directors and managers honestly assess risk and reward and accept for the corporation the highest risk adjusted returns available that are above the firm's cost of capital.

But directors will tend to deviate from this rational acceptance of corporate risk *if* in authorizing the corporation to undertake a risky investment, the directors must assume some degree of personal risk relating to *ex post facto* claims of derivative liability for any resulting corporate loss.

Corporate directors of public companies typically have a very small proportionate ownership interest in their corporations and little or no incentive compensation. Thus, they enjoy (as residual owners) only a very small proportion of any "upside" gains earned by the corporation on risky investment projects. If, however, corporate directors were to be found liable for a corporate loss from a risky project on the ground that the investment was too risky (foolishly risky! stupidly risky! egregiously risky! —you supply the adverb), their liability would be joint and several for the whole loss (with I suppose a right of contribution). Given the scale of operation of modern public corporations, this stupefying disjunction between risk and reward for corporate directors threatens undesirable effects. Given this disjunction, only a very small probability of director liability based on "negligence," "inattention," "waste," etc., could induce a board to avoid authorizing risky investment projects to any extent! Obviously, it is in the shareholders' economic interest to offer sufficient protection to directors from liability for negligence, etc., to allow directors to conclude that, as a practical matter, there is risk that, if they act in good faith and meet minimal proceduralist standards of attention, they can face liability as a result of a business loss.

The law *protects shareholder investment interests* against the uneconomic consequences that the presence of such second-guessing risk would have on director action and shareholder wealth in a number of ways. It authorizes corporations to pay for director and officer liability insurance and authorizes corporate indemnification in a broad range of cases, for example. But the first protection against a threat of sub-optimal risk acceptance is the so-called business judgment rule. That "rule" in effect provides that where a director is independent and disinterested, there can be no liability for corporate loss, unless the facts are such that no person could possibly authorize such a transaction if he or she were attempting in good faith to meet their duty. *Saxe v. Brady,* Del. Ch., 184 A.2d 602 (1962).

Thus, for example it does not state a claim to allege that: (1) Hart caused the corporation to pay $125,000 to a consultant for the design of a new logo and packaging. On what possible basis might a corporate officer or director be put to the expense of defending such a claim? Nothing is alleged except that an expenditure of corporate funds for a corporate purpose was made. Whether that expenditure was wise or foolish, low risk or high risk is of no concern to this Court. What is alleged certainly does not bring the allegation to within shouting distance of the *Saxe v. Brady* principle. (2) Nor does an allegation that defendants acquiesced in a reckless commission structure "in order to build volume" state a claim; it alleges no conflicting interest or improper motivation, nor does it state facts that might come within the *Saxe v. Brady* principle. It alleges only an ordinary business decision with a pejorative characterization added. (3) The allegation of "duplication" of existing product research facilities similarly simply states a matter that falls within ordinary business judgment; that plaintiff regards the decision as unwise, foolish, or even stupid in the circumstances is not legally significant; indeed that others may look back on it and agree that it was stupid is legally unimportant, in my opinion. (4) That the terms of the purchase of "Steak-umms" seem to plaintiff unwise (especially when compared to the terms of a 1980 transaction involving that product) again fail utterly to state any legal claim. No self-interest, nor facts possibly disclosing improper motive or judgment satisfying the waste standard are alleged. Similarly, (5) the allegations of corporate loss resulting from harm to customer relations by delivery of poor product and (6) harm to supplier relations by poor payment practices, again state nothing that constitutes a legal claim. Certainly these allegations state facts that, if true, constitute either mistakes, poor judgment, or reflect hard choices facing a cash-pressed company, but where is the allegation of conflicting interest or suspect motivation? In the absence of such, where are the facts that, giving the pleader all reasonable inferences in his favor, might possibly make the *Saxe v. Brady* principle applicable? There are none. Nothing is alleged other than poor business practices. To permit the possibility of director liability on that basis would be very destructive of shareholder welfare in the long-term.

A similar analysis holds for the allegations concerning a contract to acquire the product "Lloyd's Ribs" (7); nothing is alleged other than that the price was excessive and the directors knew (or recklessly didn't know) that "the company could not afford such a transaction." . . .

For the foregoing reason Count IV of the amended complaint will be dismissed. . . .

Questions

1. What bad business decisions did defendants make? Why did the court nonetheless dismiss the case?

2. What is the policy behind the business judgment rule?

3. What recourse does a shareholder who disagrees with a board decision have?

As discussed in the above case, to rebut the business judgment rule with respect to a board decision, a plaintiff must plead and prove that a majority of directors (1) were interested, (2) lacked independence, (3) were inadequately informed, or (4) acted in bad faith.[2] We discuss item (3) next in the duty of care context and then items (1), (2), and (4) in the duty of loyalty context.

As Chancellor Allen alludes to, if the plaintiff fails to rebut the rule, the decision will be upheld unless it cannot be attributed to any rational business purpose. Courts apply the waste standard to determine whether a decision was irrational. To meet this standard, a plaintiff "must shoulder the burden of proving that the [decision] was 'so one sided that no business person of ordinary, sound judgment could conclude that the corporation has received adequate consideration.' A claim of waste will arise only in the rare, 'unconscionable case where directors irrationally squander or give away corporate assets.'"[3] As indicated in *Gagliardi* and as remains true today, no plaintiff has ever been awarded money damages by a Delaware court on a waste claim.

If a plaintiff successfully rebuts the business judgment rule, the burden shifts to the defendant directors to prove that the challenged decision was fair to the corporation.

Exercise 10.1

In September 2011, Netflix Inc. announced that its board of directors had approved splitting its streaming and DVD rental business into two separate businesses. Netflix would continue to handle the streaming business and Qwikster, a new wholly owned subsidiary, would handle the DVD rental business. This plan was not well received by Netflix customers, and Netflix stock promptly dropped 25 percent. The Netflix board scrapped the plan three weeks later, but Netflix stock did not recover. Das, a Netflix shareholder, is furious about the whole episode and thus consults you about a possible cause of action under state corporate law against the board for its "idiotic" decision and her likelihood of success. What do you tell her?

---

2. The Duty of Care

The duty of care requires a board to be adequately informed when making a decision. In other words, the focus of the duty of care is on the decision-making

---

2. Some courts also throw fraud and illegality into the mix, but this sort of conduct would undoubtedly constitute acting in bad faith so it really adds nothing.

3. *In re Walt Disney Co. Derivative Litigation*, 906 A.2d 27, 73 (Del. 2006) (citations omitted).

process as opposed to the substance of the decision itself. The next case discusses the Delaware law standard for determining whether a board was adequately informed.

Smith v. Van Gorkom
488 A.2d 858 (Del. 1985)

HORSEY, Justice (for the majority):

This appeal from the Court of Chancery involves a class action brought by shareholders of the defendant Trans Union Corporation ("Trans Union" or "the Company"), originally seeking rescission of a cash-out merger of Trans Union into the defendant New T Company ("New T"), a wholly-owned subsidiary of the defendant, Marmon Group, Inc. ("Marmon"). Alternate relief in the form of damages is sought against the defendant members of the Board of Directors of Trans Union, New T, and Jay A. Pritzker and Robert A. Pritzker, owners of Marmon.

Following trial, the former Chancellor granted judgment for the defendant directors by unreported letter opinion dated July 6, 1982. . . . Judgment was based on [the finding] that the Board of Directors had acted in an informed manner so as to be entitled to protection of the business judgment rule in approving the cash-out merger. . . . The plaintiffs appeal. . . .

I.

The nature of this case requires a detailed factual statement. The following facts are essentially uncontradicted:

A

Trans Union was a publicly-traded, diversified holding company, the principal earnings of which were generated by its railcar leasing business. During the period here involved, the Company had a cash flow of hundreds of millions of dollars annually. However, the Company had difficulty in generating sufficient taxable income to offset increasingly large investment tax credits (ITCs). Accelerated depreciation deductions had decreased available taxable income against which to offset accumulating ITCs. The Company took these deductions, despite their effect on usable ITCs, because the rental price in the railcar leasing market had already impounded the purported tax savings.

In the late 1970's, together with other capital-intensive firms, Trans Union lobbied in Congress to have ITCs refundable in cash to firms which could not fully utilize the credit. During the summer of 1980, defendant Jerome W. Van Gorkom, Trans Union's Chairman and Chief Executive Officer, testified and lobbied in Congress for refundability of ITCs and against further accelerated depreciation. By the end of August, Van Gorkom was convinced that Congress would neither accept the refundability concept nor curtail further accelerated depreciation.

Beginning in the late 1960's, and continuing through the 1970's, Trans Union pursued a program of acquiring small companies in order to increase available taxable income. In July 1980, Trans Union Management prepared the annual revision of the Company's Five Year Forecast. This report was presented to the Board of Directors at its July, 1980 meeting. The report projected an annual income growth of about 20%. The report also concluded that Trans Union would have about $195 million in spare cash between 1980 and 1985, "with the surplus growing rapidly from 1982 onward." The report referred to the ITC situation as a "nagging problem" and, given that problem, the leasing company "would still appear to be constrained to a tax breakeven." The report then listed four alternative uses of the projected 1982-1985 equity surplus: (1) stock repurchase; (2) dividend increases; (3) a major acquisition program; and (4) combinations of the above. The sale of Trans Union was not among the alternatives. The report emphasized that, despite the overall surplus, the operation of the Company would consume all available equity for the next several years, and concluded: "As a result, we have sufficient time to fully develop our course of action."

B

On August 27, 1980, Van Gorkom met with Senior Management of Trans Union. Van Gorkom reported on his lobbying efforts in Washington and his desire to find a solution to the tax credit problem more permanent than a continued program of acquisitions. Various alternatives were suggested and discussed preliminarily, including the sale of Trans Union to a company with a large amount of taxable income.

Donald Romans, Chief Financial Officer of Trans Union, stated that his department had done a "very brief bit of work on the possibility of a leveraged buy-out." This work had been prompted by a media article which Romans had seen regarding a leveraged buy-out by management. The work consisted of a "preliminary study" of the cash which could be generated by the Company if it participated in a leveraged buy-out. As Romans stated, this analysis "was very first and rough cut at seeing whether a cash flow would support what might be considered a high price for this type of transaction."

On September 5, at another Senior Management meeting which Van Gorkom attended, Romans again brought up the idea of a leveraged buy-out as a "possible strategic alternative" to the Company's acquisition program. Romans and Bruce S. Chelberg, President and Chief Operating Officer of Trans Union, had been working on the matter in preparation for the meeting. According to Romans: They did not "come up" with a price for the Company. They merely "ran the numbers" at $50 a share and at $60 a share with the "rough form" of their cash figures at the time. Their "figures indicated that $50 would be very easy to do but $60 would be very difficult to do under those figures." This work did not purport to establish a fair price for either the Company or 100% of the stock. It was intended to determine the cash flow needed to service the debt that would "probably" be incurred in a leveraged buy-out, based on "rough calculations" without "any benefit of experts to identify what the limits were to that, and so forth." These computations were not considered extensive and no conclusion was reached.

At this meeting, Van Gorkom stated that he would be willing to take $55 per share for his own 75,000 shares. He vetoed the suggestion of a leveraged buy-out by Management, however, as involving a potential conflict of interest for Management. Van Gorkom, a certified public accountant and lawyer, had been an officer of Trans Union for 24 years, its Chief Executive Officer for more than 17 years, and Chairman of its Board for 2 years. It is noteworthy in this connection that he was then approaching 65 years of age and mandatory retirement.

For several days following the September 5 meeting, Van Gorkom pondered the idea of a sale. He had participated in many acquisitions as a manager and director of Trans Union and as a director of other companies. He was familiar with acquisition procedures, valuation methods, and negotiations; and he privately considered the pros and cons of whether Trans Union should seek a privately or publicly-held purchaser.

Van Gorkom decided to meet with Jay A. Pritzker, a well-known corporate takeover specialist and a social acquaintance. However, rather than approaching Pritzker simply to determine his interest in acquiring Trans Union, Van Gorkom assembled a proposed per share price for sale of the Company and a financing structure by which to accomplish the sale. Van Gorkom did so without consulting either his Board or any members of Senior Management except one: Carl Peterson, Trans Union's Controller. Telling Peterson that he wanted no other person on his staff to know what he was doing, but without telling him why, Van Gorkom directed Peterson to calculate the feasibility of a leveraged buy-out at an assumed price per share of $55. Apart from the Company's historic stock market price,[4] and Van Gorkom's long association with Trans Union, the record is devoid of any competent evidence that $55 represented the per share intrinsic value of the Company.

Having thus chosen the $55 figure, based solely on the availability of a leveraged buy-out, Van Gorkom multiplied the price per share by the number of shares outstanding to reach a total value of the Company of $690 million. Van Gorkom told Peterson to use this $690 million figure and to assume a $200 million equity contribution by the buyer. Based on these assumptions, Van Gorkom directed Peterson to determine whether the debt portion of the purchase price could be paid off in five years or less if financed by Trans Union's cash flow as projected in the Five Year Forecast, and by the sale of certain weaker divisions identified in a study done for Trans Union by the Boston Consulting Group ("BCG study"). Peterson reported that, of the purchase price, approximately

---

4. [FN 5] The common stock of Trans Union was traded on the New York Stock Exchange. Over the five year period from 1975 through 1979, Trans Union's stock had traded within a range of a high of $39-1/2 and a low of $24-1/4. Its high and low range for 1980 through September 19 (the last trading day before announcement of the merger) was $38-1/4 –$29-1/2.

$50-80 million would remain outstanding after five years. Van Gorkom was disappointed, but decided to meet with Pritzker nevertheless.

Van Gorkom arranged a meeting with Pritzker at the latter's home on Saturday, September 13, 1980. Van Gorkom prefaced his presentation by stating to Pritzker: "Now as far as you are concerned, I can, I think, show how you can pay a substantial premium over the present stock price and pay off most of the loan in the first five years. . . . If you could pay $55 for this Company, here is a way in which I think it can be financed."

Van Gorkom then reviewed with Pritzker his calculations based upon his proposed price of $55 per share. Although Pritzker mentioned $50 as a more attractive figure, no other price was mentioned. However, Van Gorkom stated that to be sure that $55 was the best price obtainable, Trans Union should be free to accept any better offer. Pritzker demurred, stating that his organization would serve as a "stalking horse" for an "auction contest" only if Trans Union would permit Pritzker to buy 1,750,000 shares of Trans Union stock at market price which Pritzker could then sell to any higher bidder. After further discussion on this point, Pritzker told Van Gorkom that he would give him a more definite reaction soon.

On Monday, September 15, Pritzker advised Van Gorkom that he was interested in the $55 cash-out merger proposal and requested more information on Trans Union. Van Gorkom agreed to meet privately with Pritzker, accompanied by Peterson, Chelberg, and Michael Carpenter, Trans Union's consultant from the Boston Consulting Group. The meetings took place on September 16 and 17. Van Gorkom was "astounded that events were moving with such amazing rapidity."

On Thursday, September 18, Van Gorkom met again with Pritzker. At that time, Van Gorkom knew that Pritzker intended to make a cash-out merger offer at Van Gorkom's proposed $55 per share. Pritzker instructed his attorney, a merger and acquisition specialist, to begin drafting merger documents. There was no further discussion of the $55 price. However, the number of shares of Trans Union's treasury stock to be offered to Pritzker was negotiated down to one million shares; the price was set at $38—75 cents above the per share price at the close of the market on September 19. At this point, Pritzker insisted that the Trans Union Board act on his merger proposal within the next three days, stating to Van Gorkom: "We have to have a decision by no later than Sunday [evening, September 21] before the opening of the English stock exchange on Monday morning." Pritzker's lawyer was then instructed to draft the merger documents, to be reviewed by Van Gorkom's lawyer, "sometimes with discussion and sometimes not, in the haste to get it finished."

On Friday, September 19, Van Gorkom, Chelberg, and Pritzker consulted with Trans Union's lead bank regarding the financing of Pritzker's purchase of Trans Union. The bank indicated that it could form a syndicate of banks that would finance the transaction. On the same day, Van Gorkom retained James Brennan, Esquire, to advise Trans Union on the legal aspects of the merger. Van

Gorkom did not consult with William Browder, a Vice-President and director of Trans Union and former head of its legal department, or with William Moore, then the head of Trans Union's legal staff.

On Friday, September 19, Van Gorkom called a special meeting of the Trans Union Board for noon the following day. He also called a meeting of the Company's Senior Management to convene at 11:00 A.M., prior to the meeting of the Board. No one, except Chelberg and Peterson, was told the purpose of the meetings. Van Gorkom did not invite Trans Union's investment banker, Salomon Brothers or its Chicago-based partner, to attend.

Of those present at the Senior Management meeting on September 20, only Chelberg and Peterson had prior knowledge of Pritzker's offer. Van Gorkom disclosed the offer and described its terms, but he furnished no copies of the proposed Merger Agreement. Romans announced that his department had done a second study which showed that, for a leveraged buy-out, the price range for Trans Union stock was between $55 and $65 per share. Van Gorkom neither saw the study nor asked Romans to make it available for the Board meeting.

Senior Management's reaction to the Pritzker proposal was completely negative. No member of Management, except Chelberg and Peterson, supported the proposal. Romans objected to the price as being too low;[5] he was critical of the timing and suggested that consideration should be given to the adverse tax consequences of an all-cash deal for low-basis shareholders; and he took the position that the agreement to sell Pritzker one million newly-issued shares at market price would inhibit other offers, as would the prohibitions against soliciting bids and furnishing inside information to other bidders. Romans argued that the Pritzker proposal was a "lock up" and amounted to "an agreed merger as opposed to an offer." Nevertheless, Van Gorkom proceeded to the Board meeting as scheduled without further delay.

Ten directors served on the Trans Union Board, five inside (defendants Bonser, O'Boyle, Browder, Chelberg, and Van Gorkom) and five outside (defendants Wallis, Johnson, Lanterman, Morgan and Reneker). All directors were present at the meeting, except O'Boyle who was ill. Of the outside directors, four were corporate chief executive officers and one was the former Dean of the University of Chicago Business School. None was an investment banker or trained financial analyst. All members of the Board were well informed about the Company and its operations as a going concern. They were familiar with the current financial condition of the Company, as well as operating and earnings projections reported in the recent Five Year Forecast. The Board generally received regular and detailed reports and was kept abreast of the accumulated investment tax credit and accelerated depreciation problem.

---

5. [FN 6] Van Gorkom asked Romans to express his opinion as to the $55 price. Romans stated that he "thought the price was too low in relation to what he could derive for the company in a cash sale, particularly one which enabled us to realize the values of certain subsidiaries and independent entities."

Van Gorkom began the Special Meeting of the Board with a twenty-minute oral presentation. Copies of the proposed Merger Agreement were delivered too late for study before or during the meeting. He reviewed the Company's ITC and depreciation problems and the efforts theretofore made to solve them. He discussed his initial meeting with Pritzker and his motivation in arranging that meeting. Van Gorkom did not disclose to the Board, however, the methodology by which he alone had arrived at the $55 figure, or the fact that he first proposed the $55 price in his negotiations with Pritzker.

Van Gorkom outlined the terms of the Pritzker offer as follows: Pritzker would pay $55 in cash for all outstanding shares of Trans Union stock upon completion of which Trans Union would be merged into New T Company, a subsidiary wholly-owned by Pritzker and formed to implement the merger; for a period of 90 days, Trans Union could receive, but could not actively solicit, competing offers; the offer had to be acted on by the next evening, Sunday, September 21; Trans Union could only furnish to competing bidders published information, and not proprietary information; the offer was subject to Pritzker obtaining the necessary financing by October 10, 1980; if the financing contingency were met or waived by Pritzker, Trans Union was required to sell to Pritzker one million newly-issued shares of Trans Union at $38 per share.

Van Gorkom took the position that putting Trans Union "up for auction" through a 90-day market test would validate a decision by the Board that $55 was a fair price. He told the Board that the "free market will have an opportunity to judge whether $55 is a fair price." Van Gorkom framed the decision before the Board not as whether $55 per share was the highest price that could be obtained, but as whether the $55 price was a fair price that the stockholders should be given the opportunity to accept or reject.

Attorney Brennan advised the members of the Board that they might be sued if they failed to accept the offer and that a fairness opinion was not required as a matter of law.

Romans attended the meeting as chief financial officer of the Company. He told the Board that he had not been involved in the negotiations with Pritzker and knew nothing about the merger proposal until the morning of the meeting; that his studies did not indicate either a fair price for the stock or a valuation of the Company; that he did not see his role as directly addressing the fairness issue; and that he and his people "were trying to search for ways to justify a price in connection with such a [leveraged buy-out] transaction, rather than to say what the shares are worth." Romans testified:

> I told the Board that the study ran the numbers at 50 and 60, and then the subsequent study at 55 and 65, and that was not the same thing as saying that I have a valuation of the company at X dollars. But it was a way—a first step towards reaching that conclusion.

Romans told the Board that, in his opinion, $55 was "in the range of a fair price," but "at the beginning of the range."

Chelberg, Trans Union's President, supported Van Gorkom's presentation and representations. He testified that he "participated to make sure that the Board members collectively were clear on the details of the agreement or offer from Pritzker"; that he "participated in the discussion with Mr. Brennan, inquiring of him about the necessity for valuation opinions in spite of the way in which this particular offer was couched"; and that he was otherwise actively involved in supporting the positions being taken by Van Gorkom before the Board about "the necessity to act immediately on this offer," and about "the adequacy of the $55 and the question of how that would be tested."

The Board meeting of September 20 lasted about two hours. Based solely upon Van Gorkom's oral presentation, Chelberg's supporting representations, Romans' oral statement, Brennan's legal advice, and their knowledge of the market history of the Company's stock,[6] the directors approved the proposed Merger Agreement. . . .

The Merger Agreement was executed by Van Gorkom during the evening of September 20 at a formal social event that he hosted for the opening of the Chicago Lyric Opera. Neither he nor any other director read the agreement prior to its signing and delivery to Pritzker. . . .

On December 19, this litigation was commenced. . . . On January 21, Management's Proxy Statement for the February 10 shareholder meeting was mailed to Trans Union's stockholders. On January 26, Trans Union's Board met and, after a lengthy meeting, voted to proceed with the Pritzker merger. The Board also approved for mailing, "on or about January 27," a Supplement to its Proxy Statement. The Supplement purportedly set forth all information relevant to the Pritzker Merger Agreement, which had not been divulged in the first Proxy Statement.

On February 10, the stockholders of Trans Union approved the Pritzker merger proposal. Of the outstanding shares, 69.9 percent were voted in favor of the merger; 7.25 percent were voted against the merger; and 22.85 percent were not voted.

II.

We turn to the issue of the application of the business judgment rule to the September 20 meeting of the Board.

The Court of Chancery concluded from the evidence that the Board of Directors' approval of the Pritzker merger proposal fell within the protection of the business judgment rule. The Court found that the Board had given sufficient time and attention to the transaction, since the directors had considered the Pritzker proposal on three different occasions, on September 20, and

---

6. [FN 9] The Trial Court stated the premium relationship of the $55 price to the market history of the Company's stock as follows:

> . . . the merger price offered to the stockholders of Trans Union represented a premium of 62% over the average of the high and low prices at which Trans Union stock had traded in 1980, a premium of 48% over the last closing price, and a premium of 39% over the highest price at which the stock of Trans Union had traded any time during the prior six years.

on October 8, 1980 and finally on January 26, 1981. On that basis, the Court reasoned that the Board had acquired, over the four-month period, sufficient information to reach an informed business judgment on the cash-out merger proposal. The Court ruled:

> . . . that given the market value of Trans Union's stock, the business acumen of the members of the board of Trans Union, the substantial premium over market offered by the Pritzkers and the ultimate effect on the merger price provided by the prospect of other bids for the stock in question, that the board of directors of Trans Union did not act recklessly or improvidently in determining on a course of action which they believed to be in the best interest of the stockholders of Trans Union.

The Court of Chancery made but one finding; i.e., that the Board's conduct over the entire period from September 20 through January 26, 1981 was not reckless or improvident, but informed. . . .

Under Delaware law, the business judgment rule is the offspring of the fundamental principle, codified in 8 Del. C. §141(a), that the business and affairs of a Delaware corporation are managed by or under its board of directors. In carrying out their managerial roles, directors are charged with an unyielding fiduciary duty to the corporation and its shareholders. The business judgment rule exists to protect and promote the full and free exercise of the managerial power granted to Delaware directors. The rule itself "is a presumption that in making a business decision, the directors of a corporation acted on an informed basis, in good faith and in the honest belief that the action taken was in the best interests of the company." *Aronson* [*v. Lewis*, 473 A.2d 805 (Del. 1984)] at 812. Thus, the party attacking a board decision as uninformed must rebut the presumption that its business judgment was an informed one.

The determination of whether a business judgment is an informed one turns on whether the directors have informed themselves "prior to making a business decision, of all material information reasonably available to them." *Id.*

Under the business judgment rule there is no protection for directors who have made "an unintelligent or unadvised judgment." *Mitchell v. Highland-Western Glass*, 167 A. 831, 833 (Del. Ch. 1933). A director's duty to inform himself in preparation for a decision derives from the fiduciary capacity in which he serves the corporation and its stockholders. Since a director is vested with the responsibility for the management of the affairs of the corporation, he must execute that duty with the recognition that he acts on behalf of others. Such obligation does not tolerate faithlessness or self-dealing. But fulfillment of the fiduciary function requires more than the mere absence of bad faith or fraud. Representation of the financial interests of others imposes on a director an affirmative duty to protect those interests and to proceed with a critical eye in assessing information of the type and under the circumstances present here.

Thus, a director's duty to exercise an informed business judgment is in the nature of a duty of care, as distinguished from a duty of loyalty. Here, there were no allegations of fraud, bad faith, or self-dealing, or proof thereof. Hence, it is presumed that the directors reached their business judgment in good faith, and considerations of motive are irrelevant to the issue before us.

The standard of care applicable to a director's duty of care has also been recently restated by this Court. In *Aronson, supra,* we stated:

> While the Delaware cases use a variety of terms to describe the applicable standard of care, our analysis satisfies us that under the business judgment rule director liability is predicated upon concepts of gross negligence. (footnote omitted)

473 A.2d at 812.

We again confirm that view. We think the concept of gross negligence is also the proper standard for determining whether a business judgment reached by a board of directors was an informed one. . . .

In the specific context of a proposed merger of domestic corporations, a director has a duty under 8 Del. C. §251(b), along with his fellow directors, to act in an informed and deliberate manner in determining whether to approve an agreement of merger before submitting the proposal to the stockholders. Certainly in the merger context, a director may not abdicate that duty by leaving to the shareholders alone the decision to approve or disapprove the agreement. . . .

It is against those standards that the conduct of the directors of Trans Union must be tested, as a matter of law and as a matter of fact, regarding their exercise of an informed business judgment in voting to approve the Pritzker merger proposal.

III. . . .

A

. . . On the record before us, we must conclude that the Board of Directors did not reach an informed business judgment on September 20, 1980 in voting to "sell" the Company for $55 per share pursuant to the Pritzker cash-out merger proposal. Our reasons, in summary, are as follows:

The directors (1) did not adequately inform themselves as to Van Gorkom's role in forcing the "sale" of the Company and in establishing the per share purchase price; (2) were uninformed as to the intrinsic value of the Company; and (3) given these circumstances, at a minimum, were grossly negligent in approving the "sale" of the Company upon two hours' consideration, without prior notice, and without the exigency of a crisis or emergency.

As has been noted, the Board based its September 20 decision to approve the cash-out merger primarily on Van Gorkom's representations. None of the directors, other than Van Gorkom and Chelberg, had any prior knowledge that the purpose of the meeting was to propose a cash-out merger of Trans Union. No members of Senior Management were present, other than Chelberg, Romans and Peterson; and the latter two had only learned of the proposed sale an hour earlier. Both general counsel Moore and former general counsel Browder attended the meeting, but were equally uninformed as to the purpose of the meeting and the documents to be acted upon.

Without any documents before them concerning the proposed transaction, the members of the Board were required to rely entirely upon Van Gorkom's 20-minute oral presentation of the proposal. No written summary of the terms of the merger was presented; the directors were given no documentation to support the adequacy of $55 price per share for sale of the Company; and the Board had before it nothing more than Van Gorkom's statement of his understanding of the substance of an agreement which he admittedly had never read, nor which any member of the Board had ever seen.

Under 8 Del. C. §141(e), "directors are fully protected in relying in good faith on reports made by officers." *Michelson v. Duncan,* Del. Ch., 386 A.2d 1144, 1156 (1978). The term "report" has been liberally construed to include reports of informal personal investigations by corporate officers. However, there is no evidence that any "report," as defined under §141(e), concerning the Pritzker proposal, was presented to the Board on September 20. Van Gorkom's oral presentation of his understanding of the terms of the proposed Merger Agreement, which he had not seen, and Romans' brief oral statement of his preliminary study regarding the feasibility of a leveraged buy-out of Trans Union do not qualify as §141(e) "reports" for these reasons: The former lacked substance because Van Gorkom was basically uninformed as to the essential provisions of the very document about which he was talking. Romans' statement was irrelevant to the issues before the Board since it did not purport to be a valuation study. At a minimum for a report to enjoy the status conferred by §141(e), it must be pertinent to the subject matter upon which a board is called to act, and otherwise be entitled to good faith, not blind, reliance. Considering all of the surrounding circumstances — hastily calling the meeting without prior notice of its subject matter, the proposed sale of the Company without any prior consideration of the issue or necessity therefor, the urgent time constraints imposed by Pritzker, and the total absence of any documentation whatsoever — the directors were duty bound to make reasonable inquiry of Van Gorkom and Romans, and if they had done so, the inadequacy of that upon which they now claim to have relied would have been apparent.

In support of the defendants' argument that their judgment as to the adequacy of $55 per share was an informed one, the directors rely on the BCG study and the Five Year Forecast. However, no one even referred to either of these studies at the September 20 meeting; and it is conceded that these materials do not represent valuation studies. Hence, these documents do not constitute evidence as to whether the directors reached an informed judgment on September 20 that $55 per share was a fair value for sale of the Company.

The defendants rely on the following factors to sustain the Trial Court's finding that the Board's decision was an informed one: (1) the magnitude of the premium or spread between the $55 Pritzker offering price and Trans Union's current market price of $38 per share; . . . ; and (4) their reliance on

Brennan's legal advice that the directors might be sued if they rejected the Pritzker proposal. . . .

(1)

A substantial premium may provide one reason to recommend a merger, but in the absence of other sound valuation information, the fact of a premium alone does not provide an adequate basis upon which to assess the fairness of an offering price. Here, the judgment reached as to the adequacy of the premium was based on a comparison between the historically depressed Trans Union market price and the amount of the Pritzker offer. Using market price as a basis for concluding that the premium adequately reflected the true value of the Company was a clearly faulty, indeed fallacious, premise, as the defendants' own evidence demonstrates.

The record is clear that before September 20, Van Gorkom and other members of Trans Union's Board knew that the market had consistently undervalued the worth of Trans Union's stock, despite steady increases in the Company's operating income in the seven years preceding the merger. The Board related this occurrence in large part to Trans Union's inability to use its ITCs as previously noted. Van Gorkom testified that he did not believe the market price accurately reflected Trans Union's true worth; and several of the directors testified that, as a general rule, most chief executives think that the market undervalues their companies' stock. Yet, on September 20, Trans Union's Board apparently believed that the market stock price accurately reflected the value of the Company for the purpose of determining the adequacy of the premium for its sale.

In the Proxy Statement, however, the directors reversed their position. There, they stated that, although the earnings prospects for Trans Union were "excellent," they found no basis for believing that this would be reflected in future stock prices. With regard to past trading, the Board stated that the prices at which the Company's common stock had traded in recent years did not reflect the "inherent" value of the Company. But having referred to the "inherent" value of Trans Union, the directors ascribed no number to it. Moreover, nowhere did they disclose that they had no basis on which to fix "inherent" worth beyond an impressionistic reaction to the premium over market and an unsubstantiated belief that the value of the assets was "significantly greater" than book value. By their own admission they could not rely on the stock price as an accurate measure of value. Yet, also by their own admission, the Board members assumed that Trans Union's market price was adequate to serve as a basis upon which to assess the adequacy of the premium for purposes of the September 20 meeting.

The parties do not dispute that a publicly-traded stock price is solely a measure of the value of a minority position and, thus, market price represents only the value of a single share. Nevertheless, on September 20, the Board assessed the adequacy of the premium over market, offered by Pritzker, solely by comparing it with Trans Union's current and historical stock price.

Indeed, as of September 20, the Board had no other information on which to base a determination of the intrinsic value of Trans Union as a going concern. As of September 20, the Board had made no evaluation of the Company designed to value the entire enterprise, nor had the Board ever previously considered selling the Company or consenting to a buy-out merger. Thus, the adequacy of a premium is indeterminate unless it is assessed in terms of other competent and sound valuation information that reflects the value of the particular business.

Despite the foregoing facts and circumstances, there was no call by the Board, either on September 20 or thereafter, for any valuation study or documentation of the $55 price per share as a measure of the fair value of the Company in a cash-out context. It is undisputed that the major asset of Trans Union was its cash flow. Yet, at no time did the Board call for a valuation study taking into account that highly significant element of the Company's assets.

We do not imply that an outside valuation study is essential to support an informed business judgment; nor do we state that fairness opinions by independent investment bankers are required as a matter of law. Often insiders familiar with the business of a going concern are in a better position than are outsiders to gather relevant information; and under appropriate circumstances, such directors may be fully protected in relying in good faith upon the valuation reports of their management.

Here, the record establishes that the Board did not request its Chief Financial Officer, Romans, to make any valuation study or review of the proposal to determine the adequacy of $55 per share for sale of the Company. On the record before us: The Board rested on Romans' elicited response that the $55 figure was within a "fair price range" within the context of a leveraged buy-out. No director sought any further information from Romans. No director asked him why he put $55 at the bottom of his range. No director asked Romans for any details as to his study, the reason why it had been undertaken or its depth. No director asked to see the study; and no director asked Romans whether Trans Union's finance department could do a fairness study within the remaining 36-hour period available under the Pritzker offer.

Had the Board, or any member, made an inquiry of Romans, he presumably would have responded as he testified: that his calculations were rough and preliminary; and, that the study was not designed to determine the fair value of the Company, but rather to assess the feasibility of a leveraged buy-out financed by the Company's projected cash flow, making certain assumptions as to the purchaser's borrowing needs. Romans would have presumably also informed the Board of his view, and the widespread view of Senior Management, that the timing of the offer was wrong and the offer inadequate.

The record also establishes that the Board accepted without scrutiny Van Gorkom's representation as to the fairness of the $55 price per share for sale of the Company—a subject that the Board had never previously considered. The Board thereby failed to discover that Van Gorkom had suggested the $55 price to Pritzker and, most crucially, that Van Gorkom had arrived at the $55 figure based on calculations designed solely to determine the feasibility of a leveraged buy-out.[7] No questions were raised either as to the tax implications of a cash-out merger or how the price for the one million share option granted Pritzker was calculated.

We do not say that the Board of Directors was not entitled to give some credence to Van Gorkom's representation that $55 was an adequate or fair price. Under §141(e), the directors were entitled to rely upon their chairman's opinion of value and adequacy, provided that such opinion was reached on a sound basis. Here, the issue is whether the directors informed themselves as to all information that was reasonably available to them. Had they done so, they would have learned of the source and derivation of the $55 price and could not reasonably have relied thereupon in good faith.

None of the directors, Management or outside, were investment bankers or financial analysts. Yet the Board did not consider recessing the meeting until a later hour that day (or requesting an extension of Pritzker's Sunday evening deadline) to give it time to elicit more information as to the sufficiency of the offer, either from inside Management (in particular Romans) or from Trans Union's own investment banker, Salomon Brothers, whose Chicago specialist in merger and acquisitions was known to the Board and familiar with Trans Union's affairs.

Thus, the record compels the conclusion that on September 20 the Board lacked valuation information adequate to reach an informed business judgment as to the fairness of $55 per share for sale of the Company. . . .

We conclude that Trans Union's Board was grossly negligent in that it failed to act with informed reasonable deliberation in agreeing to the Pritzker merger proposal on September 20. . . .

We hold, therefore, that the Trial Court committed reversible error in applying the business judgment rule in favor of the director defendants in this case.

On remand, the Court of Chancery shall conduct an evidentiary hearing to determine the fair value of the shares represented by the plaintiffs' class, based on the intrinsic value of Trans Union on September 20, 1980. . . . Thereafter, an award of damages may be entered to the extent that the fair value of Trans Union exceeds $55 per share.

REVERSED and REMANDED for proceedings consistent herewith.

---

7. [FN 19] As of September 20 the directors did not know: that Van Gorkom had arrived at the $55 figure alone, and subjectively, as the figure to be used by Controller Peterson in creating a feasible structure for a leveraged buy-out by a prospective purchaser; that Van Gorkom had not sought advice, information or assistance from either inside or outside Trans Union directors as to the value of the Company as an entity or the fair price per share for 100 percent of its stock; that Van Gorkom had not consulted with the Company's investment bankers or other financial analysts; that Van Gorkom had not consulted with or confided in any officer or director of the Company except Chelberg; and that Van Gorkom had deliberately chosen to ignore the advice and opinion of the members of his Senior Management group regarding the adequacy of the $55 price.

Questions

1. What is the board decision at issue?
2. Why are plaintiffs suing?
3. What is the legal basis for their suit?
4. Why did the plaintiffs lose at the trial court level?
5. Why did plaintiffs win on appeal?
6. What did Trans Union's board do wrong?
7. Does the court think the board made a bad decision?
8. What are the consequences of losing the case for the directors?

As *Van Gorkom* makes clear, the standard for determining whether a board was adequately informed when making a decision is gross negligence. Later Delaware opinions have defined gross negligence in this context as a "'reckless indifference to or a deliberate disregard of the whole body of stockholders' or actions which are 'without the bounds of reason,'"[8] and noted that pleading it successfully "requires the articulation of facts that suggest a *wide* disparity between the process the directors used to ensure the integrity of the company's financial statements and that which would have been rational."[9]

3. Exculpation Provisions

Van Gorkom sent shockwaves through the boardrooms of corporate America. It was the first time in memory that the directors of a public company were held personally liable for breach of the duty of care. One of the purported consequences of the decision was that it made it much more difficult and expensive for corporations to obtain director and officer liability insurance (D&O insurance for short),[10] presumably because insurers now viewed writing these policies as involving substantially more risk. This gave rise to concerns that quality individuals would not be willing to serve on the boards of corporations who were not able to procure the insurance, or if still willing to serve on such a board, would "be deterred from making entrepreneurial decisions."[11]

The Delaware legislature quickly responded to these concerns. In June of 1986, less than 18 months after the court issued its opinion in *Van Gorkom*,

---

8. *Walt Disney Co. Derivative Litigation*, 907 A.2d 693 (Del. Ch. 2005) (quoting *Tomczak v. Morton Thiokol, Inc.*, 1990 WL 42607, at *12 (Del. Ch. Apr. 5, 1990)).

9. *Id.* at 750 n.429 (quoting *Guttman v. Huang*, 823 A.2d 492, 507 n.39 (Del. Ch. 2003) (emphasis in original).

10. D&O insurance provides a director or officer with insurance protection in the event he or she gets sued for breach of fiduciary duties and his or her company is unable to cover the related costs (legal fees, settlement, judgment, etc.). D&O insurance is covered in more detail in Section D.2 below.

11. Legislative Synopsis to S. 533, 133d Del. Gen. Assembly (1986).

Delaware's governor signed into law a bill that, among other things, amended DGCL §102 to add subsection (b)(7). This subsection provides as follows:

(b) In addition to the matters required to be set forth in the certificate of incorporation by subsection (a) of this section, the certificate of incorporation may also contain any or all of the following matters: . . .

(7) A provision eliminating or limiting the personal liability of a director to the corporation or its stockholders for monetary damages for breach of fiduciary duty as a director, provided that such provision shall not eliminate or limit the liability of a director: (i) For any breach of the director's duty of loyalty to the corporation or its stockholders; (ii) for acts or omissions not in good faith or which involve intentional misconduct or a knowing violation of law; (iii) under §174 of this title [director liability for unlawful payment of dividends]; or (iv) for any transaction from which the director derived an improper personal benefit. No such provision shall eliminate or limit the liability of a director for any act or omission occurring prior to the date when such provision becomes effective. All references in this paragraph to a director shall also be deemed to refer to such other person or persons, if any, who, pursuant to a provision of the certificate of incorporation in accordance with §141(a) of this title, exercise or perform any of the powers or duties otherwise conferred or imposed upon the board of directors by this title.[12]

The subsection essentially allows a corporation to opt out of having its directors be personally liable for monetary damages for breach of the duty of care. A corporation opts out by including a provision, commonly called an exculpation provision, in its charter along the lines of the following:

ARTICLE XI

(A) To the fullest extent permitted by the General Corporation Law of Delaware, as the same may be amended from time to time, a director of the Corporation shall not be personally liable to the Corporation or its stockholders for monetary damages for breach of fiduciary duty as a director. If the General Corporation Law of Delaware is hereafter amended to authorize, with the approval of a corporation's stockholders, further reductions in the liability of the Corporation's directors for breach of fiduciary duty, then a director of the Corporation shall not be liable for any such breach to the fullest extent permitted by the General Corporation Law of Delaware, as so amended.

(B) Any repeal or modification of the foregoing provisions of this Article XI shall not adversely affect any right or protection of a director of the Corporation with respect to any acts or omissions of such director occurring prior to such repeal or modification.

---

12. The analogous provision under the MBCA is § 2.02(b)(4) which was added in 1990.

Thus, the directors of a corporation that were grossly negligent in their decision-making process and therefore breached the duty of care are nonetheless not personally liable for monetary damages if the corporation has an exculpation provision in its charter. In other words, had §102(b)(7) been in effect pre-*Van Gorkom*, and had Trans Union had an exculpation provision in its charter, its directors would not have been personally liable even though they breached the duty of care. Most Delaware corporations amended their charters to add exculpation provisions shortly after §102(b)(7) went into effect, and practitioners immediately began including these provisions as a matter of course in the certificates of incorporation of new Delaware corporations.

The presence of an exculpation provision in a corporation's charter forecloses a claim against directors for monetary damages for breach of the duty of care. In fact, if a complaint seeking monetary damages alleges only a breach of the duty of care (as opposed to, for example, also alleging a breach of the duty of loyalty), a court is likely to dismiss it on summary judgment, that is, without deciding whether the director's decision-making process was grossly negligent. Note, however, that an exculpation provision does not apply to a breach of duty of care claim seeking equitable relief instead of monetary damages. Thus, for example, a plaintiff may be able to get a court to enjoin a merger if the plaintiff can successfully argue, before the merger is closed, that the board was inadequately informed when it decided to approve the merger.

Question

A corporation in which you own a small amount of stock wants to amend its charter to add an exculpation provision. Would you vote in favor of the amendment?

4. The Duty of Loyalty

The duty of loyalty addresses the agency problem head on. Broadly speaking, it requires a director to act in the best interests of the corporation. The Delaware Supreme Court elaborated on the duty of loyalty in *Guth v. Loft*.

> Corporate officers and directors are not permitted to use their position of trust and confidence to further their private interests. While technically not trustees, they stand in a fiduciary relation to the corporation and its stockholders. A public policy, existing through the years, and derived from a profound knowledge of human characteristics and motives, has established a rule that demands of a corporate officer or director, peremptorily and inexorably, the most scrupulous observance of his duty, not only affirmatively to protect the interests of the corporation committed to his charge, but also to refrain from doing anything that would work injury to the corporation, or to deprive it of profit or advantage

which his skill and ability might properly bring to it, or to enable it to make in the reasonable and lawful exercise of its powers. The rule that requires an undivided and unselfish loyalty to the corporation demands that there shall be no conflict between duty and self-interest.[13]

The duty of loyalty is implicated in a number of different contexts, mainly, conflicting interest transactions, failure to provide adequate oversight, failure to act in good faith, and usurpation of a corporate opportunity.

a. Conflicting Interest Transactions

A conflicting interest transaction is any transaction between a director and the corporation. For example, say you are a director of XYZ, Inc. and have been trying to sell your vacation home in Aspen, Colorado. You convince XYZ to buy the property from you for use as a corporate retreat, so you and XYZ's CFO negotiate the price. This is obviously a conflict of interest between you and XYZ—it is in your best interest to get as high a price as possible for the home, but it is in XYZ's best interest to pay as low a price as possible. Thus, it raises concern that you will put your own self-interest ahead of the interests of the corporation, using your position and influence in the process, in violation of the duty of loyalty.

Historically, the common law rule was that any transaction between a corporation and a director was voidable at the option of the corporation or its shareholders, regardless of the merits of the transaction. This rule eventually shifted to provide that such a transaction was not per se voidable so long as it was (1) approved by a majority of the corporation's disinterested directors following full disclosure *and* (2) fair to the corporation. State legislatures later further shifted the rule by adopting statutory provisions (see, e.g., DGCL §144) establishing that a conflicting interest transaction was not per se voidable if (1) a majority of informed disinterested directors approved the transaction, (2) a majority of informed disinterested shareholders approved the transaction, *or* (3) the transaction was fair to the corporation.

This shift toward more leniency reflects the fact that there is nothing inherently wrong with a director engaging in a transaction with his or her corporation. In fact, in some situations, it may be quite beneficial for the corporation. For example, when a corporation is facing hard times and desperately needs to raise financing, a director may be the only one willing to provide the financing on reasonable terms or at all, because he or she has a strong interest in the company succeeding or more confidence than the marketplace in the company's prospects for success. Hence, the law should not discourage these types of transactions as the historical common law rule arguably did.

[Handwritten margin note: transaction b/w director/corp not voidable if: RULE]

---

13. *Guth v. Loft, Inc.*, 5 A.2d 503, 510 (Del. 1939).

Note, however, that statutory provisions such as DGCL §144 have a narrow focus: They shield director conflicting interest transactions from per se voidability. <u>They do not shield the director(s) who engaged in the transaction from a breach of duty of loyalty claim</u>. The framework for analyzing whether a conflict of interest transaction constitutes a breach of the duty of loyalty is left to common law in many states. In Delaware, it shakes out as follows:

- Technically, the starting point for any breach of fiduciary duty analysis is the business judgment rule. In the context of a conflicting interest transaction, however, all a plaintiff needs to do to rebut the rule is to plead and prove that the director did in fact enter into the transaction because courts then consider the director interested (recall from above that interestedness is one way to rebut the business judgment rule). Typically, a defendant simply stipulates to the transaction so there is no need for a court to spend much time, if any, addressing application of the business judgment rule.
- The director then has the burden of proving the transaction was fair to the corporation.
- If the director meets this burden, the director did not breach the duty of loyalty. If the director fails to meet it, the director breached the duty of loyalty and is personally liable for damages. Thus, for example, if the sale of your Aspen vacation home is found to be a breach of the duty of loyalty, the court will determine the amount by which the corporation overpaid, and order you to pay that amount to the corporation.
- A director can avoid having to prove fairness by having the transaction approved by a fully informed majority of disinterested and independent directors or stockholders. Such an approval (sometimes called a "cleansing device") invokes the business judgment rule. In this context, the effect of invoking the business judgment rule is to place the burden on the plaintiff to prove the transaction constituted waste. If the plaintiff fails to carry this burden, the plaintiff loses. In other words, the court would never examine the fairness of the transaction. If the plaintiff carries this extremely heavy burden, the court would then examine fairness. Presumably, the director will be found to have breached the duty of loyalty, because it is hard to imagine a transaction that constituted waste yet was fair to the corporation, and will be personally liable to the corporation for damages.

    Given the difficulty of meeting the waste standard, plaintiffs instead typically focus their efforts on defeating the alleged cleansing device. Specifically, they argue the directors or shareholders were not fully informed, disinterested, and/or independent.
- Note that per DGCL §102(b)(7), an exculpation provision cannot apply to a breach of duty of loyalty, so it is not relevant to the analysis.

Now let's look at the tests for fairness (a/k/a "entire fairness" or "intrinsic fairness"), disinterestedness, and independence, as well as what constitutes being fully informed.

(1) Fairness

The Delaware test for fairness was aptly summarized by the court in *Boyer v. Wilmington Materials, Inc.*[14] as follows:

> It is a well-settled principle of Delaware law that where directors stand on both sides of a transaction, they have "the burden of establishing its entire fairness, sufficient to pass the test of careful scrutiny by the courts." *Weinberger v. UOP, Inc.*, Del. Supr., 457 A.2d 701, 710 (1983) ("There is no 'safe harbor' for such divided loyalties in Delaware."). Directors will be found to have acted with entire fairness where they "demonstrate their utmost good faith *and* the most scrupulous inherent fairness of the bargain." *Id*. . . .
>
> The concept of entire fairness has two components: fair dealing and fair price. *See Weinberger*, Del. Supr., 457 A.2d at 711. Fair dealing "embraces questions of when the transaction was timed, how it was initiated, structured, negotiated, disclosed to the directors, and how the approvals of the directors and the stockholders were obtained." *Id.* Fair price "relates to the economic and financial considerations of the proposed merger, including all relevant factors: assets, market value, earnings, future prospects, and any other elements that affect the intrinsic or inherent value of a company's stock." *Id.* In making a determination as to the entire fairness of a transaction, the Court does not focus on one component over the other, but examines all aspects of the issue as a whole. *Id.*

(2) Disinterestedness (Or, When Is a Director Interested?)

Disinterestedness goes to whether or not a director or shareholder has an interest in the transaction at issue. The sale of your Aspen vacation home to the corporation for whom you are a director provides a classic example of being interested (and therefore not disinterested), because, as the courts would say, you are on both sides of the deal. More broadly,

> [a] director is considered interested where he or she will receive a personal financial benefit from a transaction that is not equally shared by the stockholders. Directorial interest also exists where a corporate decision will have a materially detrimental impact on a director, but not on the corporation and the stockholders. In such circumstances, a director cannot be expected to exercise his or her independent business judgment without being influenced by the adverse personal consequences resulting from the decision.[15]

---

14. 754 A.2d 881 (1999).
15. *Rales v. Blasband*, 634 A.2d 927, 936 (Del. 1993).

[handwritten margin note: interested director ✱ RULE]

For a director to be interested because of receipt of a benefit, the benefit to be received by a director must be material to that director. Specifically, it must be "significant enough '*in the context of the director's economic circumstances, as to have made it improbable that the director could perform her fiduciary duties to the . . . shareholders without being influenced by her overriding personal interest.*'"[16]

Additionally, a court may consider a director interested in a transaction even if he or she is not directly involved in the transaction. For example, a number of courts have found a director interested in a transaction between the director's corporation and an entity in which the director has a significant financial interest or between the director's corporation and a close relative of the director.

(3) Independence

[handwritten margin mark: ✱]

Independence goes to whether or not a director or stockholder can exercise independent judgment with respect to a decision as opposed to simply voting in accordance with the conflicted director's wishes. Put differently, "[i]ndependence means that a director's decision is based on the corporate merits of the subject before the board rather than extraneous considerations or influences."[17]

To establish lack of independence, a plaintiff must show that a director or shareholder is so "beholden" to the conflicted director that his or her discretion is "sterilized." This can be difficult to do because "personal friendships, without more; outside business relationships, without more; and approving of or acquiescing in the challenged transactions, without more, are each insufficient" to establish a lack of independence.[18] However, "financial ties, familial affinity, a particularly close or intimate personal or business affinity or . . . evidence that in the past the relationship caused the director to act non-independently vis à vis an interested director" may be sufficient.[19]

(4) Fully Informed

To be fully informed in this context, the directors or stockholders must be furnished all material information concerning the conflicting interest transaction at issue. This includes information about how the director is conflicted. A fact is considered material "if there is a substantial likelihood that a reasonable shareholder [or director] would consider it important in deciding how to vote."[20]

---

16. *Orman v. Cullman*, 794 A.2d 5, 23 (Del. Ch. 2002), quoting *In re General Motors Class H Shareholders Litig.*, 734 A.2d 611, 617 (Del. Ch. 1999) (emphasis added).

17. *Rales*, 634 A.2d at 927, 936.

18. *Beam v. Stewart*, 845 A.2d 1040, 1051 (Del. 2004).

19. *Id.*

20. *Rosenblatt v. Getty Oil Co.*, 493 A.2d 929 (Del. 1985), quoting *TSC Industries, Inc. v. Northway, Inc.*, 426 U.S. 438, 449 (1976).

Exercise 10.2

Innoclub, Inc., a Delaware corporation, is a leading nanotech company. The company was founded three years ago by Kuchar and has grown quickly. Kuchar is CEO and president of Innoclub. Innoclub's board of directors consists of the following individuals:

1. Kuchar
2. Alonso (Innoclub's chief financial officer)
3. Baker (Kuchar's brother-in-law)
4. Cruz (Kuchar's cousin)
5. Donos (Kuchar's high school football coach)
6. Els (Kuchar's hairdresser)
7. Fowler (Kuchar's chauffeur)

Kuchar is short on cash so he decides to sell his collection of Salvador Dali paintings. Kuchar acquired the paintings over the last five years for a total of $1.5 million. The collection was appraised two years ago at $2 million. Kuchar decides that Innoclub should buy the collection to jazz up its corporate headquarters. Innoclub buys the collection from Kuchar for $3 million. The transaction was handled on behalf of Innoclub by Alonso. Prior to closing, the transaction was unanimously approved by a board committee consisting of Baker, Cruz, Donos, Els, and Fowler. Thereafter, the full board unanimously approved the transaction.

Innoclub's Certificate of Incorporation and Bylaws simply track the default provisions of the DGCL except that Innoclub's Certificate of Incorporation contains the following provision:

> To the fullest extent permitted by the General Corporation Law of Delaware, as the same may be amended from time to time, a director of the Corporation shall not be personally liable to the Corporation or its stockholders for monetary damages for breach of fiduciary duty as a director. If the General Corporation Law of Delaware is hereafter amended to authorize, with the approval of a corporation's stockholders, further reductions in the liability of the Corporation's directors for breach of fiduciary duty, then a director of the Corporation shall not be liable for any such breach to the fullest extent permitted by the General Corporation Law of Delaware, as so amended.

Watson, a disgruntled Innoclub shareholder, finds out about the above transaction and hires you to bring a breach of fiduciary duty claim against Kuchar. Analyze the case. Include in your analysis any additional information you may require and explain why you need it.

b. The Duty to Monitor/Provide Oversight

Part of a board of directors' duties is to monitor, or provide oversight of, the corporation's business. Thus, when a corporation loses money because of misconduct by one or more employees, it is not uncommon for the board to get sued for failure to provide adequate oversight. In other words, the plaintiff alleges that had the board been fulfilling its oversight function, the misconduct would not have occurred and the corporation would not have lost the money. The next case, *Caremark*, provides an example of this sort of fact pattern and is regarded as the leading case on the duty of oversight. (In fact, judges and lawyers typically refer to oversight claims as "*Caremark*" claims.)

To set the stage, the case involves a derivative suit, which is where a shareholder sues on behalf of the corporation. (We'll discuss these suits in more detail in Section A.6 below.) For reasons we will discuss, the legal system imposes special procedural requirements on derivate suits, that is, requirements not applicable to regular litigation. Among these requirements is that any settlement of the suit must be approved by the court. The opinion in *Caremark* involves the approval of a proposed derivative suit settlement.

In re Caremark International Inc. Derivative Litigation
698 A.2d 959 (Del. Ch. 1996)

ALLEN, Chancellor.

Pending is a motion pursuant to Chancery Rule 23.1 to approve as fair and reasonable a proposed settlement of a consolidated derivative action on behalf of Caremark International, Inc. ("Caremark"). The suit involves claims that the members of Caremark's board of directors (the "Board") breached their fiduciary duty of care to Caremark in connection with alleged violations by Caremark employees of federal and state laws and regulations applicable to health care providers. As a result of the alleged violations, Caremark was subject to an extensive four year investigation by the United States Department of Health and Human Services and the Department of Justice. In 1994 Caremark was charged in an indictment with multiple felonies. It thereafter entered into a number of agreements with the Department of Justice and others. Those agreements included a plea agreement in which Caremark pleaded guilty to a single felony of mail fraud and agreed to pay civil and criminal fines. Subsequently, Caremark agreed to make reimbursements to various private and public parties. In all, the payments that Caremark has been required to make total approximately $250 million.

This suit was filed in 1994, purporting to seek on behalf of the company recovery of these losses from the individual defendants who constitute the board of directors of Caremark. The parties now propose that it be settled and, after notice to Caremark shareholders, a hearing on the fairness of the proposal was held on August 16, 1996. . . .

Legally, evaluation of the central claim made entails consideration of the legal standard governing a board of directors' obligation to supervise or monitor corporate performance. For the reasons set forth below I conclude, in light of the discovery record, that there is a very low probability that it would be determined that the directors of Caremark breached any duty to appropriately monitor and supervise the enterprise. Indeed the record tends to show an active consideration by Caremark management and its Board of the Caremark structures and programs that ultimately led to the company's indictment and to the large financial losses incurred in the settlement of those claims. It does not tend to show knowing or intentional violation of law. Neither the fact that the Board, although advised by lawyers and accountants, did not accurately predict the severe consequences to the company that would ultimately follow from the deployment by the company of the strategies and practices that ultimately led to this liability, nor the scale of the liability, gives rise to an inference of breach of any duty imposed by corporation law upon the directors of Caremark.

I. BACKGROUND

For these purposes I regard the following facts, suggested by the discovery record, as material. Caremark, a Delaware corporation with its headquarters in Northbrook, Illinois, was created in November 1992 when it was spun-off from Baxter International, Inc. ("Baxter") and became a publicly held company listed on the New York Stock Exchange. The business practices that created the problem pre-dated the spin-off. During the relevant period Caremark was involved in two main health care business segments, providing patient care and managed care services. As part of its patient care business, which accounted for the majority of Caremark's revenues, Caremark provided alternative site health care services, including infusion therapy, growth hormone therapy, HIV/AIDS-related treatments and hemophilia therapy. Caremark's managed care services included prescription drug programs and the operation of multi-specialty group practices.

A. Events Prior to the Government Investigation

A substantial part of the revenues generated by Caremark's businesses is derived from third party payments, insurers, and Medicare and Medicaid reimbursement programs. The latter source of payments are subject to the terms of the Anti-Referral Payments Law ("ARPL") which prohibits health care providers from paying any form of remuneration to induce the referral of Medicare or Medicaid patients. From its inception, Caremark entered into a variety of agreements with hospitals, physicians, and health care providers for advice and services, as well as distribution agreements with drug manufacturers, as had its predecessor prior to 1992. Specifically, Caremark did have a practice of entering into contracts for services (e.g., consultation agreements and research grants) with physicians at least some of whom prescribed or recommended services or products that Caremark provided to Medicare recipients and other patients. Such contracts were not prohibited by the ARPL but they obviously raised a possibility of unlawful "kickbacks."

As early as 1989, Caremark's predecessor issued an internal "Guide to Contractual Relationships" ("Guide") to govern its employees in entering into contracts with physicians and hospitals. The Guide tended to be reviewed annually by lawyers and updated. Each version of the Guide stated as Caremark's and its predecessor's policy that no payments would be made in exchange for or to induce patient referrals. But what one might deem a prohibited *quid pro quo* was not always clear. Due to a scarcity of court decisions interpreting the ARPL, however, Caremark repeatedly publicly stated that there was uncertainty concerning Caremark's interpretation of the law. . . .

B. Government Investigation and Related Litigation

In August 1991, the [United States Department of Health and Human Services] Office of the Inspector General ("OIG") initiated an investigation of Caremark's predecessor. Caremark's predecessor was served with a subpoena requiring the production of documents, including contracts between Caremark's predecessor and physicians (Quality Service Agreements ("QSAs")). Under the QSAs, Caremark's predecessor appears to have paid physicians fees for monitoring patients under Caremark's predecessor's care, including Medicare and Medicaid recipients. Sometimes apparently those monitoring patients were referring physicians, which raised ARPL concerns.

In March 1992, the Department of Justice ("DOJ") joined the OIG investigation and separate investigations were commenced by several additional federal and state agencies.

C. Caremark's Response to the Investigation

During the relevant period, Caremark had approximately 7,000 employees and ninety branch operations. It had a decentralized management structure. By May 1991, however, Caremark asserts that it had begun making attempts to centralize its management structure in order to increase supervision over its branch operations.

The first action taken by management, as a result of the initiation of the OIG investigation, was an announcement that as of October 1, 1991, Caremark's predecessor would no longer pay management fees to physicians for services to Medicare and Medicaid patients. Despite this decision, Caremark asserts that its management, pursuant to advice, did not believe that such payments were illegal under the existing laws and regulations.

During this period, Caremark's Board took several additional steps consistent with an effort to assure compliance with company policies concerning the ARPL and the contractual forms in the Guide. In April 1992, Caremark published a fourth revised version of its Guide apparently designed to assure that its agreements either complied with the ARPL and regulations or excluded Medicare and Medicaid patients altogether. In addition, in September 1992, Caremark instituted a policy requiring its regional officers, Zone Presidents, to approve each contractual relationship entered into by Caremark with a physician.

Although there is evidence that inside and outside counsel had advised Caremark's directors that their contracts were in accord with the law, Caremark recognized that some uncertainty respecting the correct interpretation of the law existed. In its 1992 annual report, Caremark disclosed the ongoing government investigations, acknowledged that if penalties were imposed on the company they could have a material adverse effect on Caremark's business, and stated that no assurance could be given that its interpretation of the ARPL would prevail if challenged.

Throughout the period of the government investigations, Caremark had an internal audit plan designed to assure compliance with business and ethics policies....

The Board appears to have been informed about ... efforts to assure compliance with the law....

D. Federal Indictments Against Caremark and Officers

On August 4, 1994, a federal grand jury in Minnesota issued a 47 page indictment charging Caremark, two of its officers (not the firm's chief officer), an individual who had been a sales employee of Genentech, Inc., and David R. Brown, a physician practicing in Minneapolis, with violating the ARPL over a lengthy period. According to the indictment, over $1.1 million had been paid to Brown to induce him to distribute Protropin, a human growth hormone drug marketed by Caremark. The substantial payments involved started, according to the allegations of the indictment, in 1986 and continued through 1993. Some payments were "in the guise of research grants," and others were "consulting agreements." The indictment charged, for example, that Dr. Brown performed virtually none of the consulting functions described in his 1991 agreement with Caremark, but was nevertheless neither required to return the money he had received nor precluded from receiving future funding from Caremark. In addition the indictment charged that Brown received from Caremark payments of staff and office expenses, including telephone answering services and fax rental expenses.

In reaction to the Minnesota Indictment and the subsequent filing of this and other derivative actions in 1994, the Board met and was informed by management that the investigation had resulted in an indictment; Caremark denied any wrongdoing relating to the indictment and believed that the OIG investigation would have a favorable outcome. Management reiterated the grounds for its view that the contracts were in compliance with law.

Subsequently, five stockholder derivative actions were filed in this court and consolidated into this action....

On September 21, 1994, a federal grand jury in Columbus, Ohio issued another indictment alleging that an Ohio physician had defrauded the Medicare program by requesting and receiving $134,600 in exchange for referrals of patients whose medical costs were in part reimbursed by Medicare in violation of the ARPL. Although unidentified at that time, Caremark was the health care provider who allegedly made such payments. The indictment also charged that the physician, Elliot Neufeld, D.O., was provided with the services of a registered nurse to work in his office at the expense of the infusion company, in addition to free office equipment.

An October 28, 1994 amended complaint in this action added allegations concerning the Ohio indictment as well as new allegations of over billing and inappropriate referral payments in connection with an action brought in Atlanta, *Booth v. Rankin.* Following a newspaper article report that federal investigators were expanding their inquiry to look at Caremark's referral practices in Michigan as well as allegations of fraudulent billing of insurers, a second amended complaint was filed in this action. The third, and final, amended complaint was filed on April 11, 1995, adding allegations that the federal indictments had caused Caremark to incur significant legal fees and forced it to sell its home infusion business at a loss. . . .

E. Settlement Negotiations

. . . Caremark began settlement negotiations with federal and state government entities in May 1995. In return for a guilty plea to a single count of mail fraud by the corporation, the payment of a criminal fine, the payment of substantial civil damages, and cooperation with further federal investigations on matters relating to the OIG investigation, the government entities agreed to negotiate a settlement that would permit Caremark to continue participating in Medicare and Medicaid programs. On June 15, 1995, the Board approved a settlement ("Government Settlement Agreement") with the DOJ, OIG, U.S. Veterans Administration, U.S. Federal Employee Health Benefits Program, federal Civilian Health and Medical Program of the Uniformed Services, and related state agencies in all fifty states and the District of Columbia. No senior officers or directors were charged with wrongdoing in the Government Settlement Agreement or in any of the prior indictments. In fact, as part of the sentencing in the Ohio action on June 19, 1995, the United States stipulated that *no senior executive of Caremark participated in, condoned, or was willfully ignorant of wrongdoing in connection with the home infusion business practices.* . . .

Settlement negotiations between the parties in this action commenced in May 1995 as well, based upon a letter proposal of the plaintiffs, dated May 16, 1995. These negotiations resulted in a memorandum of understanding ("MOU"), dated June 7, 1995, and the execution of the Stipulation and Agreement of Compromise and Settlement on June 28, 1995, which is the subject of this action. The MOU, approved by the Board on June 15, 1995, required the Board to adopt several resolutions, discussed below, and to create a new compliance committee. The Compliance and Ethics Committee has been reporting to the Board in accord with its newly specified duties. . . .

F. The Proposed Settlement of This Litigation

In relevant part the terms upon which these claims asserted are proposed to be settled are as follows:

1. That Caremark, undertakes that it and its employees, and agents not pay any form of compensation to a third party in exchange for the referral of a patient to a Caremark facility or service or the prescription of drugs marketed or distributed by Caremark for which reimbursement may be sought from Medicare, Medicaid, or a similar state reimbursement program;

2. That Caremark, undertakes for itself and its employees, and agents not to pay to or split fees with physicians, joint ventures, any business combination in which Caremark maintains a direct financial interest, or other health care providers with whom Caremark has a financial relationship or interest, in exchange for the referral of a patient to a Caremark facility or service or the prescription of drugs marketed or distributed by Caremark for which reimbursement may be sought from Medicare, Medicaid, or a similar state reimbursement program;

3. That the full Board shall discuss all relevant material changes in government health care regulations and their effect on relationships with health care providers on a semi-annual basis;

4. That Caremark's officers will remove all personnel from health care facilities or hospitals who have been placed in such facility for the purpose of providing remuneration in exchange for a patient referral for which reimbursement may be sought from Medicare, Medicaid, or a similar state reimbursement program;

5. That every patient will receive written disclosure of any financial relationship between Caremark and the health care professional or provider who made the referral;

6. That the Board will establish a Compliance and Ethics Committee of four directors, two of which will be non-management directors, to meet at least four times a year to effectuate these policies and monitor business segment compliance with the ARPL, and to report to the Board semi-annually concerning compliance by each business segment; and

7. That corporate officers responsible for business segments shall serve as compliance officers who must report semi-annually to the Compliance and Ethics Committee and, with the assistance of outside counsel, review existing contracts and get advanced approval of any new contract forms.

II. LEGAL PRINCIPLES

A. Principles Governing Settlements of Derivative Claims

... [T]his Court is now required to exercise an informed judgment whether the proposed settlement is fair and reasonable in the light of all relevant factors. On an application of this kind, this Court attempts to protect the best interests of the corporation and its absent shareholders all of whom will be barred from future litigation on these claims if the settlement is approved. The parties proposing the settlement bear the burden of persuading the court that it is in fact fair and reasonable.

B. Directors' Duties to Monitor Corporate Operations

The complaint charges the director defendants with breach of their duty of attention or care in connection with the on-going operation of the corporation's business. The claim is that the directors allowed a situation to develop and continue which exposed the corporation to enormous legal liability and that in so doing they violated a duty to be active monitors of corporate performance. The complaint thus does not charge either director self-dealing or the more difficult loyalty-type problems arising from cases of suspect director motivation, such as entrenchment or sale of control contexts. The theory here advanced is possibly the most difficult theory in corporation law upon which a plaintiff might hope to win a judgment. . . .

[One] class of cases in which director liability for inattention is theoretically possible entail[s] circumstances in which a loss eventuates not from a decision but, from unconsidered inaction. Most of the decisions that a corporation, acting through its human agents, makes are, of course, not the subject of director attention. Legally, the board itself will be required only to authorize the most significant corporate acts or transactions: mergers, changes in capital structure, fundamental changes in business, appointment and compensation of the CEO, etc. As the facts of this case graphically demonstrate, ordinary business decisions that are made by officers and employees deeper in the interior of the organization can, however, vitally affect the welfare of the corporation and its ability to achieve its various strategic and financial goals. . . . [This] raise[s] the question, what is the board's responsibility with respect to the organization and monitoring of the enterprise to assure that the corporation functions within the law to achieve its purposes?

Modernly this question has been given special importance by an increasing tendency, especially under federal law, to employ the criminal law to assure corporate compliance with external legal requirements, including environmental, financial, employee and product safety as well as assorted other health and safety regulations. In 1991, pursuant to the Sentencing Reform Act of 1984, the United States Sentencing Commission adopted Organizational Sentencing Guidelines which impact importantly on the prospective effect these criminal sanctions might have on business corporations. The Guidelines set forth a uniform sentencing structure for organizations to be sentenced for violation of federal criminal statutes and provide for penalties that equal or often massively exceed those previously imposed on corporations. The Guidelines offer powerful incentives for corporations today to have in place compliance programs to detect violations of law, promptly to report violations to appropriate public officials when discovered, and to take prompt, voluntary remedial efforts.

In 1963, the Delaware Supreme Court in *Graham v. Allis-Chalmers Mfg. Co.*, addressed the question of potential liability of board members for losses experienced by the corporation as a result of the corporation having violated the anti-trust laws of the United States. There was no claim in that case that the directors knew about the behavior of subordinate employees of the corporation that had resulted in the liability. Rather, as in this case, the claim asserted was that the directors *ought to have known* of it and if they had known they would have been under a duty to bring the corporation into compliance with the law and thus save the corporation from the loss. The Delaware Supreme Court concluded that, under the facts as they appeared, there was no basis to find that the directors had breached a duty to be informed of the ongoing operations of the firm. In notably colorful terms, the court stated that "absent cause for suspicion there is no duty upon the directors to install and operate a corporate system of espionage to ferret out wrongdoing which they have no reason to suspect exists." The Court found that there were no grounds for suspicion in that case and, thus, concluded that the directors were blamelessly unaware of the conduct leading to the corporate liability.

How does one generalize this holding today? Can it be said today that, absent some ground giving rise to suspicion of violation of law, that corporate directors have no duty to assure that a corporate information gathering and reporting systems exists which represents a good faith attempt to provide senior management and the Board with information respecting material acts, events or conditions within the corporation, including compliance with applicable statutes and regulations? I certainly do not believe so. I doubt that such a broad generalization of the *Graham* holding would have been accepted by the Supreme Court in 1963. The case can be more narrowly interpreted as standing for the proposition that, absent grounds to suspect deception, neither corporate boards nor senior officers can be charged with wrongdoing simply for assuming the integrity of employees and the honesty of their dealings on the company's behalf.

A broader interpretation of *Graham v. Allis-Chalmers* — that it means that a corporate board has no responsibility to assure that appropriate information and reporting systems are established by management — would not, in any event, be accepted by the Delaware Supreme Court in 1996, in my opinion. In stating the basis for this view, I start with the recognition that in recent years the Delaware Supreme Court has made it clear — especially in its jurisprudence concerning takeovers, from *Smith v. Van Gorkom* through *Paramount Communications v. QVC* the seriousness with which the corporation law views the role of the corporate board. Secondly, I note the elementary fact that relevant and timely *information* is an essential predicate for satisfaction of the board's supervisory and monitoring role under Section 141 of the Delaware General Corporation Law. Thirdly, I note the potential impact of the federal organizational sentencing guidelines on any business organization. Any rational person attempting in good faith to meet an organizational governance responsibility would be bound to take into account this development and the enhanced penalties and the opportunities for reduced sanctions that it offers.

In light of these developments, it would, in my opinion, be a mistake to conclude that our Supreme Court's statement in *Graham* concerning "espionage" means that corporate boards may satisfy their obligation to be reasonably informed concerning the corporation, without assuring themselves that information and reporting systems exist in the organization that are reasonably designed to provide to senior management and to the board itself timely, accurate information sufficient to allow management and the board, each within its scope, to reach informed judgments concerning both the corporation's compliance with law and its business performance.

Obviously the level of detail that is appropriate for such an information system is a question of business judgment. And obviously too, no rationally designed information and reporting system will remove the possibility that the corporation will violate laws or regulations, or that senior officers or directors may nevertheless sometimes be misled or otherwise fail reasonably to detect acts material to the corporation's compliance with the law. But it is important that the board exercise a good faith judgment that the corporation's information and reporting system is in concept and design adequate to assure the board that appropriate information will come to its attention in a timely manner as a matter of ordinary operations, so that it may satisfy its responsibility.

Thus, I am of the view that a director's obligation includes a duty to attempt in good faith to assure that a corporate information and reporting system, which the board concludes is adequate, exists, and that failure to do so under some circumstances may, in theory at least, render a director liable for losses caused by non-compliance with applicable legal standards. I now turn to an analysis of the claims asserted with this concept of the directors duty of care, as a duty satisfied in part by assurance of adequate information flows to the board, in mind.

III. ANALYSIS OF THIRD AMENDED COMPLAINT AND SETTLEMENT

A. The Claims

On balance, after reviewing an extensive record in this case, including numerous documents and three depositions, I conclude that this settlement is fair and reasonable. In light of the fact that the Caremark Board already has a functioning committee charged with overseeing corporate compliance, the changes in corporate practice that are presented as consideration for the settlement do not impress one as very significant. Nonetheless, that consideration appears fully adequate to support dismissal of the derivative claims of director fault asserted, because those claims find no substantial evidentiary support in the record and quite likely were susceptible to a motion to dismiss in all events.

In order to show that the Caremark directors breached their duty of care by failing adequately to control Caremark's employees, plaintiffs would have to show either (1) that the directors knew or (2) should have known that violations of law were occurring and, in either event, (3) that the directors took no steps in a good faith effort to prevent or remedy that situation, and (4) that such failure proximately resulted in the losses complained of. . . .

1. *Knowing violation for statute:* Concerning the possibility that the Caremark directors knew of violations of law, none of the documents submitted for review, nor any of the deposition transcripts appear to provide evidence of it. Certainly the Board understood that the company had entered into a variety of contracts with physicians, researchers, and health care providers and it was understood that some of these contracts were with persons who had prescribed treatments that Caremark participated in providing. The board was informed that the company's reimbursement for patient care was frequently from government funded sources and that such services were subject to the ARPL. But the Board appears to have been informed by experts that the company's practices while contestable, were lawful. There is no evidence that reliance on such reports was not reasonable. . . .

2. *Failure to monitor:* Since it does appears that the Board was to some extent unaware of the activities that led to liability, I turn to a consideration of the other potential avenue to director liability that the pleadings take: director inattention or "negligence." Generally where a claim of directorial liability for corporate loss is predicated upon ignorance of liability creating activities within the corporation, as in *Graham* or in this case, in my opinion only a sustained or systematic failure of the board to exercise oversight—such as an utter failure to attempt to assure a reasonable information and reporting system exists—will establish the lack of good faith that is a necessary condition to liability. Such a test of liability—lack of good faith as evidenced by sustained or systematic failure of a director to exercise reasonable oversight—is quite high. But, a demanding test of liability in the oversight context is probably beneficial to corporate shareholders as a class, as it is in the board decision context, since it makes board service by qualified persons more likely, while continuing to act as a stimulus to *good faith performance of duty* by such directors.

Here the record supplies essentially no evidence that the director defendants were guilty of a sustained failure to exercise their oversight function. To the contrary, insofar as I am able to tell on this record, the corporation's information systems appear to have represented a good faith attempt to be informed of relevant facts. If the directors did not know the specifics of the activities that lead to the indictments, they cannot be faulted. . . .

IV. ATTORNEYS' FEES

The various firms of lawyers involved for plaintiffs seek an award of $1,025,000 in attorneys' fees and reimbursable expenses. . . .

In this case no factor points to a substantial fee, other than the amount and sophistication of the lawyer services required. There is only a modest substantive benefit produced; in the particular circumstances of the government activity there was realistically a very slight contingency faced by the attorneys at the time they expended time. The services rendered required a high degree of sophistication and expertise. I am told that at normal hourly billing rates approximately $710,000 of time was expended by the attorneys.

In these circumstances, I conclude that an award of a fee determined by reference to the time expended at normal hourly rates plus a premium of 15 percent of that amount to reflect the limited degree of real contingency in the undertaking, is fair. Thus I will award a fee of $816,000 plus $53,000 of expenses advanced by counsel.

Questions

1. What did Caremark's directors allegedly do wrong?
2. When are directors liable for failure to monitor?
3. Did the Caremark board breach its duty to monitor?
4. Who benefitted most from this suit?

You may have noticed that Chancellor Allen characterized a failure to monitor as a breach of the duty of care. This is because until fairly recently the duty to monitor was generally viewed as a component of the duty of care. In the 2006 case *Stone v. Ritter*, however, the Delaware Supreme Court stated as follows:

> We hold that *Caremark* articulates the necessary conditions predicate for director oversight liability: (a) the directors utterly failed to implement any reporting or information system or controls; *or* (b) having implemented such a system or controls, consciously failed to monitor or oversee its operations thus disabling themselves from being informed of risks or problems requiring their attention. In either case, imposition of liability requires a showing that the directors knew that they were not discharging their fiduciary obligations. Where directors fail to act in the face of a known duty to act, thereby demonstrating a conscious disregard for their responsibilities, *they breach their duty of loyalty* by failing to discharge that fiduciary obligation in good faith.[21]

A consequence of shifting the duty of oversight from a component of care to a component of loyalty is that an exculpation provision will no longer protect directors from monetary damages for breach of the duty of oversight. When it comes to potential personal liability of directors, however, this may not be as significant as it appears. As Chancellor Allen said in *Caremark*, a failure to provide oversight claim "is possibly the most difficult theory in corporation law upon which a plaintiff might hope to win a judgment."[22] Further, post-*Stone* it is even more difficult for a plaintiff to prevail on such a claim because, as indicated in the above quote, *Stone* added a knowledge element to the mix. Thus,

---

21. *Stone v. Ritter*, 911 A.2d 362, 370 (Del. 2006) (emphasis added).
22. *In re Caremark Int'l Deriv. Litig.*, 698 A.2d 959 (Del. Ch. 1996).

a plaintiff has to now prove a sustained or systematic failure of the board to provide oversight and that such failure was done knowingly.

c. *The Duty of Good Faith*

The duty of good faith became much more prominent following a 1993 opinion by the Delaware Supreme Court designating it, along with the duties of care and loyalty, as part of a "triad" of fiduciary duties owed by corporate directors.[23] The duty of good faith played an important role in high-profile litigation against the board of directors of the Walt Disney Company that commenced in 1997.

The case arose out of Disney's employment relationship with Michael Ovitz. Ovitz was a founder and leading partner of Creative Artists Agency, the premier talent agency in the country, and was regarded as one of the most powerful agents in Hollywood. Disney hired Ovitz as president in August 1995 in anticipation of his eventually succeeding Michael Eisner as Disney's chief executive officer. Shortly thereafter, however, Eisner concluded that Ovitz was a poor fit for Disney and thus fired him in December 1996. Notably, Disney decided to treat Ovitz's firing as a "non-fault" termination, which meant that under his employment agreement Ovitz was entitled to a severance package worth approximately $130 million, a package he would not have been entitled to if Disney had terminated him for good cause.[24]

In January 1997, several Disney shareholders brought derivative suits in the Delaware Court of Chancery claiming, among other things, that the Disney board of directors breached its fiduciary duties when it (1) approved Ovitz's employment agreement, and (2) later agreed to a "non-fault" termination of his employment agreement. The Court of Chancery dismissed the complaint "for failure to set forth particularized facts creating a reasonable doubt that the director defendants were disinterested and independent or that their conduct was protected by the business judgment rule."[25] On appeal, the Delaware Supreme Court agreed, but "in the interests of justice" remanded the case to the Court of Chancery to allow the plaintiffs to file an amended complaint.[26]

The plaintiffs filed a new complaint, and this time the Court of Chancery did not dismiss it in part because "[a] fair reading of the new complaint . . . gives rise to a reason to doubt whether the board's actions were taken honestly and in good faith. . . ."[27] The case proceeded to trial with Chancellor William Chandler

---

23. *See Cede & Co. v. Technicolor, Inc.*, 634 A.2d 345, 361 (Del. 1993).
24. Under his employment agreement, Disney could terminate Ovitz for "good cause" only if he committed gross negligence or malfeasance.
25. *Brehm v. Eisner*, 746 A.2d 244, 248 (Del. 2000).
26. *Id.*
27. *In re Walt Disney Co. Derivative Litigation*, 825 A.2d 275 (Del. Ch. 2003).

ultimately determining that the Disney board "did not breach their fiduciary duties . . . ."[28] He therefore entered judgment in favor of the defendants.

The plaintiffs once again appealed, arguing, among other things, that "directors violate their duty of good faith if they are making material decisions without adequate information and without adequate deliberation."[29] In essence, the plaintiffs were asking the court to consider a breach of the duty of care as a breach of the duty of good faith as well. This was necessary for their case because Disney's charter contains an exculpation provision. Thus, to get around it the plaintiffs needed to come up with some argument as to why the directors acted in bad faith. (There apparently were no facts they could point at to support a breach of duty of loyalty claim.)

The Chancery Court opinion defined bad faith as follows:

> Upon long and careful consideration, I am of the opinion that the concept of *intentional dereliction of duty, a conscious disregard for one's responsibilities,* is an appropriate (although not the only) standard for determining whether fiduciaries have acted in good faith. Deliberate indifference and inaction *in the face of a duty to act* is, in my mind, conduct that is clearly disloyal to the corporation. It is the epitome of faithless conduct.[30]

Hence, the plaintiffs argued that this definition was erroneous, and the Delaware Supreme Court took the opportunity to elaborate on the issue as follows.

> This case . . . is one in which the duty to act in good faith has played a prominent role, yet to date is not a well-developed area of our corporate fiduciary law. Although the good faith concept has recently been the subject of considerable scholarly writing, which includes articles focused on this specific case, the duty to act in good faith is, up to this point relatively uncharted. Because of the increased recognition of the importance of good faith, some conceptual guidance to the corporate community may be helpful. For that reason we proceed to address the merits of the appellants' . . . argument.
>
> The precise question is whether the Chancellor's articulated standard for bad faith corporate fiduciary conduct—intentional dereliction of duty, a conscious disregard for one's responsibilities—is legally correct. In approaching that question, we note that the Chancellor characterized that definition as "*an* appropriate (*although not the only*) standard for determining whether fiduciaries have acted in good faith." That observation is accurate and helpful, because as a matter of simple logic, at least three different categories of fiduciary behavior are candidates for the "bad faith" pejorative label.
>
> The first category involves so-called "subjective bad faith," that is, fiduciary conduct motivated by an actual intent to do harm. That such conduct constitutes classic, quintessential bad faith is a proposition so well accepted in the

---

28. *In re Walt Disney Co. Derivative Litigation*, 907 A.2d 693, 697 (Del. Ch. 2005).

29. *In re Walt Disney Co. Derivative Litigation*, 906 A.2d 27, 63 (Del. 2006).

30. *In re Walt Disney Co. Derivative Litigation*, 907 A.2d 693, 755 (Del. Ch. 2005) (italics in original, footnotes omitted).

liturgy of fiduciary law that it borders on axiomatic. We need not dwell further on this category, because no such conduct is claimed to have occurred, or did occur, in this case.

The second category of conduct, which is at the opposite end of the spectrum, involves lack of due care — that is, fiduciary action taken solely by reason of gross negligence and without any malevolent intent. In this case, appellants assert claims of gross negligence to establish breaches not only of director due care but also of the directors' duty to act in good faith. Although the Chancellor found, and we agree, that the appellants failed to establish gross negligence, to afford guidance we address the issue of whether gross negligence (including a failure to inform one's self of available material facts), without more, can also constitute bad faith. The answer is clearly no.

From a broad philosophical standpoint, that question is more complex than would appear, if only because (as the Chancellor and others have observed) "issues of good faith are (to a certain degree) inseparably and necessarily intertwined with the duties of care and loyalty. . . ." But, in the pragmatic, conduct-regulating legal realm which calls for more precise conceptual line drawing, the answer is that grossly negligent conduct, without more, does not and cannot constitute a breach of the fiduciary duty to act in good faith. The conduct that is the subject of due care may overlap with the conduct that comes within the rubric of good faith in a psychological sense, but from a legal standpoint those duties are and must remain quite distinct. Both our legislative history and our common law jurisprudence distinguish sharply between the duties to exercise due care and to act in good faith, and highly significant consequences flow from that distinction.

The Delaware General Assembly has addressed the distinction between bad faith and a failure to exercise due care (*i.e.,* gross negligence) in two separate contexts. The first is Section 102(b)(7) of the DGCL, which authorizes Delaware corporations, by a provision in the certificate of incorporation, to exculpate their directors from monetary damage liability for a breach of the duty of care. That exculpatory provision affords significant protection to directors of Delaware corporations. The statute carves out several exceptions, however, including most relevantly, "for acts or omissions not in good faith. . . ." Thus, a corporation can exculpate its directors from monetary liability for a breach of the duty of care, but not for conduct that is not in good faith. To adopt a definition of bad faith that would cause a violation of the duty of care automatically to become an act or omission "not in good faith," would eviscerate the protections accorded to directors by the General Assembly's adoption of Section 102(b)(7).

A second legislative recognition of the distinction between fiduciary conduct that is grossly negligent and conduct that is not in good faith, is Delaware's indemnification statute, found at 8 Del. C. §145. To oversimplify, subsections (a) and (b) of that statute permit a corporation to indemnify (*inter alia*) any person who is or was a director, officer, employee or agent of the corporation against expenses (including attorneys' fees), judgments, fines and amounts paid in settlement of specified actions, suits or proceedings, where (among other things): (i) that person is, was, or is threatened to be made a party to that action, suit or proceeding, and (ii) that person "acted in good faith and in a manner the person reasonably believed to be in or not opposed to the best interests of the corporation. . . ." Thus, under Delaware statutory law a director or officer of a corporation can be indemnified for liability (and litigation expenses) incurred by reason of a violation of the duty of care, but not for a violation of the duty to act in good faith.

Section 145, like Section 102(b)(7), evidences the intent of the Delaware General Assembly to afford significant protections to directors (and, in the case of Section 145, other fiduciaries) of Delaware corporations. To adopt a definition that conflates the duty of care with the duty to act in good faith by making a violation of the former an automatic violation of the latter, would nullify those legislative protections and defeat the General Assembly's intent. There is no basis in policy, precedent or common sense that would justify dismantling the distinction between gross negligence and bad faith.

The invariant policy of Delaware legislation on indemnification is to "promote the desirable end that corporate officials will resist what they consider unjustified suits and claims, secure in the knowledge that their reasonable expenses will be borne by the corporation they have served if they are vindicated." Folk, On Delaware General Corporation Law sec. 145 (2001). Beyond that, its larger purpose is "to encourage capable men to serve as corporate directors, secure in the knowledge that expenses incurred by them in upholding their honesty and integrity as directors will be borne by the directors they serve." *Id.*

That leaves the third category of fiduciary conduct, which falls in between the first two categories of (1) conduct motivated by subjective bad intent and (2) conduct resulting from gross negligence. This third category is what the Chancellor's definition of bad faith—intentional dereliction of duty, a conscious disregard for one's responsibilities—is intended to capture. The question is whether such misconduct is properly treated as a non-exculpable, nonindemnifiable violation of the fiduciary duty to act in good faith. In our view it must be, for at least two reasons.

First, the universe of fiduciary misconduct is not limited to either disloyalty in the classic sense (*i.e.,* preferring the adverse self-interest of the fiduciary or of a related person to the interest of the corporation) or gross negligence. Cases have arisen where corporate directors have no conflicting self-interest in a decision, yet engage in misconduct that is more culpable than simple inattention or failure to be informed of all facts material to the decision. To protect the interests of the corporation and its shareholders, fiduciary conduct of this kind, which does not involve disloyalty (as traditionally defined) but is qualitatively more culpable than gross negligence, should be proscribed. A vehicle is needed to address such violations doctrinally, and that doctrinal vehicle is the duty to act in good faith. The Chancellor implicitly so recognized in his Opinion, where he identified different examples of bad faith as follows:

> The good faith required of a corporate fiduciary includes not simply the duties of care and loyalty, in the narrow sense that I have discussed them above, but all actions required by a true faithfulness and devotion to the interests of the corporation and its shareholders. A failure to act in good faith may be shown, for instance, where the fiduciary intentionally acts with a purpose other than that of advancing the best interests of the corporation, where the fiduciary acts with the intent to violate applicable

positive law, or where the fiduciary intentionally fails to act in the face of a known duty to act, demonstrating a conscious disregard for his duties. There may be other examples of bad faith yet to be proven or alleged, but these three are the most salient.

Those articulated examples of bad faith are not new to our jurisprudence. Indeed, they echo pronouncements our courts have made throughout the decades.

Second, the legislature has also recognized this intermediate category of fiduciary misconduct, which ranks between conduct involving subjective bad faith and gross negligence. Section 102(b)(7)(ii) of the DGCL expressly denies money damage exculpation for "acts or omissions not in good faith or which involve intentional misconduct or a knowing violation of law." By its very terms that provision distinguishes between "intentional misconduct" and a "knowing violation of law" (both examples of subjective bad faith) on the one hand, and "acts . . . not in good faith," on the other. Because the statute exculpates directors only for conduct amounting to gross negligence, the statutory denial of exculpation for "acts . . . not in good faith" must encompass the intermediate category of misconduct captured by the Chancellor's definition of bad faith.

For these reasons, we uphold the Court of Chancery's definition as a legally appropriate, although not the exclusive, definition of fiduciary bad faith. We need go no further. To engage in an effort to craft (in the Court's words) "a definitive and categorical definition of the universe of acts that would constitute bad faith" would be unwise and is unnecessary to dispose of the issues presented on this appeal.[31]

The court left open the question of "whether the fiduciary duty of good faith is a duty that, like the duties of care and loyalty, can serve as an independent basis for imposing liability upon corporate officers and directors."[32] It, however, answered the question later that year in *Stone v. Ritter*, stating that the requirement to act in good faith is a "subsidiary element" of the duty of loyalty.[33] The court then elaborated on what this means:

This view of a failure to act in good faith results in two additional doctrinal consequences. First, although good faith may be described colloquially as part of a "triad" of fiduciary duties that includes the duties of care and loyalty, the obligation to act in good faith does not establish an independent fiduciary duty that stands on the same footing as the duties of care and loyalty. Only the latter two duties, where violated, may directly result in liability, whereas a failure to act in good faith may do so, but indirectly. The second doctrinal consequence is that the fiduciary duty of loyalty is not limited to cases involving a financial or other cognizable fiduciary conflict of interest. It also encompasses cases where the fiduciary fails to act in good faith.[34]

---

31. *In re Walt Disney Co. Derivative Litigation*, 906 A.2d 27, 63-67 (Del. 2006).
32. *Id.* at 67 n.112.
33. *Stone v. Ritter*, 911 A.2d 362, 369 (Del. 2006).
34. *Id.* at 370.

d. Usurping a Corporate Opportunity

A director usurps a corporate opportunity when the director takes for him- or herself a business opportunity that should have gone to the corporation. For example, say Deeb is a director of Bulla Inc., which is engaged in the business of purchasing rundown homes, rehabbing and then reselling them. Deeb learns that a widow in his neighborhood has passed away, and her children want to quickly sell her house. Deeb buys the house for himself at a great price, rehabs it, and flips it for $100,000 profit. Deeb has likely usurped a Bulla corporate opportunity and therefore breached the duty of loyalty he owes to Bulla as a director. Buying the house himself was obviously in his own best interest as opposed to the best interest of Bulla since had he notified Bulla of the opportunity presumably it would have taken it and made the $100,000.

Assume the same facts as above but instead of flipping houses Bulla manufactures solar panels. In this situation, it is unlikely that Deeb's house deal was a corporate opportunity of Bulla. Just because owes a duty of loyalty to Bulla does not mean he has to pass on to Bulla all business opportunities he comes across. Flipping houses has nothing to do with manufacturing solar panels, so it seems completely fine that Deeb took the deal for himself.

Based on the limited facts above, these situations appear clear cut, but many factual situations are not. As a result, courts have developed various tests to determine whether a business opportunity is one that belongs to the corporation and therefore if taken by a director or officer may give rise to a loyalty breach. The Delaware Supreme Court elaborated on its test in *Broz v. Cellular Information Systems, Inc.*:[35]

> The doctrine of corporate opportunity represents but one species of the broad fiduciary duties assumed by a corporate director or officer. A corporate fiduciary agrees to place the interests of the corporation before his or her own in appropriate circumstances. In light of the diverse and often competing obligations faced by directors and officers, however, the corporate opportunity doctrine arose as a means of defining the parameters of fiduciary duty in instances of potential conflict. The classic statement of the doctrine is derived from the venerable case of *Guth v. Loft, Inc.* In *Guth,* this Court held that:
>
>> if there is presented to a corporate officer or director a business opportunity which the corporation is financially able to undertake, is, from its nature, in the line of the corporation's business and is of practical advantage to it, is one in which the corporation has an interest or a reasonable expectancy, and, by embracing the opportunity, the self-interest of the officer or director will be brought into conflict with that of the corporation, the law will not permit him to seize the opportunity for himself. *Guth,* 5 A.2d at 510-11.
>
> The corporate opportunity doctrine, as delineated by *Guth* and its progeny, holds that a corporate officer or director may not take a business

---

35. 673 A.2d 148 (Del. 1996).

opportunity for his own if: (1) the corporation is financially able to exploit the opportunity; (2) the opportunity is within the corporation's line of business; (3) the corporation has an interest or expectancy in the opportunity; and (4) by taking the opportunity for his own, the corporate fiduciary will thereby be placed in a position inimicable to his duties to the corporation. The Court in *Guth* also derived a corollary which states that a director or officer *may* take a corporate opportunity if: (1) the opportunity is presented to the director or officer in his individual and not his corporate capacity; (2) the opportunity is not essential to the corporation; (3) the corporation holds no interest or expectancy in the opportunity; and (4) the director or officer has not wrongfully employed the resources of the corporation in pursuing or exploiting the opportunity. *Guth,* 5 A.2d at 509.

Thus, the contours of this doctrine are well established. It is important to note, however, that the tests enunciated in *Guth* and subsequent cases provide guidelines to be considered by a reviewing court in balancing the equities of an individual case. No one factor is dispositive and all factors must be taken into account insofar as they are applicable. Cases involving a claim of usurpation of a corporate opportunity range over a multitude of factual settings. Hard and fast rules are not easily crafted to deal with such an array of complex situations. As this Court noted in *Johnston v. Greene,* Del. Supr., 121 A.2d 919 (1956), the determination of "[w]hether or not a director has appropriated for himself something that in fairness should belong to the corporation is 'a factual question to be decided by reasonable inference from objective facts.'" *Id.* at 923 (quoting *Guth,* 5 A.2d at 513).[36]

A corporation's line of business generally includes activities to which it has "fundamental knowledge, practical experience and the ability to pursue" and that are consistent with the corporation's "reasonable needs and aspirations for expansion."[37] For the "interest or expectancy" factor to be met "there must be some tie between [the transaction at issue] and the nature of the corporate business."[38] An example would be if the corporation was planning to pursue the specific or similar type of transaction.

As for how a director or officer should approach a business opportunity the director or officer wants to pursue for him- or herself, the *Broz* court provided as follows:

> The teaching of *Guth* and its progeny is that the director or officer must analyze the situation *ex ante* to determine whether the opportunity is one rightfully belonging to the corporation. If the director or officer believes, based on one of the factors articulated above, that the corporation is not entitled to the opportunity, then he may take it for himself. Of course, presenting the opportunity to the board creates a kind of "safe harbor" for the director, which removes the specter of a *post hoc* judicial determination that the director or officer has improperly usurped a corporate opportunity. Thus, presentation avoids the possibility that

---

36. *Id.* at 154-55.
37. *Guth v. Loft. Inc.,* 5 A.2d 503, 514 (Del. 1939).
38. *Broz,* 673 A.2d at 156 (quoting *Johnston v. Greene,* 121 A.2d 919 (Del. Ch. 1956).

an error in the fiduciary's assessment of the situation will create future liability for breach of fiduciary duty. It is not the law of Delaware that presentation to the board is a necessary prerequisite to a finding that a corporate opportunity has not been usurped.[39]

In 2000, the Delaware legislature added subsection (17) to §122 of the DGCL, which provides as follows:

> Every corporation created under this chapter shall have power to:
> (17) Renounce, in its certificate of incorporation or by action of its board of directors, any interest or expectancy of the corporation in, or in being offered an opportunity to participate in, specified business opportunities or specified classes or categories of business opportunities that are presented to the corporation or 1 or more of its officers, directors or stockholders.

The legislature added the subsection to eliminate uncertainty created by *Siegman v. Tri-Star Pictures, Inc.*,[40] which cast doubt on the validity of a charter provision limiting director liability for usurping a corporate opportunity.

Here is an example of a §122(17) provision from the certificate of incorporation of Jive Software, Inc.

> The corporation renounces any interest or expectancy of the corporation in, or in being offered an opportunity to participate in, or in being informed about, an Excluded Opportunity. An "Excluded Opportunity" is any matter, transaction or interest that is presented to, or acquired, created or developed by, or which otherwise comes into the possession of, (i) any director of the corporation who is not an employee of the corporation or any of its subsidiaries, or (ii) any holder of Preferred Stock or any affiliate, partner, member, director, stockholder, employee, agent or other related person of any such holder, other than someone who is an employee of the corporation or any of its subsidiaries (collectively, "Covered Persons"), unless such matter, transaction or interest is presented to, or acquired, created or developed by, or otherwise comes into the possession of, a Covered Person expressly and solely in such Covered Person's capacity as a director of the corporation.

Exercise 10.3

From 1991 to 2010, Harris was a director of Northeast Harbor Golf Club, Inc. (the Club), a Delaware corporation. The Club owns and operates an 18-hole golf course in Northeast Harbor, Maine. Throughout her time on the board, the Club had continuous financial difficulties. Occasionally, the board discussed develop-

---

39. *Id.* at 157.
40. 1989 WL 48746 (Del. Ch. 1989).

ing various parcels of real estate it owned surrounding the golf course to raise money, but never did so, despite Harris being in favor of such actions.

In 2006, because he knew she was affiliated with the Club, a man contacted Harris regarding property adjacent to the golf course that was for sale. She told individual board members of her intentions to purchase the land at the time but did not formally disclose the purchase until 2007, saying she had no current plans to develop the land.

In 2008, she began making plans to develop homes on the property. A majority of the board took no action, but some board members formed an organization to oppose the development. In 2010, there was increasing concern regarding her development, and she was asked to resign from the board.

1. The board is considering suing Harris. They consult you about a possible cause of action under state corporate law and the likelihood of success. What do you tell them?
2. Assume Harris sought your advice on how to proceed in 2006 when she was contemplating buying the property. What advice would you have given her?
3. How would your analysis change if the Club has the same §122(17) provision in its charter as Jive Software?

5. The Duty of Disclosure

The duty of disclosure, or candor, gets its own subsection because it is derived from both the duty of care and loyalty. As the Delaware Supreme Court observed in *Malone v. Brincat*, "the duty of disclosure is, and always has been, a specific application of the general fiduciary duty owed by directors."[41] The duty "obligates directors to provide the stockholders with accurate and complete information material to a transaction or other corporate event that is being presented to them for action."[42] More generally, whenever directors communicate with stockholders they are required to do so honestly.[43] The state law duty of disclosure is not particularly well developed because stockholders typically bring false or misleading disclosure claims under federal securities laws, in particular §10(b) and Rule 10b-5 under the Securities Exchange Act of 1934, which is discussed in Chapter 13.

---

41. 722 A.2d 5, 10 (Del. 1988).
42. *Id.*
43. *Id.*

6. Fiduciary Duty Litigation

When it comes to a breach of fiduciary duty claim against directors, oftentimes it is the corporation, as opposed to its stockholders, that is directly harmed, and therefore the corporation and not its stockholders that has standing to sue. The problem, of course, is that the board controls whether a corporation sues, and the board is unlikely to initiate a suit against itself or a subset of directors. That is where derivative suits come into play. As mentioned above, a derivative suit is a suit initiated by a stockholder on behalf of the corporation. Courts developed the concept to allow a stockholder to pursue a cause of action of the corporation when those in charge of the corporation have refused to do so. Note that because the claim belongs to the corporation, any recovery goes to the corporation and not the stockholder-plaintiff.

Courts and legislatures have erected a number of procedural requirements with respect to derivative suits largely to curb plaintiffs' firms from bringing unmeritorious claims, or strike suits. Plaintiffs' firms bring strike suits because of their nuisance value. They figure a corporation is likely to settle the suit regardless of the merits to avoid the expense and disruption of protracted litigation. Thus, they recruit a stockholder to serve as nominal plaintiff, file suit, and then negotiate a settlement with the corporation that includes a nice payment to the plaintiffs' firm for its time and expense in bringing the suit.

In Delaware, special procedural requirements for derivative suits are specified in the following Court of Chancery rule:

Rule 23.1. Derivative actions by shareholders.

(a) In a derivative action brought by one or more shareholders or members to enforce a right of a corporation or of an unincorporated association, the corporation or association having failed to enforce a right which may properly be asserted by it, the complaint shall allege that the plaintiff was a shareholder or member at the time of the transaction of which the plaintiff complains or that the plaintiff's share or membership thereafter devolved on the plaintiff by operation of law. The complaint shall also allege with particularity the efforts, if any, made by the plaintiff to obtain the action the plaintiff desires from the directors or comparable authority and the reasons for the plaintiff's failure to obtain the action or for not making the effort.

(b) Each person seeking to serve as a representative plaintiff on behalf of a corporation or unincorporated association pursuant to this Rule shall file with the Register in Chancery an affidavit stating that the person has not received, been promised or offered and will not accept any form of compensation, directly or indirectly, for prosecuting or serving as a representative party in the derivative action in which the person or entity is a named party except (i) such fees, costs or other payments as the Court expressly approves to be paid to or on behalf of such person, or (ii) reimbursement, paid by such person's attorneys, of actual and reasonable out-of-pocket expenditures incurred directly in connection with the prosecution of the action. The affidavit required by this subpart shall be filed within 10 days after the earliest of the affiant filing the complaint, filing a motion to intervene in the action or filing a motion seeking appointment as a representative party in the action. An affidavit provided pursuant to this sub-part shall not be construed to be a waiver of the attorney-client privilege.

(c) The action shall not be dismissed or compromised without the approval of the Court, and notice by mail, publication or otherwise of the proposed dismissal or compromise shall be given to shareholders or members in such manner as the Court directs; except that if the dismissal is to be without prejudice or with prejudice to the plaintiff only, then such dismissal shall be ordered without notice thereof if there is a showing that no compensation in any form has passed directly or indirectly from any of the defendants to the plaintiff or plaintiff's attorney and that no promise to give any such compensation has been made. At the time that any party moves or otherwise applies to the Court for approval of a compromise of all or any part of a derivative action, each representative plaintiff in such action shall file with the Register in Chancery a further affidavit in the form required by subpart (b) of this rule.

a. The Demand Requirement

While much could be said about the various requirements of Rule 23.1, we are going to focus on the demand requirement because it is typically at the heart of a breach of fiduciary duty derivative suit. This requirement is reflected in the last sentence of subsection (a) of 23.1 and can be stated as follows: Prior to bringing a derivative claim, a stockholder must (1) make a demand on the corporation's board of directors to pursue the claim, or (2) include in the derivative action complaint particularized facts as to why making a demand would be futile.

The Delaware Supreme Court explained the policy behind the demand requirement in *Aronson v. Lewis*:

> By its very nature the derivative action impinges on the managerial freedom of directors. Hence, the demand requirement of Chancery Rule 23.1 exists at the threshold, first to insure that a stockholder exhausts his intracorporate remedies, and then to provide a safeguard against strike suits. Thus, by promoting this form of alternate dispute resolution, rather than immediate recourse to litigation, the demand requirement is a recognition of the fundamental precept that directors manage the business and affairs of corporations.[44]

(1) Demand Futility

Aronson established the following test for determining when demand is futile in a derivative suit challenging a board decision:

---

44. *Aronson v. Lewis*, 473 A.2d 805, 811-12 (Del. 1984).

[I]n determining demand futility the Court of Chancery in the proper exercise of its discretion must decide whether, under the particularized facts alleged, a reasonable doubt is created that: (1) the directors are disinterested and independent and (2) the challenged transaction was otherwise the product of a valid exercise of business judgment.[45]

The Delaware Supreme Court later clarified that the above two-prong test is disjunctive, meaning a plaintiff must only meet one of the prongs for demand to be excused.[46] In other words, the "and" right before the "(2)" should have been an "or."

Prong (1) of *Aronson* should look familiar because we discussed disinterestedness and independence above in the context of conflicting interest transactions. In the demand futility context, the question is whether a reasonable doubt exists as to the disinterestedness and independence of a majority of the board in responding to a demand, if the plaintiff had made one. The tests for disinterestedness and independence are essentially the same as those discussed above. Thus, demand will be excused if the complaint alleges particularized facts that, if proved, would show, for example, that (a) a majority of the board has a direct and substantial financial interest in the challenged transaction, or (b) a majority of the board is so beholden to an interested party that it cannot exercise independent judgment with respect to the demand. Note that merely being named as a defendant in the derivative suit at issue does not render a director interested.[47]

To meet prong (2) of *Aronson*, a plaintiff has to plead particularized facts creating a reasonable doubt that a majority of the board was (a) adequately informed when making the challenged decision or, (b) honestly and good faith believed that the challenged decision was in the best interests of the corporation. As explained by the court in *Khan v. Tremont*, the second prong of *Aronson* is "directed to extreme cases in which despite the appearance of independence and disinterest a decision is so extreme or curious as to itself raise a legitimate ground to justify further inquiry and judicial review."[48]

The test for demand futility with respect to a failure to provide oversight, or *Caremark*, claim was established by *Rales v. Blasband*[49] as follows:

whether or not the particularized factual allegations of a derivative stockholder complaint create a reasonable doubt that, as of the time the complaint was filed, the board of directors could have properly exercised its independent and disinterested business judgment in responding to a demand. If the derivative plaintiff satisfies this burden, then demand will be excused as futile.[50]

---

45. *Id.* at 814.
46. See *Brehm v. Eisner*, 746 A.2d 244, 256 (Del. 2000).
47. *Aronson*, 473 A.2d at 818.
48. *Kahn v. Tremont Corp.*, 1994 WL 162613, at *6 (Del. Ch. 1994).
49. *Rales v. Blasband*, 634 A.2d 927 (Del. 1993).
50. *Id.* at 934.

In other words, it is basically prong (1) of the *Aronson* test. Prong (2) of *Aronson* is inapplicable because in the *Caremark* context there is no board decision at issue.

Note that a court determines demand futility based solely on the plaintiff's complaint. In other words, plaintiffs are not entitled to discovery. As a result, plaintiffs will often find it difficult to meet the particularization requirement. Most plaintiffs nonetheless conclude that it is better to go the demand futility route than to make a demand. This is because courts have held that by making a demand a plaintiff tacitly admits that a majority of the board is disinterested and independent with respect to evaluating the demand. Thus, if the board rejects the demand (as expected), the plaintiff is basically left with claiming the board's decision to reject the demand was irrational, that is, the plaintiff has to meet the waste standard, or was made in bad faith. Most plaintiffs will conclude that they are more likely to succeed by arguing lack of disinterestedness or independence than waste or bad faith.

The next case involves application of both the *Aronson* and *Rales* tests. It also serves somewhat as a summation of current Delaware director fiduciary duty law.

In re Goldman Sachs Group, Inc. Shareholder Litigation
2011 WL 4826104 (Del. Ch. 2011)

GLASSCOCK, Vice Chancellor.

The Delaware General Corporation Law is, for the most part, enabling in nature. It provides corporate directors and officers with broad discretion to act as they find appropriate in the conduct of corporate affairs. It is therefore left to Delaware case law to set a boundary on that otherwise unconstrained realm of action. The restrictions imposed by Delaware case law set this boundary by requiring corporate officers and directors to act as faithful fiduciaries to the corporation and its stockholders. Should these corporate actors perform in such a way that they are violating their fiduciary obligations — their core duties of care or loyalty — their faithless acts properly become the subject of judicial action in vindication of the rights of the stockholders. Within the boundary of fiduciary duty, however, these corporate actors are free to pursue corporate opportunities in any way that, in the exercise of their business judgment on behalf of the corporation, they see fit. It is this broad freedom to pursue opportunity on behalf of the corporation, in the myriad ways that may be revealed to creative human minds, that has made the corporate structure a supremely effective engine for the production of wealth. Exercising that freedom is precisely what directors and officers are elected by their shareholders to do. So long as such individuals act within the boundaries of their fiduciary duties, judges are ill-suited by training (and should be disinclined by temperament) to secondguess the business decisions of those chosen by the stockholders to fulfill precisely that function. This case, as in so many corporate matters considered by this Court, involves whether actions taken by certain director defendants fall outside of the fiduciary boundaries existing under Delaware case law—and are therefore subject to judicial oversight—or whether the acts complained of are within those broad boundaries, where a law-trained judge should refrain from acting.

This matter is before me on a motion to dismiss, pursuant to Court of Chancery Rule 23.1, for failure to make a pre-suit demand upon the board.... The Plaintiffs contend that Goldman's compensation structure created a divergence of interest between Goldman's management and its stockholders. The Plaintiffs allege that because Goldman's directors have consistently based compensation for the firm's management on a percentage of net revenue, Goldman's employees had a motivation to grow net revenue at any cost and without regard to risk.

The Plaintiffs allege that under this compensation structure, Goldman's employees would attempt to maximize short-term profits, thus increasing their bonuses at the expense of stockholders' interests. The Plaintiffs contend that Goldman's employees would do this by engaging in highly risky trading practices and by over-leveraging the company's assets. If these practices turned a profit, Goldman's employees would receive a windfall; however, losses would fall on the stockholders.

The Plaintiffs allege that the Director Defendants breached their fiduciary duties by approving the compensation structure discussed above. Additionally, the Plaintiffs claim that the payments under this compensation structure constituted corporate waste. Finally, the Plaintiffs assert that this compensation structure led to overly-risky business decisions and unethical and illegal practices, and that the Director Defendants failed to satisfy their oversight responsibilities with regard to those practices.

The Defendants seek dismissal of this action on the grounds that the Plaintiffs have failed to make a pre-suit demand on the board.... For the reasons stated below, I find that the Plaintiffs' complaint must be dismissed.

I. FACTS

The facts below are taken from the second amended complaint. All reasonable inferences are drawn in the Plaintiffs' favor.

A. Parties

Co-Lead plaintiffs Southeastern Pennsylvania Transportation Authority and International Brotherhood of Electrical Workers Local 98 Pension Fund ("the Plaintiffs") are stockholders of Goldman Sachs Group, Inc. ("Goldman"), and have continuously held Goldman stock during all relevant times.

Defendant Goldman is a global financial services firm which provides investment banking, securities, and investment management services to consumers, businesses, and governments. Goldman is a Delaware corporation with its principal executive offices in New York, NY.

The complaint also names fourteen individual current and former directors and officers of Goldman as defendants: Lloyd C. Blankfein, Gary D. Cohn,

John H. Bryan, Claes Dahlback, Stephen Friedman, William W. George, Rajat K. Gupta, James A. Johnson, Lois D. Juliber, Lakshmi N. Mittal, James J. Schiro, Ruth J. Simmons, David A. Viniar, and J. Michael Evans (together with Goldman, "the Defendants").

Blankfein, Cohn, Bryan, Dahlback, Friedman, George, Gupta, Johnson, Juliber, Mittal, Schiro, and Simmons are current and former directors of Goldman, and are collectively referred to as the "Director Defendants." Evans and Viniar are officers of the company; Evans, Viniar, Cohn, and Blankfein are collectively referred to as the "Executive Officer Defendants." Bryan, Dahlback, Friedman, George, Gutpa, Johnson, Juliber, Mittal, and Schiro served as members of the Board's Audit Committee (collectively, the "Audit Committee Defendants"). Finally, defendants Byran, Dahlback, Friedman, George, Gutpa, Johnson, Juliber, Mittal, Schiro, and Simmons served as members of the Board's Compensation Committee, and are collectively referred to as the "Compensation Committee Defendants."

B. Background

Goldman engages in three principal business segments: investment banking, asset management and securities services, and trading and principal investments. The majority of Goldman's revenue comes from the trading and principal investment segment. In that segment Goldman engages in market making, structuring and entering into a variety of derivative transactions, and the proprietary trading of financial instruments.

Since going public in 1999, Goldman's total assets under management and common stockholder equity have substantially increased. In 1999, Goldman had $258 billion of assets under management and $10 billion of common shareholder equity. By 2010, those numbers had grown to $881 billion of assets under management and $72.94 billion of common shareholder equity. Corresponding with this increase in assets under management and common shareholder equity was a hike in the percentage of Goldman's revenue that was generated by the trading and principal investment segment. In 1999, the trading and principal investment segment generated 43% of Goldman's revenue; by 2007 the segment generated over 76% of Goldman's revenue.

As the revenue generated by the trading and principal investment segment grew, so did the trading department's stature within Goldman. The traders "became wealthier and more powerful in the bank." The Plaintiffs allege that the compensation for these traders was not based on performance and was unjustifiable because Goldman was doing "nothing more than compensat[ing] employees for results produced by the vast amounts of shareholder equity that Goldman ha[d] available to be deployed."

C. Compensation

Goldman employed a "pay for performance" philosophy linking the total compensation of its employees to the company's performance. Goldman has used a Compensation Committee since at least 2006 to oversee the development and implementation of its compensation scheme. The Compensation Committee was responsible for reviewing and approving the Goldman executives' annual compensation. To fulfill their charge, the Compensation Committee consulted with senior management about management's projections of net revenues and the proper ratio of compensation and benefits expenses to net revenues (the "compensation ratio"). Additionally, the Compensation Committee compared Goldman's compensation ratio to that of Goldman's competitors such as Bear Stearns, Lehman Brothers, Merrill Lynch, and Morgan Stanley. The Compensation Committee would then approve a ratio and structure that Goldman would use to govern Goldman's compensation to its employees.

The Plaintiffs allege that from 2007 through 2009, the Director Defendants approved a management-proposed compensation structure that caused management's interests to diverge from those of the stockholders. According to the Plaintiffs, in each year since 2006 the Compensation Committee approved the management-determined compensation ratio, which governed "the total amount of funds available to compensate all employees including senior executives," without any analysis. Although the total compensation paid by Goldman varied significantly each year, total compensation as a percentage of net revenue remained relatively constant. Because management was awarded a relatively constant percentage of total revenue, management could maximize their compensation by increasing Goldman's total net revenue and total stockholder equity. The Plaintiffs contend that this compensation structure led management to pursue a highly risky business strategy that emphasized short term profits in order to increase their yearly bonuses.

D. Business Risk

The Plaintiffs allege that management achieved Goldman's growth "through extreme leverage and significant uncontrolled exposure to risky loans and credit risks." The trading and principal investment segment is the largest contributor to Goldman's total revenues; it is also the segment to which Goldman commits the largest amount of capital. The Plaintiffs argue that this was a risky use of Goldman's assets, pointing out that Goldman's Value at Risk (VAR) increased between 2007 and 2009, and that in 2007 Goldman had a leverage ratio of 25 to 1, exceeding that of its peers.

The Plaintiffs charge that this business strategy was not in the best interest of the stockholders, in part, because the stockholders did not benefit to the same degree that management did. Stockholders received roughly 2 percent of the revenue generated in the form of dividends—but if the investment went south, it was the stockholders' equity at risk, not that of the traders.

The Plaintiffs point to Goldman's performance in 2008 as evidence of these alleged diverging interests. In that year, "the Trading and Principal Investment segment produced $9.06 billion in net revenue, but as a result of discretionary bonuses paid to employees *lost* more than $2.7 billion." This contributed to

Goldman's 2008 net income falling by $9.3 billion. The Plaintiffs contend that, but for a cash infusion from Warren Buffett, federal government intervention and Goldman's conversion into a bank holding company, Goldman would have gone into bankruptcy.

The Plaintiffs acknowledge that during this time Goldman had an Audit Committee in charge of overseeing risk. The Audit Committee's purpose was to assist the board in overseeing "the Company's management of market, credit, liquidity, and other financial and operational risks." The Audit Committee was also required to review, along with management, the financial information that was provided to analysts and ratings agencies and to discuss "management's assessment of the Company's market, credit, liquidity and other financial and operational risks, and the guidelines, policies and processes for managing such risks."

In addition to having an Audit Committee in place, Goldman managed risk associated with the trading and principal investment section by hedging its positions—sometimes taking positions opposite to the clients that it was investing with, advising, and financing. Since 2002, Goldman has acknowledged that possible conflicts could occur and that it seeks to "manage" these conflicts. The Plaintiffs allege that if the Audit Committee had been properly functioning, the board should have been forewarned about conflicts of interest between Goldman and its clients.

The Plaintiffs contend that these conflicts of interest came to a head during the mortgage and housing crisis. In December 2006, Goldman's CFO, in a meeting with Goldman's mortgage traders and risk managers, concluded that the firm was over-exposed to the subprime mortgage market and decided to reduce Goldman's overall exposure. In 2007, as the housing market began to decline, a committee of senior executives, including Viniar, Cohn, and Blankfein, took an active role in monitoring and overseeing the mortgage unit. The committee's job was to examine mortgage products and transactions while protecting Goldman against risky deals. The committee eventually decided to take positions that would allow Goldman to profit if housing prices declined. When the subprime mortgage markets collapsed, not only were Goldman's long positions hedged, Goldman actually profited more from its short positions than it lost from its long positions. The Plaintiffs allege that Goldman's profits resulted from positions that conflicted with its clients' interests to the detriment of the company's reputation.

As an example of these conflicts of interest, the Plaintiffs point to the infamous Abacus transaction. In the Abacus transaction, hedge fund manager John Paulson, a Goldman client, had a role in selecting the mortgages that would ultimately be used to back a collateralized debt obligation (CDO). Paulson took a short position that would profit if the CDO fell in value. Goldman sold the long positions to other clients without disclosing Paulson's involvement. On April 16, 2010, the SEC charged Goldman and a Goldman employee with fraud for their actions related to the Abacus transaction. On July 14, 2010, Goldman settled the case with the SEC and agreed to pay a civil penalty of $535 million and to disgorge the $15 million in profits it made on the transaction. Goldman also agreed to review its internal processes related to mortgage securities transactions.

To demonstrate further examples of conflicts of interest, the Plaintiffs rely on a April 26, 2010 memorandum, from Senators Carl Levin and Tom Coburn to the Members of the Permanent Subcommittee on Investigations, entitled "Wall Street and the Financial Crisis: The Role of Investment Banks" ("Permanent Subcommittee Report"), that highlighted three mortgage-related products that Goldman sold to its clients. These transactions involved synthetic CDOs, where Goldman sold long positions to clients while Goldman took the short positions. Unlike the Abacus transaction, these three transactions did not end with SEC involvement, but the Plaintiffs allege that investors who lost money are "reviewing their options, including possibly bringing lawsuits."

E. The Plaintiffs' Claims

The Plaintiffs allege that the Director Defendants breached their fiduciary duties by (1) failing to properly analyze and rationally set compensation levels for Goldman's employees and (2) committing waste by "approving a compensation ratio to Goldman employees in an amount so disproportionately large to the contribution of management, as opposed to capital as to be unconscionable."

The Plaintiffs also allege that the Director Defendants violated their fiduciary duties by failing to adequately monitor Goldman's operations and by "allowing the Firm to manage and conduct the Firm's trading in a grossly unethical manner."

II. LEGAL STANDARDS

The Plaintiffs have brought this action derivatively on behalf of Goldman "to redress the breaches of fiduciary duty and other violations of law by [the] Defendants." The Defendants have moved to dismiss, pursuant to Court of Chancery Rule 23.1, for failure to make a pre-suit demand upon the board. . . .

C. Demand Futility

If, as here, a stockholder does not first demand that the directors pursue the alleged cause of action, he must establish that demand is excused by satisfying "stringent [pleading] requirements of factual particularity" by "set[ting] forth particularized factual statements that are essential to the claim" in order to demonstrate that making demand would be futile. Pre-suit demand is futile if a corporation's board is "deemed incapable of making an impartial decision regarding the pursuit of the litigation."

Under the two-pronged test, first explicated in *Aronson,* when a plaintiff challenges a conscious decision of the board, a plaintiff can show demand futility by alleging particularized facts that create a reasonable doubt that either (1) the directors are disinterested and independent or (2) "the challenged transaction was otherwise the product of a valid exercise of business judgment."

On the other hand, when a plaintiff complains of board *inaction,* "there is no 'challenged transaction,' and the ordinary *Aronson* analysis does not apply." Instead, the board's inaction is analyzed under *Rales v. Blasband.* Under the *Rales* test, a plaintiff must plead particularized facts that "create a reasonable doubt that, as of the time the complaint [was] filed, the board of directors could have properly exercised its independent and disinterested business judgment in responding to a demand."

Here, the Plaintiffs concede that they have not made demand upon Goldman's board of directors, but they assert that such demand would be futile for numerous reasons. First, they argue that Goldman's board of directors is interested or lacks independence because of financial ties between the Director Defendants and Goldman. Next, they allege that there is a reasonable doubt as to whether the board's compensation structure was the product of a valid exercise of business judgment. The Plaintiffs further assert that there is a substantial likelihood that the Director Defendants will face personal liability for the dereliction of their duty to oversee Goldman's operations.

I evaluate the Plaintiffs' claims involving active decisions by the board under *Aronson.* I evaluate the Plaintiffs' oversight claims against the Director Defendants for the failure to monitor Goldman's operations under *Rales.*

III. ANALYSIS

A. *Approval of the Compensation Scheme*

The Plaintiffs challenge the Goldman board's approval of the company's compensation scheme on three grounds. They allege (1) that the majority of the board was interested or lacked independence when it approved the compensation scheme, (2) the board did not otherwise validly exercise its business judgment, and (3) the board's approval of the compensation scheme constituted waste. Because the approval of the compensation scheme was a conscious decision by the board, the Plaintiffs must satisfy the *Aronson* test to successfully plead demand futility. I find that under all three of their challenges to the board's approval of the compensation scheme, the Plaintiffs have failed to adequately plead demand futility.

1. *INDEPENDENCE AND DISINTERESTEDNESS OF THE BOARD*

A plaintiff successfully pleads demand futility under the first prong of *Aronson* when he alleges particularized facts that create a reasonable doubt that "a 'majority' of the directors could [have] impartially consider[ed] a demand" either because they were interested or lacked independence, as of the time that suit was filed.[51] Generally, "[a] director's interest may be shown by demonstrating a potential personal benefit or detriment to the director as a result of the

---

51. [FN 71] *Beneville v. York,* 769 A.2d 80, 82 (Del. Ch. 2000).

decision."[52] A director is independent if the "director's decision is based on the corporate merits of the subject before the board rather than extraneous considerations or influences."[53]

When the complaint was originally filed, Goldman's board had 12 directors: Blankfein, Cohn, Bryan, Dahlback, Friedman, George, Gupta, Johnson, Juliber, Mittal, Schiro, and Simmons. The Plaintiffs fail to allege that George and Schiro were interested or lacked independence. It can be assumed that Blankfein and Cohn, as officials of Goldman, would be found to be interested or lack independence. Therefore, the Plaintiffs must satisfy *Aronson* with respect to at least four of the remaining eight directors.

The Plaintiffs argue that demand is excused because a majority of the Director Defendants lacked independence or were interested as a result of significant financial relationships with Goldman. The Plaintiffs contend that directors Bryan, Friedman, Gupta, Johnson, Juliber, and Simmons were interested because the private Goldman Sachs Foundation ("the Goldman Foundation") has made contributions to charitable organizations that the directors were affiliated with. The Plaintiffs assert that directors Dahlback, Friedman, and Mittal were interested because of financial interactions with Goldman.

Below I provide the specific allegations found in the complaint about the Director Defendants. Since the Plaintiffs do not allege that the Director Defendants (aside from Blankfein and Cohn) were interested in the compensation decisions, I analyze whether the director lacks independence.

a. Directors and Charitable Contributions

i. John H. Bryan

Bryan has served as a Goldman director since 1999. He was also a member of Goldman's Audit Committee and Goldman's Compensation Committee. His charitable works included chairing a successful campaign to raise $100 million for the renovation of the Chicago Lyric Opera House and Orchestra Hall, and acting as a life trustee of the University of Chicago. The Plaintiffs state that part of Bryan's responsibility, as a trustee, was to raise money for the University. The Plaintiffs note that Goldman has made "substantial contributions" to the campaign to renovate the Chicago Lyric Opera House and Orchestra Hall and that the Goldman Foundation donated $200,000 to the University in 2006 and allocated an additional $200,000 in 2007.

The Plaintiffs allege that because Goldman and the Goldman Foundation have assisted Bryan in his fund raising responsibilities, Bryan lacks independence.

This Court has previously addressed directorial independence and charitable contributions. *Hallmark*[54] involved a special committee member who served on a variety of charitable boards where the charity received donations from the

---

52. [FN 72] *Beam v. Stewart*, 845 A.2d 1040, 1049 (Del. 2004).
53. [FN 73] *Aronson v. Lewis*, 473 A.2d 805, 816 (Del. 1984).
54. [FN 83] *S. Muoio & Co. LLC v. Hallmark Entm't Inv. Co.*, 2011 WL 863007 (Del. Ch. Mar. 9, 2011).

defendant corporation. The *Hallmark* Court noted that, even though part of the member's role was to act as a fund raiser, the member did not receive a salary for his work and did not actively solicit donations from the defendant corporation; therefore, the plaintiff failed to sufficiently show that the member was incapable of "exercising independent judgment."

This Court also addressed charitable contributions in *J.P. Morgan.*[55] In that case, the plaintiff challenged the independence of a director who was the President and a trustee of the American Natural History Museum, another director who was a trustee of the American Natural History Museum, and a director who was the President and CEO of the United Negro College Fund. The plaintiff alleged that because the defendant corporation made donations to these organizations and was a significant benefactor, the directors lacked independence. The Court decided that without additional facts showing, for instance, how the donations would affect the decision making of the directors or what percentage of the overall contribution was represented by the corporation's donations, the plaintiff had failed to demonstrate that the directors were not independent.

In the case at bar, nothing more can be inferred from the complaint than the facts that the Goldman Foundation made donations to a charity that Bryan served as trustee, that part of Bryan's role as a trustee was to raise money, and that Goldman made donations to another charity where Bryan chaired a renovation campaign. The Plaintiffs do not allege that Bryan received a salary for either of his philanthropic roles, that the donations made by the Goldman Foundation or Goldman were the result of active solicitation by Bryan, or that Bryan had other substantial dealings with Goldman or the Goldman Foundation. The Plaintiffs do not provide the ratios of the amounts donated by Goldman, or the Goldman Foundation, to overall donations, or any other information demonstrating that the amount would be material to the charity. Crucially, the Plaintiffs fail to provide any information on how the amounts given influenced Bryan's decision-making process. Because the complaint lacks such particularized details, the Plaintiffs have failed to create a reasonable doubt as to Bryan's independence.

ii. Rajat K. Gupta

Gupta has served as a Goldman director since 2006. He was also a member of Goldman's Audit Committee and Goldman's Compensation Committee. Gupta is chairman of the board of the Indian School of Business, to which the Goldman Foundation has donated $1.6 million since 2002. Gupta is also a member of the dean's advisory board of Tsinghua University School of Economics and Management, to which the Foundation has donated at least $3.5 million since 2002. Finally, Gupta is a member of the United Nations Commission on the Private Sector and Development and he is a special advisor to the UN Secretary General on UN Reform. Since 2002, the Foundation has donated around $1.6

---

55. [FN 85] *In re J.P. Morgan Chase & Co. S'holder Litig.*, 906 A.2d 808, 808.

million to the Model UN program. The Plaintiffs allege that as "a member of these boards and commission, it is part of Gupta's job to raise money."

The Plaintiffs challenge to Gupta's independence fails for reasons similar to Bryan's. The Plaintiffs allegations only provide information that shows that Gupta was engaged in philanthropic activities and that the Goldman foundation made donations to charities to which Gupta had ties. The Plaintiffs do not mention the materiality of the donations to the charities or any solicitation on the part of Gupta. The Plaintiffs do not state how Gupta's decision-making was altered by the donations. Without such particularized allegations, the Plaintiffs fail to raise a reasonable doubt that Gupta was independent.

iii. James A. Johnson

Johnson has served as a Goldman director since 1999. He was also a member of Goldman's Audit Committee and Goldman's Compensation Committee. Johnson is an honorary trustee of the Brookings Institution. The Plaintiffs allege that part of Johnson's role as a trustee is to raise money and that the Foundation donated $100,000 to the Brookings Institution in 2006.

Again the Plaintiffs fail to provide any information other than that a director was affiliated with a charity and the Goldman Foundation made a donation to that charity. Without more, the Plaintiffs fail to provide particularized factual allegations that create a reasonable doubt in regards to Johnson's independence.

iv. Lois D. Juliber

Juliber has served as a Goldman director since 2004. She was also a member of Goldman's Audit Committee and Goldman's Compensation Committee. Juliber is a member of the board of Girls Incorporated, a charitable organization, to which the Plaintiffs contend that the Goldman Foundation donated $400,000 during 2006 and 2007. The Plaintiffs allege that part of Juliber's job as a Girls Incorporated board member is to raise money.

For the same reasons that the Plaintiffs' allegations fall short for directors Bryan, Gupta, and Johnson, the Plaintiffs' allegations fall short here. The Plaintiffs do not plead facts sufficient to create a reasonable doubt whether Juliber was independent.

v. Ruth J. Simmons

Simmons has served as a Goldman director since 2000. She was also a member of Goldman's Compensation Committee. Simmons is President of Brown University, and the Plaintiffs allege that part of her job is to raise money for the University. The Plaintiffs note that "[t]he [Goldman] Foundation has pledged funding in an undisclosed amount to share in the support of a position of Program Director at The Swearer Center for Public Service at Brown University," and so far $200,000 has been allocated to this project.

Simmons differs from the other directors in that, rather than sitting on a charitable board, as the other defendants do, Simmons' livelihood as President of Brown University does directly depend on her fundraising abilities; however, the Plaintiffs fail to allege particularized factual allegations that create a reasonable doubt that Simmons was independent.

The Plaintiffs provide the amount donated to Brown University, but do not give any additional information showing the materiality of the donation to Brown University. The Plaintiffs do not provide the percentage this amount represented of the total amount raised by Brown, or even how this amount was material to the Swearer Center. Additionally, the Plaintiffs' allegations do not provide information that Simmons actively solicited this amount or how this or potential future donations would affect Simmons. The facts pled are insufficient to raise the inference that Simmons feels obligated to the foundation or Goldman management. Consequently, the factual allegations pled by the Plaintiffs fail to raise a reasonable doubt that, despite Simmons's position as President of Brown University, she remained independent.

b. Directors with Other Alleged Interests

The Plaintiffs allege that three directors have, in addition (in the case of Mr. Friedman) to charitable connections to Goldman or the Goldman Foundation, business dealings with Goldman that render them dependent for purposes of the first prong of the *Aronson* analysis. Having already found that a majority of the Goldman board was independent, I could simply omit analysis of the independence of these directors under *Aronson*. I will briefly address the Plaintiffs' contentions with respect to the directors below.

i. Stephen Friedman

Friedman has served as a Goldman director since 2005. He was also a member of Goldman's Audit Committee and Goldman's Compensation Committee. The Plaintiffs allege that Friedman lacks independence for two reasons. First, the Plaintiffs allege that Friedman is not independent because of his philanthropic work and Goldman's advancement thereof. Second, the Plaintiffs allege that Friedman is not independent due to his business dealings with Goldman.

Friedman is an emeritus trustee of Columbia University. The Plaintiffs contend that part of his job as a trustee is to raise money for Columbia University and that since 2002 the Goldman foundation has donated at least $765,000 to Columbia University

Taken by themselves, the facts pled, concerning Friedman's charitable connection to the Goldman Foundation, are insufficient to create a reasonable doubt that Friedman was independent. Similar to the Plaintiffs' other allegations concerning defendants with charitable connections to the Goldman Foundation, the Plaintiffs only allege that Friedman is a trustee of Columbia University, that part of his job as a trustee is to raise money, and that the Foundation has donated money to the University. The complaint fails to allege that

Friedman solicited money from the Goldman Foundation, that he receives any salary for his work as trustee, or that he had any substantial dealings with the Goldman Foundation.

Besides their allegations concerning Friedman's charitable endeavors, the Plaintiffs also allege that Goldman "*has* invested at least $670 million in funds managed by Friedman." This is the entirety of the pleadings regarding Friedman's business involvement with Goldman. Contrary to the contentions in the Plaintiffs' Answering Brief, the complaint does not allege that Friedman relies on the management of these funds for his livelihood; that contention, if buttressed by factual allegations in the complaint, might reasonably demonstrate lack of independence. The complaint is insufficient, as written, for that purpose.

ii. Claes Dahlback

Dahlback has served as a Goldman director since 2003. He was also a member of Goldman's Audit Committee and Goldman's Compensation Committee. Besides serving on Goldman's board, Dahlback is a senior advisor to an entity described in the complaint as "Investor AB." The Plaintiffs note that Goldman has invested more than $600 million in funds to which Dahlback is an adviser (presumably, but not explicitly, Investor AB). The Plaintiffs contend that because Dahlback had substantial financial relationships with Goldman, he lacked independence.

The Plaintiffs' allegations regarding Dahlback are sparse and tenuous. "[T]he complaint contains no allegations of fact tending to show that [any] fees paid were material to [Dahlback]." The Plaintiffs only note that Dahlback is an advisor to Investor AB, and that Goldman has invested more than $600 million in funds with an entity to which Dahlback is an advisor. Contrary to the statements by the Plaintiffs in the answering brief, the complaint does not allege that Dahlback's "livelihood depends on his full-time job as an advisor." The Plaintiffs fail to allege that Dahlback derives a substantial benefit from being an advisor to Investor AB, that Dahlback solicited funds from Goldman, that Investor AB received funds because of Dahlback's involvement, or any other fact that would tend to raise a reasonable doubt that Dahlback's future employment with Investor AB is independent of Goldman's investment. As with defendant Friedman, the pleadings are insufficient to raise a reasonable doubt as to Dahlback's independence.

iii. Lakshmi N. Mittal

Mittal has served as a Goldman director since 2008. He was also a member of Goldman's Audit Committee and Goldman's Compensation Committee. Mittal is the chairman and CEO of ArcelorMittal. The Plaintiffs allege that "Goldman has arranged or provided billions of euros in financing to his company" and that "[d]uring 2007 and 2008 alone, the Company had made loans to AcelorMittal [sic] in the aggregate amount of 464 million euros."

Goldman is an investment bank. The fact "[t]hat it provided financing to large . . . companies should come as no shock to anyone. Yet this is all that the plaintiffs allege." The Plaintiffs fail to plead facts that show anything other than a series of market transactions occurred between ArcelorMittal and Goldman. For instance, the Plaintiffs have not alleged that ArcelorMittal is receiving a discounted interest rate on the loans from Goldman, that Mittal was unable to receive financing from any other lender, or that loans from Goldman compose a substantial part of ArcelorMittal's funding. The pleadings fail to raise a reasonable doubt as to the independence of Mittal.

B. Otherwise the Product of a Valid Exercise of Business Judgment

Having determined that the Plaintiffs have not pled particularized factual allegations that raise a reasonable doubt as to a majority of the Director Defendants' disinterestedness and independence, I must now apply the second prong of *Aronson* and determine whether the Plaintiffs have pled particularized facts that raise a reasonable doubt that Goldman's compensation scheme was otherwise the product of a valid exercise of business judgment. To successfully plead demand futility under the second prong of *Aronson,* the Plaintiffs must allege "particularized facts sufficient to raise (1) a reason to doubt that the action was taken honestly and in good faith or (2) a reason to doubt that the board was adequately informed in making the decision."[56] Goldman's charter has an 8 Del. C. §102(b)(7) provision, providing that the directors are exculpated from liability except for claims based on "bad faith" conduct; therefore, the Plaintiffs must also plead particularized facts that demonstrate that the directors acted with scienter; i.e., there was an "intentional dereliction of duty" or "a conscious disregard" for their responsibilities, amounting to bad faith.[57]

The Plaintiffs assert that the Director Defendants owed "a fiduciary duty to assess continually Goldman's compensation scheme to ensure that it reasonably compensated employees and reasonably allocated the profit of Goldman's activities according to the contributions of shareholder capital and the employees of the Company." The Plaintiffs contend that the entire compensation structure put in place by the Director Defendants was done in bad faith and that the Director Defendants were not properly informed when making compensation awards. I find that the Plaintiffs have not provided particularized factual allegations that raise a reasonable doubt whether the process by which Goldman's compensation scheme allocated profits between the employees and shareholders was implemented in good faith and on an informed basis.

1. Good Faith

"[A] failure to act in good faith requires conduct that is qualitatively different from, and more culpable than, the conduct giving rise to a violation of the

---

56. [FN 127] *J.P. Morgan,* 906 A.2d at 824 (quoting *In re Walt Disney Co. Derivative Litig.,* 825 A.2d 275, 286 (Del. Ch. 2003) (*Disney II*)).

57. [FN 128] *In re Walt Disney Co. Derivative Litig.,* 907 A.2d 693, 755 (Del. Ch. 2005) (*Disney III*).

fiduciary duty of care (i.e., gross negligence)."[58] Examples of this include situations where the fiduciary intentionally breaks the law, "where the fiduciary intentionally acts with a purpose other than that of advancing the best interests of the corporation," or "where the fiduciary intentionally fails to act in the face of a known duty to act, demonstrating a conscious disregard for his duties."[59] While this is not an exclusive list, "these three are the most salient."[60]

The third category above falls between "conduct motivated by subjective bad intent," and "conduct resulting from gross negligence."[61] "Conscious disregard" involves an "intentional dereliction of duty" which is "more culpable than simple inattention or failure to be informed of all facts material to the decision."[62]

The Plaintiffs' main contention is that Goldman's compensation scheme itself was approved in bad faith. The Plaintiffs allege that "[n]o person acting in good faith on behalf of Goldman consistently could approve the payment of between 44 percent and 48 percent of net revenues to Goldman's employees year in and year out" and that accordingly the Director Defendants abdicated their duties by engaging in these "practices that overcompensate management." The complaint is entirely silent with respect to any individual salary or bonus; the Plaintiffs' allegation is that the scheme so misaligns incentives that it cannot have been the product of a good faith board decision.

The Plaintiffs' problems with the compensation plan structure can be summarized as follows: Goldman's compensation plan is a positive feedback loop where employees reap the benefits but the stockholders bear the losses. Goldman's plan incentivizes employees to leverage Goldman's assets and engage in risky behavior in order to maximize yearly net revenue and their yearly bonuses. At the end of the year, the remaining revenue that is not paid as compensation, with the exception of small dividend payments to stockholders, is funneled back into the company. This increases the quantity of assets Goldman employees have available to leverage and invest. Goldman employees then start the process over with a greater asset base, increase net revenue again, receive even larger paychecks the next year, and the cycle continues. At the same time, stockholders are only receiving a small percentage of net revenue as dividends; therefore, the majority of the stockholders' assets are simply being cycled back into Goldman for the Goldman employees to use.

The stockholders' and Goldman employees' interests diverge most notably, argue the Plaintiffs, when there is a drop in revenue. If net revenues fall, the stockholders lose their equity, but the Goldman employees do not share this loss.

The decision as to how much compensation is appropriate to retain and incentivize employees, both individually and in the aggregate, is a core function

---

58. [FN 131] *Stone v. Ritter*, 911 A.2d 362, 369 (Del. 2006).
59. [FN 132] *In re Walt Disney Co. Derivative Litig.*, 906 A.2d 27, 67 (Del. 2006) (*Disney IV*).
60. [FN 133] *Id.*
61. [FN 134] *Id.* at 66.
62. [FN 135] *Id.*

of a board of directors exercising its business judgment. The Plaintiffs' pleadings fall short of creating a reasonable doubt that the Directors Defendants have failed to exercise that judgment here. The Plaintiffs acknowledge that the compensation plan authorized by Goldman's board, which links compensation to revenue produced, was intended to align employee interests with those of the stockholders and incentivize the production of wealth. To an extent, it does so: extra effort by employees to raise corporate revenue, if successful, is rewarded. The Plaintiffs' allegations mainly propose that the compensation scheme implemented by the board does not perfectly align these interests; and that, in fact, it may encourage employee behavior incongruent with the stockholders' interest. This may be correct, but it is irrelevant. The fact that the Plaintiffs may desire a different compensation scheme does not indicate that equitable relief is warranted. Such changes may be accomplished through directorial elections, but not, absent a showing unmet here, through this Court.

Allocating compensation as a percentage of net revenues does not make it virtually inevitable that management will work against the interests of the stockholders. Here, management was only taking a percentage of the net revenues. The remainder of the net revenues was funneled back into the company in order to create future revenues; therefore, management and stockholder interests were aligned. Management would increase its compensation by increasing revenues, and stockholders would own a part of a company which has more assets available to create future wealth.

The Plaintiffs' focus on percentages ignores the reality that over the past 10 years, in absolute terms, Goldman's net revenue and dividends have substantially increased. Management's compensation is based on net revenues. Management's ability to generate that revenue is a function of the total asset base, which means management has an interest in maintaining that base (owned, of course, by the Plaintiffs and fellow shareholders) in order to create future revenues upon which its future earnings rely.

The Plaintiffs argue that there was an intentional dereliction of duty or a conscious disregard by the Director Defendants in setting compensation levels; however, the Plaintiffs fail to plead with particularity that any of the Director Defendants had the scienter necessary to give rise to a violation of the duty of loyalty. The Plaintiffs do not allege that the board failed to employ a metric to set compensation levels; rather, they merely argue that a different metric, such as comparing Goldman's compensation to that of hedge fund managers rather than to compensation at other investment banks, would have yielded a better result. But this observance does not make the board's decision self-evidently wrong, and it does not raise a reasonable doubt that the board approved Goldman's compensation structure in good faith.

2. ADEQUATELY INFORMED

The Plaintiffs also contend that the board was uninformed in making its compensation decision. "Pre-suit demand will be excused in a derivative suit only if the . . . particularized facts in the complaint create a reasonable doubt that the informational component of the directors' decisionmaking process, *measured by concepts of gross negligence,* included consideration of all material information reasonably available."[63] Here, Goldman's charter has a 8 Del. C. §102(b)(7) provision, so gross negligence, by itself, is insufficient basis upon which to impose liability. The Plaintiffs must allege particularized facts creating a reasonable doubt that the directors acted in good faith.

The Plaintiffs allege that the Director Defendants fell short of this reasonableness standard in several ways. They point out that the Director Defendants never "analyzed or assessed the extent to which management performance, as opposed to the ever-growing shareholder equity and assets available for investment, has contributed to the generation of net revenues." The Plaintiffs also argue that because the amount of stockholder equity and assets available for investment was responsible for the total revenue generated, the Director Defendants should have used other metrics, such as compensation levels at shareholder funds and hedge funds, to decide compensation levels at Goldman. The Plaintiffs allege that Goldman's performance, on a risk adjusted basis, lagged behind hedge fund competitors, yet the percentage of net revenue awarded did not substantially vary, and that the Director Defendants never adequately adjusted compensation in anticipation of resolving future claims.

Nonetheless, the Plaintiffs acknowledge that Goldman has a compensation committee that reviews and approves the annual compensation of Goldman's executives. The Plaintiffs also acknowledge that Goldman has adopted a "pay for performance" philosophy, that Goldman represents as a way to align employee and shareholder interests. The Plaintiffs further acknowledge that Goldman's compensation committee receives information from Goldman's management concerning Goldman's net revenues and the ratio of compensation and benefits expenses to net revenues. Finally, the Plaintiffs note that the compensation committee reviewed information relating to the compensation ratio of Goldman's "core competitors that are investment banks (Bear Stearns, Lehman Brothers, Merrill Lynch, and Morgan Stanley)."

Rather than suggesting that the Director Defendants acted on an uninformed basis, the Plaintiffs' pleadings indicate that the board adequately informed itself before making a decision on compensation. The Director Defendants considered other investment bank comparables, varied the total percent and the total dollar amount awarded as compensation, and changed the total amount of compensation in response to changing public opinion. None of the Plaintiffs' allegations suggests gross negligence on the part of the Director Defendants, and the conduct described in the Plaintiffs' allegations certainly does not rise to the level of bad faith such that the Director Defendants would lose the protection of an 8 Del. C. §102(b)(7) exculpatory provision.

At most, the Plaintiffs' allegations suggest that there were other metrics not considered by the board that might have produced better results. The business

---

63. [FN 142] *Brehm v. Eisner,* 746 A.2d 244, 259 (Del. 2000).

judgment rule, however, only requires the board to *reasonably* inform itself; it does not require perfection or the consideration of every conceivable alternative. The factual allegations pled by the Plaintiffs, therefore, do not raise a reasonable doubt that the board was informed when it approved Goldman's compensation scheme.

3. WASTE

The Plaintiffs also contend that Goldman's compensation levels were unconscionable and constituted waste. To sustain their claim that demand would be futile, the Plaintiffs must raise a reasonable doubt that Goldman's compensation levels were the product of a valid business judgment. Specifically, to excuse demand on a waste claim, the Plaintiffs must plead particularized allegations that "overcome the general presumption of good faith by showing that the board's decision was so egregious or irrational that it could not have been based on a valid assessment of the corporation's best interests."[64]

"[W]aste entails an exchange of corporate assets for consideration so disproportionately small as to lie beyond the range at which any reasonable person might be willing to trade."[65] Accordingly, if "there is any *substantial* consideration received by the corporation, and if there is a *good faith judgment* that in the circumstances the transaction is worthwhile, there should be no finding of waste."[66] The reason being, "[c]ourts are ill-fitted to attempt to weigh the 'adequacy' of consideration under the waste standard or, ex post, to judge appropriate degrees of business risk."[67] Because of this, "[i]t is the essence of business judgment for a board to determine if a particular individual warrant[s] large amounts of money."[68]

The Plaintiffs' waste allegations revolve around three premises: that Goldman's pay per employee is significantly higher than its peers, that Goldman's compensation ratios should be compared to hedge funds and other shareholder funds to reflect Goldman's increasing reliance on proprietary trading as opposed to traditional investment banking services, and that Goldman's earnings and related compensation are only the result of risk taking.

The Plaintiffs consciously do not identify a particular individual or person who received excessive compensation, but instead focus on the average compensation received by each of Goldman's 31,000 employees. The Plaintiffs allege that "Goldman consistently allocated and distributed anywhere from two to six times the amounts that its peers distributed to each employee," and the Plaintiffs provide comparisons of Goldman's average pay per employee to firms such as Morgan Stanley, Bear Stearns, Merrill Lynch, Citigroup, and Bank of America. The Plaintiffs note that these firms are investment banks, but do

---

64. [FN 152] *In re Citigroup Inc. S'holder Derivative Litig.*, 964 A.2d 106, 136 (Del. Ch. 2009) (quoting *White v. Panic*, 783 A.2d 543, 554 n.36 (Del. 2001)).

65. [FN 153] *Lewis v. Vogelstein*, 699 A.2d 327, 336 (Del. Ch. 1997).

66. [FN 154] *Id.*

67. [FN 155] *Id.*

68. [FN 156] *Brehm*, 746 A.2d at 263 (internal quotations omitted).

not provide any indication of why these firms are comparable to Goldman or their respective primary areas of business. The Plaintiffs do not compare trading segment to trading segment or any other similar metric. A broad assertion that Goldman's board devoted more resources to compensation than did other firms, standing alone, is not a particularized factual allegation creating a reasonable doubt that Goldman's compensation levels were the product of a valid business judgment.

The Plaintiffs urge that, in light of Goldman's increasing reliance on proprietary trading, Goldman's employees' compensation should be compared against a hedge fund or other shareholder fund. The Plaintiffs allege that Goldman's compensation scheme is equal to 2 percent of net assets and 45 percent of the net income produced, but a typical hedge fund is only awarded 2 percent of net assets and 20 percent of the net income produced. The Plaintiffs paradoxically assert that "no hedge fund manager may command compensation for managing assets at the annual rate of 2 percent of net assets and 45 percent of net revenues," but then immediately acknowledge that in fact there are hedge funds that have such compensation schemes. It is apparent to me from the allegations of the complaint that while the majority of hedge funds may use a "2 and 20" compensation scheme, this is not the exclusive method used to set such compensation. Even if I were to conclude that a hedge fund or shareholder fund would be an appropriate yardstick with which to measure Goldman's compensation package and "even though the amounts paid to defendants exceeded the industry average," I fail to see a "shocking disparity" between the percentages that would render them "legally excessive."[69]

In the end, while the Goldman employees may not have been doing, in the words of the complaint and Defendant Blankfein, "God's Work," the complaint fails to present facts that demonstrate that the work done by Goldman's 31,000 employees was of such limited value to the corporation that no reasonable person in the directors' position would have approved their levels of compensation. Absent such facts, these decisions are the province of the board of directors rather than the courts. Without examining the payment to a specific individual, or group of individuals, and what was specifically done in exchange for that payment, I am unable to determine whether a transaction is "so one sided that no business person of ordinary, sound judgment could conclude that the corporation has received adequate consideration."[70]

The closest the Plaintiffs come to pleading waste with any factual particularity is in regards to the payment to the Trading and Principal Investment segment in 2008. The Plaintiffs allege that in 2008 "the Trading and Principal Investments segment produced $9.06 billion in net revenue, but, as a result of discretionary bonuses paid to employees, lost more than $2.7 billion for the [stockholders]." The Plaintiffs' allegations, however, are insufficient to raise a

---

69. [FN 163] *Saxe v. Brady*, 184 A.2d 602, 610 (Del. Ch. 1962).
70. [FN 167] *Brehm*, 746 A.2d at 263 (quoting *In re Walt Disney Co. Deriv. Litig.*, 731 A.2d 342, 362 (Del. Ch. 1998) (*Disney I*)).

reasonable doubt that Goldman's compensation levels in this segment were the product of a valid business judgment. As a strictly pedagogic exercise, imagine a situation where one half of the traders lost money, and the other half made the same amount of money, so that the firm broke even. Even if no bonus was awarded to the half that lost money, a rational manager would still want to award a bonus to the half that did make money in order to keep that talent from leaving. Since net trading gains were $0, these bonuses would cause a net loss, but there would not be a waste of corporate assets because there was adequate consideration for the bonuses. Without specific allegations of unconscionable transactions and details regarding who was paid and for what reasons they were paid, the Plaintiffs fail to adequately plead demand futility on the basis of waste.

Finally, the Plaintiffs herald the fact that during the sub-prime crisis the Director Defendants continued to allocate similar percentages of net revenue as compensation while the firm was engaged in risky transactions; however, "there should be no finding of waste, even if the fact finder would conclude *ex post* that the transaction was unreasonably risky. Any other rule would deter corporate boards from the optimal rational acceptance of risk."[71] Because this complaint lacks a particular pleading that an individual or group of individuals was engaged in transactions so unconscionable that no rational director could have compensated them, the Plaintiffs have failed to raise a reasonable doubt that the compensation decisions were not the product of a valid business judgment.

D. The Plaintiffs' Caremark Claim

In addition to the claims addressed above, the Plaintiffs assert that the board breached its duty to monitor the company as required under *Caremark*.[72] Because this claim attacks a failure to act, rather than a specific transaction, the *Rales* standard applies. The *Rales* standard addresses whether the "board that would be addressing the demand can impartially consider its merits without being influenced by improper considerations."[73] To properly plead demand futility under *Rales*, a plaintiff must allege particularized facts which create a reasonable doubt that "the board of directors could have properly exercised its independent and disinterested business judgment in responding to a demand."[74]

"Under *Rales*, defendant directors who face a *substantial* likelihood of personal liability are deemed interested in the transaction and thus cannot make an impartial decision."[75] A simple allegation of potential directorial liability is

---

71. [FN 169] *Lewis*, 699 A.2d at 336.
72. [FN 170] *In re Caremark Int'l Inc. Derivative Litig.*, 698 A.2d 959 (Del. Ch. 1996).
73. [FN 172] *Rales*, 634 A.2d at 934.
74. [FN 173] *Id.*
75. [FN 174] *In re Dow Chem. Co. Derivative Litig.*, 2010 WL 66769, at *12 (internal quotations omitted; emphasis added); *Guttman v. Huang*, 823 A.2d 492, 501 (Del. Ch. 2003) ("[I]f the directors face a 'substantial likelihood' of personal liability, their ability to consider a demand impartially is compromised under *Rales*, excusing demand.").

insufficient to excuse demand, else the demand requirement itself would be rendered toothless, and directorial control over corporate litigation would be lost. The likelihood of directors' liability is significantly lessened where, as here, the corporate charter exculpates the directors from liability to the extent authorized by 8 Del. C. §102(b)(7). Because Goldman's charter contains such a provision, shielding directors from liability for breaches of the duty of care (absent bad faith) "a serious threat of liability may only be found to exist if the plaintiff pleads a *non-exculpated* claim against the directors based on particularized facts."[76] This means that "plaintiffs must plead particularized facts showing bad faith in order to establish a substantial likelihood of personal directorial liability."[77]

The Plaintiffs' contentions that the Director Defendants face a substantial likelihood of personal liability are based on oversight liability, as articulated by then-Chancellor Allen in *Caremark*. In *Caremark*, Chancellor Allen held that a company's board of directors could not "satisfy [its] obligation to be reasonably informed . . . without assuring [itself] that information and reporting systems exist[ed] in the organization."[78] These systems are needed to provide the board with accurate information so that the board may reach "informed judgments concerning both the corporation's compliance with law and its business performance."[79] A breach of oversight responsibilities is a breach of the duty of loyalty, and thus not exculpated under section 102(b)(7).

To face a substantial likelihood of oversight liability for a *Caremark* claim, the Director Defendants must have "(a) . . . utterly failed to implement any reporting or information system or controls" (which the Plaintiffs concede is not the case here); "*or* (b) having implemented such a system or controls, consciously failed to monitor or oversee its operations thus disabling themselves from being informed of risks or problems requiring their attention."[80] Furthermore, "where a claim of directorial liability for corporate loss is predicated upon ignorance of liability creating activities within the corporation . . . only a sustained or systematic failure of the board to exercise oversight—such as an utter failure to attempt to assure a reasonable information and reporting system [exists]—will establish the lack of good faith that is a necessary condition to liability."[81]

The Plaintiffs specifically contend that the Director Defendants created a compensation structure that caused management's interests to diverge from the stockholders' interests. As a result, management took risks which eventually led to unethical behavior and illegal conduct that exposed Goldman to fi-

---

76. [FN 176] *Guttman*, 823 A.2d at 501.
77. [FN 177] *In re Dow Chem. Co. Derivative Litig.*, 2010 WL 66769, at *12; *see also Citigroup*, 964 A.2d at 124-25.
78. [FN 178] *Caremark*, 698 A.2d at 970.
79. [FN 179] *Id.*
80. [FN 180] *Stone v. Ritter*, 911 A.2d 362, 370 (Del. 2006).
81. [FN 181] *Caremark*, 698 A.2d at 971; *see also Stone*, 911 A.2d at 370 ("Where directors fail to act in the face of a known duty to act, thereby demonstrating a conscious disregard for their responsibilities, they breach their duty of loyalty by failing to discharge that fiduciary obligation in good faith.").

nancial liability. According to the Plaintiffs, after the Director Defendants created Goldman's compensation structure, they had a duty to ensure protection from abuses by management, which were allegedly made more likely due to the form of that structure. Instead of overseeing management, however, the Director Defendants abdicated their oversight responsibilities.

Unlike the original and most subsequent *Caremark* claims, where plaintiffs alleged that liability was predicated on a failure to oversee corporate conduct leading to violations of law, the Plaintiffs here argue that the Director Defendants are also liable for oversight failure relating to Goldman's business performance. Because the oversight of legal compliance and the oversight of business risk raise distinct concerns, I shall examine those issues separately.

1. *UNLAWFUL CONDUCT*

As described above, the Plaintiffs must plead particularized facts suggesting that the board failed to implement a monitoring and reporting system or consciously disregarded the information provided by that system. Here, the Plaintiffs assert that the Goldman employees engaged in unethical trading practices in search of short term revenues. Although the Plaintiffs' allegations fall short of the florid contentions about the corporation made elsewhere, the Plaintiffs provide examples, based on the Permanent Subcommittee report, of conduct they believe was unethical and harmful to the company. The Plaintiffs argue that the Director Defendants should have been aware of purportedly unethical conduct such as securitizing high risk mortgages, shorting the mortgage market, using naked credit default swaps, and "magnifying risk" through the creation of synthetic CDOs. The Plaintiffs also allege that Goldman's trading business often put Goldman in potential conflicts of interest with its own clients and that the Director Defendants were aware of this and have embraced this goal.

Illegal corporate conduct is not loyal corporate conduct. "[A] fiduciary of a Delaware corporation cannot be loyal to a Delaware corporation by knowingly causing it to seek profit by violating the law."[82] The "unethical" conduct the Plaintiffs allege here, however, is not the type of wrongdoing envisioned by *Caremark*. The conduct at issue here involves, for the most part, *legal* business decisions that were firmly within management's judgment to pursue. There is nothing intrinsic in using naked credit default swaps or shorting the mortgage market that makes these actions illegal or wrongful. These are actions that Goldman managers, presumably using their informed business judgment, made to hedge the Corporation's assets against risk or to earn a higher return. Legal, if risky, actions that are within management's discretion to pursue are not "red flags" that would put a board on notice of unlawful conduct.

Similarly, securitizing and selling high risk mortgages is not illegal or wrongful per se. The Plaintiffs take issue with actions where Goldman continued to sell mortgage related products to its clients while profiting from the decline of

---

82. [FN 190] *In re Massey Energy*, 2011 WL 2176479 at *20 (Del. Ch. May 31, 2011).

the mortgage market. In particular, the Plaintiffs point to three transactions where Goldman took the short side of synthetic CDOs while simultaneously being long on the underlying reference assets, or sold a long position while being, itself, short.

The three transactions referenced by the Plaintiffs as "disloyal and unethical trading practices" are not sufficient pleadings of wrongdoing or illegality necessary to establish a *Caremark* claim—the only inferences that can be made are that Goldman had risky assets and that Goldman made a business decision, involving risk, to sell or hedge these assets. The Hudson Mezzanine 2006-1 and Anderson Mezzanine Funding 2007-1 were synthetic CDOs that referenced RMBS securities. Timberwolf I was a "hybrid cash/synthetic CDO squared" where "a significant portion of the referenced assets were CDO securities." Goldman structured all three securities and took short positions because it was trying to reduce its mortgage holdings. All three securities eventually were downgraded, and the investors who had taken long positions lost money. The fact that another party would make money from such a decline was obvious to those investors—inherent in the structure of a synthetic CDO is that another party is taking a short position. The Plaintiffs' allegations can be boiled down to the fact that these three securities lost money when Goldman may have had a conflict of interest. Though these transactions involved risk, including a risk of damaging the company's reputation, these are not "red flags" that would give rise to an actionable *Caremark* claim—reputational risk exists in any business decision.

To act in bad faith, there must be scienter on the part of the defendant director. The Plaintiffs argue that, as Goldman increased its proprietary trading, the Director Defendants were aware of the possible conflicts of interest and that the conflicts had to be addressed. The three transactions referenced by the Plaintiffs do not indicate that the Director Defendants "acted inconsistent[ly] with [their] fiduciary duties [or], most importantly, that the director[s] *knew* [they were] so acting."[83] A conflict of interest may involve wrongdoing, but is not wrongdoing itself. An active management of conflicts of interest is not an abdication of oversight duties, and an inference cannot be made that the Director Defendants were acting in bad faith.

The Plaintiffs also posit the theory that the credit rating agencies were beholden to Goldman and that Goldman unduly influenced them to give higher credit ratings to certain products. These allegations are purely conclusory. The complaint is silent as to any mechanism (other than that inherent in the relationship of a credit agency to a large financial player) by which Goldman coerced or colluded with the ratings agencies or (more to the point in a *Caremark* context) that the Director Defendants disregarded any such actions in bad faith.

The heart of the Plaintiffs' *Caremark* claim is in the allegation that Goldman's "trading practices have subjected the Firm to civil liability, via, inter alia,

---

83. [FN 197] *In re Massey Energy*, 2011 WL 2176479, at *22 (Del. Ch. May 31, 2011).

an SEC investigation and lawsuit." Once the legal, permissible business decisions are removed, what the Plaintiffs are left with is a single transaction that Goldman settled with the SEC.

In 2007 Goldman designed a CDO, Abacus 2007-AC1, with input from the hedge fund founder John Paulson. The Plaintiffs allege that Paulson helped select a set of mortgages that would collateralize the CDO and then took a short position, betting that the same mortgages would fall in value. The Plaintiffs point out that meanwhile Goldman was selling long positions in the CDO without disclosing Paulson's role in selecting the underlying collateral or Paulson's short position. The Plaintiffs allege that "Goldman's clients who took long positions in Abacus 2007-AC 1 lost their entire $1 billion investment." As a result, on April 16, 2010 the SEC charged Goldman and a Goldman Vice President with fraud for their roles in creating and marketing Abacus 2007-AC 1. On July 14, 2010, Goldman settled the case with the SEC. As part of the settlement, Goldman agreed to disgorge its profits on the Abacus transaction, pay a large civil penalty, and evaluate various compliance programs.

The Abacus transaction, with its disclosure problems, is unique. The complaint does not plead with factual particularity that the other highlighted transactions contain disclosure omissions similar to Abacus, and the Abacus transaction on its own cannot demonstrate the willful ignorance of "red flags" on the part of the Defendants that might lead to a reasonable apprehension of liability. Though the Plaintiffs allege that the "Abacus deals are likely just the tip of the iceberg," conclusory statements are not particularized pleadings. The single Abacus transaction without more is insufficient to provide a reasonable inference of bad faith on the part of the Director Defendants.

2. BUSINESS RISK

Part of the Plaintiffs' *Caremark* claim stems from the Director Defendants' oversight of Goldman's business practices. As a preliminary matter, this Court has not definitively stated whether a board's *Caremark* duties include a duty to monitor business risk. In *Citigroup*, then-Chancellor Chandler posited that "it may be possible for a plaintiff to meet the burden under some set of facts."[84] Indeed, the *Caremark* court seemed to suggest the possibility of such a claim:

[I]t would . . . be a mistake to conclude that . . . corporate boards may satisfy their obligation to be reasonably informed concerning the corporation without assuring themselves that information and reporting systems exist in the organization that are reasonably designed to provide to senior management and to the board itself timely, accurate information sufficient to allow management and the board, each within its scope, to reach informed judgments concerning both the corporation's compliance with law *and its business performance*.[85]

---

84. [FN 208] *Citigroup*, 964 A.2d at 126.
85. [FN 209] *Caremark*, 698 A.2d at 970 (emphasis added).

As was the case in *Citigroup*, however, the facts pled here do not give rise to a claim under *Caremark*, and thus I do not need to reach the issue of whether the duty of oversight includes the duty to monitor business risk.

As the Court observed in *Citigroup*, "imposing *Caremark*-type duties on directors to monitor business risk is fundamentally different" from imposing on directors a duty to monitor fraud and illegal activity.[86] Risk is "the chance that a return on an investment will be different than expected."[87] Consistent with this, "a company or investor that is willing to take on more risk can earn a higher return."[88] The manner in which a company "evaluate[s] the trade-off between risk and return" is "[t]he essence of . . . business judgment."[89] The Plaintiffs here allege that Goldman was over-leveraged, engaged in risky business practices, and did not set enough money aside for future losses. As a result, the Plaintiffs assert, Goldman was undercapitalized, forcing it to become a bank holding company and to take on an onerous loan from Warren Buffett.

Although the Plaintiffs have molded their claims with an eye to the language of *Caremark*, the essence of their complaint is that I should hold the Director Defendants "personally liable for making (or allowing to be made) business decisions that, in hindsight, turned out poorly for the Company." If an actionable duty to monitor business risk exists, it cannot encompass any substantive evaluation by a court of a board's determination of the appropriate amount of risk. Such decisions plainly involve business judgment.

The Plaintiffs' remaining allegations in essence seek to hold the Director Defendants "personally liable to the Company because they failed to fully recognize the risk posed by subprime securities." The Plaintiffs charge that the entire board was aware of, or should have been aware of, "the details of the trading business of Goldman and failed to take appropriate action." The Plaintiffs note that "[a]s the housing market began to fracture in early 2007, a committee of senior Goldman executives . . . including Defendants Viniar, Cohn, and Blankfein and those helping to manage Goldman's mortgage, credit and legal operations, took an active role in overseeing the mortgage unit." "[This] committee's job was to vet potential new products and transactions, being wary of deals that exposed Goldman to too much risk." This committee eventually decided that housing prices would decline and decided to take a short position in the mortgage market. The Plaintiffs contend that the Director Defendants were "fully aware of the extent of Goldman's RMBS and CDO securities market activities." The Plaintiffs point out that the Director Defendants were informed about the business decisions Goldman made during the year including an "intensive effort to not only reduce its mortgage risk exposure, but profit from high risk RMBS and CDO Securities incurring losses." The Plaintiffs further allege that because of this the Director Defendants "understood that these efforts involved

---

86. [FN 210] *Citigroup*, 964 A.2d at 131.
87. [FN 211] *Id.* at 126.
88. [FN 212] *Id.*
89. [FN 213] *Id.*

very large amounts of Goldman's capital that exceeded the Company's Value-at-Risk measures." Finally, the Plaintiffs allege that the practices allowed by the board, including transactions in which Goldman's risk was hedged, imposed reputational risk upon the corporation.

Thus, the Plaintiffs do not plead with particularity anything that suggests that the Director Defendants acted in bad faith or otherwise consciously disregarded their *oversight* responsibilities in regards to Goldman's business risk. Goldman had an Audit Committee in place that was "charged with assisting the Board in its oversight of the Company's management of market, credit liquidity and other financial and operational risks." The Director Defendants exercised their business judgment in choosing and implementing a risk management system that they presumably believed would keep them reasonably informed of the company's business risks. As described in detail above, the Plaintiffs admit that the Director Defendants were "fully aware of the extent of Goldman's RMBS and CDO securities market activities."

"Oversight duties under Delaware law are not designed to subject directors, even expert directors, to *personal liability* for failure to predict the future and to properly evaluate business risk."[90] No reasonable inference can be made from the pleadings that the Director Defendants consciously disregarded their duty to be informed about business risk (assuming such a duty exists). On the contrary, the pleadings suggest that the Director Defendants kept themselves reasonably informed and fulfilled their duty of oversight in good faith. Good faith, not a good result, is what is required of the board.

Goldman's board and management made decisions to hedge exposure during the deterioration of the housing market, decisions that have been roundly criticized in Congress and elsewhere. Those decisions involved taking objectively large risks, including particularly reputational risks. The outcome of that risk-taking may prove ultimately costly to the corporation. The Plaintiffs, however, have failed to plead with particularity that the Director Defendants consciously and in bad faith disregarded these risks; to the contrary, the facts pled indicate that the board kept itself informed of the risks involved. The Plaintiffs have failed to plead facts showing a substantial likelihood of liability on the part of the Director Defendants under *Caremark*.

IV. CONCLUSION

The Delaware General Corporation law affords directors and officers broad discretion to exercise their business judgment in the fulfillment of their obligations to the corporation. Consequently, Delaware's case law imposes fiduciary duties on directors and officers to ensure their loyalty and care toward the corporation. When an individual breaches these duties, it is the proper function of this Court to step in and enforce those fiduciary obligations.

---

90. [FN 229] *Citigroup*, 964 A.2d at 131.

Here, the Plaintiffs allege that the Director Defendants violated fiduciary duties in setting compensation levels and failing to oversee the risks created thereby. The facts pled in support of these allegations, however, if true, support only a conclusion that the directors made poor business decisions. Through the business judgment rule, Delaware law encourages corporate fiduciaries to attempt to increase stockholder wealth by engaging in those risks that, in their business judgment, are in the best interest of the corporation "without the debilitating fear that they will be held personally liable if the company experiences losses."[91] The Plaintiffs have failed to allege facts sufficient to demonstrate that the directors were unable to properly exercise this judgment in deciding whether to bring these claims. Since the Plaintiffs have failed to make a demand upon the Corporation, this matter must be dismissed. . . .

For the foregoing reasons, the Defendants' motion to dismiss is granted, and the Plaintiffs' claims are dismissed with prejudice.

An Order has been entered consistent with this Opinion.

Questions

1. What arguments did the plaintiffs make for why demand was futile with respect to their claims based on the board's approval of the company's compensation scheme? Why did the court reject these arguments?
2. What arguments did the plaintiffs make for why demand was futile with respect to their *Caremark* claims? Why did the court reject these arguments?
3. In hindsight, should plaintiffs have made a demand on the board to bring the suit?

(2) Special Litigation Committees

Even if a court finds that making a demand was futile and therefore excused, the plaintiff is still not out of the woods. This is because the board is likely to respond by appointing a special litigation committee, or SLC. An SLC is a board committee composed of directors the board has determined are disinterested and independent when it comes to the derivative suit. If there are not any directors on the existing board that meet these criteria, the board will simply increase its size (this may involve amending the corporation's bylaws), fill the resulting vacancies with individuals who meet the criteria, and appoint them to the SLC. The board will empower the SLC to investigate the plaintiff's allegations and determine whether proceeding with the suit is in the corporation's best interest. After conducting an investigation, the SLC then decides whether the

---

91. [FN 231] *Id.* at 139.

corporation should pursue, attempt to settle, or move to dismiss the suit. If it decides that the corporation should pursue the suit, the SLC will normally take control of it, meaning the stockholder-plaintiff is out. More often than not, an SLC will conclude that proceeding is not in the corporation's best interest and will thus move on behalf of the corporation to dismiss the suit.

The court in *Biondi v. Scrushy* described the policy behind SLCs as follows:

> One of the obvious purposes for forming a special litigation committee is to promote confidence in the integrity of corporate decision making by vesting the company's power to respond to accusations of serious misconduct by high officials in an impartial group of independent directors. By forming a committee whose fairness and objectivity cannot be reasonably questioned, giving them the resources to retain advisors, and granting them the freedom to do a thorough investigation and to pursue claims against wrongdoers, the company can assuage concern among its stockholders and retain, through the SLC, control over any claims belonging to the Company itself.[92]

A decision by an SLC to move for dismissal is *not* afforded the protection of the business judgment rule. Instead, in deciding whether to grant the motion, a court applies the following two-step test articulated by the Delaware Supreme Court in *Zapata Corp. v. Maldonado*:[93]

> First, the Court should inquire into the independence and good faith of the committee and the bases supporting its conclusions. Limited discovery may be ordered to facilitate such inquiries. The corporation should have the burden of proving independence, good faith and a reasonable investigation, rather than presuming independence, good faith and reasonableness. If the Court determines either that the committee is not independent or has not shown reasonable bases for its conclusions, or, if the Court is not satisfied for other reasons relating to the process, including but not limited to the good faith of the committee, the Court shall deny the corporation's motion. If, however, the Court is satisfied under Rule 56 standards that the committee was independent and showed reasonable bases for good faith findings and recommendations, the Court may proceed, in its discretion, to the next step.
>
> The second step provides, we believe, the essential key in striking the balance between legitimate corporate claims as expressed in a derivative stockholder suit and a corporation's best interests as expressed by an independent investigating committee. The Court should determine, applying its own independent business judgment, whether the motion should be granted. This means, of course, that instances could arise where a committee can establish its independence and sound bases for its good faith decisions and still have the corporation's motion denied. The second step is intended to thwart instances where corporate actions meet the criteria of step one, but the result does not appear to satisfy its spirit, or where corporate actions would simply prematurely terminate a stockholder grievance deserving of further consideration in the corporation's interest. The

---

92. *Biondi v. Scrushy*, 820 A.2d 1148, 1156 (Del. Ch. 2003).
93. 430 A.2d 779 (Del. 1980).

Court of Chancery of course must carefully consider and weigh how compelling the corporate interest in dismissal is when faced with a non-frivolous lawsuit. The Court of Chancery should, when appropriate, give special consideration to matters of law and public policy in addition to the corporation's best interests.

If the Court's independent business judgment is satisfied, the Court may proceed to grant the motion, subject, of course, to any equitable terms or conditions the Court finds necessary or desirable.[94]

While courts in other states had applied the business judgment rule when reviewing SLC motions to dismiss, the *Zapata* court concluded doing so was too deferential to the board. The court reasoned as follows:

> At the risk of stating the obvious, the problem is relatively simple. If, on the one hand, corporations can consistently wrest bona fide derivative actions away from well-meaning derivative plaintiffs through the use of the committee mechanism, the derivative suit will lose much, if not all, of its generally-recognized effectiveness as an intra-corporate means of policing boards of directors. If, on the other hand, corporations are unable to rid themselves of meritless or harmful litigation and strike suits, the derivative action, created to benefit the corporation, will produce the opposite, unintended result. It thus appears desirable to us to find a balancing point where bona fide stockholder power to bring corporate causes of action cannot be unfairly trampled on by the board of directors, but the corporation can rid itself of detrimental litigation. . . .

> [T]he question has been treated by other courts as one of the "business judgment" of the board committee. If a "committee, composed of independent and disinterested directors, conducted a proper review of the matters before it, considered a variety of factors and reached, in good faith, a business judgment that (the) action was not in the best interest of (the corporation)," the action must be dismissed. The issues become solely independence, good faith, and reasonable investigation. The ultimate conclusion of the committee, under that view, is not subject to judicial review.

> We are not satisfied, however, that acceptance of the "business judgment" rationale at this stage of derivative litigation is a proper balancing point. While we admit an analogy with a normal case respecting board judgment, it seems to us that there is sufficient risk in the realities of a situation like the one presented in this case to justify caution beyond adherence to the theory of business judgment. . . .

> [N]otwithstanding our conviction that Delaware law entrusts the corporate power to a properly authorized committee, we must be mindful that directors are passing judgment on fellow directors in the same corporation and fellow directors, in this instance, who designated them to serve both as directors and committee members. The question naturally arises whether a "there but for the grace of God go I" empathy might not play a role. And the further question arises whether inquiry as to independence, good faith and reasonable investigation is sufficient safeguard against abuse, perhaps subconscious abuse. . . .

---

94. *Id.* at 788-89.

We thus steer a middle course between those cases which yield to the independent business judgment of a board committee and this case as determined below which would yield to unbridled plaintiff stockholder control. . . .[95]

b. Direct vs. Derivative

One way for a plaintiff to avoid dealing with the demand requirement, an SLC, and other vagaries of Rule 23.1 is to bring a direct as opposed to a derivative suit. In a direct suit, the plaintiff asserts that he or she was directly harmed by the directors' breach of fiduciary duty and therefore is suing in his or her individual capacity for redress of this harm and not on behalf of the corporation. Because this would not be a derivative suit but instead regular litigation (in this context, we would call it a direct suit), Rule 23.1 would not apply, and any recovery would go to the plaintiff and not the corporation. Thus, it is fairly common for a plaintiff to frame its complaint as a direct rather than derivative suit. It is also fairly common for the defendant directors to respond by claiming that the suit can only be brought derivatively and therefore that the complaint should be dismissed for failure to comply with Rule 23.1. As a result, there is a fair amount of case law addressing how to distinguish a direct claim from a derivative claim. The next case sets forth the Delaware test.

Tooley v. Donaldson, Lufkin & Jenrette, Inc.
845 A.2d 1031 (Del. 2004)

VEASEY, Chief Justice:

Plaintiff-stockholders brought a purported class action in the Court of Chancery, alleging that the members of the board of directors of their corporation breached their fiduciary duties by agreeing to a 22-day delay in closing a proposed merger. Plaintiffs contend that the delay harmed them due to the lost time-value of the cash paid for their shares. The Court of Chancery granted the defendants' motion to dismiss on the sole ground that the claims were, "at most," claims of the corporation being asserted derivatively. They were, thus, held not to be direct claims of the stockholders, individually. Thereupon, the Court held that the plaintiffs lost their standing to bring this action when they tendered their shares in connection with the merger.

Although the trial court's legal analysis of whether the complaint alleges a direct or derivative claim reflects some concepts in our prior jurisprudence, we believe those concepts are not helpful and should be regarded as erroneous. We set forth in this Opinion the law to be applied henceforth in determining whether a stockholder's claim is derivative or direct. That issue must turn *solely* on the following questions: (1) who suffered the alleged harm (the corporation or the

---

95. *Id.* at 786-88.

suing stockholders, individually); and (2) who would receive the benefit of any recovery or other remedy (the corporation or the stockholders, individually)?

To the extent we have concluded that the trial court's analysis of the direct vs. derivative dichotomy should be regarded as erroneous, we view the error as harmless in this case because the complaint does not set forth *any* claim upon which relief can be granted. In its opinion, the Court of Chancery properly found on the facts pleaded that the plaintiffs have no separate contractual right to the alleged lost time-value of money arising out of extensions in the closing of a tender offer. These extensions were made in connection with a merger where the plaintiffs' right to any payment of the merger consideration had not ripened at the time the extensions were granted. No other individual right of these stockholders having been asserted in the complaint, it was correctly dismissed.

In affirming the judgment of the trial court as having correctly dismissed the complaint, we reverse only its dismissal with prejudice. We remand this action to the Court of Chancery with directions to amend its order of dismissal to provide that: (a) the action is dismissed for failure to state a claim upon which relief can be granted; and (b) the dismissal is without prejudice. Thus, plaintiffs will have an opportunity to replead, if warranted under Court of Chancery Rule 11.

FACTS

Patrick Tooley and Kevin Lewis are former minority stockholders of Donaldson, Lufkin & Jenrette, Inc. (DLJ), a Delaware corporation engaged in investment banking. DLJ was acquired by Credit Suisse Group (Credit Suisse) in the Fall of 2000. Before that acquisition, AXA Financial, Inc. (AXA), which owned 71 percent of DLJ stock, controlled DLJ. Pursuant to a stockholder agreement between AXA and Credit Suisse, AXA agreed to exchange with Credit Suisse its DLJ stockholdings for a mix of stock and cash. The consideration received by AXA consisted primarily of stock. Cash made up one-third of the purchase price. Credit Suisse intended to acquire the remaining minority interests of publicly-held DLJ stock through a cash tender offer, followed by a merger of DLJ into a Credit Suisse subsidiary.

The tender offer price was set at $90 per share in cash. The tender offer was to expire 20 days after its commencement. The merger agreement, however, authorized two types of extensions. First, Credit Suisse could unilaterally extend the tender offer if certain conditions were not met, such as SEC regulatory approvals or certain payment obligations. Alternatively, DLJ and Credit Suisse could agree to postpone acceptance by Credit Suisse of DLJ stock tendered by the minority stockholders.

Credit Suisse availed itself of both types of extensions to postpone the closing of the tender offer. The tender offer was initially set to expire on October 5, 2000, but Credit Suisse invoked the five-day unilateral extension provided in the agreement. Later, by agreement between DLJ and Credit Suisse, it postponed the merger a second time so that it was then set to close on November 2, 2000.

Plaintiffs challenge the second extension that resulted in a 22-day delay. They contend that this delay was not properly authorized and harmed minority stockholders while improperly benefitting AXA. They claim damages representing the time-value of money lost through the delay.

THE DECISION OF THE COURT OF CHANCERY

The order of the Court of Chancery dismissing the complaint, and the Memorandum Opinion upon which it is based, state that the dismissal is based on the plaintiffs' lack of standing to bring the claims asserted therein. Thus, when plaintiffs tendered their shares, they lost standing under Court of Chancery Rule 23.1, the contemporaneous holding rule. The ruling before us on appeal is that the plaintiffs' claim is derivative, purportedly brought on behalf of DLJ. The Court of Chancery, relying upon our confusing jurisprudence on the direct/derivative dichotomy, based its dismissal on the following ground: "Because this delay affected all DLJ shareholders equally, plaintiffs' injury was not a special injury, and this action is, thus, a derivative action, at most."

Plaintiffs argue that they have suffered a "special injury" because they had an alleged contractual right to receive the merger consideration of $90 per share without suffering the 22-day delay arising out of the extensions under the merger agreement. But the trial court's opinion convincingly demonstrates that plaintiffs had no such contractual right that had ripened at the time the extensions were entered into:

> *Here, it is clear that plaintiffs have no separate contractual right to bring a direct claim, and they do not assert contractual rights under the merger agreement.* First, the merger agreement specifically disclaims any persons as being third party beneficiaries to the contract. Second, any contractual shareholder right to payment of the merger consideration did not ripen until the conditions of the agreement were met. The agreement stated that Credit Suisse Group was not required to accept any shares for tender, or could extend the offer, under certain conditions — one condition of which included an extension or termination by agreement between Credit Suisse Group and DLJ. *Because Credit Suisse Group and DLJ did in fact agree to extend the tender offer period, any right to payment plaintiffs could have did not ripen until this newly negotiated period was over. The merger agreement only became binding and mutually enforceable at the time the tendered shares ultimately were accepted for payment by Credit Suisse Group.* It is at that moment in time, November 3, 2000, that the company became bound to purchase the tendered shares, making the contract mutually enforceable. *DLJ stockholders had no individual contractual right to payment until November 3, 2000, when their tendered shares were accepted for payment.* Thus, they have no contractual basis to challenge a delay in the closing of the tender offer up until November 3. *Because this is the date the tendered shares were accepted for payment, the contract was not breached and plaintiffs do not have a contractual basis to bring a direct suit.*

Moreover, no other individual right of these stockholder-plaintiffs was alleged to have been violated by the extensions.

That conclusion could have ended the case because it portended a definitive ruling that plaintiffs have no claim whatsoever on the facts alleged. But the defendants chose to argue, and the trial court chose to decide, the standing issue, which is predicated on an assertion that this claim is a derivative one asserted on behalf of the corporation, DLJ.

The Court of Chancery correctly noted that "[t]he Court will independently examine the nature of the wrong alleged and any potential relief to make its own determination of the suit's classification. . . . Plaintiffs' classification of the suit is not binding."[96] The trial court's analysis was hindered, however, because it focused on the confusing concept of "special injury" as the test for determining whether a claim is derivative or direct. The trial court's premise was as follows:

> In order to bring a *direct* claim, a plaintiff must have experienced some "special injury." [citing *Lipton v. News Int'l*, 514 A.2d 1075, 1079 (Del. 1986)]. A special injury is a wrong that "is separate and distinct from that suffered by other shareholders, . . . or a wrong involving a contractual right of a shareholder, such as the right to vote, or to assert majority control, which exists independently of any right of the corporation." [citing *Moran v. Household Int'l Inc.*, 490 A.2d 1059, 1070 (Del. Ch. 1985), *aff'd* 500 A.2d 1346 (Del. 1986 [1985])].

In our view, the concept of "special injury" that appears in some Supreme Court and Court of Chancery cases is not helpful to a proper analytical distinction between direct and derivative actions. We now disapprove the use of the concept of "special injury" as a tool in that analysis.

THE PROPER ANALYSIS TO DISTINGUISH BETWEEN DIRECT AND DERIVATIVE ACTIONS

The analysis must be based solely on the following questions: Who suffered the alleged harm—the corporation or the suing stockholder individually—and who would receive the benefit of the recovery or other remedy? This simple analysis is well imbedded in our jurisprudence, but some cases have complicated it by injection of the amorphous and confusing concept of "special injury."

The Chancellor, in the very recent *Agostino* case,[97] correctly points this out and strongly suggests that we should disavow the concept of "special injury." In a scholarly analysis of this area of the law, he also suggests that the inquiry should be whether the stockholder has demonstrated that he or she has suffered an injury that is not dependent on an injury to the corporation. In the context of a claim for breach of fiduciary duty, the Chancellor articulated the inquiry as follows: "Looking at the body of the complaint and considering the nature

---

96. [FN 5] *Tooley v. Donaldson Lufkin and Jenrette*, No. Civ. A. 18414-NC, 2003 WL 203060, at *3 (Del. Ch. Jan. 21, 2003).

97. [FN 8] *Agostino v. Hicks*, No. Civ. A. 20020-NC, 2004 WL 443987 (Del. Ch. March 11, 2004).

of the wrong alleged and the relief requested, has the plaintiff demonstrated that he or she can prevail without showing an injury to the corporation?"[98] We believe that this approach is helpful in analyzing the first prong of the analysis: what person or entity has suffered the alleged harm? The second prong of the analysis should logically follow.

A BRIEF HISTORY OF OUR JURISPRUDENCE

The derivative suit has been generally described as "one of the most interesting and ingenious of accountability mechanisms for large formal organizations."[99] It enables a stockholder to bring suit on behalf of the corporation for harm done to the corporation. Because a derivative suit is being brought on behalf of the corporation, the recovery, if any, must go to the corporation. A stockholder who is directly injured, however, does retain the right to bring an individual action for injuries affecting his or her legal rights as a stockholder. Such a claim is distinct from an injury caused to the corporation alone. In such individual suits, the recovery or other relief flows directly to the stockholders, not to the corporation.

Determining whether an action is derivative or direct is sometimes difficult and has many legal consequences, some of which may have an expensive impact on the parties to the action. For example, if an action is derivative, the plaintiffs are then required to comply with the requirements of Court of Chancery Rule 23.1, that the stockholder: (a) retain ownership of the shares throughout the litigation; (b) make presuit demand on the board; and (c) obtain court approval of any settlement. Further, the recovery, if any, flows only to the corporation. The decision whether a suit is direct or derivative may be outcome-determinative. Therefore, it is necessary that a standard to distinguish such actions be clear, simple and consistently articulated and applied by our courts.

In *Elster v. American Airlines, Inc.,*[100] the stockholder sought to enjoin the grant and exercise of stock options because they would result in a dilution of her stock personally. In *Elster,* the alleged injury was found to be derivative, not direct, because it was essentially a claim of mismanagement of corporate assets. Then came the complication in the analysis: The Court held that where the alleged injury is to both the corporation *and* to the stockholder, the stockholder must allege a "special injury" to maintain a direct action. The Court did not

---

98. [FN 9] *Agostino,* 2004 WL 443987, at *7. The Chancellor further explains that the focus should be on the person or entity to whom the relevant duty is owed. *Id.* at *7 n.54. As noted in *Agostino, id.,* this test is similar to that articulated by the American Law Institute (ALI), a test that we cited with approval in *Grimes v. Donald,* 673 A.2d 1207 (Del. 1996). The ALI test is as follows:

> A direct action may be brought in the name and right of a holder to redress an injury sustained by, or enforce a duty owed to, the holder. An action in which the holder can prevail without showing an injury or breach of duty to the corporation should be treated as a direct action that may be maintained by the holder in an individual capacity.

2 American Law Institute, Principles of Corporate Governance: Analysis and Recommendations §7.01(b) at 17.

99. [FN 10] *Kramer v. Western Pacific Industries, Inc.,* 546 A.2d at 351 (quoting R. Clark, *Corporate Law* 639-40 (1986)).

100. [FN 13] 100 A.2d 219, 222 (Del. Ch. 1953).

define "special injury," however. By implication, decisions in later cases have interpreted *Elster* to mean that a "special injury" is alleged where the wrong is inflicted upon the stockholder alone or where the stockholder complains of a wrong affecting a particular right. Examples would be a preemptive right as a stockholder, rights involving control of the corporation or a wrong affecting the stockholder, qua individual holder, and not the corporation.

In *Bokat v. Getty Oil Co.,*[101] a stockholder of a subsidiary brought suit against the director of the parent corporation for causing the subsidiary to invest its resources wastefully, resulting in a loss to the subsidiary. The claim in *Bokat* was essentially for mismanagement of corporate assets. Therefore, the Court held that any recovery must be sought on behalf of the corporation, and the claim was, thus, found to be derivative.

In describing how a court may distinguish direct and derivative actions, the *Bokat* Court stated that a suit must be maintained derivatively if the injury falls equally upon all stockholders. Experience has shown this concept to be confusing and inaccurate. It is confusing because it appears to have been intended to address the fact that an injury to the corporation tends to diminish each share of stock equally because corporate assets or their value are diminished. In that sense, the *indirect* injury to the stockholders arising out of the harm to the corporation comes about solely by virtue of their stockholdings. It does not arise out of any independent or direct harm to the stockholders, individually. That concept is also inaccurate because a direct, individual claim of stockholders that does not depend on harm to the corporation can also fall on all stockholders equally, without the claim thereby becoming a derivative claim.

In *Lipton v. News International, Plc.,*[102] this Court applied the "special injury" test. There, a stockholder began acquiring shares in the defendant corporation presumably to gain control of the corporation. In response, the defendant corporation agreed to an exchange of its shares with a friendly buyer. Due to the exchange and a supermajority voting requirement on certain stockholder actions, the management of the defendant corporation acquired a veto power over any change in management.

The *Lipton* Court concluded that the critical analytical issue in distinguishing direct and derivative actions is whether a "special injury" has been alleged. There, the Court found a "special injury" because the board's manipulation worked an injury upon the plaintiff-stockholder unlike the injury suffered by other stockholders. That was because the plaintiff-stockholder was actively seeking to gain control of the defendant corporation. Therefore, the Court found that the claim was direct. Ironically, the Court could have reached the same correct result by simply concluding that the manipulation directly and individually harmed the stockholders, without injuring the corporation.

---

101. [FN 15] 262 A.2d 246 (Del. 1970).
102. [FN 17] *Lipton v. News International, Plc.,* 514 A.2d 1075, 1078 (Del. 1986).

In *Kramer v. Western Pacific Industries, Inc.*,[103] this Court found to be derivative a stockholder's challenge to corporate transactions that occurred six months immediately preceding a buy-out merger. The stockholders challenged the decision by the board of directors to grant stock options and golden parachutes to management. The stockholders argued that the claim was direct because their share of the proceeds from the buy-out sale was reduced by the resources used to pay for the options and golden parachutes. Once again, our analysis was that to bring a direct action, the stockholder must allege something other than an injury resulting from a wrong to the corporation. We interpreted *Elster* to require the court to determine the nature of the action based on the "nature of the wrong alleged" and the relief that could result. That was, and is, the correct test. The claim in *Kramer* was essentially for mismanagement of corporate assets. Therefore, we found the claims to be derivative. That was the correct outcome.

In *Grimes v. Donald*,[104] we sought to distinguish between direct and derivative actions in the context of employment agreements granted to certain officers that allegedly caused the board to abdicate its authority. Relying on the *Elster* and *Kramer* precedents that the court must look to the nature of the wrong and to whom the relief will go, we concluded that the plaintiff was not seeking to recover any damages for injury to the corporation. Rather, the plaintiff was seeking a declaration of the invalidity of the agreements on the ground that the board had abdicated its responsibility to the stockholders. Thus, based on the relief requested, we affirmed the judgment of the Court of Chancery that the plaintiff was entitled to pursue a direct action.

Grimes was followed by *Parnes v. Bally Entertainment Corp.*, which held, among other things, that the injury to the stockholders must be "independent of any injury to the corporation."[105] As the Chancellor correctly noted in *Agostino*, neither *Grimes* nor *Parnes* applies the purported "special injury" test.

Thus, two confusing propositions have encumbered our caselaw governing the direct/derivative distinction. The "special injury" concept, applied in cases such as *Lipton*, can be confusing in identifying the nature of the action. The same is true of the proposition that stems from *Bokat*—that an action cannot be direct if all stockholders are equally affected or unless the stockholder's injury is separate and distinct from that suffered by other stockholders. The proper analysis has been and should remain that stated in *Grimes*[,] *Kramer* and *Parnes*. That is, a court should look to the nature of the wrong and to whom the relief should go. The stockholder's claimed direct injury must be independent of any alleged injury to the corporation. The stockholder must demonstrate that the duty breached was owed to the stockholder and that he or she can prevail without showing an injury to the corporation.

---

103. [FN 19] 546 A.2d 348, 352 (Del. 1988).
104. [FN 22] 673 A.2d 1207, 1213 (Del. 1996).
105. [FN 25] 722 A.2d 1243, 1245 (Del. 1999).

STANDARD TO BE APPLIED IN THIS CASE

In this case it cannot be concluded that the complaint alleges a derivative claim. There is no derivative claim asserting injury to the corporate entity. There is no relief that would go the corporation. Accordingly, there is no basis to hold that the complaint states a derivative claim.

But, it does not necessarily follow that the complaint states a direct, individual claim. While the complaint purports to set forth a direct claim, in reality, it states no claim at all. The trial court analyzed the complaint and correctly concluded that it does not claim that the plaintiffs have any rights that have been injured. Their rights have not yet ripened. The contractual claim is nonexistent until it is ripe, and that claim will not be ripe until the terms of the merger are fulfilled, including the extensions of the closing at issue here. Therefore, there is no direct claim stated in the complaint before us.

Accordingly, the complaint was properly dismissed. But, due to the reliance on the concept of "special injury" by the Court of Chancery, the ground set forth for the dismissal is erroneous, there being no derivative claim. That error is harmless, however, because, in our view, there is no direct claim either.

CONCLUSION

For purposes of distinguishing between derivative and direct claims, we expressly disapprove both the concept of "special injury" and the concept that a claim is necessarily derivative if it affects all stockholders equally. In our view, the tests going forward should rest on those set forth in this opinion.

We affirm the judgment of the Court of Chancery dismissing the complaint, although on a different ground from that decided by the Court of Chancery. We reverse the dismissal with prejudice and remand this matter to the Court of Chancery to amend the order of dismissal: (a) to state that the complaint is dismissed on the ground that it does not state a claim upon which relief can be granted; and (b) that the dismissal is without prejudice.

Because our determination that there is no valid claim whatsoever in the complaint before us was not argued by the defendants and was not the basis of the ruling of the Court of Chancery, the interests of justice will be best served if the dismissal is without prejudice, and plaintiffs have an opportunity to replead if they have a basis for doing so under Court of Chancery Rule 11. This result — permitting plaintiffs to replead — is unusual, but not unprecedented. . . .

Questions

1. What remedy are the plaintiffs seeking? Why? What is the legal basis for their claim?
2. What's the test for determining whether a claim is direct or derivative?
3. Was the claim in *Tooley* direct or derivative?

Exercise 10.4

For items 1 through 5 below, determine whether the suit would be direct or derivative.

1. The Certificate of Incorporation of XYZ Corp. requires the corporation to pay Class A shareholders twice the dividend of Class B shareholders. This year, however, XYZ Corp. paid the same amount of dividends to shareholders of both classes. Anderson, a Class A shareholder, sues.
2. Birkenstock is a director of XYZ Corp. He is also the sole shareholder of HIJ Co. XYZ agrees to buy HIJ for $5 million. Croc is a shareholder of XYZ and thinks XYZ is overpaying for HIJ. She sues Birkenstock and the other board members of XYZ for breach of fiduciary duties.
3. The board of directors of XYZ Corp. entered into a merger transaction with B Corp. Under the terms of the merger agreement, XYZ Corp. merged into B Corp. and the shareholders of XYZ were cashed out at $55 per share. After the merger had been completed, Tuba, a shareholder of XYZ, was unhappy with the transaction. She sues the board for breach of its fiduciary duty.
4. Ranum, the CEO of Matrix Development Inc. (MDI), purchased a parcel of property adjoining a shopping center owned by MDI. Porch, a shareholder of MDI, is unhappy with the transaction and sues Ranum for breach of fiduciary duty.
5. Chumba Inc. is fined $100 million by the EPA for dumping hazardous waste. Ralston, a Chumba stockholder, sues the Chumba board for failure to provide adequate oversight.

---

7. The MBCA Approach to Director Fiduciary Duties

Unlike the DGCL, the MBCA codifies much of director fiduciary duties law. This includes provisions regarding the standards of conduct and liability, conflicting interest transactions, usurping a corporate opportunity, and shareholder derivative suits.

a. Standards of Conduct and Liability

The standards of conduct for directors are set forth in MBCA §8.30, which provides:

(a) Each member of the board of directors, when discharging the duties of a director, shall act: (1) in good faith, and (2) in a manner the director reasonably believes to be in the best interests of the corporation.

(b) The members of the board of directors or a committee of the board, when becoming informed in connection with their decision-making function or devoting attention to their oversight function, shall discharge their duties with the care that a person in a like position would reasonably believe appropriate under similar circumstances. . . .

The above provisions more or less track Delaware law with the duty of loyalty reflected in subsection (a) and the duty of care in subsection (b).

MBCA §8.31 sets forth the standards of liability for directors, that is, when a director will be liable for failure to comply with §8.30. It is based on "the extensive body of decisional law dealing with liability of directors to the corporation or its shareholders."[106] Under §8.31(a)(2), as is the case under Delaware law (mainly, the business judgment rule), a plaintiff claiming that directors breached their fiduciary duties in approving a transaction has the initial burden of proving the approval process was inadequate or tainted. Unlike under Delaware law, however, overcoming this burden does not shift to the defendant directors the burden to prove "entire fairness." Instead, under §8.31(b)(1), a plaintiff seeking money damages also has to prove that "harm to the corporation or its shareholders has been suffered" and that "the harm suffered was proximately caused by the director's challenged conduct."

b. Conflicting Interest Transactions

Subchapter 8F of the MBCA contains detailed provisions addressing director's conflicting interest transactions (§§8.60-8.63). It establishes a framework similar to Delaware's for analyzing the propriety of these transactions but includes much of the detail in the statute as opposed to leaving it to case law.

Section 8.61 lays out the basic framework. It provides as follows:

> (a) A transaction effected or proposed to be effected by the corporation (or by an entity controlled by the corporation) may not be the subject of equitable relief, or give rise to an award of damages or other sanctions against a director of the corporation, in a proceeding by a shareholder or by or in the right of the corporation, on the ground that the director has an interest respecting the transaction, if it is not a director's conflicting interest transaction.
>
> (b) A director's conflicting interest transaction may not be the subject of equitable relief, or give rise to an award of damages or other sanctions against a director of the corporation, in a proceeding by a shareholder or by or in the right of the corporation, on the ground that the director has an interest respecting the transaction, if:
>
> (1) directors' action respecting the transaction was taken in compliance with section 8.62 at any time; or
>
> (2) shareholders' action respecting the transaction was taken in compliance with section 8.63 at any time; or

---

106. MBCA Intro. at xxviii.

(3) the transaction, judged according to the circumstances at the relevant time, is established to have been fair to the corporation.

Section 8.60 defines "director's conflicting interest transaction" as follows:

"Director's conflicting interest transaction" means a transaction effected or proposed to be effected by the corporation (or by an entity controlled by the corporation) (i) to which, at the relevant time, the director is a party; or (ii) respecting which, at the relevant time, the director had knowledge and a material financial interest known to the director; or (iii) respecting which, at the relevant time, the director knew that a related person was a party or had a material financial interest.

Section 8.60 also defines "relevant time," "material financial interest," and "related person." Note that under §8.61(a), any transaction that falls outside of the definition of "director's conflicting interest transaction" is not subject to challenge, even if a director has an interest in the transaction.

Section 8.62 specifies the requirements for valid director approval. Among other things, the transaction must be approved by the affirmative vote of "qualified directors" after "required disclosure." "Qualified director" is defined in §1.43, and "required disclosure" is defined in §8.60.

Section 8.63 specifies the requirement for valid shareholder approval. Among other things, the transaction must be approved by a majority of votes cast by the holders of all "qualified shares" following "required disclosure." "Qualified shares" is defined in §8.63(c).

Subchapter 8F reflects a decision by the drafters of the MBCA to establish bright-line tests for analyzing director conflicting interest transactions as opposed to leaving them to the courts. The drafters explained their decision as follows:

Bright-line provisions of any kind represent a trade-off between the benefits of certainty, and the danger that some transactions or conduct that fall outside the area circumscribed by the bright-lines may be so similar to the transactions and conduct that fall within the area that different treatment may seem anomalous. Subchapter F reflected the considered judgment that in corporate matters, where planning is critical, the clear and important efficiency gains that result from certainty through defining director's conflict-of-interest transactions clearly exceeded any potential and uncertain efficiency losses that might occasionally follow from excluding other director's transactions from judicial review for fairness on conflict-of-interest grounds.[107]

---

107. MBCA Subch. F. Intro. Cmt. 1.

> **Exercise 10.5**
>
> 1. Redo Exercise 10.1 assuming Netflix is incorporated in a state that has adopted the current version of the MBCA verbatim. Also assume that Netflix has an exculpation provision in its charter. Make sure you point to statutory provisions that support your analysis.
> 2. Redo Exercise 10.2 assuming Innoclub is incorporated in a state that has adopted the current version of the MBCA verbatim. Also assume that Innoclub has an exculpation provision in its charter. Make sure you point to statutory provisions that support your analysis.

c. Usurping a Corporate Opportunity

MBCA §8.70 provides a safe harbor for a director contemplating taking a business opportunity that may constitute a "corporate opportunity" and thus potentially give rise to a breach of duty of loyalty claim for usurping a corporate opportunity. The provision shields a director from such liability if, before taking the opportunity, the director brings it to the attention of the corporation, discloses all material facts concerning the opportunity known to the director, and either a majority of qualified directors or qualified shares disclaim the corporation's interest in the opportunity.

d. Shareholder Derivative Suits

MBCA Subchapter 7D addresses shareholder derivative suits. The requirements for bringing such a suit are similar to those in Delaware with the exception of the demand requirement. Under §7.42, a shareholder cannot commence a derivative suit until he or she has (1) made a written demand on the corporation to bring the suit, and (2) 90 days has run from the date of the demand, the corporation has rejected the demand, or waiting 90 days would result in irreparable injury to the corporation. This is known as the universal demand requirement because there is no demand futility exception; a written demand is required in all cases.

According to the Official Comment to §7.42:

> This approach has been adopted for two reasons. First, even though no director may be independent, the demand will give the board of directors the opportunity to re-examine the act complained of in the light of a potential lawsuit and take corrective action. Secondly, the provision eliminates the time and expense of the litigants and the court involved in litigating the question whether demand is required.

B. FIDUCIARY DUTIES OF OFFICERS

Officers owe the same fiduciary duties to the corporation as directors. In Delaware, this is pursuant to case law.[108] Under the MBCA, it is pursuant to statute (§8.42). Recall that officers are agents of the corporation so they owe fiduciary duties to the corporation (the principal) under agency law too.

One open issue under Delaware law is whether the business judgment rule applies to decisions made by officers. A federal court applying Delaware law stated that "[t]he business judgment rule applies only to directors of a corporation and not to officers,"[109] but no Delaware court has addressed the issue. The business judgment rule does appear to apply to offices under the MBCA. First, §8.42(d) states that "[w]hether an officer who does not comply with this section shall have liability will depend in such instance on applicable law, including those principles of §8.31 that have relevance." Recall that §8.31 provides the standard of liability for directors and at least partially codifies the business judgment rule. Furthermore, the Official Comment to §8.42 states that "the business judgment rule will normally apply to decisions within an officer's discretional authority." This area of law is not well developed because very few judicial opinions have had occasion to address breach of fiduciary duties by an officer.

Note that under both the DGCL and MBCA, an exculpation provision can only apply to directors and not officers. The corporate law statutes of a handful of states do nonetheless allow exculpation provisions to cover officers.[110]

C. FIDUCIARY DUTIES OF CONTROLLING SHAREHOLDERS

Under corporate common law, a controlling shareholder owes fiduciary duties to the corporation and its other shareholders. The issue comes up most often in the duty of loyalty context where a controlling shareholder enters into a transaction with the corporation. For example, say you are the controlling shareholder of XYZ, Inc. and you convince XYZ to buy your Aspen, Colorado vacation home from you. This transaction raises the same sort of concerns as we discussed above when you were a director of XYZ, specifically that you will use your influence as controlling shareholder to cause XYZ to overpay for the property.

The next case discusses the threshold issue of whether someone is a controlling shareholder. This issue can be outcome determinative because only a controlling shareholder owes the corporation and its other shareholders fiduciary

---

108. *See Gantler v. Stephens*, 965 A.2d 695, 708 ("officers of Delaware corporations, like directors, owe fiduciary duties of care and loyalty, and . . . the fiduciary duties of officers are the same as those of directors").
109. *Platt v. Richardson*, No. 88-0144, 1989 WL 159584, at *2 (M.D. Pa. June 6, 1989).
110. These states include Louisiana, Maryland, New Hampshire, and New Jersey.

duties. In other words, a non-controlling shareholder cannot be liable to the corporation or other shareholders for breach of fiduciary duty because it owes them no fiduciary duties.

Superior Vision Services, Inc. v. ReliaStar Life Insurance Company
2006 WL 2521426 (2006)

NOBLE, Vice Chancellor.

I. INTRODUCTION

A company agreed with its investors that it would not pay dividends; it has now concluded that it does not like the consequences of its agreement. The prohibition against the payment of dividends may be waived if the holders of two-thirds of its shares agree. Although the board of directors has authorized the payment of dividends, some dividends have not been paid because one investor, which owns 44 percent of the stock in the company, refuses to waive the contractual prohibition. The company—not the other investors who would have received the dividends if paid—brings this action and charges the investor who refuses to waive the contractual prohibition with breach of fiduciary duty as a "controlling" shareholder ... because, according to the company, there is no good reason for not acquiescing in the payment of dividends. Before the Court is the non-waiving investor's motion to dismiss.

II. BACKGROUND

Plaintiff Superior Vision Services, Inc. ("SVS") is a privately-held Delaware corporation that provides vision insurance to its customers. Pursuant to a series of Stock Purchase Agreements, SVS issued shares to its various investors, including Defendant ReliaStar Life Insurance Company ("ReliaStar"), SVS's largest investor and holder of 44 percent of its stock.

The Agreements prohibit payment of any dividend. Specifically, Section 8.4 of the Agreements provides:

> *Limitation on Dividends; Redemption. The Company will not pay any dividend* or make any distribution with respect to any of its equity securities or redeem or repurchase any of its equity securities except for required redemptions of the Series A Stock and/or Series B stock and repurchases, approved by the Company's board of directors pursuant to the Stockholders' Agreement.

The prohibition against payment of dividends may be waived. Section 12.8 governs waivers of the Agreements' terms, including waivers of the dividend prohibition contained in Section 8.4. Under Section 12.8, "[w]ith the written consent of such Investors owning at least two-thirds of the Purchased Securities then owned by such Investors, the obligations of the Company under this Agreement may be waived." As a result of ReliaStar's 44 percent ownership interest, the prohibition against dividend payments (Section 8.4) may only be waived with ReliaStar's consent.

The SVS Board has considered, and voted on, a proposed dividend payment on three occasions: (1) October 8, 2004, (2) May 6, 2005, and (3) July 25, 2005. SVS contends that ReliaStar's response in these instances demonstrates that "[i]t is ReliaStar's practice to withhold its consent to dividends in order to strong-arm individual stockholders or SVS to further its own agenda." . . .

III. CONTENTIONS

Frustrated by ReliaStar's failure to consent to the dividend payment, SVS petitioned this Court for declaratory relief. In particular, SVS seeks: (1) a declaration that, subject to compliance with 8 Del. C. §170, SVS is entitled to pay [a proposed dividend]; [and] (2) a declaration that ReliaStar breached the fiduciary duties it owes to SVS . . . .

With respect to SVS's fiduciary duty claim, ReliaStar argues that . . . it is not a "controlling shareholder" and, thus, does not owe fiduciary duties. . . .

IV. ANALYSIS

. . . SVS presents a remarkably unconventional cause of action. In this instance, it is the corporation — not its shareholders — alleging breach of fiduciary duty by an allegedly controlling shareholder. More importantly, SVS has not alleged any wrongdoing by ReliaStar through its designated directors; rather, the alleged harm stems *solely* from the purported abuse of ReliaStar's contractual right to withhold its consent and, thus, effectively to veto any dividend payments in contravention of its fiduciary obligations as a controlling shareholder. Specifically, SVS contends that: ReliaStar owes a fiduciary duty to SVS and its stockholders with respect to the exercise of rights under the Agreements; ReliaStar, in violation of Delaware law, has knowingly, recklessly and in bad faith violated its duties of good faith, care, and candor owed; and ReliaStar has breached its fiduciary duties by, among other things, withholding its consent to the payment of dividends without any economic justification or other bona fide reason.

A shareholder owes fiduciary duties in two instances: (1) when it is a "majority shareholder," owning more than 50 percent of the shares, or (2) when it "exercises control over the business affairs of the corporation." ReliaStar holds a 44 percent interest in SVS; thus, fiduciary obligations will result only if it is deemed a "controlling shareholder."

"[T]o be deemed a controlling stockholder for purposes of imposing fiduciary obligations, the plaintiff must establish the *actual exercise* of control over the corporation's conduct by that otherwise minority stockholder."[111] In order to append the label of "controlling shareholder," pervasive control over the corporation's actions is not required; indeed, a plaintiff "can survive

---

111. [FN 34] *Weinstein Enters. v. Orloff*, 870 A.2d 499, 507 (Del. 2005) (emphasis in original).

the motion to dismiss by alleging actual control with regard to the particular transaction that is being challenged."[112] ReliaStar is a significant shareholder in SVS; it has the power to preclude the payment of dividends; and, in fact, it has prevented the payment of dividends. Thus, it has exercised "actual control" with regard to the payment of dividends. SVS, however, has not alleged that ReliaStar controlled the Board; in fact, the Board, including ReliaStar's designees, unanimously approved the Policy for payment of dividends. The question here is whether the actual control must be over the Board or whether separately negotiated contract rights can supply the requisite degree of control.

Delaware case law has focused on control of the board. For example, in *In re Western National Corp. Shareholders Litigation,* the Court inquired as to whether the significant shareholder "in fact, exercise[d] actual control over the board of directors during the course of a particular transaction."[113] In *Kahn v. Lynch Communications Systems, Inc.,*[114] a 43% minority shareholder (Alcatel) was deemed a controlling shareholder of Lynch Communications Systems ("Lynch") because of its influence over the Lynch board. As the Court observed, "[t]he [Lynch] management and independent directors disagreed with Alcatel on several important issues. However, when Alcatel made its position clear, and reminded the other directors of its significant stockholdings, Alcatel prevailed."[115] Similarly, in *Williamson v. Cox Communications, Inc.,* minority shareholders, with their designated members of the board constituting less than a majority, were able to benefit from the ongoing commercial relationships the company had with those shareholders to override the board's independent judgment (or so it was alleged).[116] Accordingly, the focus of the inquiry has been on the *de facto* power of a significant (but less than majority) shareholder, which, when coupled with other factors, gives that shareholder the ability to dominate the corporate decision-making process. The concern is that the significant shareholder will use its power to obtain (or compel) favorable actions by the board to the ultimate detriment of other shareholders.

ReliaStar, by contrast, draws its power from a previously (and, at least from the Complaint, fairly) negotiated contract. It is not influencing or controlling

---

112. [FN 35] *Williamson v. Cox Commc'ns, Inc.,* 2006 WL 1586375, at *4 (Del. Ch. June 5, 2006).

113. [FN 38] 2000 WL 710192, at *20 (Del. Ch. May 22, 2000). The Court in *Western National* noted that, in order for a significant shareholder to be deemed a controlling shareholder, there must be "a judicial finding of actual control over the *business and affairs of the corporation.*" 2000 WL 710192, at *8 (emphasis in original). That view may be pertinent for two reasons. First, the reference to the "business and affairs" of the corporation suggests something broader than one corporate act, such as the payment of a dividend. If so, SVS would be required to allege that ReliaStar's control was more extensive, reaching beyond the payment of dividends. It has not done so. Second, the "business and affairs" of a Delaware corporation are under the direction of the board pursuant to 8 Del. C. §141(a), as noted by the Court in *Western National;* that suggests that questions of control by a significant shareholder should be assessed at the board level in terms of whether the board's capacity to exercise its judgment independently has been impaired. SVS, of course, has not challenged the conduct of its directors.

114. [FN 39] 638 A.2d 1110 (Del. 1994).

115. [FN 40] *Id.* at 1114.

116. [FN 41] *Williamson,* 2006 WL 1586375, at *5.

any action by the Board; indeed, the Board has taken the action that it saw fit—approving dividends. ReliaStar does, however, have a contractual right that allows it to prevent implementation of the corporate dividend policy adopted by the Board. Under SVS's view, any significant shareholder who, because of a contractual right, effectively blocks a particular corporate action would be considered a "controlling shareholder" with respect to that action. In essence, any strong contractual right, duly obtained by a significant shareholder (a somewhat elusive term in itself), would be limited by and subject to fiduciary duty concerns. In substance, SVS asks the Court to engraft upon ReliaStar's specific and fairly negotiated contractual rights a limitation that ReliaStar cannot just consider its interests whenever it decides whether to waive (or not) any provision which it obtained during the process of negotiating the Agreement. Here, ReliaStar is alleged to have taken advantage of its contractual rights for its own purposes. Without more, that is not sufficient to allege that ReliaStar is a "controlling shareholder" bound by fiduciary obligations.

In sum, a significant shareholder, who exercises a duly-obtained contractual right that somehow limits or restricts the actions that a corporation otherwise would take, does not become, without more, a "controlling shareholder" for that particular purpose. There may be circumstances where the holding of contractual rights, coupled with a significant equity position and other factors, will support the finding that a particular shareholder is, indeed, a "controlling shareholder," especially if those contractual rights are used to induce or to coerce the board of directors to approve (or refrain from approving) certain actions. That confluence of factors is not alleged to be present in this matter and, accordingly, ReliaStar may not fairly be deemed a "controlling shareholder" with respect to the payment of dividends by SVS. With that conclusion, SVS's claim against ReliaStar for breach of fiduciary duty fails. . . .

V. CONCLUSION

For the foregoing reasons, the Amended Complaint will be dismissed under Court of Chancery Rule 12(b)(6). An implementing order will be entered.

Questions

1. Who is ReliaStar? What did it allegedly do wrong?
2. What is the test for determining whether someone is a controlling shareholder?
3. What is SVS's argument for why ReliaStar is a controlling shareholder of SVS? Why does the court reject this argument?
4. What are the consequences of being a controlling shareholder?

Note that the opinion above makes a distinction between a majority share-holder and a controlling shareholder. Since both owe the corporation and other shareholders fiduciary duties, my use of the term "controlling shareholder" en-compasses a majority shareholder.

The framework for analyzing whether a controlling shareholder conflicting interest transaction constitutes a breach of the duty of loyalty is as follows:

- The controlling shareholder has the burden of proving the transaction was fair to the corporation.
- If the controlling shareholder meets this burden, it did not breach the duty of loyalty. If it fails to meet it, it breached the duty of loyalty and is liable for damages. Thus, for example, if the sale of your Aspen vacation home is found to be a breach of the duty of loyalty, the court will deter-mine the amount by which the corporation overpaid for your vacation home, and order you to pay that amount to the corporation.
- A controlling shareholder can avoid having to prove fairness by having the transaction approved by a fully informed majority of disinterested and independent directors or a majority of disinterested stockholders (often referred to as a "majority of the minority" vote). Such an approval (sometimes called a "cleansing device") shifts the burden to the plaintiff to prove that the transaction was unfair to the corporation. If the plaintiff meets its burden, the controlling shareholder breached the duty of loyalty and is liable for damages. Note that this burden shift differs from when a cleansing device is used in the director conflicting interest transaction context. As discussed above, in that context, a cleansing device invokes the business judgment rule.

Courts have also endorsed as a cleansing device the use of a committee com-posed of outside directors to negotiate the transaction with the controlling stockholder. However:

> [t]he mere existence of an independent special committee . . . does not itself shift the burden. At least two factors are required. First, the majority sharehold-er must not dictate the terms of the [transaction]. Second, the special committee must have real bargaining power that it can exercise with the majority share-holder on an arms length basis.[117]

The next case addresses at what point in a proceeding (pre- or post-trial) a court is to determine whether a burden shifting occurred.

---

117. *Kahn v. Lynch*, 638 A.2d 1110, 1117 (quoting *Rabkin v. Olin Corp.*, 1990 WL 47648, at 14-15 (1990), citations omitted).

Americas Mining Corporation v. Theriault
51 A.3d 1213 (Del. 2012)

HOLLAND, Justice.

This is an appeal from a post-trial decision and final judgment of the Court of Chancery awarding more than $2 billion in damages and more than $304 million in attorneys' fees. The Court of Chancery held that the defendants-appellants, Americas Mining Corporation ("AMC"), the subsidiary of Southern Copper Corporation's ("Southern Peru") controlling shareholder, and affiliate directors of Southern Peru (collectively, the "Defendants"), breached their fiduciary duty of loyalty to Southern Peru and its minority stockholders by causing Southern Peru to acquire the controller's 99.15% interest in a Mexican mining company, Minera México, S.A. de C.V. ("Minera"), for much more than it was worth, i.e., at an unfair price.

The Plaintiff challenged the transaction derivatively on behalf of Southern Peru. The Court of Chancery found the trial evidence established that the controlling shareholder, Grupo México, S.A.B. de C.V. ("Grupo Mexico"), through AMC, "extracted a deal that was far better than market" from Southern Peru due to the ineffective operation of a special committee (the "Special Committee"). To remedy the Defendants' breaches of loyalty, the Court of Chancery awarded the difference between the value Southern Peru paid for Minera ($3.7 billion) and the amount the Court of Chancery determined Minera was worth ($2.4 billion). The Court of Chancery awarded damages in the amount of $1.347 billion plus pre- and post-judgment interest, for a total judgment of $2.0316 billion. The Court of Chancery also awarded the Plaintiff's counsel attorneys' fees and expenses in the amount of 15% of the total judgment, which amounts to more than $304 million. . . .

FACTUAL BACKGROUND

The controlling stockholder in this case is Grupo México, S.A.B. de C.V. The NYSE-listed mining company is Southern Peru Copper Corporation. The Mexican mining company is Minera México, S.A. de C.V.

In February 2004, Grupo Mexico proposed that Southern Peru buy its 99.15% stake in Minera. At the time, Grupo Mexico owned 54.17% of Southern Peru's outstanding capital stock and could exercise 63.08% of the voting power of Southern Peru, making it Southern Peru's majority stockholder.

Grupo Mexico initially proposed that Southern Peru purchase its equity interest in Minera with 72.3 million shares of newly-issued Southern Peru stock. This "indicative" number assumed that Minera's equity was worth $3.05 billion, because that is what 72.3 million shares of Southern Peru stock were worth then in cash. By stark contrast with Southern Peru, Minera was almost wholly owned by Grupo Mexico and therefore had no market-tested value.

Because of Grupo Mexico's self-interest in the merger proposal, Southern Peru formed a "Special Committee" of disinterested directors to "evaluate" the transaction with Grupo Mexico. The Special Committee spent eight months in an awkward back and forth with Grupo Mexico over the terms of the deal before approving Southern Peru's acquisition of 99.15% of Minera's stock in exchange for 67.2 million newly-issued shares of Southern Peru stock (the "Merger") on October 21, 2004. That same day, Southern Peru's board of directors (the "Board") unanimously approved the Merger and Southern Peru and Grupo Mexico entered into a definitive agreement (the "Merger Agreement"). On October 21, 2004, the market value of 67.2 million shares of Southern Peru stock was $3.1 billion. When the Merger closed on April 1, 2005, the value of 67.2 million shares of Southern Peru had grown to $3.75 billion.

This derivative suit was then brought against the Grupo Mexico subsidiary that owned Minera, the Grupo Mexico-affiliated directors of Southern Peru, and the members of the Special Committee, alleging that the Merger was entirely unfair to Southern Peru and its minority stockholders.

The crux of the Plaintiff's argument is that Grupo Mexico received something demonstrably worth more than $3 billion (67.2 million shares of Southern Peru stock) in exchange for something that was not worth nearly that much (99.15% of Minera). The Plaintiff points to the fact that Goldman, which served as the Special Committee's financial advisor, never derived a value for Minera that justified paying Grupo Mexico's asking price, but instead relied on a "relative" valuation analysis that involved comparing the discounted cash flow ("DCF") values of Southern Peru and Minera, and a contribution analysis that improperly applied Southern Peru's own market EBITDA multiple (and even higher multiples) to Minera's EBITDA projections, to determine an appropriate exchange ratio to use in the Merger. The Plaintiff claims that, because the Special Committee and Goldman abandoned the company's market price as a measure of the true value of the give, Southern Peru substantially overpaid in the Merger.

The Defendants remaining in the case are Grupo Mexico and its affiliate directors who were on the Southern Peru Board at the time of the Merger. These Defendants assert that Southern Peru and Minera are similar companies and were properly valued on a relative basis. In other words, the defendants argue that the appropriate way to determine the price to be paid by Southern Peru in the Merger was to compare both companies' values using the same set of assumptions and methodologies, rather than comparing Southern Peru's market capitalization to Minera's DCF value. The Defendants do not dispute that shares of Southern Peru stock could have been sold for their market price at the time of the Merger, but they contend that Southern Peru's market price did not reflect the fundamental value of Southern Peru and thus could not appropriately be compared to the DCF value of Minera. . . .

BURDEN SHIFTING ANALYSIS

The Defendants . . . [argue] . . . that the Court of Chancery committed reversible error by failing to determine which party bore the burden of proof before trial. The Defendants submit that the Court of Chancery further erred by ultimately allocating the burden to the Defendants, because the Special Committee was independent, was well-functioning, and did not rely on the controlling shareholder for the information that formed the basis for its recommendation.

When a transaction involving self-dealing by a controlling shareholder is challenged, the applicable standard of judicial review is entire fairness, with the defendants having the burden of persuasion. In other words, the defendants bear the burden of proving that the transaction with the controlling stockholder was entirely fair to the minority stockholders. In the Court of Chancery and on appeal, both the Plaintiff and the Defendants agree that entire fairness is the appropriate standard of judicial review for the Merger. . . .

In *Kahn v. Lynch Communication Systems, Inc.*,[118] this Court held that when the entire fairness standard applies, the defendants may shift the burden of persuasion by one of two means: first, they may show that the transaction was approved by a well-functioning committee of independent directors; or second, they may show that the transaction was approved by an informed vote of a majority of the minority shareholders. Nevertheless, even when an interested cash-out merger transaction receives the informed approval of a majority of minority stockholders or a well-functioning committee of independent directors, an entire fairness analysis is the only proper standard of review. Accordingly, "[r]egardless of where the burden lies, when a controlling shareholder stands on both sides of the transaction the conduct of the parties will be viewed under the more exacting standard of entire fairness as opposed to the more deferential business judgment standard."[119]

In *Emerald Partners v. Berlin*,[120] we noted that "[w]hen the standard of review is entire fairness, ab initio, director defendants can move for summary judgment on either the issue of entire fairness or the issue of burden shifting."[121] In this case, the Defendants filed a summary judgment motion, arguing that the Special Committee process shifted the burden of persuasion under the preponderance standard to the Plaintiff. The Court of Chancery found the summary judgment record was insufficient to determine that question of burden shifting prior to trial.

Lynch and its progeny set forth what is required of an independent committee for the defendants to obtain a burden shift. In this case, the Court of Chancery recognized that, in *Kahn v. Tremont Corp.*,[122] this Court held that "[t]o obtain the benefit of a burden shifting, the controlling shareholder must do more than establish a perfunctory special committee of outside directors."[123] Rather, the special committee must "function in a manner which indicates that the controlling shareholder did not dictate the terms of the transaction and

---

118. [FN 22] *Kahn v. Lynch Commc'n Sys., Inc.*, 638 A.2d 1110 (Del. 1994).
119. [FN 25] *Kahn v. Tremont Corp.*, 694 A.2d 422, 428 (citation omitted).
120. [FN 26] *Emerald Partners v. Berlin*, 787 A.2d 85 (Del. 2001).
121. [FN 27] *Id.* at 98-99.
122. [FN 29] *Kahn v. Tremont Corp.*, 694 A.2d 422 (Del. 1997).
123. [FN 30] *Id.* at 429 (citation omitted).

that the committee exercised real bargaining power 'at an arms-length.'"[124] In this case, the Court of Chancery properly concluded that:

> A close look at *Tremont* suggests that the [burden shifting] inquiry must focus on how the special committee actually negotiated the deal—was it "well functioning"[125]—rather than just how the committee was set up. The test, therefore, seems to contemplate a look back at the substance, and efficacy, of the special committee's negotiations, rather than just a look at the composition and mandate of the special committee.

The Court of Chancery expressed its concern about the practical implications of such a factually intensive burden shifting inquiry because it is "deeply enmeshed" in the ultimate entire fairness analysis.

> Subsuming within the burden shift analysis questions of whether the special committee was substantively effective in its negotiations with the controlling stockholder—questions fraught with factual complexity—will, absent unique circumstances, guarantee that the burden shift will rarely be determinable on the basis of the pretrial record alone. If we take seriously the notion, as I do, that a standard of review is meant to serve as the framework through which the court evaluates the parties' evidence and trial testimony in reaching a decision, and, as important, the framework through which the litigants determine how best to prepare their cases for trial, it is problematic to adopt an analytical approach whereby the burden allocation can only be determined in a post-trial opinion, after all the evidence and all the arguments have been presented to the court.

We agree with these thoughtful comments. However, the general inability to decide burden shifting prior to trial is directly related to the reason why entire fairness remains the applicable standard of review even when an independent committee is utilized, i.e., "because the underlying factors which raise the specter of impropriety can never be completely eradicated and still require careful judicial scrutiny."[126]

This case is a perfect example. The Court of Chancery could not decide whether to shift the burden based upon the pretrial record. After hearing all of the evidence presented at trial, the Court of Chancery found that, although the independence of the Special Committee was not challenged, "from inception, the Special Committee fell victim to a controlled mindset and allowed Grupo Mexico to dictate the terms and structure of the merger." The Court of Chancery concluded that "although the Special Committee members were

---

124. [FN 31] *Id.* (citation omitted).
125. [FN 32] *Id.* at 428.
126. [FN 36] *Kahn v. Tremont Corp.*, 694 A.2d at 428 (citing *Weinberger v. UOP, Inc.*, 457 A.2d at 710). See also *In re Cox Commc'ns, Inc. S'holders Litig.*, 879 A.2d 604, 617 (Del. Ch. 2005) ("All in all, it is perhaps fairest and more sensible to read *Lynch* as being premised on a sincere concern that mergers with controlling stockholders involve an extraordinary potential for the exploitation by powerful insiders of their informational advantages and their voting clout.").

competent businessmen and may have had the best of intentions, they allowed themselves to be hemmed in by the controlling stockholder's demands."

We recognize that there are practical problems for litigants when the issue of burden shifting is not decided until after the trial. For example, "in order to prove that a burden shift occurred because of an effective special committee, the defendants must present evidence of a fair process. Because they must present this evidence affirmatively, they have to act like they have the burden of persuasion throughout the entire trial court process."[127] That is exactly what happened in this case.

Delaware has long adhered to the principle that the controlling shareholders have the burden of proving an interested transaction was entirely fair. However, in order to encourage the use of procedural devices that foster fair pricing, such as special committees and minority stockholder approval conditions, this Court has provided transactional proponents with what has been described as a "modest procedural benefit—the shifting of the burden of persuasion on the ultimate issue of entire fairness to the plaintiffs—if the transaction proponents proved, in a factually intensive way, that the procedural devices had, in fact, operated with integrity."[128] We emphasize that in *Cox*, the procedural benefit of burden shifting was characterized as "modest."

Once again, in this case, the Court of Chancery expressed uncertainty about whether "there is much, if any, practical implication of a burden shift." According to the Court of Chancery, "[t]he practical effect of the *Lynch* doctrine's burden shift is slight. One reason why this is so is that shifting the burden of persuasion under a preponderance standard is not a major move, if one assumes ... that the outcome of very few cases hinges on what happens if ... the evidence is in equipoise."[129]

In its post-trial opinion, the Court of Chancery found that the burden of persuasion remained with the Defendants, because the Special Committee was not "well functioning." The trial judge also found, "however, that this determination matters little because I am not stuck in equipoise about the issue of fairness. Regardless of who bears the burden, I conclude that the Merger was unfair to Southern Peru and its stockholders."

Nothing in the record reflects that a different outcome would have resulted if either the burden of proof had been shifted to the Plaintiff, or the Defendants had been advised prior to trial that the burden had not shifted. The record reflects that, by agreement of the parties, each witness other than the Plaintiff's expert was called in direct examination by the Defendants, and then was cross-examined by the Plaintiff. The Defendants have not identified any decision they might have made differently, if they had been advised prior to trial that the burden of proof had not shifted.

127. [FN 38] *In re Cysive, Inc. S'holders Litig.*, 836 A.2d at 549.
128. [FN 40] *In re Cox Commc'ns, Inc. S'holders Litig.*, 879 A.2d at 617.
129. [FN 41] *In re Cysive, Inc. S'holders Litig.*, 836 A.2d 531, 548 (Del. Ch. 2003).

The Court of Chancery concluded that this is not a case where the evidence of fairness or unfairness stood in equipoise. It found that the evidence of unfairness was so overwhelming that the question of who had the burden of proof at trial was irrelevant to the outcome. That determination is supported by the record. The Court of Chancery committed no error by not allocating the burden of proof before trial, in accordance with our prior precedents. In the absence of a renewed request by the Defendants during trial that the burden be shifted to the Plaintiff, the burden of proving entire fairness remained with the Defendants throughout the trial. The record reflects that is how the trial in this case was conducted.

Nevertheless, we recognize that the purpose of providing defendants with the opportunity to seek a burden shift is not only to encourage the use of special committees, but also to provide a reliable pretrial guide for the parties regarding who has the burden of persuasion. Therefore, which party bears the burden of proof must be determined, if possible, before the trial begins. The Court of Chancery has noted that, in the interest of having certainty, "it is unsurprising that few defendants have sought a pretrial hearing to determine who bears the burden of persuasion on fairness" given "the factually intense nature of the burden-shifting inquiry" and the "modest benefit" gained from the shift.

The failure to shift the burden is not outcome determinative under the entire fairness standard of review. We have concluded that, because the only "modest" effect of the burden shift is to make the plaintiff prove unfairness under a preponderance of the evidence standard, the benefits of clarity in terms of trial presentation outweigh the costs of continuing to decide either during or after trial whether the burden has shifted. Accordingly, we hold prospectively that, if the record does not permit a pretrial determination that the defendants are entitled to a burden shift, the burden of persuasion will remain with the defendants throughout the trial to demonstrate the entire fairness of the interested transaction.

The Defendants argue that if the Court of Chancery rarely determines the issue of burden shifting on the basis of a pretrial record, corporations will be dissuaded from forming special committees of independent directors and from seeking approval of an interested transaction by an informed vote of a majority of the minority shareholders. That argument underestimates the importance of either or both actions to the process component—fair dealing—of the entire fairness standard. This Court has repeatedly held that any board process is materially enhanced when the decision is attributable to independent directors. Accordingly, judicial review for entire fairness of how the transaction was structured, negotiated, disclosed to the directors, and approved by the directors will be significantly influenced by the work product of a properly functioning special committee of independent directors. Similarly, the issue of how stockholder approval was obtained will be significantly influenced by the affirmative vote of a majority of the minority stockholders.

A fair process usually results in a fair price. Therefore, the proponents of an interested transaction will continue to be incentivized to put a fair dealing process in place that promotes judicial confidence in the entire fairness of the transaction price. Accordingly, we have no doubt that the effective use of a properly functioning special committee of independent directors and the informed conditional approval of a majority of minority stockholders will continue to be integral parts of the best practices that are used to establish a fair dealing process. . . .

CONCLUSION

The judgment of the Court of Chancery, awarding more than $2 billion in damages and more than $304 million in attorneys' fees, is affirmed.

Questions

1. At what point in the proceedings did the trial court determine whether the burden shifted? Why? Why do Defendants take issue with the timing of this determination?
2. What is the rule for when a trial court is to determine whether the burden has shifted?
3. Why does the court characterize the procedural benefit of burden shifting as modest? How is this characterization relevant to the case?

D. INDEMNIFICATION AND INSURANCE

Even if a plaintiff prevails on a claim against a director or officer and is awarded monetary damages, these damages will not necessarily be paid by the defendant(s). It depends on whether payment of the damages qualifies for indemnification and/or is covered by the corporation's directors and officers liability (D&O) insurance.

1. Indemnification

Indemnification is when a corporation pays the litigation costs and expenses of directors and officers from suits arising out of their corporate service. It is expressly allowed by statute.[130] The basic policy behind allowing indemnification is to prevent a person from turning down the opportunity to be a director or officer out of fear of getting saddled with large legal bills from lawsuits.

Corporate law statutes provide for both mandatory and permissive indemnification. Generally speaking, a corporation is required to indemnify a director

---

130. *See, e.g.*, DGCL §145; MBCA Chap. 8F.

or officer who is sued in such capacity and wins the suit on the merits.[131] A corporation is permitted, but not statutorily required, to indemnify a director or officer who was unsuccessful on the merits, provided the person acted in good faith and in a manner he or she reasonably believed to be in the best interests of the corporation.[132] With respect to a criminal proceeding, the person must also have had no reasonable cause to believe that his or her conduct was unlawful.[133] Permissive indemnification includes payment of attorneys' fees, judgments, monetary settlements, and fines. For derivative suits, permissible indemnification is limited to the payment of expenses (i.e., attorneys' fees) and in some states (including Delaware) doing so requires court approval.[134]

Directors and officers typically insist as a condition to working for a corporation that the corporation contractually agree to indemnify them to the full extent allowed by law. This is typically done pursuant to an indemnification agreement between the director or officer and the corporation. Here is some sample language from an indemnification agreement of a Delaware corporation (the director or officer is the "Indemnitee"):

---

3. <u>Proceedings Other Than Proceedings by or in the Right of the Company</u>. If in connection with or by reason of Indemnitee's Corporate Status Indemnitee was, is, or is threatened to be made, a party to or a participant in any Proceeding (as hereinafter defined) other than a Proceeding by or in the right of the Company to procure a judgment in its favor, the Company shall, to the fullest extent permitted by law, indemnify Indemnitee with respect to, and hold Indemnitee harmless from and against, all losses, liabilities, judgments, fines, penalties, costs amounts paid in settlement, Expenses and other amounts (including all interest, assessments and other charges paid or payable in connection with or in respect of such amounts paid in settlement) reasonably incurred by Indemnitee or on behalf of Indemnitee in connection with such Proceeding or any claim, issue or matter therein, if Indemnitee acted in good faith and in a manner Indemnitee reasonably believed to be in, or not opposed to, the best interests of the Company and, with respect to any criminal Proceeding, had no reasonable cause to believe Indemnitee's conduct was unlawful.

4. <u>Proceedings by or in the Right of the Company</u>. If by reason of Indemnitee's Corporate Status Indemnitee was, is, or is threatened to be made a party to or a participant in any Proceeding by or in the right of the Company to procure a judgment in its favor, the Company shall, to the fullest extent permitted by law, indemnify Indemnitee with respect to, and hold Indemnitee harmless from and against, all Expenses reasonably incurred by Indemnitee or on behalf of Indemnitee in connection with such Proceeding if Indemnitee acted in good faith and

---

131. *See, e.g.*, DGCL §145(c); MBCA §§8.52 & §8.56(c).
132. *See, e.g.*, DGCL §145(a); MBCA §§8.51 & 8.56.
133. *See id.*
134. *See* DGCL §145(b); MBCA §8.51(d)(1).

in a manner Indemnitee reasonably believed to be in, or not opposed to, the best interests of the Company; provided, however, that indemnification against such Expenses shall be made in respect of any claim, issue or matter in such Proceeding as to which Indemnitee shall have been adjudged by a court of competent jurisdiction to be liable to the Company only if (and only to the extent that) the Court of Chancery of the State of Delaware or other court in which such Proceeding shall have been brought or is pending shall determine that despite such adjudication of liability and in light of all circumstances such indemnification may be made. . . .

"Corporate Status" describes the status of a person by reason of such person's past, present or future service as a director or officer of the Company. . . .

"Expenses" shall mean all reasonable direct and indirect costs, fees and expenses of any type or nature whatsoever and shall specifically include, without limitation, all reasonable attorneys' fees, retainers, court costs, transcript costs, fees and costs of experts, witness fees, travel expenses, duplicating costs, printing and binding costs, telephone charges, postage, delivery service fees, and all other disbursements or expenses of the types customarily incurred in connection with prosecuting, defending, preparing to prosecute or defend, investigating, being or preparing to be a witness, in, or otherwise participating in, a Proceeding, including, but not limited to, the premium for appeal bonds, attachment bonds or similar bonds and all interest, assessments and other charges paid or payable in connection with or in respect of any such Expenses, and shall also specifically include, without limitation, all reasonable attorneys' fees and all other expenses incurred by or on behalf of Indemnitee in connection with preparing and submitting any requests or statements for indemnification, advancement, contribution or any other right provided by this Agreement. Expenses, however, shall not include amounts paid in settlement by Indemnitee or the amounts of judgments or fines against Indemnitee. . . .

"Proceeding" includes any actual, threatened, pending or completed action, suit, arbitration, alternate dispute resolution mechanism, investigation, inquiry, administrative hearing or any other actual, threatened, pending or completed proceeding, whether brought by or in the right of the Company or otherwise and whether civil, criminal, administrative or investigative in nature, in which Indemnitee was, is, may be or will be involved as a party, witness or otherwise, by reason of Indemnitee's Corporate Status or by reason of any action taken by Indemnitee or of any inaction on Indemnitee's part while acting as director or officer of any Mattress Firm Entity (in each case whether or not he is acting or serving in any such capacity or has such status at the time any liability or expense is incurred for which indemnification or advancement of Expenses can be provided under this Agreement).

Corporate law statutes also allow a corporation to advance litigation expenses to directors and officers.[135] In order to make advances, however, the director or officer must furnish the corporation an undertaking to repay advanced amounts if it is ultimately determined that he or she was not entitled to

---

135. *See* DGCL §145(c); MBCA §§8.53 & 8.56(a).

indemnification.[136] Advancement is normally addressed in an indemnification agreement. Here is sample language from the same indemnification agreement as the above language:

> 8. <u>Advancement of Expenses</u>. The Company shall, to the fullest extent permitted by law, pay on a current and as-incurred basis all Expenses incurred by Indemnitee in connection with any Proceeding in any way connected with, resulting from or relating to Indemnitee's Corporate Status. Such Expenses shall be paid in advance of the final disposition of such Proceeding, without regard to whether Indemnitee will ultimately be entitled to be indemnified for such Expenses. Upon submission of a request for advancement of Expenses pursuant to Section 9(c) of this Agreement, Indemnitee shall be entitled to advancement of Expenses as provided in this Section 8, and such advancement of Expenses shall continue until such time (if any) as there is a final non-appealable judicial determination that Indemnitee is not entitled to indemnification. . . .
>
> 9. <u>Indemnification Procedures</u>. . . .
>   (c) <u>Request for Advancement; Request for Indemnification</u>.
>   (i) To obtain advancement of Expenses under this Agreement, Indemnitee shall submit to the Company a written request therefor, together with such invoices or other supporting information as may be reasonably requested by the Company and reasonably available to Indemnitee, and, only to the extent required by applicable law which cannot be waived, and a written undertaking to repay amounts advanced. Any such repayment obligation shall be unsecured and shall not bear interest. Advancement shall be made without regard to Indemnitee's ability to repay amounts advanced. The Company shall make advance payment of Expenses to Indemnitee no later than twenty (20) days after receipt of the written request for advancement (and each subsequent request for advancement) by Indemnitee. If, at the time of receipt of any such written request for advancement of Expenses, the Company has director and officer insurance policies in effect, the Company will promptly notify the relevant insurers in accordance with the procedures and requirements of such policies. The Company shall thereafter keep such director and officer insurers informed of the status of the Proceeding or other claim, as appropriate to secure coverage of Indemnitee for such claim. . . .

Exercise 10.6

Assume Watson prevails against Kuchar on the merits in the breach of fiduciary duty claim he brought on behalf of Innoclub for the sale of Kuchar's Salvador Dali collection to Innoclub (see Exercise 10.2). Kuchar incurs $300,000 in legal

---

136. *See id.*

> fees defending the case and is ordered by the court to pay Innoclub $500,000, because that is the amount the court determined Innoclub overpaid for the collection. Assume Innoclub is incorporated in Delaware.
>
> 1. Assume Kuchar and Innoclub are not parties to an indemnification agreement. Is Innoclub required to indemnify Kuchar? Is Innoclub permitted to indemnify Kuchar? If so, how much could it pay him? What advice would you give the board when considering and acting on the indemnification question?
> 2. Assume Kuchar settled the suit for $300,000 prior to a decision on the merits and incurred $100,000 in legal fees in the process. Is Innoclub required or permitted to reimburse him for these amounts?
> 3. Assume Kuchar and Innoclub are parties to an indemnification agreement containing the above sample language. Is Innoclub required to indemnify Kuchar? If so, for how much? What about if Kuchar settled the suit for $300,000 prior to a decision on the merits and incurred $100,000 in legal fees in the process? If so, for how much?

2. Directors and Officers Liability Insurance

Corporate law statutes expressly allow corporations to purchase insurance to protect directors and officers against liabilities arising out of their corporate service.[137] This type of insurance is referred to as directors and officers liability insurance, or D&O insurance for short. A typical D&O insurance policy supplies two types of coverage, known as "Side A" and "Side B." Side A coverage provides directors and officers with insurance protection when indemnification is not available, either because indemnification by the corporation is not legally permitted under the circumstances or the corporation is financially unable to meet its indemnification obligations. Side B coverage reimburses a corporation for amounts it pays out fulfilling its indemnification obligations. Thus, with Side B coverage, a corporation is essentially contractually transferring its indemnification obligations to the insurer.

The coverage, limits, premium amount, and other details of a D&O policy are determined by negotiations between the corporation, usually with the aid of an insurance broker, and the insurance company. Policies normally provide coverage for loss arising from claims first made during the policy period alleging wrongful acts by a director or officer. Policies usually define "wrongful act" as an actual or alleged act, error or omission, misleading statement, or breach of duty. However, D&O policies typically specifically exclude from coverage losses relating to (1) fraudulent or criminal misconduct, and (2) profits or remuneration to which the director or officer was not legally entitled.

137. *See, e.g.,* DGCL §145(g); MBCA §8.57.

D&O insurance is normally addressed in an indemnification agreement. Here is sample language from the same indemnification agreement as the indemnification and advancement provisions above:

> The Company shall use its reasonable best efforts to purchase and maintain a policy or policies of insurance with reputable insurance companies with A.M. Best ratings of "A" or better, providing Indemnitee with coverage for any liability asserted against, and incurred by, Indemnitee or on Indemnitee's behalf by reason of Indemnitee's Corporate Status, or arising out of Indemnitee's status as such, whether or not the Company would have the power to indemnify Indemnitee against such liability. Such insurance policies shall have coverage terms and policy limits at least as favorable to Indemnitee as the insurance coverage provided to any other director or officer of the Company. If the Company has such insurance in effect at the time it receives from Indemnitee any notice of the commencement of an action, suit, proceeding or other claim, the Company shall give prompt notice of the commencement of such action, suit, proceeding or other claim to the insurers in accordance with the procedures set forth in the policy. The Company shall thereafter take all necessary or desirable action to cause such insurers to pay, on behalf of Indemnitee, all amounts payable as a result of such action, suit, proceeding or other claim in accordance with the terms of such policy. The Company shall continue to provide such insurance coverage to Indemnitee for a period of at least six (6) years after Indemnitee ceases to serve as a director or officer or any other present Corporate Status.

· CHAPTER ELEVEN ·

RETURN ON INVESTMENT

People buy stock in corporations with the hope of earning a return on the investment. There are basically two ways for them to do so: (1) through the receipt of distributions, and (2) by selling the stock to someone else for more than they paid. In this chapter, we discuss the associated legal issues.

A. DISTRIBUTIONS

A distribution is a transfer of money or other property by a corporation to its owners. There are two types of distributions: dividends and repurchases. A dividend is the transfer of cash or other property (except the corporation's own shares) by a corporation to its shareholders pro rata based on the number of shares owned. For example, say a corporation has 10,000 shares of common stock outstanding. You own 4,000 of the shares and I own 6,000. The corporation decides it wants to distribute $20,000 to its shareholders so it declares a $2.00 per share cash dividend on its common stock. Because you own 4,000 shares, the corporation sends you a check for $8,000 (4,000 × $2.00), and because I own 6,000, the corporation sends me a check for $12,000 (6,000 × $2.00). The declaration and payment of a dividend requires board approval, and the board has broad discretion in deciding whether or not to declare a dividend.

A repurchase is when a corporation buys back shares from its shareholders. If a corporation repurchases the same percentage of shares from each shareholder, the effect is the same as if it paid a dividend. Continuing the example from above, say that the corporation decides it wants to distribute the $20,000 to you and me by means of a repurchase instead of a dividend. Thus, it buys back 10 percent, or 400 of your shares at $20.00 per share and 10 percent, or 600 of my shares for $20.00 per share. As a result, the corporation sends you a check for $8,000 and your shareholdings drop from 4,000 to 3,600.

Likewise, the corporation sends me a check for $12,000 and my shareholdings drop from 6,000 to 5,400. After these transactions, you end up with $8,000 in your pocket and own 40 percent (3,600/9,000) of the corporation's outstanding stock, the same result as if the corporation paid out the $20,000 as dividends. You now own fewer shares, but because the corporation now has fewer shares outstanding, your percentage ownership remains the same. Shareholders may prefer to receive distributions through repurchases as opposed to dividends for tax reasons that are beyond the scope of this course. Note that a shareholder generally has to agree to sell his or her shares back to the corporation; the corporation cannot force the shareholder to do so. Exceptions include when the terms of the shares as set forth in the corporation's charter provide the corporation with the right to buy back the shares (often called a call right) or the shareholder has contractually agreed to sell shares back to the corporation upon the happening of specified events pursuant to a buy-sell or similar agreement.

As with dividends, the repurchase of shares requires board approval. Unlike dividends, however, a corporation is not statutorily required to repurchase shares proportionately from its shareholders.[1] Continuing with the example from above, instead of purchasing 400 shares from you and 600 shares from me, the corporation could purchase zero shares from you and 1,000 shares from me. This would result in me receiving the entire $20,000. Although you would not receive any cash, you would benefit somewhat from this transaction because your percentage ownership of the corporation would increase from 40 percent (4,000/10,000) to 44.44 percent (4,000/9,000).

1. Statutory Restrictions

While a board has broad latitude to choose not to make a distribution, its discretion to pay a dividend or repurchase shares is constrained by statute. For example, MBCA §6.40(c) provides as follows:

> No distribution may be made if, after giving it effect:
>   (1) the corporation would not be able to pay its debts as they become due in the usual course of business; or
>   (2) the corporation's total assets would be less than the sum of its total liabilities plus (unless the articles of incorporation permit otherwise) the amount that would be needed, if the corporation were to be dissolved at the time of the distribution, to satisfy the preferential rights upon dissolution of shareholders whose preferential rights are superior to those receiving the distribution.

---

1. Note that the case law in some states imposes an equal opportunity rule with respect to repurchases in the close corporation context. Under this rule, a corporation has to provide all of its shareholders the opportunity to participate ratably in a repurchase.

Subsection (1) is called the equity insolvency test. A corporation is considered insolvent if it is unable to pay its debts as they become due. Thus, if a corporation will be insolvent after paying a proposed dividend or making a proposed repurchase, it is not permitted to do so. It is left to the board to determine whether this will be the case. Comment 2 to §6.40 provides the following guidance for applying the equity insolvency test:

> In most cases involving a corporation operating as a going concern in the normal course, information generally available will make it quite apparent that no particular inquiry concerning the equity insolvency test is needed. While neither a balance sheet nor an income statement can be conclusive as to this test, the existence of significant shareholders' equity and normal operating conditions are of themselves a strong indication that no issue should arise under that test. Indeed, in the case of a corporation having regularly audited financial statements, the absence of any qualification in the most recent auditor's opinion as to the corporation's status as a "going concern," coupled with a lack of subsequent adverse events, would normally be decisive.
>
> It is only when circumstances indicate that the corporation is encountering difficulties or is in an uncertain position concerning its liquidity and operations that the board of directors or, more commonly, the officers or others upon whom they may place reliance under section 8.30(b), may need to address the issue. Because of the overall judgment required in evaluating the equity insolvency test, no one or more "bright line" tests can be employed. However, in determining whether the equity insolvency test has been met, certain judgments or assumptions as to the future course of the corporation's business are customarily justified, absent clear evidence to the contrary. These include the likelihood that (a) based on existing and contemplated demand for the corporation's products or services, it will be able to generate funds over a period of time sufficient to satisfy its existing and reasonably anticipated obligations as they mature, and (b) indebtedness which matures in the near-term will be refinanced where, on the basis of the corporation's financial condition and future prospects and the general availability of credit to businesses similarly situated, it is reasonable to assume that such refinancing may be accomplished. To the extent that the corporation may be subject to asserted or unasserted contingent liabilities, reasonable judgments as to the likelihood, amount, and time of any recovery against the corporation, after giving consideration to the extent to which the corporation is insured or otherwise protected against loss, may be utilized. There may be occasions when it would be useful to consider a cash flow analysis, based on a business forecast and budget, covering a sufficient period of time to permit a conclusion that known obligations of the corporation can reasonably be expected to be satisfied over the period of time that they will mature.

Subsection (2) is called the balance sheet test because it involves comparing a corporation's total assets to its total liabilities, both of which are balance sheet items. If after paying a proposed dividend or making a proposed repurchase, a corporation's liabilities plus the liquidation preferences of any preferred stock it has outstanding would exceed a corporation's assets, it is not permitted to do so. Again, it is left to the board to determine whether this will be the case. Notably, the board is not restricted to the values placed on assets by the corporation's balance sheet, as these often reflect historical costs less depreciation and not current market values. The board is free to revalue the corporation's assets for purposes of the balance sheet test as long as it is reasonable under the circumstances to do so.

A number of non-MBCA states use the legal capital test instead of the equity insolvency and balance sheet tests for regulating dividends. For example, DGCL §170(a) provides as follows:

> The directors of every corporation, subject to any restrictions contained in its certificate of incorporation, may declare and pay dividends upon the shares of its capital stock either (1) out of its surplus . . . or (2) in case there shall be no such surplus, out of its net profits for the fiscal year in which the dividend is declared and/or the preceding fiscal year.

The concept of surplus is a bit convoluted. It equals the excess of the net assets of a corporation less the amount of its "capital" (see DGCL §154). Net assets equals the corporation's total assets minus its total liabilities. A corporation's capital for these purposes (sometimes called "legal capital" to distinguish it from capital in the sense that we used the word in Chapter 8) consists of the number of shares it has issued multiplied by their par value. Additionally, the board may specify any portion of consideration received for the shares in excess of par value as capital if it so chooses. For shares with no par value, capital consists of the amount of consideration designated as such by the board. If the board fails to designate what part of the consideration is capital, the entire amount of consideration is deemed capital. Typically, a corporation will want to minimize the amount of consideration received for its shares that is designated as capital.

Let's look at an example. Assume a corporation's outstanding capital stock consists of 100,000 shares of common stock, par value $0.01. When it sold these shares, the board chose not to specify any additional amount as capital. The corporation's total assets equal $500,000, and its total liabilities equal $300,000. Under the legal capital test, it would be able to pay out an aggregate of $199,000 in dividends computed as follows:

$500,000 total assets – $300,000 total liabilities – $1,000 capital = $199,000.

I computed capital by multiplying 100,000 (the number of shares the corporation has issued) by the shares' par value of $0.01.

Clause (2) of DGCL §170(a) is referred to as the "nimble dividend" provision. It allows a corporation to pay a dividend even if the corporation has no

Example

or negative surplus, up to the amount of the corporation's net profits for the fiscal year in which the dividend is paid or the preceding fiscal year. The DGCL does not define the term "net profits" so it is left to the board to determine, in its business judgment.

Delaware uses a similar restriction on repurchases. Specifically, DGCL §160 prohibits a corporation from repurchasing shares if its capital is impaired or the proposed repurchase would cause its capital to be impaired. Essentially, this means a corporation can repurchase shares so long as it has adequate surplus to cover the aggregate repurchase price. Note that there is no equivalent to the nimble dividend rule for repurchases.

The purpose of statutory restrictions on making distributions is to prevent a board from draining the corporation of assets to the detriment of creditors. Creditors, of course, are concerned about money flowing out of a corporation to its shareholders, because it means the corporation has less money to pay its debts. Lenders such as banks, however, do not rely on statutory dividend restrictions for protection in part because these statutes allow a corporation to pay out dividends until it is on the brink of insolvency. Instead, a lender will include a negative covenant in its loan agreement with a corporation prohibiting the corporation from paying any dividends without the consent of the lender.

2. Director Liability

Statutory distribution restrictions are negatively reinforced by provisions imposing personal liability on directors for dividends paid in violation of the restrictions. For example, MBCA §8.33(a) provides:

> A director who votes for or assents to a distribution in excess of what may be authorized and made pursuant to section 6.40(a) . . . is personally liable to the corporation for the amount of the distribution that exceeds what could have been distributed without violating section 6.40(a) . . . if the party asserting liability establishes that when taking the action the director did not comply with section 8.30.

Section 8.30, among other things, requires a director to make decisions on an informed basis, in good faith, and in a manner the director reasonably believes to be in the best interests of the corporation. Thus, as long as a director votes in favor of a dividend in compliance with these standards, he or she will not be personally liable, even it is later proven that the dividend was paid in violation of §6.40(a).

In light of provisions such as §8.33(a), if there is any question as to whether a dividend or repurchase is permitted under the applicable distribution restriction statute, the board will purchase a solvency opinion from an investment banking firm. The chosen firm analyzes a corporation's finances and renders an opinion to the board that the applicable statutory restriction does not prohibit the company from making the proposed distribution. If a suit ever arises against the directors under a provision such as §8.33(a), they can then point to the solvency opinion as evidence that they acted on an informed basis and in good faith. In a sense, a solvency opinion serves as insurance against director liability for wrongful payment of a dividend.

Questions

1. Why would a Delaware corporation want to minimize the amount of consideration received for its shares that is designated as capital?
2. How does a solvency opinion serve as insurance against director liability for wrongful payment of a dividend?

Exercise 11.1

In answering these problems, refer to the financial statements of XYZ Corp. on the next page. Assume that XYZ is governed by the MBCA and has 100,000 shares of common stock outstanding.

1. On January 3 of 2012, XYZ convinces a hedge fund to loan it $1 million dollars, which XYZ intends to immediately pay out to its shareholders as a dividend. The loan carries an interest rate of 15 percent. All interest and principal on the loan is due and payable in one lump sum in two years. Can XYZ legally pay the contemplated dividend? Assuming it can, list the corporate law steps it must take to do so.
2. Assume instead that XYZ decides to pay out the $1 million to Sjostrom, its controlling shareholder, by buying back some of his stock. Can XYZ legally do this? Assuming it can, list the corporate law steps it must take to do so.
3. Assume that in addition to the common stock XYZ has outstanding, it also just created and issued 5,000 shares of Series A Preferred Stock with terms identical to those of Riffpad's Series A Preferred (see Chapter 8). XYZ's board has authorized the payment of $1 million in dividends. How is the $1 million divided up between the common and preferred?
4. An XYZ director is nervous about personal liability if she votes in favor of the proposed dividend. She asks you for advice on what she can do to minimize this risk. What do you tell her?

BALANCE SHEET OF XYZ CORP.
December 31, 2011

Assets:

Cash:	$50,000
Accounts receivable:	2,000
Pre-paid expenses:	1,500
Inventory:	7,000
Equipment:	30,000
Less depreciation:	5,500
Building:	105,000
Less depreciation:	20,000
Land:	60,000
TOTAL ASSETS:	**230,000**

Liabilities:

Accounts payable:	3,000
Rent payable:	4,000
Wages payable:	8,000
Advance payments:	2,000
Bank loan:	57,000
TOTAL LIABILITIES:	**74,000**

Owners' Equity:

Capital:	100,000
Retained earnings:	56,000
TOTAL OWNER'S EQUITY:	156,000
TOTAL LIABILITIES AND OWNERS EQUITY:	**$230,000**

INCOME STATEMENT OF XYZ CORP.
January 1 – December 31, 2011

Revenues:	$345,000
Costs of goods sold:	143,000
Gross profit (loss):	202,000
Other expenses:	
Wages:	102,000
Utilities:	9,500
Depreciation:	7,000
Rent:	52,000
Advertising:	1,000
Interest on bank loan:	3,000
Other gains (losses):	(1,500)
Income (loss) before income tax:	26,000
Income tax:	5,000
NET INCOME (LOSS):	**21,000**

CASH FLOW STATEMENT OF XYZ CORP.
January 1 – December 31, 2011

Cash flow from operating activities:	
Cash from customers:	$349,000
Cash used for operations:	310,000
Net cash from operations:	39,000
Cash flow from investing activities:	
Cash from investing:	1,000
Cash used for investing:	4,500
Net cash from investing:	(3,500)
Cash flow from financing activities:	
Cash from financing:	10,000
Cash used for financing:	6,000
Net cash from financing:	4,000
Net increase in cash:	39,500
Cash at beginning of period:	10,500
Cash at end of period:	$50,000

B. SALES

In addition to distributions, you can make money on an equity investment by selling all or some of your shares to someone for more than you paid. In this subsection, we discuss state statutory rules and federal Securities Act compliance for transferring shares.

1. State Statutory Rules

The default rule under corporate law is that shares of stock are freely transferable. This means that you can sell your shares to anybody, anytime, and at any price. The person purchasing your shares is then entitled to vote the shares, receive dividends, etc. Free transferability is what makes possible secondary trading markets, such as the New York Stock Exchange and NASDAQ Stock Market.

Corporate law statutes allow corporations to impose transfer restrictions on their shares.[2] Closely held corporations in particular generally do not want freely transferable shares and therefore routinely impose transfer restrictions. A common transfer restriction they impose is a right of first refusal. Basically, it requires a shareholder who is planning to sell some or all of her shares to first offer the shares to the corporation and/or other shareholders before selling them to a third party. The idea is to provide the other shareholders a means to control with whom they are co-owners. Here is sample language:

Right of First Refusal.

(a) No Shareholder shall sell, transfer, pledge, encumber, hypothecate, or otherwise dispose of any of his shares or any right or interest in them without obtaining prior written consent of the Company and each other Shareholder, unless the Shareholder shall first have given written notice ("Offer Notice") to the Company specifying the name and address of the proposed transferee and the number of shares to be transferred, the price per share, and the terms of payment. For 30 days following delivery of the Offer Notice to the Company, it shall have the option, but not the obligation, to purchase all or any part of the shares at the price and on the terms stated in the Offer Notice (the "Offering Price"). To exercise its option, the Company must give the Shareholder written notice to that effect within the 30-day period. The Company shall pay the Offering Price in the manner provided in the terms of sale to the proposed transferee.

(b) If the Company does not exercise its option on all Shares set forth in the Offer Notice, the Shareholder shall furnish the Offer Notice to the Company's other Shareholders, who shall, for a period of 30 days after receiving the Offer Notice, have the option, but not the obligation, to purchase any Shares not purchased by

---

2. *See* DGCL §202; MBCA §6.27.

the Company at the Offering Price on the same terms and conditions specified in the Offer Notice. Within such 30-day period after receiving the Offer Notice, any Shareholder desiring to acquire some or all of the Shares offered shall deliver to the Company a written election to purchase the Shares or a specified number of them. If the total number of Shares specified in the elections exceeds the number of available Shares, each Shareholder shall have priority, up to the number of Shares specified in his election notice, to purchase the available Shares, in the same proportion that the number of the Company's Shares that he holds bears to the total number of the Company's Shares held by all Shareholders electing to purchase. The Shares not purchased on such a priority basis shall be allocated in one or more successive allocations to those Shareholders electing to purchase more than the number of Shares to which they have a priority right, up to the number of Shares specified in their respective notices, in the proportion that the number of Shares held by each of them bears to the number of Shares held by all of them. Within 10 days after the mailing of the notice to the Shareholders, the Company shall notify each Shareholder of the number of Shares as to which his election was effective, and the Shareholder shall meet the terms and conditions of the purchase within the 45-day period specified above.

If the Company and the remaining Shareholders do not purchase all the Shares set forth in the Offer Notice within the prescribed time periods, all the Shares may be transferred to the proposed transferee on the terms specified in the Offer Notice, at any time within 10 days after expiration of the 45-day period specified above. The transferee will hold the Shares subject to the provisions of this Agreement. No transfer of the Shares shall be made after the end of the 10-day period, nor shall any change in the terms of transfer be permitted without a new Offer Notice and compliance with the requirements of this paragraph. Any transfer by any Shareholder in violation of this paragraph 3 shall be null and void and of no effect.

Transfer restrictions are normally specified in a written agreement among the corporation and its shareholders (typically called a "shareholders' agreement" or "buy-sell agreement"), although they are sometimes contained in a corporation's charter or bylaws. A transfer restriction is binding on a transferee of shares if the restriction is noted conspicuously on the front or back of the stock certificate representing the transferred shares or if the transferee has knowledge of the restriction. Here is a sample "legend" printed on the back of a stock certificate for shares subject to transfer restrictions specified in a shareholders' agreement:

The shares represented by this certificate are subject to the provisions of a Shareholders' Agreement dated December 8, 2009, which Agreement is available for inspection at the principal office of the Corporation. Such provisions provide, among other things, that, except as otherwise provided in such Agreement, the shares represented by this certificate are not assignable or transferable, in whole or in part.

The legend is in bold to meet the conspicuous requirement of the statute.[3]

Manifestly unreasonable restrictions are invalid, regardless of a conspicuous legend or knowledge. The next case discusses the test for determining reasonableness.

F.B.I. Farms, Inc. v. Moore
798 N.E.2d 440 (2003)

BOEHM, Justice.

We hold that as a general proposition, restrictions on corporate share transfers may require approval of the transfer by the corporation's Board of Directors, at least in a family-owned corporation. Although generally valid against purchasers with notice of them, such restrictions may not prevent a creditor from foreclosing a lien on the shares, but a purchaser who buys at a foreclosure sale with notice of the restrictions acquires the shares subject to the restrictions. We also hold that if shares are subject to a right of first refusal, and the holder of the right has notice of the foreclosure, the holder cannot exercise the right against a purchaser at a foreclosure sale after the purchaser has taken title to the shares without objection from the holder of the rights.

FACTUAL AND PROCEDURAL BACKGROUND

F.B.I. Farms, Inc., was formed in 1976 by Ivan and Thelma Burger, their children, Linda and Freddy, and the children's spouses. Each of the three couples transferred a farm and related machinery to the corporation in exchange for common stock in the corporation. At the time, Birchell Moore was married to Linda. Linda and Moore deeded a jointly-owned 180-acre farm to F.B.I., and 2,507 shares were issued to Moore and one to Linda. These 2,508 shares represented approximately fourteen percent of the capitalization of F.B.I.

In 1977, the Board of Directors of F.B.I. consisted of Moore, Ivan, Freddy and Linda. The minutes of a 1977 meeting of the Board recite that the following restrictions on the transfer of shares were "adopted":

1) No stock of said corporation shall be transferred, assigned and/or exchanged or divided, unless or until approved by the Directors thereof;

2) That if any stock be offered for sale, assigned and/or transferred, the corporation should have the first opportunity of purchasing the same at no more than the book value thereof;

3) Should said corporation be not interested, and could not economically offer to purchase said stock, any stockholder of record should be given the next opportunity to purchase said stock, at a price not to exceed the book value thereof;

---

3. *See id.*

4) That if the corporation was not interested in the stock, and any stock-holders were not interested therein, then the same could be sold to any blood member of the family. Should they be desirous of purchasing the same, then at not more than the book value thereof.

Linda's marriage to Moore was dissolved in 1982. As part of the dissolution proceedings, Linda was awarded all of the F.B.I. shares and Moore was awarded a monetary judgment in the amount of $155,889.80, secured by a lien on Linda's shares.

F.B.I. filed for bankruptcy protection in 1989 and emerged from Chapter 11 Bankruptcy in 1991. Moore's judgment against Linda remained unsatisfied, and in April 1998 he sought a writ of execution of his lien. . . . Moore obtained the writ of execution in June 1999. . . . A sheriff's sale went forward and in February 2000 Moore purchased all 2,924 shares owned by Linda at the time for $290,450.67.

In December 2000 Moore instituted this suit against F.B.I., its shareholders, and Linda seeking a declaratory judgment . . . that the shares were unencumbered by restrictions and were freely transferable. . . . The trial court granted Moore's motion for partial summary judgment, finding . . . (3) the restriction in paragraph one of the agreement requiring approval by F.B.I.'s directors for a share transfer was "manifestly unreasonable"; and, (4) the provision in paragraph four of the agreement giving "blood members" the option to purchase after the corporation and shareholders was "manifestly unreasonable" and unenforceable. . . .

On appeal, the Court of Appeals held that the transfer restrictions barred only voluntary transfers. Because the sheriff's sale effectuated an involuntary transfer of Linda's shares, Moore, as the purchaser of the shares, acquired the shares. Although the court found that future transfers of stock would be subject to the restrictions in Moore's hands, it also affirmed the trial court's finding that the two disputed restrictions were manifestly unreasonable. The court reasoned that the several tumultuous years of dispute between the parties rendered the restriction requiring director approval before transfer unreasonable, and the reference to "blood members" of the family was sufficiently ambiguous that that restriction was unenforceable. We granted transfer. . . .

I. TRANSFER RESTRICTIONS

A. General Principles

Most of the issues in this case are resolved by the Indiana statute governing share transfer restrictions. Indiana Code section 23-1-26-8 essentially mirrors Model Business Corporation Act §6.27, which authorizes restrictions on the transfer of shares. The Indiana statute reads as follows:

> (a) The articles of incorporation, bylaws, an agreement among shareholders, or an agreement between shareholders and the corporation may impose restrictions on the transfer or registration of transfer of shares of any class or series of shares of the corporation. A restriction does not affect shares issued before the

restriction was adopted unless the holders of the shares are parties to the restriction agreement or voted in favor of the restrictions.

(b) A restriction on the transfer or registration of transfer of shares is valid and enforceable against the holder or a transferee of the holder if the restriction is authorized by this section and its existence is noted conspicuously on the front or back of the certificate or is contained in the information statement required by section 7(b) [Ind. Code 23-1-26-7(b)] of this chapter. Unless so noted, a restriction is not enforceable against a person without knowledge of the restriction.

(c) A restriction on the transfer or registration of transfer of shares is authorized:

(1) to maintain the corporation's status when it is dependent on the number or identity of its shareholders;

(2) to preserve exemptions under federal or state securities law; or

(3) for any other reasonable purpose.

(d) A restriction on the transfer or registration of transfer of shares may, among other things:

(1) obligate the shareholder first to offer the corporation or other persons (separately, consecutively, or simultaneously) an opportunity to acquire the restricted shares;

(2) obligate the corporation or other persons (separately, consecutively, or simultaneously) to acquire the restricted shares;

(3) require the corporation, the holders of any class of its shares, or another person to approve the transfer of the restricted shares, if the requirement is not manifestly unreasonable; or

(4) prohibit the transfer of the restricted shares to designated persons or classes of persons, if the prohibition is not manifestly unreasonable. . . .

Corporate shares are personal property. At common law, any restriction on the power to alienate personal property was impermissible. Despite this doctrine, Indiana, like virtually all jurisdictions, allows corporations and their shareholders to impose restrictions on transfers of shares. The basic theory of these statutes is to permit owners of a corporation to control its ownership and management and prevent outsiders from inserting themselves into the operations of the corporation. Chief Justice Holmes stated the matter succinctly a century ago: "Stock in a corporation is not merely property. It also creates a personal relation analogous otherwise than technically to a partnership. . . . [T]here seems to be no greater objection to retaining the right of choosing one's associates in a corporation than in a firm." *Barrett v. King*, 181 Mass. 476, 63 N.E. 934, 935 (1902). As applied to a family-owned corporation, this remains valid today.

Transfer restrictions are treated as contracts either between shareholders or between shareholders and the corporation.[4] Apart from any statutory

---

4. [FN 1] The Indiana statute provides that restrictions are valid if included in the articles, the bylaws, an agreement among shareholders or an agreement between the corporation and shareholders. None of these was done here. However, no one challenges the restrictions as defective in their initial adoption. At least as to Moore, who approved them as a director and had actual knowledge of them, under these circumstances, the restrictions constitute a contract as to all of those shareholders who approved the adoption of the restrictions.

requirements, restrictions on transfer are to be read, like any other contract, to further the manifest intention of the parties. Because they are restrictions on alienation and therefore disfavored, the terms in the restrictions are not to be expanded beyond their plain and ordinary meaning.

For a party to be bound by share transfer restrictions, that party must have notice of the restrictions. Here, the restrictions on transfer of F.B.I. shares were neither "noted conspicuously" on the certificates nor contained in the information statement referred to in Indiana Code 23-1-26-8(b), but there is no doubt that Moore, the buyer at the sheriff's sale, had notice of the restrictions. He was therefore bound by them.

Finally, a closely held corporation is a "corporation in which all of the outstanding stock is held by just a few individuals, or by a small group of persons belonging to a single family." J.R. Kemper, *Validity of "Consent Restraint" on Transfer of Shares of Close Corporation*, 69 A.L.R.3d 1327, 1328 (1976). In 1977, F.B.I. plainly fell within that description; it was owned by six individuals, all members of a single family. Closely held corporations have a viable interest in remaining the organization they envision at incorporation and transfer restrictions are an appropriate means of maintaining the status quo.

B. Rights of First Refusal

Paragraphs (2) and (3) of the restrictions created rights of first refusal in F.B.I. and its shareholders. A transfer in violation of restrictions is voidable at the insistence of the corporation. F.B.I. and its shareholders argue that Moore should have been obliged to offer the shares to the corporation or a shareholder pursuant to those provisions. Moore responds, and the Court of Appeals agreed, that he was not a shareholder until he purchased the shares at the sheriff's sale. He contends he therefore had no power to offer the shares. This misses the point that before Linda could transfer her shares, she was obliged to offer them to F.B.I. and the other shareholders. Moore was on notice of that requirement. Moore, as the buyer, had the right to demand that Linda initiate the process to exercise or waive the right to first refusal.

Thus, if the corporation had insisted on its right of first refusal, Linda would have been obliged to sell to F.B.I. (or its shareholders). And Moore, as a buyer on notice of the restrictions, had the right to insist that that process go forward. But the corporation and its shareholders were aware of the sheriff's sale and did nothing to assert the right of first refusal. They cannot sit back and let the sale go forward, await future events, then claim a right to purchase on the same terms as Moore. In sum, F.B.I. and its shareholders had rights of first refusal, but failed to exercise them. As a result, the sale to Moore proceeded as if the shares had been offered and the corporation refused the opportunity. To hold otherwise would be to give F.B.I. and its shareholders a perpetual option to purchase but no obligation to do so. Having failed to demand their right to buy at the time of the sale, the rights of first refusal gave them no ability to upset the sale conducted by the sheriff.

C. Restrictions on Transfer with Board Approval

The restrictions "adopted" in paragraphs (1) and (4) are more problematic. Indiana's statute, reflecting the common law, requires that restrictions on share transfers be reasonable. I.C. §23-1-26-8(c)(3), (d)(3), and (d)(4). The general common law doctrine surrounding evaluation of the reasonableness of restrictions is well established. A restriction is reasonable if it is designed to serve a legitimate purpose of the party imposing the restraint and the restraint is not an absolute restriction on the recipient's right of alienability. The Indiana statute is somewhat more generous in allowing restrictions on classes of buyers unless "manifestly unreasonable." Several factors are relevant in determining the reasonableness of any transfer restriction, including the size of the corporation, the degree of restraint upon alienation; the time the restriction was to continue in effect, the method to be used in determining the transfer price of shares, the likelihood of the restriction's contributing to the attainment of corporate objectives, the possibility that a hostile stockholder might injure the corporation, and the probability of the restriction's promoting the best interests of the corporation. At one extreme, a restriction that merely prescribes procedures that must be observed before stock may be transferred is not unreasonable. At the other end of the spectrum, restrictions that are fraudulent, oppressive, unconscionable, or the result of a breach of the fiduciary duty that shareholders in a close corporation owe to one another, will not be upheld. The restrictions on F.B.I.'s shares, like most, are somewhere in the middle. They impose substantive limitations on transfer, but are not alleged to be the result of fraud or breach of fiduciary duty.

The trial court, in its order granting partial summary judgment, concluded that the restriction precluding transfer without Board approval was reasonable at the time that it was adopted, but the lengthy and difficult history between the parties had rendered the restriction unreasonable. Under basic contract law principles, the reasonableness of a term of a contract is evaluated at the time of its adoption. The same is true of share transfer restrictions. As a result, evaluating the reasonableness of the restrictions in light of subsequent developments is inappropriate. For that reason, we do not agree that the restriction requiring director approval became unreasonable based upon events and disputes within the family that occurred after the restrictions had been adopted. To be sure, the parties find themselves in a difficult dispute as is sometimes the case in a family business following a dissolution. But when F.B.I. was formed and the family farms were effectively pooled, the shareholders agreed that the Board would be permitted to restrict access to the shares. To the extent that restriction devalues the shares in the hands of any individual shareholder by reason of lack of transferability, it is the result of the bargain they struck. The policy behind enforcement of these restrictions is to encourage entering into formal partnerships by permitting all parties to have confidence they will not involuntarily end up with an undesired co-venturer. Presumably for that reason, the statute permits a restriction that requires a transferee to be approved by the Board of Directors, and to that extent may severely limit transferability.

A "consent restriction" such as this has been considered unreasonable by some courts. However, the General Assembly has allowed precisely this type of restriction in Indiana Code section 23-1-26-8(d)(3). That section provides that transfer restrictions may require the approval of "the corporation, the holders of any class of its shares, or another person" before the shares may be transferred. Board approval is one permissible way of implementing approval by "the Corporation" under this section.

D. Restrictions on Transfer Except to "Blood Members of the Family"

We also find the "blood-member" restriction to be enforceable as protecting a viable interest. These are family farmers in corporate form. It is apparent from the nature of the corporation that the Burger family had an interest in maintaining ownership and operation of F.B.I. in the hands of family members. Although one may quibble with the terminology, and there may be some individuals where status as blood members is debatable, we think it plain enough that all parties to this dispute either are or are not blood members of the Burger family. All are either direct descendants of Ivan or spouses of Ivan or of one of his children. . . .

III. RESTRICTIONS AS APPLIED TO INVOLUNTARY TRANSFERS

The Court of Appeals held that the restrictions on Linda's shares did not apply by their terms to the sheriff's sale and, as a result, did not bar the sheriff's sale to Moore. We agree that Moore acquired the shares at the sheriff's sale, but not because the restrictions were inapplicable by their terms.

The Court of Appeals relied on cases stating that involuntary transfers fall within the terms of a restriction only if the language of the restrictions specifically identifies them. This doctrine has been developed largely in cases involving intestate transfers by a decedent, and in marriage dissolution proceedings where a transfer is made to a spouse.

The sheriff's sale where Moore purchased Linda's shares was an involuntary transfer. Transfers ordered incident to marriage dissolutions and transfers under intestate law may also be deemed involuntary. We think the governing principle is not the same for all forms of "involuntary" transfers. The language of the restrictions in this case does not specifically refer to involuntary transfers of any kind. Rather, it seems to contemplate restricting all transfers, voluntary and involuntary, by providing that no stock of the corporation should be "transferred, assigned, exchanged, divided, or sold" without complying with the restrictions. The intent of the parties is thus rather plain: to restrict ownership to the designated group, and to preclude transfer by any means. The question is whether that intent should be permitted to prevail in the face of countervailing policies.

Transfer by intestacy is in some sense involuntary, but it may also be viewed as a voluntary act of the decedent who had the option to leave a will. If a transfer could not be made by gift during lifetime, for example, to an offspring regarded by other shareholders as an undesirable partner, we see no reason to permit it at death by the decedent's choice to die intestate. There are, however, forms of involuntary transfers that a private agreement may not prevent because the agreement would unreasonably interfere with the rights of third parties. In a dissolution, the interests of the spouse require permitting transfer over the stated intent of the parties. Similarly, creditors of the shareholder cannot be stymied by a private agreement that renders foreclosure of a lien impossible. For that reason, we agree with the trial court that the sheriff's sale transferred the shares to Moore despite the restrictions. Transfer restrictions cannot preclude transfer in a foreclosure sale and thereby leave creditors without recourse. This does not turn on a doctrine of construction. Rather we hold that requiring an explicit bar specifically naming transfer by intestacy or by testamentary disposition should not be necessary. If the language purports to bar all transfers, and by its terms would apply to intestacy, devise or any other means of transfer, it should be given effect unless the restriction violates some policy.

Although we agree with Moore that he could purchase the shares at the sale, it is also the case that he purchased the shares with knowledge of the restrictions. We conclude that he could not acquire more property rights than were possessed by Linda as his seller. The shares in Linda's hands were valued with restrictions in place, and therefore it is not unfair to her creditors that a purchaser at a foreclosure sale acquire the disputed shares subject to the same restrictions, and with whatever lessened value that produces. To be sure, the effect of such a restriction may be to make the shares unmarketable to any buyer. But the creditor retains the option to bid at the sale and, if successful, succeed to the shareholders' interest. The creditor then gets the assets the debtor used to secure the underlying obligation. If the creditor wants collateral free of restrictions, the creditor must negotiate for that at the outset of the arrangement.

CONCLUSION...

We ... uphold the trial court's finding that the transfer restrictions did not prevent the sheriff's sale, and that the transfer restrictions remain applicable to the shares in Moore's hands. We reverse the trial court's ruling that the two disputed transfer restrictions are unreasonable and therefore unenforceable, and find that the director-approval and blood-member restrictions are reasonable and enforceable. The case is remanded for further proceedings consistent with this opinion.

Questions

1. Why is Moore seeking a declaratory judgment?
2. What is the test for determining whether a transfer restriction is manifestly unreasonable?

3. What were the transfer restrictions involved in the above case? Were any of them manifestly unreasonable?
4. Would the case have come out differently if the F.B.I. transfer restrictions specifically prohibited transfers via a sheriff's sale?
5. Assume you were hired by Moore in 1977 to review F.B.I.'s transfer restrictions prior to their adoption. What changes to them would you recommend?

2. Federal Securities Law Compliance

As mentioned in Chapter 8, §5 of the Securities Act of 1933 makes it unlawful to sell a security unless the sale is registered with the SEC or is exempt from registration. Consequently, every sale of securities, whether or not it is made by the issuer of the securities, must be registered or exempt. This includes the sale of securities from one investor to another (what the SEC calls a "resale"), even if the seller bought the shares on an exchange.

a. Section 4(a)(1) and Rule 144

Typically, a resale is exempt from registration under §4(a)(1) of the Securities Act. Section 4(a)(1) exempts from registration "transactions by any person other than an issuer, underwriter, or dealer." Thus, when you go to E*Trade's website to sell the 100 shares of Microsoft you own to help cover your law school tuition, you are relying on §4(a)(1) for compliance with §5, whether you know it or not, because you (presumably) are not an issuer, underwriter, or dealer. The overwhelming majority of resales of public company securities (what the SEC calls "trading transactions") are made in reliance on §4(a)(1).

Section 4(a)(1), however, is not available for the *immediate* resale of securities sold to an investor in an exempt offering or private placement. (The SEC refers to such securities as "restricted.") This is because §2(a)(11) of the Securities Act defines the term "underwriter," among other things, as "any person who has purchased from an issuer with a view to . . . the distribution of any security." Under SEC interpretations, anyone who sells restricted securities is presumed to be an underwriter unless the sale is made in compliance with Securities Act Rule 144. The reason this matters is that §4(a)(1) is not available for a reseller who falls under the definition of underwriter.

Rule 144 sets forth conditions under which a person who sells restricted securities "shall be deemed not to be an underwriter of those securities within the meaning of Section 2(a)(11) of the [Securities] Act."[5] Thus, if a person sells restricted securities in compliance with Rule 144, he or she falls outside the

---

5. Rule 144(b), 17 C.F.R. §230.144(b).

definition of underwriter and can therefore rely on §4(a)(1) for the resale (assuming the person is not an issuer or dealer).

Rule 144 essentially requires investors to hold restricted securities at a minimum for six months or one year before reselling, depending on whether the issuer is a public or private company. Rule 144 includes much more elaborate provisions for a resale by an "affiliate" of the issuer (an officer, director, or 10 percent or greater shareholder). Among other things, restrictions on affiliate resales last indefinitely and limit the number of securities an affiliate can sell during any three-month period. We will leave other details regarding affiliate resales to your Securities Regulation class.

Companies are required to inform investors in their private placements of these restrictions. They are also required to put a "legend" on the certificates representing the securities that specifies that the securities may not be sold unless the transaction is registered or the seller furnishes the issuer an opinion of counsel that the proposed sale is exempt from registration. Here is a sample legend printed on the back of a stock certificate representing shares issued in a private placement:

> The shares of stock represented by this certificate have not been registered under either the Securities Act of 1933 or applicable state securities laws and may not be sold, transferred, assigned, offered, pledged or otherwise distributed for value unless there is an effective registration statement under such Act and such laws covering such securities, or the Company receives an opinion of counsel acceptable to the Company stating that such sale, transfer, assignment, offer, pledge or other distribution for value is exempt from the registration and prospectus delivery requirements of such Act and such laws.

Restricted securities can also be resold outside of Rule 144 under the so-called Section 4(a)(1-1/2) exemption—an exemption that does not actually appear in the Securities Act, but has long been recognized by the SEC. The exemption permits the resale of restricted securities "so long as some of the established criteria for sales under both Section 4[(a)](1) and Section 4[(a)](2) of the [Securities] Act are satisfied."[6] Specifically, when selling restricted securities under §4(a)(1-1/2), a reseller claims he or she is not an underwriter because the resale does not involve a distribution, and therefore the resale transaction is exempt under §4(a)(1). Courts and the SEC have equated the term "distribution" with public offering. Therefore, the analysis of whether a resale involves a distribution is based on §4(a)(2) as interpreted by *Ralston Purina* and its progeny. This approach is conceptually sound but can be difficult to apply in practice because of the §4(a)(2) jurisprudence mishmash. Hence, to

---

6. *See* Employee Benefit Plans, Securities Act Release No. 6188, 19 SEC Docket 465, 496 n.178 (Feb. 1, 1980).

avoid the mishmash, the standard advice is instead to sell in compliance with Rule 144.

Question

What is the significance of an investor falling under the Securities Act definition of underwriter?

b. Registration Rights

In light of these restrictions, venture capitalists and angel investors often insist on getting registration rights as part of making an investment in a company. Registration rights are contractual promises by a company to register the resale of securities by investors with the SEC. If the resale is registered, it does not have to be made in compliance with Rule 144. Below are provisions from a venture capital investment term sheet regarding registration rights.

Registrable Securities:	All shares of Common Stock issuable upon conversion of the Series A Preferred will be deemed "**Registrable Securities**."
Demand Registration:	Upon earliest of (i) three years after the Closing; or (ii) six months following an initial public offering ("**IPO**"), persons holding 25 percent of the Registrable Securities may request two (consummated) registrations by the Company of their shares. The aggregate offering price for such registration may not be less than $10 million. A registration will count for this purpose only if (i) all Registrable Securities requested to be registered are registered and (ii) it is closed, or withdrawn at the request of the Investors (other than as a result of a material adverse change to the Company).
Piggyback Registration:	The holders of Registrable Securities will be entitled to "piggyback" registration rights on all registration statements of the Company, subject to the right, however, of the Company and its underwriters to reduce the number of shares proposed to be registered to a minimum of 30 percent on a pro rata basis and to complete reduction on an IPO at the underwriter's discretion. In all events, the shares to be registered by holders of Registrable Securities will be reduced only after all other stockholders' shares are reduced.
Expenses:	The registration expenses (exclusive of stock transfer taxes, underwriting discounts and commissions) will be borne by the Company. The Company will also pay the reasonable fees and expenses, not to exceed $30,000, of one special counsel to represent all the participating stockholders.

3. Secondary Trading Markets

Outstanding shares of public companies are traded among investors in secondary markets. There are two types of secondary markets in the United States: exchanges and over-the-counter (OTC) markets.

a. Exchanges

The two principal U.S. stock exchanges are the New York Stock Exchange (NYSE) and the NASDAQ Stock Market. A brief overview of each is provided below.

(1) NYSE

The NYSE (also known as the "Big Board") was founded in 1792 and is arguably the most prestigious market in which a company can have its stock traded. Historically, all NYSE trading took place on the trading floor of the exchange, located in New York City, where brokerage firms would phone in customer orders to floor brokers who executed trades face to face with another floor broker or a specialist (an employee of a firm who has agreed to maintain an orderly market in a particular stock). Today the bulk of trades on the NYSE are executed via computers.

A company has to apply to have its shares listed for trading on the NYSE. The NYSE will only approve an application if the company, among other things, meets the NYSE's initial listing standards. The following table from the NYSE website summarizes these standards.[7]

Distribution & Size Criteria *Must meet all 3 of the following:*	
Round-lot Holders[8]	400 U.S.
Public Shares[9]	1,100,000 outstanding
Market Value of Public Shares: IPOs, Spin-offs, Carve-outs, Affiliates All Other Listings	$40 million $100 million
Stock Price Criteria All issuers must have a $4 stock price at the time of listing	

---

7. *See* http://www.nyse.com/regulation/nyse/1147474807344.html.

8. Round-lot holders are shareholders with 100 shares or more. This includes record and beneficial owners.

9. Public shares equals total number of shares outstanding less shares held directly or indirectly by directors, officers, or any person who is the beneficial owner of more than 10 percent of the total shares outstanding of the company.

Financial Criteria
Must meet 1 of the following standards:

Alternative #1 — Earnings Test

Aggregate pre-tax income for the last 3 years	$10 million
Minimum in each of the 2 most recent years Third year must be positive	$2 million
OR	
Aggregate pre-tax income for the last 3 years	$12 million
Minimum in the most recent year	$5 million
Minimum in the next most recent year	$2 million

Alternative #2a — Valuation with Cash Flow

Global Market Capitalization	$500 million
Revenues (most recent 12-month period)	$100 million
Adjusted Cash Flow:	
Aggregate for the last 3 years All 3 years must be positive	$25 million

Alternative #2b — Pure Valuation with Revenues

Global Market Capitalization	$750 million
Revenues (most recent fiscal year)	$75 million

Alternative #3 — Affiliated Company
*For new entities with a parent or affiliated company
    listed on the NYSE*

Global Market Capitalization	$500 million
Operating History	12 months

Parent or affiliate is a listed company in good
    standing; Company's parent or affiliated company
    retains control of the entity or is under common
    control with the entity.	

Alternative #4 — Assets and Equity

Global Market Capitalization	$150 million
Total Assets	$75 million
Stockholders' Equity	$50 million

The NYSE also has "continued listing standards" a company is required to meet, or risk having its shares delisted from the exchange. Among other things, a company's shares are subject to delisting if:

- the company has less than 400 stockholders;
- the company has less than 1,200 stockholders and the average monthly trading volume of its shares for the most recent 12 months is less than 100,000 shares;
- the company has less than 600,000 publicly held shares;[10] or
- the company's average closing share price is less than $1.00 over a consecutive 30-trading-day period.

Financial continued listing standards vary depending on the financial criteria alternative a company relied on to meet the initial listing standards. For example, a company that listed under Financial Criteria, Alternative #1 may be delisted if its average global market capitalization over a consecutive 30-trading-day period is less than $50 million and its total stockholder equity is less than $50 million or its average global market capitalization over a consecutive 30-trading-day period is less than $15 million.

In addition to meeting the above standards, a company also has to pay a listing fee and annual fee for the privilege of having its shares traded on the NYSE. The listing fee for the first time a company lists common shares is $50,000 plus $.00032 per share, subject to a $125,000 minimum and a $250,000 maximum. The annual fee for listing a single class of common stock is the greater of $0.00093 per share and $38,000.

As of 2012, approximately 2,800 companies had securities listed on the NYSE. Among these companies are 3M, AT&T, Boeing, Coca-Cola, ExxonMobil, General Electric, IBM, JPMorgan Chase, McDonalds, Merck, Wal-Mart, and Walt Disney.

(2) NASDAQ

The NASDAQ Stock Market (NASDAQ) was founded in 1971. Unlike the NYSE, NASDAQ does not have a physical trading floor. Instead, all trading occurs electronically via computers. NASDAQ was originally an OTC market but became an exchange in 2006 by registering as such with the SEC.

NASDAQ is currently comprised of three different market tiers—the Global Select Market, the Global Market (formerly known as the National Market System or NMS), and the Capital Market (formerly known as the SmallCap Market). Each tier has different initial listing requirements composed of criteria similar to those of the NYSE.[11] A company must meet at least

---

10. Total publicly held shares equals total number of shares outstanding less shares held directly or indirectly by directors, officers, or any person who is the beneficial owner of more than 10 percent of the total shares outstanding of the company.

11. For a summary of these requirements, see NASDAQ OMX Initial Listing Guide (Sept. 2012) *available at* https://listingcenter.nasdaqomx.com/assets/initialguide.pdf.

one set of all of the same numbered items in each box and the items in the boxes without numbers.

Each market tier also has continued listing standards a company is required to meet or risk having its shares delisted from the tier. All tiers require listed companies to maintain a $1.00 minimum bid price and at least 400 total shareholders. Other criteria vary by tier.[12]

Similar to the NYSE, a company has to pay NASDAQ an entry fee and annual fee for the privilege of having its shares traded on one of its markets. For the Global Select Market and the Global Market, the entry fee ranges from $125,000 for companies with 30 million shares outstanding or less to $225,000 for companies with over 100 million shares outstanding. For the Capital Market, the entry fee is $50,000 for companies with 15 million shares outstanding or less and $75,000 for companies with over 15 million shares outstanding.

As of 2012, approximately 3,200 companies had securities listed on NAS-DAQ. Among these companies are Amazon.com, Apple, Cisco, Dell, eBay, Google, Microsoft, Oracle, Starbucks, Whole Foods, and Yahoo!.

Question

Can a company that has lost money every year since its inception list its shares on the NYSE?

b. OTC Markets

OTC markets are decentralized networks of brokers through which securities not listed on an exchange are traded. Originally, OTC trading occurred through telephone calls between brokers, but now most of it is done via computer networks. The two principal OTC networks are the OTC Bulletin Board and OTC Link.

(1) OTC Bulletin Board

The OTC Bulletin Board (OTCBB for short) is an electronic quotation system owned and operated by the Financial Industry Regulatory Authority (FINRA for short), the quasi-governmental self-regulatory organization that oversees all securities firms doing business in the United States.[13] The OTCBB has

---

12. For a summary of these standards, see NASDAQ OMX Continued Listing Guide (Sept. 2012) at 3-4, *available at* https://listingcenter.nasdaqomx.com/assets/continuedguide.pdf.

13. These firms were overseen by the National Association of Securities Dealers, Inc. (NASD) up until July 2007 when the NASD was consolidated with the member regulation, enforcement, and arbitration functions of the NYSE to create FINRA.

no listing requirements. In fact, companies do not technically list shares on it. Instead, brokerage firms apply to quote, or make a market in, a particular company's securities. The OTCBB charges these firms $6.00 per month for each security in which they make a market. Only securities of companies subject to periodic reporting requirements of the SEC (we discuss these requirements in Chapter 13), banking, or insurance regulators can be quoted on the OTCBB.

(2) OTC Link

OTC Link is operated by OTC Market Groups, Inc. and is billed as "the world's largest electronic interdealer quotation system for broker-dealers to trade unlisted securities."[14] It is the successor to the Pink Sheets, an OTC securities quotation service dating back to 1904 that at one time disseminated quotes on pink paper.

OTC Link is comprised of three tiers—OTCQX, OTCQB, and OTC Pink. OTCQX is the highest tier and has listing requirements, including a minimum bid price of $0.10 per share, and at least 50 round-lot shareholders. There are no listing requirements for the OTCQB, but only securities of companies subject to periodic reporting requirements of the SEC or banking regulators and that are current in their reporting can be in the tier. The OTC Pink tier has no listing or reporting requirements. As with the OTCBB, companies do not technically list their shares on OTC Link. Instead, brokerage firms apply to quote, or make a market in, a particular company's securities.

c. Choosing a Secondary Market

As you probably figured out, there is a definite hierarchy when it comes to secondary trading markets. At one time, it was undisputed that the NYSE was at the top. In the last few decades, however, NASDAQ has pulled equal with or arguably surpassed the NYSE on the hierarchy, at least when it comes to listings by technology companies. Both the NYSE and NASDAQ are part of larger for-profit companies and thus fiercely compete for listings. Competition is likely what caused NASDAQ to create its Global Select Market so that it could boast of operating the market with "the highest initial listing standards of any exchange in the world."[15]

In any event, a company wants its stock traded on the most active market possible, because it will be easier for its shareholders to buy and sell its shares. An active market is one where a significant number of a company's shares change hands, or trade, every trading day. Thus, if the average daily volume

---

14. http://www.otcmarkets.com/home.
15. http://www.nasdaq.com/about/Top_Tier_Splash.stm.

in a company's shares is 3 million, there will be plenty of buyers when you go to sell your 10,000 shares, which means you should be able to do so almost instantaneously at the quoted price. Conversely, if the average daily volume in a stock is only 5,000 shares, your order to sell 10,000 shares may take several days to complete, or fill. Furthermore, you will likely get less than the price quoted when you submitted your order, because the laws of supply and demand will cause the price to drop. (The demand is 5,000 but your order is supplying 10,000.) The NYSE and the NASDAQ Global Select/Global Market provide comparable market activity or depth, so a company cannot really go wrong choosing between them. Technology companies are probably biased in favor of NASDAQ because NASDAQ has successfully marketed itself as the exchange of choice for these sorts of companies. Older-line businesses likely lean toward the NYSE.

A company that does not meet the NYSE or NASDAQ Global Select/Global Market listing requirements looks next to the NASDAQ Capital Market. If it does not meet those listing requirements, historically it would seek market makers to quote its stock on the OTCBB and only look to OTC Link as a last resort. However, competition between the OTCBB and OTC Link has heated up in recent years, and some companies now prefer at least the OTCQX over the OTCBB.

d. Stock Splits

A company's stock price will fluctuate in trading on the secondary market as investors' views on the company's future performance change. As a result, a company may become concerned that its stock price is either too high or too low. While a high stock price is a good thing, it may mean that the shares are too expensive for small investors because you generally have to buy a minimum of 100 shares, or a round lot. Thus, if you have $10,000 to invest, you will not be able to use it for shares trading at $200.00 per share because you would need $20,000 to buy the 100 share minimum. A stock price that is too low is a big concern for an exchange-traded company because of the minimum bid price continued listing requirement. As mentioned above, both the NYSE and NASDAQ have a $1.00 per share minimum. This is where stock splits come into play, and there are two types—forward and reverse.

(1) Forward Stock Splits

A forward stock split (often just called a stock split) is when a company divides, or splits, its outstanding shares into more shares. Effecting one will reduce the price at which a company's stock trades immediately after the split. For example, say Sjo Co. has 5 million shares of common stock outstanding, and these shares are currently trading on the NASDAQ Global Market at

$90.00 per share. As a result, Sjo Co.'s market capitalization is $450 million (5,000,000 × $90.00). Sjo Co. wants to lower its stock price to the $45 per share range, so it effects a 2-for-1 stock split. This means that for every one share Sjo Co. had outstanding before the split, it now has two, and therefore its outstanding shares went from 5 million to 10 million shares. As a result, if you owned 100 Sjo Co. shares pre-split, post-split you will own 200 shares. You pay nothing for these additional shares, and Sjo Co. receives nothing. All Sjo Co. has done is cut the "pie" into more slices. Pre-split, the pie was worth $450 million and cut into 5 million pieces (or shares). Post-split, the pie is still worth $450 million because it is the exact same pie, but it is now cut into 10 million pieces (or shares). The individual pieces are now 50 percent smaller than they were before, so they are worth 50 percent less, that is, $45 instead of $90 each. However, you still own the same amount of pie because you own 100 additional shares, that is, pre-split you owned $9,000 worth of stock (100 × $90.00), and post-split you own $9,000 of stock (200 × $45.00).

A company can effect a forward stock split either through a share dividend[16] or by amending its charter. Continuing our example from above, if Sjo Co. went the share dividend route, its board would declare a one share per share dividend, which would mean that Sjo Co. would issue each shareholder one additional share for every one he or she owned. These additional shares would come from Sjo Co.'s authorized but unissued shares, assuming Sjo Co. has enough remaining. If it does not, it will need to amend its charter to increase its authorized shares in order to effect the share dividend. Such a charter amendment normally requires shareholder approval. MBCA §10.05(4)(b), however, allows the board of a corporation with only one class of shares outstanding to amend a charter without shareholder approval "to increase the number of authorized shares of the class to the extent necessary to permit the issuance of shares as a share dividend." Note that Delaware does not have an analogous provision.

Now let's look at the charter amendment route. Assume Article Fourth of Sjo Co.'s charter provides as follows:

> The total number of shares of capital stock which the Corporation shall have authority to issue is 50,000,000, all of which shares shall be common stock having a par value of $0.01 per share.

To effect a split through a charter amendment, Sjo Co.'s board would adopt a resolution along the lines of the following and submit it for approval by Sjo Co.'s shareholders:

---

16. *See* DGCL §173; MBCA §6.23.

> RESOLVED, that Article Fourth of the Corporation's Certificate of Incorporation is hereby amended as follows:
>
> "FOURTH: The total number of shares of capital stock which the Corporation shall have authority to issue is 100,000,000, all of which shares shall be common stock having a par value of $0.005 per share."
>
> At the time this amendment becomes effective, each share of common stock of par value $0.01 per share then issued and outstanding shall be changed and re-classified into two fully paid and nonassessable shares of common stock of a par value of $0.005. The capital account of the corporation shall not be increased or decreased by such reclassification. To reflect the reclassification, each certificate representing a share of common stock par value $0.01 then issued and outstanding shall be canceled, and the holder of record of each such certificate shall be entitled to receive a new certificate representing two shares of common stock of a par value of $0.005.

Notice that the resolution doubles the number of authorized shares and cuts their par value in half. Cutting par value proportionately is standard practice in a legal capital state, so that the corporation does not have to reduce its surplus and increase its legal capital in connection with the split.

Questions

1. From a corporate formalities standpoint, is it easier to effect a stock split through a stock dividend or a charter amendment?
2. What is the logic behind MBCA §10.05(4)(b)?
3. Say you own 1,000 shares in a corporation that has announced a 6-for-1 stock split. How many shares will you own post-split?

(2) Reverse Stock Splits

A reverse stock split is when a corporation combines its outstanding shares into fewer shares, and effecting one will increase the price at which a corporation's stock trades immediately after the split. Below is a press release put out by NextWave Wireless Inc. on June 18, 2010 announcing a reverse stock split.

NEXTWAVE ANNOUNCES 1-FOR-7 REVERSE STOCK SPLIT, EFFECTIVE JUNE 21, 2010

SAN DIEGO—(BUSINESS WIRE)—NextWave Wireless Inc. (NASDAQ: WAVE—News) (the "Company") today announced that it has filed a certificate of amendment to its Amended and Restated Certificate of Incorporation to effect a 1-for-7 reverse stock split that will become effective at 12:01 A.M. Eastern Time on Monday, June 21, 2010. The primary purpose of the reverse stock split is to raise the per share trading price of the Company's common stock to better enable the Company to maintain the listing of its common stock on The NASDAQ Stock Market LLC (NASDAQ). It is expected that NASDAQ will append a "D" to the Company's ticker symbol to indicate the completion of the reverse split and that after a 20-day period following the reverse split, the ticker symbol will revert to "WAVE."

At the effective time of the reverse stock split, every 7 shares of the Company's pre-split common stock, par value $0.001 per share, will automatically be reclassified as and converted into 1 share of post-split common stock, par value $0.007 share. The number of authorized shares of the Company's common stock will be reduced accordingly by a ratio of 1-for-7. Outstanding stock incentive awards will also be adjusted to give effect to the reverse split and the shares available for future grants will be proportionately reduced.

The Company has retained its transfer agent, Computershare Shareholder Services ("Computershare"), to act as exchange agent for the reverse stock split. Computershare will notify the Company's stockholders of record that held paper share certificates as of the effective time to transmit outstanding share certificates to Computershare, and Computershare will issue new book entry statements of holding representing 1 share of post-split common stock for every 7 shares held of record as of the effective time. Stockholders that currently hold shares in book entry form will receive updated statements of holding reflecting the reverse split and need not take any action. In settlement of fractional shares that might arise as a result of the reverse split, the Company will cause Computershare to make a cash payment based on the average closing sales price of the Company's common stock as reported on The Nasdaq Global Market for the ten trading days immediately preceding the effective time.

In order to maintain the Company's listing on NASDAQ, on or before July 21, 2010, the Company's common stock must have a closing bid price of $1.00 or more for a minimum of ten prior consecutive trading days. If the Company is unable to meet this requirement, the NASDAQ Listing Qualifications Panel will issue a final determination to delist and suspend trading of the Company's common stock. The reverse stock split is intended to raise the bid price of the common stock to satisfy the $1.00 minimum bid price requirement. However, there can be no assurance that the reverse stock split will have the desired effect of sufficiently raising the common stock price. The effect of a reverse stock split upon the market price of the common stock cannot be predicted with any certainty. The market price of the common stock may vary based on other factors that are unrelated to the number of shares outstanding, including the Company's future performance. We also cannot assure you that the common stock will not be delisted due to a failure to meet other continued listing requirements even if after the reverse stock split the market price per share of the common stock remains in excess of $1.00. If a delisting from NASDAQ were to occur, the Company may seek to have the common stock traded on the OTC Bulletin Board or in the "pink sheets." These alternative markets are generally considered to be less efficient and liquid than The NASDAQ Global Market.

NextWave's stock closed at $0.28 on June 18, 2010 (the last trading day before the reverse split), and traded as high as $1.98 on June 21, 2010, the effective date of the reverse split, so it had the desired effect. Unfortunately for NextWave, its stock did not remain above a dollar for long, and was thus delisted by NASDAQ on July 23, 2010. NextWave's stock now trades on the OTCQB.

As described in the NextWave press release, a corporation effects a reverse split by amending its charter. Here is the text of the charter amendment adopted by NextWave:

CERTIFICATE OF AMENDMENT TO AMENDED AND RESTATED CERTIFICATE OF INCORPORATION OF NEXTWAVE WIRELESS INC.

NextWave Wireless Inc. (the "Corporation"), a corporation organized and existing under the laws of the State of Delaware, hereby certifies as follows:

FIRST: The name of the corporation is NextWave Wireless Inc.

SECOND: The Corporation's original Certificate of Incorporation was filed with the Secretary of State of Delaware on June 29, 2006.

THIRD: The first paragraph of Article IV of the Corporation's Amended and Restated Certificate of Incorporation is hereby amended to read in its entirety as follows:

The Corporation is authorized to issue two classes of stock to be designated, respectively, "Common Stock" and "Preferred Stock." The total number of shares of Common Stock which this corporation has authority to issue is fifty seven million, one hundred forty two thousand, eight hundred fifty seven (57,142,857) with a par value of $0.007 per share. The total number of shares of Preferred Stock which this corporation has authority to issue is twenty-five million (25,000,000) with a par value of $0.001 per share.

FOURTH: The following is hereby added at the end of Article IV of the Corporation's Amended and Restated Certificate of Incorporation:

Reverse Stock Split

On the effective date of the amendment revising Article IV and adding this paragraph to Article IV pursuant to the General Corporation Law of the State of Delaware (the "Effective Date"), each share of Common Stock, par value $0.001

per share (the "Old Common Stock"), issued and outstanding immediately before the Effective Date, shall be and hereby is, reclassified as and changed into one-seventh (1/7) of a share of Common Stock, par value $0.007 per share (the "New Common Stock"). Each outstanding stock certificate which immediately before the Effective Date represented one or more shares of Old Common Stock shall thereafter, automatically and without the necessity of surrendering the same for exchange, represent the number of whole shares of New Common Stock determined by multiplying the number of shares of Old Common Stock represented by such certificate immediately prior to the Effective Date by one-seventh (1/7), and shares of Old Common Stock held in uncertificated form shall be treated in the same manner. No fractional shares of New Common Stock will be issued, and stockholders who would otherwise be entitled to receive one or more fractional shares of New Common Stock shall instead receive a cash payment equal to the fair value, as determined by the Board of Directors, of such fractional shares as of the Effective Date.

FIFTH: This Amendment to the Corporation's Amended and Restated Certificate of Incorporation was duly adopted by unanimous consent of the Board of Directors of the Corporation, who have been duly elected and qualified, in accordance with the provisions of Section 242 of the DGCL.

SIXTH: The effective date of this Amendment will be Monday, June 21, 2010 at 12:01 A.M.

IN WITNESS WHEREOF, NextWave Wireless Inc. has caused this Certificate of Amendment to be signed by its Executive Vice President and Chief Financial Officer this 18th day of June, 2010.

NEXTWAVE WIRELESS INC.

By: /s/ Francis J. Harding
Name: Francis J. Harding
Title: Executive Vice President and
          Chief Financial Officer

Prior to the above amendment, the first paragraph of Article IV of Next-Wave's charter read as follows:

The Corporation is authorized to issue two classes of stock to be designated, respectively, "Common Stock" and "Preferred Stock." The total number of shares which the Corporation is authorized to issue is four hundred twenty-five million (425,000,000) shares. Four hundred million (400,000,000) shares shall be Common Stock, par value $0.001 per share. Twenty-five million (25,000,000) shares shall be Preferred Stock, par value $0.001 per share.

As you can see, NextWave decreased its authorized shares of Common Stock and increased their par value, both by a factor of seven, as is standard practice for a reverse split.

The language in the certificate amendment addressing fractional shares is to deal with the situation where a shareholder owns a number of shares pre-split that is not divisible by seven. For example, say you owned 100 shares of NextWave pre-split. This would equate to 14.29 shares post-split. Corporations are allowed to issue fractional shares or instead essentially buy them back for cash.[17] NextWave opted for the latter (as is standard), which means post-split you own 14 shares of NextWave and will get a check for around $0.50 instead of 0.29 of a share.

Question

Why do you think NextWave decided on a 7-for-1 reverse split as opposed to some other number?

---

17. See DGCL §155; MBCA §6.04.

· CHAPTER TWELVE ·

MINORITY SHAREHOLDER PROTECTIONS

Default corporate law rules provide little protection to minority shareholders. Among other things, a minority shareholder (1) has no right to be employed by the corporation or participate in management, (2) cannot compel the corporation to pay dividends or buy back shares, and (3) has insufficient voting power to elect even a single director. These drawbacks are magnified in the private company context, given there is no public market for the corporation's shares, and therefore a minority shareholder is essentially locked into the investment.

Savvy investors are well aware of the plight of a minority shareholder, and thus negotiate for various protections as a condition to making a minority investment in a private company. We discuss some of these protections below. Then we cover the limited number of immutable protections built into corporate law statutes, as well as common law protections imposed by some courts. We close with an overview of buy-sell agreements.

A. NEGOTIATED PROTECTIONS

1. Cumulative Voting and Other Board-Related Provisions

As discussed in Chapter 9, the default corporate law rule is that directors are elected by straight voting, which means a majority shareholder will be able to elect the entire board, regardless of how minority shareholders vote. (You may want to reread section B.3. of Chapter 9 to refresh your memory regarding straight voting.) Corporate law statutes, however, provide for cumulative voting. Under both the MBCA and DGCL, a corporation can opt in to cumulative voting by including a statement to that effect in its charter.[1] For example, DGCL §214 provides:

> The certificate of incorporation of any corporation may provide that at all elections of directors of the corporation, or at elections held under specified circumstances, each holder of stock or of any class or classes or of a series or series thereof shall be entitled to as many votes as shall equal the number of votes which (except for such provision as to cumulative voting) such holder would be entitled to cast for the election of directors with respect to such holder's shares of stock multiplied by the number of directors to be elected by such holder, and that such holder may cast all of such votes for a single director or may distribute them among the number to be voted for, or for any 2 or more of them as such holder may see fit.

Cumulative voting provides some protection to a minority shareholder, because it may result in him or her being able to elect one or more directors, a possibility not afforded by straight voting.

Here is a formula, X, for figuring out the number of directors a shareholder has the voting power to elect under cumulative voting (assuming one vote per share and no fractional shares):

$$X = \frac{S}{T}(D + 1)$$

S = total number of shares owned by the shareholder
D = number of board seats up for election
T = total number of shares the corporation has outstanding

You then take the result and round it down to the nearest whole number.

Let's look at an example. Doza Co. has 500,000 shares issued and outstanding and a non-staggered board of five directors that is elected by cumulative voting. You own 200,000 of these shares and I own 300,000 of these shares. How many Doza directors can you elect? Plugging these numbers into the above formula looks like this:

$$X = \frac{200,000}{500,000}(5 + 1) = 2.4$$

Rounding the result down to the nearest whole number gives us two. In other words, you own enough Doza shares to be assured of electing two of the five Doza directors.

---

1. *See* DGCL §214; MBCA §7.28. Note that cumulative voting is the default rule under the corporate code of some states. A corporation incorporated in one of these states can (and normally does) opt out of cumulative voting by including a statement to that effect in its charter.

So how should you spread your votes among your preferred candidates? Since you own 200,000 shares and there are five seats up for election, you have a total of 1,000,000 votes (200,000 x 5) you can cast on one or more candidates. Based on the above formula, you know that you can elect two but not three directors (assuming I vote correctly). You could just cast 500,000 votes on each of your preferred candidates. However, it is probably better if you cast the minimum number of votes on each of your two candidates necessary to ensure that they win and the balance of your votes on a third candidate in case I misvote. The following formula specifies the minimum number of votes, V, that must be cast on a director to ensure he or she is elected:

$$V = \frac{(T - S)D}{(D - X) + 1} + 1$$

You fill in the "X" with the number of directors the previous formula indicated you have sufficient votes to elect. You then round the result down to the nearest whole number. Thus, continuing with the Doza Co. example, using the formula to figure out the number of votes you would need to put on each of your two candidates would look like this:

$$V = \frac{(500,000 - 200,000)5}{(5 - 2) + 1} + 1 = 375,001$$

The result came out as a whole number so there is nothing to round down. Thus, you should cast 375,001 votes on each of your two candidates and your remaining 249,998 votes on a third candidate.

Now let's look at how the Doza voting is likely to play out. Again, five directors are up for election and you have enough votes to elect two of them. You intend to elect A and B to the board. I use the same formulas as you and determine that I have enough votes to elect three candidates and that I need to cast 333,334 votes on each of my three candidates to ensure they win.[2] I intend to elect J, K, and L to the board. Hence, the voting will look like this:

Candidate	Votes Received
A	375,001
B	375,001
C	249,998

---

2. Here are the calculations for me. Number of directors I can elect: [300,000(5+1)]/500,000=3.6 which we round down to 3. Number of votes I should cast on each of the 3 directors: [(500,000-300,000)5]/[(5-3)+1] + 1=333,334.

Candidate	Votes Received
J	333,334
K	333,334
L	333,334
M	249,999
N	249,999

As discussed in Chapter 9, the default rule is that directors are elected by a plurality voting standard, meaning the candidates receiving the most votes win. Let's assume Doza has not opted out of this default rule. Here, the candidates receiving the most votes are A, B, J, K, and L. In other words, you picked two directors and I picked three directors, just as the formulas predicted. You cast some votes on C just in case I misvoted. I likewise cast some votes on M and N just in case you misvoted.

Of course, had Doza not opted in to cumulative voting meaning straight voting applied, I would have cast 300,000 votes on each of J, K, L, M, and N; and you would have cast 100,000 votes on each of A, B, C, D, and E. (D and E are your fourth, and fifth choices, respectively, for directors.) Hence, the top vote-getters would have been J, K, L, M, and N, meaning I would have elected the entire board.

A more straightforward way than cumulative voting for a minority shareholder to ensure he or she gets to select one or more members of the board of directors is to insist on just that as a condition to making the minority investment. For example, when negotiating with me concerning your investment in Doza Co., instead of requiring that I amend Doza's charter to provide for cumulative voting so that you would have the power to elect two Doza directors, you could have just required me to contractually agree to vote my shares for two director candidates to be chosen by you.

In addition to being simpler than cumulative voting, this approach also provides you with better protection. This is because, as mentioned in Chapter 9, a corporation can undermine the effect of cumulative voting by implementing a staggered board. For example, if Doza staggered its board into three classes, you no longer would have enough shares to elect two directors. This is because at most there would only be two seats up for election each year. As a result, the calculation of how many directors you could elect would be:

$$X = \frac{200,000}{500,000} \ (2 + 1) = 1.2, \text{ yielding 1 after rounding.}$$

Furthermore, my contractual obligation to vote for your two nominees is impervious to dilution. Thus, you would still get to pick two of the members of the Doza board even if Doza issued me another 1,000,000 shares. This would not be the case under cumulative voting because the calculation of how many directors you can elect would be:

$$X = \frac{200,000}{1,500,000}(5 + 1) = 0.8, \text{yielding 0 after rounding.}$$

A contractual commitment of this sort would normally be reflected in a voting agreement (also known as a pooling agreement). A voting agreement is simply an agreement between two or more shareholders as to the voting of shares.[3]

In addition to board representation, a minority investor may also insist on a particular frequency of board meetings (e.g., monthly or quarterly). Otherwise, he or she runs the risk of the corporation undercutting the effect of board representation by rarely holding board meetings. A minority investor may also require that his or her director be included on every board committee to prevent the corporation from delegating everything possible to a board committee whose membership does not include the investor's director to again undercut the effect of board representation.

Exercise 12.1

Assume the following facts:

- WKS Corp. has 1,000 shares of common stock outstanding.
- You own 450 and I own 550 of these shares.
- The WKS board consists of seven directors, all of whom are up for election.
- WKS is a Delaware corporation and its charter provides for cumulative voting.
- Your preferred director candidates, in order of preference are A, B, C, D, E, F, and G.
- My preferred director candidates in order of preference are H, I, J, K, L, M, and N.

1. How many directors can you elect? How many can I elect?
2. How should you cast your votes? How should I cast my votes?

---

2. Preemptive Rights

Preemptive rights give an existing shareholder the opportunity to purchase a proportionate part of to-be-issued shares before they are offered to other persons. Such purchase enables a shareholder to avoid having his or her ownership percentage in a corporation diluted down by new issuances.

---

3. The statutory provisions on point for a voting agreement are DGCL §218(c) and MBCA §7.31.

Let's look at an example to give you a better sense of this. Continuing with Doza Co. from above, assume Doza Co. is planning to issue me 300,000 shares of common stock to raise additional capital. Before the issuance, you own 200,000 out of Doza's 500,000 outstanding shares or 40 percent. If all 300,000 shares are issued to me, post-issuance you will own 200,000 out of 800,000 outstanding shares, or 25 percent. In other words, the issuance will dilute down your ownership percentage in Doza from 40 percent to 25 percent. If you're entitled to preemptive rights, however, Doza will first have to offer you your proportionate share of the 300,000 shares before they can issue them to me. Since your ownership percentage is 40 percent, you'd be entitled to buy 120,000 shares (300,000 x .40) on the same terms Doza intends to sell to me. If you do so, Doza will have to reduce the shares to be sold to me by 120,000 to 180,000. After the issuances, you will own 320,000 out of 800,000, or 40 percent. In other words, because you exercised your preemptive rights, your ownership percentage has not been diluted down.

Under both the MBCA and DGCL, all a corporation needs to do to afford its shareholders preemptive rights is to include a statement to that effect in its charter.[4] In other words, the default rule is that shareholders have no preemptive rights.

It is fairly common for a corporation to provide shareholders with the equivalent of preemptive rights via contract instead of a charter provision. Lawyers refer to these rights as "rights of first refusal" presumably to distinguish them from statutory preemptive rights. However, they are basically the same thing as preemptive rights. A corporation may go the contractual route because (1) there are fewer formalities associated with entering into a contract as compared to amending its charter, and (2) it only needs to grant the rights to select shareholders. For example, let's say when you invested in Doza Co., you did not negotiate for preemptive rights. Doza has convinced a new investor, Baez, to buy some shares, but one of her conditions to the investment is getting preemptive rights. Instead of amending its charter to provide Baez with these rights, which would mean you would get them too (essentially for nothing), Doza can contractually agree to give Baez the option to purchase her proportionate share of any new Doza issuances.

Exercise 12.2

Assume the following facts:

- WKS Corp. has 1,000 shares of common stock outstanding.
- You own 450 and I own 550 of these shares.
- WKS is an MBCA corporation and its charter provides for preemptive rights.

---

4. MBCA §6.30(h); DGCL §102(b)(3).

WKS is planning the following:
  (a) Issuing 200 shares of common stock to an investor in exchange for cash.
  (b) Issuing 300 shares of common stock to me in exchange for intellectual property I developed.
  (c) Issuing a promissory note to a lender in exchange for cash. The note is convertible into 100 shares of common stock.
  (d) Issuing 100 shares of stock to me in exchange for serving as a director.
  (e) Issuing a consultant options to purchase 100 shares of common stock for cash in exchange for consulting services provided to WKS.

  1. Which of the above issuances trigger preemptive rights?
  2. For those issuances that trigger preemptive rights, how many of the securities are you entitled to buy as a result?
  3. What exactly does WKS need to do to comply with your preemptive rights?
  4. Redo Questions 1 through 3 assuming WKS is a Delaware corporation.

3. Veto Rights

Veto rights give a shareholder the right to prevent a corporation from taking a specified action. Veto rights can be either explicit or implicit. We saw an example of explicit veto rights back in Chapter 8, Section B.2.e — protective provisions sometimes included in the terms of preferred stock. In that example, the corporation, among other things, cannot declare or pay a dividend, liquidate or dissolve, sell its assets, or engage in a merger without the approval of at least a majority of the outstanding shares of Series A Preferred. In other words, the owners of Series A Preferred can effectively veto any of those actions by not voting in favor of them.

Implicit veto rights result from higher quorum or voting requirements. For example, continuing with Doza Co. from above, assume that as a condition to your investment you required Doza to amend its charter to increase the voting standard for shareholder action to 61 percent of outstanding shares. (This is known as a supermajority voting requirement.) Here is sample charter language doing just that:

Action on a matter (other than the election of directors) by the shareholders is approved if at least 61 percent of the voting power of the then-outstanding shares of stock vote in favor of the action.

Since you own 200,000 of Doza's 500,000 outstanding shares, or 40 percent, you will be able to prevent Doza from getting the requisite vote of shareholders. In other words, you have veto power over any action that requires shareholder approval (charter amendments, a sale or dissolution of Doza, etc.). Of course, to prevent me from diluting you down below 40 percent, you better have negotiated for preemptive rights or veto rights over additional issuances of shares.

4. Employment Rights

It is fairly common for a person to make a minority investment in a closely held corporation with the expectation that the corporation will employ him or her. As mentioned above, stock ownership does not come with employment rights. Thus, a minority investor that has an expectation of employment better get a contractual commitment to that effect at the time of investment. The contract should address, at a minimum, the position, duties, compensation, fringe benefits, and circumstances under which employment may be terminated.

5. Buyout Obligations

Under statutory default rules, neither the corporation nor its shareholders have any obligation to buy out a shareholder who wants to exit his or her investment. In the private company context, this means minority shareholders are essentially locked in because there is no public market for their shares; there is little interest among third parties in buying minority stakes in private companies; and, as discussed in Chapter 11, the corporation will likely have imposed transfer restrictions on the shares. To address this lock-in, a minority investor can negotiate for a provision that requires the corporation or other shareholders to buy out the minority investors upon the happening of certain events. Normally, a majority shareholder is not going to agree to a broad buyout obligation because the point of taking on a minority investor is often to raise permanent capital for the corporation. It is fairly common, however, for a corporation to agree to buy out a shareholder upon death. Here's sample language:

> Following the death of a Shareholder, the Corporation will purchase all of the shares owned by the deceased Shareholder, and the personal representative of the estate of the deceased Shareholder must sell the shares to the Corporation.

A majority shareholder is willing to agree to such a provision, because he or she doesn't want the shares to pass to some unknown or undesirable person upon the settlement of the deceased shareholder's estate. (Notice that the above language not only obligates the corporation to purchase, but also obligates the estate to sell.) Also, the corporation can buy life insurance on the shareholder to ensure it has the cash for the buyout when the time comes. In addition to the above language, the relevant document will also address how the buyout price is to be determined and when the transaction is to close. We discuss the valuation issue below in the context of buy-sell agreements.

6. Dividend Policy

As discussed in Chapter 11, the default rule is that the payment of dividends is left to the discretion of the board of directors. As a result, a minority shareholder generally cannot force the board to declare a dividend, even if the corporation is making money hand over fist. Thus, it behooves a minority investor to negotiate a dividend policy in connection with his or her investment. Here's a sample dividend policy provision:

> The Corporation will pay cash dividends to its Shareholders within 45 days of the end of each fiscal year of the Corporation in an amount equal to at least 75 percent of the net income of the Corporation for that fiscal year less any reasonable provision for working capital requirements the Board determines appropriate.

7. Documenting Minority Shareholder Protections

Negotiated minority shareholder protections are typically documented in one of three ways: a charter provision, a bylaws provision, or a shareholders' agreement provision. The location of the provision is sometimes dictated by statute. For example, as mentioned above, under both the MBCA and DGCL, a corporation opts in to cumulative voting through a charter provision. Thus, if a minority investor insists on cumulative voting, it would need to be reflected in the corporation's charter. Absent a specific statutory requirement, there is a lot of flexibility as to in which document a particular provision can be located. A corporation's preference, however, is usually to document the protections via a shareholders' agreement (sometimes called an "investors' rights agreement"). This is because, as mentioned earlier, a corporation typically wants to minimize what it includes in its charter since a charter is (1) a public document, and (2) more difficult and costly to amend than its bylaws or a shareholders' agreement. As for bylaws versus a shareholders' agreement, a corporation typically prefers to keep investor-specific provisions out of its bylaws so that its bylaws are more plain vanilla, in part because it will likely need to furnish them to various third parties.

A shareholders' agreement is simply a contract between two or more of the coroporation's shareholders and oftentimes the corporation as well. You get to work with a basic shareholders' agreement in the next exercise.

Historically, courts would sometimes invalidate various types of shareholders' agreements as inconsistent with the applicable corporate law statute. For example, in *Long Park, Inc. v. Trenton-New Brunswick Theatres Co.*, 77 N.E.2d 633

(N.Y. 1948), the court invalidated a shareholders' agreement of a New Jersey corporation because the agreement vested all managerial authority in a single shareholder, and was therefore inconsistent with the New Jersey statutory requirement that "[t]he business of the corporation shall be managed by its board of directors."

Recognizing the importance of shareholders' agreements to private ordering of closely held corporations, state legislatures responded by adding provisions to their states' corporate codes validating shareholders' agreements. The relevant MBCA provision is §7.32, which was added to the MBCA in 1990. As explained in the Historical Background to the section:

> Section 7.32 validates agreements among close corporation shareholders that establish a "private order" otherwise inconsistent with one or more provisions of the Model Act. Its approach in accomplishing this is concrete and pragmatic: it provides that seven general types of arrangements among close corporation shareholders will be valid as to the adopting shareholders and their transferees even though these arrangements expressly or arguably conflict with the governing business corporation statute.
>
> As adopted, section 7.32 expressly validates, among other classic types of close corporation shareholder arrangements, those eliminating or restricting the discretion or power of boards; permitting disproportionate distributions; appointing specific persons as directors or officers notwithstanding otherwise applicable shareholder or board prerogatives; providing for weighted or other nonstandard voting; permitting customized business arrangements among shareholders and directors and their corporations; and requiring corporate dissolution upon the occurrence of specified events or acts.

For a shareholders' agreement to fall within §7.32, among other things, it must be set forth in (1) the corporation's charter or bylaws "and approved by all persons who are shareholders at the time of the agreement" or (2) "in a written agreement that is signed by all persons who are shareholders at the time of the agreement and is made known to the corporation."[5] Furthermore, the existence of the agreement must be "noted conspicuously on the front or back of each certificate for outstanding shares or on the information statement required by section 6.26(b)."[6]

A shareholders' agreement does not have to comply with §7.32 to be enforceable. As the Official Comment to the section states:

> Section 7.32 supplements the other provisions of the Model Act. If an agreement is not in conflict with another section of the Model Act, no resort need be made to section 7.32, with its requirement of unanimity. For example, special provisions can be included in the articles of incorporation or bylaws with less than unanimous shareholder agreement so long as such provisions are not in conflict

---

5. MBCA §7.32(b)(1).
6. *Id.* §7.32(c). An "information statement" is a document a corporation is required to furnish to shareholders who it issued shares without certificates. Such shares are referred to as "uncertificated."

with other provisions of the Act. Similarly, section 7.32 would not have to be relied upon to validate typical buy-sell agreements among two or more shareholders or the covenants and other terms of a stock purchase agreement entered into in connection with the issuance of shares by a corporation.

Hence, §7.32 is a safe harbor for shareholders' agreements that contain provisions that conflict or may conflict with the governing corporate law statute. In other words, a shareholders' agreement that does not comply with §7.32 is not necessarily invalid.

The analogous provision under the DGCL is §350. This section provides that a written agreement between shareholders of a close corporation is not invalid "on the ground that it so relates to the conduct of the business and affairs of the corporation as to restrict or interfere with the discretion or powers of the board of directors."[7]

Exercise 12.3

Below is a proposed Shareholders' Agreement drafted by Beckman's counsel. Assume WKS is a Delaware corporation and its charter does not provide for cumulative voting or preemptive rights.

1. You represent Sjostrom. What comments do you have on the agreement?
2. Why didn't Beckman include preemptive rights?
3. What's the purpose of section 5 of the Agreement?

SHAREHOLDERS' AGREEMENT

This Shareholders' Agreement (this "**Agreement**") is dated March 9, 2008 between Nancy G. Beckman ("**Beckman**") and William K. Sjostrom, Jr. ("**Sjostrom**"), (collectively, the "**Shareholders**"), and WKS Corp. (the "**Company**").

Background

A. Simultaneously with the signing of this Agreement, Beckman is making a minority investment in the Company's common stock.

B. To induce Beckman to make such investment, the Company and Sjostrom, its majority shareholder, have agreed to execute this agreement, which provides various rights to Beckman.

---

7. DGCL §350.

Accordingly, the parties agree as follows:

1. Board of Directors

1.1 <u>Size of Board</u>. Sjostrom agrees to vote, or cause to be voted, all shares of common stock of the Company (the "**Shares**") owned by him, or over which he has voting control, from time to time and at all times, in whatever manner as shall be necessary to ensure that the size of the Company's board of directors (the "**Board**") shall be set and remain at two directors.

1.2 <u>Board Composition</u>. Sjostrom agrees to vote, or cause to be voted, all Shares owned by him, or over which he has voting control, from time to time and at all times, in whatever manner as shall be necessary to ensure that at each annual or special meeting of stockholders at which an election of directors is held or pursuant to any written consent of the stockholders, one person designated by Beckman shall be elected to the Board (the "**Beckman Director**").

1.3 <u>Removal of Board Members</u>. Sjostrom also agrees to vote, or cause to be voted, all Shares owned by him, or over which he has voting control, from time to time and at all times, in whatever manner as shall be necessary to ensure that:

(a) the Beckman Director may not be removed from office unless (i) such removal is directed or approved by Beckman;

(b) any vacancies created by the resignation, removal or death of the Beckman Director shall be filled pursuant to the provisions of this Section 1; and

(c) the Beckman Director shall be removed upon Beckman's request.

Sjostrom agrees to execute any written consents required to perform the obligations of this Agreement, and the Company agrees at the request of Beckman to call a special meeting of stockholders for the purpose of electing directors.

1.4 <u>Matters Requiring Beckman Director Approval.</u> The Company shall not, without approval of the Board of Directors, which approval must include the affirmative vote of the Beckman Director:

(a) make any loan or advance to Sjostrom or any affiliate of Sjostrom;

(b) hire, terminate, or change the compensation of the executive officers, including approving any option grants or stock awards to executive officers;

(c) change the principal business of the Company, enter new lines of business, or exit the current line of business;

(d) effect any voluntary liquidation or dissolution of the Company;

(e) effect any sale, lease, assignment, transfer or other conveyance of all or substantially all of the assets of the Company, or any consolidation or merger involving the Company, or any reclassification or other change of any stock, or any recapitalization of the Company;

(f) create any Board committee; or

(g) issue any security.

1.5 Meetings. The Board of Directors shall meet at least quarterly in accordance with an agreed-upon schedule. The Company shall reimburse the Beckman Director for all reasonable out-of-pocket travel expenses incurred (consistent with the Company's travel policy) in connection with attending Board meetings.

2. Information and Observer Rights.

2.1 Information. The Company shall deliver to Beckman:

(a) as soon as practicable, but in any event within 90 days after the end of each fiscal year of the Company, (i) a balance sheet as of the end of such year, (ii) statements of income and of cash flows for such year, and (iii) a statement of stockholders' equity as of the end of such year, all such financial statements audited and certified by independent public accountants of regionally recognized standing selected by Beckman;

(b) as soon as practicable, but in any event within forty-five (45) days after the end of each of the first three (3) quarters of each fiscal year of the Company, unaudited statements of income and of cash flows for such fiscal quarter, and an unaudited balance sheet as of the end of such fiscal quarter, all prepared in accordance with GAAP;

(c) as soon as practicable, but in any event 30 days before the end of each fiscal year, a budget and business plan for the next fiscal year (collectively, the "**Budget**"), prepared on a monthly basis, including balance sheets, income statements, and statements of cash flow for such months and, promptly after prepared, any other budgets or revised budgets prepared by the Company;

(d) such other information relating to the financial condition, business, prospects, or corporate affairs of the Company as Beckman may from time to time request.

2.2 Inspection. The Company shall permit Beckman to visit and inspect the Company's properties; examine its books of account and records; and discuss the Company's affairs, finances, and accounts with its officers, during normal business hours of the Company as may be reasonably requested by Beckman.

3. Employment with the Company.

3.1 Beckman Employment. The Company will employ Beckman on the terms and conditions set forth in this Agreement.

3.2 <u>Position</u>. Beckman will be the vice president of sales for the Company and in such capacity will supervise, direct, and control the Company's sales operations and will perform such specific duties as the Board may from time to time request.

3.3 <u>Compensation</u>. The Company shall pay Beckman a salary of $20,000.00 per month. Such salary will be adjusted for the calendar year following the date of this Agreement, and for each succeeding calendar year thereafter, to reflect changes in the cost of living. Effective January 1st of the year following the date of this agreement, and January 1st of each succeeding calendar year, the Shareholders' compensation will be increased by a percentage equal to the percentage increase in the United States Department of Labor, Bureau of Labor Statistics, Consumer Price Index (1982/84 = 100), All Urban Consumers, All Items, U.S. City Average for the one-year period ending September 30 of the immediately preceding calendar year.

3.4 <u>Fringe Benefits</u>. In addition to salary, the Company will provide Beckman with group health insurance for herself and immediate family members and with $1 million of group term life insurance.

3.5 <u>Vacations</u>. Beckman, as an employee, will be entitled to a vacation of 12 weeks during each calendar year. Unused vacation will carry over from year to year.

3.6 <u>Illness</u>. Beckman will receive full compensation for any period during which she is unable to perform her duties as a result of illness or injury.

4. <u>Put Options</u>.

4.1 <u>Death</u>. For the 180 days immediately following Beckman's death, the personal representative of Beckman's estate shall have the option to require the Company to buy all Shares formerly owned by Beckman at the price and on the terms provided for in this Section 4. In the event of Beckman's death, unless the context otherwise requires, the term "Beckman" in the Agreement shall be deemed to include such personal representative.

4.2 <u>Disability</u>. For the 180 days immediately following the disability of Beckman, Beckman shall have the option to require the Company to buy all of her Shares at the price and on the terms provided in this Section 4. For purposes of this Agreement, Beckman will be considered disabled if she is (i) eligible for benefits for more than 50 percent disability under any group or individual disability insurance policy (as confirmed by an insurance company), or (ii) unable to perform on a full-time basis for a period of 90 consecutive days the essential functions of her position with the Company.

4.3 <u>Termination of Employment</u>. For 180 days following the termination of Beckman's employment with the Company for any reason, Beckman shall have the option to require the Company to buy all of her Shares at the price and on the terms provided in this Agreement.

4.4 <u>Exercise</u>. A put option under this Section 4 shall be exercised, if at all, by delivery of written notice of exercise to the Company within the above-prescribed period.

4.5 <u>Purchase Price</u>. The purchase price for Shares sold under this Section 4 shall be the value per share determined by appraisal as of the last day of the month immediately preceding the exercise of the option and shall be based on the greater of the Company's liquidation or going concern value. The appraiser shall be selected by Beckman and the cost of the appraisal shall be paid by the Company. The appraiser shall not apply a marketability or minority discount in determining the price per share.

4.6 <u>Payment Terms</u>. The Company shall pay Beckman 50 percent of the purchase price when the sale of Shares is closed. The remaining balance of the purchase price will be paid in accordance with the terms of a promissory note of the Company providing that the principal amount is payable in two equal annual installments, including interest on the unpaid balance at the prime rate of interest as quoted in the *Wall Street Journal* for the last business day prior to the closing plus 2 percent. The first installment will be due one year after the closing, and the second installment will be due on the same day of the next year. The promissory note will provide that if any installment is not paid when due, the holder may declare the entire remaining balance, together with all accrued interest, immediately due and payable. Full or partial prepayment of the promissory note will be permitted at any time, provided that any partial payment will not affect the amount or regularity of payments coming due thereafter. Payment of the promissory note will be secured by a stock pledge agreement in a form reasonably acceptable to Beckman. The collateral will be the Shares being purchased or their equivalent.

5. <u>Tag-Along Right</u>.

If Sjostrom proposes to sell any of his Shares, he must give written notice of the sale to Beckman, at least 30 days prior to its closing. The notice must indicate the percentage of the total number of shares of the Company held by Sjostrom that will be sold or transferred and the proposed price and terms. Within 20 days after receipt of this notice, Beckman may elect to sell the same percentage of her Shares at the price and on the terms specified in the notice; provided, however, that if Sjostrom is proposing to sell Shares amounting to a majority stake in the Company, Beckman may elect to sell all of her Shares at the price and on the terms specified in the notice. If Beckman makes such election, Sjostrom must purchase or otherwise acquire the shares in a transaction closed simultaneously with Sjostrom's sale of Shares unless the person purchasing Sjostrom's shares agrees to purchase Beckman's shares in the same transaction.

6. <u>General Provisions</u>.

6.1 <u>Entire Agreement</u>. This Agreement is the final, complete, and exclusive statement of the parties' agreement on the matters contained in this Agreement and supersedes all prior communications, understandings, and agreements between the parties related thereto.

6.2 <u>Modification and Waiver</u>. No purported amendment, modification, or waiver of any provision of this Agreement shall be binding unless set forth in a writing signed by both parties (in the case of amendments and modifications) or by the party to be charged (in the case of waivers). Any waiver shall be limited to the circumstance or event specifically referenced in the written waiver document and shall not be deemed a waiver of any other term of this Agreement or of the same circumstance or event upon any recurrence thereof.

6.3 <u>Governing Law</u>. This Agreement shall be governed by and construed in accordance with the laws of the State of Arizona without regard to the rules of conflict of laws of such state or any other jurisdiction.

6.4 <u>Successors and Assigns</u>. This Agreement shall be binding upon and be enforceable by the parties to this Agreement and their respective heirs, legal representatives, successors and assigns, who are obligated to take any action which may be necessary or proper to carry out the purpose and intent hereof.

6.5 <u>Notices</u>. All notices and other communications given or made pursuant to this Agreement shall be in writing and shall be deemed effectively given upon the earlier of actual receipt or: (i) personal delivery to the party to be notified; (ii) when sent, if sent by electronic mail or facsimile during the recipient's normal business hours, and if not sent during normal business hours, then on the recipient's next business day; (iii) five (5) days after having been sent by registered or certified mail, return receipt requested, postage prepaid; or (iv) one (1) business day after the business day of deposit with a nationally recognized overnight courier, freight prepaid, specifying next-day delivery, with written verification of receipt. All notices permitted or required hereunder shall be in writing and shall be deemed to have been delivered when received if hand delivered (including delivery by commercial or private messenger with signed receipt) or two days after depositing, if placed in the U.S. mails for delivery by registered or certified mail, return receipt requested, postage prepaid, and addressed to the appropriate party at the address set forth on the first page hereof. Addresses may be changed by written notice given pursuant to this section.

6.6 <u>Consent to Specific Performance</u>. The parties hereto acknowledge that it is impossible to measure in money the damages which would accrue to a party by reason of failure to perform any of the obligations hereunder. Therefore, if any party shall institute any action or proceeding to enforce the provisions hereof, any party against whom such action or proceeding is brought hereby waives any claim or defense therein that the plaintiff has an adequate remedy at law.

To evidence the parties' agreement to this Agreement's provisions, they have executed and delivered this Agreement on the date set forth in the preamble.

WKS Corp.

By:_____

Its:_____

_____

William K. Sjostrom, Jr.

_____

Nancy G. Beckman

B. IMMUTABLE STATUTORY PROTECTIONS

In this section we cover the limited number of mandatory statutory provisions that can be viewed as protecting minority shareholders.

1. Inspection Rights

Both the MBCA and DGCL afford shareholders rights to inspect a corporation's books and records. Specifically, MBCA §16.02(a) entitles a shareholder to inspect and copy, among other things, the corporation's charter, bylaws, shareholder meeting minutes from the last three years, written communications from the corporation to its shareholders from the last three years, and a list of current directors and officers. Additionally, per MBCA §16.02(c) a shareholder can inspect and copy excerpts from board meeting minutes, accounting records, and the shareholder list provided the shareholder seeks to do so in good faith and for a proper purpose and the records the shareholder wants to inspect are connected to the purpose. The Official Comment to §16.02 provides that "[a] 'proper purpose' means a purpose that is reasonably relevant to the demanding shareholder's interest as a shareholder."

Section 220 is the analogous DGCL provision. Under this section, shareholders have the right to inspect and copy for any proper purpose "[t]he corporation's stock ledger, a list of its stockholders, and its other books and records." Section 220(b) defines "proper purpose" as "a purpose reasonably related to such person's interest as a stockholder."

Wholly separate from inspection rights, MBCA §16.20 requires a corporation to deliver annual financial statements to its shareholders "[w]ithin 120 days after the close of each fiscal year." There is no analogous provision under the DGCL.

Finally, both the DGCL and MBCA allow a director to examine the corporation's books and records for a purpose reasonably related to the performance of his or her duties as a director.[8] This right accentuates the value of a minority shareholder being able to elect him- or herself to a corporation's board through cumulative voting or other negotiated provision, even though having a single member on a board (assuming a board size of at least three directors) confers no actual control.

2. Judicial Dissolution for Oppression

MBCA §14.30(a)(2) provides for dissolution of a corporation in a proceeding by a shareholder "if it is established that: . . . (iii) the directors or those in control of the corporation have acted, are acting, or will act in a manner that is illegal, oppressive, or fraudulent." Thus, a minority shareholder who believes he or she is being mistreated by a majority shareholder can bring a suit for dissolution and argue the mistreatment amounts to oppression. The next case discusses the definition of oppression.

Balvik v. Sylvester
411 N.W.2d 383 (N.D. 1987)

VANDE WALLE, Justice.

This is an appeal from a district court judgment dissolving Weldon Corporation [Weldon] and appointing a liquidating receiver to dispose of its assets. We affirm in part, reverse in part, and remand with directions.

In November 1979 Elmer Balvik and Thomas Sylvester formed a partnership, Weldon Electric, for the purpose of engaging in the electrical contracting business. Balvik contributed $8,000 and a vehicle worth $2,000, and Sylvester contributed $25,000 to the partnership's assets. Although Sylvester's contribution under the terms of the articles of partnership was 70 percent, and Balvik's was 30 percent, both partners had an equal vote and equal rights in the management of the business.

The parties continued operating the business as a partnership until 1984, when, at Sylvester's urging, they decided to incorporate. Stock was issued to

---

8. *See* DGCL §220(d); MBCA §16.05.

Balvik and Sylvester in proportion to their partnership ownership interests, with Sylvester receiving 70 percent and Balvik receiving 30 percent of the stock. Sylvester and his wife and Balvik and his wife were the four directors of the corporation, with Sylvester being elected president and Balvik being elected vice-president. The bylaws of the corporation provided that a shareholder was entitled to one vote for each share of stock owned; thus Balvik held only a minority voice in the management of the corporation. The bylaws also provided that the "sale of shares of stock by any shareholder shall be as [set] forth in a 'Buy-Sell Agreement' entered into by the shareholders." Although the subject of the "buy-sell agreement" was discussed on various occasions by the parties and an attorney had prepared a "stock redemption agreement" for their consideration, no separate agreements were executed by the parties.

In 1985 problems arose between the parties concerning their differences in philosophy of management of the corporation. Sylvester wanted excess profits reinvested into the corporation while Balvik wanted them withdrawn and paid out as bonuses or dividends. Sylvester also questioned Balvik's job performance. According to Balvik, during August 1985 he was fired as an employee of the corporation. According to Sylvester, Balvik was removed from his position as the foreman on a job the corporation was performing for the Ladish Malting Company in Spiritwood, but was not "fired" from his position with the corporation. In any event, Balvik no longer came to work for the corporation and began drawing unemployment benefits. He subsequently obtained employment at the Ladish Malting Company.

In October 1985, Balvik brought this action seeking Weldon's dissolution or, in the alternative, that he be paid the "true value" of his stock. He also sought punitive damages. Balvik alleged that Sylvester had breached a fiduciary duty he owed to Balvik and that Sylvester had been guilty of oppression and malice by discharging him from employment with the corporation. Balvik also alleged other instances of misconduct by Sylvester and asserted that he had "reasonable expectations . . . that he would be treated as a partner, furnished employment and not discharged merely because he did not hold an equal amount of stock."

In January 1986 Weldon held its annual shareholders meeting. On the strength of Sylvester's 70 percent of the voting shares, the bylaws were amended to reduce the number of directors from four to three, and to reduce the number needed for a quorum from three to two. Sylvester, his wife, and Peter Sylvester were voted in as the new directors of the corporation. The directors then voted in Peter Sylvester as the new vice-president, removing Balvik from that office. It does not appear from the record that Weldon has declared a dividend or that Balvik has received any money from the corporation since August 1985.

The trial court ruled in favor of Balvik, finding that Sylvester had discharged Balvik from his employment with the corporation and had discharged Balvik and his wife as members of the board of directors, leaving Balvik without any benefit from his 30-percent ownership in the corporation. The court concluded that Sylvester, through a series of acts culminating with the January 1986 shareholders meeting, effectively prevented Balvik "from participating in the management or operation of Weldon Corporation, thus constituting 'oppressive' behavior under Sec. 10-21-16, N.D.C.C., and establishing sufficient grounds for the dissolution of Weldon Corporation." This appeal followed.

The issue on appeal is whether Sylvester's actions amounted to "oppressive" conduct under §10-21-16(1)(b), N.D.C.C., sufficient to justify the forced dissolution of Weldon. . . .

"Oppressive" conduct is not defined in the statute or in the Model Business Corporation Act, from which our statute was derived. Courts construing the Model Act have noted that there are no specific elements necessary for a finding of oppression, but that it is an expansive term that is used to cover a multitude of situations dealing with improper conduct which is neither "illegal" nor "fraudulent." As the court stated in *White v. Perkins*, 213 Va. 129, 189 S.E.2d 315, 319 (1972):

> "The word 'oppressive,' as used in the statute does not carry an essential inference of imminent disaster; it can contemplate a continuing course of conduct. The word does not necessarily savor of fraud, and the absence of 'mismanagement, or misapplication of assets,' does not prevent a finding that the conduct of the dominant directors or officers has been oppressive. It is not synonymous with 'illegal' and 'fraudulent.'"

The statutory concept of oppressive conduct, and the broad and imprecise definitions of the term given by the courts, is best understood by examining the nature and characteristics of close corporations. The typical attributes of a close corporation are that: (1) the shareholders are few in number, often only two or three; (2) the shareholders usually live in the same geographical area, know each other, and are well acquainted with each other's business skills; (3) all or most of the shareholders are active in the business, usually serving as directors or officers or as key participants in some managerial capacity; and (4) there is no established market for the corporate stock. 1 F. O'Neal and R. Thompson, *O'Neal's Close Corporations* §1.07 (3d ed. 1987). Thus it is generally understood that, in addition to supplying capital and labor to a contemplated enterprise and expecting a fair return, parties comprising the ownership of a close corporation expect to be actively involved in its management and operation. One leading commentator observed:

> Unlike the typical shareholder in a publicly held corporation, who may be simply an investor or a speculator and does not desire to assume the responsibilities of management, the shareholder in a close corporation considers himself or herself as a co-owner of the business and wants the privileges and powers that go with ownership. Employment by the corporation is often the shareholder's principal or sole source of income. As a matter of fact, providing for employment may have been the principal reason why the shareholder participated in organizing the corporation. Even if shareholders in a close corporation anticipate an ultimate profit from the sale of shares, they usually expect (or perhaps

should expect) to receive any immediate return in the form of salaries as officers or employees of the corporation rather than in the form of dividends on their stock. Earnings of a close corporation, often are distributed in major part in salaries, bonuses and retirement benefits, a fact which illustrates how some business policies in a close corporation are more likely than in a publicly held corporation to be determined by tax consequences. 1 F. O'Neal and R. Thompson, *supra*, at p. 25. [Footnotes omitted.]

The limited market for stock in a close corporation and the natural reluctance of potential investors to purchase a noncontrolling interest in a close corporation that has been marked by dissension can result in a minority shareholder's interest being held "hostage" by the controlling interest, and can lead to situations where the majority "freeze out" minority shareholders by the use of oppressive tactics.

> Freeze-outs are actions taken by the controlling shareholders to deprive a minority shareholder of her interest in the business or a fair return on her investment. A variety of freeze-out techniques exist, with the withholding of dividends being by far the most commonly applied technique. This technique is often combined with the discharge of the minority shareholder from employment and removal of the minority shareholder from the board of directors. If the minority shareholder is employed by the corporation full time, as is typical, and if she relies on her salary as her primary means of obtaining a return on her investment, as is typical, she is suddenly left with little or no income and little or no return on her investment. The controlling shareholders may effectively deprive the minority shareholder of every economic benefit that she derives from the corporation. Meanwhile, the controlling shareholders may continue to receive a substantial return based on their continuing employment with the corporation. The minority shareholder's investment serves only to ensure the success of the corporation for the benefit of the controlling shareholders.

D. MacDonald, *Corporate Behavior and the Minority Shareholder: Contrasting Interpretations of Section 10-19.1-115 of the North Dakota Century Code*, 62 N.D. L. Rev. 155, 164-65 (1986) (Footnotes omitted).

Because of the predicament in which minority shareholders in a close corporation are placed by a "freeze out" situation, courts have analyzed alleged "oppressive" conduct by those in control in terms of "fiduciary duties" owed by the majority shareholders to the minority and the "reasonable expectations" held by the minority shareholders in committing their capital and labor to the particular enterprise. . . .

Recognizing that a minority shareholder who reasonably expects that ownership in the corporation would entitle him to a job, a share of corporate earnings, and a place in corporate management would be "oppressed" in a very real sense when the majority seeks to defeat those expectations and there exists no effective means of salvaging the investment, the court in *Matter of Kemp & Beatley, Inc., supra,* 64 N.Y.2d at 73, 484 N.Y.S.2d at 805, 473 N.E.2d at 1179, held that a complaining shareholder's "reasonable expectations" can be used as a means of identifying and measuring conduct alleged to be oppressive. The court stated that "oppression should be deemed to arise only when the majority conduct substantially defeats expectations that, objectively viewed, were both reasonable under the circumstances and were central to the petitioner's decision to join the venture," and further explained: "A court considering a petition alleging oppressive conduct must investigate what the majority shareholders knew, or should have known, to be the petitioner's expectations in entering the particular enterprise. Majority conduct should not be deemed oppressive simply because the petitioner's subjective hopes and desires in joining the venture are not fulfilled. Disappointment alone should not necessarily be equated with oppression."

Measuring the conduct alleged to be oppressive in this case in light of the "fiduciary duty" and "reasonable expectation" concepts, we cannot say that the trial court erred in finding that Sylvester's cumulative actions amounted to "oppression" within the meaning of §10-21-16(1)(b), N.D.C.C. Balvik quit his former job to join Sylvester in the new business enterprise, making a relatively substantial investment in the process. It is apparent from the record that Balvik's involvement with Weldon constituted his primary, if not sole, source of livelihood and that he quite reasonably expected to be actively involved in the operations of the business. Due mainly to the different business philosophies of Balvik and Sylvester, disputes often arose regarding the handling of the corporation's profits. Balvik was ultimately fired as an employee of the corporation, thus destroying the primary mode of return on his investment. Any slim hope of gaining a return on his investment and remaining involved in the operations of the business was dashed when Sylvester removed Balvik as a director and officer of the corporation. Since that time Balvik has apparently received nothing from the corporation, and considering Sylvester's inclination to reinvest profits in the corporation, the possibility of a declaration of dividends in the near future appears remote. We find little relevance in whether Sylvester discharged Balvik from employment for cause, or in the fact that Balvik's removal as a director and officer of the corporation occurred only after Balvik brought the instant suit. The ultimate effect of these actions is that Balvik clearly has been "frozen out" of a business in which he reasonably expected to participate. As a result, Balvik is entitled to relief.

We have recognized that forced dissolution of a corporation is a drastic remedy which should be invoked with extreme caution and only when justice requires it. In a sense, a forced dissolution allows minority shareholders to exercise retaliatory "oppression" against the majority. Although §10-21-16, N.D.C.C., mentions only dissolution as a remedy for oppressive conduct, we agree with those courts which have interpreted their similar statutory counterparts to allow alternative equitable remedies not specifically stated in the statute. In *Baker v. Commercial Body Builders, Inc.,* 507 P.2d 387, 395-96 (Or. 1973) the court stated:

Depending upon the facts of the case and the nature of the problem involved, various alternative remedies may be appropriate. Among those suggested are the following:

"(a) The entry of an order requiring dissolution of the corporation at a specified future date, to become effective only in the event that the stockholders fail to resolve their differences prior to that date;

"(b) The appointment of a receiver, not for the purposes of dissolution, but to continue the operation of the corporation for the benefit of all the stockholders, both majority and minority, until differences are resolved or 'oppressive' conduct ceases;

"(c) The appointment of a 'special fiscal agent' to report to the court relating to the continued operation of the corporation, as a protection to its minority stockholders, and the retention of jurisdiction of the case by the court for that purpose;

"(d) The retention of jurisdiction of the case by the court for the protection of the minority stockholders without appointment of a receiver or 'special fiscal agent';

"(e) The ordering of an accounting by the majority in control of the corporation for funds alleged to have been misappropriated;

"(f) The issuance of an injunction to prohibit continuing acts of 'oppressive' conduct and which may include the reduction of salaries or bonus payments found to be unjustified or excessive;

"(g) The ordering of affirmative relief by the required declaration of a dividend or a reduction and distribution of capital;

"(h) The ordering of affirmative relief by the entry of an order requiring the corporation or a majority of its stockholders to purchase the stock of the minority stockholders at a price to be determined according to a specified formula or at a price determined by the court to be a fair and reasonable price;

"(i) The ordering of affirmative relief by the entry of an order permitting minority stockholders to purchase additional stock under conditions specified by the court;

"(j) An award of damages to minority stockholders as compensation for any injury suffered by them as the result of 'oppressive' conduct by the majority in control of the corporation." [Footnotes omitted.]

Under the circumstances, we believe the trial court abused its discretion in ordering the extreme remedy of dissolution. Weldon is apparently an on-going business and, under the facts presented, ordering its dissolution and liquidation is unduly harsh. Balvik, in his complaint, sought as an alternative remedy that "the Defendant pay to the Plaintiff the true value of his stock in the Corporation . . . ." This is similar to alternative remedy (h) listed above and, we believe, is the appropriate remedy here. Consequently, we remand this case for the entry of an order requiring either Weldon or Sylvester to purchase Balvik's stock at a price determined by the court to be the fair value thereof. The court may conduct any further proceedings it deems necessary for resolution of the issue. The parties are, of course, free to agree to other alternative methods of resolving this dispute.

We affirm the trial court's determination that Sylvester's conduct was oppressive under §10-21-16(1)(b), N.D.C.C., but we reverse the trial court's order of dissolution and remand the case for further proceedings.

***

Questions

1. What is the definition of oppression?
2. How was Balvik oppressed?
3. What remedy did the court award? What's the statutory support for this remedy?

In 1990, §14.34 was added to the MBCA. This section allows the corporation or one or more of its shareholders to purchase at fair value all of the shares of a shareholder petitioning for judicial dissolution. As the Official Comment to the section explains:

> The proceeding for judicial dissolution has become an increasingly important remedy for minority shareholders of closely held corporations who believe that the value of their investment is threatened by reason of circumstances or conduct described in section 14.30(2). If the petitioning shareholder proves one or more grounds under section 14.30(2), he is entitled to some form of relief but many courts have hesitated to award dissolution, the only form of relief explicitly provided, because of its adverse effects on shareholders, employees, and others who may have an interest in the continuation of the business.
>
> Commentators have observed that it is rarely necessary to dissolve the corporation and liquidate its assets in order to provide relief: the rights of the petitioning shareholder are fully protected by liquidating only his interest and paying the fair value of his shares while permitting the remaining shareholders to continue the business. In fact, it appears that most dissolution proceedings result in a buyout of one or another of the disputants' shares either pursuant to a statutory buyout provision or a negotiated settlement. . . . Accordingly, section 14.34 affords an orderly procedure by which a dissolution proceeding under section 14.30(2) can be terminated upon payment of the fair value of the petitioner's shares.

The DGCL has no analogous provision to MBCA §14.30(a)(2)(iii) or §14.34.

Exercise 12.4

Tanaka is a minority shareholder in a closely held corporation. He believes he is being oppressed, so wants to be bought out. Assume the MBCA applies. Make a list of questions to ask Tanaka so that you can provide him with the best advice.

---

3. Judicial Dissolution for Deadlock

Deadlock occurs when a corporation's board is evenly divided on an issue and is therefore unable to make decisions. It most often occurs at corporations with boards comprised of an even number of directors, with half elected by one group of shareholders and half elected by another group of shareholders. Of course, shareholders can break a board deadlock by amending the corporation's bylaws to add another director or removing a director. However, neither avenue will be a possibility if shareholders are also evenly divided on the issue. The MBCA's remedy for deadlock is judicial dissolution. Specifically, MBCA §14.30(a)(2) provides for dissolution of a corporation

in a proceeding by a shareholder if it is established that:

(i) the directors are deadlocked in the management of the corporate affairs, the shareholders are unable to break the deadlock, and irreparable injury to the corporation is threatened or being suffered, or the business and affairs of the corporation can no longer be conducted to the advantage of the shareholders generally, because of the deadlock; . . . [or]

(iii) the shareholders are deadlocked in voting power and have failed, for a period that includes at least two consecutive annual meeting dates, to elect successors to directors whose terms have expired . . . .

Note that a buyout right under MBCA §14.34 is also triggered by a petition for dissolution because of deadlock.

As alluded to in *Balvik*, judicial dissolution is a blunt remedy, especially when it comes to a corporation with an ongoing successful business. It is also slow and expensive. Thus, it is fairly common for shareholders to include language in a shareholders' agreement to resolve a deadlock, especially when ownership is split 50/50 between two shareholders. A common approach is a so-called shotgun provision. Here is sample language:

---

3. SHOTGUN PROVISION

3.1 <u>Deadlock Triggering Event</u>. In the event that Shareholders, acting as the board of directors of the Company or as the sole shareholders of the Company, are unable, due to a fifty-fifty (50-50) vote on a resolution, to take action upon a resolution duly presented to the directors or shareholders of the Company and such inability continues for a period of fifteen (15) days, then either Shareholder may initiate the deadlock procedures provided in Section 3.2 below.

3.2 <u>Deadlock Procedures</u>.

(a) <u>Initiation</u>. Upon the occurrence of the triggering event described in Section 3.1 and so long as the deadlock continues, either Shareholder (the "**Initiator**") may submit to the other (the "**Recipient**") a written notice (hereinafter

---

the "**Proposal**") setting forth a price and payment terms on which the Initiator would either (i) purchase all of the Stock owned by the Recipient or (ii) sell all of his Stock to the Recipient, and containing such other terms and conditions as are provided for in Section 3.3 below.

(b) <u>Option by Recipient</u>. The Recipient shall have, for a period of thirty (30) days following receipt of the Proposal, an option (the "**Recipient Option**") to either (i) purchase all of the Stock of the Initiator at the price and upon the payment terms set forth in the Proposal, or (ii) require the Initiator to purchase, at the price and upon the payment terms set forth in the Proposal, all of the Stock owned by the Recipient. Neither the option to purchase all of the Stock of the Initiator nor the option to require the Initiator to purchase all of the Stock of the Recipient shall be transferable. The Recipient Option shall be exercised by delivering to the Initiator, within such thirty (30) day period, a written notice, signed by the Recipient, of his intention to purchase the Initiator's Stock or sell his Stock to the Initiator, as the case may be.

(c) <u>Option by Initiator</u>. If the Recipient fails to deliver the notice to the Initiator within such thirty (30) day period, the Initiator shall have, for an additional period of thirty (30) days, an option (the "**Initiator Option**") to purchase all of the Stock of the Recipient at the price set forth in the Proposal. The Initiator Option shall not be transferable, and shall be exercised by delivering to the Recipient, within such additional thirty (30) day period, a written notice, signed by the Initiator, of his intention to buy. If the Initiator does not deliver to the Recipient notice of his intention to purchase within such period, the Initiator shall not submit to the Recipient any further offers under subsection (a) hereof for a period of three (3) months from and after the expiration of said thirty (30) day period.

3.3 <u>Terms of the Proposal</u>. The Proposal shall establish the price per share at which the Stock of either party may be purchased or sold (the "**Purchase Price**") and the payment terms and may establish such additional terms for the purchase and sale of the Stock as may be reasonably incidental to such purchase and sale. Either Shareholder purchasing all of the other Shareholder's Stock may elect to have the Company redeem the selling Shareholder's Stock provided the purchasing Shareholder personally guarantees the payment of the Purchase Price for such Stock.

A shotgun provision resolves a deadlock by taking out one of the sides. The beauty of the provision is that the initiating shareholder's offer is highly likely to be fair, because the shareholder does not know whether he or she will be buying or selling at the offered price.

C. HEIGHTENED FIDUCIARY DUTIES

Courts in many states have imposed common law heightened fiduciary duties on close corporation shareholders, as exemplified by the next case.

Wilkes v. Springside Nursing Home, Inc.
353 N.E.2d 657 (Mass. 1976)

On August 5, 1971, the plaintiff (Wilkes) filed a bill in equity for declaratory
judgment in the Probate Court for Berkshire County, naming as defendants T.
Edward Quinn (Quinn), Leon L. Riche (Riche), the First Agricultural National
Bank of Berkshire County and Frank Sutherland MacShane as executors under
the will of Lawrence R. Connor (Connor), and the Springside Nursing Home,
Inc. (Springside or the corporation). Wilkes alleged that he, Quinn, Riche and
Dr. Hubert A. Pipkin (Pipkin) entered into a partnership agreement in 1951,
prior to the incorporation of Springside, which agreement was breached in
1967 when Wilkes's salary was terminated and he was voted out as an officer
and director of the corporation. Wilkes sought, among other forms of relief,
damages in the amount of the salary he would have received had he continued
as a director and officer of Springside subsequent to March, 1967.

A judge of the Probate Court referred the suit to a master, who, after a lengthy
hearing, issued his final report in late 1973. Wilkes's objections to the master's
report were overruled after a hearing, and the master's report was confirmed
in late 1974. A judgment was entered dismissing Wilkes's action on the merits.
We granted direct appellate review. On appeal, Wilkes argued in the alternative
that (1) he should recover damages for breach of the alleged partnership agreement; and (2) he should recover damages because the defendants, as majority
stockholders in Springside, breached their fiduciary duty to him as a minority
stockholder by their action in February and March, 1967.

We conclude that the master's findings were warranted by the evidence and
that his report was properly confirmed. However, we reverse so much of the
judgment as dismisses Wilkes's complaint and order the entry of a judgment
substantially granting the relief sought by Wilkes under the second alternative
set forth above.

A summary of the pertinent facts as found by the master is set out in the
following pages. . . .

In 1951 Wilkes acquired an option to purchase a building and lot located on
the corner of Springside Avenue and North Street in Pittsfield, Massachusetts,
the building having previously housed the Hillcrest Hospital. Though Wilkes
was principally engaged in the roofing and siding business, he had gained a
reputation locally for profitable dealings in real estate. Riche, an acquaintance
of Wilkes, learned of the option, and interested Quinn (who was known to
Wilkes through membership on the draft board in Pittsfield) and Pipkin (an

acquaintance of both Wilkes and Riche) in joining Wilkes in his investment. The four men met and decided to participate jointly in the purchase of the building and lot as a real estate investment which, they believed, had good profit potential on resale or rental.

The parties later determined that the property would have its greatest potential for profit if it were operated by them as a nursing home. Wilkes consulted his attorney, who advised him that if the four men were to operate the contemplated nursing home as planned, they would be partners and would be liable for any debts incurred by the partnership and by each other. On the attorney's suggestion, and after consultation among themselves, ownership of the property was vested in Springside [Nursing Home, Inc.], a corporation organized under Massachusetts law.

Each of the four men invested $1,000 and subscribed to ten shares of $100 par value stock in Springside. At the time of incorporation it was understood by all of the parties that each would be a director of Springside and each would participate actively in the management and decision making involved in operating the corporation. It was, further, the understanding and intention of all the parties that, corporate resources permitting, each would receive money from the corporation in equal amounts as long as each assumed an active and ongoing responsibility for carrying a portion of the burdens necessary to operate the business.

The work involved in establishing and operating a nursing home was roughly apportioned, and each of the four men undertook his respective tasks. Initially, Riche was elected president of Springside, Wilkes was elected treasurer, and Quinn was elected clerk. Each of the four was listed in the articles of organization as a director of the corporation.

At some time in 1952, it became apparent that the operational income and cash flow from the business were sufficient to permit the four stockholders to draw money from the corporation on a regular basis. Each of the four original parties initially received $35 a week from the corporation. As time went on the weekly return to each was increased until, in 1955, it totalled $100.

In 1959, after a long illness, Pipkin sold his shares in the corporation to Connor, who was known to Wilkes, Riche and Quinn through past transactions with Springside in his capacity as president of the First Agricultural National Bank of Berkshire County. Connor received a weekly stipend from the corporation equal to that received by Wilkes, Riche and Quinn. He was elected a director of the corporation but never held any other office. He was assigned no specific area of responsibility in the operation of the nursing home but did participate in business discussions and decisions as a director and served additionally as financial adviser to the corporation.

In 1965 the stockholders decided to sell a portion of the corporate property to Quinn who, in addition to being a stockholder in Springside, possessed an interest in another corporation which desired to operate a rest home on the property. Wilkes was successful in prevailing on the other stockholders of

Springside to procure a higher sale price for the property than Quinn apparently anticipated paying or desired to pay. After the sale was consummated, the relationship between Quinn and Wilkes began to deteriorate.

The bad blood between Quinn and Wilkes affected the attitudes of both Riche and Connor. As a consequence of the strained relations among the parties, Wilkes, in January of 1967, gave notice of his intention to sell his shares for an amount based on an appraisal of their value. In February of 1967 a directors' meeting was held and the board exercised its right to establish the salaries of its officers and employees. A schedule of payments was established whereby Quinn was to receive a substantial weekly increase and Riche and Connor were to continue receiving $100 a week. Wilkes, however, was left off the list of those to whom a salary was to be paid. The directors also set the annual meeting of the stockholders for March, 1967.

At the annual meeting in March, Wilkes was not reelected as a director, nor was he reelected as an officer of the corporation. He was further informed that neither his services nor his presence at the nursing home was wanted by his associates.

The meetings of the directors and stockholders in early 1967, the master found, were used as a vehicle to force Wilkes out of active participation in the management and operation of the corporation and to cut off all corporate payments to him. Though the board of directors had the power to dismiss any officers or employees for misconduct or neglect of duties, there was no indication in the minutes of the board of directors' meeting of February, 1967, that the failure to establish a salary for Wilkes was based on either ground. The severance of Wilkes from the payroll resulted not from misconduct or neglect of duties, but because of the personal desire of Quinn, Riche and Connor to prevent him from continuing to receive money from the corporation. Despite a continuing deterioration in his personal relationship with his associates, Wilkes had consistently endeavored to carry on his responsibilities to the corporation in the same satisfactory manner and with the same degree of competence he had previously shown. Wilkes was at all times willing to carry on his responsibilities and participation if permitted so to do and provided that he receive his weekly stipend.

1. We turn to Wilkes's claim for damages based on a breach of the fiduciary duty owed to him by the other participants in this venture. In light of the theory underlying this claim, we do not consider it vital to our approach to this case whether the claim is governed by partnership law or the law applicable to business corporations. This is so because, as all the parties agree, Springside was at all times relevant to this action, a close corporation as we have recently defined such an entity in *Donahue v. Rodd Electrotype Co. of New England, Inc.*, 328 N.E.2d 505 (Mass. 1975).

In *Donahue*, we held that "stockholders in the close corporation owe one another substantially the same fiduciary duty in the operation of the enterprise that partners owe to one another." Id. at 515. As determined in previous decisions of this court, the standard of duty owed by partners to one another is one of "utmost good faith and loyalty." *Cardullo v. Landau*, 105 N.E.2d 843 (Mass. 1952), and cases cited. Thus, we concluded in *Donahue*, with regard to "their actions relative to the operations of the enterprise and the effects of that operation on the rights and investments of other stockholders," "(s)tockholders in close corporations must discharge their management and stockholder responsibilities in conformity with this strict good faith standard. They may not act out of avarice, expediency or self-interest in derogation of their duty of loyalty to the other stockholders and to the corporation." 328 N.E.2d at 515.

In the *Donahue* case we recognized that one peculiar aspect of close corporations was the opportunity afforded to majority stockholders to oppress, disadvantage or "freeze out" minority stockholders. In *Donahue* itself, for example, the majority refused the minority an equal opportunity to sell a ratable number of shares to the corporation at the same price available to the majority. The net result of this refusal, we said, was that the minority could be forced to "sell out at less than fair value, 328 N.E.2d at 515, since there is by definition no ready market for minority stock in a close corporation.

"Freeze outs," however, may be accomplished by the use of other devices. One such device which has proved to be particularly effective in accomplishing the purpose of the majority is to deprive minority stockholders of corporate offices and of employment with the corporation. This "freeze-out" technique has been successful because courts fairly consistently have been disinclined to interfere in those facets of internal corporate operations, such as the selection and retention or dismissal of officers, directors and employees, which essentially involve management decisions subject to the principle of majority control.

The denial of employment to the minority at the hands of the majority is especially pernicious in some instances. A guaranty of employment with the corporation may have been one of the "basic reason(s) why a minority owner has invested capital in the firm." Symposium—The Close Corporation, 52 Nw. U. L. Rev. 345, 392 (1957). The minority stockholder typically depends on his salary as the principal return on his investment, since the "earnings of a close corporation . . . are distributed in major part in salaries, bonuses and retirement benefits." 1 F. H. O'Neal, Close Corporations §1.07 (1971). Other noneconomic interests of the minority stockholder are likewise injuriously affected by barring him from corporate office. Such action severely restricts his participation in the management of the enterprise, and he is relegated to enjoying those benefits incident to his status as a stockholder. In sum, by terminating a minority stockholder's employment or by severing him from a position as an officer or director, the majority effectively frustrate the minority stockholder's purposes in entering on the corporate venture and also deny him an equal return on his investment.

The *Donahue* decision acknowledged, as a "natural outgrowth" of the case law of this Commonwealth, a strict obligation on the part of majority stockholders in a close corporation to deal with the minority with the utmost good faith and loyalty. On its face, this strict standard is applicable in the instant case. The distinction between the majority action in *Donahue* and the majority action in this case is more one of form than of substance. Nevertheless, we are concerned that untempered application of the strict good faith standard enunciated in *Donahue* to cases such as the one before us will result in the imposition of limitations on legitimate action by the controlling group in a close corporation which will unduly hamper its effectiveness in managing the corporation in the best interests of all concerned. The majority, concededly, have certain rights to what has been termed "selfish ownership" in the corporation which should be balanced against the concept of their fiduciary obligation to the minority.

Therefore, when minority stockholders in a close corporation bring suit against the majority alleging a breach of the strict good faith duty owed to them by the majority, we must carefully analyze the action taken by the controlling stockholders in the individual case. It must be asked whether the controlling group can demonstrate a legitimate business purpose for its action. In asking this question, we acknowledge the fact that the controlling group in a close corporation must have some room to maneuver in establishing the business policy of the corporation. It must have a large measure of discretion, for example, in declaring or withholding dividends, deciding whether to merge or consolidate, establishing the salaries of corporate officers, dismissing directors with or without cause, and hiring and firing corporate employees.

When an asserted business purpose for their action is advanced by the majority, however, we think it is open to minority stockholders to demonstrate that the same legitimate objective could have been achieved through an alternative course of action less harmful to the minority's interest. If called on to settle a dispute, our courts must weigh the legitimate business purpose, if any, against the practicability of a less harmful alternative.

Applying this approach to the instant case it is apparent that the majority stockholders in Springside have not shown a legitimate business purpose for severing Wilkes from the payroll of the corporation or for refusing to reelect him as a salaried officer and director. The master's subsidiary findings relating to the purpose of the meetings of the directors and stockholders in February and March, 1967, are supported by the evidence. There was no showing of misconduct on Wilkes's part as a director, officer or employee of the corporation which would lead us to approve the majority action as a legitimate response to the disruptive nature of an undesirable individual bent on injuring or destroying the corporation. On the contrary, it appears that Wilkes had always accomplished his assigned share of the duties competently, and that he had never indicated an unwillingness to continue to do so.

It is an inescapable conclusion from all the evidence that the action of the majority stockholders here was a designed "freeze out" for which no legitimate business purpose has been suggested. Furthermore, we may infer that a design to pressure Wilkes into selling his shares to the corporation at a price below their value well may have been at the heart of the majority's plan.

In the context of this case, several factors bear directly on the duty owed to Wilkes by his associates. At a minimum, the duty of utmost good faith and loyalty would demand that the majority consider that their action was in disregard of a long-standing policy of the stockholders that each would be a director of the corporation and that employment with the corporation would go hand in hand with stock ownership; that Wilkes was one of the four originators of the nursing home venture; and that Wilkes, like the others, had invested his capital and time for more than fifteen years with the expectation that he would continue to participate in corporate decisions. Most important is the plain fact that the cutting off of Wilkes's salary, together with the fact that the corporation never declared a dividend, assured that Wilkes would receive no return at all from the corporation.

2. The question of Wilkes's damages at the hands of the majority has not been thoroughly explored on the record before us. Wilkes, in his original complaint, sought damages in the amount of the $100 a week he believed he was entitled to from the time his salary was terminated up until the time this action was commenced. However, the record shows that, after Wilkes was severed from the corporate payroll, the schedule of salaries and payments made to the other stockholders varied from time to time. In addition, the duties assumed by the other stockholders after Wilkes was deprived of his share of the corporate earnings appear to have changed in significant respects. Any resolution of this question must take into account whether the corporation was dissolved during the pendency of this litigation.

Therefore our order is as follows: So much of the judgment as dismisses Wilkes's complaint and awards costs to the defendants is reversed. The case is remanded to the Probate Court for Berkshire County for further proceedings concerning the issue of damages. Thereafter a judgment shall be entered declaring that Quinn, Riche and Connor breached their fiduciary duty to Wilkes as a minority stockholder in Springside, and awarding money damages therefor. Wilkes shall be allowed to recover from Riche, the estate of T. Edward Quinn and the estate of Lawrence R. Connor, ratably, according to the inequitable enrichment of each, the salary he would have received had he remained an officer and director of Springside. In considering the issue of damages the judge on remand shall take into account the extent to which any remaining corporate funds of Springside may be diverted to satisfy Wilkes's claim.

So ordered.

Questions

1. What fiduciary duties do the shareholders of a close corporation owe each other? What is the policy behind imposing these duties?

2. As a result of these duties, what do the majority shareholders have to demonstrate when a minority shareholder brings suit claiming a breach? How can a minority shareholder respond?
3. Did the defendants breach their fiduciary duties? Why or why not?
4. In hindsight, what could the defendants have done differently to avoid this litigation? What could Wilkes have done differently?

Note that the duty of utmost good faith and loyalty described in the above case is more rigorous than the fiduciary duties owed by a controlling share-holder to a non-controlling shareholder discussed in Chapter 10. This heightened duty, however, applies only to shareholders of a "close corporation." In *Donahue*, the court stated that a close corporation is "typified by: (1) a small number of stockholders; (2) no ready market for the corporate stock; and (3) substantial majority stockholder participation in the management, direction and operations of the corporation."[9]

A majority of courts that have addressed the issue have imposed heightened fiduciary duties on close corporation shareholders. The Delaware Supreme Court, however, has refused to do so. Specifically, in *Nixon v. Blackwell*,[10] the court stated as follows:

> We wish to address one further matter which was raised at oral argument before this Court: Whether there should be any special, judicially-created rules to "protect" minority stockholders of closely-held Delaware corporations.
>
> The case at bar points up the basic dilemma of minority stockholders in receiving fair value for their stock as to which there is no market and no market valuation. It is not difficult to be sympathetic, in the abstract, to a stockholder who finds himself or herself in that position. A stockholder who bargains for stock in a closely-held corporation and who pays for those shares (unlike the plaintiffs in this case who acquired their stock through gift) can make a business judgment whether to buy into such a minority position, and if so on what terms. One could bargain for definitive provisions of self-ordering permitted to a Delaware corporation through the certificate of incorporation or by-laws by reason of the provisions in 8 Del. C. §§102, 109, and 141(a). Moreover, in addition to such mechanisms, a stockholder intending to buy into a minority position in a Delaware corporation may enter into definitive stockholder agreements, and such agreements may provide for elaborate earnings tests, buy-out provisions, voting trusts, or other voting agreements.
>
> The tools of good corporate practice are designed to give a purchasing minority stockholder the opportunity to bargain for protection before parting with consideration. It would do violence to normal corporate practice and our corporation law to fashion an ad hoc ruling which would result in a court-imposed stockholder buy-out for which the parties had not contracted. In 1967, when the Delaware General Corporation Law was significantly revised, a new Subchapter XIV entitled "Close Corporations; Special Provisions," became a part of that law

---

9. 328 N.E.2d 505 at 511.
10. 626 A.2d 1366 (Del. 1993).

for the first time. While these provisions were patterned in theory after close corporation statutes in Florida and Maryland, "the Delaware provisions were unique and influenced the development of similar legislation in a number of other states . . . ." *See* Ernest L. Folk, III, Rodman Ward, Jr., and Edward P. Welch, 2 *Folk on the Delaware General Corporation Law* 404 (1988). Subchapter XIV is a narrowly constructed statute which applies only to a corporation which is designated as a "close corporation" in its certificate of incorporation, and which fulfills other requirements, including a limitation to 30 on the number of stockholders, that all classes of stock have to have at least one restriction on transfer, and that there be no "public offering." 8 Del. C. §342. Accordingly, subchapter XIV applies only to "close corporations," as defined in section 342. "Unless a corporation elects to become a close corporation under this subchapter in the manner prescribed in this subchapter, it shall be subject in all respects to this chapter, except this subchapter." 8 Del. C. §341. The corporation before the Court in this matter, is not a "close corporation." Therefore it is not governed by the provisions of Subchapter XIV.

One cannot read into the situation presented in the case at bar any special relief for the minority stockholders in this closely held, but not statutory "close corporation" because the provisions of Subchapter XIV relating to close corporations and other statutory schemes preempt the field in their respective areas. It would run counter to the spirit of the doctrine of independent legal significance, and would be inappropriate judicial legislation for this Court to fashion a special judicially-created rule for minority investors when the entity does not fall within those statutes, or when there are no negotiated special provisions in the certificate of incorporation, by-laws, or stockholder agreements.

The last two paragraphs of the above block quote may give you the impression that the DGCL's close corporation provisions provide special protection to minority shareholders of a statutory close corporation. They, however, do not. *Nixon* perhaps can be read to leave the door open for a Delaware court to impose heightened fiduciary duties on a statutory close corporation. However, to date, it has not happened.

Delaware is one of roughly 20 states with statutory provisions specifically designed for close corporations. About half of these states take the same approach as Delaware and require a corporation to elect to be governed by the provisions, usually by including a statement to that effect in its charter. Lawyers typically refer to a corporation that has made such an election as a statutory close corporation to distinguish it from a close corporation in the *Donahue* sense that has not made an election. In other states, close corporation provisions apply to any corporation meeting the statutory definition of a close corporation. Notably, the Massachusetts corporate statute does not contain close corporation provisions.

D. BUY-SELL AGREEMENTS

Buy-sell agreements are standard among closely held corporations where all shareholders participate in the business. They (1) restrict an owner's rights to transfer shares, and (2) specify how shares are to be transferred following a shareholder's death, disability, etc. As mentioned in Chapter 11, transfer restrictions are customary with closely held corporations, because they allow shareholders to control with whom they are co-owners. Provisions triggered by death, disability, etc. provide an owner (or the owner's estate) with liquidity for his or her shares when the owner no longer participates in the business and therefore loses the associated income. These provisions also prevent a non-participating owner (or estate) from continuing to hold a stake in the business. Buy-sell provisions can be included in a corporation's charter or bylaws, but the most common approach is to include them in a shareholders' agreement (oftentimes it is titled "Buy-Sell Agreement").

Shareholders typically enter into a buy-sell agreement at the same time or shortly after the corporation is incorporated. At this point, relations among shareholders are harmonious as they are all excited about the new business. They realize that it is in each of their best interest to restrict transfer and address upfront what happens to a shareholder's shares if he or she dies, becomes disabled, etc. Furthermore, because no shareholder will know at this point whether he or she will be a buyer or seller under a buy-sell agreement, the provisions of the agreement will invariably be drafted so both buyers and sellers are treated fairly.

The key parts of a buy-sell agreement are described below. Note that buy-sell agreements raise various tax and estate planning issues that are beyond the scope of this book.

1. Blanket Prohibition on Transfers

A buy-sell agreement normally begins with a blanket prohibition on share transfers except as allowed by the agreement. Here is sample language:

> No Shareholder may transfer any Shares except as permitted under this Agreement. Any purported transfer of Shares in violation of this Agreement is void.

The agreement will typically include a broad definition of transfer that includes a sale, gift, exchange, or pledge of the shares, whether voluntary, involuntary, or by operation of the law.

2. Right of First Refusal or First Offer

A buy-sell agreement will often allow for transfers in compliance with a right of first refusal or first offer in the corporation or its shareholders. A right of first refusal requires a shareholder who has found a third party to buy some or all of his or her shares to first offer the shares to the corporation or its other shareholders on the same terms the third party has agreed to. The corporation or other shareholders then have a specified period of time to buy the shares on those terms. If they choose not to, the selling shareholder may sell his or her shares to the third party.

A right of first offer allows a selling shareholder to offer his or her shares to the corporation or other shareholders on terms determined by the selling shareholder. If the offer is not accepted, the selling shareholder may then sell the shares to a third party on terms no better (for the third party) than those offered to the right holders. Thus, unlike a right of first refusal, a selling shareholder can trigger a right of first offer, and thus the ability to sell his or her shares if the offer is declined, without first securing an offer from a third party. An advantage of this approach (at least from the selling shareholder's perspective) is that it will likely be easier for a selling shareholder to find a buyer. Specifically, if transfer is subject to a right of first refusal instead of first offer, prospective buyers may be reluctant to spend the time negotiating terms and obtaining financing for the purchase, given that he or she will lose the deal if the corporation or its other shareholders exercise their rights of first refusal. On the flip side, a right of first offer may compel the corporation or other shareholders to buy out a selling shareholder out of concern of his or her shares ending up in undesirable hands, even though a third-party buyer may never have emerged.

3. Obligations to Sell and Buy

The heart of a buy-sell agreement is the provisions requiring a shareholder to sell, and the corporation or other shareholders to buy, a shareholder's shares following the occurrence of a specified "triggering" event. Triggering events commonly include a shareholder's death, disability, or termination of employment with the corporation. The agreement will state who is obligated to buy—the corporation or the other shareholders. Alternatively, it may give the corporation the option to purchase with the other shareholders required to purchase if the corporation does not exercise its option. Furthermore, the agreement could provide for optional instead of mandatory repurchase depending on the triggering event. For example, it is somewhat common for an agreement to provide for mandatory repurchase upon the death, disability, or firing of a shareholder, but optional repurchase following a shareholder's voluntary termination of his or her employment with the corporation.

The price at which a shareholder's shares are to change hands following a triggering event will be addressed in the agreement. The three most common ways to handle price are as follows:

(1) Appraised price: The agreement provides that the price will be determined by an appraiser. The agreement will typically specify who the appraiser is to be or how the appraiser is to be selected. A common approach is to have the buyer and seller each appoint an appraiser. Each of them then does an appraisal of the corporation to determine the value of the shares. If their appraisals diverge (as is invariably the case), the two appraisers then select a third appraiser to decide which appraisal to use.

(2) Stipulated price: The agreement requires the shareholders to periodically agree on a value for the corporation's shares. The price for a transaction is then determined by multiplying the latest value by the number of shares being sold. An agreement going this route will normally provide for an appraised price as a backup in the event the shareholders failed to agree on an updated price as required by the agreement.

(3) Formula price: The agreement specifies a formula to be used to determine the price. For example, the agreement could specify that price is to be determined by multiplying the corporation's most recent year EBITDA (earnings before interest, taxes, depreciation, and amortization) by five and then by the percentage of outstanding shares being sold.

If a corporation is obligated to buy out a shareholder upon his or her death or disability, it will often purchase life and disability insurance on each shareholder to fund the obligation. This is, in part, to avoid having to come up with cash for the purchase at a time when the corporation may be in turmoil from the death or disability of a key participant in the business.

· CHAPTER THIRTEEN ·

PUBLIC COMPANY REGULATION

As mentioned earlier, a public company is subject to additional regulation under federal securities laws, principally the Securities Exchange Act of 1934 (Exchange Act), and under the rules of the exchange (if any) on which its shares are listed. Below we discuss the three most prominent sets of rules: disclosure requirements, proxy voting regulations, and corporate governance listing standards. We close by examining the prohibition of insider trading.

A. DISCLOSURE REQUIREMENTS

The Exchange Act requires public companies to prepare and file with the SEC annual, quarterly, and current reports. The policy behind this requirement is to provide investors access to information they can use to make informed trading decisions (the reports are accessible on the SEC's website shortly after filing). In this context, a public company is one that has securities registered under the Exchange Act. A company is required to register securities under the Exchange Act if (1) the securities are listed on a national securities exchange;[1] (2) the company has $10 million or more in total assets and a class of equity securities held of record by (a) 2,000 or more persons, or (b) 500 or more persons who are not accredited investors;[2] or (3) the company has filed a registration statement under the Securities Act that became effective.[3] Thus, pretty much any company with publicly traded securities will have to register the securities

---

1. *See* Exchange Act §12(b).
2. *See id.* §12(g)(1)(A) and Rule 12g-1. Persons holding of record securities issued under certain registration exemptions are not counted for purposes of the 2,000 and 500 triggers. *See* Exchange Act §12(g)(5) & (6). Up until 2012, the held of record trigger was 500 persons but was changed by Congress as part of the Jumpstart Our Business Startups Act, Pub. L. 112-106, 126 Stat. 306 (2012).
3. *See id.* §15(d).

under the Exchange Act and thereby become subject to the Exchange Act's disclosure requirements.[4]

1. Annual Reports

The contents of a company's annual report is dictated by SEC Form 10-K, and, as a result, many attorneys refer to the report simply as a "10-K." Among other things, a 10-K must include or incorporate by reference a description of the company's business, risk factors, audited financial statements for the fiscal year, management's discussion and analysis (MD&A) of the issuer's financial condition and results of operation for the fiscal year, and information concerning executive compensation. "Incorporate by reference" means that the required information is not actually set forth in the document but instead it contains a cross reference to some other SEC filing by the company that contains (or will contain) the required information. For example, it is common for a company's 10-K to incorporate by reference to its proxy statement (we discuss proxy statements in Section 8.B below) the required information regarding executive compensation. Here is sample language from Yahoo!'s 2010 10-K doing just that:

Item 11. *Executive Compensation*

The information required by this item is incorporated by reference to Yahoo!'s Proxy Statement for its 2011 Annual Meeting of Shareholders to be filed with the SEC within 120 days after the end of the fiscal year ended December 31, 2010.

The reference to "Item 11" comes from Form 10-K, which specifies various numbered "items" that need to be in the report. Item 11 addresses executive compensation.

The due date for a company's 10-K depends on the company's "filer" status. The 10-K of a "large accelerated filer" is due 60 days after fiscal year end, for an "accelerated filer," it is due 75 days after fiscal year end, and for all other companies it is due 90 days after fiscal year end. A "large accelerated filer" is a company with, among other things, an aggregate worldwide market value of voting and non-voting common equity held by its non-affiliates of $700 million or more.[5] An "accelerated filer" is a company with, among other things, an

---

4. I say "pretty much" because it is possible for a company to have publicly traded securities that are not registered under the Exchange Act. For example, a company could have sold stock to investors unaffiliated with the company a year or more ago in one or more private placements. A market maker could then start quoting the stock on OTC Pink. In this situation, the securities would not be listed on a national securities exchange (OTC Pink is not one) and the company would not have filed a registration under the Securities Act. Thus, as long as the company has fewer than 2,000 shareholders and 500 non-accredited shareholders (and it can take steps to ensure this is the case), it will not have to register its shares under the Exchange Act even though they are publicly traded.

5. *See* Exchange Act Rule 12b-2.

aggregate worldwide market value of voting and non-voting common equity held by its non-affiliates of $75 million or more, but less than $700 million. A public company that is neither a large accelerated filer nor an accelerated filer is sometimes referred to as a "non-accelerated filer."

2. Quarterly Reports

A public company is required to file quarterly reports after the end of each of its first three quarters of every fiscal year. The contents of a company's quarterly report is dictated by SEC Form 10-Q, and, as a result, many attorneys refer to the report simply as a "10-Q." Among other things, a 10-Q must include or incorporate by reference unaudited quarterly financial statements and MD&A with respect to quarterly results. The 10-Q due date is 40 days after fiscal quarter end for large accelerated and accelerated filers and 45 days after fiscal quarter end for all other filers.

3. Current Reports

A public company is required to file a current report generally within four business days after the occurrence of various events. The triggering events and contents of current reports are dictated by SEC Form 8-K, and, as a result, many attorneys refer to the report simply as an "8-K." Triggering events include entering into or terminating a material definitive agreement; entering into bankruptcy or receivership; completing an acquisition or disposition of assets; creating a direct financial obligation or an obligation under an off-balance sheet arrangement of a company; receiving of notice of delisting or failure to satisfy continued listing standards; selling equity securities in a transaction not registered under the Securities Act; materially modifying rights of security holders; resignation or dismissal of the company's outside accounting firm; a change in control of the company; departure of directors or certain officers; election of directors; appointment of certain officers; entry into compensatory arrangement with certain officers; amendments to the company's charter or bylaws; changing the company's fiscal year; temporary suspension of trading under the company's employee benefit plans; amendments to the company's code of ethics, or waiver of a code of ethics provision; and submitting matters to a vote of security holders. The report must include detailed information about the event, as specified in the form.

4. Sarbanes-Oxley Act of 2002

Congress passed the Sarbanes-Oxley Act of 2002 (SOX) in the wake of the massive accounting frauds discovered at Enron and WorldCom in the early 2000s. The stated purpose of SOX was "[t]o protect investors by improving the accuracy and reliability of corporate disclosures made pursuant to the securities laws."[6] In that regard, SOX included various provisions to address the content, timing, and reliability of 10-Ks, 10-Qs, and 8-Ks.

As for content, the most infamous provision is undoubtedly §404. Section 404(a) directed the SEC to adopt rules requiring firms' 10-Ks to include an internal control report that "state[s] the responsibility of management for establishing and maintaining an adequate internal control structure and procedures for financial reporting" and "contain[s] an assessment . . . of the effectiveness of the internal control structure and procedures of the issuer for financial reporting."[7] The SEC adopted elaborate rules under the Exchange Act implementing §404(a) in June 2003. SOX §404(b) requires firms' auditors to "attest to, and report on, the assessment made by the management of the issuer."[8] In March 2004, the Public Company Accounting Oversight Board, a board created by SOX §101 to oversee the auditors of public companies, adopted Audit Standard No. 2, which provides extensive guidelines and rules for auditing a firm's internal controls in connection with providing the required attestation and report. Section 404 is infamous because compliance with its dictates is costly—a 2008 survey found that compliance costs averaged $1.66 million per U.S. accelerated filer—and many believe these costs easily outweigh §404's benefits, especially when it comes to smaller public companies. As a result, the Dodd-Frank Wall Street Reform and Consumer Protection Act (briefly discussed below) permanently exempted non-accelerated filers from compliance with SOX §404(b).

As for timing of disclosure, §409 of SOX amended the Exchange Act to require public companies to "disclose to the public on a rapid and current basis such additional information concerning material changes in the financial condition or operations of the issuer . . . as the [SEC] determines, by rule, is necessary or useful for the protection of investors and in the public interest."[9] In response, the SEC expanded the list of events that trigger a public company's obligation to file an 8-K. The SEC also decreased the filing deadline for 8-K from five or 15 calendar days (depending on the triggering event) following the triggering event to four business days for most events.

SOX included several provisions relating to the reliability of disclosure. Section 302 requires senior officers to certify in each 10-K and 10-Q that they have reviewed the report, that the report is free of misstatements of material fact or misleading omissions of material fact, and that the report fairly presents the financial condition and results of operation of the company. Additionally, signing officers must certify that they are responsible for establishing and maintaining the company's internal controls, have evaluated the effectiveness of such controls, and disclosed to the company's auditor and audit committee all significant deficiencies in the design or operation of such controls.

---

6. Sarbanes-Oxley Act of 2002, Pub. L. 107-204, Preamble, 116 Stat. 745, 745 (2002).
7. *Id.* §404(a).
8. *Id.* §404(b).
9. *Id.* §409.

Similarly, SOX §906 requires a company's chief executive officer and chief financial officer to certify in each annual and quarterly report "that information contained in the periodic report fairly presents, in all material respects, the financial condition and results of operations of the issuer."[10] An erroneous certification can lead to personal liability for the certifier, and hence a certifier has a strong incentive to ensure reliability of the reports. In fact, §906 provides for criminal fines of up to $1 million and jail time of up to ten years for a knowingly false certification, and $5 million and 20 years for a willfully and knowingly false certification.

Exercise 13.1

Go to www.sec.gov,[11] pull up the latest Form 8-K for Facebook, Inc., and answer the following questions:

1. What is the date of the report?
2. What event(s) did Facebook report?
3. Who signed the report on behalf of Facebook?

---

5. Section 10(b) and Rule 10b-5

A public company's disclosure obligations are negatively reinforced by Exchange Act §10(b) and Rule 10b-5 promulgated thereunder.[12] Specifically, a company faces potential liability under §10(b)/Rule 10b-5 if its Exchange Act reports or other information it releases to the marketplace are not accurate and complete.

As explained by the Supreme Court in *Dura Pharmaceuticals, Inc. v. Broudo*:

> ... Section 10(b) of the Securities Exchange Act of 1934 forbids (1) the "use or employ[ment] ... of any ... deceptive device," (2) "in connection with the purchase or sale of any security," and (3) "in contravention of" Securities and Exchange Commission "rules and regulations." Commission Rule 10b-5 forbids, among other things, the making of any "untrue statement of a material fact"

---

10. *Id.* §906.

11. Here's what you do once you are at sec.gov: click on "FILINGS," click on "Search for Company Filings," click on "Company or fund name, ticker symbol . . . ," type "facebook" into the "Company name:" box, click on "Find Companies," scroll down the list until you find the first 8-K that appears under the "Filings" column, click on the corresponding "Documents" button in the next column over, and click on the link to the right of "FORM 8-K."

12. Rule 10b-5 provides, in relevant part:

> It shall be unlawful for any person, directly or indirectly, by the use of any means or instrumentality of interstate commerce, or of the mails or of any facility of any national securities exchange . . . (b) To make any untrue statement of a material fact or to omit to state a material fact necessary in order to make the statements made, in the light of the circumstances under which they were made, not misleading . . . in connection with the purchase or sale of any security.

or the omission of any material fact "necessary in order to make the statements made . . . not misleading."

The courts have implied from these statutes and Rule a private damages action, which resembles, but is not identical to, common law tort actions for deceit and misrepresentation. And Congress has imposed statutory requirements on that private action.

In cases involving publicly traded securities and purchases or sales in public securities markets, the action's basic elements include:

(1) a material misrepresentation (or omission);
(2) scienter, that is, a wrongful state of mind;
(3) a connection with the purchase or sale of a security;
(4) reliance, often referred to in cases involving public securities markets (fraud-on-the-market cases) as "transaction causation"[;]
(5) economic loss; and
(6) "loss causation," that is, a causal connection between the material misrepresentation and the loss.[13]

Each of these six elements is discussed below.

Note that §10(b)/Rule 10b-5 is very broad in its reach. It applies not just to Exchange Act reports but to any public statements made by a company by whatever means (e.g., press releases, blog posts, tweets). Furthermore, §10(b)/Rule 10b-5 applies to misstatements and omission by both public and private companies, although it comes up most often in the public company context. Additionally, as the above quote mentions, courts have recognized an implied private cause of action under §10(b)/Rule 10b-5. In other words, both the government and private plaintiffs can and do bring suits under these provisions. Suits brought by private plaintiffs are normally class actions.

a. Materiality

A misstatement or omission of fact is not actionable under §10(b)/Rule 10b-5 unless it is material. A fact is material if there is a substantial likelihood that a reasonable investor would consider it important in making an investment decision (this is known as the *TSC Industries* standard after the Supreme Court case that established it).[14] An omitted fact is material if there is "a substantial likelihood that the disclosure of the omitted fact would have been viewed by the

---

13. 544 U.S. 336, 341 (2005).

14. *See TSC Indus., Inc. v. Northway, Inc.*, 426 U.S. 438, 449 (1976) ("An omitted fact is material if there is a substantial likelihood that a reasonable shareholder would consider it important in deciding how to vote."). *TSC Industries* technically established the definition of "material fact" for purposes of §14a-9 of the Exchange Act, which applies to misstatements or omissions in proxy solicitation materials. Subsequent cases have adopted the same standard for Rule 10b-5. *See Basic Inc. v. Levinson*, 485 U.S. 224, 232 ("We now expressly adopt the TSC Industries standard of materiality for the §10(b) and Rule 10b-5 context.").

reasonable investor as having significantly altered the 'total mix' of information made available."[15]

Determining materiality is a fact-intensive inquiry that "requires delicate assessments of the inferences a 'reasonable [investor]' would draw from a given set of facts and the significance of those inferences to him, and these assessments are peculiarly ones for the trier of fact."[16] Hence, "[o]nly if the established omissions are 'so obviously important to an investor, that reasonable minds cannot differ on the question of materiality' is the ultimate issue of materiality appropriately resolved 'as a matter of law' by summary judgment."[17]

In the next case, the Supreme Court refines the *TSC Industries* standard for application to an event that is contingent or speculative in nature.

Basic Inc. v. Levinson
485 U.S. 224 (1988)

BLACKMUN, J.

This case requires us to apply the materiality requirement of §10(b) of the Securities Exchange Act of 1934 and the Securities and Exchange Commission's Rule 10b-5, promulgated thereunder, in the context of preliminary corporate merger discussions. . . .

I

Prior to December 20, 1978, Basic Incorporated was a publicly traded company primarily engaged in the business of manufacturing chemical refractories for the steel industry. As early as 1965 or 1966, Combustion Engineering, Inc., a company producing mostly alumina-based refractories, expressed some interest in acquiring Basic, but was deterred from pursuing this inclination seriously because of antitrust concerns it then entertained. In 1976, however, regulatory action opened the way to a renewal of Combustion's interest. The "Strategic Plan," dated October 25, 1976, for Combustion's Industrial Products Group included the objective: "Acquire Basic Inc. $30 million."

Beginning in September 1976, Combustion representatives had meetings and telephone conversations with Basic officers and directors, including petitioners here, concerning the possibility of a merger. During 1977 and 1978, Basic made three public statements denying that it was engaged in merger negotiations.[18] On December 18, 1978, Basic asked the New York Stock Exchange

---

15. *TSC Indus., Inc.*, 426 U.S. at 449.
16. *Id.* at 450.
17. *Id.* (quoting *Johns Hopkins University v. Hutton*, 422 F.2d 1124, 1129 (4th Cir. 1970)).
18. [FN 4] On October 21, 1977, after heavy trading and a new high in Basic stock, the following news item appeared in the *Cleveland Plain Dealer*:

"[Basic] President Max Muller said the company knew no reason for the stock's activity and that no negotiations were under way with any company for a merger. He said Flintkote recently denied Wall

to suspend trading in its shares and issued a release stating that it had been "approached" by another company concerning a merger. On December 19, Basic's board endorsed Combustion's offer of $46 per share for its common stock, and on the following day publicly announced its approval of Combustion's tender offer for all outstanding shares.

Respondents are former Basic shareholders who sold their stock after Basic's first public statement of October 21, 1977, and before the suspension of trading in December 1978. Respondents brought a class action against Basic and its directors, asserting that the defendants issued three false or misleading public statements and thereby were in violation of §10(b) of the 1934 Act and of Rule 10b-5. Respondents alleged that they were injured by selling Basic shares at artificially depressed prices in a market affected by petitioners' misleading statements and in reliance thereon. . . .

[T]he District Court granted summary judgment for the defendants. It held that, as a matter of law, any misstatements were immaterial: there were no negotiations ongoing at the time of the first statement, and although negotiations were taking place when the second and third statements were issued, those negotiations were not "destined, with reasonable certainty, to become a merger agreement in principle."

The United States Court of Appeals for the Sixth Circuit . . . reversed the District Court's summary judgment, and remanded the case. . . . In the Court of Appeals' view, Basic's statements that no negotiations were taking place, and that it knew of no corporate developments to account for the heavy trading activity, were misleading. With respect to materiality, the court rejected the argument that preliminary merger discussions are immaterial as a matter of law, and held that "once a statement is made denying the existence of any discussions, even discussions that might not have been material in absence of the denial are material because they make the statement made untrue." 786 F.2d, at 749. . . .

We granted certiorari . . . to resolve the split . . . among the Courts of Appeals as to the standard of materiality applicable to preliminary merger discussions. . . .

II

The 1934 Act was designed to protect investors against manipulation of stock prices. See S. Rep. No. 792, 73d Cong., 2d Sess., 1-5 (1934). Underlying

---

Street rumors that it would make a tender offer of $25 a share for control of the Cleveland-based maker of refractories for the steel industry." App. 363.

On September 25, 1978, in reply to an inquiry from the New York Stock Exchange, Basic issued a release concerning increased activity in its stock and stated that "management is unaware of any present or pending company development that would result in the abnormally heavy trading activity and price fluctuation in company shares that have been experienced in the past few days."

On November 6, 1978, Basic issued to its shareholders a "Nine Months Report 1978." This Report stated: "With regard to the stock market activity in the Company's shares we remain unaware of any present or pending developments which would account for the high volume of trading and price fluctuations in recent months." *Id.*, at 403.

the adoption of extensive disclosure requirements was a legislative philosophy: "There cannot be honest markets without honest publicity. Manipulation and dishonest practices of the market place thrive upon mystery and secrecy." H.R. Rep. No. 1383, 73d Cong., 2d Sess., 11 (1934). This Court "repeatedly has described the 'fundamental purpose' of the Act as implementing a 'philosophy of full disclosure.' "*Santa Fe Industries, Inc. v. Green*, 430 U.S. 462, 477-478 (1977), quoting *SEC v. Capital Gains Research Bureau, Inc.*, 375 U.S. 180, 186 (1963). . . .

The Court previously has addressed various positive and common-law requirements for a violation of §10(b) or of Rule 10b-5. The Court also explicitly has defined a standard of materiality under the securities laws, see *TSC Industries, Inc. v. Northway, Inc.*, 426 U.S. 438 (1976), concluding in the proxy-solicitation context that "[a]n omitted fact is material if there is a substantial likelihood that a reasonable shareholder would consider it important in deciding how to vote." Id., at 449. Acknowledging that certain information concerning corporate developments could well be of "dubious significance," *id.*, at 448, the Court was careful not to set too low a standard of materiality; it was concerned that a minimal standard might bring an overabundance of information within its reach, and lead management "simply to bury the shareholders in an avalanche of trivial information—a result that is hardly conducive to informed decisionmaking." *Id.*, at 448-449. It further explained that to fulfill the materiality requirement "there must be a substantial likelihood that the disclosure of the omitted fact would have been viewed by the reasonable investor as having significantly altered the 'total mix' of information made available." *Id.*, at 449. We now expressly adopt the *TSC Industries* standard of materiality for the §10(b) and Rule 10b-5 context.

III

The application of this materiality standard to preliminary merger discussions is not self-evident. Where the impact of the corporate development on the target's fortune is certain and clear, the *TSC Industries* materiality definition admits straightforward application. Where, on the other hand, the event is contingent or speculative in nature, it is difficult to ascertain whether the "reasonable investor" would have considered the omitted information significant at the time. Merger negotiations, because of the ever-present possibility that the contemplated transaction will not be effectuated, fall into the latter category.[19]

A

Petitioners urge upon us a Third Circuit test for resolving this difficulty. Under this approach, preliminary merger discussions do not become material until "agreement-in-principle" as to the price and structure of the transaction has been reached between the would-be merger partners. By definition, then, information

---

19. [FN 9] We do not address here any other kinds of contingent or speculative information, such as earnings forecasts or projections.

concerning any negotiations not yet at the agreement-in-principle stage could be withheld or even misrepresented without a violation of Rule 10b-5.

Three rationales have been offered in support of the "agreement-in-principle" test. The first derives from the concern expressed in *TSC Industries* that an investor not be overwhelmed by excessively detailed and trivial information, and focuses on the substantial risk that preliminary merger discussions may collapse: because such discussions are inherently tentative, disclosure of their existence itself could mislead investors and foster false optimism. The other two justifications for the agreement-in-principle standard are based on management concerns: because the requirement of "agreement-in-principle" limits the scope of disclosure obligations, it helps preserve the confidentiality of merger discussions where earlier disclosure might prejudice the negotiations; and the test also provides a usable, bright-line rule for determining when disclosure must be made.

None of these policy-based rationales, however, purports to explain why drawing the line at agreement-in-principle reflects the significance of the information upon the investor's decision. The first rationale, and the only one connected to the concerns expressed in *TSC Industries*, stands soundly rejected, even by a Court of Appeals that otherwise has accepted the wisdom of the agreement-in-principle test. "It assumes that investors are nitwits, unable to appreciate — even when told — that mergers are risky propositions up until the closing." *Flamm v. Eberstadt*, 814 F.2d, at 1175. Disclosure, and not paternalistic withholding of accurate information, is the policy chosen and expressed by Congress. We have recognized time and again, a "fundamental purpose" of the various Securities Acts, "was to substitute a philosophy of full disclosure for the philosophy of caveat emptor and thus to achieve a high standard of business ethics in the securities industry." *SEC v. Capital Gains Research Bureau, Inc.*, 375 U.S., at 186, 84 S. Ct., at 280. The role of the materiality requirement is not to "attribute to investors a child-like simplicity, an inability to grasp the probabilistic significance of negotiations," *Flamm v. Eberstadt*, 814 F.2d, at 1175, but to filter out essentially useless information that a reasonable investor would not consider significant, even as part of a larger "mix" of factors to consider in making his investment decision.

The second rationale, the importance of secrecy during the early stages of merger discussions, also seems irrelevant to an assessment whether their existence is significant to the trading decision of a reasonable investor. To avoid a "bidding war" over its target, an acquiring firm often will insist that negotiations remain confidential, and at least one Court of Appeals has stated that "silence pending settlement of the price and structure of a deal is beneficial to most investors, most of the time." *Flamm v. Eberstadt*, 814 F.2d, at 1177.

We need not ascertain, however, whether secrecy necessarily maximizes shareholder wealth — although we note that the proposition is at least disputed as a matter of theory and empirical research—for this case does not concern the timing of a disclosure; it concerns only its accuracy and completeness. We face here the narrow question whether information concerning the existence and status of preliminary merger discussions is significant to the reasonable investor's trading decision. Arguments based on the premise that some disclosure would be "premature" in a sense are more properly considered under the rubric of an issuer's duty to disclose. The "secrecy" rationale is simply inapposite to the definition of materiality.

The final justification offered in support of the agreement-in-principle test seems to be directed solely at the comfort of corporate managers. A bright-line rule indeed is easier to follow than a standard that requires the exercise of judgment in the light of all the circumstances. But ease of application alone is not an excuse for ignoring the purposes of the Securities Acts and Congress' policy decisions. Any approach that designates a single fact or occurrence as always determinative of an inherently fact-specific finding such as materiality, must necessarily be overinclusive or underinclusive. . . .

We therefore find no valid justification for artificially excluding from the definition of materiality information concerning merger discussions, which would otherwise be considered significant to the trading decision of a reasonable investor, merely because agreement-in-principle as to price and structure has not yet been reached by the parties or their representatives. . . .

C

Even before this Court's decision in *TSC Industries*, the Second Circuit had explained the role of the materiality requirement of Rule 10b-5, with respect to contingent or speculative information or events, in a manner that gave that term meaning that is independent of the other provisions of the Rule. Under such circumstances, materiality "will depend at any given time upon a balancing of both the indicated probability that the event will occur and the anticipated magnitude of the event in light of the totality of the company activity." *SEC v. Texas Gulf Sulphur Co.*, 401 F.2d, at 849. Interestingly, neither the Third Circuit decision adopting the agreement-in-principle test nor petitioners here take issue with this general standard. Rather, they suggest that with respect to preliminary merger discussions, there are good reasons to draw a line at agreement on price and structure.

In a subsequent decision, the late Judge Friendly, writing for a Second Circuit panel, applied the *Texas Gulf Sulphur* probability/magnitude approach in the specific context of preliminary merger negotiations. After acknowledging that materiality is something to be determined on the basis of the particular facts of each case, he stated:

> Since a merger in which it is bought out is the most important event that can occur in a small corporation's life, to wit, its death, we think that inside information, as regards a merger of this sort, can become material at an earlier stage than would be the case as regards lesser transactions — and this even though the mortality rate of mergers in such formative stages is doubtless high." *SEC v. Geon Industries, Inc.*, 531 F.2d 39, 47-48 (1976).

We agree with that analysis.

Whether merger discussions in any particular case are material therefore depends on the facts. Generally, in order to assess the probability that the event will occur, a factfinder will need to look to indicia of interest in the transaction at the highest corporate levels. Without attempting to catalog all such possible factors, we note by way of example that board resolutions, instructions to investment bankers, and actual negotiations between principals or their intermediaries may serve as indicia of interest. To assess the magnitude of the transaction to the issuer of the securities allegedly manipulated, a factfinder will need to consider such facts as the size of the two corporate entities and of the potential premiums over market value. No particular event or factor short of closing the transaction need be either necessary or sufficient by itself to render merger discussions material.[20]

As we clarify today, materiality depends on the significance the reasonable investor would place on the withheld or misrepresented information. The fact-specific inquiry we endorse here is consistent with the approach a number of courts have taken in assessing the materiality of merger negotiations. Because the standard of materiality we have adopted differs from that used by both courts below, we remand the case for reconsideration of the question whether a grant of summary judgment is appropriate on this record....

Questions

1. Who are the respondents and what is their claim?
2. What were the alleged misstatements?
3. Why did the district court conclude the misstatements were immaterial?
4. What test does the Court say applies to determine whether the misstatements were material? Why does the Court go with this test instead of the *TSC Industries* test?
5. In light of this case, what would you advise a client who is involved in preliminary merger discussions to do in response to a media inquiry regarding whether the client is involved in merger discussions?

---

20. [FN 17] To be actionable, of course, a statement must also be misleading. Silence, absent a duty to disclose, is not misleading under Rule 10b-5. "No comment" statements are generally the functional equivalent of silence.

It has been suggested that given current market practices, a "no comment" statement is tantamount to an admission that merger discussions are underway. That may well hold true to the extent that issuers adopt a policy of truthfully denying merger rumors when no discussions are underway, and of issuing "no comment" statements when they are in the midst of negotiations. There are, of course, other statement policies firms could adopt; we need not now advise issuers as to what kind of practice to follow, within the range permitted by law. Perhaps more importantly, we think that creating an exception to a regulatory scheme founded on a prodisclosure legislative philosophy, because complying with the regulation might be "bad for business," is a role for Congress, not this Court.

b. Scienter

The Supreme Court imposed a scienter requirement for a §10(b)/Rule 10b-5 cause of action in *Ernst & Ernst* v. *Hochfelder*.[21] Under this requirement, a plaintiff must prove that the defendant made the misstatement or omission with scienter. The Court described scienter as "a mental state embracing intent to deceive, manipulate or defraud."[22] Lower courts have since uniformly held that recklessness suffices, although the Supreme Court has never said one way or the other. Courts have defined reckless conduct for purposes of §10(b)/Rule 10b-5 as:

> a highly unreasonable [misstatement or] omission, involving not merely simple, or even inexcusable negligence, but an extreme departure from the standards of ordinary care, and which presents a danger of misleading buyers or sellers that is either known to the defendant or is so obvious that the actor must have been aware of it.[23]

In 1995, Congress passed the Private Securities Litigation Reform Act (PLSRA) in an effort "to curb frivolous lawyer driven [§10(b)/Rule 10b-5] litigation."[24] Among other things, the PLSRA amended the Exchange Act to require a §10(b)/Rule 10b-5 plaintiff to plead "with particularity facts giving rise to a strong inference that the defendant acted with the required state of mind[, that is, scienter]."[25] The PLSRA, did not, however, specify what constitutes a "strong inference." The Supreme Court addressed the issue in *Tellabs, Inc. v. Makor Issues & Rights, Ltd.,* ruling that in order to qualify as "strong," "an inference of scienter must be more than merely plausible or reasonable — it must be cogent and at least as compelling as any opposing inference of nonfraudulent intent."[26]

You may be wondering how a corporation can act with scienter given it has no mind of its own. Judge Posner addressed so-called corporate scienter in *Makor Issues & Rights, Ltc. v. Tellabs Inc.*:

> There are two competing inferences (always assuming of course that the plaintiffs are able to prove the allegations of the complaint). One is that the company knew (or was reckless in failing to realize, but we shall not have to discuss that possibility separately) that the statements were false, and material to investors. The other is that although the statements were false and material, their falsity was the result of innocent, or at worst careless, mistakes at the executive level. Suppose a clerical worker in the company's finance department accidentally overstated the company's earnings and the erroneous figure got reported in

---

21. 425 U.S. 185, 213-14 (1976).
22. Id. at 193, n.12.
23. *Sundstrand Corp. v. Sun Chem. Corp.*, 553 F.2d 1033, 1045 (7th Cir. 1977) (quoting *Franke v. Midwestern Okla. Dev. Auth.*, 428 F. Supp. 719, 725 (W.D. Okla. 1976), *vacated on other grounds*, 619 F.2d 856 (10th Cir. 1980)).
24. *Tellabs, Inc. v. Makor Issues & Rights, Ltd.*, 551 U.S. 308, 313-14 (2007).
25. Exchange Act §21D(b)(2), 15 U.S.C. §78u-4(b)(2).
26. *Tellabs, Inc.*, 551 U.S. at 313-14.

good faith up the line to . . . senior management, who then included the figure in their public announcements. Even if senior management had been careless in failing to detect the error, there would be no corporate scienter. Intent to deceive is not a corporate attribute — though not because "collective intent" or "shared purpose" is an oxymoron. It is not. A panel of judges does not have a single mind, but if all the judges agree on the decision of a case, the decision can properly be said to represent the collective intent of the panel, though the judges who join an opinion to make it unanimous may not agree with everything said in it.

The problem with inferring a collective intent to deceive behind the act of a corporation is that the hierarchical and differentiated corporate structure makes it quite plausible that a fraud, though ordinarily a deliberate act, could be the result of a series of acts none of which was both done with scienter and imputable to the company by the doctrine of respondeat superior. Someone low in the corporate hierarchy might make a mistake that formed the premise of a statement made at the executive level by someone who was at worst careless in having failed to catch the mistake. A routine invocation of respondeat superior, which would impute the mistake to the corporation provided only that it was committed in the course of the employee's job rather than being "a frolic of his own," *Joel v. Morrison*, 6 C. & P. 501, 172 Eng. Rep. 1338 (1834), would, if applied to a securities fraud that requires scienter, attribute to a corporation a state of mind that none of its employees had. To establish corporate liability for a violation of Rule 10b-5 requires "look[ing] to the state of mind of the individual corporate official or officials who make or issue the statement (or order or approve it or its making or issuance, or who furnish information or language for inclusion therein, or the like) rather than generally to the collective knowledge of all the corporation's officers and employees acquired in the course of their employment." *Southland Securities Corp. v. INSpire Ins. Solutions, Inc.*, 365 F.3d 353, 366 (5th Cir. 2004) (footnote omitted). A corporation is liable for statements by employees who have apparent authority to make them.

Suppose the false communication by the low-level employee to his superiors had been deliberate. Suppose he was embezzling tens of millions of dollars, and by concealing the embezzlement greatly exaggerated his corporation's assets. Suppose he even knew that as a result the corporation would misrepresent its assets to investors. Nevertheless, even if his superiors were careless in failing to detect the embezzlement, the corporation would not be guilty of fraud, since the malefactor's acts of embezzling and concealing the embezzlement would not be acts on behalf of the corporation; deliberate wrongs by an employee are not imputed to his employer unless they are not only within the scope of his employment but in attempted furtherance of the employer's goals.

c. A Connection with the Purchase or Sale of a Security

Courts have interpreted the "in connection with" language to include false or misleading statements that were made "in a manner reasonably calculated to influence the investing public."[27] The statements do not even have to be

---

27. *SEC v. Texas Gulf Sulphur Co.*, 401 F.2d 833, 862 (2d Cir. 1968).

specifically directed to investors as long as they were "disseminated in a medium upon which a reasonable investor would rely . . . ."[28] This is what gives §10(b)/Rule 10b-5 its broad reach. As mentioned above, it applies not just to Exchange Act reports but to any public statements made by a company by whatever means (e.g., press releases, blog posts, tweets).

d. Reliance

A §10(b)/Rule 10b-5 plaintiff must prove reliance (also called transaction causation). To do so, the plaintiff must show that the material misstatement or omission of defendant was a substantial factor in causing plaintiff's purchase or sale of a security. In a §10(b)/Rule 10b-5 suit against a public company, however, a plaintiff's reliance will often be presumed under the fraud-on-the-market theory. This theory was endorsed by the Supreme Court in the *Basic* case. The part of the opinion discussing the theory follows.

Basic Inc. v. Levinson
485 U.S. 224 (1988)

[The facts of *Basic* are set forth in Section A.5.a above as part of the portion of the opinion addressing materiality.] . . .

IV

A

We turn to the question of reliance and the fraud-on-the-market theory. Succinctly put:

> The fraud on the market theory is based on the hypothesis that, in an open and developed securities market, the price of a company's stock is determined by the available material information regarding the company and its business. . . . Misleading statements will therefore defraud purchasers of stock even if the purchasers do not directly rely on the misstatements. . . . The causal connection between the defendants' fraud and the plaintiffs' purchase of stock in such a case is no less significant than in a case of direct reliance on misrepresentations. *Peil v. Speiser*, 806 F.2d 1154, 1160-1161 (CA3 1986).

Our task, of course, is not to assess the general validity of the theory, but to consider whether it was proper for the courts below to apply a rebuttable presumption of reliance, supported in part by the fraud-on-the-market theory. . . .

---

28. *S.E.C. v. Pirate Investor LLC*, 580 F.3d 233, 249 (4th Cir. 2009).

This case required resolution of several common questions of law and fact concerning the falsity or misleading nature of the three public statements made by Basic, the presence or absence of scienter, and the materiality of the misrepresentations, if any. In their amended complaint, the named plaintiffs alleged that in reliance on Basic's statements they sold their shares of Basic stock in the depressed market created by petitioners. Requiring proof of individualized reliance from each member of the proposed plaintiff class effectively would have prevented respondents from proceeding with a class action, since individual issues then would have overwhelmed the common ones. The District Court found that the presumption of reliance created by the fraud-on-the-market theory provided "a practical resolution to the problem of balancing the substantive requirement of proof of reliance in securities cases against the procedural requisites of [Federal Rule of Civil Procedure] 23." The District Court thus concluded that with reference to each public statement and its impact upon the open market for Basic shares, common questions predominated over individual questions, as required by Federal Rules of Civil Procedure 23(a)(2) and (b)(3).

Petitioners and their amici complain that the fraud-on-the-market theory effectively eliminates the requirement that a plaintiff asserting a claim under Rule 10b-5 prove reliance. They note that reliance is and long has been an element of common-law fraud and argue that because the analogous express right of action includes a reliance requirement, see, e.g., §18(a) of the 1934 Act, as amended, 15 U.S.C. §78r(a), so too must an action implied under §10(b).

We agree that reliance is an element of a Rule 10b-5 cause of action. Reliance provides the requisite causal connection between a defendant's misrepresentation and a plaintiff's injury. There is, however, more than one way to demonstrate the causal connection. Indeed, we previously have dispensed with a requirement of positive proof of reliance, where a duty to disclose material information had been breached, concluding that the necessary nexus between the plaintiffs' injury and the defendant's wrongful conduct had been established. See *Affiliated Ute Citizens v. United States*, 406 U.S., at 153-154, 92 S. Ct., at 1472....

The modern securities markets, literally involving millions of shares changing hands daily, differ from the face-to-face transactions contemplated by early fraud cases, and our understanding of Rule 10b-5's reliance requirement must encompass these differences.

> In face-to-face transactions, the inquiry into an investor's reliance upon information is into the subjective pricing of that information by that investor. With the presence of a market, the market is interposed between seller and buyer and, ideally, transmits information to the investor in the processed form of a market price. Thus the market is performing a substantial part of the valuation process performed by the investor in a face-to-face transaction. The market is acting as the unpaid agent of the investor, informing him that given all the information available to it, the value of the stock is worth the market price.

In re LTV Securities Litigation, 88 F.R.D. 134, 143 (N.D. Tex. 1980).

B

Presumptions typically serve to assist courts in managing circumstances in which direct proof, for one reason or another, is rendered difficult. The courts below accepted a presumption, created by the fraud-on-the-market theory and subject to rebuttal by petitioners, that persons who had traded Basic shares had done so in reliance on the integrity of the price set by the market, but because of petitioners' material misrepresentations that price had been fraudulently depressed. Requiring a plaintiff to show a speculative state of facts, i.e., how he would have acted if omitted material information had been disclosed, or if the misrepresentation had not been made, would place an unnecessarily unrealistic evidentiary burden on the Rule 10b-5 plaintiff who has traded on an impersonal market.

Arising out of considerations of fairness, public policy, and probability, as well as judicial economy, presumptions are also useful devices for allocating the burdens of proof between parties. The presumption of reliance employed in this case is consistent with, and, by facilitating Rule 10b-5 litigation, supports, the congressional policy embodied in the 1934 Act. In drafting that Act, Congress expressly relied on the premise that securities markets are affected by information, and enacted legislation to facilitate an investor's reliance on the integrity of those markets:

> No investor, no speculator, can safely buy and sell securities upon the exchanges without having an intelligent basis for forming his judgment as to the value of the securities he buys or sells. The idea of a free and open public market is built upon the theory that competing judgments of buyers and sellers as to the fair price of a security brings [sic] about a situation where the market price reflects as nearly as possible a just price. Just as artificial manipulation tends to upset the true function of an open market, so the hiding and secreting of important information obstructs the operation of the markets as indices of real value.

H.R. Rep. No. 1383, at 11.

The presumption is also supported by common sense and probability. Recent empirical studies have tended to confirm Congress' premise that the market price of shares traded on well-developed markets reflects all publicly available information, and, hence, any material misrepresentations. It has been noted that "it is hard to imagine that there ever is a buyer or seller who does not rely on market integrity. Who would knowingly roll the dice in a crooked crap game?" *Schlanger v. Four-Phase Systems Inc.*, 555 F. Supp. 535, 538 (S.D.N.Y. 1982). Indeed, nearly every court that has considered the proposition has concluded that where materially misleading statements have been disseminated into an impersonal, well-developed market for securities, the reliance of individual plaintiffs on the integrity of the market price may be presumed. Commentators generally have applauded the adoption of one variation or another of the fraud-on-the-market theory. An investor who buys or sells stock at the price set by the market does so in reliance on the integrity of that price. Because most publicly available information is reflected in market price, an investor's reliance on any public material misrepresentations, therefore, may be presumed for purposes of a Rule 10b-5 action.

C

The Court of Appeals found that petitioners "made public, material misrepresentations and [respondents] sold Basic stock in an impersonal, efficient market. Thus the class, as defined by the district court, has established the threshold facts for proving their loss." 786 F.2d, at 751. The court acknowledged that petitioners may rebut proof of the elements giving rise to the presumption, or show that the misrepresentation in fact did not lead to a distortion of price or that an individual plaintiff traded or would have traded despite his knowing the statement was false.

Any showing that severs the link between the alleged misrepresentation and either the price received (or paid) by the plaintiff, or his decision to trade at a fair market price, will be sufficient to rebut the presumption of reliance. For example, if petitioners could show that the "market makers" were privy to the truth about the merger discussions here with Combustion, and thus that the market price would not have been affected by their misrepresentations, the causal connection could be broken: the basis for finding that the fraud had been transmitted through market price would be gone. Similarly, if, despite petitioners' allegedly fraudulent attempt to manipulate market price, news of the merger discussions credibly entered the market and dissipated the effects of the misstatements, those who traded Basic shares after the corrective statements would have no direct or indirect connection with the fraud. Petitioners also could rebut the presumption of reliance as to plaintiffs who would have divested themselves of their Basic shares without relying on the integrity of the market. For example, a plaintiff who believed that Basic's statements were false and that Basic was indeed engaged in merger discussions, and who consequently believed that Basic stock was artificially underpriced, but sold his shares nevertheless because of other unrelated concerns, e.g., potential antitrust problems, or political pressures to divest from shares of certain businesses, could not be said to have relied on the integrity of a price he knew had been manipulated.

Questions

1. What is the fraud-on-the-market theory? What does it have to do with whether a plaintiff relied on a misstatement or omission?
2. What does a plaintiff need to show to meet the reliance element under the theory?
3. How can a defendant rebut the presumption of reliance?

Courts typically apply the five factors set forth in *Cammer v. Bloom*, 711 F. Supp. 1264 (D.N.J. 1989), to determine whether shares of stock trade in an efficient market. These factors are (1) the stock's trading volume; (2) the number of analysts following the issuer; (3) the number of market makers for the stock; (4) the eligibility of the issuer to file a Form S-3 registration statement; and (5) the stock price's reaction to unexpected new events.

e. Economic Loss

This element requires a plaintiff to prove actual economic loss as a result of the fraud. A classic example would be a plaintiff who bought stock at $20.00 per share and then sold it at $15.00 per share after the price dropped following a company announcement that it overstated earnings.

f. Loss Causation

Finally, a plaintiff must prove loss causation. Specifically, "a plaintiff must prove 'that the economic harm that it suffered occurred as a result of the alleged misrepresentations' and that 'the damage suffered was a foreseeable consequence of the misrepresentation.'"[29]

B. PROXY VOTING REGULATIONS

As discussed in Chapter 9, shareholders have the right to vote on certain corporate actions (electing directors, charter amendments, mergers, etc.). In the public company context, shareholder voting almost always takes place at a shareholders' meeting as opposed to through written consent. Recall that a quorum of shares (typically a majority of outstanding shares) must be present, in person or by proxy, before the shareholders may vote on any matter at a shareholders' meeting. For most public company shareholders, in person attendance at a shareholders' meeting is an inefficient use of time — often the meeting site is geographically inconvenient or the shareholder's investment in the corporation represents a small percentage of a diversified portfolio so it does not make sense for the shareholder to attend. Hence, quorum requirements necessitate that public companies solicit shareholder proxies for their shareholders' meetings. As a result, the overwhelming majority of shareholders vote by proxy pursuant to the proxy materials furnished to them by the company. Consequently, these proxy materials are of central importance to shareholder voting at public companies.

---

29. *Rothman v. Gregor*, 220 F.3d 81, 95 (2d Cir. 2000) (quoting *Citibank, N.A. v. K-H Corp.*, 968 F.2d 1489, 1495 (2d Cir. 1992)).

1. Proxy Statement and Card

Appreciating this importance, Congress empowered the SEC through §14(a) of the Exchange Act to regulate the solicitation of proxies by public corporations. "The purpose of [§]14(a) is to prevent management or others from obtaining authorization for corporate action by means of deceptive or inadequate disclosure in proxy solicitation."[30] Thus, SEC rules require a public corporation to furnish its shareholders with a detailed disclosure document called a proxy statement whenever it solicits proxies. The proxy statement is designed to provide shareholders with relevant information regarding the matters up for vote for which proxies are solicited. For example, a proxy statement relating to the election of directors must include biographical information about the nominees, their stock and option holdings in the corporation, and with respect to incumbent directors, when they first became directors and whether they failed to attend at least 75 percent of board and applicable committee meetings. The proxy statement must also include detailed information about director compensation and transactions between any directors and the corporation during the past year.

Recall that voting by proxy is when a shareholder appoints an agent who will be attending the shareholders' meeting to vote the shareholder's shares on his or her behalf at the meeting. This appointment is typically made pursuant to a proxy card furnished by the company to its shareholders along with the company's proxy statement. SEC proxy regulations specify requirements for the proxy card. For example, the card must set forth the name of the proxy and on whose behalf proxy appointments are solicited. Furthermore, the card may not confer authority to vote for a nominee not listed in the proxy statement or to vote at more than one meeting. Below is a sample card.

If a company's management solicits proxies for the election of directors at an annual meeting (which is almost always the case), the solicitation materials must be accompanied or preceded by an annual report to security holders. Thus, the standard package of company proxy materials for an annual meeting consists of a proxy statement, a proxy card, and an annual report. A company can simply use its 10-K to meet the annual report requirement, but many companies prefer to use something slicker that includes color pictures, graphs, etc. Corporate attorneys refer to such a document as a "glossy annual report." A company that does not want to incur the time and expense to produce a glossy annual report will normally at least overlay its 10-K with a CEO letter to shareholders. Corporate attorneys refer to this approach as a "10-K wrap."[31]

---

30. *J.I. Case Co. v. Borak*, 377 U.S. 426, 431 (1964).
31. Sjostrom sometimes performs a "10-K" rap at his law school's talent show.

Google

Admission Ticket

C123456789

000000000.000000 ext   000000000.000000 ext
000000000.000000 ext   000000000.000000 ext
000000000.000000 ext   000000000.000000 ext

Electronic Voting Instructions

You can vote by internet or telephone!
Available 24 hours a day, 7 days a week!

Instead of mailing your proxy, you may choose one of the two voting methods outlined below to vote your proxy.

VALIDATION DETAILS ARE LOCATED BELOW IN THE TITLE BAR.

Proxies submitted by the internet or telephone must be received by 1:00 a.m., Central Time, on June 2, 2011.

Vote by internet
- Log on to the internet and go to www.envisionreports.com/goog
- Click on Annual Meeting.
- Follow the steps outlined on the secure website.

Vote by telephone
- Call toll free 1-800-652-VOTE (8683) within the United States, Canada & Puerto Rico any time on a touch tone telephone. There is NO CHARGE to you for the call.
- Follow the instructions provided by the recorded message.

Using a **black ink** pen, mark your votes with an **X** as shown in this example. Please do not write outside the designated areas.   [X]

Annual Meeting Proxy Card

1234 5678 9012 345

▼ IF YOU HAVE NOT VOTED VIA THE INTERNET OR TELEPHONE, FOLD ALONG THE PERFORATION, DETACH AND RETURN THE BOTTOM PORTION IN THE ENCLOSED ENVELOPE. ▼

A Election of Directors — The Board of Directors recommends a vote FOR the listed nominees.

1. Nominees:

	For	Withhold		For	Withhold		For	Withhold
01 - Larry Page	☐	☐	02 - Sergey Brin	☐	☐	03 - Eric E. Schmidt	☐	☐
04 - L. John Doerr	☐	☐	05 - John L. Hennessy	☐	☐	06 - Ann Mather	☐	☐
07 - Paul S. Otellini	☐	☐	08 - K. Ram Shriram	☐	☐	09 - Shirley M. Tilghman	☐	☐

B Proposals — The Board of Directors recommends a vote FOR Proposals 2, 3, and 4, every 3 YRS for Proposal 5, and AGAINST Proposals 6, 7, and 8.

	For	Against	Abstain
2. The ratification of Ernst & Young LLP as Google's independent registered public accounting firm for the fiscal year ending December 31, 2011.	☐	☐	☐
3. The approval of an amendment to Google's 2004 Stock Plan to increase the number of authorized shares of Class A common stock issuable under the plan by 1,500,000.	☐	☐	☐
4. The approval of 2010 compensation awarded to named executive officers.	☐	☐	☐

	3 Yrs	2 Yrs	1 Yr	Abstain
5. The frequency of future stockholder advisory votes regarding compensation awarded to named executive officers.	☐	☐	☐	☐

	For	Against	Abstain
6. A stockholder proposal regarding the formation of a board committee on sustainability, if properly presented at the meeting.	☐	☐	☐
7. A stockholder proposal regarding the adoption of a simple majority voting standard for stockholder matters, if properly presented at the meeting.	☐	☐	☐
8. A stockholder proposal regarding a conflict of interest and code of conduct compliance report, if properly presented at the meeting.	☐	☐	☐

IF VOTING BY MAIL, YOU MUST COMPLETE SECTIONS A - D ON BOTH SIDES OF THIS CARD.

C 1234567890   JNT
1UPX   1 1 4 0 9 5 1

MR A SAMPLE (THIS AREA IS SET UP TO ACCOMMODATE 140 CHARACTERS) MR A SAMPLE AND MR A SAMPLE AND MR A SAMPLE AND MR A SAMPLE AND MR A SAMPLE AND MR A SAMPLE AND

01AZNF

Exercise 13.2

Go to www.sec.gov,[32] pull up the latest proxy statement for Apple, Inc. (it will be labeled "DEF 14A"), and answer the following questions (the questions are written as if the meeting already occurred. If it has not, mentally change the verb tenses):

1. What was the date, time, and location of Apple's annual meeting of shareholders?
2. What items were up for a vote at the meeting?
3. How did the board recommend shareholders should vote?
4. What are the different ways by which an Apple shareholder can vote?
5. How many directors did Apple have, and how many of them were up for election?
6. At the end of the filing is a copy of the Annual Meeting Proxy Card. What is the effect of a shareholder signing the card but not filling in any of the boxes?
7. How much did Apple's non-employee directors receive in compensation for the applicable year?
8. As far as Apple knows, who is its largest shareholder?
9. How much did Apple's CEO make for the applicable year?
10. Who was Apple's auditor, and how much did Apple pay it in audit fees for the year?
11. Assume you own 100 shares of Apple's common stock. Would you take the time to read its proxy statement and fill out and send in your proxy card?

---

2. Proxy Solicitation and Voting Process

The actual solicitation and voting process is a bit convoluted as explained in the following excerpt from an SEC concept release.

———————————————•———————————————

Concept Release on the U.S. Proxy System
Release Nos. 34-62495; IA-3052; IC-29340
Securities and Exchange Commission (July 14, 2010) . . .

II. THE CURRENT PROXY DISTRIBUTION AND VOTING PROCESS

A fundamental tenet of state corporation law is that shareholders have the right to vote their shares to elect directors and to approve or reject major corporate transactions at shareholder meetings. Under state law, shareholders can

---

32. Here's what you do once you are at sec.gov: click on "FILINGS," click on "Search for Company Filings," click on "Company or fund name, ticker symbol ...," type "apple" into the "Company name" box, click on "Find Companies," click on the CIK number to the left of APPLE INC, scroll down the list until you find the first "DEF 14A" that appears under the "Filings" column, click on the corresponding "Documents" button in the next column over, and click on the link to the right of "DEFINITIVE PROXY STATEMENT."

appoint a proxy to vote their shares on their behalf at shareholder meetings, and the major national securities exchanges generally require their listed companies to solicit proxies for all meetings of shareholders. Because most shareholders do not attend public company shareholder meetings in person, voting occurs almost entirely by the use of proxies that are solicited before the shareholder meeting, thereby resulting in the corporate proxy becoming "the forum for shareholder suffrage."[33] Issuers with a class of securities registered under Section 12 of the Securities Exchange Act of 1934 ("Exchange Act") . . . are required to comply with the federal proxy rules in Regulation 14A when soliciting proxies from shareholders.

A. Types of Share Ownership and Voting Rights

The proxy solicitation process starts with the determination of who has the right to receive proxy materials and vote on matters presented to shareholders for a vote at shareholder meetings. The method for making this determination depends on the way the shares are owned. There are two types of security holders in the U.S. — registered owners and beneficial owners.

1. Registered Owners

Registered owners (also known as "record holders") have a direct relationship with the issuer because their ownership of shares is listed on records maintained by the issuer or its transfer agent. State corporation law generally vests the right to vote and the other rights of share ownership in registered owners. Because registered owners have the right to vote, they also have the authority to appoint a proxy to act on their behalf at shareholder meetings.

Registered owners can hold their securities either in certificated form or in electronic (or "book-entry") form through a direct registration system ("DRS"), which enables an investor to have his or her ownership of securities recorded on the books of the issuer without having a physical securities certificate issued. Under DRS, an investor can electronically transfer his or her securities to a broker-dealer to effect a transaction without the risk, expense, or delay associated with the use of securities certificates. Investors holding their securities in DRS retain the rights of registered owners, without having the responsibility of holding and safeguarding securities certificates.

2. Beneficial Owners

The vast majority of investors in shares issued by U.S. companies today are beneficial owners, which means that they hold their securities in book-entry form through a securities intermediary, such as a broker-dealer or bank. This is often referred to as owning in "street name." A beneficial owner does not own the securities directly. Instead, as a customer of the securities intermediary, the beneficial owner has an entitlement to the rights associated with ownership of the securities.[34]

---

33. [FN 22] *Roosevelt v. E.I duPont de Nemours & Co.*, 958 F.2d 416, 422 (D.C. Cir. 1992).
34. [FN 31] The rights and interests that a customer has against a securities intermediary's property are created by the agreements between the customer and the securities intermediary, as well as by the UCC, as

B. The Process of Soliciting Proxies

The following diagram illustrates the flow of proxy materials that typically occurs during a solicitation. The steps illustrated in the diagram and descriptions of the relevant parties are discussed below.

Diagram 1: The Flow of Proxy Materials

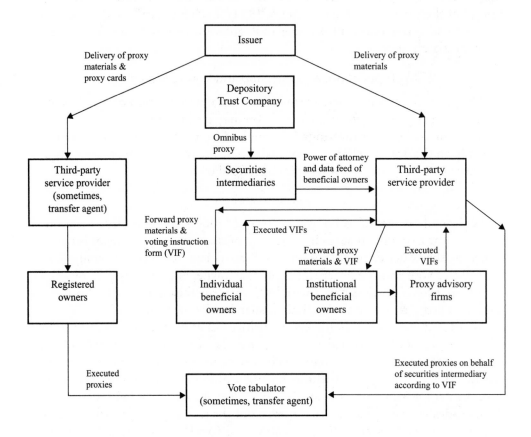

1. Distributing Proxy Materials to Registered Owners

It is a relatively simple process for an issuer to send proxy materials to registered owners because their names and addresses are listed in the issuer's records, which are usually maintained by a transfer agent. As the left side of Diagram 1 illustrates, proxy materials are sent directly from the issuer through its transfer

---

adopted in the relevant jurisdiction. Under the UCC, beneficial owners have a "securities entitlement" to the fungible bulk of securities held by the broker-dealer or bank. An "entitlement holder" is defined as a person identified in the records of a securities intermediary as the person having a security entitlement against the securities intermediary. UCC 8-503 (1994). A securities intermediary is obligated to provide the entitlement holder with all of the economic and governance rights that comprise the financial asset and that the entitlement holder can look only to that intermediary for performance of the obligations. *See generally* UCC 8-501 *et seq.* (1994).

agent or third-party proxy service provider to all registered owners in paper or electronic form.[35] Registered owners execute the proxy card and return it to the issuer's transfer agent or vote tabulator for tabulation.

2. Distributing Proxy Materials to Beneficial Owners

As the right side of Diagram 1 illustrates, the process of distributing proxy materials to beneficial owners is more complicated than it is for registered owners. The indirect system of ownership in the U.S. permits securities intermediaries to hold securities for their customers, and there can be multiple layers of securities intermediaries leading to one beneficial owner. This potential for multiple tiers of securities intermediaries presents a number of challenges in the distribution of proxy materials.

a. The Depository Trust Company

In most cases, the chain of ownership for beneficially owned securities of U.S. companies begins with the Depository Trust Company ("DTC"), a registered clearing agency acting as a securities depository.[36] Most large U.S. broker-dealers and banks are DTC participants, meaning that they deposit securities with, and hold those securities through, DTC. DTC's nominee, Cede & Co., appears in an issuer's stock records as the sole registered owner of securities deposited at DTC. DTC holds the deposited securities in "fungible bulk," meaning that there are no specifically identifiable shares directly owned by DTC participants. Rather, each participant owns a pro rata interest in the aggregate number of shares of a particular issuer held at DTC. Correspondingly, each customer of a DTC participant — such as an individual investor — owns a pro rata interest in the shares in which the DTC participant has an interest.

Once an issuer establishes a date for the shareholder meeting and a record date for shareholders entitled to vote on matters presented at the meeting, it sends a formal announcement of these dates to DTC, which DTC forwards to all of its participants. The issuer then requests from DTC a "securities position listing" as of the record date, which identifies the participants having a position in the issuer's securities and the number of securities held by each participant.

---

35. [FN 32] Commission rules provide, generally, that proxy materials can be provided electronically to shareholders who have affirmatively consented to electronic delivery. See Use of Electronic Media for Delivery Purposes, Release No. 33-7233 (Oct. 6, 1995) [60 Fed. Reg. 53,458]. In addition, the Commission has adopted the notice and access model that permits issuers to send shareholders a Notice of Internet Availability of Proxy Materials in lieu of the traditional paper packages including the proxy statement, annual report and proxy card. See Notice and Access Release. These two concepts work in tandem. Although an issuer electing to send a Notice in lieu of a full package generally would be required to send a paper copy of that Notice, it may send that Notice electronically to a shareholder who has provided an affirmative consent to electronic delivery.

36. [FN 33] DTC provides custody and book-entry transfer services of securities transactions in the U.S. market involving equities, corporate and municipal debt, money market instruments, American depositary receipts, and exchange-traded funds. In accordance with its rules, DTC accepts deposits of securities from its participants (i.e., broker-dealers and banks), credits those securities to the depositing participants' accounts, and effects book-entry movements of those securities. For more information about DTC, see http://www.dtcc.com/about/subs/dtc.php.

DTC must promptly respond by providing the issuer with a list of the number of shares in each DTC participant's account as of the record date. The record date securities position listing establishes the number of shares that a participant is entitled to vote through its DTC proxy.

For each shareholder meeting, DTC executes an "omnibus proxy"[37] transferring its right to vote the shares held on deposit to its participants. In this manner, broker-dealer and bank participants in DTC obtain the right to vote directly the shares that they hold through DTC.

b. Securities Intermediaries: Broker-Dealers and Banks

Once the issuer identifies the DTC participants holding positions in its securities, it is required to send a search card to each of those participants, as well as other securities intermediaries that are registered owners, to determine whether they are holding shares for beneficial owners and, if so, the number of sets of proxy packages needed to be forwarded to those beneficial owners. This process may involve multiple tiers of securities intermediaries holding securities on behalf of other securities intermediaries, with search cards distributed to each securities intermediary in the chain of ownership.

Commission rules require broker-dealers to respond to the issuer within seven business days with the approximate number of customers of the broker-dealer who are beneficial owners of the issuer's securities. The Commission's rules also require banks to follow a similar process except that banks must respond to the issuer within one business day with the names and addresses of all respondent banks and must respond within seven business days with the approximate number of customers of the bank who are beneficial owners of shares.

Once the search card process is complete, the issuer should know the approximate number of beneficial owners owning shares through each securities intermediary. The issuer must then provide the securities intermediary, or its third-party proxy service provider, with copies of its proxy materials (including, if applicable, a Notice of Internet Availability of Proxy Materials) for forwarding to those beneficial owners. The securities intermediary must forward these proxy materials to beneficial owners no later than five business days after receiving such materials. Securities intermediaries are entitled to reasonable reimbursement for their costs in forwarding these materials.

Instead of receiving and executing a proxy card (as registered owners receive and do), the beneficial owner receives a "voting instruction form" or "VIF" from the securities intermediary, which permits the beneficial owner to instruct the securities intermediary how to vote the beneficially owned shares. Although the VIF does not give the beneficial owner the right to attend the meeting, a beneficial owner typically can attend the meeting by requesting the appropriate documentation from the securities intermediary.

---

37. [FN 41] Rather than issue each participant a separate proxy to vote its shares, DTC drafts a single proxy (the "omnibus proxy") granting to each of the multiple participants listed in the proxy the right to vote the number of shares attributed to it in the omnibus proxy.

C. Proxy Voting Process

Once the proxy materials have been distributed to the registered owners and beneficial owners of the securities, the means by which shareholders vote their shares differs. As Diagram 1 illustrates, registered owners execute the proxy card and return it to the vote tabulator, either by mail, by phone, or through the Internet. Beneficial owners, on the other hand, indicate their voting instructions on the VIF and return it to the securities intermediary or its proxy service provider, either by mail, by phone, or through the Internet. The securities intermediary, or its proxy service provider, tallies the voting instructions that it receives from its customers. . . . [T]he securities intermediary, or its proxy service provider, then executes and submits to the vote tabulator a proxy card for all securities held by the securities intermediary's customers.

In certain situations, a broker-dealer may use its discretion to vote shares if it does not receive instructions from the beneficial owner of the shares. Historically, broker-dealers were generally permitted to vote shares on uncontested matters, including uncontested director elections, without instructions from the beneficial owner. The NYSE recently revised this rule to prohibit broker-dealers from voting uninstructed shares with regard to any election of directors.

D. The Roles of Third Parties in the Proxy Process

Issuers, securities intermediaries, and shareholders often retain third parties to perform a number of proxy-related functions, including forwarding proxy materials, collecting voting instructions, voting shares, soliciting proxies, tabulating proxies, and analyzing proxy issues.

1. Transfer Agents

Issuers are required to maintain a record of security holders for state law purposes and often hire a transfer agent to maintain that record. Transfer agents, as agents of the issuer, are obliged to confirm to a vote tabulator (if the transfer agent does not itself perform the tabulation function) matters such as the amount of shares outstanding, as well as the identity and holdings of registered owners entitled to vote. Transfer agents are required to register with the Commission, which inspects and currently regulates some of their functions.

2. Proxy Service Providers

To facilitate the proxy material distribution and voting process for beneficial owners, securities intermediaries typically retain a proxy service provider to perform a number of processing functions, including forwarding the proxy materials by mail or electronically and collecting voting instructions.[38] To enable the proxy service provider to perform these functions, the securities intermediary gives the service provider an electronic data feed of a list of beneficial owners

---

38. [FN 57] A single proxy service provider, Broadridge Financial Services, Inc. ("Broadridge"), states that it currently handles over 98% of the U.S. market for such proxy vote processing services. *See* http://www.broadridge.com/investor-communications/us/institutions/proxy-disclosure.asp.

and the number of shares held by each beneficial owner on the record date. The proxy service provider, on behalf of the intermediary, then requests the appropriate number of proxy material sets from the issuer for delivery to the beneficial owners. Upon receipt of the packages, the proxy service provider, on behalf of the intermediary, mails either the proxy materials with a VIF, or a Notice of Internet Availability of Proxy Materials, to beneficial owners. Although we do not directly regulate such proxy service providers, our regulations governing the proxy process-related obligations of securities intermediaries apply to the way in which proxy service providers perform their services because they act as agents for, and on behalf of, those intermediaries and typically vote proxies on behalf of those intermediaries pursuant to a power of attorney.

3. Proxy Solicitors

Issuers sometimes hire third-party proxy solicitors to identify beneficial owners holding large amounts of the issuers' securities and to telephone shareholders to encourage them to vote their proxies consistent with the recommendations of management. This often occurs when there is a contested election of directors, and issuer's management and other persons are competing for proxy authority to vote securities in the election (commonly referred to as a "proxy contest"). In addition, an issuer may hire a proxy solicitor in uncontested situations when voting returns are expected to be insufficient to meet state quorum requirements or when an important matter is being considered. Issuers and other soliciting persons are required to disclose the use of such services and estimated costs for such services in their proxy statements.

4. Vote Tabulators

Under many state statutes, an issuer must appoint a vote tabulator (sometimes called "inspectors of elections" or "proxy tabulators") to collect and tabulate the proxy votes as well as votes submitted by shareholders in person at a meeting.[39] We understand that often the issuer's transfer agent will act as the vote tabulator because most major transfer agents have the infrastructure to communicate with registered holders, proxy service providers, and securities intermediaries, while also being able to reconcile the identity of voters that are registered owners and the number of votes to the issuer's records. However, sometimes the issuer will hire an independent third party to perform this function, often to certify important votes. The vote tabulator is ultimately responsible for determining that the correct number of votes has been submitted by each registered owner. In addition, proxies submitted by securities intermediaries that are not registered owners, but have been granted direct voting rights through DTC's omnibus proxy, are reconciled with DTC's securities position listing. Although the Commission does regulate transfer agents (which often serve as vote tabulators) in their roles as transfer agents, the Commission does

---

39. [FN 60] *See, e.g.,* Del. Code Ann. tit. 8, §231; Model Bus. Corp. Act §7.29.

not currently regulate vote tabulators or the function of tabulating proxies by transfer agents.

5. Proxy Advisory Firms

Institutional investors typically own securities positions in a large number of issuers. Therefore, they are presented annually with the opportunity to vote on many matters and often must exercise fiduciary responsibility in voting. Some institutional investors may retain an investment adviser to manage their investments, and may also delegate proxy voting authority to that adviser. To assist them in their voting decisions, investment advisers (or institutional investors if they retain voting authority) frequently hire proxy advisory firms to provide analysis and voting recommendations on matters appearing on the proxy. In some cases, proxy advisory firms are given authority to execute proxies or voting instructions on behalf of their client. Some proxy advisory firms also provide consulting services to issuers on corporate governance or executive compensation matters, such as helping to develop an executive compensation proposal to be submitted for shareholder approval. Some proxy advisory firms may also qualitatively rate or score issuers, based on judgments about the issuer's governance structure, policies, and practices. . . .

Questions

1. What does the Depository Trust Company do?
2. What does a proxy solicitor do? When would a company hire one?
3. What does a proxy advisory firm do?
4. What is a VIF? How is it different than a proxy card? — VIF = proxy card
5. If you own shares in a public company, will you receive a VIF or a proxy card?
6. Who mails you the company's proxy materials? What is included in the mailing?

3. Shareholder Proposals

Recognizing that few shareholders actually attend the annual shareholders' meetings of public companies and therefore it is not possible for a shareholder to bring a proposal to the shareholder body from the floor of the meeting, since the 1940s SEC rules have required public companies to include in their proxy materials those shareholder proposals that meet certain qualifications. These qualifications are specified in Rule 14a-8 under the Exchange Act and include both procedural and substantive requirements. To be eligible to submit a proposal, the proponent must have continually held a minimum of $2,000 or 1 percent of the corporation's stock during the preceding year. The length of the proposal is limited to 500 words. Proposals submitted for consideration during annual meetings generally must be submitted at least four months prior to the anniversary of the mailing date of the previous year's proxy materials.

Rule 14a-8 provides 13 substantive grounds under which a corporation may exclude a proposal from its proxy materials (see Rule 14a-(8)(i)(1)-(13)). For example, a corporation may exclude a proposal that is not a proper subject for action by shareholders under state law, relates to ordinary business operations, or has already been substantially implemented by the company.

If a corporation intends to exclude a proposal, it typically files a no-action letter request with the SEC explaining why the corporation believes the proposal is excludable. After the SEC grants or denies the request, the company will generally include or exclude the proposal in conformance with the SEC's decision. Infrequently, a proponent of a proposal that the company and the SEC deem excludable will thereafter seek a court order compelling the company to include the proposal, or, as in the next case, the company may launch a preemptive strike and seek a declaratory judgment that the proposal is excludable.

Apache Corporation v. New York City Employees' Retirement System
621 F. Supp. 2d 444 (S.D. Tex. 2008)

GRAY H. MILLER, District Judge.

Pending before the court are plaintiff Apache Corporation's Original Complaint seeking a declaratory judgment and application for a preliminary injunction. The court combined the hearing on Apache's request for injunctive relief with trial on the merits pursuant to Rule 65(a)(2) of the Federal Rules of Civil Procedure. The court has carefully reviewed the application, all responsive and supplemental pleadings, declarations and other record evidence, arguments of counsel, and the applicable law. For the reasons discussed below, the court finds that Apache properly excluded defendants' proposal from proxy materials mailed to Apache's shareholders. Therefore, judgment will be entered in favor of Apache and against the defendants. As Apache has succeeded on the merits of its declaratory judgment action, the parties have agreed that the court need not address Apache's request for injunctive relief.

BACKGROUND

Apache is a Delaware corporation, with its principal office and principal place of business in Houston, Texas. Apache is an independent energy company that explores for, develops, and produces natural gas, crude oil, and natural gas liquids. Defendants New York City Employees' Retirement System, New York City Teachers' Retirement System, New York City Police Pension Fund, New

York City Fire Department Pension Fund, New York City Board of Education Retirement System (collectively, "Funds"), and Office of the Comptroller of the City of New York ("NYC Comptroller") are five New York pension funds and New York's chief fiscal and chief auditing officer, the custodian and trustee of the Funds. Each defendant's principal office and principal place of business are in New York City, New York.

On October 29, 2007, NYC Comptroller submitted to Apache, pursuant to Section 14(a) of the Securities Exchange Act of 1934, a shareholder proposal ("Proposal") for inclusion in the company's proxy statement to be mailed in advance of Apache's May 8, 2008, annual shareholders' meeting. The Proposal reads:

SEXUAL ORIENTATION
Submitted By William C. Thompson, Jr., Comptroller, City of New York, on behalf of the Boards of Trustees of the New York City Pension Funds

WHEREAS, corporations with non-discrimination policies relating to sexual orientation have a competitive advantage to recruit and retain employees from the widest talent pool;

Employment discrimination on the basis of sexual orientation diminishes employee morale and productivity;

The company has an interest in preventing discrimination and resolving complaints internally so as to avoid costly litigation and damage its reputation as an equal opportunity employer;

Atlanta, Seattle, Los Angeles, and San Francisco have adopted legislation restricting business with companies that do not guaranteed equal treatment for lesbian and gay employees and similar legislation is pending in other jurisdictions;

The company has operations in and makes sales to institutions in states and cities which prohibit discrimination on the basis of sexual orientation;

A recent National Gay and Lesbian Taskforce study has found that 16%-44% of gay men and lesbians in twenty cities nationwide experienced workplace harassment or discrimination based on their sexual orientation;

National public opinion polls consistently find more than three-quarters of the American people support equal rights in the workplace for gay men, lesbians, and bisexuals;

A number of Fortune 500 corporations have implemented non-discrimination policies encompassing the following principles:

1) Discrimination based on sexual orientation and gender identity will be prohibited in the company's employment policy statement.

2) The company's non-discrimination policy will be distributed to all employees.

3) There shall be no discrimination based on any employee's actual or perceived health condition, status, or disability.

4) There shall be no discrimination in the allocation of employee benefits on the basis of sexual orientation or gender identity.

5) Sexual orientation and gender identity issues will be included in corporate employee diversity and sensitivity programs.

6) There shall be no discrimination in the recognition of employee groups based on sexual orientation or gender identity.

7) Corporate advertising policy will avoid the use of negative stereotypes based on sexual orientation or gender identity.

8) There shall be no discrimination in corporate advertising and marketing policy based on sexual orientation or gender identity.

9) There shall be no discrimination in the sale of goods and services based on sexual orientation or gender identity, and

10) There shall be no policy barring on corporate charitable contributions to groups and organizations based on sexual orientation.

RESOLVED: The Shareholders request that management implement equal employment opportunity policies based on the aforementioned principles prohibiting discrimination based on sexual orientation and gender identity.

STATEMENT: By implementing policies prohibiting discrimination based on sexual orientation and gender identity, the Company will ensure a respectful and supportive atmosphere for all employees and enhance its competitive edge by joining the growing ranks of companies guaranteeing equal opportunity for all employees.

Apache refused to include the proposal in its proxy materials and on January 3, 2008, pursuant to Rule 14a-8(j), Apache requested a no-action letter from the Securities and Exchange Commission's ("SEC") Division of Corporation Finance. Apache asserted that the Proposal relates to the company's ordinary business operations and, therefore, is properly excludable from the proxy materials pursuant to Rule 14a-8(i)(7). Both Apache and defendants extensively briefed the SEC on their respective positions. On March 5, 2008, the SEC's Division of Corporation Finance issued a no-action letter. The SEC found,

> The proposal requests that management implement equal employment opportunity polices [sic] based on principles specified in the proposal prohibiting discrimination based on sexual orientation and gender identity.
>
> There appears to be some basis for your view that Apache may exclude the proposal under rule 14a-8(i)(7). We note in particular that some of the principles relate to Apache's ordinary business operations. Accordingly, we will not recommend enforcement action to the Commission if Apache omits the proposal from its proxy materials in reliance on rule 14a-8(i)(7).

On March 31, 2008, Apache sent out notice of its annual meeting of stockholders and proxy statement. The proxy statement did not include the Proposal.

On April 8, 2008, Apache filed a declaratory judgment action in this court. Apache seeks a declaration that it properly excluded the Proposal pursuant to

Rule 14a-8(i)(7). The next day, defendants filed a parallel lawsuit in the Southern District of New York. On April 10, 2008, Apache moved this court for a temporary restraining order. After a hearing, this court declined to issue a TRO. Instead, the court scheduled a hearing on Apache's application for injunctive relief and consolidated the hearing with a trial on the merits. On April 17, 2008, the Honorable Colleen McMahon stayed the parallel New York action.

ANALYSIS

To resolve this dispute, the court must determine whether Apache properly excluded the Proposal from its proxy statement. . . .

Apache seeks to exclude the Proposal based on the Rule 14a-8(i)(7), 17 C.F.R. §240.14a-8(i)(7), exception. Rule 14a-8 requires, under certain circumstances, a public company to include "a shareholder's proposal in its proxy statement and identify the proposal in its form of proxy when the company holds an annual or special meeting of shareholders." 17 C.F.R. §240.14a-8. If the shareholder submits a proposal in accordance with controlling regulations, the company must include the proposal in its proxy materials unless it is properly excludable for the substantive reasons listed in Rule 14a-8(i). See 17 C.F.R. §240.14a-8(i). Prior to excluding the proposal, Rule 14a-8(j) requires the company to "file its reasons with the Commission no later than 80 calendar days before it files its definitive proxy statement and form of proxy with the Commission." 17 C.F.R. §240.14a-8(j). The company must show that the proposal fits within one or more of Rule 14a-8(i)'s exceptions. See *Austin v. Consolidated Edison Co. of N.Y.*, 788 F. Supp. 192, 194 (S.D.N.Y.1992); Solicitation of Proxies, 19 Fed. Reg. 246, 246 (Jan. 1, 1954) ("The rule places the burden of proof upon the management to show that a particular security holder's proposal is not a proper one for inclusion in management's proxy material.").

Rule 14a-8(i)(7) permits exclusion of a proposal if it "deals with a matter relating to the company's ordinary business operations." 17 C.F.R. §240.14a-8(i)(7). The term "ordinary business operations" escapes formal definition. To gleam [sic] its scope, courts look to SEC guidance and state law. In adopting Rule 14a-8(i)(7), the SEC stated:

> the term "ordinary business operations" has been deemed on occasion to include certain matters which have significant policy, economic or other implications inherent in them. For instance, a proposal that a utility company not construct a proposed nuclear power plant has in the past been considered excludable. . . . In retrospect, however, it seems apparent that the economic and safety considerations attendant to nuclear power plants are of such magnitude that a determination whether to construct one is not an "ordinary" business matter. Accordingly, proposals of that nature, as well as others that have major implications, will in the future be considered beyond the realm of an issuer's ordinary business operations. . . .

Adoption of Amendments Relating to Proposals by Security Holders ("1976 Release"), 41 Fed. Reg. 52,994, 52,998 (December 3, 1976). Accordingly, only "business matters that are mundane in nature and do not involve any substantial policy" considerations may be omitted under the "ordinary business" exception. Id.

The policy underlying the ordinary business exclusion rests on two central considerations. The first relates to the subject matter of the proposal. Certain tasks are so fundamental to management's ability to run a company on a day-to-day basis that they could not, as a practical matter, be subject to direct shareholder oversight. Examples include the management of the workforce, such as the hiring, promotion, and termination of employees, decisions on production quality and quantity, and the retention of suppliers. However, proposals relating to such matters but focusing on sufficiently significant social policy issues (e.g., significant discrimination matters) generally would not be considered to be excludable, because the proposals would transcend the day-to-day business matters and raise policy issues so significant that it would be appropriate for a shareholder vote.

The second consideration relates to the degree to which the proposal seeks to "micro-manage" the company by probing too deeply into matters of a complex nature upon which shareholders, as a group, would not be in a position to make an informed judgment. This consideration may come into play in a number of circumstances, such as where the proposal involves intricate detail, or seeks to impose specific time-frames or methods for implementing complex policies.

Amendments to Rules on Shareholder Proposals ("1998 Release"), 63 Fed. Reg. 29106, 29108 (May 28, 1998).[40] As to the second factor, the SEC explained that the determination "will be made on a case-by-case basis, taking into account factors such as the nature of the proposal and the circumstances of the company to which it is directed." Id. at 29109.

A clear reading of the 1998 Release informs this court's analysis. To read the guidance as directing proper exclusion of shareholder proposals only when those proposals do not implicate a significant social policy would make much of the statement superfluous and most of the no-action letters presented to the court by the parties incorrect.[41] Because such a directive cannot be gleamed [sic]

---

40. [FN 6] In 1992, the SEC issued a no-action letter to Cracker Barrel ruling that all employment-related stockholder proposals raising social policy issues would be excludable under the ordinary business exception. Cracker Barrel Old Country Stores, Inc., SEC No-Action Letter, 1997 WL 384740 (October 13, 1992). In the 1998 Release, the SEC reversed its prior ruling:

> Reversal of the Cracker Barrel no-action position will result in a return to a case-by-case analytical approach. In making distinctions in this area, the [SEC] will continue to apply the applicable standard for determining when a proposal relates to "ordinary business." The standard, originally articulated in the [SEC]'s 1976 release, provided an exception for certain proposals that raise significant social policy issues.

1998 Release, 63 Fed. Reg. at 29108.

41. [FN 7] Defendants argue that their Proposal implicates a significant social policy that transcends the ordinary business exception. Defendants urge that the 1998 Release arose from the Commission's recognition of the significance of avoiding employment discrimination based on sexual orientation — the policy at issue in this case. Defendants, therefore, conclude that the Commission's reversal of the *Cracker Barrel* decision

from the release language, the court finds that it must first determine whether the Proposal implicates a significant policy issue. A proposal that does not concern a significant policy issue but nevertheless implicates the ordinary business operations of a company is properly excludable under Rule 14a-8(i)(7). However, a proposal concerning the ordinary business operations of a company that implicates a significant policy issue is only excludable under Rule 14a-8(i)(7) if it "seeks to 'micro-manage' the company by probing too deeply into matters of a complex nature upon which shareholders, as a group, would not be in a position to make an informed judgment." 1998 Release, 63 Fed. Reg. at 29108. As one court explained, "management cannot exercise its specialized talents effectively if corporate investors assert the power to dictate the minutiae of daily business decisions." *Med. Comm. for Human Rights*, 432 F.2d at 679, vacated as moot, 404 U.S. 403, 92 S. Ct. 577, 30 L. Ed. 2d 560 (1972).

The court now turns to the Proposal. The "resolved" paragraph provides, "The Shareholders request that management implement equal employment opportunity policies based on the aforementioned principles prohibiting discrimination based on sexual orientation and gender identity." Defendants now argue that the enumerated principles merely illustrate how various Fortune 500 corporations implemented non-discrimination policies. Nevertheless, a plain reading dictates the construction of the request. The shareholders seek that the company implement policies based on a list of principles. It is those principles that determine the employment opportunity policies, and not vice versa.[42] Specifically, Apache directs the court to the following principles:

---

is, by itself, a fully sufficient basis for denying exclusion of the Proposal under Rule 14a-8(i)(7). Had the defendants drafted the Proposal to simply request that Apache add sexual orientation to its existing anti-discrimination policy and deleted the principles, the court would be inclined to agree with the defendants. But, the proposal goes well beyond that. Defendants further argue that any reliance on the SEC's no-action letter is misplaced. Because the letter "refuses" to analyze the significance of the underlying social policy, the finding of "some basis for [the] view that Apache may exclude the proposal under rule 14a-8(i)(7)" "'contravenes the 1976 Release's explicit recognition that all proposals could be seen as involving some aspect of day-to-day business operations.'" (Dkt. 19 (quoting *Wal-Mart Stores, Inc.,* 821 F. Supp. at 890)). Defendants argue that because the *Wal-Mart* court noted that all proposals could be viewed as effecting at least some aspect of ordinary business operations, whether a proposal implicates significant social policy is the dispositive inquiry.

Conversely, Apache contends that defendants' interpretation of Rule 14a-8(i)(7) would make the exception ineffectual. The court can posit circumstances where even under defendants' interpretation, Rule 14a-8(i)(7) would function to exclude proposals addressing ordinary business matters without significant social policy implications. Nevertheless, defendants' interpretation would promote submission of proposals dealing with ordinary business matters yet cabined in social policy concern. Although the proposal exclusion process would be significantly simplified, the court finds defendants' interpretation unwise. The SEC reversed *Cracker Barrel* because it found the hard and fast rule it promulgated failed to adhere to the guidance issued in the 1976 Release. Defendants' interpretation of Rule 14a-8(i)(7) is inappropriate for the same reason.

42. [FN 8] Defendants argue that the enumerated principles are merely examples, not integral to the Proposal. But, the defendants sought to have the Proposal included in the proxy statement in its entirety. Therefore, because a plain reading of the Proposal indicates that the principles are indeed indispensable, and because the Proposal requests that the management of Apache "implement . . . policies based on the aforementioned principles . . . ," the court finds defendants' argument unconvincing and without merit. To permit revision of the proposal at this late stage would conflict with proposal submission regulations. *See* 17 C.F.R. §240.14a-8(c), -8(e)(2).

Principle (4) There shall be no discrimination in the allocation of employee benefits on the basis of sexual orientation or gender identity;

Principle (7) Corporate advertising policy will avoid the use of negative stereotypes based on sexual orientation or gender identity;

Principle (8) There shall be no discrimination in corporate advertising and marketing policy based on sexual orientation or gender identity;

Principle (9) There shall be no discrimination in the sale of goods and services based on sexual orientation or gender identity; and,

Principle (10) There shall be no policy barring on corporate charitable contributions to groups and organizations based on sexual orientation.

With these in mind, the Proposal seeks to have Apache implement policies incorporating sexual orientation and gender identity into the company's employee benefits allocation, corporate advertising and marketing activities, sales activities, and charitable contributions.

Undoubtedly, advertising and marketing, sale of goods and services, and charitable contributions are ordinary business matters. Yet, the defendants, through the Proposal, seek to have Apache implement equal employment opportunity policies which incorporate anti-discrimination directives based on sexual orientation and gender identity into such activities. The court finds that only principles one through six are directed at discrimination in employment. To consider the remaining four principles as implicating employment discrimination would be a far stretch. Instead, principles seven through ten aim at discrimination in Apache's business conduct as it relates to advertising, marketing, sales, and charitable contributions. Therefore, because these principles do not implicate the social policy underlying the Proposal, and because the Proposal must be read with all of its parts, the Proposal is properly excludable under Rule 14a-8(i)(7).

Even were the court to find that principles seven through ten implicate the underlying social policy, the Proposal seeks to micromanage the company to an unacceptable degree. Shareholders, as a group, are not sufficiently involved in the day-to-day operations of Apache's business to fully appreciate its complex nature. For example, shareholders, as a group, are not positioned to make informed judgments as to the propriety of certain sales and purchases. Similarly, the complex implications stemming from the proposed principle forbidding discrimination in the sale of goods and services based on sexual orientation or gender identity preclude provident judgment on the part of the shareholders. It would be imprudent to effectively cede control over such day-to-day decisions, traditionally within the purview of a company's executives and officers, to the shareholders. The aforementioned concerns are enhanced by the principle's implicit requirement that Apache determine whether its customers and suppliers discriminate on the basis of sexual orientation or gender identity. Such an inquiry is impractical and unreasonable, and the determination as to its propriety should properly remain with the company's management.

CONCLUSION

For the foregoing reasons, the court finds that pursuant to Rule 14a-8(i)(7), Apache properly excluded the Proposal from the proxy statement mailed to its shareholders. . . .

Questions

1. What proposal did Mr. Thompson want included in Apache's proxy materials?
2. On what basis did Apache argue it can exclude it? Why do you think Apache wants to exclude it?
3. What is the test for determining whether the proposal falls within the exclusion asserted by Apache?
4. If Apache included Mr. Thompson's proposal in its proxy materials and it received overwhelming approval at the shareholders' meeting, would Apache's board be required to implement the proposal?
5. Why do you think Mr. Thompson submitted the proposal?
6. Assume you own 100 shares of Apache. Are you glad Apache litigated whether it could exclude Mr. Thompson's proposal?
7. How many shares of Apache would you need to own to meet the ownership requirement for submitting a proposal for inclusion in its next proxy statement? By when would you need to send in your proposal?

Notice that Mr. Thompson worded the proposal as a request ("The Shareholders *request* that management implement . . .") as opposed to a directive such as "management shall implement. . . ." This is because, as mentioned above, Rule 14a-8 allows a company to exclude a proposal that "is not a proper subject for action by shareholders under the laws of the jurisdiction of the company's organization."[43] As you know from Chapter 9, under state corporate law, managerial authority is vested in a corporation's board of directors, not its shareholders. Thus, a shareholder proposal telling management what to do is generally improper under state law and therefore excludable. The standard way around this exclusion is to do what Mr. Thompson did — word the proposal as a request or recommendation (these types of proposals are commonly called "precatory proposals"). Unfortunately for Mr. Thompson, his proposal was excluded on other grounds. Note that even if Apache had included the proposal in its proxy materials, and it received a majority of votes cast, Apache management would not be legally required to follow it.

---

43. Rule 14(a)-8(i)(1).

There are two broad categories of shareholder proposals: social issues and corporate governance. Mr. Thompson's proposal falls under the social issues category and is a fairly common type of proposal in recent years. Other common social issue proposals include those on political contributions, climate change, human rights, and sustainability. Common examples of corporate governance proposals include those to repeal staggered boards, eliminate supermajority voting provisions, separate the roles of CEO and chairman, and rescind poison pills (we discuss poison pills in Chapter 14).

4. Say-on-Pay

Say-on-pay was imposed on public companies by Congress as part of the Dodd-Frank Wall Street Reform and Consumer Protection Act that President Obama signed into law in July 2010. Congress passed Dodd-Frank in the wake of the global financial crisis of the late-2000s. While much of Dodd-Frank deals with the regulation of financial institutions and instruments, it included a few provisions relating to corporate governance, and say-on-pay is one of them. Specifically, Dodd-Frank §951 amended the Exchange Act to include §14A. This section requires all companies subject to SEC proxy rules to hold a shareholder advisory vote on (1) the compensation of the companies' most highly compensated executive officers (referred to as say-on-pay vote); (2) the frequency of say-on-pay votes (annually, biennially, or triennially); and (3) certain golden parachute compensation arrangements. By advisory, I mean that the vote is not binding on the corporation; the corporation can go forward with its proposed compensation even if its shareholders voted it down.[44]

5. Public Company Director Elections

Public companies hold in total over 13,000 shareholders' meetings each year, the principal purpose of which is to elect directors. Given the regulation and complexity of the proxy solicitation process and the fact that one of the few things shareholders get to vote on is the election of directors, you may have assumed that these elections are meaningful, but you would be wrong. The outcome of almost all of these elections is a foregone conclusion—the individuals selected by the existing board win. This is because the company controls the de facto election ballot (its proxy materials) and uses this control to ensure people of the board's choosing are elected. Specifically, it only includes in the proxy statement and on the proxy card a slate of directors equal to the number of seats up for election. There is no requirement that a corporation's proxy materials provide a means for shareholders to write in candidates, and few, if

---

44. *See* Exchange Act §14A(c) (providing that a say-on-pay vote "shall not be binding on the issuer or the board of directors of an issuer, and may not be construed . . . as overruling a decision by such issuer or board of directors . . .").

any, corporations provide this option. Thus, it is generally not possible for a shareholder to use the corporation's proxy card to instruct the proxy to vote for someone other than a nominee listed on the card.

SEC proxy regulations do require that the card contain a box shareholders can check to withhold authority to vote for a particular nominee or nominees (a "withhold authority" box), or, if given effect under applicable state law, to vote against a particular nominee or nominees. Hence, a shareholder could attempt to communicate dissatisfaction with a director or directors up for re-election by marking the "withhold authority" or "against" box. However, if a company uses a plurality voting standard, the default standard for the election of directors under state corporate law, the outcome of a board election will not be impacted by "withheld" or "against" votes, even if they represent a majority of shares. This is because under a plurality standard the candidates that receive the largest number of votes win. In an uncontested election, the only individuals who receive any votes are those listed on the corporation's proxy card and ballot.[45] Since the number of names listed will equal the number of seats up for election, each listed person is guaranteed to be among the top (and only) vote getters and therefore guaranteed to be elected (assuming a quorum). Under a plurality standard, even if all non-management shareholders check the "withhold authority" box on the proxy card or abstain from voting at the annual meeting, management will vote the shares it controls in favor of the slate, and the slate will still be elected, even if management votes only a single share.

To be sure, a disgruntled shareholder, or insurgent, could create a contested election by putting forth additional candidates or an entire alternative slate. However, because companies are generally not required to include shareholder nominated candidates in their proxy materials and therefore do not do it, the only realistic way for a disgruntled shareholder to put forth alternative candidates is by independently soliciting proxies from a corporation's shareholders. In such an event, shareholders would receive two sets of proxy materials—one set from the corporation and one set from the insurgent, thereby giving shareholders a choice of competing slates. But proxy contests for the election of directors outside of the takeover context are extremely rare, occurring on average at less than one-tenth of 1 percent of elections in any given year.

There are several explanations for the dearth of electoral proxy contests. The first is cost: A proxy contest will typically cost an insurgent between five and ten million dollars. While the board will use the corporate coffers to fund its proxy campaign, including fending off any insurgent challenges, an insurgent must fund its campaign out of its own pocket, and the insurgent will be reimbursed by the corporation only if it wins. A proxy contest is expensive because the insurgent will have to prepare and distribute proxy materials and, as discussed below, overcome shareholder apathy and other impediments. As a result, the insurgent will need to retain attorneys, investment bankers, public

---

45. A corporation distributes a ballot to shareholders and proxies in attendance at the annual meeting for them to cast their votes.

relations advisors, proxy solicitors, and financial printers. These professionals' fees quickly add up. Additionally, an incumbent board does not sit idly by in the face of a proxy contest. It may initiate litigation against the insurgent, alleging federal proxy rule violations. At the same time, the insurgent may have to initiate litigation against the corporation or inspector of elections; for example, the insurgent may sue to obtain access to corporate records or challenge the invalidation of proxy cards. Such litigation will add to the insurgent's costs.

If the insurgent prevails, the costs it incurred will likely be reimbursed by the corporation. But only about one-third of electoral proxy contests launched outside of the takeover context are successful. Hence, an insurgent must consider the benefits of victory in light of the probability of failure. Also relevant is the insurgent's ownership percentage of the target corporation. If an insurgent owns 5 percent of the target, it will capture only 5 percent of the increase in firm value (if any) resulting from a successful proxy contest, notwithstanding the fact that the insurgent incurred and risked 100 percent of the cost. The remaining 95 percent of value will be conferred upon the firm's other shareholders, even though they funded none of the costs of the proxy contest. This "free rider" problem discourages shareholders from launching proxy contests. Instead, many shareholders will hold out for the opportunity to "free ride" on a fellow shareholder's proxy contest.

Related to cost are collective action difficulties inherent in public corporation shareholder voting. In the face of a proxy contest, a rational shareholder will choose to become informed about an insurgent's slate only if the benefits of doing so outweigh the costs. Most shareholders will conclude that the opportunity cost of reading the insurgent's proxy statement exceeds the expected benefit of an informed vote. Therefore, the rational shareholder will remain uninformed and vote for the incumbents by default. Even if a shareholder concludes that the expected benefit of becoming informed outweighs the cost, he or she is still unlikely to act because of the "free rider" problem. Realizing that his or her vote is unlikely to be outcome determinative, the shareholder will choose to avoid the cost of becoming informed. Instead, the shareholder will try to free ride on the efforts of other shareholders and still capture the benefits of informed collective action. Of course, other shareholders are likely to implement the same strategy and likewise remain uninformed. In such a case, no collective action will be taken and no benefits will be captured.

Additionally, even if shareholders are informed, many will be reluctant to vote for the insurgents. Shareholders may be suspicious of the insurgent's motives, uncertain as to whether the corporation will perform better under the insurgent's team, or decide to stick with the devil they know. Furthermore, some institutional investors may be reluctant to vote against the incumbents because of business concerns. For example, a vote by an insurance company against an incumbent board is likely to jeopardize any existing and future business with that corporation and will be poorly received by incumbents at other companies.

As a result of the above factors, most shareholders are predisposed to vote for incumbents. An insurgent's slate may not even receive the votes of disgruntled shareholders. These shareholders are more likely to follow the "Wall Street Rule," that is, sell their shares prior to the vote, thereby eliminating the need to incur information costs or to assume risk with respect to the insurgent.

With many public companies, an insurgent will have to deal with a staggered board. A corporation with a staggered board typically divides its directors into three groups, and only one group comes up for election each year. Thus, if a corporation has a three-group staggered board, only one-third of its board seats would come up for election each year. Therefore, to win a majority of board seats, an insurgent would have to mount and win two electoral proxy contests in three years. This increases an insurgent's costs because it doubles the number of required solicitations and stretches the insurgent's campaign over more than one year. Even shareholders who deem the insurgent's slate superior to that of the incumbents may be reluctant to vote for the insurgent because of the required two rounds of elections. Voting in the insurgent's slate in the first round puts the board in limbo for a year. During this year, the incumbents retain control but they are aware that they will soon lose their positions. The entire board will have to deal with the internal divisions and friction caused by having one-third of the board composed of a competing faction.

The bottom line is that an insurgent will encounter an expensive uphill battle in an electoral proxy contest. The insurgent will have to spend heavily to overcome rational shareholder apathy and other impediments with less than a 50/50 chance of success. Many would-be insurgents are likely to do nothing or sell out instead of fighting because insurgents are reimbursed only if they prevail, and even if they prevail, they have to share the spoils with all other shareholders. Thus, it is not surprising that so few electoral proxy contests are launched and that even fewer are successful. The end result is that in the vast majority of cases the election of directors is a charade—incumbent victory is a foregone conclusion.

This state of affairs has not gone unnoticed, and various proposals have been made over the years to make director elections more meaningful. Recently, two proposals have gained significant traction: (1) implementing a majority voting standard for the election of directors, and (2) allowing shareholders to include nominees in corporations' proxy materials.

a. Majority Voting

Historically, almost all public companies stuck with the default plurality standard for director elections. In 2005, however, activist shareholders began pressuring companies to adopt majority voting, mostly through Rule 14a-8 proposals. This so-called majority vote movement proved quite successful. By late 2007, 66 percent of S&P 500 companies and 57 percent of Fortune 500 companies had adopted some form of majority voting.[46]

---

46. *See* Claudia H. Allen, Study of Majority Voting in Director Elections i (Nov. 12, 2007), *available at* http://www.ngelaw.com/files/upload/majoritystudy111207.pdf.

While there are several different means by which a company can implement majority voting, the most common one is through a bylaw provision. Here is sample language from the bylaws of Yahoo! Inc., which implemented majority voting in 2007:

3.3   Election, Qualification and Term of Office of Directors.

Except as provided in Section 3.4 of these Bylaws [Section 3.4 addresses director resignations and vacancies], directors shall be elected by a "majority of votes cast" (as defined herein) at each annual meeting of stockholders to hold office until the next annual meeting, unless the election is contested, in which case directors shall be elected by a plurality of votes cast. An election shall be contested if, as determined by the Board of Directors, the number of nominees exceeds the number of directors to be elected. Each director, including a director elected to fill a vacancy, shall hold office until his or her successor is elected and qualified or until his or her earlier death, resignation (including resignation pursuant to the resignation policy set forth in the Corporation's Corporate Governance Guidelines) or removal. For the purposes of this Section, a "majority of votes cast" means that the number of shares voted "for" a director exceeds the number of votes cast "against" that director. . . .

In connection with approving the above provision, the Yahoo! board also approved the following amendment to Yahoo!'s Corporate Governance Guidelines:

Prior to each election of directors at an annual meeting, each director nominee is required to submit to the Board an irrevocable letter of resignation from the Board and all committees thereof, which will become effective if that director does not receive a majority of votes cast (as defined in the Amended Bylaws) and upon acceptance of the letter by the Board.

The Nominating and Corporate Governance Committee of the Board will recommend to the Board the action to be taken with respect to any resignation, the Board will determine whether to accept the resignation within 90 days from certification of the election results, and the Board's explanation of its decision will be promptly disclosed in a Current Report on Form 8-K filed with the Securities and Exchange Commission.

A nominee may not participate in the decision-making process of the Nominating and Corporate Governance Committee or of the Board with respect to his or her own resignation. If a majority of the members of the Nominating and Corporate Governance Committee does not receive a majority of votes cast, then the independent directors who did receive a majority of votes cast will consider the tendered resignations.

Yahoo! added the above language to its Corporate Governance Guidelines in light of the so-called holdover rule. The holdover rule provides that a director remains in office until his or her successor is elected.[47] The policy justification for the holdover rule is to ensure that "the power of the board of directors to act continues uninterrupted even though an annual shareholders' meeting is not held or the shareholders are deadlocked and unable to elect directors at the meeting."[48] The practical effect of the holdover rule is that an incumbent director who does not receive the requisite majority vote in an uncontested election would nonetheless remain on the board since no successor will have been elected. Thus, unless the holdover rule is addressed, majority voting has little bite. Yahoo! took the standard approach of requiring each director to submit a letter of resignation whose effect is contingent on failing to receive the requisite vote. This essentially gives the board the power, through private contract, to remove a director who was not reelected and thereby abrogate the holdover rule (a board does not otherwise have this power). Both the DGCL and MBCA were amended in 2006 to expressly give effect to these sorts of resignation letters.[49]

Exercise 13.3

Assume Yahoo! Inc., a Delaware corporation, has 1.24 billion shares outstanding and that 700 million of those shares are represented at Yahoo!'s 2011 annual meeting. Assume ten seats are up for election and that all directors, with exception of Smith, are incumbents, that is, they were elected to the board last year. The voting was as follows:

Candidate	For	Against	Abstain
Bartz	700,000,000	0	0
Bostock	699,500,000	100,000	400,000
Hart	700,000,000	0	0
James	700,000,000	0	0
Joshi	699,500,000	100,000	400,000
Kenny	699,500,000	100,000	400,000
Kem	100,000,000	200,000,000	400,000,000
Smith	100,000,000	200,000,000	400,000,000
Wilson	700,000,000	0	0
Yang	300,000,000	300,000,000	100,000,000

1. Which individuals were elected to the board?
2. What happens now with respect to Kem and Yang?

---

47. *See* DGCL §141(b); MBCA §8.05(e).
48. Mod. Bus. Corp. Act Ann. §8.05 Offic. Cmt.
49. *See* DGCL §141(b); MBCA §8.07(b).

b. Proxy Access

"Proxy access" is shorthand for allowing shareholders to include director nominees in a corporation's proxy materials. Under such a regime, the existing board would still put forth a slate of directors equal to the number of seats up for election but shareholders could also put forth additional candidates whom the corporation would have to include in its proxy materials. Thus, the frequency of contested elections would presumably increase because no longer would a shareholder have to incur the significant expense of independently soliciting proxies but could instead piggyback on the company's proxy materials.

(1) Rule 14a-11

Shareholder activists have been clamoring for decades for proxy access, and it looked like the clamoring had paid off in 2010 with the SEC's adoption of Rule 14a-11 under the Exchange Act. Rule 14a-11 required public companies to include in their proxy materials board candidates nominated by eligible shareholders unless applicable state law (i.e., the corporate statute of the company's state of incorporation) or the company's governing documents prohibited shareholders from nominating directors. The Business Roundtable and U.S. Chamber of Commerce, however, challenged the Rule in court. In July 2011, the D.C. Circuit found that the SEC violated the Administrative Procedure Act in adopting the Rule and thus vacated it.[50] The SEC did not appeal the decisions, and it is unknown when, or if, the SEC will re-propose a proxy access rule.

Note that Dodd-Frank Act §971 amended §14(a) of the Exchange Act to explicitly empower the SEC to adopt proxy access rules. Congress included this section in the Act to foreclose arguments by proxy access opponents that the SEC lacks the authority to adopt proxy access rules.

(2) Access Bylaws

Recall that under corporate law statutes shareholders have the power to unilaterally amend a corporation's bylaws.[51] Given the lack of success in securing SEC mandated proxy access, shareholder activists have sought to use this power to implement proxy access bylaw provisions at individual companies through Rule 14a-8 shareholder proposals. Here is an example of such a proposal submitted in 2007 for inclusion in the proxy materials of Verizon Communications Inc.

---

50. *See Business Roundtable v. SEC*, 647 F.3d 1144 (D.C. Cir. 2011).
51. *See, e.g.,* DGCL §109(a); MBCA §10.20(a).

RESOLVED, pursuant to Section 7.06 of the Bylaws of Verizon Communications Inc., the stockholders hereby amend the Bylaws to add the following to Section 4.12(c) of Article IV, permitting shareholders to nominate candidates for election to the Board under limited circumstances:

"Notwithstanding the above, the corporation shall include in its proxy materials for a meeting of shareholders at which directors are to be elected the name, together with the Disclosure and Statement (as defined in this section), of any person nominated for election to the Board of Directors by a shareholder or group thereof that satisfies the requirements of this section 4.12(c) (the 'Nominator'), and allow shareholders to vote with respect to such nominee on the corporation's proxy card. Each Nominator may nominate up to two candidates for election at a meeting.
    A Nominator must:
    (a) have beneficially owned 3% or more of the corporation's outstanding common stock ('Required Shares') continuously for at least two years;
    (b) provide written notice received by the secretary of the corporation within the time period specified in this section 4.12(c) containing (i) with respect to the nominee, (A) the information required by such section and (B) such nominee's consent to being named in the proxy statement and to serving as a director if elected; and (ii) with respect to the Nominator, proof of ownership of the Required Shares; and
    (c) execute an undertaking that it agrees to (i) assume all liability stemming from any legal or regulatory violation arising out of the Nominator's communications with the corporation's shareholders, including, without limitation, the Disclosure and Statement; (ii) to the extent it uses soliciting material other than the corporation's proxy materials, comply with all applicable laws and regulations, including, without limitation, the SEC's Rule 14a-12.
    The Nominator may furnish a statement, not to exceed 500 words, in support of the nominee's candidacy (the 'Statement') at the time the Disclosure is submitted. The Board of Directors shall adopt a procedure for timely resolving disputes over whether notice of a nomination was timely given and whether the Disclosure and Statement comply with this section 4.12 and any applicable SEC rules."

Historically, the SEC allowed companies to exclude these sort of proposals under the "Relates to election" exclusion of Rule 14a-8(i)(8). Furthermore, many argued that this type of shareholder-enacted bylaw provision violated state corporate law because it impinged on the board's authority to manage the business and affairs of the corporation and thus was also excludable under the "Improper under state law" exclusion of Rule 14a-8(i)(1). Both of these impediments have now been removed. Specifically, in 2010 the SEC narrowed Rule 14a-8(i)(8) so that the "Relates to election" exclusion no longer applies to a shareholder proposal to amend a company's bylaws to provide for proxy access. On the state law front, in 2009 both the DGCL and MBCA were amended to specifically authorize proxy access bylaw provisions.[52]

---

52. *See* DGCL §112; MBCA §2.06(c)(1).

Questions

1. Assuming the above resolution passed, how many Verizon shares would you need to own to qualify as a Nominator and for how long do you have to have owned the shares?
2. Assuming the above resolution passed and you meet the share requirements, how many of your nominees does Verizon have to include in its proxy materials?

C. CORPORATE GOVERNANCE LISTING STANDARDS

As mentioned earlier, the NYSE and NASDAQ have listing standards a company has to meet in order for its securities to be traded on one of these exchanges. In addition to the quantitative standards we discussed in Chapter 11, these standards include certain corporate governance requirements, most of which were put in effect in the wake of the massive accounting frauds discovered at Enron and WorldCom in the early 2000s. In fact, SOX included several provisions requiring the exchanges to adopt various corporate governance requirements, but most of these were already in the works prior to the adoption of SOX. Following are the most prominent of the NYSE's corporate governance requirements. NASDAQ's requirements are very similar.

Independent Directors. A majority of directors on a listed company's board of directors must be independent.[53] For a director to be considered independent, the board must affirmatively determine "that the director has no material relationship with the listed company (either directly or as a partner, shareholder or officer of an organization that has a relationship with the company)."[54] In addition, a director is not considered independent if:

- "The director is, or has been within the last three years, an employee of the listed company, or an immediate family member is, or has been within the last three years, an executive officer, of the listed company."
- "The director has received, or has an immediate family member who has received, during any twelve-month period within the last three years, more than $120,000 in direct compensation from the listed company, other than director and committee fees and pension or other forms of deferred compensation for prior service (provided such compensation is not contingent in any way on continued service)."
- "(A) The director is a current partner or employee of a firm that is the listed company's internal or external auditor; (B) the director has an immediate family member who is a current partner of such a firm; (C) the director has an immediate family member who is a current employee of such a firm and personally works on the listed company's audit; or (D) the

53. NYSE Listed Co. Man. §303A.01.
54. *Id.* §303A.01(a).

director or an immediate family member was within the last three years a partner or employee of such a firm and personally worked on the listed company's audit within that time."

- "The director or an immediate family member is, or has been within the last three years, employed as an executive officer of another company where any of the listed company's present executive officers at the same time serves or served on that company's compensation committee."
- "The director is a current employee, or an immediate family member is a current executive officer, of a company that has made payments to, or received payments from, the listed company for property or services in an amount which, in any of the last three fiscal years, exceeds the greater of $1 million, or 2% of such other company's consolidated gross revenues."[55]

Executive Sessions. A listed company's board must hold regular executive sessions of its non-management directors without management present.[56] It should also hold at least one executive session per year limited solely to its independent directors.

Nominating/Corporate Governance Committee. A listed company must have a nominating/corporate governance committee comprised entirely of independent directors.[57] The committee's purpose, at a minimum, must be to "identify individuals qualified to become board members, consistent with criteria approved by the board, and to select, or to recommend that the board select, the director nominees for the next annual meeting of shareholders; develop and recommend to the board a set of corporate governance guidelines applicable to the corporation; and oversee the evaluation of the board and management."[58]

Compensation Committee. A listed company must have a compensation committee comprised entirely of independent directors.[59] The committee, at a minimum, must have direct responsibility to:

- "review and approve corporate goals and objectives relevant to CEO compensation, evaluate the CEO's performance in light of those goals and objectives, and, either as a committee or together with the other independent directors (as directed by the board), determine and approve the CEO's compensation level based on this evaluation";
- "make recommendations to the board with respect to non-CEO executive officer compensation, and incentive-compensation and equity-based plans that are subject to board approval"; and
- prepare the compensation committee report required by SEC rules to be included in the company's proxy statement.[60]

---

55. *Id.* §303A.02(b).
56. *Id.* §303A.03.
57. *Id.* §303A.04.
58. *Id.* §303A.04(b).
59. *Id.* §303A.05.
60. *Id.* §303A.05(b).

Audit Committee. A listed company must have an audit committee comprised entirely of directors that meet the NYSE definition of independence and the independence criteria specified in Exchange Act Rule 10A-3(b)(1).[61] Under Rule 10A-3(b)(1), a director is considered independent if he or she has not accepted any consulting, advisory, or other compensatory fee from the company other than for board service; and is not an affiliated person of the company or one of its subsidiaries (an affiliated person is generally an executive officer or 10 percent or greater shareholder of the company at issue). The committee must be comprised of at least three directors, all of whom are financially literate (as determined by the company's board in its business judgment) and at least one of whom has accounting or related financial expertise.

The committee's responsibilities must include, among other things, to:

- "assist board oversight of (1) the integrity of the listed company's financial statements, (2) the listed company's compliance with legal and regulatory requirements, (3) the independent auditor's qualifications and independence, and (4) the performance of the listed company's internal audit function and independent auditors";
- prepare the audit committee report required by SEC rules to be included in the company's proxy statement;
- "be directly responsible for the appointment, compensation, retention and oversight of the work of any registered public accounting firm engaged (including resolution of disagreements between management and the auditor regarding financial reporting) for the purpose of preparing or issuing an audit report or performing other audit, review or attest services for the [company], and each such registered public accounting firm must report directly to the audit committee";
- "establish procedures for . . . [t]he receipt, retention, and treatment of complaints received by the [company] regarding accounting, internal accounting controls, or auditing matters; and . . . [t]he confidential, anonymous submission by employees of the listed issuer of concerns regarding questionable accounting or auditing matters";
- "have the authority to engage independent counsel and other advisers, as it determines necessary to carry out its duties" and receive funding from the company to compensate such outside legal, accounting or other advisors;
- "at least annually, obtain and review a report by the independent auditor describing: the firm's internal quality-control procedures; any material issues raised by the most recent internal quality-control review, or peer review, of the firm, or by any inquiry or investigation by governmental or professional authorities, within the preceding five years, respecting one or more independent audits carried out by the firm, and any steps taken to

---

61. *Id.* §303A.06.

deal with any such issues; and (to assess the auditor's independence) all relationships between the independent auditor and the listed company";

- "meet to review and discuss the listed company's annual audited financial statements and quarterly financial statements with management and the independent auditor, including reviewing the listed company's specific disclosures under 'Management's Discussion and Analysis of Financial Condition and Results of Operations'";
- "discuss the listed company's earnings press releases, as well as financial information and earnings guidance provided to analysts and rating agencies";
- "discuss policies with respect to risk assessment and risk management";
- "meet separately, periodically, with management, with internal auditors (or other personnel responsible for the internal audit function) and with independent auditors";
- "review with the independent auditor any audit problems or difficulties and management's response";
- "set clear hiring policies for employees or former employees of the independent auditors"; and
- "report regularly to the board of directors."[62]

Corporate Governance Guidelines. A listed company must adopt and disclose corporate governance guidelines.[63] These guidelines must address the following subjects:

- director qualification standards,
- director responsibilities,
- director access to management and independent advisors,
- director compensation,
- director orientation and continuing education,
- management succession, and
- annual board performance evaluation.

Code of Business Conduct and Ethics. A listed company must adopt and disclose a code of business conduct and ethics for directors, officers, and employees, and promptly disclose any waivers of the code for directors or executive officers.[64] The code should address the following:

- conflicts of interest,
- corporate opportunities,
- confidentiality,
- fair dealing,

---

62. *Id.* §303A.07.
63. *Id.* §303A.09.
64. *Id.* §303A.10.

- protection and proper use of listed company assets,
- compliance with laws, rules, and regulation (including insider trading laws), and
- encouraging the reporting of any illegal or unethical behavior.

Additionally, the code must provide that any waiver of it for executive officers or directors may be made only by the board or a board committee.

D. INSIDER TRADING

Federal securities laws, principally §10(b) and Rule 10b-5 as interpreted by the courts, prohibit buying or selling a security, in breach of a fiduciary duty or other relationship of trust or confidence, on the basis of material, nonpublic information about the security, or, what corporate lawyers refer to as insider trading. In this section, we discuss the two principal theories of insider trading, classical and misappropriation. Also discussed are Rule 14e-3 and tipper/tippee liability.

1. Classical Theory

The classical theory of insider trading prohibits trading on the basis of material, nonpublic information in violation of a duty to disclose arising from a relationship of trust and confidence between the trader and those with whom he traded. For purposes of the theory, a relationship of trust and confidence exists between the shareholders of a corporation and those insiders who have obtained confidential information by reason of their positions with that corporation.

The term "insiders" encompasses both actual and constructive insiders. An actual insider is a person whom obtains nonpublic information concerning a company as a result of his or her position as an officer, director, employee, or agent of the company. A constructive insider is a person whom obtains nonpublic information concerning a company as a result of a temporary association with the company with an expectation by the company that the person will keep the disclosed information confidential. Examples of constructive insiders include lawyers, accountants, and investment bankers retained by the company.

2. Misappropriation Theory

The Supreme Court adopted the misappropriation theory of insider trading in 1997 in *United States v. O'Hagan*.[65] The theory prohibits trading on the basis

---

65. 521 U.S. 642 (1997).

of material nonpublic information obtained in breach of a duty of trust or confidence owed by the trader to the information source.

O'Hagan was a partner of a law firm that represented Grand Met PLC in connection with its proposed takeover of Pillsbury Company, a Minneapolis-based public company that produced flour, Green Giant foods, and Haagen-Dazs ice cream. At the time, Pillsbury's stock was trading around $39.00 per share. O'Hagan did not work on the Grand Met representation but learned of its impending takeover attempt. Knowing that Grand Met would have to offer a substantial premium over $39.00 per share to successfully complete the take-over and that Pillsbury stock would therefore jump significantly when Grand Met publicly announced its intent to acquire Pillsbury, O'Hagan purchased 5,000 shares of common stock and 2,500 Pillsbury call options prior to Grand Met's public announcement. Grand Met then announced it was seeking to ac-quire Pillsbury at $60.00 per share, which immediately caused Pillsbury's stock price to jump to just under that figure. Shortly thereafter, O'Hagan sold his Pillsbury shares and call options, making around $4.3 million in the process. The SEC investigated O'Hagan, and the Justice Department indicted him for insider trading, among other things.

The problem with the insider trading charge was that the classical theory did not apply because O'Hagan was not a Pillsbury insider. Thus the Justice Department asked the Supreme Court to expand insider trading liability by adopting the misappropriation theory. The Court obliged.

A key issue in applying the misappropriation theory is determining the cir-cumstances that give rise to a duty of trust or confidence. *O'Hagan* shed little light on this issue beyond finding that a partner and his or her law firm are gen-erally in a relationship of trust or confidence. In 2000, the SEC adopted Rule 10b5-2 in an effort to provide some certainty on the issue. The Rule provides a non-exclusive definition of circumstances in which a person has a duty of trust or confidence for purposes of the misappropriation theory. Specifically, Rule 10b5-2 provides that a duty of trust or confidence exists under the following circumstances: (1) when a person agrees to maintain information in confidence; (2) when parties have a "history, pattern, or practice of sharing confidences"; or (3) when a person receives material nonpublic information from a spouse, par-ent, child, or sibling.

3. Rule 14e-3

Rule 14e-3(a) under the Securities Exchange Act of 1934 prohibits a person from trading while in possession of material nonpublic information concern-ing a tender offer. A tender offer is one of several methods by which a bidder can acquire a publicly traded company (the target). Under this acquisition method, the bidder offers to buy out target's shareholders, typically at a premium to what target's shares are then trading. For example, say target's shares are cur-rently trading at $10.00 per share. Bidder knows that target's shareholders will be unlikely to sell unless it offers to pay substantially more than $10.00, so it decides to offer $15.00 per share. As soon as bidder's offer is publicly disclosed, target's share price will immediately rise from $10.00 to just under $15.00.[66] Thus, someone who knows about bidder's plans before the plans are publicly disclosed could make a quick profit by buying target stock at $10.00 and then selling at just under $15.00 following public disclosure of the tender offer. Note that Grand Met's acquisition of Pillsbury was structured as a tender offer, so O'Hagan was prosecuted and convicted under Rule 14e-3 in addition to the misappropriation theory.

Unlike the classical and misappropriation theory, Rule 14e-3 applies even if the trader did not breach a fiduciary duty or other relationship of trust or confidence when trading. However, the Rule only applies if a tender offer was involved. In other words, if an acquisition is structured as a merger or asset purchase (these acquisition methods are discussed in Chapter 14) instead of a tender offer, Rule 14e-3 does not apply.

4. Tipper/Tippee Liability

In the realm of insider trading, a "tipper" is a person who discloses material, nonpublic information (a "tip") to another individual. A "tippee" is a person who trades on the basis of the tip. Depending on the facts, both a tipper and a tippee may be liable for insider trading under the classical theory, the misappropriation theory, or Rule 14e-3.

Under the classical theory, both a tipper and tippee are liable for insider trading if (1) tipper passed material nonpublic information concerning a company in which tipper is an insider in breach of a fiduciary duty owed by tipper to the company, and (2) tippee knew or had reason to know of tipper's breach of duty. For these purposes, the requisite breach of duty exists only if tipper personally benefitted, directly or indirectly, from disclosing the information to tippee.

Under the misappropriation theory, both a tipper and tippee are liable for insider trading if (1) tipper passed material nonpublic information concerning a company in breach of a fiduciary duty owed by tipper to the information source, and (2) tippee knew or had reason to know of tipper's breach of duty. As with tipper/tippee liability under the classical theory, most courts require the tipper to have received a personal benefit from passing the tip, although a few courts have held receipt of a personal benefit is not required for tipper/tippee liability under the misappropriation theory.

Rule 14e-3(c) expressly prohibits a person from passing a tip relating to a tender offer under circumstances in which it is reasonably foreseeable that the person receiving the tip will trade on the information.[67] Hence, the tippee will

---

66. Target's shares normally do not start trading at or above $15.00 out of concern that bidder will change its mind and withdraw the offer.

67. *See* Rule 14e-3(d).

be liable under section (a) of Rule 14e-3 for trading while in possession of material nonpublic information concerning a tender offer, and the tipper will be liable under section (c) for passing the tip.

Exercise 13.4

1. Rob is a sixth year associate at a big New York City law firm and is on his first date with Amber at a trendy restaurant in SoHo. While sitting at dinner, Rob's cell phone rings. It is Omar, a junior associate at Rob's firm, calling Rob to update him on the Jetix deal. The Jetix deal refers to the acquisition by Makusi Corp. of Jetix Co., a publicly traded company. Rob's firm represents Makusi, and Rob is the point person on the deal.

   Trying to impress Amber ("Amber, look, I'm a big-shot attorney working on a high-powered deal that you'll soon be reading about in the paper"), Rob purposely mentions to Omar that Makusi will be acquiring Jetix at a substantial premium over the then prevailing market price of Jetix's stock knowing that Amber is listening. Amber calls it a night with Rob following dinner (notwithstanding the phone call, she was not particularly impressed).

   The next morning, Amber calls her broker and has him buy for her account 1,000 shares of Jetix. Amber also tells her roommate Kathy that Jetix is going to be taken over and that Kathy should buy some of its stock. Kathy immediately calls her broker and instructs him to buy 500 shares of Jetix for her account.

   That afternoon, Rob treats his dad Rupert to lunch for Rupert's 60th birthday. Rob gives his dad a birthday card in which Rob has written, "A special birthday tip for you—buy Jetix stock." Rupert reads the card and then calls his broker and has her buy 3,000 shares of Jetix stock for his account.

   Three days later, Jetix and Makusi issue a joint press release announcing that Makusi will be acquiring 100 percent of Jetix for $30 per share through a merger of Jetix into a newly created wholly owned subsidiary of Makusi. The price of Jetix promptly rises from $20.00 to $29.50.

   Are any of the above individuals guilty of illegal insider trading?

2. You are a student at the Rogers College of Law. While flying back to school after spring break, you overhear two strangers discussing the acquisition of Raytheon by Boeing at a 40 percent premium over Raytheon's market price. You go home and Google Raytheon and Boeing and find no mention anywhere of the acquisition. You call your broker and have her buy you 1,000 shares of Raytheon. The deal is announced two days later, and Raytheon's stock price jumps $20. You sell your shares for a quick $20,000 profit. Have you violated the federal prohibition against insider trading?

· CHAPTER FOURTEEN ·

MERGERS AND ACQUISITIONS
INTRODUCTION

Oftentimes when a corporation wants to add to its product lines or enter new markets, instead of starting from scratch, it just buys a corporation that already makes the desired products or is in the desired markets. The purchase of one corporation by another, or an M&A transaction, is a complicated subject matter that cannot be covered in a single chapter (or even a single course). Thus, this chapter provides only an introduction to the principal legal issues involved when one corporation acquires another.

Acquisitions can be divided into two categories: friendly and hostile. An acquisition is friendly if the board of directors of the corporation to be acquired ("target") is in favor of the sale. An acquisition is hostile if the board of directors of the target is against being acquired by the pursuing corporation ("bidder"). We first focus on friendly deals and then cover additional issues raised by hostile deals.

A. FRIENDLY ACQUISITIONS

A friendly acquisition, or deal, is typically structured in one of four ways: an asset purchase, stock purchase, merger, or share exchange. Below is an overview of each of these structures and then a discussion of considerations that drive the choice of structure.

1. Asset Purchase

As the name indicates, if a deal is structured as an asset purchase, bidder acquires target's business by buying target's assets. For example, say Clare's Conery, Inc. (CCI) has agreed to be acquired by National Ice Cream Corp. (NICC) through an asset purchase. CCI would sell its assets (equipment, inventory, furniture, trademarks, etc.) and assign its contracts (lease agreement, ice cream supply agreement, etc.) to NICC in exchange for the deal consideration negotiated by CCI and NICC. Deal consideration, regardless of deal structure, can consist of cash, bidder stock, bidder debt, or a combination of any of the foregoing. As part of the deal, NICC may also agree to assume some of CCI's liabilities (such as CCI's bank loan), and this would be factored into the deal price. In other words, if NICC agrees to assume CCI's $80,000 bank loan as part of the deal, NICC will pay $80,000 less for CCI's assets than it otherwise would have.

The specific assets target is selling to bidder, specific liabilities bidder is assuming from target, and the amount and composition of the deal consideration will be specified in an "Asset Purchase Agreement" signed by bidder and target. Under state corporate law, target's board of directors and shareholders (assuming the sale constitutes all or substantially all of target's assets) have to approve the deal.[1] The voting requirement for target shareholder approval varies by state. The requirement under the MBCA is more votes for than against. The requirement under the DGCL is a majority of outstanding shares. Bidder board approval is not technically required under corporate law statutes but is required under agency law if the transaction is out of the ordinary course of bidder's business. Regardless, both target's and bidder's attorneys will insist on bidder board approval so that there is no question as to whether the officer signing the asset purchase agreement on behalf of bidder had the authority to do so.

Target remains in existence after the deal, but it no longer owns any business assets because it has sold them to bidder. In other words, post-deal target is basically a shell corporation whose only asset is the deal consideration. Thus, following the deal, target typically dissolves pursuant to the applicable state corporate law dissolution statute, which involves paying off its creditors and distributing its remaining assets, that is, the deal consideration, to its shareholders.

Below is a diagram of an acquisition structured as an asset purchase. For this and the other diagrams in this chapter, "B" stands for bidder, and "T" stands for target.

---

1. *See, e.g.,* DGCL §271(a); MBCA §12.02(a) & (b).

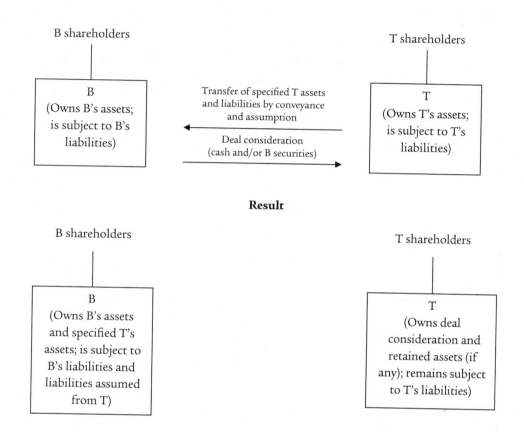

2. Stock Purchase

As the name indicates, if a deal is structured as a stock purchase, bidder acquires target's business by buying all of target's outstanding stock. Thus, if the CCI/NICC deal is structured as a stock purchase, NICC would buy all of CCI's outstanding shares from CCI's shareholders. This deal would be documented by a "Stock Purchase Agreement" signed by NICC and each of CCI's shareholders, as well as CCI. The agreement will specify the deal consideration, or how much and in what form NICC is paying each CCI shareholder for his or her shares.

A target does not technically need to be a party to a stock purchase agreement because the transaction is between bidder and target's shareholders and not target itself. Bidder, however, will want target to make various representations and warranties concerning its business in the stock purchase agreement and will therefore require target to be a party to the agreement. Agency law and the parties' attorneys will require the boards of both bidder and target to approve the deal. Target's shareholders, however, do not get a formal vote on the deal because they are each making their own individual decision of whether to sell their target stock to bidder. (If one or more target shareholders refuses to sell, bidder and target will likely then just go with a different deal structure.)

Given bidder acquires all of target's outstanding stock, post-deal, target ends up as a wholly owned subsidiary of bidder. A wholly owned subsidiary is a corporation (or other entity) 100 percent of whose stock is owned by another corporation (or other entity) (often called the "parent" company). In other words, bidder has acquired target's business by acquiring control through 100 percent stock ownership of target. Target's shareholders pre-deal no longer own any stock in target because they have sold it to bidder in exchange for the deal consideration.

Below is a diagram of an acquisition structured as a stock purchase.

STOCK PURCHASE

Transaction

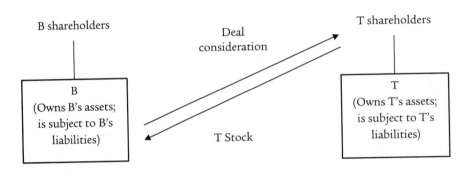

Result

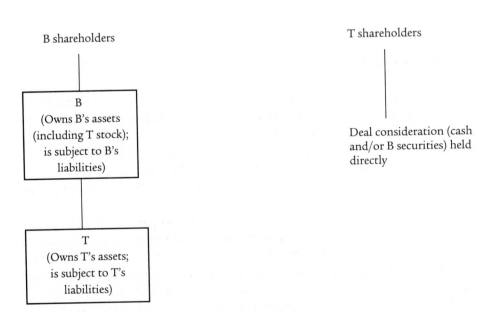

3. Merger

A merger is entirely a function of state corporate law. In other words, a bidder can acquire a target through a merger only because state corporate law statutes include merger provisions. These provisions dictate the steps a bidder and target must complete to merge and the legal effect of merging. The basic steps are (1) approval of a plan of merger by the board of directors of bidder and target, (2) approval of the plan of merger by target's shareholders, and (3) filing of articles of merger with the secretary of state.

There are three different types of mergers: (1) direct merger, (2) forward triangular merger, and (3) reverse triangular merger. The type of merger the parties have decided on is set forth in the plan of merger (lawyers actually typically title it "Agreement and Plan of Merger") as is the deal consideration target's shareholders will receive upon consummation of the merger.

a. Direct Merger

In a direct merger, target merges with and into bidder. Pursuant to the merger statute and as specified in the agreement and plan of merger, upon consummation of the merger: (1) target's assets and liabilities are transferred to bidder by operation of law, (2) target's outstanding shares are converted into the deal consideration specified in the agreement and plan of merger, and (3) target ceases to exist.

Below is a diagram of an acquisition structured as a direct merger.

MERGER

Transaction

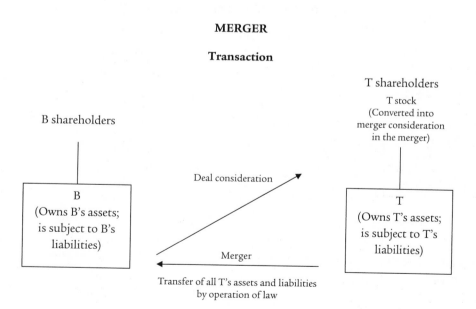

Result

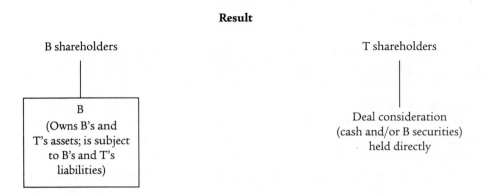

b. *Forward Triangular Merger*

In a forward triangular merger, target merges with and into a newly created wholly owned subsidiary of bidder ("merger sub"). Pursuant to the merger statute and as specified in the agreement and plan of merger, upon consummation of the merger: (1) target's assets and liabilities are transferred to merger sub by operation of law, (2) target's outstanding shares are converted into the deal consideration specified in the agreement and plan of merger, and (3) target ceases to exist. As a result, target's business ends up in a wholly owned subsidiary of bidder.

Below is a diagram for a deal structured as a forward triangular merger. In this diagram and the next one, "S" stands for merger sub.

FORWARD TRIANGULAR MERGER

Transaction

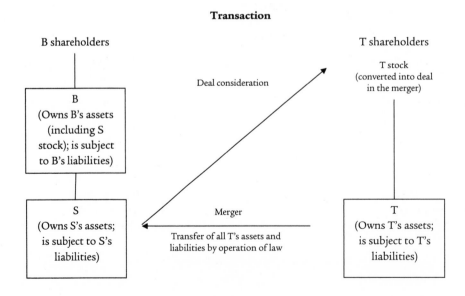

Result

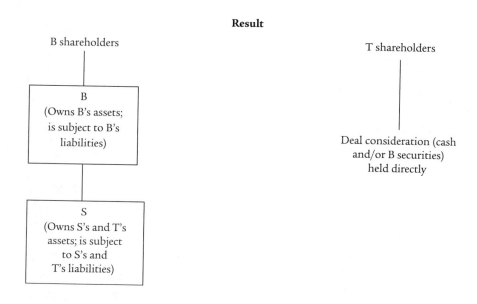

B shareholders

B
(Owns B's assets;
is subject to B's
liabilities)

S
(Owns S's and T's
assets; is subject
to S's and
T's liabilities)

T shareholders

Deal consideration (cash
and/or B securities)
held directly

c. Reverse Triangular Merger

In a reverse triangular merger, merger sub merges with and into target. Pursuant to the merger statute and as specified in the agreement and plan of merger, upon consummation of the merger: (1) target's outstanding shares are converted into the deal consideration specified in the agreement and plan of merger, (2) merger sub's outstanding shares, all of which are owned by bidder, are converted into target common stock, and (3) merger sub ceases to exist. As a result, target ends up as a wholly owned subsidiary of bidder.

Below is a diagram for a deal structured as a reverse triangular merger.

REVERSE TRIANGULAR MERGER

Transaction

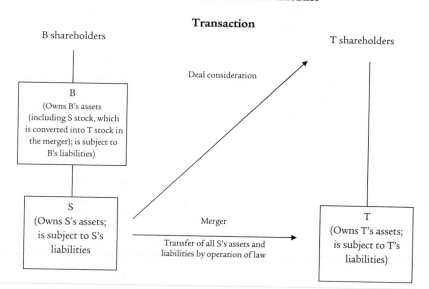

B shareholders

T shareholders

B
(Owns B's assets
(including S stock, which
is converted into T stock in
the merger); is subject to
B's liabilities)

Deal consideration

S
(Owns S's assets;
is subject to S's
liabilities

Merger

Transfer of all S's assets and
liabilities by operation of law

T
(Owns T's assets;
is subject to T's
liabilities)

Result

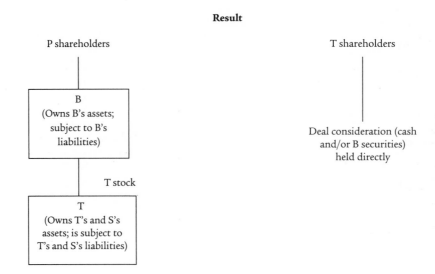

4. Share Exchange

As with a merger, a share exchange is entirely a function of state corporate law. In other words, a bidder can acquire a target through a share exchange only because the MBCA and thus many state corporate law statutes include share exchange provisions. The DGCL, however, does not provide for a share exchange. Thus, if either bidder or target is incorporated in Delaware (or some other state that does not provide for a share exchange), the parties cannot structure the deal as a share exchange.

Share exchange provisions dictate the steps a bidder and target must complete to effect a share exchange and the legal consequences of doing so. The basic steps are (1) approval of a plan of share exchange by the board of directors of bidder and target, (2) approval of the plan of share exchange by target's shareholders, and (3) filing of articles of share exchange with the secretary of state, basically the same steps as a merger.

In a share exchange, bidder acquires all of the outstanding stock of target by operation of the law in exchange for the deal consideration, which it pays directly to target's shareholders. As a result, target ends up as a wholly owned subsidiary of bidder. This is very similar to what happens in a stock purchase. The difference between the two is that with a share exchange, instead of each shareholder deciding individually whether or not to sell his or her shares to bidder, target shareholders vote on the deal. If enough shares vote in favor of the deal (the voting requirement under the MBCA is more votes for than against), all shareholders have to participate. In other words, a shareholder cannot refuse to sell his or her shares to bidder.

Below is a diagram for a deal structured as a share exchange.

SHARE EXCHANGE

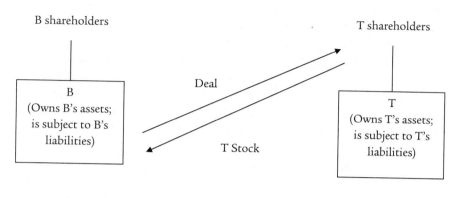

Result

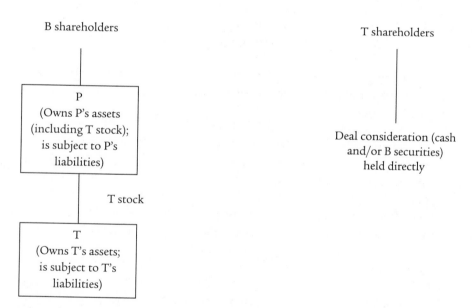

5. Structuring Considerations

In this subsection we discuss the primary considerations that drive the choice of deal structure and consideration (cash, stock, mix of both, etc.).

a. Target Liabilities

All corporations incur liabilities in the normal course of operations. Examples include bank loans, accounts payable, wages payable, and taxes payable.

Bidder will not be concerned about these liabilities because they will be reflected in the deal price. For example, if post-closing bidder (or a bidder subsidiary) will be liable on a $2 million target loan, bidder will pay $2 million less for target than it otherwise would have.

Bidder will be concerned about contingent liabilities. A contingent liability is a liability that may or may not come into being depending on whether some future event occurs. A pending lawsuit is a classic example of a contingent liability. The corporation will be liable for any judgment if it loses the lawsuit but obviously not if it wins. It is difficult for the parties to agree on a price reduction with respect to a contingent liability because it is often hard to estimate the chance of it coming to fruition and how much it will be if it does.

Bidder will also be concerned about unknown liabilities of target. These are liabilities that may emerge in the future from target's past business operations, but it is unknown if they actually will. Thus, they cannot be quantified at the time of bidder's acquisition of target. Examples of unknown liabilities include environmental and product liability claims.

The basic ground rules with respect to target's liabilities are as follows:

- If target merges directly into bidder, that is, the deal is structured as a direct merger, bidder succeeds by operation of law to all the liabilities of target, known, contingent, and unknown.
- If bidder purchases target's stock (whether through a stock purchase or a share exchange), bidder does not itself assume target's liabilities; but since bidder has become the 100 percent owner of target, and since target remains subject to all of its pre-existing known, contingent, and unknown liabilities, bidder will be seriously concerned about those liabilities.
- A forward or reverse triangular merger accomplishes basically the same thing as bidder's acquisition of target's stock, as far as target's liabilities are concerned. Whether target merges into merger sub or merger sub merges into target, target's liabilities end up in a wholly owned subsidiary of bidder.
- If bidder acquires target's assets, then (subject to exceptions discussed below) bidder can specifically list in the asset purchase agreement for the deal the target liabilities it is and is not assuming. Typically, an asset purchase agreement will provide that bidder is not assuming any unknown liabilities of target. Here is sample language.

Subject to the terms and conditions set forth in this Agreement, at the Closing, Purchaser shall assume from Seller and thereafter pay, perform, or discharge in accordance with their terms only those liabilities listed on <u>Schedule 1.4</u>. Except as specifically provided in this Agreement, Purchaser shall not assume, or otherwise be responsible or liable for or obligated with respect to, any liabilities or obligations of Seller, whether actual or contingent, accrued or unaccrued, matured or unmatured, liquidated or unliquidated, or known or unknown, whether arising out of occurrences prior to, on or after the Closing Date. Without limiting the foregoing, Purchaser shall not assume nor bear any responsibility of any kind whatsoever with respect to, and specifically disclaims any liability for: (a) All environmental claims related to, associated with or arising out of the ownership, operation, use or control of the Acquired Assets, or environmental conditions existing on, or as a result of the operations of, the Acquired Assets, before or as of the Closing Date, whether arising under environmental laws, or in any way arising in connection with the presence, release or threatened release of any contaminant at, on, to or from (i) the Acquired Assets, including, but not limited to, surface water, air, soil or groundwater thereon, thereunder or adjacent thereto or (ii) any real property at which contaminants generated by operations of the Acquired Assets were sent prior to the Closing Date; and (b) all warranty or product liability claims related to, associated with or arising out of the ownership, operation, use or control of the Acquired Assets existing on, or as a result of the operations of, the Acquired Assets, before or as of the Closing Date.

Schedule 1.4 referenced in the above language will list the liabilities of target ("Seller" in the above language) bidder ("Purchaser" in the above language) is assuming. This list will likely consist only of known liabilities that have been reflected in the purchase price. The disclaimer of liability language is a bit of overkill, but bidder's lawyers will want to make it crystal clear that bidder assumes nothing that is not listed on Schedule 1.4.

As indicated above, the only way for bidder to (potentially) avoid unwanted liabilities of target is to structure the deal as an asset purchase. If bidder is concerned about target's liabilities but for other reasons it is not feasible to structure the deal as an asset purchase, bidder should at least not merge target directly into itself. In other words, it should avoid structuring the deal as a direct merger but should instead use a structure in which target's liabilities end up in a bidder subsidiary. Bidder can achieve this through a stock purchase, share exchange (if available), or a triangular merger. Then, if catastrophic liabilities emerge later, bidder will hopefully at least be able to shield the rest of its business from these liabilities.

Avoiding liabilities by structuring a deal as an asset purchase is by no means bulletproof. For example, federal and state environmental laws impose liability on a landowner for contamination even if it occurred prior to when the owner acquired the land. In other words, even if the asset purchase agreement explicitly disclaimed liabilities arising out of target's pre-deal violations of environmental laws (as the language in the above box does), bidder may nonetheless be held liable. The same thing is true for liabilities arising out of target's violation of certain employment laws. The next case discusses when an asset buyer can be held liable on product liability claims against target.

Ray v. Alad Corporation
560 P.2d 3 (Cal. 1977)

WRIGHT, Associate Justice.

Claiming damages for injury from a defective ladder, plaintiff asserts strict tort liability against defendant Alad Corporation (Alad II) which neither manufactured nor sold the ladder but prior to plaintiff's injury succeeded to the business of the ladder's manufacturer, the now dissolved "Alad Corporation" (Alad I), through a purchase of Alad I's assets for an adequate cash consideration. Upon acquiring Alad I's plant, equipment, inventory, trade name, and good will, Alad II continued to manufacture the same line of ladders under the "Alad" name, using the same equipment, designs, and personnel, and soliciting Alad I's customers through the same sales representatives with no outward indication of any change in the ownership of the business. The trial court entered summary judgment for Alad II and plaintiff appeals. . . .

Plaintiff alleges in his complaint that on March 24, 1969, he fell from a defective ladder in the laundry room of the University of California at Los Angeles while working for the contracting company by which he was employed. . . .

It is undisputed that the ladder involved in the accident was not made by Alad II and there was testimony that the ladder was an "old" model manufactured by Alad I. Hence the principal issue addressed by the parties' submissions on the motion for summary judgment was the presence or absence of any factual basis for imposing any liability of Alad I as manufacturer of the ladder upon Alad II as successor to Alad I's manufacturing business.

Prior to the sale of its principal business assets, Alad I was in "the specialty ladder business" and was known among commercial and industrial users of ladders as a "top quality manufacturer" of that product. On July 1, 1968, Alad I sold to Lighting Maintenance Corporation (Lighting) its "stock in trade, fixtures, equipment, trade name, inventory and goodwill" and its interest in the real property used for its manufacturing activities. The sale did not include Alad I's cash, receivables, unexpired insurance, or prepaid expenses. As part of the sale transaction Alad I agreed "to dissolve its corporate existence as soon as practical and (to) assist and cooperate with Lighting in the organization of a new corporation to be formed by Lighting under the name 'ALAD CORPORATION.'" Concurrently with the sale the principal stockholders of Alad I, Mr. and Mrs. William S. Hambly, agreed for a separate consideration not to compete with the purchased business for 42 months and to render nonexclusive consulting services during that period. By separate agreement Mr. Hambly was employed as a salaried consultant for the initial five months. There was ultimately paid to Alad I and the Hamblys "total cash consideration in excess of $207,000.00 plus interest for the assets and goodwill of ALAD (I)."

The only provisions in the sale agreement for any assumption of Alad I's liabilities by Lighting were that Lighting would (1) accept and pay for materials previously ordered by Alad I in the regular course of its business and (2) fill uncompleted orders taken by Alad I in the regular course of its business and hold Alad I harmless from any damages or liability resulting from failure to do so. The possibility of Lighting's or Alad II's being held liable for defects in products manufactured or sold by Alad I was not specifically discussed nor was any provision expressly made therefor.

On July 2, 1968, the day after acquiring Alad I's assets, Lighting filed and thereafter published a certificate of transacting business under the fictitious name of "Alad Co." Meanwhile Lighting's representatives had formed a new corporation under the name of "Stern Ladder Company." On August 30, 1968, there was filed with the Secretary of State (1) a certificate of winding up and dissolution of "Alad Corporation" (Alad I) and (2) a certificate of amendment to the articles of Stern Ladder Company changing its name to "Alad Corporation" (Alad II). The dissolution certificate declared that Alad I "has been completely wound up . . . (its) known debts and liabilities have been actually paid . . . (and its) known assets have been distributed to the shareholders." In due course Lighting transferred all the assets it had purchased from Alad I to Alad II in exchange for all of Alad II's outstanding stock.

The tangible assets acquired by Lighting included Alad I's manufacturing plant, machinery, offices, office fixtures and equipment, and inventory of raw materials, semifinished goods, and finished goods. These assets were used to continue the manufacturing operations without interruption except for the closing of the plant for about a week "for inventory." The factory personnel remained the same, and identical "extrusion plans" were used for producing the aluminum components of the ladders. The employee of Lighting designated as the enterprise's general manager as well as the other previous employees of Lighting were all without experience in the manufacture of ladders. The former general manager of Alad I, Mr. Hambly, remained with the business as a paid consultant for about six months after the takeover.

The "Alad" name was used for all ladders produced after the change of management. Besides the name, Lighting and Alad II acquired Alad I's lists of customers, whom they solicited, and continued to employ the salesman and manufacturer's representatives who had sold ladders for Alad I. Aside from a redesign of the logo, or corporate emblem, on the letterheads and labels, there was no indication on any of the printed materials to indicate that a new company was manufacturing Alad ladders, and the manufacturer's representatives were not instructed to notify customers of the change.

Our discussion of the law starts with the rule ordinarily applied to the determination of whether a corporation purchasing the principal assets of another corporation assumes the other's liabilities. As typically formulated the rule states that the purchaser does not assume the seller's liabilities unless (1) there is an express or implied agreement of assumption, (2) the transaction amounts to a consolidation or merger of the two corporations, (3) the purchasing corporation is a mere continuation of the seller, or (4) the transfer of assets to the purchaser is for the fraudulent purpose of escaping liability for the seller's debts.

If this rule were determinative of Alad II's liability to plaintiff it would require us to affirm the summary judgment. None of the rule's four stated grounds for imposing liability on the purchasing corporation is present here. There was no express or implied agreement to assume liability for injury from defective products previously manufactured by Alad I. Nor is there any indication or contention that the transaction was prompted by any fraudulent purpose of escaping liability for Alad I's debts.

With respect to the second stated ground for liability, the purchase of Alad I's assets did not amount to a consolidation or merger. This exception has been invoked where one corporation takes all of another's assets without providing any consideration that could be made available to meet claims of the other's creditors or where the consideration consists wholly of shares of the purchaser's stock which are promptly distributed to the seller's shareholders in conjunction with the seller's liquidation. In the present case the sole consideration given for Alad I's assets was cash in excess of $207,000. Of this amount Alad I was paid $70,000 when the assets were transferred and at the same time a promissory note was given to Alad I for almost $114,000. Shortly before the dissolution of Alad I the note was assigned to the Hamblys, Alad I's principal stockholders, and thereafter the note was paid in full. The remainder of the consideration went for closing expenses or was paid to the Hamblys for consulting services and their agreement not to compete. There is no contention that this consideration was inadequate or that the cash and promissory note given to Alad I were not included in the assets available to meet claims of Alad I's creditors at the time of dissolution. Hence the acquisition of Alad I's assets was not in the nature of a merger or consolidation for purposes of the aforesaid rule.

Plaintiff contends that the rule's third stated ground for liability makes Alad II liable as a mere continuation of Alad I in view of Alad II's acquisition of all Alad I's operating assets, its use of those assets and of Alad I's former employees to manufacture the same line of products, and its holding itself out to customers and the public as a continuation of the same enterprise. However, California decisions holding that a corporation acquiring the assets of another corporation is the latter's mere continuation and therefore liable for its debts have imposed such liability only upon a showing of one or both of the following factual elements: (1) no adequate consideration was given for the predecessor corporation's assets and made available for meeting the claims of its unsecured creditors; (2) one or more persons were officers, directors, or stockholders of both corporations. There is no showing of either of these elements in the present case. . . .

We therefore conclude that the general rule governing succession to liabilities does not require Alad II to respond to plaintiff's claim. In considering whether a special departure from that rule is called for by the policies underlying strict tort liability for defective products, we note the approach taken by the United States Supreme Court in determining whether an employer acquiring and continuing to operate a going business succeeds to the prior operator's obligations to employees and their bargaining representatives imposed by federal labor law. Although giving substantial weight to the general rules of state law making succession to the liabilities of an acquired going business dependent on the form and circumstances of the acquisition, the court refuses to be bound by these rules where their application would unduly thwart the public policies underlying the applicable labor law. Similarly we must decide whether the policies underlying strict tort liability for defective products call for a special exception to the rule that would otherwise insulate the present defendant from plaintiff's claim.

The purpose of the rule of strict tort liability "is to insure that the costs of injuries resulting from defective products are borne by the manufacturers that put such products on the market rather than by the injured persons who are powerless to protect themselves." (*Greenman v. Yuba Power Products, Inc.* (1963) 59 Cal. 2d 57, 63, 27 Cal. Rptr. 697, 701, 377 P.2d 897, 901.) However, the rule "does not rest on the analysis of the financial strength or bargaining power of the parties to the particular action. It rests, rather, on the proposition that '[t]he cost of an injury and the loss of time or health may be an overwhelming misfortune to the person injured, and a needless one for the risk of injury can be insured by the manufacturer and distributed among the public as a cost of doing business.' (*Escola v. Coca Cola Bottling Co.*, 24 Cal. 2d 453, 462, 150 P.2d 436 (concurring opinion).)" (*Seeley v. White Motor Co.* (1965) 63 Cal. 2d 9, 18-19, 45 Cal. Rptr. 17, 23, 403 P.2d 145, 151.) Thus, "the paramount policy to be promoted by the rule is the protection of otherwise defenseless victims of manufacturing defects and the spreading throughout society of the cost of compensating them." (*Price v. Shell Oil Co.* (1970) 2 Cal. 3d 245, 251, 85 Cal. Rptr. 178, 181, 466 P.2d 722, 725.) Justification for imposing strict liability upon a successor to a manufacturer under the circumstances here presented rests upon (1) the virtual destruction of the plaintiff's remedies against the original manufacturer caused by the successor's acquisition of the business, (2) the successor's ability to assume the original manufacturer's risk-spreading role, and (3) the fairness of requiring the successor to assume a responsibility for defective products that was a burden necessarily attached to the original manufacturer's good will being enjoyed by the successor in the continued operation of the business. We turn to a consideration of each of these aspects in the context of the present case.

We must assume for purposes of the present proceeding that plaintiff was injured as a result of defects in a ladder manufactured by Alad I and therefore could assert strict tort liability against Alad I under the rule of *Greenman v. Yuba Power Products, Inc., supra*, 59 Cal. 2d 57, 27 Cal. Rptr. 697, 377 P.2d 897. However, the practical value of this right of recovery against the original manufacturer was vitiated by the purchase of Alad I's tangible assets, trade name and good will on behalf of Alad II and the dissolution of Alad I within two months thereafter in accordance with the purchase agreement. The injury giving rise to plaintiff's claim against Alad I did not occur until more than six months after the filing of the dissolution certificate declaring that Alad I's "known debts and liabilities have been actually paid" and its "known assets have been distributed to its shareholders." This distribution of assets was perfectly proper as there was no requirement that provision be made for claims such as plaintiff's that had not yet come into existence. Thus, even if plaintiff could obtain a judgment on his claim against the dissolved and assetless Alad I he would face formidable and probably insuperable obstacles in attempting to obtain satisfaction of the judgment from former stockholders or directors.

The record does not disclose whether Alad I had insurance against liability on plaintiff's claim. Although such coverage is not inconceivable products liability insurance is usually limited to accidents or occurrences taking place while the policy is in effect. Thus the products liability insurance of a company that has gone out of business is not a likely source of compensation for injury from a product the company previously manufactured.

These barriers to plaintiff's obtaining redress from the dissolved Alad I set him and similarly situated victims of defective products apart from persons entitled to recovery against a dissolved corporation on claims that were capable of being known at the time of its dissolution. Application to such victim of the general rule that immunizes Alad I's successor from the general run of its debts would create a far greater likelihood of complete denial of redress for a legitimate claim than would the rule's application to most other types of claimants. Although the resulting hardship would be alleviated for those injured plaintiffs in a position to assert their claims against an active and solvent retail dealer who sold the defective product by which they were injured, the retailer would in turn be cut off from the benefit of rights against the manufacturer.

While depriving plaintiff of redress against the ladder's manufacturer, Alad I, the transaction by which Alad II acquired Alad I's name and operating assets had the further effect of transferring to Alad II the resources that had previously been available to Alad I for meeting its responsibilities to persons injured by defects in ladders it had produced. These resources included not only the physical plant, the manufacturing equipment, and the inventories of raw material, work in process, and finished goods, but also the know-how available through the records of manufacturing designs, the continued employment of the factory personnel, and the consulting services of Alad I's general manager. With these facilities and sources of information, Alad II had virtually the same capacity as Alad I to estimate the risks of claims for injuries from defects in previously manufactured ladders for purposes of obtaining insurance coverage or planning self-insurance. Moreover, the acquisition of the Alad enterprise gave Alad II the opportunity formerly enjoyed by Alad I of passing on to purchasers of new "Alad" products the costs of meeting these risks. Immediately after the takeover it was Alad II, not Alad I, which was in a position to promote the "paramount policy" of the strict products liability rule by "spreading throughout society . . . the cost of compensating (otherwise defenseless victims of manufacturing defects)" (*Price v. Shell Oil Co., supra*, 2 Cal. 3d 245, 251, 85 Cal. Rptr. 178, 182, 466 P.2d 722, 726).

Finally, the imposition upon Alad II of liability for injuries from Alad I's defective products is fair and equitable in view of Alad II's acquisition of Alad I's trade name, good will, and customer lists, its continuing to produce the same line of ladders, and its holding itself out to potential customers as the same enterprise. This deliberate albeit legitimate exploitation of Alad I's established reputation as a going concern manufacturing a specific product line gave Alad II a substantial benefit which its predecessor could not have enjoyed without the burden of potential liability for injuries from previously manufactured units. Imposing this liability upon successor manufacturers in the position of Alad II not only causes the one "who takes the benefit (to) bear the burden" (Civ. Code, §3521) but precludes any windfall to the predecessor that might otherwise result from (1) the reflection of an absence of such successor liability in an enhanced price paid by the successor for the business assets and (2) the liquidation of the predecessor resulting in avoidance of its responsibility for subsequent injuries from its defective products. By taking over and continuing the established business of producing and distributing Alad ladders, Alad II became "an integral part of the overall producing and marketing enterprise that should bear the cost of injuries resulting from defective products" (*Vandermark v. Ford Motor Co., supra*, 61 Cal. 2d 256, 262, 37 Cal. Rptr. 896, 899, 391 P.2d 168, 171).

We therefore conclude that a party which acquires a manufacturing business and continues the output of its line of products under the circumstances here presented assumes strict tort liability for defects in units of the same product line previously manufactured and distributed by the entity from which the business was acquired. . . .

The judgment is reversed.

Questions

1. Why is plaintiff suing?
2. What is defendant's argument for why it is not liable?
3. What are the four exceptions the court discusses to the rule that a purchaser of assets does not assume target's liabilities? Do any of them apply in this case? Why or why not?
4. What is the product line exception?
5. In light of this case, what should defendant have done differently in connection with the purchase of Alad I's assets?

A majority of courts in other states that have considered the issue have declined to add the product line exception adopted by the *Ryan* court.

b. Target's Contracts

A target will normally be a party to a large number of agreements, some of which, while not critical, are on favorable economic terms. The price bidder is willing to pay for target will be impacted by whether bidder will be able to step into the shoes of target on these agreements. Under contract law, the general default rule is that a contract is assignable. In other words, if the contract is silent on the issue, target will be able to transfer it to bidder in the transaction. Contracts drafted by lawyers, however, typically are not silent on the issue. A standard provision included in the "General" or "Miscellaneous" section of a contract (typically, the last section of a contract) is a non-assignment clause.

Below are two examples of non-assignment clauses from a building lease agreement. Assume that target is the Renter, bidder wants the benefit of the lease, but Owner would like to get out of the lease because it could now charge a much higher rate of rent. In other words, Owner will not consent to the lease being assigned to bidder.

Example 1:

Renter may not assign without the prior written consent of Owner, its rights, duties or obligations under this Agreement to any person or entity, in whole or in part.

Example 2:

Renter has neither the right nor the power to assign any of its rights or delegate any of its duties under this Agreement by operation of the law or otherwise without the prior written consent of Owner. Any attempt to assign or delegate without Owner's consent is void.

Under both of these examples, bidder will not be able to step into the shoes of target if the deal is structured as an asset purchase. This is because with an asset purchase, for bidder to get the benefit of a target contract, target has to assign the contract to bidder, but here Owner will not consent to the assignment as required by the agreement. (Owner is probably more than willing for bidder to take over the lease if bidder agrees to a higher rent.)

The analysis is different if the transaction is structured as a direct or forward triangular merger. In a merger, all target's assets and liabilities are transferred to bidder (or a subsidiary of bidder) by operation of the law pursuant to the merger statute. This includes target's contractual rights and obligations. Thus, bidder would step into the shoes of target on the lease if it contained the Example 1 non-assignment clause. The same is not true, however, if the lease contained the Example 2 non-assignment clause. This is because Example 2 states that the Agreement is not assignable *"by operation of the law* or otherwise. . . ."* Courts have held that including the italicized language in a non-assignment clause prevents a contract from being transferred in a merger.

Bidder and target can, however, easily structure around an Example 2-type non-assignment clause. They just have to go with a structure where target survives as a legal entity post-deal, that is, a reverse triangular merger, stock purchase, or share exchange (if available). This is because under one of these structures nothing is being transferred or assigned by target. All of the assets and liabilities of target (including its rights and obligations under its contracts) remain in target. The acquisition is instead affected by the ownership of target changing from its shareholders to bidder.

Good transactional attorneys are well aware of this loophole, and thus know to close it, if so desired, by also including a change-of-control provision in the contracts they draft. Here is sample language:

Owner may terminate this Agreement at any time following a Change of Control of Renter.

A "**Change of Control**" means the occurrence of any of the following events: (i) the consummation of a merger or consolidation of Renter with or into any corporation or other entity; (ii) the sale or other disposition of all or substantially all of Renter's assets; or (iii) any "person" (as such term is used in Sections 13(d) and 14(d) of the Securities Exchange Act of 1934, as amended) becoming the "beneficial owner" (as defined in Rule 13d-3 under said Act), directly or indirectly, of securities of Renter representing fifty percent (50%) or more of the total voting power represented by Renter's then outstanding voting securities.

There is no structuring around the above provision because it is triggered by a "Change of Control," which is defined to encompass any acquisition of Renter, regardless of structure.

Note that under federal law, intellectual property rights are not assignable, even indirectly through a transaction structure where target survives, without the consent of the owner. Thus, there is no structuring around getting the consent of a third party who, for example, has licensed patented technology to target, even if the license agreement is silent on assignment and does not include a change of control provision.

Bidder's counsel will review all of target's material contracts as part of bidder's due diligence process to determine what they provide regarding assignment and whether they contain change of control provisions. Bidder may have target contact its counterparties to contracts with change of control provisions to see whether they will consent to the contract being assigned to bidder in connection with target's sale to bidder.

c. Tax

Acquisitions raise a number of tax issues for both bidder and target. This section provides a brief overview of the federal income tax consequences to target shareholders, perhaps the most prominent tax issue. The sale of target will be a taxable event for target's shareholders unless the deal qualifies as a tax-free reorganization.

(1) Taxable Deals

For tax purposes, with the exception of a deal structured as an asset purchase, target shareholders are treated as having sold their target stock in exchange for the deal consideration. Thus, if the deal is taxable, a target shareholder will have to recognize a gain in the year the deal closed to the extent the deal consideration he or she received exceeds the shareholder's basis in his or her target stock (generally, what the shareholder paid for the stock). If a target shareholder owned his or her target stock for more than one year prior to closing, the gain will typically qualify as a long-term capital gain.

If the deal is taxable and structured as an asset purchase, target will recognize tax at the corporate level to the extent the deal consideration exceeded target's basis in the assets it sold. If target is liquidated following the transaction (which is typically the case), target shareholders will be treated as having sold their target stock in exchange for the liquidating distribution to them. Thus, a target shareholder will have to recognize a gain in the year of the distribution to the extent the deal consideration he or she received exceeded the shareholder's basis in his or her target stock.

(2) Tax-Free Reorganizations

A deal qualifies as a tax-free reorganization if it meets the criteria for one of the types of "reorganization" specified in §368(a) of the Internal Revenue Code (IRC), and (2) satisfies the three additional judicially imposed requirements. Generally speaking, a deal will not qualify as a tax-free reorganization unless a significant portion of the deal consideration consists of bidder stock. Assuming the deal does qualify, a target shareholder will not have to recognize gain with respect to the bidder stock the shareholder received in the transaction until he or she sells the stock. Thus, it is somewhat of a misnomer to label a deal as tax-free. Target shareholders will have to pay tax, it is just that tax relating to the receipt of bidder stock is deferred. Hence, it would be more accurate to refer to the deal as a tax-deferred reorganization.

Below is a brief description of the criteria for the different deal structures to qualify as a "reorganization" under §368.

A deal qualifies as an *"A" reorganization* if it falls under IRC §368(a)(1)(A). To fall under this section, the deal must be structured as a direct, forward triangular, or reverse triangular merger. For a direct merger and a forward triangular merger, at least 40 percent of the deal consideration must consist of bidder stock, that is, voting or non-voting common or preferred stock. The balance can include cash, property, or debt securities (what tax people refer to as "boot"). For a reverse triangular merger, at least 80 percent of the deal consideration must consist of bidder *voting* stock. Thus, up to 20 percent of the deal consideration can be boot but the bidder stock issued to target shareholders must include voting rights.

A deal qualifies as a **"B" reorganization** if it falls under IRC §368(a)(1)(B). To fall under this section, the deal must be structured as a stock purchase (including a share exchange) where bidder acquires at least 80 percent of the voting power of target. Furthermore, the deal consideration must consist solely of bidder voting stock. In other words, boot is not allowed nor is non-voting stock.

A deal qualifies as a **"C" reorganization** if it falls under IRC §368(a)(1)(C). To fall under this section, the deal must be structured as an asset purchase where bidder acquires at least 90 percent of target's assets. Furthermore, at least 80 percent of the deal consideration must consist of bidder voting stock, meaning up to 20 percent of the deal consideration can consist of boot. If the deal consideration does include boot (e.g., cash or non-voting stock), the value of any target liabilities bidder assumes are considered boot as well and thus count toward the 20 percent cap. Additionally, target generally must liquidate and distribute the deal consideration to target shareholders immediately following the acquisition.

The three judicially imposed requirements are (1) continuity of interest, (2) continuity of business enterprise, and (3) business purposes. Continuity of interest generally requires that target shareholders receive a substantial ownership interest in bidder. Continuity of business enterprise requires bidder to continue at least one of the target's significant historic businesses or use a significant portion of the target's historic business assets in a business. Business purpose requires that the transaction had a bona fide business reason other than tax savings.

As mentioned above, if the deal qualifies as a tax-free reorganization, target shareholders do not have to recognize a gain with respect to the bidder stock they received in the deal until they sell the stock. They do, however, have to recognize gains in the year the deal closed with respect to any boot received in the deal. The bottom line is that a deal cannot be tax free if the deal consideration consists solely of cash. There can, however, be a cash component, depending on deal structure. More cash is allowed in an A reorganization than a C reorganization (with the exception of a reverse triangular merger); boot is not allowed at all in a B reorganization.

Question

Why might T shareholders be opposed to the sale of T being structured so that it is tax free?

d. Voting Concerns

As touched on above, with the exception of a stock purchase, target shareholders get to vote on a deal regardless of structure. Even with a stock purchase, each individual shareholder gets to decide whether or not to participate. Thus, there is no structuring around a deal that does not have the support of target shareholders owning a majority of shares.

It is a different story when it comes to the shareholders of bidder, and there is variance between the MBCA and DGCL. Under the MBCA, whether bidder's shareholders get to vote on the proposed acquisition of target turns on how much stock, if any, bidder will be issuing in the deal. Specifically, MBCA §6.21(f)(1)(ii) requires a bidder shareholder vote on the deal if bidder will be issuing shares equal to more than 20 percent of its outstanding voting power pre-deal. For example, say bidder has 1,000,000 shares of common stock outstanding and has agreed to acquire target for 250,000 shares of common stock. Bidder's common stock is currently worth $10 per share so 250,000 shares equates to $2,500,000. Bidder shareholders would get to vote on this deal because bidder will be issuing shares equal to more than 20 percent of its pre-deal voting power (250,000/1,000,000 = .25 or 25%). If instead the deal consideration was, for example, 150,000 shares and $1,000,000 in cash, bidder's shareholders would not get to vote on the deal. In other words, under the MBCA, whether bidder shareholders get to vote depends on the type and amount of deal consideration.

The DGCL has a similar 20 percent rule, but it only applies to a deal structured as a direct merger.[2] It does not apply to a triangular merger because the Delaware merger statute affords a shareholder vote, if at all, only to the shareholders of a corporation party to the merger. With a triangular merger, bidder is not a party to the merger; the parties are target and merger sub. Hence, under Delaware law there are several ways to structure a deal so that it does not require a bidder vote, including going with an asset purchase, triangular merger, stock purchase, or using cash consideration in a direct merger.

e. Appraisal Rights

Appraisal rights afford shareholders who vote against specified corporate actions the option of having their shares bought back by the corporation for cash at fair value as determined by a court. The actions triggering appraisal rights for target shareholders under the MBCA include a merger, share exchange, and sale of all or substantially all of the corporation's assets.[3] In contrast, only a merger triggers appraisal rights under the DGCL.

Appraisal rights came into being for historical reasons. Specifically, at one time state corporate statutes required a proposed sale of a corporation to be

---

2. *See* DGCL §251(f).
3. *See* MBCA §13.02(a).

unanimously approved by its shareholders. This proved unworkable because it meant a single shareholder could block the sale. Thus, states moved to a majority shareholder voting standard coupled with appraisal rights. The appraisal rights piece was put in to provide shareholders who are against a deal for whatever reason (they think the price is too low, the deal consideration is in stock and they do not want to be a bidder shareholder, etc.) the option of getting cashed out of their investments at a price determined by an objective third party.

Under both the DGCL and MBCA, bidder shareholders generally are not entitled to appraisal rights even if they get to vote on the acquisition. One exception is if the deal is structured as a direct merger and the deal consideration consists of greater than 20 percent of bidder's outstanding stock pre-deal.

Both the MBCA and DGCL include a so-called market out exception. Under this exception (subject to some limited exceptions), appraisal rights are not available for shares that are traded on a national securities exchange. In other words, if target's shares are traded on the NYSE or NASDAQ, its shareholders do not get appraisal rights in connection with the sale of the company.

The MBCA provides the following explanation for the market out exception:

> Chapter 13 provides a limited exception to appraisal rights for those situations where shareholders can either accept the consideration offered in the appraisal-triggering transaction or can obtain the fair value of their shares by selling them in the market. This provision is predicated on the theory that where an efficient market exists, the market price will be an adequate proxy for the fair value of the corporation's shares, thus making appraisal unnecessary. Furthermore, after the corporation announces an appraisal-triggering action, the market operates at maximum efficiency with respect to that corporation's shares because interested parties and market professionals evaluate the offer and competing offers may be generated if the original offer is deemed inadequate. Moreover, the market exception reflects an evaluation that the uncertainty, costs and time commitment involved in any appraisal proceeding are not warranted where shareholders can sell their shares in an efficient, fair and liquid market. For these reasons, approximately half of the states have enacted market exceptions to their appraisal statutes.[4]

Appraisal rights may become a prominent structuring consideration if it appears rights, if available, will be asserted with respect to a significant number of target's shares, especially if bidder is tight on cash. This is because if the deal is structured as anything other than an asset purchase, it will essentially be bidder cashing out target's shareholders following an appraisal proceeding since the proceeding will be concluded post-closing, at which point bidder will be responsible for target's liabilities. Structuring around appraisal rights is easy if target is a Delaware corporation because the DGCL does not afford target shareholders appraisal rights in a deal structured as an asset purchase. The same is not true under the MBCA, but an asset purchase helps in that situation

---

4. *Id.* Offic. Cmt. 2.

too since target survives the transaction and is still owned by target's shareholders. Hence, bidder will not be involved in the appraisal proceeding.

Concerns over shareholders' exercising appraisal rights also come into play if the deal is to be structured as a tax-free reorganization. This is because cash paid to shareholders who have asserted appraisal rights may count as "boot," and having too much boot can disqualify a transaction from being tax free.

Note that neither the DGCL nor MBCA provides for appraisal rights if the deal is structured as a stock purchase. The problem, however, of using a stock purchase when it appears that some target shareholders are not in favor of the deal is that there is a good chance they will not participate. In such a case, target ends up as a less than wholly owned subsidiary of bidder, which is not ideal for bidder from a legal standpoint because it will then owe these shareholders fiduciary duties since bidder has become a controlling shareholder of target. Bidder can follow up the transaction with a "squeeze-out" merger (see Section B.1.a below) but this adds to the transaction costs of the deal.

Exercise 14.1

B Inc. has agreed to acquire substantially all the assets of T Inc. in exchange for $90 million in B common stock and $10 million in non-voting B preferred stock. B will also assume $20 million in T debt in connection with the deal. Does the deal qualify as a tax-free reorganization? If not, what could be changed so it does?

Exercise 14.2

B Corp., an MBCA corporation, has agreed to acquire T Corp. in a reverse triangular merger. The deal consideration is comprised of a mix of B common stock and debt securities. B's common stock is traded on OTC Bulletin Board. B currently has 100 million shares outstanding and roughly 10,000 shareholders. B will be issuing 25 million shares of common stock in the deal. T is also an MBCA corporation, and its shares are traded on NASDAQ.

1. Do B's shareholders get to vote on the deal? What about T's shareholders?
2. Are B's shareholders entitled to appraisal rights with respect to the deal? What about T's shareholders?

Make sure you note the specific statutory provisions that support your answers to the above questions.

Exercise 14.3

B, a Delaware corporation, manufactures video games, among other things. T, a Delaware corporation, is a video game development company. B has agreed to acquire T for 5,000,000 shares of B common stock. T had asked for at least a portion of the deal consideration to consist of cash, but B declined because B is currently short on cash.

T was started three years ago by two college roommates and has been financed by venture capitalists. T also has $3 million in bank debt on its books. T's most important asset is a lucrative long-term contract with Microsoft for the development of 15 games for the X-Box game system over a period of ten years. While the first game developed by T under the contract was a success, the second game was a flop, and as a result, Microsoft has expressed its displeasure with the contract. The contract provides that it may not be assigned by operation of law or otherwise without Microsoft's prior written consent.

Each T founder owns 2,000,000 shares of common stock, VC Fund I owns 1,000,000 shares of T Series A Preferred Stock, VC Fund II owns 1,000,000 shares of T Series B Preferred Stock and VC Fund III owns 1,000,000 shares of T Series C Preferred Stock. Each share of T preferred stock is entitled to one vote on any matter submitted to the T shareholders and votes with common as a single class. T's board of directors consists of five members—the two founders and a representative of each VC Fund. The VC Fund III board member has indicated that she does not support T's acquisition by B under the above terms and will therefore vote against the deal and assert appraisal rights. B has indicated to you that, given its cash situation, if appraisal rights are asserted by 10 percent or more of T's shares B will not be able to go forward with the deal.

1. How do you recommend that B structure the deal?
2. What will be the tax consequences to T shareholders?

B. HOSTILE ACQUISITIONS

A hostile acquisition, or takeover, is the label given to an acquisition where target's board of directors is against target being acquired by bidder. In this section we discuss deal structure options for a hostile takeover, defensive tactics target can implement to thwart a hostile takeover attempt, fiduciary duties of target's directors in the hostile takeover context, and state anti-takeover statutes.

1. Deal Structure Options

Given all but one of the deal structures discussed above requires target board approval that obviously will not be forthcoming, bidder is left with two choices for a hostile takeover: launching a tender offer or a proxy fight. (Note that generally only a public corporation can be acquired against the will of its board of directors, so in this section assume that target is public.)

a. Tender Offer

In this context, a tender offer is a deal structured as a stock purchase that includes some or all of the following factors:

> (1) Active and widespread solicitation of public shareholders for the shares of an issuer; (2) solicitation made for a substantial percentage of the issuer's stock; (3) offer to purchase made at a premium over the prevailing market price; (4) terms of the offer are firm rather than negotiable; (5) offer contingent on the tender of a fixed number of shares, often subject to a fixed maximum number to be purchased; (6) offer open only for a limited period of time; (7) offeree subjected to pressure to sell his stock; [and (8)] public announcements of a purchasing program concerning the target company precede or accompany rapid accumulation of a large amount of target company's securities.[5]

Basically, bidder bypasses target's board of directors and goes directly to its shareholders.

Tender offers are regulated under the Exchange Act. The regulations impose the following structural requirements:

- 20-day minimum offering period;
- tendering shareholders can revoke their tenders at any time during offering period;
- if the tender offer is oversubscribed, that is, more shares are tendered than bidder has offered to buy, bidder must buy shares pro rata from each tendering shareholder;
- bidder's offer must be open to all shareholders; and
- all shareholders must get the best price offered by bidder (this requirement comes into play when bidder raises its offering price to get more target shareholders to tender).

Furthermore, the Exchange Act requires bidder to furnish target's shareholders a disclosure document regarding bidder and the tender offer.

A hostile bidder's tender offer is normally for the number of shares that will result in bidder owning a majority of target's outstanding shares (bidder often buys some target shares on the open market prior to officially launching its tender offer). Even if a tender offer is for all of target's stock not owned by bidder, not every target shareholder will tender. Thus, a hostile tender of-

---

5. *SEC v. Carter Hawley Hale Stores, Inc.*, 760 F.2d 945, 950 (9th Cir. 1985) (quoting *Wellman v. Dickinson*, 475 F. Supp. 783 (S.D.N.Y. 1979)).

fer is routinely followed by a so-called squeeze-out merger. Specifically, bidder will cause target to be merged with a subsidiary of bidder in exchange for deal consideration equivalent to what bidder offered in the tender offer. Upon closing of the merger, target shareholders that did not tender will be taken out by virtue of the merger statute, and target will end up being a wholly owned subsidiary of bidder. Bidder can cause target to merge because following the tender offer it is target's majority shareholder. Thus, it can replace target's directors with its own people who will approve the merger and is assured of getting the requisite target shareholder approval of the merger because it will vote its target shares in favor of it. To protect against a later claim of controlling shareholder breach of fiduciary duty, bidder will normally not go forward with a squeeze-out merger unless a majority of target's minority shareholders also approve the merger.

Exercise 14.4

Draw a diagram along the lines of the ones from Section A above (Friendly Acquisitions) for a bidder's acquisition of target through a tender offer for a majority of target stock followed by a squeeze-out merger of non-tendering target shareholders.

---

b. Proxy Fight

In a proxy fight, bidder seeks to take over target's board of directors by getting its people elected to fill a majority of board seats. Taking over target's board puts all deal structuring options on the table because the board will no longer be opposed to the takeover. This method is called a proxy fight because, as discussed in Chapter 13, for public companies the overwhelming majority of shareholder voting occurs via proxy. Thus, in advance of the target's next board of directors' election, bidder will send target's shareholders proxy materials soliciting their proxies to vote in favor of bidder's slate of directors. This means that target's shareholders will receive two sets of proxy materials—one set from target soliciting proxies for the slate of directors selected by target and bidder's set putting forth an alternative slate. Bidder and target will then engage in essentially a political campaign trying to convince target shareholders to use its respective proxy card.

If bidder does not want to wait for target's next annual election of directors, it could perhaps launch a proxy fight to remove target's board of directors and immediately elect bidder's replacement. Alternatively, it could perhaps seek written consents from shareholders for the same purposes.

2. Defensive Measures

A target can implement a number of different measures to make it more difficult for a hostile bidder to succeed. This section discusses two of the most prominent defenses: the poison pill and the staggered board.

a. Poison Pill

A poison pill is the colloquial name for a shareholders' rights plan adopted by a corporation's board of directors to make a hostile tender offer for a corporation's shares prohibitively expensive. To give you a sense of the specifics of a poison pill, below is an excerpt from a Form 8-K of Navistar International Corporation regarding the stockholder rights plan it adopted in June 2012:

ITEM 1.01 ENTRY INTO A MATERIAL DEFINITIVE AGREEMENT

On June 19, 2012, the Board of Directors (the "Board") of Navistar International Corporation, a Delaware corporation (the "Company"), authorized and declared a dividend distribution of one right (a "Right") for each outstanding share of the common stock of the Company, par value $0.10 per share (the "Common Stock"), to stockholders of record at the close of business on June 29, 2012 (the "Record Date"). Each Right entitles the registered holder to purchase from the Company a unit consisting of one one-thousandth of a share (a "Unit") of a newly authorized series of Junior Participating Preferred Stock, Series A, par value $1.00 per share (the "Preferred Stock"), at a purchase price of $140.00 per Unit, subject to adjustment (the "Purchase Price"). The complete terms of the Rights are set forth in a Rights Agreement (the "Rights Agreement"), dated as of June 19, 2012, between the Company and Computershare Shareowner Services LLC, as Rights Agent.

Rights Certificates; Exercise Period

Initially, the Rights will be attached to all shares of Common Stock then outstanding, and no separate rights certificates ("Rights Certificates") will be distributed. Subject to certain exceptions specified in the Rights Agreement, the Rights will separate from the Common Stock and a distribution date (a "Distribution Date") will occur upon the earlier of (i) 10 business days following a public announcement that a person or group of affiliated or associated persons (an "Acquiring Person") has acquired beneficial ownership of fifteen percent (15%) or more of the outstanding shares of Common Stock (the "Stock Acquisition Date"), other than as a result of repurchases of stock by the Company or certain inadvertent actions by certain stockholders or (ii) 10 business days (or such later date as the Board shall determine) following the commencement of a tender offer or exchange offer that would result in a person or group becoming an Acquiring Person. For purposes of the Rights Agreement, beneficial ownership is defined to include ownership of derivative securities.

Until a Distribution Date, (i) the Rights will be evidenced by the certificates for the Common Stock (or, in the case of shares reflected on the direct registration system, by the notations in the book-entry account system) and will only be transferable with such Common Stock, (ii) new Common Stock certificates issued after the Record Date will contain a legend incorporating the Rights Agreement by reference and (iii) the surrender for transfer of any certificates for Common Stock outstanding will also constitute the transfer of the Rights associated with the Common Stock represented by such certificates. Pursuant to the Rights Agreement, the Company reserves the right to require prior to the occurrence of a Triggering Event (as defined below) that, upon any exercise of Rights, a number of Rights be exercised so that only whole shares of Preferred Stock will be issued.

The Rights are not exercisable until a Distribution Date and will expire at 5:00 P.M., New York City time on June 18, 2013, unless such date is extended or the Rights are earlier redeemed, exchanged or terminated.

As soon as practicable after a Distribution Date, Rights Certificates will be mailed to holders of record of the Common Stock as of the close of business on a Distribution Date and, thereafter, the separate Rights Certificates alone will represent the Rights. Except as otherwise determined by the Board, only shares of Common Stock issued prior to a Distribution Date will be issued with Rights.

Flip-in Trigger

In the event that a person or group of affiliated or associated persons becomes an Acquiring Person, except pursuant to an offer for all outstanding shares of Common Stock which the independent directors determine to be fair and not inadequate and to otherwise be in the best interests of the Company and its stockholders after receiving advice from one or more investment banking firms, each holder of a Right will thereafter have the right to receive, upon exercise, Common Stock (or, in certain circumstances, cash, property or other securities of the Company) having a value equal to two times the exercise price of the Right. Notwithstanding the foregoing, following the occurrence of the event set forth in this paragraph, all Rights that are, or (under certain circumstances specified in the Rights Agreement) were, beneficially owned by any Acquiring

Person will be null and void. However, Rights are not exercisable following the occurrence of the event set forth above until such time as the Rights are no longer redeemable by the Company as set forth below. Any person who, together with its affiliates and associates, beneficially owns 15% or more of the outstanding shares of Common Stock as of the time of the first public announcement of the Rights Agreement (an "Exempt Person") shall not be deemed an Acquiring Person, but only for so long as such person, together with its affiliates and associates, does not become the beneficial owner of any additional shares of Common Stock while such person is an Exempt Person. A person will cease to be an Exempt Person if such person, together with such person's affiliates and associates, becomes the beneficial owner of less than 15% of the outstanding shares of Common Stock.

Flip-over Trigger

In the event that, at any time following the Stock Acquisition Date, (i) the Company engages in a merger or other business combination transaction in which the Company is not the surviving corporation, (ii) the Company engages in a merger or other business combination transaction in which the Company is the surviving corporation and the Common Stock of the Company is changed or exchanged, or (iii) 50% or more of the Company's assets, cash flow or earning power is sold or transferred, each holder of a Right (except Rights which have previously been voided as set forth above) shall thereafter have the right to receive, upon exercise, common stock of the acquiring company having a value equal to two times the exercise price of the Right. The events set forth in this paragraph and in the second preceding paragraph are referred to as the "Triggering Events."

Exchange Feature

At any time after a person becomes an Acquiring Person and prior to the acquisition by such person or group of fifty percent (50%) or more of the outstanding Common Stock, the Board may exchange the Rights (other than Rights owned by such person or group which have become void), in whole or in part, at an exchange ratio of one share of Common Stock, or one one-thousandth of a share of Preferred Stock (or of a share of a class or series of the Company's preferred stock having equivalent rights, preferences and privileges), per Right (subject to adjustment).

Equitable Adjustments

The Purchase Price payable, and the number of Units of Preferred Stock or other securities or property issuable, upon exercise of the Rights are subject to adjustment from time to time to prevent dilution (i) in the event of a dividend on the Preferred Stock payable in shares of Preferred Stock, a subdivision or split of outstanding shares of Preferred Stock, a combination or consolidation of Preferred Stock into a smaller number of shares through a reverse stock split or otherwise, or reclassification of the Preferred Stock, (ii) if holders of the Preferred Stock are granted certain rights, options or warrants to subscribe for Preferred Stock or convertible securities at less than the current market price of the Preferred Stock, or (iii) upon the distribution to holders of the Preferred Stock of cash (excluding regular quarterly cash dividends), assets, evidences of indebtedness or of subscription rights or warrants (other than those referred to above).

With certain exceptions, no adjustment in the Purchase Price will be required until cumulative adjustments amount to at least 1% of the Purchase Price. No fractional Units will be issued and, in lieu thereof, an adjustment in cash will be made based on the market price of the Preferred Stock on the last trading date prior to the date of exercise.

Redemption Rights

At any time until ten business days following the Stock Acquisition Date, the Company may redeem the Rights in whole, but not in part, at a price of $0.001 per Right (payable in cash, Common Stock or other consideration deemed appropriate by the Board). Immediately upon the action of the Board ordering redemption of the Rights, the Rights will terminate and the only right of the holders of Rights will be to receive the $0.001 redemption price.

Miscellaneous

Until a Right is exercised, the holder thereof, as such, will have no separate rights as a stockholder of the Company, including, without limitation, the right to vote or to receive dividends in respect of Rights. While the distribution of the Rights will not be taxable to stockholders or to the Company, stockholders may, depending upon the circumstances, recognize taxable income in the event that the Rights become exercisable for Common Stock (or other consideration) of the Company or for common stock of the acquiring company or in the event of the redemption of the Rights as set forth above.

Amendment

Any of the provisions of the Rights Agreement may be amended by the Board prior to a Distribution Date. After a Distribution Date, the provisions of the Rights Agreement may be amended by the Board in order to cure any ambiguity, to make changes which do not adversely affect the interests of holders of Rights, or to shorten or lengthen any time period under the Rights Agreement. Notwithstanding the foregoing, no amendment may be made at such time as the Rights are not redeemable.

Anti-Takeover Effects

The Rights may have certain anti-takeover effects. The Rights may cause substantial dilution to any person or group that attempts to acquire the Company without the approval of the Board. As a result, the overall effect of the Rights may be to render more difficult or discourage a merger, tender offer or other business combination involving the Company that is not supported by the Board.

Questions

1. Under what situations is Navistar's poison pill triggered?
2. What happens upon triggering of the pill?
3. If you were a Navistar shareholder, would you be in favor of or opposed to its board implementing a poison pill? Why?

A board of directors can adopt a shareholders' rights plan without shareholder approval because corporate law statutes empower the board to issue rights.[6] Navistar's certificate includes blank check preferred stock, and thus its board was able to have the rights exercisable for a new class of preferred stock it created in connection with the rights plan. If Navistar did not have blank check preferred, the board of directors could still adopt a poison pill, but the rights would have to be exercisable for common stock.

A poison pill essentially eliminates the possibility of target being taken over through a hostile tender offer. Furthermore, given a board can adopt a poison pill without shareholder approval, a corporation can quickly put one in place in the face of a hostile tender offer attempt.

Note that poison pills are redeemable at the option of the company (as is the case with the Navistar pill described above). This allows a company to remove the pill for a friendly deal. It also means that a bidder can remove the pill through a successful electoral proxy fight to take over the board (that is where a staggered board comes into play, as we discuss in the next subsection). In other words, a poison pill does not protect target from a bidder launching a proxy fight. Target lawyers tried to close this gap by including dead-hand and slow-hand provisions in shareholders' rights plans. A dead-hand provision allowed a pill to be redeemed only by directors in office at the time the poison pill was adopted. A slow-hand provision restricted a newly elected board from

---

6. *See* DGCL §157(a); MBCA §6.24(a).

redeeming the pill for a specified period of time (typically six months). The Delaware Supreme Court has invalidated both dead-hand and slow-hand provisions as impermissibly impinging on the authority of a newly elected board to manage the business and affairs of the corporation.

b. Staggered Board

Recall from Chapter 9 that a corporation can choose to stagger, or classify, its board so that terms of only a portion of its directors expire in a particular year. A staggered board serves as a powerful defense against a bidder launching an electoral proxy contest. Specifically, a corporation will stagger its directors into three groups (the maximum allowed), and thus only one-third of its board seats will come up for election each year. Therefore, to win a majority of board seats through a proxy fight, a bidder would have to mount and win two electoral proxy contests in two years. This increases the cost of the proxy fight because it doubles the number of required solicitations and stretches the bidder's campaign over more than one year. It also decrease the odds of the bidder ultimately succeeding because even shareholders who are in favor of bidder acquiring target may be reluctant to vote for bidder's slate because of the required two rounds of elections. Voting in the bidder's slate in the first round puts the board in limbo for a year. During this year, the incumbents retain control but they are aware that they will soon lose their positions. The entire board will have to deal with the internal divisions and friction caused by having one-third of the board composed of a competing faction. Given these factors, many bidders will conclude it does not make sense to pursue a proxy fight. Hence, the odds of one being launched against a target with a staggered board are greatly reduced. Put differently, a staggered board does not make it impossible for a bidder to launch and win an electoral proxy fight. It just makes the fight more expensive and time consuming, and therefore less likely to occur.

A company will typically reinforce the anti-takeover effect of a staggered board by making it difficult for shareholders to remove a director other than by voting someone else in when he or she is up for election. Thus, it will include provisions in its governing documents (1) allowing directors to be removed only for cause,[7] (2) restricting the ability of shareholders to call a special meeting (in case they want to do so to remove the board and elect a new one), and (3) eliminating the ability of shareholders to act through written consent (so they cannot remove the board and elect a new one through written consent).

---

7. This is not necessary for a Delaware corporation because DGCL §141(k)(1) provides that unless the corporation's charter provides otherwise, a director of a corporation with a staggered board can only be removed for cause.

Question

If you were a small shareholder of a public corporation, would you want the corporation to have a staggered board? Why?

3. Fiduciary Duties

As established by the next case, a target board decision to implement defensive measures in the face of a hostile takeover attempt is subject to enhanced scrutiny to ensure the decision was made consistent with the directors' fiduciary duties.

Unocal Corp. v. Mesa Petroleum
493 A.2d 946 (Del. 1985)

MOORE, Justice.

We confront an issue of first impression in Delaware—the validity of a corporation's self-tender for its own shares which excludes from participation a stockholder making a hostile tender offer for the company's stock.

The Court of Chancery granted a preliminary injunction to the plaintiffs, Mesa Petroleum Co., Mesa Asset Co., Mesa Partners II, and Mesa Eastern, Inc. (collectively "Mesa"),[8] enjoining an exchange offer of the defendant, Unocal Corporation (Unocal) for its own stock. The trial court concluded that a selective exchange offer, excluding Mesa, was legally impermissible. We cannot agree with such a blanket rule. The factual findings of the Vice Chancellor, fully supported by the record, establish that Unocal's board, consisting of a majority of independent directors, acted in good faith, and after reasonable investigation found that Mesa's tender offer was both inadequate and coercive. Under the circumstances the board had both the power and duty to oppose a bid it perceived to be harmful to the corporate enterprise. On this record we are satisfied that the device Unocal adopted is reasonable in relation to the threat posed, and that the board acted in the proper exercise of sound business judgment. We will not substitute our views for those of the board if the latter's decision can be "attributed to any rational business purpose." *Sinclair Oil Corp. v. Levien*, Del. Supr., 280 A.2d 717, 720 (1971). Accordingly, we reverse the decision of the Court of Chancery and order the preliminary injunction vacated.

I.

The factual background of this matter bears a significant relationship to its ultimate outcome.

---

8. [FN 1] T. Boone Pickens, Jr., is President and Chairman of the Board of Mesa Petroleum and President of Mesa Asset and controls the related Mesa entities.

On April 8, 1985, Mesa, the owner of approximately 13% of Unocal's stock, commenced a two-tier "front loaded" cash tender offer for 64 million shares, or approximately 37%, of Unocal's outstanding stock at a price of $54 per share. The "back-end" was designed to eliminate the remaining publicly held shares by an exchange of securities purportedly worth $54 per share. However, pursuant to an order entered by the United States District Court for the Central District of California on April 26, 1985, Mesa issued a supplemental proxy statement to Unocal's stockholders disclosing that the securities offered in the second-step merger would be highly subordinated, and that Unocal's capitalization would differ significantly from its present structure. Unocal has rather aptly termed such securities "junk bonds."[9]

Unocal's board consists of eight independent outside directors and six insiders. It met on April 13, 1985, to consider the Mesa tender offer. Thirteen directors were present, and the meeting lasted nine and one-half hours. The directors were given no agenda or written materials prior to the session. However, detailed presentations were made by legal counsel regarding the board's obligations under both Delaware corporate law and the federal securities laws. The board then received a presentation from Peter Sachs on behalf of Goldman Sachs & Co. (Goldman Sachs) and Dillon, Read & Co. (Dillon Read) discussing the bases for their opinions that the Mesa proposal was wholly inadequate. Mr. Sachs opined that the minimum cash value that could be expected from a sale or orderly liquidation for 100% of Unocal's stock was in excess of $60 per share. In making his presentation, Mr. Sachs showed slides outlining the valuation techniques used by the financial advisors, and others, depicting recent business combinations in the oil and gas industry. The Court of Chancery found that the Sachs presentation was designed to apprise the directors of the scope of the analyses performed rather than the facts and numbers used in reaching the conclusion that Mesa's tender offer price was inadequate.

Mr. Sachs also presented various defensive strategies available to the board if it concluded that Mesa's two-step tender offer was inadequate and should be opposed. One of the devices outlined was a self-tender by Unocal for its own

9. [FN 3] Mesa's May 3, 1985 supplement to its proxy statement states:

(i) following the Offer, the Purchasers would seek to effect a merger of Unocal and Mesa Eastern or an affiliate of Mesa Eastern (the "Merger") in which the remaining Shares would be acquired for a combination of subordinated debt securities and preferred stock; (ii) the securities to be received by Unocal shareholders in the Merger would be subordinated to $2,400 million of debt securities of Mesa Eastern, indebtedness incurred to refinance up to $1,000 million of bank debt which was incurred by affiliates of Mesa Partners II to purchase Shares and to pay related interest and expenses and all then-existing debt of Unocal; (iii) the corporation surviving the Merger would be responsible for the payment of all securities of Mesa Eastern (including any such securities issued pursuant to the Merger) and the indebtedness referred to in item (ii) above, and such securities and indebtedness would be repaid out of funds generated by the operations of Unocal; (iv) the indebtedness incurred in the Offer and the Merger would result in Unocal being much more highly leveraged, and the capitalization of the corporation surviving the Merger would differ significantly from that of Unocal at present; and (v) in their analyses of cash flows provided by operations of Unocal which would be available to service and repay securities and other obligations of the corporation surviving the Merger, the Purchasers assumed that the capital expenditures and expenditures for exploration of such corporation would be significantly reduced.

stock with a reasonable price range of $70 to $75 per share. The cost of such a proposal would cause the company to incur $6.1-6.5 billion of additional debt, and a presentation was made informing the board of Unocal's ability to handle it. The directors were told that the primary effect of this obligation would be to reduce exploratory drilling, but that the company would nonetheless remain a viable entity.

The eight outside directors, comprising a clear majority of the thirteen members present, then met separately with Unocal's financial advisors and attorneys. Thereafter, they unanimously agreed to advise the board that it should reject Mesa's tender offer as inadequate, and that Unocal should pursue a self-tender to provide the stockholders with a fairly priced alternative to the Mesa proposal. The board then reconvened and unanimously adopted a resolution rejecting as grossly inadequate Mesa's tender offer. Despite the nine and one-half hour length of the meeting, no formal decision was made on the proposed defensive self-tender.

On April 15, the board met again with four of the directors present by telephone and one member still absent. This session lasted two hours. Unocal's Vice President of Finance and its Assistant General Counsel made a detailed presentation of the proposed terms of the exchange offer. A price range between $70 and $80 per share was considered, and ultimately the directors agreed upon $72. The board was also advised about the debt securities that would be issued, and the necessity of placing restrictive covenants upon certain corporate activities until the obligations were paid. The board's decisions were made in reliance on the advice of its investment bankers, including the terms and conditions upon which the securities were to be issued. Based upon this advice, and the board's own deliberations, the directors unanimously approved the exchange offer. Their resolution provided that if Mesa acquired 64 million shares of Unocal stock through its own offer (the Mesa Purchase Condition), Unocal would buy the remaining 49% outstanding for an exchange of debt securities having an aggregate par value of $72 per share. The board resolution also stated that the offer would be subject to other conditions that had been described to the board at the meeting, or which were deemed necessary by Unocal's officers, including the exclusion of Mesa from the proposal (the Mesa exclusion). Any such conditions were required to be in accordance with the "purport and intent" of the offer.

Unocal's exchange offer was commenced on April 17, 1985, and Mesa promptly challenged it by filing this suit in the Court of Chancery. On April 22, the Unocal board met again and was advised by Goldman Sachs and Dillon Read to waive the Mesa Purchase Condition as to 50 million shares. This recommendation was in response to a perceived concern of the shareholders that, if shares were tendered to Unocal, no shares would be purchased by either offeror. The directors were also advised that they should tender their own Unocal stock into the exchange offer as a mark of their confidence in it.

Another focus of the board was the Mesa exclusion. Legal counsel advised that under Delaware law Mesa could only be excluded for what the directors reasonably believed to be a valid corporate purpose. The directors' discussion centered on the objective of adequately compensating shareholders at the "back-end" of Mesa's proposal, which the latter would finance with "junk bonds." To include Mesa would defeat that goal, because under the proration aspect of the exchange offer (49%) every Mesa share accepted by Unocal would displace one held by another stockholder. Further, if Mesa were permitted to tender to Unocal, the latter would in effect be financing Mesa's own inadequate proposal. . . .

[O]n April 22, 1985, Mesa amended its complaint in this action to challenge the Mesa exclusion. . . .

After the May 8 hearing the Vice Chancellor issued an unreported opinion on May 13, 1985 granting Mesa a preliminary injunction. Specifically, the trial court noted that "[t]he parties basically agree that the directors' duty of care extends to protecting the corporation from perceived harm whether it be from third parties or shareholders." The trial court also concluded in response to the second inquiry in the Supreme Court's May 2 order, that "[a]lthough the facts, . . . do not appear to be sufficient to prove that Mesa's principle objective is to be bought off at a substantial premium, they do justify a reasonable inference to the same effect."

As to the third and fourth questions posed by this Court, the Vice Chancellor stated that they "appear to raise the more fundamental issue of whether directors owe fiduciary duties to shareholders who they perceive to be acting contrary to the best interests of the corporation as a whole." While determining that the directors' decision to oppose Mesa's tender offer was made in a good faith belief that the Mesa proposal was inadequate, the court stated that the business judgment rule does not apply to a selective exchange offer such as this.

On May 13, 1985 the Court of Chancery certified this interlocutory appeal to us as a question of first impression, and we accepted it on May 14. The entire matter was scheduled on an expedited basis.

II.

The issues we address involve these fundamental questions: Did the Unocal board have the power and duty to oppose a takeover threat it reasonably perceived to be harmful to the corporate enterprise, and if so, is its action here entitled to the protection of the business judgment rule?

Mesa contends that the discriminatory exchange offer violates the fiduciary duties Unocal owes it. Mesa argues that because of the Mesa exclusion the business judgment rule is inapplicable, because the directors by tendering their own shares will derive a financial benefit that is not available to all Unocal stockholders. Thus, it is Mesa's ultimate contention that Unocal cannot establish that the exchange offer is fair to all shareholders, and argues that the Court of Chancery was correct in concluding that Unocal was unable to meet this burden.

Unocal answers that it does not owe a duty of "fairness" to Mesa, given the facts here. Specifically, Unocal contends that its board of directors reasonably and in good faith concluded that Mesa's $54 two-tier tender offer was coercive and inadequate, and that Mesa sought selective treatment for itself. Furthermore, Unocal argues that the board's approval of the exchange offer was made in good faith, on an informed basis, and in the exercise of due care. Under these circumstances, Unocal contends that its directors properly employed this device to protect the company and its stockholders from Mesa's harmful tactics.

III.

We begin with the basic issue of the power of a board of directors of a Delaware corporation to adopt a defensive measure of this type. Absent such authority, all other questions are moot. Neither issues of fairness nor business judgment are pertinent without the basic underpinning of a board's legal power to act.

The board has a large reservoir of authority upon which to draw. Its duties and responsibilities proceed from the inherent powers conferred by 8 Del. C. §141(a), respecting management of the corporation's "business and affairs." Additionally, the powers here being exercised derive from 8 Del. C. §160(a), conferring broad authority upon a corporation to deal in its own stock. From this it is now well established that in the acquisition of its shares a Delaware corporation may deal selectively with its stockholders, provided the directors have not acted out of a sole or primary purpose to entrench themselves in office.

Finally, the board's power to act derives from its fundamental duty and obligation to protect the corporate enterprise, which includes stockholders, from harm reasonably perceived, irrespective of its source. Thus, we are satisfied that in the broad context of corporate governance, including issues of fundamental corporate change, a board of directors is not a passive instrumentality.

Given the foregoing principles, we turn to the standards by which director action is to be measured. In *Pogostin v. Rice*, Del. Supr., 480 A.2d 619 (1984), we held that the business judgment rule, including the standards by which director conduct is judged, is applicable in the context of a takeover. Id. at 627. The business judgment rule is a "presumption that in making a business decision the directors of a corporation acted on an informed basis, in good faith and in the honest belief that the action taken was in the best interests of the company." *Aronson v. Lewis*, Del. Supr., 473 A.2d 805, 812 (1984) (citations omitted). A hallmark of the business judgment rule is that a court will not substitute its judgment for that of the board if the latter's decision can be "attributed to any rational business purpose." *Sinclair Oil Corp. v. Levien*, Del. Supr., 280 A.2d 717, 720 (1971).

When a board addresses a pending takeover bid it has an obligation to determine whether the offer is in the best interests of the corporation and its shareholders. In that respect a board's duty is no different from any other responsibility it shoulders, and its decisions should be no less entitled to the respect they otherwise would be accorded in the realm of business judgment. There are, however, certain caveats to a proper exercise of this function. Because of the omnipresent specter that a board may be acting primarily in its own interests, rather than those of the corporation and its shareholders, there is an enhanced duty which calls for judicial examination at the threshold before the protections of the business judgment rule may be conferred.

This Court has long recognized that:

> We must bear in mind the inherent danger in the purchase of shares with corporate funds to remove a threat to corporate policy when a threat to control is involved. The directors are of necessity confronted with a conflict of interest, and an objective decision is difficult.

Bennett v. Propp, Del. Supr., 187 A.2d 405, 409 (1962). In the face of this inherent conflict directors must show that they had reasonable grounds for believing that a danger to corporate policy and effectiveness existed because of another person's stock ownership. *Cheff v. Mathes*, 199 A.2d at 554-55. However, they satisfy that burden "by showing good faith and reasonable investigation. . . ." Id. at 555. Furthermore, such proof is materially enhanced, as here, by the approval of a board comprised of a majority of outside independent directors who have acted in accordance with the foregoing standards.

IV.

A.

In the board's exercise of corporate power to forestall a takeover bid our analysis begins with the basic principle that corporate directors have a fiduciary duty to act in the best interests of the corporation's stockholders. *Guth v. Loft, Inc.*, Del. Supr., 5 A.2d 503, 510 (1939). As we have noted, their duty of care extends to protecting the corporation and its owners from perceived harm whether a threat originates from third parties or other shareholders. But such powers are not absolute. A corporation does not have unbridled discretion to defeat any perceived threat by any Draconian means available.

The restriction placed upon a selective stock repurchase is that the directors may not have acted solely or primarily out of a desire to perpetuate themselves in office. *See Cheff v. Mathes*, 199 A.2d at 556; *Kors v. Carey*, 158 A.2d at 140. Of course, to this is added the further caveat that inequitable action may not be taken under the guise of law. *Schnell v. Chris-Craft Industries, Inc.*, Del. Supr., 285 A.2d 437, 439 (1971). The standard of proof established in *Cheff v. Mathes* . . . is designed to ensure that a defensive measure to thwart or impede a takeover is indeed motivated by a good faith concern for the welfare of the corporation and its stockholders, which in all circumstances must be free of any fraud or other misconduct. *Cheff v. Mathes*, 199 A.2d at 554-55. However, this does not end the inquiry.

B.

A further aspect is the element of balance. If a defensive measure is to come within the ambit of the business judgment rule, it must be reasonable in relation to the threat posed. This entails an analysis by the directors of the nature of the takeover bid and its effect on the corporate enterprise. Examples of such concerns may include: inadequacy of the price offered, nature and timing of the offer, questions of illegality, the impact on "constituencies" other than shareholders (i.e., creditors, customers, employees, and perhaps even the community generally), the risk of nonconsummation, and the quality of securities being offered in the exchange. While not a controlling factor, it also seems to us that a board may reasonably consider the basic stockholder interests at stake, including those of short term speculators, whose actions may have fueled the coercive aspect of the offer at the expense of the long term investor.[10] Here, the threat posed was viewed by the Unocal board as a grossly inadequate two-tier coercive tender offer coupled with the threat of greenmail.

Specifically, the Unocal directors had concluded that the value of Unocal was substantially above the $54 per share offered in cash at the front end. Furthermore, they determined that the subordinated securities to be exchanged in Mesa's announced squeeze out of the remaining shareholders in the "back-end" merger were "junk bonds" worth far less than $54. It is now well recognized that such offers are a classic coercive measure designed to stampede shareholders into tendering at the first tier, even if the price is inadequate, out of fear of what they will receive at the back end of the transaction. Wholly beyond the coercive aspect of an inadequate two-tier tender offer, the threat was posed by a corporate raider with a national reputation as a "greenmailer."[11]

In adopting the selective exchange offer, the board stated that its objective was either to defeat the inadequate Mesa offer or, should the offer still succeed, provide the 49% of its stockholders, who would otherwise be forced to accept "junk bonds," with $72 worth of senior debt. We find that both purposes are valid.

However, such efforts would have been thwarted by Mesa's participation in the exchange offer. First, if Mesa could tender its shares, Unocal would effectively be subsidizing the former's continuing effort to buy Unocal stock at $54 per share. Second, Mesa could not, by definition, fit within the class of shareholders being protected from its own coercive and inadequate tender offer.

---

10. [FN 11] There has been much debate respecting such stockholder interests. One rather impressive study indicates that the stock of over 50 percent of target companies, who resisted hostile takeovers, later traded at higher market prices than the rejected offer price, or were acquired after the tender offer was defeated by another company at a price higher than the offer price. Moreover, an update by Kidder Peabody & Company of this study, involving the stock prices of target companies that have defeated hostile tender offers during the period from 1973 to 1982 demonstrates that in a majority of cases the target's shareholders benefited from the defeat. The stock of 81% of the targets studied has, since the tender offer, sold at prices higher than the tender offer price. When adjusted for the time value of money, the figure is 64%. The thesis being that this strongly supports application of the business judgment rule in response to takeover threats....

11. [FN 13] The term "greenmail" refers to the practice of buying out a takeover bidder's stock at a premium that is not available to other shareholders in order to prevent the takeover. The Chancery Court noted that "Mesa has made tremendous profits from its takeover activities although in the past few years it has not been successful in acquiring any of the target companies on an unfriendly basis." Moreover, the trial court specifically found that the actions of the Unocal board were taken in good faith to eliminate both the inadequacies of the tender offer and to forestall the payment of "greenmail."

Thus, we are satisfied that the selective exchange offer is reasonably related to the threats posed. It is consistent with the principle that "the minority stockholder shall receive the substantial equivalent in value of what he had before." *Sterling v. Mayflower Hotel Corp.*, Del. Supr., 93 A.2d 107, 114 (1952). This concept of fairness, while stated in the merger context, is also relevant in the area of tender offer law. Thus, the board's decision to offer what it determined to be the fair value of the corporation to the 49% of its shareholders, who would otherwise be forced to accept highly subordinated "junk bonds," is reasonable and consistent with the directors' duty to ensure that the minority stockholders receive equal value for their shares.

V.

Mesa contends that it is unlawful, and the trial court agreed, for a corporation to discriminate in this fashion against one shareholder. It argues correctly that no case has ever sanctioned a device that precludes a raider from sharing in a benefit available to all other stockholders. However, as we have noted earlier, the principle of selective stock repurchases by a Delaware corporation is neither unknown nor unauthorized. The only difference is that heretofore the approved transaction was the payment of "greenmail" to a raider or dissident posing a threat to the corporate enterprise. All other stockholders were denied such favored treatment, and given Mesa's past history of greenmail, its claims here are rather ironic.

However, our corporate law is not static. It must grow and develop in response to, indeed in anticipation of, evolving concepts and needs. Merely because the General Corporation Law is silent as to a specific matter does not mean that it is prohibited. See *Providence and Worcester Co. v. Baker*, Del. Supr., 378 A.2d 121, 123-124 (1977). In the days when *Cheff*, *Bennett*, *Martin* and *Kors* were decided, the tender offer, while not an unknown device, was virtually unused, and little was known of such methods as two-tier "front-end" loaded offers with their coercive effects. Then, the favored attack of a raider was stock acquisition followed by a proxy contest. Various defensive tactics, which provided no benefit whatever to the raider, evolved. Thus, the use of corporate funds by management to counter a proxy battle was approved. Litigation, supported by corporate funds, aimed at the raider has long been a popular device.

More recently, as the sophistication of both raiders and targets has developed, a host of other defensive measures to counter such ever mounting threats has evolved and received judicial sanction. These include defensive charter amendments and other devices bearing some rather exotic, but apt, names: Crown Jewel, White Knight, Pac Man, and Golden Parachute. Each has highly selective features, the object of which is to deter or defeat the raider.

Thus, while the exchange offer is a form of selective treatment, given the nature of the threat posed here the response is neither unlawful nor unreasonable. If the board of directors is disinterested, has acted in good faith and with due care, its decision in the absence of an abuse of discretion will be upheld as a proper exercise of business judgment.

To this Mesa responds that the board is not disinterested, because the directors are receiving a benefit from the tender of their own shares, which because of the Mesa exclusion, does not devolve upon all stockholders equally. See *Aronson v. Lewis*, Del. Supr., 473 A.2d 805, 812 (1984). However, Mesa concedes that if the exclusion is valid, then the directors and all other stockholders share the same benefit. The answer of course is that the exclusion is valid, and the directors' participation in the exchange offer does not rise to the level of a disqualifying interest. . . .

Nor does this become an "interested" director transaction merely because certain board members are large stockholders. As this Court has previously noted, that fact alone does not create a disqualifying "personal pecuniary interest" to defeat the operation of the business judgment rule. *Cheff v. Mathes*, 199 A.2d at 554.

Mesa also argues that the exclusion permits the directors to abdicate the fiduciary duties they owe it. However, that is not so. The board continues to owe Mesa the duties of due care and loyalty. But in the face of the destructive threat Mesa's tender offer was perceived to pose, the board had a supervening duty to protect the corporate enterprise, which includes the other shareholders, from threatened harm.

Mesa contends that the basis of this action is punitive, and solely in response to the exercise of its rights of corporate democracy. Nothing precludes Mesa, as a stockholder, from acting in its own self-interest. However, Mesa, while pursuing its own interests, has acted in a manner which a board consisting of a majority of independent directors has reasonably determined to be contrary to the best interests of Unocal and its other shareholders. In this situation, there is no support in Delaware law for the proposition that, when responding to a perceived harm, a corporation must guarantee a benefit to a stockholder who is deliberately provoking the danger being addressed. There is no obligation of self-sacrifice by a corporation and its shareholders in the face of such a challenge.

Here, the Court of Chancery specifically found that the "directors' decision [to oppose the Mesa tender offer] was made in the good faith belief that the Mesa tender offer is inadequate." Given our standard of review under *Levitt v. Bouvier*, Del. Supr., 287 A.2d 671, 673 (1972), and *Application of Delaware Racing Association*, Del. Supr., 213 A.2d 203, 207 (1965), we are satisfied that Unocal's board has met its burden of proof. *Cheff v. Mathes*, 199 A.2d at 555.

VI.

In conclusion, there was directorial power to oppose the Mesa tender offer, and to undertake a selective stock exchange made in good faith and upon a reasonable investigation pursuant to a clear duty to protect the corporate enterprise. Further, the selective stock repurchase plan chosen by Unocal is reasonable in relation to the threat that the board rationally and reasonably believed was posed by Mesa's inadequate and coercive two-tier tender offer. Under those circumstances the board's action is entitled to be measured by the standards of the business judgment rule. Thus, unless it is shown by a preponderance of the evidence that the directors' decisions were primarily based on perpetuating themselves in office, or some other breach of fiduciary duty such as fraud, over-reaching, lack of good faith, or being uninformed, a Court will not substitute its judgment for that of the board.

In this case that protection is not lost merely because Unocal's directors have tendered their shares in the exchange offer. Given the validity of the Mesa exclusion, they are receiving a benefit shared generally by all other stockholders except Mesa. In this circumstance the test of *Aronson v. Lewis*, 473 A.2d at 812, is satisfied. See also *Cheff v. Mathes*, 199 A.2d at 554. If the stockholders are displeased with the action of their elected representatives, the powers of corporate democracy are at their disposal to turn the board out. *Aronson v. Lewis*, Del. Supr., 473 A.2d 805, 811 (1984). See also 8 Del. C. §§141(k) and 211(b).

With the Court of Chancery's findings that the exchange offer was based on the board's good faith belief that the Mesa offer was inadequate, that the board's action was informed and taken with due care, that Mesa's prior activities justify a reasonable inference that its principle objective was greenmail, and implicitly, that the substance of the offer itself was reasonable and fair to the corporation and its stockholders if Mesa were included, we cannot say that the Unocal directors have acted in such a manner as to have passed an "unintelligent and unadvised judgment." *Mitchell v. Highland-Western Glass Co.*, Del. Ch., 167 A. 831, 833 (1933). The decision of the Court of Chancery is therefore REVERSED, and the preliminary injunction is VACATED.

Questions

1. What did Mesa offer Unocal shareholders in the tender offer?
2. How did Unocal respond?
3. What test applies to determine the validity of a board decision to implement a takeover defense in response to a takeover attempt?
4. Why isn't the decision simply reviewed under the business judgment rule?
5. Did the court uphold the decision of Unocal's board? Why?
6. What is greenmail? What does it have to do with this case?

In 1986, the SEC amended Rule 13e-4(f)(8)(i) under the Exchange Act to provide that an issuer tender offer must be open to all security holders. This is known as the "all-holders" rule and would have prevented Unocal from excluding Mesa from its self-tender offer, had it been in effect. At the same time, the SEC also adopted Rule 14d-10, which includes an all-holders rule applicable to non-issuer tender offers.

A corporation's board is generally allowed to "just say no" in the face of take-over overtures, even if a bidder or bidders have offered a substantial premium over the current market value of the target's stock. Of course, the board has to believe, after deliberation, that saying no is in the best interest of the corporation, and any defensive measures it implements to ward off the bidders have to pass muster under *Unocal*.

If, however, the board decides to sell the company and multiple buyers express interest, it may be prohibited from favoring one buyer over another, as established by the next case.

Revlon, Inc. v. MacAndrews
506 A.2d 173 (Del. 1985)

MOORE, Justice.

In this battle for corporate control of Revlon, Inc. (Revlon), the Court of Chancery enjoined certain transactions designed to thwart the efforts of Pantry Pride, Inc. (Pantry Pride) to acquire Revlon. The defendants are Revlon, its board of directors, and Forstmann Little & Co. and the latter's affiliated limited partnership (collectively, Forstmann). The injunction barred consummation of an option granted Forstmann to purchase certain Revlon assets (the lock-up option), a promise by Revlon to deal exclusively with Forstmann in the face of a takeover (the no-shop provision), and the payment of a $25 million cancellation fee to Forstmann if the transaction was aborted. The Court of Chancery found that the Revlon directors had breached their duty of care by entering into the foregoing transactions and effectively ending an active auction for the company. The trial court ruled that such arrangements are not illegal per se under Delaware law, but that their use under the circumstances here was impermissible. We agree. *See MacAndrews & Forbes Holdings, Inc. v. Revlon, Inc.*, Del. Ch., 501 A.2d 1239 (1985). Thus, we granted this expedited interlocutory appeal to consider for the first time the validity of such defensive measures in the face of an active bidding contest for corporate control. Additionally, we address for the first time the extent to which a corporation may consider the impact of a takeover threat on constituencies other than shareholders. *See Unocal Corp. v. Mesa Petroleum Co.*, Del. Supr., 493 A.2d 946, 955 (1985).

In our view, lock-ups and related agreements are permitted under Delaware law where their adoption is untainted by director interest or other breaches of fiduciary duty. The actions taken by the Revlon directors, however, did not meet this standard. Moreover, while concern for various corporate constituencies is proper when addressing a takeover threat, that principle is limited by the requirement that there be some rationally related benefit accruing to the stockholders. We find no such benefit here.

Thus, under all the circumstances we must agree with the Court of Chancery that the enjoined Revlon defensive measures were inconsistent with the directors' duties to the stockholders. Accordingly, we affirm.

I.

The somewhat complex maneuvers of the parties necessitate a rather detailed examination of the facts. The prelude to this controversy began in June 1985, when Ronald O. Perelman, chairman of the board and chief executive officer of Pantry Pride, met with his counterpart at Revlon, Michel C. Bergerac, to discuss a friendly acquisition of Revlon by Pantry Pride. Perelman suggested a price in the range of $40-50 per share, but the meeting ended with Bergerac dismissing those figures as considerably below Revlon's intrinsic value. All subsequent Pantry Pride overtures were rebuffed, perhaps in part based on Mr. Bergerac's strong personal antipathy to Mr. Perelman.

Thus, on August 14, Pantry Pride's board authorized Perelman to acquire Revlon, either through negotiation in the $42-$43 per share range, or by making a hostile tender offer at $45. Perelman then met with Bergerac and outlined Pantry Pride's alternate approaches. Bergerac remained adamantly opposed to such schemes and conditioned any further discussions of the matter on Pantry Pride executing a standstill agreement prohibiting it from acquiring Revlon without the latter's prior approval.

On August 19, the Revlon board met specially to consider the impending threat of a hostile bid by Pantry Pride. At the meeting, Lazard Freres, Revlon's investment banker, advised the directors that $45 per share was a grossly inadequate price for the company. Felix Rohatyn and William Loomis of Lazard Freres explained to the board that Pantry Pride's financial strategy for acquiring Revlon would be through "junk bond" financing followed by a break-up of Revlon and the disposition of its assets. With proper timing, according to the experts, such transactions could produce a return to Pantry Pride of $60 to $70 per share, while a sale of the company as a whole would be in the "mid 50" dollar range. Martin Lipton, special counsel for Revlon, recommended two defensive measures: first, that the company repurchase up to 5 million of its nearly 30 million outstanding shares; and second, that it adopt a Note Purchase Rights Plan. Under this plan, each Revlon shareholder would receive as a dividend one Note Purchase Right (the Rights) for each share of common stock, with the Rights entitling the holder to exchange one common share for a $65 principal Revlon note at 12% interest with a one-year maturity. The Rights would become effective whenever anyone acquired beneficial ownership of 20% or more of Revlon's shares, unless the purchaser acquired all the company's stock for cash at $65 or more per share. In addition, the Rights would not be available to the acquiror, and prior to the 20% triggering event the Revlon board could redeem the rights for 10 cents each. Both proposals were unanimously adopted.

Pantry Pride made its first hostile move on August 23 with a cash tender offer for any and all shares of Revlon at $47.50 per common share and $26.67 per preferred share, subject to (1) Pantry Pride's obtaining financing for the purchase, and (2) the Rights being redeemed, rescinded or voided.

The Revlon board met again on August 26. The directors advised the stockholders to reject the offer. Further defensive measures also were planned. On

August 29, Revlon commenced its own offer for up to 10 million shares, exchanging for each share of common stock tendered one Senior Subordinated Note (the Notes) of $47.50 principal at 11.75% interest, due 1995, and one-tenth of a share of $9.00 Cumulative Convertible Exchangeable Preferred Stock valued at $100 per share. Lazard Freres opined that the notes would trade at their face value on a fully distributed basis. Revlon stockholders tendered 87 percent of the outstanding shares (approximately 33 million), and the company accepted the full 10 million shares on a pro rata basis. The new Notes contained covenants which limited Revlon's ability to incur additional debt, sell assets, or pay dividends unless otherwise approved by the "independent" (non-management) members of the board.

At this point, both the Rights and the Note covenants stymied Pantry Pride's attempted takeover. The next move came on September 16, when Pantry Pride announced a new tender offer at $42 per share, conditioned upon receiving at least 90% of the outstanding stock. Pantry Pride also indicated that it would consider buying less than 90%, and at an increased price, if Revlon removed the impeding Rights. While this offer was lower on its face than the earlier $47.50 proposal, Revlon's investment banker, Lazard Freres, described the two bids as essentially equal in view of the completed exchange offer.

The Revlon board held a regularly scheduled meeting on September 24. The directors rejected the latest Pantry Pride offer and authorized management to negotiate with other parties interested in acquiring Revlon. Pantry Pride remained determined in its efforts and continued to make cash bids for the company, offering $50 per share on September 27, and raising its bid to $53 on October 1, and then to $56.25 on October 7.

In the meantime, Revlon's negotiations with Forstmann and the investment group Adler & Shaykin had produced results. The Revlon directors met on October 3 to consider Pantry Pride's $53 bid and to examine possible alternatives to the offer. Both Forstmann and Adler & Shaykin made certain proposals to the board. As a result, the directors unanimously agreed to a leveraged buyout by Forstmann. The terms of this accord were as follows: each stockholder would get $56 cash per share; management would purchase stock in the new company by the exercise of their Revlon "golden parachutes"; Forstmann would assume Revlon's $475 million debt incurred by the issuance of the Notes; and Revlon would redeem the Rights and waive the Notes covenants for Forstmann or in connection with any other offer superior to Forstmann's. The board did not actually remove the covenants at the October 3 meeting, because Forstmann then lacked a firm commitment on its financing, but accepted the Forstmann capital structure, and indicated that the outside directors would waive the covenants in due course. Part of Forstmann's plan was to sell Revlon's Norcliff Thayer and Reheis divisions to American Home Products for $335 million. Before the merger, Revlon was to sell its cosmetics and fragrance division to Adler & Shaykin for $905 million. These transactions would facilitate the purchase by Forstmann or any other acquiror of Revlon.

When the merger, and thus the waiver of the Notes covenants, was announced, the market value of these securities began to fall. The Notes, which originally traded near par, around 100, dropped to 87.50 by October 8. One director later reported (at the October 12 meeting) a "deluge" of telephone calls from irate noteholders, and on October 10 the Wall Street Journal reported threats of litigation by these creditors.

Pantry Pride countered with a new proposal on October 7, raising its $53 offer to $56.25, subject to nullification of the Rights, a waiver of the Notes covenants, and the election of three Pantry Pride directors to the Revlon board. On October 9, representatives of Pantry Pride, Forstmann and Revlon conferred in an attempt to negotiate the fate of Revlon, but could not reach agreement. At this meeting Pantry Pride announced that it would engage in fractional bidding and top any Forstmann offer by a slightly higher one. It is also significant that Forstmann, to Pantry Pride's exclusion, had been made privy to certain Revlon financial data. Thus, the parties were not negotiating on equal terms.

Again privately armed with Revlon data, Forstmann met on October 11 with Revlon's special counsel and investment banker. On October 12, Forstmann made a new $57.25 per share offer, based on several conditions. The principal demand was a lock-up option to purchase Revlon's Vision Care and National Health Laboratories divisions for $525 million, some $100-$175 million below the value ascribed to them by Lazard Freres, if another acquiror got 40% of Revlon's shares. Revlon also was required to accept a no-shop provision. The Rights and Notes covenants had to be removed as in the October 3 agreement. There would be a $25 million cancellation fee to be placed in escrow, and released to Forstmann if the new agreement terminated or if another acquiror got more than 19.9% of Revlon's stock. Finally, there would be no participation by Revlon management in the merger. In return, Forstmann agreed to support the par value of the Notes, which had faltered in the market, by an exchange of new notes. Forstmann also demanded immediate acceptance of its offer, or it would be withdrawn. The board unanimously approved Forstmann's proposal because: (1) it was for a higher price than the Pantry Pride bid, (2) it protected the noteholders, and (3) Forstmann's financing was firmly in place. The board further agreed to redeem the rights and waive the covenants on the preferred stock in response to any offer above $57 cash per share. The covenants were waived, contingent upon receipt of an investment banking opinion that the Notes would trade near par value once the offer was consummated.

Pantry Pride, which had initially sought injunctive relief from the Rights plan on August 22, filed an amended complaint on October 14 challenging the lock-up, the cancellation fee, and the exercise of the Rights and the Notes covenants. Pantry Pride also sought a temporary restraining order to prevent Revlon from placing any assets in escrow or transferring them to Forstmann. Moreover, on October 22, Pantry Pride again raised its bid, with a cash offer of $58 per share conditioned upon nullification of the Rights, waiver of the covenants, and an injunction of the Forstmann lock-up.

On October 15, the Court of Chancery prohibited the further transfer of assets, and eight days later enjoined the lock-up, no-shop, and cancellation fee provisions of the agreement. The trial court concluded that the Revlon directors had breached their duty of loyalty by making concessions to Forstmann, out of concern for their liability to the noteholders, rather than maximizing the sale price of the company for the stockholders' benefit.

II.

Preliminary injunction RULE

To obtain a preliminary injunction, a plaintiff must demonstrate both a reasonable probability of success on the merits and some irreparable harm which will occur absent the injunction. Additionally, the Court shall balance the conveniences of and possible injuries to the parties.

A.

We turn first to Pantry Pride's probability of success on the merits. The ultimate responsibility for managing the business and affairs of a corporation falls on its board of directors. In discharging this function the directors owe fiduciary duties of care and loyalty to the corporation and its shareholders. These principles apply with equal force when a board approves a corporate merger pursuant to 8 Del. C. §251(b); and of course they are the bedrock of our law regarding corporate takeover issues. While the business judgment rule may be applicable to the actions of corporate directors responding to takeover threats, the principles upon which it is founded—care, loyalty and independence—must first be satisfied.

BJR RULE

If the business judgment rule applies, there is a "presumption that in making a business decision the directors of a corporation acted on an informed basis, in good faith and in the honest belief that the action taken was in the best interests of the company." *Aronson v. Lewis*, 473 A.2d 805, 812 (1984). However, when a board implements anti-takeover measures there arises "the omnipresent specter that a board may be acting primarily in its own interests, rather than those of the corporation and its shareholders . . .". *Unocal Corp. v. Mesa Petroleum Co.*, 493 A.2d at 954. This potential for conflict places upon the directors the burden of proving that they had reasonable grounds for believing there was a danger to corporate policy and effectiveness, a burden satisfied by a showing of good faith and reasonable investigation. *Id.* at 955. In addition, the directors must analyze the nature of the takeover and its effect on the corporation in order to ensure balance—that the responsive action taken is reasonable in relation to the threat posed. *Id.*

B.

#1

The first relevant defensive measure adopted by the Revlon board was the Rights Plan which would be considered a "poison pill" in the current language of corporate takeovers—a plan by which shareholders receive the right to be bought out by the corporation at a substantial premium on the occurrence of a stated triggering event. By 8 Del. C. §§141 and 122(13), the board clearly had the power to adopt the measure. Thus, the focus becomes one of reasonableness and purpose.

The Revlon board approved the Rights Plan in the face of an impending hostile takeover bid by Pantry Pride at $45 per share, a price which Revlon reasonably concluded was grossly inadequate. Lazard Freres had so advised the directors, and had also informed them that Pantry Pride was a small, highly leveraged company bent on a "bust-up" takeover by using "junk bond" financing to buy Revlon cheaply, sell the acquired assets to pay the debts incurred, and retain the profit for itself. In adopting the Plan, the board protected the shareholders from a hostile takeover at a price below the company's intrinsic value, while retaining sufficient flexibility to address any proposal deemed to be in the stockholders' best interests.

To that extent the board acted in good faith and upon reasonable investigation. Under the circumstances it cannot be said that the Rights Plan as employed was unreasonable, considering the threat posed. Indeed, the Plan was a factor in causing Pantry Pride to raise its bids from a low of $42 to an eventual high of $58. At the time of its adoption the Rights Plan afforded a measure of protection consistent with the directors' fiduciary duty in facing a takeover threat perceived as detrimental to corporate interests. Far from being a "showstopper," . . . the measure spurred the bidding to new heights, a proper result of its implementation.

Although we consider adoption of the Plan to have been valid under the circumstances, its continued usefulness was rendered moot by the directors' actions on October 3 and October 12. At the October 3 meeting the board redeemed the Rights conditioned upon consummation of a merger with Forstmann, but further acknowledged that they would also be redeemed to facilitate any more favorable offer. On October 12, the board unanimously passed a resolution redeeming the Rights in connection with any cash proposal of $57.25 or more per share. Because all the pertinent offers eventually equalled or surpassed that amount, the Rights clearly were no longer any impediment in the contest for Revlon. This mooted any question of their propriety under *Moran* or *Unocal*.

C.

The second defensive measure adopted by Revlon to thwart a Pantry Pride #2 takeover was the company's own exchange offer for 10 million of its shares. The directors' general broad powers to manage the business and affairs of the corporation are augmented by the specific authority conferred under 8 Del. C. §160(a), permitting the company to deal in its own stock. However, when exercising that power in an effort to forestall a hostile takeover, the board's actions are strictly held to the fiduciary standards outlined in *Unocal*. These standards require the directors to determine the best interests of the corporation and its stockholders, and impose an enhanced duty to abjure any action that is motivated by considerations other than a good faith concern for such interests.

The Revlon directors concluded that Pantry Pride's $47.50 offer was grossly inadequate. In that regard the board acted in good faith, and on an informed basis, with reasonable grounds to believe that there existed a harmful threat to the corporate enterprise. The adoption of a defensive measure, reasonable in relation to the threat posed, was proper and fully accorded with the powers, duties, and responsibilities conferred upon directors under our law.

D.

when it all went south

However, when Pantry Pride increased its offer to $50 per share, and then to $53, it became apparent to all that the break-up of the company was inevitable. The Revlon board's authorization permitting management to negotiate a merger or buyout with a third party was a recognition that the company was for sale. The duty of the board had thus changed from the preservation of Revlon as a corporate entity to the maximization of the company's value at a sale for the stockholders' benefit. This significantly altered the board's responsibilities under the *Unocal* standards. It no longer faced threats to corporate policy and effectiveness, or to the stockholders' interests, from a grossly inadequate bid. The whole question of defensive measures became moot. The directors' role changed from defenders of the corporate bastion to auctioneers charged with getting the best price for the stockholders at a sale of the company.

III.

This brings us to the lock-up with Forstmann and its emphasis on shoring up the sagging market value of the Notes in the face of threatened litigation by their holders. Such a focus was inconsistent with the changed concept of the directors' responsibilities at this stage of the developments. The impending waiver of the Notes covenants had caused the value of the Notes to fall, and the board was aware of the noteholders' ire as well as their subsequent threats of suit. The directors thus made support of the Notes an integral part of the company's dealings with Forstmann, even though their primary responsibility at this stage was to the equity owners.

The original threat posed by Pantry Pride—the break-up of the company— had become a reality which even the directors embraced. Selective dealing to fend off a hostile but determined bidder was no longer a proper objective. Instead, obtaining the highest price for the benefit of the stockholders should have been the central theme guiding director action. Thus, the Revlon board could not make the requisite showing of good faith by preferring the noteholders and ignoring its duty of loyalty to the shareholders. The rights of the former already were fixed by contract. The noteholders required no further protection, and when the Revlon board entered into an auction-ending lock-up agreement with Forstmann on the basis of impermissible considerations at the expense of the shareholders, the directors breached their primary duty of loyalty.

Revlon Breach of duty

The Revlon board argued that it acted in good faith in protecting the noteholders because *Unocal* permits consideration of other corporate constituencies.

Although such considerations may be permissible, there are fundamental limitations upon that prerogative. A board may have regard for various constituencies in discharging its responsibilities, provided there are rationally related benefits accruing to the stockholders. However, such concern for non-stockholder interests is inappropriate when an auction among active bidders is in progress, and the object no longer is to protect or maintain the corporate enterprise but to sell it to the highest bidder.

Revlon also contended that by *Gilbert v. El Paso Co.*, Del. Ch., 490 A.2d 1050, 1054-55 (1984), it had contractual and good faith obligations to consider the noteholders. However, any such duties are limited to the principle that one may not interfere with contractual relationships by improper actions. Here, the rights of the noteholders were fixed by agreement, and there is nothing of substance to suggest that any of those terms were violated. The Notes covenants specifically contemplated a waiver to permit sale of the company at a fair price. The Notes were accepted by the holders on that basis, including the risk of an adverse market effect stemming from a waiver. Thus, nothing remained for Revlon to legitimately protect, and no rationally related benefit thereby accrued to the stockholders. Under such circumstances we must conclude that the merger agreement with Forstmann was unreasonable in relation to the threat posed.

A lock-up is not per se illegal under Delaware law. Its use has been approved in an earlier case. *Thompson v. Enstar Corp.*, Del. Ch., [509] A.2d [822] (1984). Such options can entice other bidders to enter a contest for control of the corporation, creating an auction for the company and maximizing shareholder profit. Current economic conditions in the takeover market are such that a "white knight" like Forstmann might only enter the bidding for the target company if it receives some form of compensation to cover the risks and costs involved. However, while those lock-ups which draw bidders into the battle benefit shareholders, similar measures which end an active auction and foreclose further bidding operate to the shareholders' detriment. . . .

The Forstmann option had a . . . destructive effect on the auction process. Forstmann had already been drawn into the contest on a preferred basis, so the result of the lock-up was not to foster bidding, but to destroy it. The board's stated reasons for approving the transactions were: (1) better financing, (2) noteholder protection, and (3) higher price. As the Court of Chancery found, and we agree, any distinctions between the rival bidders' methods of financing the proposal were nominal at best, and such a consideration has little or no significance in a cash offer for any and all shares. The principal object, contrary to the board's duty of care, appears to have been protection of the noteholders over the shareholders' interests.

While Forstmann's $57.25 offer was objectively higher than Pantry Pride's $56.25 bid, the margin of superiority is less when the Forstmann price is adjusted for the time value of money. In reality, the Revlon board ended the auction in return for very little actual improvement in the final bid. The principal benefit went to the directors, who avoided personal liability to a class of creditors to whom the board owed no further duty under the circumstances. Thus, when a board ends an intense bidding contest on an insubstantial basis, and where a significant by-product of that action is to protect the directors against a perceived threat of personal liability for consequences stemming from the adoption of previous defensive measures, the action cannot withstand the enhanced scrutiny which *Unocal* requires of director conduct.

In addition to the lock-up option, the Court of Chancery enjoined the no-shop provision as part of the attempt to foreclose further bidding by Pantry Pride. The no-shop provision, like the lock-up option, while not per se illegal, is impermissible under the *Unocal* standards when a board's primary duty becomes that of an auctioneer responsible for selling the company to the highest bidder. The agreement to negotiate only with Forstmann ended rather than intensified the board's involvement in the bidding contest.

It is ironic that the parties even considered a no-shop agreement when Revlon had dealt preferentially, and almost exclusively, with Forstmann throughout the contest. After the directors authorized management to negotiate with other parties, Forstmann was given every negotiating advantage that Pantry Pride had been denied: cooperation from management, access to financial data, and the exclusive opportunity to present merger proposals directly to the board of directors. Favoritism for a white knight to the total exclusion of a hostile bidder might be justifiable when the latter's offer adversely affects shareholder interests, but when bidders make relatively similar offers, or dissolution of the company becomes inevitable, the directors cannot fulfill their enhanced *Unocal* duties by playing favorites with the contending factions. Market forces must be allowed to operate freely to bring the target's shareholders the best price available for their equity. Thus, as the trial court ruled, the shareholders' interests necessitated that the board remain free to negotiate in the fulfillment of that duty. . . .

IV.

Having concluded that Pantry Pride has shown a reasonable probability of success on the merits, we address the issue of irreparable harm. The Court of Chancery ruled that unless the lock-up and other aspects of the agreement were enjoined, Pantry Pride's opportunity to bid for Revlon was lost. The court also held that the need for both bidders to compete in the marketplace outweighed any injury to Forstmann. Given the complexity of the proposed transaction between Revlon and Forstmann, the obstacles to Pantry Pride obtaining a meaningful legal remedy are immense. We are satisfied that the plaintiff has shown the need for an injunction to protect it from irreparable harm, which need outweighs any harm to the defendants.

V.

In conclusion, the Revlon board was confronted with a situation not uncommon in the current wave of corporate takeovers. A hostile and determined bidder sought the company at a price the board was convinced was inadequate. The initial defensive tactics worked to the benefit of the shareholders, and thus the board was able to sustain its *Unocal* burdens in justifying those measures. However, in granting an asset option lock-up to Forstmann, we must conclude that under all the circumstances the directors allowed considerations other than the maximization of shareholder profit to affect their judgment, and followed a course that ended the auction for Revlon, absent court intervention, to the ultimate detriment of its shareholders. No such defensive measure can be sustained when it represents a breach of the directors' fundamental duty of care. In that context the board's action is not entitled to the deference accorded it by the business judgment rule. The measures were properly enjoined. The decision of the Court of Chancery, therefore, is

AFFIRMED.

Questions

1. What defenses did Revlon implement to ward off Pantry Pride?
2. What test applies to determine the validity of the Revlon board's decisions to implement these defenses?
3. What are *Revlon* duties? Why were they triggered here?
4. What did the Revlon board do wrong?
5. What is the policy behind *Revlon* duties?

A key question concerning *Revlon* is under what circumstances a board's role changes "from defenders of the corporate bastion to auctioneers charged with getting the best price for the stockholders at a sale of the company." In *Arnold v. Society for Savings Bancorp, Inc.*, the Delaware Supreme Court answered this question as follows:

> The directors of a corporation "have the obligation of acting reasonably to seek the transaction offering the best value reasonably available to the stockholders," *Paramount Communications, Inc. v. QVC Network, Inc.*, Del. Supr., 637 A.2d 34, 43 (1994), in at least the following three scenarios: (1) "when a corporation initiates an active bidding process seeking to sell itself or to effect a business reorganization involving a clear break-up of the company," *Paramount Communications, Inc. v. Time Inc.*, Del. Supr., 571 A.2d 1140, 1150 (1990); (2) "where, in response to a bidder's offer, a target abandons its long-term strategy and seeks an alternative transaction involving the break-up of the company," *id.*; or (3) when approval of a transaction results in a "sale or change of control," *QVC*, 637 A.2d at 42-43, 47. In the latter situation, there is no "sale or change in control" when "'[c]ontrol of both [companies] remain[s] in a large, fluid, changeable and changing market.'" *Id.* at 47.[12]

---

12. 650 A.2d 1270, 1289-90 (Del. 1994).

The effect of the last sentence of the above quote is that (3) does not apply if target is to be acquired for bidder *stock* by a bidder that does not have a controlling shareholder. In other words, a bidder without a controlling shareholder is controlled by "a large, fluid, changeable and changing market."

The word "stock" is emphasized because several Chancery Court opinions have stated that (3) applies and thus *Revlon* is triggered when target is acquired for cash even if bidder does not have a controlling shareholder. Below is an excerpt from one such opinion, *In re Smurfit-Stone Container Corp. Shareholder Litigation*,[13] which addresses whether *Revlon* applies to a deal where target is acquired for a mix of cash and bidder stock by a bidder without a controlling shareholder.

a. Business Judgment Rule or *Revlon*?

Under §141(a) of the Delaware General Corporation Law, a corporation's board of directors is empowered to manage the business and affairs of the corporation. The business judgment rule ("BJR"), a deferential standard of review, reflects the common law's recognition of §141(a). In short, it is a "presumption that in making a business decision the directors of a corporation acted on an informed basis, in good faith and in the honest belief that the action taken was in the best interests of the company." This standard of review is respectful to director prerogatives to manage the business of a corporation; in cases where it applies, courts must give "great deference" to directors' decisions and, as long as the Court can discern a rational business purpose for the decision, it must "not invalidate the decision . . . examine its reasonableness, [or] substitute [its] views for those of the board . . . ."[14]

In limited circumstances, however, the Delaware Supreme Court has imposed special obligations of reasonableness on boards of corporations who oversee the sale of control of their corporation. When a board leads its corporation into so-called *Revlon* territory, its subsequent actions will be reviewed by this Court not under the deferential BJR standard, but rather under the heightened standard of reasonableness. In addition, and as discussed in greater detail below, the Board's fiduciary obligations shift to obtaining the best value reasonably available to the target's stockholders.

While the differences between directors' obligations under business judgment and *Revlon* review are not insignificant, the standard of review is not necessarily outcome determinative. Nonetheless, "absent a limited set of circumstances as defined under *Revlon*, a board of directors, while always required to act in an informed manner, is not under any *per se* duty to maximize shareholder value in the short term. . . ."[15] Therefore, a question of much ongoing debate, and one to

---

13. 2011 WL 2028076, *11-*16 (Del. Ch. 2011) (unpublished).

14. [FN 84] *Paramount Commc'ns Inc. v. QVC Network Inc.*, 637 A.2d 34, 45 n.17 (Del. 1994) (internal quotation marks omitted); see also, e.g., *Liquid Audio, Inc.*, 813 A.2d at 1127-28; *Emerald P'rs*, 787 A.2d at 90-91.

15. [FN 88] *Paramount Commc'ns, Inc. v. Time Inc.*, 571 A.2d 1140, 1150 (Del. 1989); *Air Prods. & Chems., Inc. v. Airgas, Inc.*, 16 A.3d 48, 101-02 (Del. Ch. 2011) ("It is not until the board is under *Revlon* that its duty 'narrow[s]' to getting the best price reasonably available for stockholders in a sale of the company."). In *Lyondell*, for example, the Supreme Court held that "*Revlon* duties do not arise simply because a company is 'in play.'" *Lyondell Chem. Co. v. Ryan*, 970 A.2d 235, 244 (Del. 2009) ("The duty to seek the best available price

which the parties devoted much ink in this case, is *when* does a corporation enter *Revlon* mode such that its directors must act reasonably to maximize short-term value of the corporation for its stockholders.

The Delaware Supreme Court has determined that a board might find itself faced with such a duty in at least three scenarios: "(1) when a corporation initiates an active bidding process seeking to sell itself or to effect a business reorganization involving a clear break-up of the company[ ]; (2) where, in response to a bidder's offer, a target abandons its long-term strategy and seeks an alternative transaction involving the break-up of the company; or (3) when approval of a transaction results in a sale or change of control[.]"[16]

Here, Plaintiffs do not allege that the Board initiated an active bidding process to sell itself or effected a reorganization involving the break-up of [target]. Nor do they argue that the Board abandoned its long-term strategy in response to a bidder's offer and sought an alternative transaction involving the break-up of the Company. Rather, they allege that *Revlon* should apply to this case because the Merger Consideration was comprised of 50% cash and 50% stock at the time the parties entered into the Agreement, which qualifies the Proposed Transaction as a "change of control" transaction. A question remains, however, as to when a mixed stock and cash merger constitutes a change of control transaction for *Revlon* purposes.

On the one hand, pure stock-for-stock transactions do not necessarily trigger *Revlon*. If, for example, the resulting entity has a controlling stockholder or stockholder group such that the target's stockholders are relegated to minority status in the combined entity, Delaware Courts have found a change of control would occur for *Revlon* purposes. But, if ownership shifts from one large unaffiliated group of public stockholders to another, that alone does not amount to a change of control. In this event, the target's stockholders' voting power will not be diminished to minority status and they are not foreclosed from an opportunity to obtain a control premium in a future change of control transaction involving the resulting entity.

On the other hand, *Revlon* will govern a board's decision to sell a corporation where stockholders will receive cash for their shares. *Revlon* applies in the latter instance because, among other things, there is no tomorrow for the corporation's present stockholders, meaning that they will forever be shut out from future profits generated by the resulting entity as well as the possibility of obtaining a control premium in a subsequent transaction. Heightened scrutiny is appropriate because of an "omnipresent specter" that a board, which may have secured a continuing interest of some kind in the surviving entity, may favor its interests over those of the corporation's stockholders.

The Supreme Court has not yet clarified the precise bounds of when *Revlon* applies in the situation where merger consideration consists of an equal or almost

---

applies only when a company embarks on a transaction—on its own initiative or in response to an unsolicited offer—that will result in a change of control."). Moreover, in *Paramount Communications v. Time*, the Supreme Court held that Time's board of directors did not enter *Revlon* mode solely by virtue of either entering into the initial merger agreement with Warner or adopting structural safety devices. See *Time Inc.*, 571 A.2d at 1142, 1151.

16. [FN 89] See, e.g., *In re Santa Fe Pac. Corp. S'holder Litig.*, 669 A.2d 59, 71 (Del. 1995) (citing *Paramount Commc'ns Inc. v. QVC Network Inc.*, 637 A.2d 34, 42-43, 47-48 (Del. 1994) (internal quotation marks and citations omitted); *Arnold v. Soc'y for Sav. Bancorp, Inc.*, 650 A.2d 1270, 1289-90 (Del. 1994).

equal split of cash and stock. Thus, to make such a determination, I evaluate the circumstances of the Proposed Transaction based on its economic implications and relevant judicial precedent.

As to judicial precedent, I note that, on a few occasions, Delaware courts have provided guidance on this issue. In *In re Santa Fe Pacific Corp.*, for example, the Supreme Court considered on a motion to dismiss the plaintiffs' claim that *Revlon* should apply to a transaction in which Burlington would acquire up to 33% of Santa Fe common shares through a tender offer (*i.e.*, cash) and then acquire the balance of Santa Fe shares through a stock-for-stock exchange. The Court declined to apply *Revlon* because it found that the plaintiffs failed to allege that the Santa Fe board decided to pursue a transaction, including the one finally settled upon, which would result in a sale of control of Santa Fe to Burlington. Notably, the Court highlighted the plaintiffs' failure to describe Burlington's capital structure, which left it with little reason to doubt that "control of Burlington and Santa Fe after the merger would [ ] remain 'in a large, fluid, changeable and changing market.'"

Similarly, in *In re Lukens Inc.*, Vice Chancellor Lamb considered a transaction in which Bethlehem Steel would acquire 100% of Lukens' common stock for a value of $25 per common share. Under the terms of the merger, which were subject to dispute on the defendants' motion to dismiss, "each Lukens shareholder would have the right to elect to receive the consideration in cash, subject to a maximum total cash payout equal to 62% of the total consideration."[17] As in *Santa Fe*, the parties disputed whether *Revlon* should control the transaction. While the Court did not have occasion to determine definitively whether *Revlon* should apply—it assumed that it did—it offered sage guidance on transactions involving both cash and stock merger consideration, which informs this Court's opinion here. Vice Chancellor Lamb opined that, though the Supreme Court had not yet established a bright line rule for what percentage of merger consideration could be cash without triggering *Revlon*, he would find that under the circumstances of the *Lukens* case *Revlon* would apply. In pertinent part, he explained as follows:

> I cannot understand how the Director Defendants were *not* obliged, in the circumstances, to seek out the best price reasonably available. The defendants argue that because over 30% of the merger consideration was shares of Bethlehem common stock, a widely held company without any controlling shareholder, *Revlon* and *QVC* do not apply. I disagree. Whether 62% or 100% of the consideration was to be in cash, the directors were obliged to take reasonable steps to ensure that the shareholders received the best price available because, in any event, for a substantial majority of the then-current shareholders, "there is no long run." . . . I do not agree with the defendants that *Santa Fe*, in which shareholders tendered 33% of their shares for cash and exchanged the remainder for common stock, controls a situation in which over 60% of the consideration is cash. . . . I take for granted . . . that a cash offer for 95% of a company's shares, for example, even if the other 5% will be exchanged for the shares of a widely held corporation, will constitute

---

17. [FN 100] *In re Lukens Inc. S'holders Litig.*, 757 A.2d 720, 725 (Del. Ch. 1999).

a change of corporate control. Until instructed otherwise, I believe that purchasing more than 60% achieves the same result.[18]

Thus far, this Court has not been instructed otherwise, and, while the stock portion of the Merger Consideration is larger than the portion in *Lukens,* I am persuaded that Vice Chancellor Lamb's reasoning applies here, as well. Defendants attempt to distinguish *Lukens* on its facts, arguing that "they offer no support to plaintiffs' position." I disagree. While the factual scenarios are not identical, there are some material similarities. Most important of these is that the Court in *Lukens* was wary of the fact that a majority of holders of Lukens common stock potentially could have elected to cash out their positions entirely, subject to the 62% total cash consideration limit. In this case, Defendants emphasize that no [target] stockholder involuntarily or voluntarily can be cashed out completely and, after consummation of the Proposed Transaction, the stockholders will own slightly less than half of [bidder]. While the facts of this case and *Lukens* differ slightly in that regard, Defendants lose sight of the fact that while no [target] stockholder will be cashed out 100%, 100% of its stockholders who elect to participate in the merger will see approximately 50% of their [target] investment cashed out. As such, like Vice Chancellor Lamb's concern that potentially there was no "tomorrow" for a substantial majority of Lukens stockholders, the concern here is that there is no "tomorrow" for approximately 50% of each stockholder's investment in [target]. That each stockholder may retain a portion of her investment after the merger is insufficient to distinguish the reasoning of *Lukens,* which concerns the need for the Court to scrutinize under *Revlon* a transaction that constitutes an end-game for all or a substantial part of a stockholder's investment in a Delaware corporation.

Defendants' other arguments, while cogent, similarly are unavailing. Citing to *Arnold,*[19] they contend that because control of [bidder] after closing will remain in a large, fluid, changing, and changeable market, [target] stockholders will retain the right to obtain a control premium in the future and, as such, the Proposed Transaction is not a change of control transaction under *Revlon.* As with their attempt to distinguish *Lukens,* Defendants assert that even though a significant part of the Merger Consideration is in cash, there is a "tomorrow" for the Company's stockholders because they will own approximately 45% of [bidder] after the merger. They aver that "[h]olding that *Revlon* applies in this type of case would require directors to behave as if there is no long run for their shareholders when in fact there is, and to pretend that shareholders will not participate in the future of the combined entity when in fact they will." This statement, however, is only half correct. While the Company's stockholders will see approximately half of their equity transformed into [bidder] equity such that they potentially can benefit from [bidder]'s future value, the other half of their investment in [target] will be cashed out. Even if [bidder] has no controlling stockholder and [target] stockholders will not be relegated to a minority status in the postmerger entity, half of their investment will be liquidated.

18. [FN 102] Id. at 732 n.25.
19. [FN 104] 650 A.2d 1270.

Citing to *Santa Fe,* Defendants note that the Supreme Court did not suggest that cashing out 33% of shares out would transform Santa Fe's transaction with Burlington into a change of control transaction. As the Court noted, the plaintiffs in that case did not allege that control of Burlington would not remain in a large, fluid, changing, and changeable market postmerger. The approximately 50% being cashed out of each stockholder's investment in [target] obviously falls between the 33% cash out that the Supreme Court held did not trigger *Revlon* in *Santa Fe* and the 62% proportion of cash consideration that Vice Chancellor Lamb determined would trigger *Revlon* in *Lukens*. Mathematically, this situation is closer to *Lukens,* but only marginally. Thus, assuming the Court's analysis in *Lukens* was correct, as I do, this case is necessarily approaching a limit in relation to the Supreme Court's holdings in *Santa Fe* and *Arnold,* which, again, involved a stock-for-stock transaction. As previously noted, however, my conclusion that *Revlon* applies here is not free from doubt.

Finally, I note that factors identified by Plaintiffs and Defendants as having been considered by Delaware courts in determining whether to apply *Revlon* review in cases like *QVC* and others are important to a robust analysis of the issue. In *QVC,* for example, the Supreme Court noted the importance of considering whether a target's stockholder's voting rights would be relegated to minority status in the surviving entity of a merger and whether such stockholders still could obtain a control premium in future transactions as part of the postmerger entity in determining whether a "change of control" had occurred. But, the fact that control of [bidder] after consummation will remain in a large pool of unaffiliated stockholders, while important, neither addresses nor affords protection to the portion of the stockholders' investment that will be converted to cash and thereby be deprived of its long-run potential.

Based on the foregoing, therefore, I conclude that Plaintiffs are likely to succeed on their argument that the approximately 50% cash and 50% stock consideration here triggers *Revlon.*

4. State Anti-Takeover Statutes

Many state corporate codes include provisions designed to impede hostile takeovers. State legislatures typically adopted these provisions following lobbying by local companies worried about, or in the midst of battling, hostile takeover attempts. Legislatures were particularly concerned that a successful bidder would close operations in the state, resulting in mass employee terminations. Below is a brief description of various state anti-takeover provisions. The specific details of these provisions vary by state. Thus, a particular state's provision may have different features than what is described below.

Control shares acquisition provisions. These provisions require a bidder to obtain approval of a majority of target's outstanding shares before acquiring a large block (e.g., 20 percent) of target stock in order to have the right to vote the shares. As a result, a bidder contemplating a hostile tender offer is essentially required to get shareholder approval before proceeding with it. The corporate law statutes of 27 states include this type of provision. The DGCL is not among them.

Business combination provisions. These provisions generally prohibit a target shareholder (or affiliate of such shareholder) from engaging in a business combination (merger, asset purchase, stock purchase, etc.) with target for a specified period of years following the date that the shareholder's percentage ownership of target's outstanding shares crosses a specified threshold. For example, DGCL §203(a) provides as follows:

> (a) Notwithstanding any other provisions of this chapter, a corporation shall not engage in any business combination with any interested stockholder for a period of 3 years following the time that such stockholder became an interested stockholder, unless:
>
> (1) Prior to such time the board of directors of the corporation approved either the business combination or the transaction which resulted in the stockholder becoming an interested stockholder;
>
> (2) Upon consummation of the transaction which resulted in the stockholder becoming an interested stockholder, the interested stockholder owned at least 85% of the voting stock of the corporation outstanding at the time the transaction commenced, excluding for purposes of determining the voting stock outstanding (but not the outstanding voting stock owned by the interested stockholder) those shares owned (i) by persons who are directors and also officers and (ii) employee stock plans in which employee participants do not have the right to determine confidentially whether shares held subject to the plan will be tendered in a tender or exchange offer; or
>
> (3) At or subsequent to such time the business combination is approved by the board of directors and authorized at an annual or special meeting of stockholders, and not by written consent, by the affirmative vote of at least 66 2/3% of the outstanding voting stock which is not owned by the interested stockholder.

The effect of this type of provision is to force a bidder who has successfully completed a hostile tender offer for a majority of target's stock to wait the specified number of years to effect a merger or other transaction to squeeze out target shareholders that did not tender unless it gets the specified shareholder approval of the transaction. The corporate law statutes of 33 states, including the DGLC, contain this type of provision.

Directors' duties provisions. These provisions, also known as "other constituency" statutes, explicitly authorize directors to consider factors other than maximizing shareholder value when deciding whether rejecting a takeover bid or fighting a hostile takeover attempt is in the best interest of the corporation. The corporate law statutes of 32 states contain this type of provision. The DGCL does not.

The application of and list of factors in these provisions vary by state. For example, Ohio's provision states as follows:

[A] director, in determining what the director reasonably believes to be in the best interests of the corporation, shall consider the interests of the corporation's shareholders and, in the director's discretion, may consider any of the following:

(1) The interests of the corporation's employees, suppliers, creditors, and customers;

(2) The economy of the state and nation;

(3) Community and societal considerations;

(4) The long-term as well as short-term interests of the corporation and its shareholders, including the possibility that these interests may be best served by the continued independence of the corporation.[20]

In contrast, Arizona's provision states as follows:

In discharging the duties of the position of director under this chapter, a director of an issuing public corporation, in considering the best interests of the corporation, shall consider the long-term as well as the short-term interests of the corporation and its shareholders including the possibility that these interests may be best served by the continued independence of the corporation. This section shall not modify the duties of the position of director in any matter outside the scope of this chapter.[21]

The above provision appears in the Arizona corporate law statute chapter that addresses corporate takeovers. In other words, the Arizona provision is limited to the takeover context. Conversely, the Ohio provision appears in the Ohio corporate law statute that specifies the duties of directors generally and thus applies to all director decisions, not just those related to takeovers.

Fair price provisions. These provisions require a bidder who has successfully completed a hostile tender offer for a majority of target's stock to pay the non-tendering shareholders a fair price in any follow up squeeze-out transaction unless the transaction receives approval of a supermajority (generally, two-thirds) of such non-tendering shares. The definition of fair price as used in these provisions is based on a formula that varies by state. For example, a number of states define fair price as the greater of (1) the highest price paid by bidder for target's shares in a specified period (e.g., five years) before the proposed squeeze-out transaction is announced, and (2) the market value per share of target's stock on the date the proposed squeeze-out transaction is announced.

The provisions are designed to prevent a bidder from using the threat of a second-step squeeze-out at a low price or for undesirable consideration as a mechanism for pressuring target shareholders into tendering. The corporate law statutes of 27 states contain this type of provision.

---

20. Ohio Rev. Code §1701.59(E).
21. Ariz. Rev. Stat. §10-2702.

Poison pill endorsement provisions. These provisions explicitly authorize the board of directors to adopt a shareholders' rights plan. Here's an example from Illinois's corporate statute:

> [A] corporation may create and issue, whether or not in connection with the issue and sale of its shares or bonds, rights or options entitling the holders thereof to purchase from the corporation, upon such consideration, terms and conditions as may be fixed by the board, shares of any class or series, whether authorized but unissued shares, treasury shares or shares to be purchased or acquired, notes of the corporation or assets of the corporation. The terms and conditions of such rights or options may include, without limitation, restrictions or conditions that preclude or limit the exercise, transfer or receipt of such rights or options by any person or persons owning or offering to acquire a specified number or percentage of the outstanding common shares or other securities of the corporation, or any transferee or transferees of any such person or persons, or that invalidate or void such rights or options held by any such person or persons or any such transferee or transferees. . . . [22]

The Delaware Supreme Court has sanctioned poison pills, so there is no need for the DGCL to contain such a provision. Other states enacted them either because of an absence of case law on the issue, or, in a few states, because of case law prohibiting the use of poison pills. The corporate law statutes of 25 states include this type of provision.

---

22. Ill. Rev. Stat. ch. 32 para 6.05.

· APPENDIX ·

INTRODUCTION TO FINANCIAL STATEMENTS

This Appendix provides a brief introduction to financial statements. Financial statements are prepared by accountants, not lawyers, but lawyers need to have at least a basic understanding of them. Corporate lawyers need to be able to read financial statements so that any issues identified in them can be explored and if necessary addressed in the deal documents, for example, acquisition agreement, loan agreement, private placement memorandum, etc. For deal and non-deal lawyers, financial statements are important in deciding whether you should take on a particular business as a client, how much to offer or demand in settlement negotiations, damages arguments (e.g., the appropriate amount of punitive damages), to name a few.

Most businesses prepare financial statements in accordance with generally accepted accounting principles, or GAAP (public companies are required to do so under SEC regulations). GAAP is a set of rules and procedures that accountants follow in preparing a company's financial statements. GAAP standards are set by the Financial Accounting Standards Board, a nonprofit organization designated by the SEC and the American Institute of Certified Public Accountants as the arbiter of GAAP.

The three principal components of financial statements are described below: (1) balance sheet, (2) income statement, and (3) cash flow statement.

A. BALANCE SHEET

A balance sheet reports the assets, liabilities, and owners' equity of a business as of a particular day. In other words, a balance sheet is a snapshot of what a business owns (its assets), what a business owes (its liabilities), and the extent to which the business's assets exceed its liabilities (its owner's equity) on a specific date (e.g., the last day of a quarter or year).

For an ice cream shop like Clare's Conery from Chapter 2, assets may include the ice cream on hand (inventory); the money in the business's checking account (cash); and the shop's freezers, scoopers, blenders, time clock, cash register, etc. (equipment). Liabilities may include money owed to ice cream vendors (accounts payable), money owed on a bank loan (notes payable), and wages owed to employees (wages payable). Owners' equity is simply the difference between a business's total assets and total liabilities, or, in equation form:

$$\text{Owners' Equity} = \text{Assets} - \text{Liabilities}$$

In fact, a balance sheet is organized based on the following rearranged version of the above equation: Assets = Liabilities + Owners' Equity. Here's a sample balance sheet for Clare's Conery, Inc. (CCI) to illustrate.

CLARE'S CONERY, INC.
BALANCE SHEET
December 31, 20xx

ASSETS	
Cash	$60,000
Accounts receivable	1,000
Prepaid expenses	500
Inventory	8,000
Equipment	50,000
Leasehold improvements	100,000
Furniture and fixtures	15,000
Accumulated depreciation	(30,000)
Total Assets	**$204,500**
LIABILITIES	
Accounts payable	5,000
Note payable	80,000
Accrued payroll	4,000
Total Liabilities	**$89,000**
STOCKHOLDERS' EQUITY	
Common stock, $0.01 par value, authorized	
10,000 shares, issued 4,000 shares	40
Additional paid in capital	99,960
Retained earnings	15,500
Total Stockholders' Equity	115,500
Total Liabilities and Stockholders' Equity	**$204,500**

Observe that in the above balance sheet "Total Assets" ($204,500) equal, or are in *balance* with, "Total Liabilities and Stockholders' Equity" ($204,500), just as the rearranged equation provides (and that is why it is called a balance sheet). If these two numbers do not equal/balance, the balance sheet contains one or more errors. In other words, they should always balance.

Note that assets are reflected on a balance sheet at "historical cost," that is, the cost that the business paid for them. For example, if CCI spends $1,000 to buy chairs for its shop, these chairs will be reflected in the furniture and fixtures line of CCI's balance sheet at $1,000. Of course, things like chairs suffer wear and tear and thus decrease in value over time. This is where depreciation comes into play, a topic we discuss below.

Here is a quick rundown of each of the line items from the CCI balance sheet above:

Cash consists of the cash CCI had in its checking account on December 31, 20xx. If CCI had money in a savings account, money market fund, a bank certificate of deposit, etc., these amounts would be included in cash too.

Accounts receivable consists of amounts owed CCI on December 31, 20xx by customers to whom CCI sold ice cream on credit.

Inventory consists of the value of ice cream and related products (cones, toppings, etc.) CCI had on hand on December 31, 20xx.

Equipment consists of the historical cost of CCI's freezers, blenders, soft serve machine, scoopers, etc. that it owned on December 31, 20xx.

Leasehold improvements appears because CCI leases (as opposed to owns) the space for its shop and remodeled (or improved) it before moving in. The figure represents what CCI paid for these improvements.

Furniture and fixtures are comprised of the historical cost of CCI's furniture (mostly tables and chairs) and removable fixtures (mostly lighting) on hand on December 31, 20xx.

Accumulated depreciation is not actually an asset but shows up in the asset portion of the balance sheet to account for the fact that certain assets like furniture and equipment decrease in value over time. It is necessary given these assets are reflected in the balance sheet at historical cost instead of current market value. We discuss depreciation more generally below in the context of the income statement.

Accounts payable is the amount CCI owed vendors (mainly, CCI's ice cream supplier) on December 31, 20xx for goods CCI had received but not yet paid for by that date. Many vendors are willing to provide customers products on credit.

Note payable reflects the principal amount of a loan owed by CCI on December 31, 20xx. CCI borrowed the money from a bank to help get its business started.

Accrued payroll is the amount CCI owed its employees for wages on December 31, 20xx for work performed prior to that date.

Common stock consists of the number of shares of common stock CCI had outstanding on December 31, 20xx multiplied by the par value of the stock.

Additional paid in capital is the amount that CCI received for the common stock it had outstanding on December 31, 20xx in excess of the stock's par value.

Retained earnings are earnings of CCI that as of December 31, 20xx it had not distributed to its shareholders.

The balance sheet for a more complicated business will have additional line items, but the basic equation of Assets = Liabilities + Owners' Equity remains the same regardless of how simple or complicated the business.

B. INCOME STATEMENT

An income statement depicts a business's financial performance over a specific period of time such as a quarter (three months) or a year. It answers the question of how much a business earned or lost over the period. The basic equation for the income statement is:

Revenue – Expenses = Net income (or loss)

Revenue is money generated by the business from the sale of products or services. Thus, for example, CCI's revenue is largely composed of money generated from the sale of ice cream. Expenses are costs incurred by the business in order to generate the revenue. For CCI, expenses include payments to its ice cream supplier, rent on its shop, and wages for its employees.

There are two methods businesses use to account for their revenue and expenses when computing net income—the cash method or the accrual method. These methods differ based on the timing of when the business recognizes (or records in its accounting records) a revenue or expense item. Under the cash method, a business does not count a sale as revenue until it receives the cash nor does it recognize an expense until it pays the bill for the expense. Thus, if CCI sells $500 of ice cream to a summer camp with the understanding that the camp will pay for the ice cream the following week, CCI does not record the sale until the summer camp pays. Likewise, if CCI buys $2,000 of ice cream on 30 days credit (meaning it doesn't have to pay its supplier the $2,000 until 30 days has run), CCI does not record this expense until it pays the $2,000 to its supplier.

Use of the accrual method is required under GAAP, so most businesses use it. Under this method, a business recognizes revenue when it delivers the goods or completes the services it provides. Likewise, a business recognizes an expense when it receives the goods or services it has ordered. Unlike the cash method, timing of payment is not relevant. Thus, continuing with the example from above, under the accrual method CCI would record the sale to the summer camp on the day it delivers the ice cream and the $2,000 ice cream expense on the day it receives the ice cream from its supplier.

Here's a sample income statement for CCI:

CLARE'S CONERY, INC.
INCOME STATEMENT
For the Year Ended December 31, 20xx

Revenue		$220,000
Cost of goods sold		<u>60,000</u>
Gross profit		160,000
Other expenses		
Wages	50,000	
Utilities	3,000	
Depreciation	8,000	
Rent	18,000	
Advertising	<u>2,000</u>	
		<u>81,000</u>
Operating income		79,000
Interest expense		<u>6,000</u>
Net income		73,000

Here is a quick rundown of some of the line items from CCI's income statement above.

Revenue is the amount of money CCI generated from sales of its products (mostly ice cream) for the year 20xx, that is, from January 1, 20xx through December 31, 20xx.

Cost of goods sold consists of the direct costs relating to the sales of CCI's products for 20xx. The amount includes the cost of ice cream, cones, toppings, etc., and wages of the counter staff.

Gross margin equals revenues minus cost of goods sold.

Depreciation is an accounting charge to reflect the use of assets such as freezers, blenders, soft serve machine, scoopers, tables, chairs, etc. by CCI during the year 20xx. It is probably easiest to explain the concept through an example. Assume CCI bought a new ice cream freezer for $6,000 in January 20xx to replace one that broke and was thrown out. CCI used this freezer during 20xx, so some dollar amount for this use should be subtracted when figuring out CCI's net income for 20xx. It would not, however, make sense to subtract the full cost of the freezer because it will be used in future years too. Thus what CCI did, as allowed by GAAP, was to divide the cost of the freezer by its useful life in years. It then included this amount in the depreciation line item on its 20xx income statement. Specifically, CCI estimated that the freezer will last for ten years (what accountants call its "useful life") at which point it will be worthless. Thus, CCI divided $6,000 by 10, which equals $600. CCI therefore included $600 in the depreciation figure on its income statement for 20xx (and will do the same for each of the nine years thereafter) to account for its use of the freezer for that year. The balance of the depreciation line item on CCI's 20xx income statement reflects the same sort of calculation for CCI's other tangible assets (soft serve machine, tables, chairs, etc.).

Operating income equals revenues minus operating expenses.

Net income equals how much money CCI made for the year. It is also referred to as profit or earnings.

Note that there is no line item on the income statement for income taxes because CCI is an S-corporation and therefore does not pay income taxes.

C. CASH FLOW STATEMENT

A cash flow statement depicts a business's cash inflows and outflows over a specific period of time. It reflects all cash that flowed into or out of the business during the specified timeframe. The concept of accrual is not applied to a cash flow statement. In other words, the fact that, for example, the company has paid for some goods but did not receive them during the specified timeframe does not matter. Cash flowed out of the business for those goods, so this outflow is reflected in the cash flow statement even though under the accrual method of accounting the undelivered goods would not be reflected in the corresponding balance sheet of the business. Here is a sample cash flow statement for CCI:

CLARE'S CONERY, INC.
CASH FLOW STATEMENT
For the Year Ended December 31, 20xx

Cash flow from operating activities	
Cash from customers	220,000
Cash used for operations	139,000
Net cash from operations	81,000
Cash flow from investing activities	
Cash from investing	500
Cash used for investing	6,000
Net cash from investing	(5,500)
Cash flow from financing activities	
Cash from financing	8,000
Cash used for financing	6,500
Net cash from financing	1,500
Net increase in cash	77,000
Cash at beginning of period	12,000
Cash at end of period	89,000

As the example above indicates, a business can have cash flow from three different sources—operating activities, investing activities, and financing activities. Operating activities include the production, sale, and delivery of a company's products. CCI's main operating activity is the sale of ice cream. Thus, its *cash from customers* line item comes mostly from ice cream sales to customers, and its *cash used for operations* comes mostly from cash CCI paid to its ice cream supplier, wages it paid to its counter staff, and rent. Investing activities reflect amounts spent on capital assets or received from the sale of capital assets. For example, CCI's *cash used from investing* is comprised of the money it spent to buy a new ice cream freezer. *Cash from investing* comes from the money CCI got for selling an old soft serve machine. Financing activities reflect cash received from selling stock or borrowing money. CCI upped its loan from the bank at the beginning of the year, so this is where its *cash from financing* line item comes from. Toward the end of the year, it paid back some of the principal it owes on the loan, so this is where its *cash used for financing* line item comes from.

Exercise A.1

Refer to the above financial statements of Clare's Conery, Inc. Assume that the following transactions were mistakenly not reflected in CCI's financial statements. For each transaction, specify which line items in the financial statements need to be changed and by how much so that the transaction is reflected.

1. CCI's ice cream supplier delivered $2,000 of ice cream on December 29. CCI paid the supplier $500 upon delivery with the $1,500 balance due in 30 days.
2. On December 31, CCI delivered $300 of ice cream to a customer for a New Year's Eve party. The customer paid for the ice cream in cash upon delivery.
3. On December 26, CCI's ice maker broke. A CCI employee went out and bought a new one for $1,000. She charged it on CCI's corporate credit card.

Exercise A.2

If you were to prepare personal financial statements, what line items would be on your balance sheet, income statement, and cash flow statement?

Exercise A.3

Review the balance sheet and income statement below and then answer the following questions.

1. What was Chipotle's biggest asset on December 31, 2011?
2. What was its biggest liability on December 31, 2011?
3. How much cash did Chipotle have on hand at the end of 2011?
4. How many shares of stock did Chipotle have outstanding on December 31, 2011? How much money did it receive for this stock?
5. How much did Chipotle make in 2011? 2010? 2009?
6. What was Chipotle's biggest expense in 2011?

CHIPOTLE MEXICAN GRILL, INC.
CONSOLIDATED BALANCE SHEET
(in thousands, except per share data)

	Year ended December 31	
	2011	2010
Assets		
Current assets:		
Cash and cash equivalents	$ 401,243	$ 224,838
Accounts receivable, net of allowance for doubtful accounts of $208 and $102 as of December 31, 2011 and 2010, respectively	8,389	5,658
Inventory	8,913	7,098
Current deferred tax asset	6,238	4,317
Prepaid expenses and other current assets	21,404	16,016
Income tax receivable	—	23,528
Investments	55,005	124,766
Total current assets	501,192	406,221
Leasehold improvements, property and equipment, net	751,951	676,881
Long term investments	128,241	—
Other assets	21,985	16,564
Goodwill	21,939	21,939
Total assets	$ 1,425,308	$ 1,121,605

Liabilities and shareholders' equity

Current liabilities:

Accounts payable	$ 46,382	$ 33,705
Accrued payroll and benefits	60,241	50,336
Accrued liabilities	46,456	38,892
Current portion of deemed landlord financing	133	121
Income tax payable	4,241	—
Total current liabilities	157,453	123,054
Deferred rent	143,284	123,667
Deemed landlord financing	3,529	3,661
Deferred income tax liability	64,381	50,525
Other liabilities	12,435	9,825
Total liabilities	381,082	310,732

Shareholders' equity:

Preferred stock, $0.01 par value, 600,000 shares authorized, no shares issued as of December 31, 2011 and 2010	—	—
Common stock, $0.01 par value, 230,000 shares authorized, 34,357 and 33,959 shares issued as of December 31, 2011 and 2010, respectively	344	340
Additional paid-in capital	676,652	594,331
Treasury stock, at cost, 3,105 and 2,885 shares at December 31, 2011 and 2010, respectively	(304,426	(240,918
Accumulated other comprehensive income	197	606
Retained earnings	671,459	456,514
Total shareholders' equity	1,044,226	810,873
Total liabilities and shareholders' equity	$ 1,425,308	$ 1,121,605

CHIPOTLE MEXICAN GRILL, INC.
CONSOLIDATED STATEMENT OF INCOME
(in thousands, except per share data)

| | Year ended December 31 | | |
	2011	2010	2009
Revenue	$ 2,269,548	$ 1,835,922	$ 1,518,417
Restaurant operating costs (exclusive of depreciation and amortization shown separately below):			
Food, beverage and packaging	738,720	561,107	466,027
Labor	543,119	453,573	385,072
Occupancy	147,274	128,933	114,218
Other operating costs	251,208	202,904	174,581
General and administrative expenses	149,426	118,590	99,149
Depreciation and amortization	74,938	68,921	61,308
Pre-opening costs	8,495	7,767	8,401
Loss on disposal of assets	5,806	6,296	5,956
Total operating expenses	1,918,986	1,548,091	1,314,712
Income from operations	350,562	287,831	203,705
Interest and other income	2,088	1,499	925
Interest and other expense	(2,945)	(269)	(405)
Income before income taxes	349,705	289,061	204,225
Provision for income taxes	(134,760)	(110,080)	(77,380)
Net income	$ 214,945	$ 178,981	$ 126,845

· INDEX ·